The Only Two Ways to Write a Story

by JOHN GALLISHAW

*A book for writers
which cites cases in the craftsmanship
of the modern short story*

NEW YORK · LONDON

G. P. PUTNAM'S SONS

The Knickerbocker Press

1928

THE ONLY TWO WAYS TO
WRITE A STORY

Copyright, 1928
by
John Gallishaw

This is a copy of the first printing

G. P. Putnam's Son

Made in the United States of America

AUTHOR'S FOREWORD

In the course of the last ten years I have seen a number of writers achieve a reputation in the field of the Modern Short-Story. Almost invariably those writers, when questioned, have told me that they studied the work of established writers in order to isolate practical standards of both form and treatment. Unconsciously, those writers have adapted to their needs the greatest forward development in modern education: the Case Method. They all agreed that their work would have been much easier had there existed, within the scope of a single volume, a series of CASES IN CRAFTSMANSHIP of the Modern Short-Story to which aspiring writers might turn with certainty that therein they would find a norm against which they might judge their own products.

In presenting the results of my search for such a norm, I am like the very enthusiastic young bayonet instructor in the British Army who always appended to the standardized phrases of his instruction upon close-quarter bayonet fighting with an enemy the phrase "and then you kicks 'im in the fyce." Questioned by an officer who overheard him, he said: "The first part I learned from an instructor; kicking 'im in the fyce is my own idea."

There is much technical instruction which has always been available in regard to the Craftsmanship of the Modern Short-Story. This volume deals primarily with the four discoveries which I conceive to be "my own idea."

Discovery No. 1. For every short-story, as indeed for every work of fiction, long or short, there is a structural or architectural norm, as definite and basic as the architect's structural concept of a building. This norm is not in any way the creation of a single personal taste; nor does its recognition in any way limit or hamper individual expression. Just as an architect realizes that a building must ordinarily have walls, a roof, and a foundation; so the short-story writer realizes that architecturally a story must have a Beginning, a Body, and an Ending.

While most writers and critics have been aware, either con-

iii

sciously or unconsciously of the existence of this architectural norm, my special contribution to the advance of short-story craftsmanship is the discovery that there is also a *functional* norm for each of the three great *structural* divisions of Beginning, Body, and Ending. The function of each division is distinct and different from the function of either of the other two; but within each division the special function remains always constant and invariable. The function of the Beginning is to present a main situation; the function of the Body is to present a struggle or conflict growing out of that main situation; the function of the Ending is to present the Conclusive Act which brings the struggle or conflict to an end.

Although I deem this discovery of the relationship of the *functional* norm to the *structural* norm to be important and helpful to craftsmen, I feel that it cannot be utilized to the fullest extent until writers have made themselves familiar with the other discoveries.

Discovery No. 2. Of paramount importance to freedom of expression for writers is the knowledge that within the large units of Beginning, Body, and Ending, there is a smaller structural unit which, for the purposes of this book, I shall call the Scene. Until a writer learns to visualize and develop every story he writes, as a series of scenes, he cannot hope for facility in plotting and presenting his material.

Discovery No. 3. There are two—and only two—distinct types of short-story: one, the story in which the central actor is called upon to accomplish some purpose; the other, the story in which the central actor is called upon to make some decision or choice. In both types of story, the structural and functional norms are the same; just as in both types, the Scene will be the unit for plotting and presentation.

Discovery No. 4. This discovery cannot be fully utilized until the writer of short-stories is fully in control of the knowledge contained in the other discoveries. Only then can he take advantage of the discovery that there are two ways of presenting or telling a story: in chronological sequence, or in anti-chronological sequence. This anti-chronological sequence is usually known as the Flashback sequence. It is especially effective in presenting the story of decision.

The student of craftsmanship will find in this book, nothing that he could not dig out for himself, as I have done, through a study of modern fiction over a period of perhaps ten years; but such a study would involve for him, as it has done for me, the examination of thousands of manuscripts. Even though he were prepared to expend the same time and energy, he would not have the opportunity, as I have had, of testing the practicability of the principles involved in these discoveries over a large number of instances.

Fortunately, my work with writers in the John Gallishaw School for Creative Writing has enabled me to prove beyond any question of doubt that the application of these principles can cut down the period of apprenticeship through which every writer must go. A large part of the gratifying success of the method of instruction has been due, I feel sure, to the use which was there made of the stories here collected as Cases in Craftsmanship.

To look up each story independently was not always possible. It was therefore suggested to me that I gather them together into a Case Book which would serve as a basic Handbook for writers; a volume to be referred to by writers for the same purpose that lawyers refer to Case Books of Law: first, to discover the basic principle of a professional problem; and, second, the special aspects of that particular problem which make it a variant from the norm, demanding unusual treatment.

Thus, for the first time, these stories are collected in a single book; and I have preceded each one with a commentary explaining why each story has been chosen, and have followed each story with a line-by-line analysis, pointing out how the individual approach of a writer toward his material makes a variant from the norm from which every short-story must derive.

This Case Book will be of greatest benefit to writers when used in conjunction with my Lectures upon the Craftsmanship of the Modern Short Story. It will, I hope, cut down for many writers the period of futile experimentation which is the penalty of unwisely directed effort, by enabling them to examine their stories objectively, with the unbiased detachment of a reader rather than a writer. For the reader is the final judge. All stories are written for him.

CONTENTS

CONTENTS

THE ONLY
TWO WAYS TO WRITE A STORY

SECTION I

STORIES OF ACCOMPLISHMENT

NOMENCLATURE

WHENEVER one person tries to make something clear to another person there instantly appears the necessity for a common nomenclature. The words must have the same meaning to both parties. Nomenclature has always been a stumbling block to any attempt to explain the processes of producing a work of fiction. Take the word "incident" as an example, or the word "meeting." Half a dozen educated people might each one give a different meaning to either of these words, and each one of the half dozen would be justified by usage and by logic in his choice. The simplest and the easiest way to avoid any misunderstanding in regard to the meaning of technical terms is to adopt for each term so used a special and limited meaning, and throughout the explanation to adhere strictly to the meaning agreed upon.

The purpose of this book is to explain to you as clearly and as simply as possible how the two kinds of stories mentioned in the Foreword: the Story of Accomplishment and the Story of Decision, are plotted and presented. This distinction between plotting and presentation is one which the writer of fiction cannot lose sight of. The two processes are at first distinct, although eventually they become almost inextricably linked together.

Plotting involves the selection and arrangement of happenings to fit the architectural norm of which I have spoken. This architectural norm is the skeletonized outline of your story to which life and reality are given by superimposing upon them the presentation unit.

Let us pause for a moment to glance at this Case Book itself, so that we may from the very beginning utilize it for the purpose for which it was intended—the illustration from the work of writers of the principles of fiction. I have chosen one of the *Adventures of Ulysses*, by Charles Lamb as illustrating the principle of both plotting and presentation. Ulysses was the king of Ithaca, who, after the siege of Troy, set out with his followers to return to Ithaca, where his wife Penelope awaited him. During the progress of his journey he met with several adventures. This *Adventure With the Cyclop* contains all of the elements of a modern short-story. It is a particularly illuminating study for the fiction writer because the plot elements are handed down from Homer; whereas the presentation is done by Charles Lamb. Plot is an outline of happenings. Presentation is an expansion of that outline so that the details of the happenings are made available to the reader. Here is an outline of the *Adventure of Ulysses With the Cyclop*.

1. Ulysses and his party inspecting the Cyclop's cave
2. are surprised there and imprisoned by the owner.
3. Ulysses, in answer to the inquiries of the Cyclop,
4. tries to impress the Cyclop as being himself form-
5. idable. The monster is unimpressed, and eats two of
6. the party. Ulysses then tries to win over the Cyclop
7. with wine. The Cyclop is won over only to the extent
8. of agreeing to eat Ulysses last of the party.
9. Ulysses then burns out the eye of the Cyclop who,
10. in his anguish, shouts aloud to the other Cyclops
11. on the outside of the cave, urging them to help him.
12. Because Ulysses first called himself No-man, when the
13. Cyclop tells his friends that No-man has caused
14. his agony, they misunderstand and go away. The Cyclop
15. rolls away the stone, and plants himself in the doorway
16. hoping to capture the party as they emerge.
17. Ulysses escapes with his party under the bellies
18. of the rams.

You will see that this occupies 18 lines in plot outline. As it is presented by Charles Lamb it occupies 425 lines. From line 426 to 467 in the Case Book there is presented a Sequel to this particular adventure of Ulysses. The adventure is over when Ulysses is permitted to escape.

If you will examine this outline you will see that even in the outline a pattern emerges. It takes this form: first, a condition or state of affairs exists. Out of this state of affairs or condition grows the necessity that Ulysses shall escape in order to evade or to avert disaster. Following this comes Ulysses' attempt to bring about the accomplishment of his purpose. At last, when the Cyclop has released the rams, we know that Ulysses has succeeded in his purpose. Finally, there is the Sequel to the accomplishment of the purpose. This, reduced to its lowest elements, is the formula for every plot of accomplishment that you will ever write.

We can therefore be safe in adopting as our norm for the Story of Accomplishment the narrative pattern as follows:

1. A condition or state of affairs.
2. The necessity for accomplishment, projecting a definite purpose.
3. The attempt or attempts to bring about that accomplishment.
4. A Conclusive Act showing that the purpose has either been accomplished or been abandoned.
5. Sequel.

In *The Cop and the Anthem*, the condition is that Soapy realizes that winter is coming on, and that it is necessary for him to secure comfortable winter quarters. The main purpose which thereafter gives the story its unity is the purpose of Soapy to secure himself ninety days on the Island. Following this come the attempts of Soapy to bring about this Ending. After a number of these attempts have met with failure, he finally succeeds. The Sequel is that by this time he has, unfortunately, changed his mind in regard to wishing to go.

In *The Escape of Mr. Trimm*, Mr. Trimm realizes that if he can escape from the handcuffs, he will be able, because he is believed dead, to resume his old life, with his booty undisturbed. This is the condition. His purpose is to escape from the handcuffs. He makes a number of attempts, which fail. Finally, he abandons his attempts completely. The Sequel is that after he gives himself up he is not particularly interested in being freed from the handcuffs.

In *Spare Parts*, Monte English is told by Sally that if he does not drive her car for her, she will have to pay certain dire penalties. He has to pilot the Vindix car from Los Angeles to St. Louis in two weeks under its own power. After a number of attempts which promise disaster because they delay the possibility of success to the whole enterprise, he at last succeeds. The Sequel is that the hero wins the girl.

In *Jake Bolton, 551*, the condition is that Jake, independent, and unused to discipline has joined up as a volunteer. He has to make good in the army. He makes a series of attempts which are unsuccessful. At last, after throwing the bomb, he abandons his attempts. The Sequel is that he succeeds and is promoted and decorated.

In *Sunk*, Jason Terwilliger is in a condition where he is desper-

5

ately in need of money. To escape from this condition, he has to kill Jake Finch. There is an attempt to overcome the difficulties lying in his way through his lack of physical strength, because his constitution has been sapped by dissipation. In the end he does succeed in killing Jake Finch.

In *Paradise Island*, Dwyer has to kill Langley. The condition bringing this necessity to the forefront is that Langley possesses certain information which may ruin his schemes. He makes an attempt, but upon perceiving the uselessness of it, he abandons it.

In *Once and Always*, Gideon Higsbee, finds himself in a position where he is unhappy because he at one time allowed a partner of his to be swindled out of ten thousand dollars. In order to achieve peace of mind he has to restore this sum with interest to his old partner. He makes an attempt which fails. He finally succeeds.

In *The Face in the Window*, Cora McBride is in dire need of money, and learns that she can secure five thousand dollars by capturing Hap Ruggam. She has to overcome and capture him. She makes an attempt to do so which fails. At last she succeeds. The Sequel is that she receives the reward for so doing.

In *Western Stuff*, the condition is that Verena Dayson realizes that she is in danger of losing her husband to another woman. She has to win back her husband from this other woman. She makes a series of attempts which fail. In the end she is successful. The Sequel is that he forgives her.

It is the central pupose of the chief actor in the story that gives to the story its narrative or plot unity. We can therefore say that not until this purpose has been apparent have you completed the Beginning of your story. The attempts growing out of that purpose will make up the Body of the story. The Conclusive Act and the Sequel will make up the Ending of the story. We are thus enabled to make three general divisions of the story and to acquire our first architectural conception of a Story of Accomplishment or Purpose.
Thus:

Block 1. The Beginning.
      (a) The condition or state of affairs.
      (b) The main purpose of a main actor.
Block 2. The Body.
      The attempt or attempts growing out of that main purpose.
Block 3. The Ending.
      (a) The Conclusive Act.
      (b) The Sequel.

As soon as a reader is made aware of a main purpose there is narrative unity to any Story of Accomplishment. This brings us at once to the question of nomenclature, as to just what is meant by narrative unity as opposed to any other kind of unity. The strict definition of narration is *an orderly recital of events*. But most people would be misled by this, because they would not think of events as having the strict and narrow meaning of *"what eventuates."* If you will keep this meaning in mind, you will be helped tremendously in understanding what is meant by narrative unity in the modern short-story built about a main purpose.

The narrative unity comes from the main purpose and what eventuates or results at the conclusion of each of the attempts which the central actor makes to bring about that main purpose. The main purpose itself eventuates from the reaction of the chief actor to the basic condition which is the first unit of the story as we have presented it in outline.

Keeping this in mind let us look at a story from the point of view of a reader. Of the three factors for consideration: the material, the writer, and the reader, the reader is the most important; because no matter how interesting the material or how competent the writer, if the story does not capture and hold the attention of the reader all the work is wasted. *A story is written in order to be read.* There is for the reader in every story a dual interest in the character and in the story: in the character and in the character's purpose. As soon as the reader is aware of a unifying central purpose for a central character he is able to phrase for himself a question which is this: "Can the main character succeed in his attempts to bring about his main purpose?" A single character is shown reacting to a certain condition or state of affairs in such a way that the reader becomes aware of a definite main purpose actuating this chief character. He then, being aware of this purpose, is able to say to himself, "Can Ulysses succeed in escaping from the Cyclop?" "Can Mr. Trimm succeed in escaping from the handcuffs?" "Can Jake Bolton succeed in making good in the army?" "Can Monte English succeed in driving the Vindix across the continent in the allotted time?"

Uncertainty as to the outcome arises at once in the mind of the reader. Professor Chauncey W. Wells of the University of California uses a very suitable descriptive term for the question which the reader asks himself at this point. Professor Wells calls it a "Narrative Question." It is this main narrative question raised in the reader's mind at the earliest possible moment that captures the reader's interest. And it is the reader's desire to know the outcome of the actor's various attempts to answer this main narrative question which holds that reader's interest until the end of the story. That is *narrative curiosity*. Just so long as there is doubt in the mind of the reader in regard to the answer to the main narrative question there is narrative curiosity or *narrative suspense*. Once this main narrative question is answered the reader's narrative curiosity ceases. Capturing narrative curiosity in a story, therefore, consists of introducing the main narrative situation or purpose which causes the reader to ask himself a Main Narrative Question. Sustaining narrative curiosity consists in making clear, at the close of each attempt, that the outcome is still in suspense.

At the close of each attempt, the writer will make clear to the reader that there is a crisis or turning point in the main narrative. These narrative turning points can be only of two kinds: 1. A turning point of furtherance, when if the story closed at that point the answer to the main narrative question would be "yes." It may be that the attempt places the main actor in a position where he is closer to success than he was before. At such a point in the story there is a turning point of furtherance. 2. On the other hand, if the attempt brings the main actor to a point where he is further than ever from success it is a turning point of hindrance. There comes eventually in every story an event that is the result of a series of attempts, or even of a single attempt, when it becomes clear to the reader that the main narrative question is answered, either affirmatively or negatively, by a Conclusive Act, which shows definitely that the purpose has either been achieved or has been abandoned.

Thus the major narrative turning points of the story are these:

1. The main purpose or Main Narrative Question. (In the Beginning.)
2. Turning points of furtherance. (In the Body.)
3. Turning points of hindrance. (In the Body.)
4. A turning point which is a Conclusive Act. (In the Ending.)

The more the outcome is left in doubt by these turning points which come at the close of attempts in the Body of the story the more plot interest there is; in other words, the more hindrances there are, the greater is the narrative curiosity.

There is another kind of curiosity which, for want of a better term I shall call "general curiosity." It is the response called forth in a reader when he asks himself, "Now why did the actor do just that thing?" A case in point you will find in the *Adventure of Ulysses* on line 226 to 243, where Ulysses chooses a stake, sharpens and hardens it in the fire, selects four men and instructs them what they are to do with this stake, and makes them perfect in their parts. You know, of course, that it has some bearing upon the outcome, but you do not know just what its use is to be. The response excited in the reader in this case is not *narrative* curiosity but *general* curiosity. The two interests may go hand in hand. Had Ulysses been caused to say to one of his men, "Now I feel that we have a way of escape," there would have been, at the close of the attempt, an *event* which would be a crisis of furtherance to the main narrative question, while at the same time the general curiosity in regard to the use to be made of the stake would still be unallayed.

Let us pause a moment and test what we have learned in order to see if it will bring about the desired result of producing a plot which will be likely to capture and hold a reader's attention,—a story outline, that is, which developed, might be accepted by some good magazine.

Assume that the condition is that a man is walking along a country road on a summer day and feels slightly thirsty. On the side of the road, about fifty yards away, is a well on the top of which is a bucket, brimming with cool water. The man's purpose is to go over and get himself a drink. You have here a condition and a purpose which are the first two elements of a story. The man walks over, and about twenty-five yards from the bucket he meets a boy and says, "Will you give me a cup so that I can get a drink of water?" The boy says, "I'm sorry, I've got to run along, but my brother will get one for you." You have here an attempt which results in a furtherance, because the man is now nearer his purpose than he was before. He goes to the brother who is only a short distance from the well and says, "Will you lend me a cup, please?" and the brother says, "No. Go and get your own cup if you want it." This is a turning point of hindrance. The man then proceeds alone to the well, lifts the bucket between his hands to his mouth, and drinks deeply. This is a Conclusive Act. There are here present all the elements of a short-story: condition, purpose, attempt, crisis of furtherance, another attempt, crisis of hindrance, a final attempt resulting in a successful Conclusive Act. The major narrative question is answered in the affirmative. If all the plot elements are present are you then

9

justified in developing the attempts, that is, filling in the details of the outline, and sending this story to a good magazine with every hope of success? The answer is, quite obviously, "No." There are two reasons for this. The first is that the condition or state of affairs is not, of itself, sufficiently dramatic to capture the reader's attention in such a way as to cause him to be interested in the outcome of the main purpose of the actor. It is not *important* enough. The second reason is that the attempts themselves are not sufficiently dramatic.

At once we see that narrative interest alone is not sufficient to make a good plot. It must in addition be dramatic. In order that you may understand these requirements, I should like you to read over the first 225 lines of the *Adventure of Ulysses with the Cyclop.* These 225 lines set forth the condition which is interesting enough to capture our attention, because it contains the promise of a difficulty to be removed, of an opponent to be overcome, and of disaster to be averted. In order to remove, or overcome or avert these varying elements, the main character must engage in conflict so that our interest is captured in the setting forth of the condition by the promise which it holds of conflict or clash. This conflict or clash between the actor and forces or conditions opposed to his purpose will grow out of the main character's attempts to overcome or remove the difficulty, to remove or overcome the opponent, and to avert disaster. The consequence is that the greater the threat of disaster, and the greater the promise of clash the more interesting the reader finds the statement of the condition. Therefore, the condition under which a main character is forced into the necessity for accomplishment *should be a condition promising conflict or threatening disaster.* Clearly, too, if, at the end of an attempt, the resulting crisis is a turning point of furtherance it is not so interesting a turning point as a turning point of hindrance. This is because the more hindrance or defeats there are the closer the hero is brought to ultimate disaster. The way to sustain interest in the turning points of the plot is to include as large a number as possible of hindering rather than furthering crises.

If the demands of your story are such that only a furthering crisis at a certain point is possible in order to bring about a meeting which will result in an extremely dramatic hindering crisis you will be wise if you will immediately indicate that although success has temporarily crowned the efforts of the actor this success is only very temporary. For example, on lines 326 to 333 of the *Adventure of Ulysses* there is a turning point of furtherance when Ulysses and his followers succeed in blinding the Cyclop. But instantly there is promise of disaster or failure of the main attempt when "he cried out in a mighty voice for his brethren the Cyclops who dwelt hardby in caverns upon hills;" and the reader learns that these other Cyclops, hearing the terrible shout, come flocking from all parts to inquire what ailed Polyphemus. Thus a *narrative* turning point of furtherance, which, from the point of view of suspense, is not so desireable as a *narrative* turning point of hindrance, is turned into, or is instantly followed by, a turning point of hindrance.

It must, however, be noted that this turning point of hindrance is not a *narrative* but a *dramatic* hindrance.

A *narrative hindrance* is a temporary defeat. A *dramatic hindrance* is the promise of ultimate defeat, even though there is a temporary triumph. *Drama*, for the short-story writer, consists of

(a) the promise of difficulties to be overcome.
(b) the promise of conflict with a new opponent.
(c) the promise of additional conflict with the same opposing force.
(d) the promise of disaster to the venture of the chief actor.

It is apparent, then, that the crises or turning points of a story may be either dramatic or narrative, or both. So it is with the attempts or meetings which intervene between the crises of the plot.

These attempts or meetings—the presentation units—may be interesting only as they lead into events which contribute dramatic or narrative interest to the plot. They may also be interesting in their own right. The less the outline of these attempts or meetings is filled in, the less they are, of themselves, interesting; and the more they must depend upon the story or plot interest to hold the reader. In such case the reader's interest is held by the event or outcome of the attempt rather than by the attempt itself. In such a story the chief interest is *plot* interest rather than *presentation* interest.

On the other hand, the more the outline is filled in and developed, the more it will be, of itself, sufficient to hold the reader's interest. Then there is *presentation* interest.

To understand fully the essential difference between an attempt or meeting introduced for the sake of advancing the plot (plot interest) as compared with an attempt or meeting introduced with the intent of holding interest upon its own account (presentation interest), I shall ask you to turn to *The Adventure of Ulysses*.

Read, first, lines 226 to 243;
Then, read lines 244 to 297.

In each of these two attempts to bring about a satisfactory outcome the very same elements occur.   In the first one the attempt is introduced by the author to carry the reader swiftly to a turning point in the plot.   He is not interested in the details of the meeting and the interchange between Ulysses and his four men, except as its occurrence eventuates in a crisis which affects the plot.

In comparison with this there is a different use of the very same elements in that portion of the Adventure occupying lines 244 to 297.   There is a meeting and an interchange between Ulysses and the Cyclop, in which Ulysses tries to persuade the Cyclop to allow him to go with a whole skin in recompense for the wine that he offers him.   Here the interchange between Ulysses and the Cyclop is in itself interesting; because it is dramatic through a clash of purposes. Ulysses' purpose to persuade the Cyclop is in dramatic clash with the Cyclop's purpose to discover Ulysses' name.   At the conclusion of this interchange the purpose of Ulysses is defeated; for the Cyclop says, "This is the kindness I will show thee No-man: I will eat thee last of all thy friends."   This is on line 294 to 297.   Thus there is presentation interest in the interchange, and *plot* interest in the result or *event* of the interchanges.   This event is a crisis of narrative *hindrance*, because the immediate purpose of the meeting or interchange is defeated; it is also a crisis of *dramatic* hindrance because it brings closer or foreshadows the ultimate disaster which threatens Ulysses' venture.

This would seem to be a good moment to discuss the make-up of the presentation unit.   Every story is made up of an alternation of presentation units and plot crises.   Together these make an architectural norm.   It is by now, I trust, evident that the presentation units are those portions of a story which are concerned primarily with the characterization of the people in the story, and particularly with the main actor in the story.

It is better for the moment to confine ourselves for illustration to those presentation units which occur in the Body of the Story, rather than to those presentation units which occur in the other divisions.   Turn first to the *Adventure of Ulysses*.   The responses of Ulysses indicated on lines 226 to 243 show him acting in such a way as to indicate what the author calls on line 233 "manly wisdom."   On lines 244 to 297 Ulysses' responses are again shown; but in addition to this there are shown the responses of the Cyclop. From lines 297 to 336 the responses are those of Ulysses and of the Cyclop.   From lines 337 to 357 the responses shown are those of the Cyclop Polyphemus and those of his brethren on the outside.

A consideration of these is ample for our purpose. They disclose that the presentation units are concerned with meetings or interchanges involving character responses that lead into plot crises. They further disclose that these responses may be the responses of any actors whatsoever in the story; and further they show that the turning points or crises may be led into through a presentation unit which includes the responses of actors other than the main actor, as in the case of the interchange between Polyphemus and his brethren on the outside of the cave, which makes up one of the presentation units.

Characterization reduced to its simplest elements is showing, by the responses to stimuli, the kind of person an actor is. In fact, this formula for characterization follows through into the most complex reaches of characterization. The character's responses can be shown by what he does, by what he says, and by what he thinks. It can be shown also by the effect of his action or his personality upon others. Anything that brings out any responses whatsoever is a stimulus to an actor in a story. It is axiomatic that no actor in a story can respond to a stimulus without becoming aware of that stimulus. So that basically, every character response of an actor to a stimulus involves a contact with or meeting with that stimulus. That is why I have said that in the presentation unit the writers will present meetings and interchanges.

A meeting does not necessarily involve an interchange, although it very often does. There are three kinds of meetings two of which are interchanges. It is essential that you learn to distinguish between these three kinds of meetings, because each one has its own special use in a presentation unit; and for that reason I am going to ask you to employ a very definite and rigid nomenclature, which will enable you to avoid any difficulty of misunderstanding as to the meaning of what I shall say in the future about any of the stories in this volume.

For the first kind of meeting, then, the one which serves to show merely the reaction of the actors to a stimulus, the stimulus not reacting upon the actor I shall ask you to employ the word *incident*. The incident is the single act of a single actor reacting to a stimulus, the stimulus itself being inactive to the extent of having no design upon the actor. From lines 99 to 102 you can find an example of what I have in mind. The stimulus is the appearance of Polyphemus. The incident is that the Greeks hide themselves in the remote parts of the cave. Sometimes a response involves a series of incidents. The actor does more than one thing.

13

If you will turn to the story *Spare Parts*, Case No. 3, and read from line 612 to 639 you will get a clearer idea of what I have in mind. The actor is Monte. The stimulus of which he becomes aware is the proposal made by Carson Kerry. On lines 637 to 639 we find the response. "He merely got up and opened the door." If we are very meticulous we can say that there are two actions of a single force: 1. Monte got up. 2. Monte opened the door. It doesn't matter a bit. The point involved is that the response is rendered in terms of incident.

If you will turn to *Paradise Island*, Case No. 7, you will find that the first three lines include the single reaction of a single force to a stimulus. The stimulus is the ditch; the single response of Dwyer is to halt. It is rendered, "Dwyer halted at the ditch." It then goes on and says, "abruptly as though an invisible hand had seized his arm. An idea rang in his brain. This would be the place to kill a man." On line 5 you become aware of a purpose, that is, that Dwyer proposes to kill a man. In this the single act of a character in responding to a stimulus has projected a main narrative purpose. If you will read from line 124 of the same story to line 144 you will see that Dwyer again becomes aware of a stimulus, but this time instead of his response projecting a major crisis, it merely leads into an interchange between him and Mrs. Dwyer. This particular interchange, which closes on line 171, is an example of the second kind of meeting, which for the purpose of clarity I shall refer to hereafter as an Episode. An *episode* is the meeting of two forces involving an interchange without clash.

In *Spare Parts*, lines 284 to 342 contain an interchange which varies from the one you have just examined in that it contains clash. For this particular kind of meeting,—an interchange, involving clash, I shall hereafter use the descriptive term *encounter*. You will recall that when I spoke of what is dramatic I said that conflict is dramatic,—conflict or clash. And you will notice that I have said here that the distinguishing quality which differentiates an Encounter from an Episode is that the Encounter is an interchange that is dramatic.

You see now that in the presentation unit you have three ways in which you can show the response of an actor to stimuli. One, the meeting where the actor is alone and responds by a series of actions. The other, in which the actor is not alone but is concerned in an interchange with somebody else. When the force is kindly the interchange is an Episode. When the force is unfriendly, and the two clash, the interchange is then dramatic, and is called an Encounter.

14

A word or two more and we shall have done forever, I trust, with nomenclature. I shall ask you to read lines 1 to 60 of the story *Spare Parts* and then turn to lines 606 to 649. Both of these are interchanges with clash and would be set down under the categories we have just discussed as Encounters. The difference between these two Encounters and the other Encounter on lines 284 to 342 is that there is in each of these other two Encounters a central unifying purpose, which is never lost sight of throughout the interchange. On lines 731 to 751 there is also an interchange, which is an Episode, which has the same unification of purpose. In this case Monte purposes to get information from the mechanic Mac. In the interchange which opens the story between Carson Kerry and Sally the purpose of Carson Kerry is to dissuade Sally from a course of conduct which she proposes to adopt. In the interchange between Carson and Monte beginning on line 606 the purpose of Carson is to persuade Monte to adopt a course of conduct, that is, to accept the bribe. You will recall that I said that whenever a purpose is apparent there is narrative interest. Whenever clash or the promise of clash is apparent there is dramatic interest, so that there may be interchanges which are narrative and interchanges which are dramatic, as well as interchanges which are both narrative and dramatic.

If one person proposes to another that that other adopt a course of conduct, the narrative unity is sustained until the reader knows whether or not the other actor has acceded to the proposal of the first one. Then that special narrative interest ceases. If during the process of the interchange, the two clash there is in addition to the narrative interest dramatic interest. If there is no clash the interest must be narrative throughout, and the interchange is episodic instead of dramatic.

You will see now that an Incident can grow into other Incidents, and a series of Incidents may result without any interchange at all. But usually such an interchange is bound to result from the accumulation of Incidents. This interchange may be episodic because no clash is involved; or it may become dramatic by the addition of clash. Therefore, we find that there is an ultimate unit called the *scene*, which involves, as a presentation unit, four steps:

1. The meeting.
2. The scene purpose, raising a minor or Scene Narrative Question.

3. The interchange, which may be either episodic or dramatic.
4. The Conclusive Act, which answers the minor or scene narrative question raised by that immediate purpose.

The interchange between Monte English and the mechanic is an episodic scene. The interchange between Monte and Carson Kerry, and the one between Carson Kerry and Sally are both dramatic scenes.

We have now completed our investigation of nomenclature and can proceed upon a ground of common understanding. Whenever the word "incident" is used it will be understood to mean the single act of a single force.

Whenever the word "episode" is used it will be understood to mean the interchange between two forces without clash.

Whenever the word "encounter" is used it will be understood to mean the interchange between two forces with clash.

Whenever the words "episodic scene" are used they will be understood to mean the friendly meeting of two forces one of whom has a purpose to which the other is not opposed.

Whenever the words "dramatic scene" are used they will be understood to mean the interchange between two actors, or an actor and a force, with clash growing out of the purpose of one actor.

With these distinctions between the different types of presentation unit clear in our minds we can establish an architectural concept that will be a norm for any Story of Accomplishment whatsoever. Individuality will be achieved by varying the number and the length of these presentation units. Such variation will be determined by the amount of material to be presented in order to make the reader aware of the plot crises. It is safe therefore to say that the author writes presentation units for the ultimate purpose of making the reader aware, at the close of each such unit, of one or more plot crises.

Architecturally then, a story is a series of blocks. Each of these is a presentation unit. The reader enjoys each for its own sake; but furnishes an additional enjoyment himself by realizing when he has finished reading each one, that it has a connection with a pattern or plot. He cannot do this until he is aware of a plot crisis. Unless the reader so responds, the writer is unsuccessful in achieving his artistic purpose.

The accompanying chart will serve as an architectural norm, showing the arrangement and proportioning of a typical short-story.

ARCHITECTURAL NORM CHART

THE BEGINNING

Condition.

- Presentation Unit No. 1, meeting or interchange. .... Promise of conflict to remove a difficulty. (Plot Crisis Type A).
- Presentation Unit No. 2, meeting or interchange. .... Promise of conflict to overcome an opponent. (Plot Crisis Type B.)
- Presentation Unit No. 3, meeting or interchange. ...... Promise of conflict to avert disaster. (Plot Crisis Type C.)

Response.

- Presentation Unit No. 4, meeting usually. .... The main actor's central purpose is clear to the reader. He phrases a main narrative question. (Plot Crisis Type D.)

THE BODY

Attempt.

- Foreshadowed conflict developed in dramatic scene. Type A. ...... Dramatic or narrative hindrance. (Plot Crisis Type E.)

Renewed Attempt.

- Foreshadowed conflict developed in dramatic scene. Type B. .... Dramatic or narrative hindrance. (Plot Crisis Type E.)

Renewed Attempt.

- Foreshadowed conflict developed in dramatic scene. Type C. .... Dramatic or narrative hindrance. (Plot Crisis Type E.

THE ENDING

The Conclusive Act.

- Meeting or interchange.

The main narrative question phrased by the reader is answered. (Plot Crisis Type F.)

The Sequel.

- Meeting or interchange.

Significance explained. (Plot Crisis Type G.)

A study of this chart will disclose certain enlightening information.

The Beginning contains two general subdivisions: the Condition or state of affairs, and the narrative response of the actor. In presenting the Beginning the author writes the necessary presentation units to make clear to the reader a Condition with dramatic possibilities. The reader on reading these presentation units becomes aware that the Condition so presented has dramatic promise, because it foreshadows conflicts.

In the chart I have chosen three such presentation units. At the close of each one I have indicated that there is a plot crisis, and that each of these plot crises differs somewhat from the others. They are all *dramatic* and not *narrative* crises.

Type A makes the reader aware of a Difficulty to be removed.

Type B makes the reader aware of an Opponent to be overcome.

Type C makes the reader aware of a Disaster to be averted.

It is from the Condition or State of Affairs, which is the first of the subdivisions of the Beginning, that the Plot acquires its *dramatic* interest. In the Beginning also, the author presents the necessary presentation units to show the *necessity for accomplishment by the chief actor*.

The reader, upon reading these units, becomes aware of a *narrative* interest. This projects the main narrative crisis of the story, which causes the reader to phrase for himself a main narrative question;

"Can A succeed in accomplishing (his purpose)?"

It is from the response of the central actor, which is the second of the sub-divisions of the Beginning, that the plot acquires its *narrative* interest. There can be no narrative interest until the reader is aware of the actor's purpose; because only when this purpose is apparent can the reader phrase for himself a main narrative question: "Can the chief actor succeed in accomplishing his purpose?" When the reader becomes aware of this purpose there is a fourth plot crisis (Type D.) It is not *dramatic*, but *narrative*.

Thus it appears that the Beginning has four plot crises; the first three, dramatic; the fourth, narrative. All of these crises come at the conclusion of presentation units. All of the crises are essential to the plot. All the Presentation Units are *not* essential. The Condition or State of Affairs may be set forth in one, two, or three presentation units. If all three *dramatic* plot crises can emerge from a single presentation unit, then one presentation unit is sufficient.

It is sometimes possible, in a single Presentation Unit to present the three dramatic plot crises of the Condition and the fourth plot or purpose crisis, which is narrative.

The norm, then, for the Beginning is:—Presentation Units necessary to set forth the Main Condition and the Chief Actor's main Purpose in such a way that the reader phrases for himself a Main Narrative Question and is aware of the Dramatic Crises which show the Promise of Conflict (a) to remove a Difficulty, (b) to overcome an Opposing Force, (c) to avert Disaster to the Main Purpose.

In the Body of the story the author writes such presentation units as will develop the conflicts foreshadowed in the Beginning by Plot Crises Types A, B, and C. Since there are three types of conflict possible I have indicated as a norm three presentation units. It will, however, be obvious that great variation is possible here.

The reader, at the close of each conflict so developed in an interchange (preferably a dramatic scene) is aware of a heightened interest in the main plot. His feeling of suspense is sustained at the close of each interchange by keeping the outcome of the main accomplishment in doubt through a plot crisis of *Hindrance*. This Hindrance (Type E Plot Crisis) may be either a *dramatic* or a *narrative* crisis. In a norm of three interchanges, in order that the expectations of the reader may be realized in respect to all three conflicts promised in the Beginning the first two attempts cannot meet with success; for such success would eliminate the necessity for the other conflicts.

Equally, if in the Beginning the Plot Crises A, B, and C have not been stressed they cannot be plausibly developed in the Body.

In the Ending, made up of the Conclusive Act and its Sequel, the author writes the necessary presentation units that will show the reader that the actor has achieved his main purpose or has abandoned it. This is the Conclusive Act.

Sometimes, where this Conclusive Act is ambiguous, the author writes an additional presentation unit or units to explain the significance of the Conclusive Act. (In many stories, no such explanation is necessary; and there is, therefore, no sequel.)

The reader, having read the presentation units containing the Conclusive Act feels his narrative curiosity satisfied. The main narrative-question he has phrased is now answered. (Plot Crisis Type F.)

Having read the presentation units which set forth the Sequel, the reader feels his general curiosity satisfied. This is Plot Crisis Type G.

The Sequel is concerned with catching up loose ends. It is frequently the equivalent of the Moral of the older stories. Sometimes a story, being written merely to entertain, has no special significance, and, therefore, no sequel. Sometimes what slight significance a story possesses may be voiced in the final words of a character which are themselves the Conclusive Act.

In studying this chart, therefore, readers must regard it as a norm against which to measure short-stories. Variation is permitted in the size and number of the Presentation Units. In size they may vary from a single incident (presented as a meeting showing the single response of an actor to a stimulus), to a prolonged dramatic scene (involving the dramatic interchange between two forces whose purposes are definitely opposed).

The number of presentation units is dependent upon the size of each one.

The length of an average short-story is from six to ten thousand words; so that in the scope of that length much variation is possible. A story may achieve its length from any one of the three great divisions of Beginning, Body, or Ending. When we come to examine the stories in this volume we shall see some illuminating examples of this variation.

Since each of these divisions may vary in length, the number of Presentation Units in each division is variable. It will depend upon two factors: upon the length of each Presentation Unit, and upon the proportionate length of the division of which it forms a part.

Two general possibilities lie open to the writer of the short-story:

1. A large number of short presentation units, in a story whose interest is chiefly in the plot.
2. A smaller number of prolonged presentation units in a story in which the interest is chiefly in the dramatic quality of the scenes, with less emphasis upon the plot.

Loosely, the difference will be that the first will be a story of plot, and the second will be a story of character. The first will hold the reader through his interest in the person who is called upon to solve the problem. These distinctions are, as I said, loose and by no means rigid. The ideal story combines the two types, having a narrative problem which is in itself interesting, no matter what actor is called upon to solve it, and in addition presenting a chief actor whose responses enliven the interchanges of the presentation units.

You will notice that upon this norm chart I have indicated a series of presentation units, and have shown that at the close of each presentation unit there is a turning point or Crisis, which in every case is called the "fifth step." This would seem to indicate that the presentation units must always be composed of the four steps which make up a complete scene, thus:

Step 1. Meeting
Step 2. Purpose of Scene
Step 3. Interchange, either episodic or dramatic
Step 4. Conclusive Act of Scene

This is not a rigid requirement. The Presentation Unit at its fullest development includes these four steps; but sometimes some steps are omitted and the turning point or Plot Crisis, which is the fifth step, is reached swiftly. It is from this Fifth Step that the plot interest comes. It is a constant factor, even though some of the first four steps may be omitted. The first four steps are concerned with *Presentation* interest, the fifth step is concerned with *Plot* interest. When presentation interest is subordinated to plot interest, the presentation units are shortened by the omission of some of the steps. The Fifth Step will be either a narrative crisis of the plot, or a dramatic crisis of the plot. If a narrative turning point, it will indicate that there is a Furtherance or Hindrance to the attempt of the main actor to achieve his purpose. If it is a dramatic turning point it will show that even though a narrative Furtherance has occurred there is a dramatic turning point which promises Conflict or Disaster.

If you will turn again to *Spare Parts*, Case No. 3 you will see what I mean. Lines 606 to 650 are the first four steps of a Scene. Lines 606 to 615 constitute the first step, which is the contact or meeting of the two forces, Kerry and Monte. Lines 619 to 633 constitute the second step, which is the scene purpose, showing that Carson hopes to persuade Monte to lose the race. Lines 634 to 649 constitute the third step, which is the interchange with clash. Lines 650 and 652 constitute the fourth step, which is the Conclusive Act, showing the reader that Carson has been forced to abandon that immediate purpose of persuading Monte to accept a bribe to lose the race.

What I want you particularly to notice is that line 652 to line 654 are the fifth step of the Scene. The fifth step is used to show the effect of the presentation unit upon the actors, particularly as it affects the outcome of the main narrative purpose. In this case the effect, or fifth step, is a dramatic crisis because it contains the promise of conflict with a dangerous opponent, that is, with a person who is likely to endanger the outcome of the main purpose of the story.

Examine with especial care also lines 655 to 673. They are an Episodic Scene because they include the steps necessary in such a presentation unit:—the meeting between Carson and the foreman; the purpose of Carson, which is to persuade the foreman to put the Vindix out of commission; an interchange, which is episodic because there is no clash; and a Conclusive Act, which is the man's statement, "All right. Leave it to me." This Episodic Scene is part of the fifth step of the preceding scene between Carson and Monte. It contributes the promise of disaster to the plot. The fifth step of this scene, therefore, begins on line 652 and ends on line 673, and it contains the promise of conflict with an opponent dangerous to the success of the whole enterprise, and a promise of disaster as well.

Thus the fifth step of a scene may be such an important turning point in the plot as to constitute *by itself* a complete presentation unit. Strictly speaking, every presentation unit after the first is part of the fifth step of that first presentation unit, because in the properly plotted story, everything which occurs should be the outgrowth of everything preceding it.

Every presentation unit has its fifth step in the plot unless the story is poorly plotted. In the plotted story there should be no presentation unit which does not lead into a fifth or plot step. The fifth or Plot Step is the effect or outcome of what has happened in the presentation unit. Thus for example, lines 674 to 730 are the fifth step of the Episodic Scene between the foreman and Carson Kerry. In analyzing stories you may be puzzled in an attempt to isolate this fifth step. You will be helped if you keep in mind that the fifth step is the outcome or the effect upon the Plot of the presentation unit, and may be itself a meeting or an interchange.

Thus your story may have plot interest or presentation interest in proportion as you stress either the fifth step or the interchange which at its highest point of development has four steps/ When it has four steps it is a Scene, and it may be dramatic just as a story is dramatic. The Dramatic Scene contains all the elements of a complete story. It is in fact a miniature short-story. It has its own scene narrative question, just as the story has its main narrative question. The complete story is made up of a number of these Scenes. Even though, sometimes, some of the steps of a scene are omitted, they cannot be omitted in all cases. Incomplete Scenes

22

are sometimes permissible, but no story can be made up entirely of incomplete Scenes. Some time in the course of your story you are going to be called upon to present a Dramatic Scene which is, as I have pointed out to you, built up from the basic structural unit of the Incident (the single act of the single force), which may be expanded gradually into:

1. Episode
2. Encounter
3. Episodic Scene
4. Dramatic Scene

Clearly then, if every story consists of a number of Scenes, in order to be able to write a short-story you must first be able to

(a) distinguish between story narrative questions and scene narrative questions,
(b) build up an Incident througn its different phases until it becomes a Dramatic Scene,
(c) present the Dramatic Scene convincingly so that the character or the actors emerge,
(d) indicate clearly to the reader at the close of each Scene, through its fifth step, even though the other steps are incomplete, the turning point or Plot Crisis which may be either dramatic or narrative.

If you depend upon the turning points of your plot for the chief interest of your story you may have in your presentation units incomplete scenes. On the other hand, if your chief interest is in the characterization of your actors you must depend for your interest largely upon the dramatic scene. Throughout each dramatic scene, through the actor's reaction to different stimuli, you will make his character clear to your reader. In the long run you will realize that characterization is everything in a story, and that your real reason for familiarizing yourself with structural devices is to acquire complete control of method in order that you may not be hampered by uncertainty as to method in rendering character through the medium of the dramatic scene in the modern short-story.

The chief aim of this book is to show you that the fundamental architectural conception of a short story is that it is a series of blocks, each block being a presentation unit which is either an incomplete scene or a dramatic scene. However, since no architectural conception of a story will *of itself* produce a story which is lifelike there must be within that architectural conception, that is, within those blocks, the breath of life which comes from convincing characterization of actors shown responding to various stimuli.

Characterization is the chief aim of the writer of the short-story. Without it his story is dead. It is made clear to the reader in presentation units, of which the dramatic scene is the highest development. For this reason, the value to you of knowing just what constitutes a scene is inestimable. A scene is a smaller unit than a complete story; yet in architectural conception it is the same. Being the same in essence as the complete story, having both narrative and dramatic interest, the dramatic scene gives you the opportunity for developing your plotting ability as well as your presentation ability. Just as the story has a Beginning, a Body, an Ending and a Sequel, so has the scene. It includes, just as the story does,

> An impression of the time, place, and social atmosphere;
> an impression of an actor's appearance;
> an impression of the various stimuli to which the actor responds.

Since the largest number of your scenes will be scenes in which the opposition to one actor is furnished by another actor, the second actor and his responses will be the stimuli to which the first one will respond. Thus the very first step in a dramatic scene of that kind will be to bring the two actors together, that is, to bring about a contact or meeting. You achieve narrative interest in this scene when you show your reader that one of the actors has a purpose. It may be to persuade the other to adopt a course of conduct. It may be to convince the other in some argument. It may be to impress the other with his own weakness or his own strength. It may be, and will very frequently be, to secure information from the other. In the so called "action-story," it will be an attempt to overcome by physical force. Just as in the story you achieve dramatic interest when you show the promise of opposition or disaster, so you achieve dramatic interest in your scene when you make clear to your reader that the second actor is opposed to the purpose of the first actor.

This promise of opposition or of clash to come makes up with the scene purpose the Beginning of the narrative scene. In plotting your dramatic scene you will keep in mind that the purpose of the first actor may grow out of the meeting with the second actor.' Ordinarily this will be the case, yet there are occasions on which the meeting will grow out of the purpose. For example, if A wishes to persuade a banker to loan him $2,000 he may go to that banker.

In this case the purpose will bring about the meeting; yet it is possible that A may not have thought of trying to borrow $2,000 from the banker until after he had met the banker who told him that money was rather easy at that particular moment. This knowledge may spur the first actor to a purpose of attempting to borrow $2,000 from the other. In that case, the purpose grew out of the meeting.

Whichever one you choose will make practically no difference in your scene. Plausibility will determine, in most cases. Yet, if the promise of opposition makes dramatic interest, it is a good idea to indicate that the opposition exists and then to indicate the purpose, so that the reader's interest will be heightened as soon as he learns that the purpose involves a clash or conflict with an opponent who is unlikely to accede to the request.

In plotting and presenting a dramatic scene you will endeavor to make the detail create the impression of being a reproduction of actual life. In giving your actor a purpose in the scene you will endeavor to reproduce the ordinary purposes which actuate people on every hand. In that way you will achieve verisimilitude, or the appearance of truth. The five purposes which I indicated in the second last paragraph are those purposes which you will find ordinarily actuate the average human being. Because this is so, the reader is able to find himself in sympathy with the actor in your story. As soon as such a common and usual purpose appears, the reader is caused to ask himself a scene narrative question.

Can actor A secure information from actor B?
Can actor A convince actor B?
Can actor A persuade actor B to adopt a course of conduct?
Can actor A impress actor B?
Can actor A overcome actor B?

Once you have enlisted the narrative interest of a reader in the scene purpose of an actor and have added dramatic interest as a hint of conflict or of failure because of the unlikelihood of the opponent agreeing with the actor, you have paved the way for the third step of your scene which is the interchange between the actor and his opponent. Because of the opposition which you have foreshadowed, it is quite evident that there will be clash in this interchange, and that it will be the kind of interchange which is an encounter.

In developing this type of interchange you will keep in mind that you have the possibility of developing both narrative and dramatic interest in that interchange. You preserve the narrative unity of that special scene by keeping the outcome of the actor's purpose in doubt. There will be no doubt, however, as to his purpose holding. The tendency of the amateur is to become so interested in the clash which ensues, that he allows the actor to lose sight of the special purpose. This, of course, the writer may do deliberately, but I am talking now about a tendency to be guarded against rather than one to be indulged.

In a scene, you achieve narrative unity by making every speech or act of actor A one which is intended to accomplish his object in the scene. Every such attempt is a Scene-Furtherance even though it does not promise success. Every speech or act of actor B will be intended to defeat the efforts or objective in the scene of actor A. Every such attempt to defeat the scene purpose is a scene hindrance.

By concentrating upon this narrative unity of the scene you almost unconsciously achieve dramatic interest in the interchange; because in order to achieve furtherance on the one hand and hindrance on the other, there must be a clash in the purposes of the two people even though there is no clash in their traits. At the close of this interchange one has either succeeded in his purpose or abandoned his purpose. In that case the Conclusive Act will show it.

Now if you will turn to the story *Once and Always*, Case No. 8, you will see from line 75 to 171 an illustration of what I mean. Lines 75 to 110 show the contact or meeting between Lemuel Gower and Gideon Higsbee, and the fact that each has responded in a different way to the three strangers indicate that they will clash in any purpose involving those three strangers. Thus you have the first step of the scene made dramatic by the promise of conflict. Immediately there grows out of this meeting or contact a purpose of one of the actors. In this case the actor whose purpose emerges is Lemuel Gower. The purpose is to persuade Gideon to adopt a course of conduct,—to go over and speak to the strangers.

From then on the interchange involves furtherances and hindrances of that purpose. Every attempt of Lemuel to bring about his purpose is a furtherance, every attempt of Gideon to defeat that purpose is a hindrance. The interchange continues to the end of line 153. On the next line the interchange is over through the Conclusive Act and speech of Lemuel when he says, "Well, if you won't speak to 'em, I will," and walks across the lobby of the Agamemnon House, "with his rubber shoes making an honest sound upon the floor." This is an example of a Scene containing the four steps which are essential to every Scene.

Lines 162 to 171 include the fifth step by showing the reflections of the actor upon what has just passed. The fifth step of any Scene is made up of the effect of the Scene upon the actor. It may involve his thoughts, it may involve action growing out of his reflections. Sometimes the reflections are omitted and the action follows without any indication of thoughts preceding it. In this case the effect is that Gideon watches Lemuel go; and he sums up his conclusions regarding what has just passed in the phrase, "Once a sucker, always a sucker."

Sometimes, in a scene, the special purpose of the actor does not immediately emerge. In the Scene which you have just examined the purpose emerges at once. But I want you now to look at another scene in which the main purpose is led up to through an interchange of conversation. This Scene you will find in the same story, *Once and Always*, on lines 917 to 1235. This Scene has its complete four steps. It has the meeting between Lemuel and Gideon. Before this in the story you have been told by the author that Gideon feels that Lemuel may be foolish enough not to take back the money, so that there is the hint of opposition. When Gideon first goes in, the main purpose does not emerge, but the interchange is concerned with his securing information from Lemuel as to his present financial status. Not until line 1114 when this information has been secured, does Gideon's real purpose emerge. He says, "And that's what I'm here for now, Lemuel, because I did know. I guess it hadn't occurred to me until the other day; but I guess I cheated you just as much as they did." From then on the interchange is concerned with Gideon's attempt to restore the money to Lemuel, and with Lemuel's arguments against taking the money. The conclusive act comes on line 1228 when Lemuel acts. "He seized Gideon's hand, and pressed something into Gideon's palm. Gideon felt it. It was the check. 'Honest Gid,' said Lemuel, 'Take it back. I couldn't keep it. I'm gettin' to be an old man Gid, and my conscience wouldn't let me.'" Thus we see the four steps of the scene completed and we see the fifth step, the effect upon the actors, is expanded into another interchange between Gideon and his friend George on lines 1236 to 1270.

Before turning to a detailed discussion of each of the stories I have chosen as a case in craftsmanship, I should like to say a word as to the reasons which dictated their choice. I have long been convinced that no one writer combines ultimate perfection in any single story. Yet I have been equally convinced that perfection comes from either presentation or plotting, that a writer's capacity may be judged by his ability to achieve his effect either through the medium of the first four steps of a scene, which is presentation, or through the medium of the fifth steps of his Scenes, which is plotting. But one thing must be clear. It is that if the fifth step is neglected in the scene, the other four steps must make up the deficiency, or, if the four steps are slighted, the deficiency must be made up in the fifth.

You will find when you examine these stories that in some cases there are present the lacks which I have pointed out. I take this occasion to make clear my position, which is, that this is not by any means a collection of "Best Short Stories." It is a collection of craftsmanlike stories by competent authors, each story selected because it contained examples which writers may well follow when they are confronted by special problems of craftsmanship.

When a lawyer is asked for an opinion upon a point of law he first determines the principle involved, and then examines the findings in cases involving this principle. Authorities upon certain phases of the law have first determined a norm for such cases and then have considered the departures from this norm which are caused by variations in special cases. Up to now we have been considering the norm of the story of accomplishment. From now on, in a detailed examination of each of the cases in this book, we shall consider the variations from that norm, so that, should you have material in mind about whose plotting and presentation you are in doubt, you may be able to turn to this book with the knowledge that you will find therein an example of a story whose author was confronted with the very same technical problems of craftsmanship which your material presents to you.

In the second section of this book we shall discuss the Story of Decision.

THE ADVENTURE OF ULYSSES WITH THE CYCLOP

BY CHARLES LAMB

My reason for including in the Case Book the story of *The Adventure of Ulysses* when he meets the Cyclop is that it serves as an excellent example of how far back into the history of the human race goes the quality of narrative interest. I want you to see that it existed as long ago as the time of Homer. This story is especially valuable as showing that the quality of narrative has not changed since that time, and that it cannot ever change. The same thing applies to the quality of drama.

Authorities upon Greek literature tell us that when they first had circulation, the various adventures of Ulysses which go to make up the complete collection known as the Odyssey were all separate adventures, not then connected through a central character. Homer's artistry brought together disconnected elements of a narrative and welded them into a coherent, unified whole. He made out of these different and disconnected adventures a centralized narrative by causing Ulysses to be, throughout the series, the central actor, and by giving Ulysses a definite central purpose which tied together all these adventures. That purpose was to return to Ithaca where his wife, Penelope, awaited him.

Except that its length rules it out, it would be possible to regard the whole series of *The Adventures of Ulysses* as a single short-story. For that reason I am taking this single adventure of Ulysses and the Cyclop, which at first stood alone as a separate tale of the prowess of an individual, in order to illustrate the basic form of narrative. It will show, especially, the difference between plot outline and presentation. In plot outline, narrative never changes, and never can change.

This particular *Adventure of Ulysses and the Cyclop* has, in its presentation, undergone at least three metamorphoses. Appearing, originally, as a folk-tale, it was developed by Homer to fit into his collection of adventures which made up his Odyssey. Chapman translated the Odyssey into English. Charles Lamb abridged this translation still further into a collection of tales which he called *The Adventures of Ulysses*. "The groundwork of the story," says Lamb, in his preface, "is as old as the Odyssey." (The text here given is from *The Works of Charles Lamb*, edited by Percy Fitzgerald, London: E. Moxon & Co., 1876.)

31

CASE No. 1

THE ADVENTURE OF ULYSSES

BY CHARLES LAMB

1 Coasting on all that night by
2 unknown and out-of-the-way
3 shores, they came by daybreak
4 to the land where the Cyclops
5 dwell, a sort of giant shepherds
6 that neither sow nor plough, but
7 the earth untilled produces for
8 them rich wheat and barley and
9 grapes; yet they have neither
10 bread nor wine, nor know the
11 arts of cultivation, nor care to
12 know them; for they live each
13 man to himself, without laws or
14 government, or anything like a
15 state or kingdom; but their
16 dwellings are in caves, on the
17 steep heads of mountains; every
18 man's household governed by
19 his own caprice, or not governed
20 at all; their wives and children
21 as lawless as themselves, none
22 caring for others, but each doing
23 as he or she thinks good. Ships
24 or boats they have none, nor
25 artificers to make them, no trade
26 or commerce, or wish to visit
27 other shores; yet they have con-
28 venient places for harbors and
29 for shipping. Here Ulysses with
30 a chosen party of twelve follow-
31 ers landed, to explore what sort
32 of men dwelt there, whether
33 hospitable and friendly to stran-
34 gers, or altogether wild and
35 savage, for as yet no dwellers
36 appeared in sight.

37 The first sight of habitation
38 which they came to was a giant's
39 cave rudely fashioned, but of a
40 size which betokened the vast
41 proportions of its owners; the
42 pillars which supported it being
43 the bodies of huge oaks or pines,
44 in the natural state of the tree,
45 and all about showed more
46 marks of strength than skill in
47 whoever built it. Ulysses, enter-
48 ing in, admired the savage con-
49 trivances and artless structure of
50 the place, and longed to see the
51 tenant of so outlandish a man-
52 sion; but well conjecturing that
53 gifts would have more avail in
54 extracting courtesy than strength
55 would succeed in forcing it, from
56 such a one as he expected to find
57 the inhabitant, he resolved to
58 flatter his hospitality with a
59 present of Greek wine, of which
60 he had store in twelve great

vessels, so strong that no one ever drank it without an infusion of twenty parts of water to one of wine, yet the fragrance of it was even then so delicious that it would have vexed a man who smelled it to abstain from tasting it; but whoever tasted it, it was able to raise his courage to the height of heroic deeds. Taking with him a goat-skin flagon full of this precious liquor, they ventured into the recesses of the cave. Here they pleased themselves a whole day with beholding the giant's kitchen, where the flesh of sheep and goats lay strewed; his dairy, where goat-milk stood ranged in troughs and pails; his pens, where he kept his live animals; but those he had driven forth to pasture with him when he went out in the morning. While they were feasting their eyes with a sight of these curiosities, their ears were suddenly deafened with a noise like the falling of a house. It was the owner of the cave, who had been abroad all day feeding his flock, as his custom was, in the mountains, and now drove them home in the evening from pasture. He threw down a pile of firewood, which he had been gathering against supper-time, before the mouth of the cave, which occasioned the crash they heard. The Grecians hid themselves in the remote parts of the cave at sight of the uncouth monster. It was Polyphemus, the largest and savagest of the Cyclops, who boasted himself to be the son of Neptune. He looked more like a mountain crag than a man, and to his brutal body he had a brutish mind answerable. He drove his flock, all that gave milk, to the interior of the cave, but left the rams and the he-goats without. Then, taking up a stone so massive that twenty oxen could not have drawn it, he placed it at the mouth of the cave to defend the entrance, and sat him down to milk his ewes and his goats; which done, he lastly kindled a fire, and throwing his great eye round the cave (for the Cyclops have no more than one eye, and that placed in the midst of their forehead), by the glimmering light he discerned some of Ulysses's men.

"Ho! guests, what are you? Merchants or wandering thieves?" he bellowed out in a voice which took from them all power of reply, it was so astounding.

Only Ulysses summoned resolution to answer, that they came neither for plunder nor traffic, but were Grecians who had lost their way, returning from Troy; which famous city, under the conduct of Agamemnon, the renowned son of Atreus, they had sacked, and laid level with the ground. Yet now they prostrated themselves humbly before his feet, whom they acknowledged to be mightier than they, and besought him that he would bestow the rites of hospitality upon them, for that Jove was the avenger of wrongs done to strangers, and would fiercely resent any injury which they might suffer.

"Fool!" said the Cyclop, "to come so far to preach to me the fear of the gods. We Cyclops care not for your Jove, whom you fable to be nursed by a goat, nor any of your blessed ones. We are stronger than they, and dare bid open battle to Jove himself, though you and all your fellows of the earth join with him." And he bade them tell him where their ship was in which they came, and whether they had any companions. But Ulysses, with a wise caution, made answer that they had no ship or companions, but were unfortunate men, whom the sea, splitting their ship in pieces, had dashed upon his coast, and they alone had escaped. He replied nothing, but gripping two of the nearest of them, as if they had been no more than children, he dashed their brains out against the earth, and, shocking to relate, tore in pieces their limbs and devoured them, yet warm and trembling, making a lion's meal of them, lapping the blood; for the Cyclops are maneaters, and esteem human flesh to be a delicacy far above goat's or kid's; though by reason of their ab-horred customs few men approach their coast, except some stragglers, or now and then a shipwrecked mariner.

At a sight so horrid, Ulysses and his men were like distracted people. He, when he had made an end of his wicked supper, drained a draught of goat's milk down his prodigious throat, and lay down and slept among his goats.

Then, Ulysses drew his sword, and half resolved to thrust it with all his might in at the bosom of the sleeping monster; but wiser thoughts restrained him, else they had there without help all perished, for none but Polyphemus himself could have removed that mass of stone which he had placed to guard the entrance. So they were constrained to abide all that night in fear.

When day came, the Cyclop awoke, and kindling a fire, made his breakfast of two other of his unfortunate prisoners; then milked his goats as he was accustomed, and pushing aside the vast stone, and shutting it again when he had done, upon the prisoners, with as much ease as a man opens and shuts a quiver's lid, he let out his flock, and drove them before him with whistlings (as sharp as winds in storms) to the mountains.

Then Ulysses, of whose strength or cunning the Cyclop seems to have had as little heed

35

229 as of an infant's, being left alone,
230 with the remnant of his men
231 which the Cyclop had not
232 devoured, gave manifest proof
233 how far manly wisdom excels
234 brutish force. He chose a stake
235 from among the wood which the
236 Cyclop had piled up for firing,
237 in length and thickness like a
238 mast, which he sharpened and
239 hardened in the fire; and selected
240 four men, and instructed them
241 what they should do with this
242 stake, and made them perfect
243 in their parts.

244 When the evening was come,
245 the Cyclop drove home his
246 sheep; and as fortune directed it,
247 either of purpose, or that his
248 memory was overruled by the
249 gods to his hurt (as in the issue
250 it proved), he drove the males
251 of his flock, contrary to his
252 custom, along with the dams
253 into the pens. Then shutting
254 to the stone of the cave, he fell
255 to his horrible supper. When he
256 had despatched two more of the
257 Grecians, Ulysses waxed bold
258 with the contemplation of his
259 project and took a bowl of
260 Greek wine, and merrily dared
261 the Cyclop to drink.

262 "Cyclop," he said, "take a
263 bowl of wine from the hand of
264 your guest: it may serve to digest
265 the man's flesh that you have
266 eaten, and show what drink our
267 ship held before it went down.
268 All I ask in recompense, if you
269 find it good, is to be dismissed in
270 a whole skin. Truly, you must
271 look to have few visitors, if you
272 observe this new custom of eat-
273 ing your guests."

274 The brute took and drank, and
275 vehemently enjoyed the taste of
276 wine, which was new to him,
277 and swilled again at the flagon,
278 and entreated for more, and
279 prayed Ulysses to tell him his
280 name, that he might bestow a
281 gift upon the man who had given
282 him such brave liquor. The
283 Cyclops, he said, had grapes, but
284 this rich juice, he swore, was
285 simply divine. Again Ulysses
286 plied him with the wine, and the
287 fool drank it as fast as he poured
288 it out, and again he asked the
289 name of his benefactor, which
290 Ulysses, cunningly dissembling
291 said, "My name is Noman: my
292 kindred and friends in my own
293 country call me Noman."

294 "Then," said the Cyclop, "this
295 is the kindness I will show thee,
296 Noman: I will eat thee last of
297 all thy friends." He had scarce
298 expressed his savage kindness,
299 when the fumes of the strong
300 wine overcame him, and he reeled
301 down upon the floor and sank
302 into a dead sleep.

303 Ulysses watched his time,
304 while the monster lay insensible;
305 and, heartening up his men,
306 they placed the sharp end of the
307 stake in the fire till it was heated
308 red-hot; and some god gave
309 them a courage beyond that
310 which they were used to have,
311 and the four men with difficulty
312 bored the sharp end of the huge

313 stake, which they had heated
314 red-hot, right into the eye of the
315 drunken cannibal; and Ulysses
316 helped to thrust it in with all his
317 might still further and further,
318 with effort, as men bore with an
319 auger, till the scalded blood
320 gushed out, and the eyeball
321 smoked, and the strings of the
322 eye cracked as the burning
323 rafter broke in it, and the eye
324 hissed as hot iron hisses when it
325 is plunged into water.

326 He, waking, roared with the
327 pain so loud that all the cavern
328 broke into claps like thunder.
329 They fled, and dispersed into
330 corners. He plucked the burn-
331 ing stake from his eye, and
332 hurled the wood madly about
333 the cave. Then he cried out
334 with a mighty voice for his
335 brethren the Cyclops, that dwelt
336 hard by in caverns upon hills.
337 They, hearing the terrible shout,
338 came flocking from all parts to
339 inquire what ailed Polyphemus,
340 and what cause he had for mak-
341 ing such horrid clamors in the
342 night-time to break their sleeps;
343 if his fright proceeded from any
344 mortal; if strength or craft had
345 given him his death-blow. He
346 made answer from within, that
347 Noman had hurt him, Noman
348 had killed him, Noman was
349 with him in the cave. They
350 replied, "If no man has hurt thee
351 and no man is with thee, then
352 thou art alone; and the evil that
353 afflicts thee is from the hand of
354 heaven, which none can resist or

help." So they left him, and 355
went their way, thinking that 356
some disease troubled him. He, 357
blind, and ready to split with 358
the anguish of the pain, went 359
groaning up and down in the 360
dark, to find the door-way; 361
which when he found, he re- 362
moved the stone, and sat in the 363
threshold, feeling if he could lay 364
hold on any man going out with 365
the sheep, which (the day now 366
breaking) were beginning to 367
issue forth to their accustomed 368
pastures. But Ulysses, whose 369
first artifice in giving himself 370
that ambiguous name had suc- 371
ceeded so well with the Cyclop, 372
was not of a wit so gross to be 373
caught by that palpable device. 374
But casting about in his mind 375
all the ways which he could 376
contrive for escape (no less than 377
all their lives depending on the 378
success), at last he thought of 379
this expedient. He made knots 380
of the osier twigs upon which the 381
Cyclop commonly slept, with 382
which he tied the fattest and 383
fleeciest of the rams together, 384
three in a rank; and under the 385
middle ram he tied a man, and 386
himself last, wrapping himself 387
fast with both his hands in the 388
rich wool of one, the fairest of 389
the flock. 390

And now the sheep began to 391
issue forth very fast; the males 392
went first, the females, un- 393
milked, stood by, bleating and 394
requiring the hand of their 395
shepherd in vain to milk them, 396

397 their full bags sore with being
398 unemptied, but he much sorer
399 with the loss of sight. Still, as
400 the males passed, he felt the
401 backs of those fleecy fools, never
402 dreaming that they carried his
403 enemies under them; so they
404 passed on till the last ram came
405 loaded with his wool and Ulysses
406 together. He stopped that ram
407 and felt him, and had his hand
408 once in the hair of Ulysses, yet
409 knew it not; and he chid the
410 ram for being last, and spoke to
411 it as if it understood him, and
412 asked it whether it did not wish
413 that its master had his eye again,
414 which the abominable Noman
415 with his execrable rout had put
416 out, when they had got him
417 down with wine; and he willed
418 the ram to tell him whereabouts
419 in the cave his enemy lurked,
420 that he might dash his brains
421 and strew them about, to ease
422 his heart of that tormenting
423 revenge which rankled in it.
424   After a deal of such foolish
425 talk to the beast, he let it go.
426   When Ulysses found himself
427 free, he let go his hold, and
428 assisted in disengaging his
429 friends. The rams which had
430 befriended them they carried off
431 with them to the ships, where
432 their companions with tears in

433 their eyes received them, as men
434 escaped from death. They plied
435 their oars and set their sails, and
436 when they were got as far off
437 from shore as a voice could
438 reach, Ulysses cried out to the
439 Cyclop: "Cyclop, thou shouldst
440 not have so much abused thy
441 monstrous strength as to
442 devour thy guests. Jove by my
443 hand sends thee requital to pay
444 thy savage inhumanity." The
445 Cyclop heard, and came forth
446 enraged, and in his anger he
447 plucked a fragment of a rock
448 and threw it with blind fury at
449 the ships. It narrowly escaped
450 lighting upon the bark in which
451 Ulysses sat, but with the fall it
452 raised so fierce an ebb as bore
453 back the ship till it almost
454 touched the shore. "Cyclop,"
455 said Ulysses, "if any ask thee
456 who imposed on thee that un-
457 sightly blemish in thine eye,
458 say it was Ulysses, son of
459 Laertes: the king of Ithaca am I
460 called, the master of cities."
461 Then they crowded sail, and beat
462 the old sea, and forth they went
463 with a forward gale; and sad for
464 fore-past losses, yet glad to have
465 escaped at any rate; till they
466 came to the isle where Æolus
467 reigned, who is god of the winds.

THE ANALYSIS

The first step in analyzing a story is to determine the amount of space devoted to each of the three major divisions of Beginning, Body, and Ending. In *The Adventure of Ulysses*, the Beginning occupies 211 lines. The Body of the story occupies lines 212 to 423, closing with the words "revenge rankled in it." The Ending of the story occupies lines 424 to 467, and includes the Conclusive Act and the Sequel. The Conclusive Act is on lines 424 to 425: "after a deal of such foolish talk to the beast, he let it go." The Sequel occupies the remainder of the lines.

The Beginning, which has as one of its functions the setting forth of the Condition or state of affairs, devotes to it the first 198 lines, ending with the words, "slept among his goats."

The function of this part of the Beginning is to acquaint the reader with the line up of forces; to indicate to him the possibilities of success or failure should an attempt be made to change this Condition; but particularly to foreshadow for him the dramatic quality of the meetings or interchanges that will take place in the Body of the story, should the hero set out to overcome difficulties, to overcome opposing forces, or to avert disaster. Let us now examine the units employed by Charles Lamb in presenting this condition or state of affairs. We will find first a series of incidents, and then a dramatic scene. Out of these grows the main purpose of Ulysses. Lines 1 to 83 comprise the incidents which show the response of Ulysses to the place in which he finds himself, closing with the words, "went out in the morning."

Following this, beginning with the words, "While they were feasting their eyes," on line 84, and continuing to line 198, concluding with the words, "among his goats," the author employs a dramatic scene between Ulysses and the Cyclop. In this scene the narrative unity is not sustained because a central purpose does not carry through the interchange. We are aware first of the purpose of the Cyclop to get information from Ulysses and his followers. Ulysses' purpose then emerges,—to impress the Cyclop. This attempt to impress does not succeed. Rather, it angers the Cyclop, who then proceeds to ask for further information which Ulysses does not furnish him. He concludes the scene by the action of killing and eating the two Greeks. The fifth step of this scene is the effect upon the actors, lines 191 to 198; as it affects Ulysses and his men; they are "like distracted people"; and as it affects the Cyclop, he is shown quite callously unconcerned, because "he lay down and slept among his goats." This fifth step then proceeds into the plot by furnishing a narrative problem which gives unity to everything throughout the story. It is the determination of Ulysses to escape. This is indicated on lines 199 to 211, together with the difficulty involved in the task. It could have been a little more plainly stated, though it is fairly evident and implied in the natural response any actor would make to such a state of affairs.

Here in a series of incidents all closely connected, and a single narrative scene, the author has set forth the main narrative problem, together with the promise of difficulty which lies in the imprisonment, the promise of conflict with a dangerous opponent, who is Polyphemus, and the danger of disaster in case the attempt should fail, which is shown by the great strength of Polyphemus, his savagery, and his cannibalistic habits.

Objection may be raised to the fact that there is no description of Ulysses. But this is not a sound objection in the light of our knowledge that this is only one of a series of adventures, and that before Ulysses was shown embarking upon these different adventures he was described. What about the requirement that the Beginning shall contain the line up of the forces which will give an indication of the capacities of the actors to carry on the combat. This requirement is quite well met. Ulysses' character and the character of the Cyclop are both shown by the way in which they react to different stimuli. It is necessary in plotting a short story that the Ending shall justify the reading of the story; that the reader shall feel that the person who is confronted by the condition which makes up the Beginning, could have solved the problem or accomplished the purpose only in the manner in which he does. Everything that an actor does in a story is his response to a stimulus, and every response of an actor to a stimulus is a characteristic or trait of his character in action. It is extremely important that you remember, in plotting your story, that the trait of character which ends the story shall be planted early in the story. If the story is ended by the use of some capacity or ability, then this capacity or ability should be planted early in the story. If the story is ended by the use of some device or some weapon, the presence of this weapon or this device should be planted early in the story. With this in mind, let us glance once more at the *Adventure of Ulysses*. Ulysses finally brings about his escape through his ingenuity and resource. Now let us see what characteristics of Ulysses are displayed by his first responses to stimuli. Ulysses is shown as cautious, because he goes first with his party of twelve to explore, in order to discover whether the dwellers are friendly and hospitable to strangers or altogether wild and savage. (See lines 29 and 36.) He is no fool; he does not rush into danger. This trait of caution is again evidenced on line 52, when although he desires to see the tenant, he conjectures that "gifts would have more avail in extracting courtesy than strength would succeed in forcing it." Here we find not only the resourcefulness, but we find also, on line 59, the weapon or device which he uses, which is the Greek wine which has a large part in bringing about the escape. We also find that Ulysses keeps in mind always that he must not give himself away to the Cyclop, and lines 133 to 173 are occupied in bringing out this trait in the character of Ulysses.

We find also that when he becomes aware of the condition, although his first impulse is courageous, wiser thoughts restrain him, because he sees in rashness the threat of disaster.

We may say therefore that this is a good Beginning because it contains all the necessary elements to foreshadow an interesting conflict of which the outcome is likely to remain in doubt. Besides this, the threat of disaster hangs over the whole story.

The greater the threat of disaster, the more interesting the story is. The wise author then, will so contrive his happenings growing out of the Beginning, that they shall culminate in a big dramatic moment when disaster seems inevitable. The simplest way to do this is to take each one of the promises which is contained in the Beginning, to form from it a meeting or interchange which will result in a defeat for that particular attempt. Thus the promise of difficulty will furnish one scene or presentation unit for the Body of the story which would result in defeat. The promise of conflict with an opponent would form another scene for the Body of the story which would again result in defeat. The accumulation of these defeats would bring the main actor in the story close to disaster. Thence would be projected the big scene of the story, which would be the development of the third of the elements in the Beginning,— the promise or threat of disaster. This big scene would inevitably be an attempt to avert this imminent disaster.

Now let us see how this norm is carried out in the *Adventure of Ulysses*. The difficulty of course, in the story, is that the Greeks are so manifestly handicapped by lack of weapons. The first attempt of Ulysses is an attempt to furnish them with weapons, and it occupies lines 226 to 243. Here we find the first weakness in the plot, because at this point it would have been so much stronger had emphasis been placed upon the outcome of the attempt as a hindrance, either dramatic or narrative. Since clearly the stake is a necessary weapon in the solution of the story, the attempt to furnish such a weapon must succeed. It will therefore be a narrative furtherance to the main purpose, but a dramatic hindrance could have been indicated had the author said, or caused one of the characters to say, that, although the weapon was there, the chances were ninety-nine out of one hundred that they would be unable to use it before the giant could exercise his strength. The fifth step could then be a colloquy between Ulysses and his followers, in which Ulysses announced his intention of reducing the giant to such a state that he would be unable to resist. This promise of conflict would then be developed into what is now the scene in the Body of the story occupying lines 244 to 297. This is a dramatic scene which could have been much stronger had it been prepared for, that is, the unity of the plot could have been strengthened. The unity of the plot can always be strengthened by making the fifth step of any attempt or presentation unit contain a hindrance and a promise of future conflict which is likely to result in disaster if the attempt is unsuccessful. The next scene then develops this promise contained in the fifth step of the preceding one. In this way the reader's interest is sustained both by the dramatic quality of the scene, and by the narrative quality of each scene by itself, in addition to being connectedly occupied by the main narrative question.

At the close of the scene between Ulysses and the Cyclop which results in a hindrance to Ulysses' main purpose, more could be made of dramatic promise of conflict were it indicated that the Cyclop did not go completely to sleep, but kept waking up and regarding Ulysses, from time to time, with suspicion, at every move of his prisoners. Interest in the ultimate outcome slumps because the prospect of success is too apparent. The conflict with the Cyclop is carried out in this scene and again in the scene where Ulysses and his followers, who are regarded as a single unit, succeed in putting out the eye of the Cyclop. This scene ends in a narrative furtherance, but it is instantly changed into a dramatic hindrance by the Cyclop's calling upon his brethren to come to his rescue. This could have been made more dramatically poignant by indicating the effect that such a shout must have had upon the Grecians, and all they must have felt upon realizing that even their gigantic effort had led only to the imminent probability of disaster. On line 387 beginning, "They, hearing the terrible shout, came flocking," and ending on line 355, "So they left him, and went their way," is a third scene of the Body which results in a narrative furtherance to the main narrative question because Ulysses here is successful in that his opponent is defeated. The weakness in the plotting of this scene is that Ulysses does not appear in it. Had

Ulysses urged the cyclops to say to his brethren, "Tell him that No-Man is here," Ulysses would then have brought about the result, whereas now it is brought about by a force not immediately acted upon by the main actor. There is, therefore, a lack of unity in the point of view which could have been avoided by causing Ulysses to be responsible for the outcome. There is also a weakness in causing the Cyclop, himself, to go to the doorway and sit on the threshold. Had Ulysses used his resourcefulness, of which he possessed a large store, the author could have then utilized the presentation unit to bring about the turning point in the plot, in such a way as to characterize the actor. Now he utilizes the presentation unit to bring about the turning point in the plot at the expense of characterizing the chief actor. Ulysses could easily have been made to taunt the Cyclop, and to challenge him to prevent Ulysses from escaping.

At the close of this scene, however, there is no question in the mind of the reader, that Ulysses is facing disaster, because although the Cyclop is blinded he is in the doorway, in such a position that he can lay hold on any man trying to go out. Thus, the fifth step of this scene is a dramatic hindrance. If you will look at the chart of this story you will see that the Beginning contains the essence of the scenes which make up the Body, with the exception of the scene between the Cyclop and his brethren. You will notice also that of the five units which now make up the Body of the story, the first one has no hindrance crisis indicated, the second, third, and fourth end in crises of hindrance, either narrative or dramatic, and that the accumulation of these hindrances brings the chief actor to the big moment of the story when it will be necessary for him to exert all his capacities in order to avert the disaster which was threatened in the Beginning.

Whenever you find that your story seems to drag in the Body you may rest assured of one of two things; either that the scenes are not in themselves interestingly dramatic, or that they do not in their crises increase the probability of disaster, and lead toward the big moment which projects the big scene of the story. This big scene is part of the Body. It is not the Ending. The Ending comes only when the reader is aware of the answer to the main narrative question. Thus, there are five scenes in the Body of this story. The first one is on lines 212 to 243; the second one is from line 244 to line 302; the third is from line 303 to line 336; the fourth is from line 337 to line 361; and the fifth is the big scene, or rather the series of incidents (it is not a scene in the strict sense),—the big presentation unit beginning on line 362 and ending on line 425. On line 425 there is also the Conclusive Act. It is what is known as a "contained" rather than an "appended" Ending. In another story I shall point out to you the difference between the contained and the appended Ending. The purpose of the writer in presenting the big scene of his story is to arouse in the reader an emotional feeling that all is about to be lost—that there is very little chance of success. The way that he can do this most effectually is to present it from the point of view and through the consciousness of the main actor. This particular series of happenings does not achieve its fullest emotional effect because the state of mind of Ulysses, as he sees the Cyclop handling the fleece of the animals, is not played up by the author. We do not, as readers, get the feeling that disaster is almost certain to ensue as we might be made to feel were we having the happenings presented to us as they affected Ulysses. A great deal could have been made of Ulysses' feeling of danger when he sees the Cyclop almost on the verge of discovering one of his companions, and the big moment in the story would have been when Ulysses felt the hand of the Cyclop touching his own hair, and believed all was lost.

This failure to develop the dramatic possibilities cannot be laid to Homer. Rather it is the fault of the translator, Charles Lamb, who tells the story objectively. We can say, in conclusion, regarding this story that it contains all the elements of a first rate modern short-story, but that they have not been developed in their presentation to the fullest possible extent.

THE COP AND THE ANTHEM

BEGINNING	Initial Condition and Main Actor's purpose are set forth.	Incidents. Soapy feels approach of winter.	1– 28	Main Narrative Question "Can Soapy succeed in securing ninety days at Blackwell's Island?"
		Soapy determines to be arrested.	29– 41	
		Condition amplified by author.	42–86	
BODY	Series of attempts of Main Actor to achieve his purpose. Attempts by opponents to prevent that achievement.	Soapy and Waiters.	87–144	Narrative Hindrance.
		Soapy (Smashes window) and policeman.	145–181	Narrative Hindrance.
		Soapy and hard-boiled waiter.	183–217	Narrative Hindrance.
		Soapy and girl.	218–288	Narrative Hindrance.
		Soapy (Yelling) and policeman.	289–324	Narrative Hindrance.
		Soapy and man with umbrella.	325–364	Narrative Hindrance.
		Soapy and condition.	365–420	
ENDING	Conclusive Act.	Soapy abandons purpose.	421–444	Main Narrative Question answered "No."
	Sequel.	Soapy and Policeman in churchyard.	445–453	Ironic Significance is shown.
		Soapy and Magistrate.	454–456	

THE COP AND THE ANTHEM

BY O. HENRY

THE story of the combined adventures of Ulysses, which make up the Odyssey, is in its totality a story of a man seeking a haven. It involves a meeting, from time to time, with a number of opponents or opposing forces, each one of which the man overcomes, until such time as he finally arrives in his haven. At the close of each such encounter, however, he is always worse off than before.

Because the story of O. Henry is a modern story of a man seeking a haven, and because it is an amusing and entertaining rather than a serious story, I have included it to show that the quality of narrative does not change; that what made good narrative in the days of Homer made good narrative in the days of O. Henry. In the Odyssey, the interest is in each of the meetings, rather than in the central narrative question of Ulysses returning to Penelope. In this particular story the interest lies in both the meetings and in the central attempt of Soapy to succeed in securing ninety days of winter on Blackwell's Island.

Now read the story, and after you have read it turn to the con ments which follow it.

CASE No. 2

THE COP AND THE ANTHEM

BY O. HENRY

On his bench in Madison Square Soapy moved uneasily. When wild geese honk high of nights, and when women without sealskin coats grow kind to their husbands, and when Soapy moves uneasily on his bench in the park, you may know that winter is near at hand.

A dead leaf fell in Soapy's lap. That was Jack Frost's card. Jack is kind to the regular denizens of Madison Square, and gives fair warning of his annual call. At the corners of four streets he hands his pasteboard to the North Wind, footman of the mansion of All Outdoors, so that the inhabitants thereof may make ready.

Soapy's mind became cognizant of the fact that the time had come for him to resolve himself into a singular Committee of Ways and Means to provide against the coming rigour. And therefore he moved uneasily on his bench.

The hibernatorial ambitions of Soapy were not of the highest. In them there were no considerations of Mediterranean cruises, of soporific Southern skies or drifting in the Vesuvian Bay. Three months on the Island was what his soul craved. Three months of assured board and bed and congenial company, safe from Boreas and bluecoats, seemed to Soapy the essence of things desirable.

For years the hospitable Blackwell's had been his winter quarters. Just as his more fortunate fellow New Yorkers had bought their tickets to Palm Beach and the Riviera each winter, so Soapy had made his humble arrangements for his annual hegira to the Island. And now the time was come. On the previous night three Sabbath newspapers, distributed beneath his coat, about his ankles and over his lap, had failed to repulse the cold as he slept on his bench near the spurting fountain in the ancient square. So the Island loomed big and timely in Soapy's mind. He scorned the provisions made in the name of charity for the city's dependents. In Soapy's opinion the Law was more benign than Philanthropy. There was an endless round of institutions, municipal and eleemosynary, on which he might set out and receive lodging and food accordant with the simple life. But to one of Soapy's proud spirits the gifts of charity are encumbered. If not in coin you must pay in humiliation of spirit for every benefit received at the hands of philanthropy. As Caesar had his Brutus, every bed of charity must have its toll of a bath, every loaf of bread its compensation of a private and personal inquisition. Wherefore it is better to be a guest of the law, which though conducted by rules, does not meddle unduly with a gentleman's private affairs.

Soapy, having decided to go to the Island, at once set about accomplishing his desire. There were many easy ways of doing this. The pleasantest was to dine luxuriously at some expensive restaurant; and then, after declaring insolvency, be handed over quietly and without uproar to a policeman. An accommodating magistrate would do the rest.

Soapy left his bench and strolled out of the square and across the level sea of asphalt, where Broadway and Fifth Avenue flow together. Up Broadway he turned, and halted at a glittering café, where are gathered together nightly the choicest products of the grape, the silkworm and the protoplasm.

Soapy had confidence in himself from the lowest button of his vest upward. He was shaven, and his coat was decent and his neat black, ready-tied four-in-hand had been presented to him by a lady missionary on Thanksgiving Day. If he could reach a table in the restaurant unsuspected success would be his. The portion of him that would show above the table would raise no doubt in the waiter's mind. A roasted mallard duck, thought Soapy, would be about the thing —with a bottle of Chablis, and then Camembert, a demi-tasse and a cigar. One dollar for the cigar would be enough. The total would not be so high as to call forth any supreme manifestation of revenge from the Café Management; and yet the meat would leave him filled and happy for the journey to his winter refuge.

But as Soapy set foot inside the restaurant door the head waiter's eye fell upon his frayed trousers and decadent shoes. Strong and ready hands turned him about and conveyed him in silence and haste to the sidewalk and averted the ignoble fate of the menaced mallard.

145 Soapy turned off Broadway.
146 It seemed that his route to the
147 coveted island was not to be an
148 epicurean one. Some other way
149 of entering limbo must be
150 thought of.

151 At a corner of Sixth Avenue
152 electric lights and cunningly
153 displayed wares behind plate-
154 glass made a shop window con-
155 spicuous. Soapy took a cobble-
156 stone and dashed it through the
157 glass. People came running
158 around the corner, a policeman
159 in the lead. Soapy stood still,
160 with his hands in his pockets,
161 and smiled at the sight of brass
162 buttons.

163 "Where's the man that done
164 that?" inquired the officer ex-
165 citedly.

166 "Don't you figure out that I
167 might have had something to
168 do with it?" said Soapy, not
169 without sarcasm, but friendly,
170 as one who greets good fortune.

171 The policeman's mind refused
172 to accept Soapy even as a clue.
173 Men who smash windows do not
174 remain to parley with the law's
175 minions. They take to their
176 heels. The policeman saw a
177 man half way down the block
178 running to catch a car. With
179 drawn club he joined in the
180 pursuit. Soapy, with disgust in
181 his heart, loafed along, twice
182 unsuccessful.

183 On the opposite side of the
184 street was a restaurant of no
185 great pretensions. It catered to
186 large appetites and modest

187 purses. Its crockery and at-
188 mosphere were thick; its soup
189 and napery thin. Into this place
190 Soapy took his accusive shoes
191 and telltale trousers without
192 challenge. At a table he sat and
193 consumed beefsteak, flapjacks,
194 doughnuts and pie. And then
195 to the waiter he betrayed the
196 fact that the minutest coin and
197 himself were strangers.

198 "Now, get busy and call a
199 cop," said Soapy. "And don't
200 keep a gentleman waiting."

201 "No cop for youse," said the
202 waiter, with a voice like butter
203 cakes and an eye like the cherry
204 in a Manhattan cocktail. "Hey,
205 Con!"

206 Neatly upon his left ear on the
207 callous pavement two waiters
208 pitched Soapy. He arose, joint
209 by joint, as a carpenter's rule
210 opens, and beat the dust from
211 his clothes. Arrest seemed but
212 a rosy dream. The Island
213 seemed very far away. A
214 policeman who stood before a
215 drug store two doors away
216 laughed and walked down the
217 street.

218 Five blocks Soapy travelled
219 before his courage permitted him
220 to woo capture again. This time
221 the opportunity presented what
222 he fatuously termed to himself
223 a "cinch." A young woman of
224 a modest and pleasing guise was
225 standing before a show window
226 gazing with sprightly interest at
227 its display of shaving mugs and
228 inkstands, and two yards from

51

229 the window a large policeman of
230 severe demeanour leaned against
231 a water plug.

232 It was Soapy's design to
233 assume the rôle of the despicable
234 and execrated "masher." The
235 refined and elegant appearance of
236 his victim and the contiguity of
237 the conscientious cop encouraged
238 him to believe that he would
239 soon feel the pleasant official
240 clutch upon his arm that would
241 insure his winter quarters on the
242 right little, tight little isle.

243 Soapy straightened the lady
244 missionary's ready - made tie,
245 dragged his shrinking cuffs into
246 the open, set his hat at a killing
247 cant and sidled toward the
248 young woman. He made eyes at
249 her, was taken with sudden
250 coughs and "hems," smiled,
251 smirked and went brazenly
252 through the impudent and con-
253 temptible litany of the
254 "masher." With half an eye
255 Soapy saw that the policeman
256 was watching him fixedly. The
257 young woman moved away a
258 few steps, and again bestowed
259 her absorbed attention upon the
260 shaving mugs. Soapy followed,
261 boldly stepping to her side,
262 raised his hat and said:

263 "Ah there, Bedelia. Don't
264 you want to come and play in
265 my yard?"

266 The policeman was still look-
267 ing. The persecuted young
268 woman had but to beckon a
269 finger and Soapy would be
270 practically en route for his

271 insular haven. Already he im-
272 agined he could feel the cozy
273 warmth of the station-house.
274 The young woman faced him
275 and, stretching out a hand,
276 caught Soapy's coat sleeve.

277 "Sure, Mike," she said joy-
278 fully, "if you'll blow me to a pail
279 of suds. I'd have spoke to you
280 sooner, but the cop was watch-
281 ing."

282 With the young woman play-
283 ing the clinging ivy to his oak
284 Soapy walked past the policeman
285 overcome with gloom. He seem-
286 ed doomed to liberty.

287 At the next corner he shook
288 off his companion and ran.

289 He halted in the district
290 where by night are found the
291 lightest streets, hearts, vows
292 and librettos. Women in furs
293 and men in greatcoats moved
294 gaily in the wintry air. A sud-
295 den fear seized Soapy that some
296 dreadful enchantment had ren-
297 dered him immune to arrest.
298 The thought brought a little of
299 panic with it, and when he came
300 upon another policeman loung-
301 ing grandly in front of a trans-
302 splendent theatre he caught at
303 the immediate straw of "dis-
304 orderly conduct."

305 On the sidewalk Soapy began
306 to yell drunken gibberish at the
307 top of his harsh voice. He
308 danced, howled, raved and other-
309 wise disturbed the welkin.

310 The policeman twirled his
311 club, turned his back to Soapy
312 and remarked to a citizen.

" 'Tis one of them Yale lads celebratin' the goose egg they give to the Hartford College. Noisy; but no harm. We've instructions to lave them be."

Disconsolate, Soapy ceased his unavailing racket. Would never a policeman lay hands on him? In his fancy the Island seemed an unattainable Arcadia. He buttoned his thin coat against the chilling wind.

In a cigar store he saw a well-dressed man lighting a cigar at a swinging light. His silk umbrella he had set by the door on entering. Soapy stepped inside, secured the umbrella and sauntered off with it slowly. The man at the cigar light followed hastily.

"My umbrella," he said, sternly.

"Oh, is it?" sneered Soapy, adding insult to petit larceny. "Well, why don't you call a policeman? I took it. Your Umbrella! Why don't you call a cop? There stands one on the corner."

The umbrella owner slowed his steps. Soapy did likewise, with a presentiment that luck would again run against him. The policeman looked at the two curiously.

"Of course," said the umbrella man—"that is—well, you know how these mistakes occur —I—if it's your umbrella I hope you'll excuse me—I picked it up this morning in a restaurant— If you recognise it as yours, why —I hope you'll——"

"Of course it's mine," said Soapy, viciously.

The ex-umbrella man retreated. The policeman hurried to assist a tall blonde in an opera cloak across the street in front of a street car that was approaching two blocks away.

Soapy walked eastward through a street damaged by improvements. He hurled the umbrella wrathfully into an excavation. He muttered against the men who wear helmets and carry clubs. Because he wanted to fall into their clutches, they seemed to regard him as a king who could do no wrong.

At length Soapy reached one of the avenues to the east where the glitter and turmoil was but faint. He set his face down this toward Madison Square, for the homing instinct survives even when the home is a park bench.

But on an unusually quiet corner Soapy came to a standstill. Here was an old church, quaint and rambling and gabled. Through one violet-stained window a soft light glowed, where, no doubt, the organist loitered over the keys, making sure of his mastery of the coming Sabbath anthem. For there drifted out to Soapy's ears sweet music that caught and held him transfixed against the convolutions of the iron fence.

The moon was above, lustrous

397 and serene; vehicles and pedes-
398 trians were few; sparrows twit-
399 tered sleepily in the eaves—for
400 a little while the scene might
401 have been a country church-
402 yard. And the anthem that the
403 organist played cemented Soapy
404 to the iron fence, for he had
405 known it well in the days when
406 his life contained such things as
407 mothers and roses and ambitions
408 and friends and immaculate
409 thoughts and collars.

410 The conjunction of Soapy's
411 receptive state of mind and the
412 influences about the old church
413 wrought a sudden and wonder-
414 ful change in his soul. He
415 viewed with swift horror the
416 pit into which he had tumbled,
417 the degraded days, unworthy
418 desires, dead hopes, wrecked
419 faculties and base motives that
420 made up his existence.

421 And also in a moment his heart
422 responded thrillingly to this
423 novel mood. An instantaneous
424 and strong impulse moved him
425 to battle with his desperate
426 fate. He would pull himself out

of the mire; he would make a 427
man of himself again; he would 428
conquer the evil that had taken 429
possession of him. There was 430
time; he was comparatively 431
young yet; he would resurrect 432
his old eager ambitions and 433
pursue them without faltering. 434
Those solemn but sweet organ 435
notes had set up a revolution 436
in him. Tomorrow he would go 437
into the roaring downtown dis- 438
trict and find work. A fur 439
importer had once offered him a 440
place as driver. He would find 441
him tomorrow and ask for the 442
position. He would be some- 443
body in the world. He would—— 444

Soapy felt a hand laid on his 445
arm. He looked quickly around 446
into the broad face of a police- 447
man. 448

"What are you doin' here?" 449
asked the officer. 450

"Nothin'," said Soapy. 451

"Then come along," said the 452
policeman. 453

"Three months on the Island," 454
said the Magistrate in the Police 455
Court the next morning. 456

THE ANALYSIS

The Beginning of this story containing the conditions and the
main narrative question occupies lines 1 to 86. This Beginning contains the condition or state of affairs and the main narrative question of the story. A slight difference in the pattern will be seen
between this and the preceding story, in which the condition came
as a block of incident and was followed by the main narrative question. In this story, lines 1 to 28 state the condition. Then lines 29
to 41 set forth the main narrative question. On lines 42 to 86
more conditions are stated, or, more accurately, more information

is given regarding the stated condition which brings about the narrative response of Soapy. An examination of this Beginning will disclose another essential difference between it and the *Adventure of Ulysses*. In the statement of conditions there is no promise of disaster because there is no indication that any difficulties are likely to place themselves in the way of the success of the hero. The author depends for the interest upon the unusualness of the main narrative purpose of the actor. On lines 110 to 122, which are now included in the Body of the story, there is indicated a difficulty which is likely to defeat his purpose,—the fact that his raiment is not above suspicion. This story is particularly interesting because within the body of the story the presentation units are not intended to excite but to entertain the reader. The story's chief interest is, that at the conclusion of each meeting the outcome is unexpected, and by its unexpectedness it forms a narrative hindrance to the main narrative question. There are six of these presentation units which are nearly all incompletely developed dramatic scenes in the Body of the story. The first of these presentation units occupies lines 87 to 144, and occurs between Soapy and the waiters who eject him without injury, thus causing a narrative hindrance by a defeat of that particular attempt. The second presentation unit is when Soapy smashes the window, and tries to convince the policeman that he broke the window. Number three is the interview between Soapy and the hard-boiled waiter, when he tries to persuade the waiter to call a cop. This occupies lines 183 to 217 and results in a narrative hindrance. The fourth presentation unit is between Soapy and the girl whom he accosts in the hope that he will be arrested. Of all the presentation units so far it is the least dramatic in its interchange. It occupies lines 218 to 288 and results in a narrative hindrance. The fifth of these presentation units is when Soapy, having made a disturbance, appeals to the policeman to arrest him. This again results in a hindrance, the whole unit occupying lines 289 to 324. The sixth and last attempt of Soapy is when he steals the umbrella from the man, and urges the man to have him arrested. This occupies lines 325 to 364, and results in a narrative hindrance.

(N.B. It is interesting to note that the minor narrative questions of these scenes fall into the categories that I mentioned in the introduction to this book; that an actor is trying to persuade another actor to adopt a course of conduct or to convince another actor that a certain state of affairs exists, etc.)

The accumulation of all these defeats brings about the big

moment in the story when disaster threatens the purpose of Soapy. Lines 365 to 409 introduce the stimulus which convinces Soapy that it is useless to proceed further in his attempts. Lines 410 to 420 show his thoughts, leading into the Conclusive Act which answers the main narrative question of the story in the negative by showing that Soapy has abandoned his purpose (421–444). Following this there comes a Sequel, lines 445 to 456, made up of the episode with the policeman, on lines 445 to 453, and of the additional sentence by the magistrate on lines 454 to 456 to three months on the Island. The Ending of the story, therefore, containing the Conclusive Act, and the Sequel, occupies lines 421 to 456.

One of my particular reasons for choosing this story was to enable you to see that even though the whole artistic purpose of the writer may change with different stories the architectural norm remains constant. You will notice that in this story there appears an element which did not occur in the previous story. It is that the sequel to this story is interesting because of its ironic significance, because it is a reversal of the original condition. The actor has failed in his purpose at the close of the story proper; he later succeeds but, ironically, he does not wish success.

This is a characteristic O. Henry story. It is not nearly so dramatic as the story of the adventure of Ulysses with the Cyclop for the reason that it is not in its main purpose sufficiently important. No group of readers could become wildly excited over the success or failure of Soapy's enterprise. The main purpose is interesting, not because of any importance which inheres in it, but because of the unusualness of such a desire on anybody's part.

SPARE PARTS

	Section	Lines	Notes
Beginning	Initial Condition and Main Actor's purpose are set forth.	Sally vs. Kerry	1– 75	
		Sally and Monte	76– 154	
		Sally and Monte	155– 283	Main Plot Crises apparent. Promises of conflict to overcome Difficulties, to remove or overcome opponents, or opposing forces, and to overcome Disaster.
		Sally and Kerry	284– 342	
		Sally and Garageman.	343– 374	
		Sally and Monte.	375– 408	
		Sally and Monte.	409– 485	Main Narrative Question: " Can Monte English succeed in driving Vindix from Los Angeles to St. Louis under its own power?"
		Sally and Kerry.	486– 562	
		Sally and Monte.	563– 605	
		Kerry and Monte.	606– 654	
		Kerry and foreman.	655– 673	
Body	Series of attempts of Main Actor to achieve his purpose, in spite of obstacles placed in the path of his success by opponents.	Foreman and Mac.	674– 730	Dramatic Hindrance.
		Mac and Monte.	731– 751	Dramatic Hindrance.
		Incidents. Monte reacts to condition.	752– 789	Monte overcomes Difficulty; Narrative Furtherance.
		Monte and Sally. (Kerry observes.)	790– 839	Friction develops. Dramatic Hindrance.
		Monte, Sally, and Kerry.	840– 887	Broken bearing; Narrative Hindrance.
		Sally and Kerry in Winslow. (5th step of 840–887.)	888– 912	No spare parts. Threat of Disaster. Narrative Hindrance.
		Incidents. Monte and condition.	913– 919	Monte overcomes Difficulty; Narrative Furtherance.
		Incidents. Effect upon Carson (5th step of 913–919.)	920– 931	Carson proposes to set pace which will ruin Vindix. Dramatic Hindrance.

58

Interchange. Kerry and Sheriff.	932– 953	Threat of arrest and delay. Dramatic Hindrance.
Incidents. Monte and condition.	954– 982	Sheriff buys liquor. Narrative Furtherance.
Incidents. Monte and condition.	983–1014	Rattling gears and chassis. Time limit close. Narrative Hindrance.
Incidents. Monte and condition.	1015–1042	Attempt presages Victory. Furtherance. Dramatic Hindrance by Kerry's knowledge that he must delay.
Monte and Kerry.		
Monte and condition. (A characterizing scene with mental struggle omitted, resulting in new condition.)	1043–1085	Kerry's accident is Furtherance.
Monte and condition.	1086–1158	Hindrance. Broken parts not replaceable.
Effect upon Carson. (5th step of 1159–1208.)	1159–1208	Furtherance. Victory in sight.
Sally and condition.	1209–1216	Hindrance. Kerry steals parts.
Kerry and Kamco General Manager.	1217–1244	Furtherance. Ally helps.
Sally and condition.	1245–1278	Hindrance. Disaster threatens.
Sally and Monte.	1279–1301	Hindrance. Vindix wrecked.
Sally and Monte.	1302–1324	Hindrance. Disaster threatens.
Sally and Monte.	1325–1392	Furtherance. Success in view.
Monte and condition.	1393–1402	Hindrance. Ultimate Disaster looms. Big Moment of Story.
	1403–1421	Furtherance. Last obstacle overcome.

BODY — Series of attempts of Main Actor to achieve his purpose, despite the obstacles placed in his path by his opponents.

Sally and Kerry. (Conclusive Act 1436–1440).	1422–1440	Main Narrative Question answered: "Yes."
Sally and Kerry. Sally and Monte.	1441–1479 1480–1483	Effect upon actors shown.

ENDING — Conclusive Act. Sequel.

SPARE PARTS

BY FRANK R. ADAMS

EVERY story of accomplishment is the story of a person who sets out to change an existing condition or state of affairs.

To set forth this initial condition which has to be changed is the function of that part of the story that we call, structurally speaking, the Beginning. The Beginning sets forth, in addition to this initial condition, the response of the chief actor to the existing condition so that the reader being aware of the stimulus and the response finds himself phrasing the main narrative question of the story.

In the two stories which precede this one the conditions set forth were, in the case of *The Adventure of Ulysses*, important; and in the case of *The Cop and the Anthem*, unusual.

Spare Parts has been included because the condition which confronts the young man is not in itself either unusual or important; but is made so by its involvements. The main purpose which emerges is not intrinsically important, but is made important synthetically. Its importance depends upon the reader being made aware of how much depends upon the success of Monte English in driving the Vindix from Los Angeles, California, to St. Louis, Missouri.

After reading the story, turn to the analysis which follows it.

CASE No. 3

"SPARE PARTS"

BY FRANK R. ADAMS

1 "But, my dear Sally, as your
2 friend, as your almost guardian,
3 as your sure-enough, bona-fide
4 suitor, I beg of you *not* to buy a
5 Vindix car!"

6 Carson Kerry was perhaps not
7 so vehement as he was pretend-
8 ing to be, but he was very much
9 in earnest at that.

10 "But I *want* a Vindix," Sally
11 insisted. "My daddy had one,
12 and *he* said it is the best car
13 made."

14 "Yes; but the Vindix is a for-
15 eign car, and your father lived
16 in New York, where there was
17 an importing agency for the Vin-
18 dix—and not in southern Cali-
19 fornia. If he broke any of the
20 parts he could replace them
21 within a reasonable time."

22 "I don't see why it should be
23 any harder to get repair parts
24 for a Vindix than it is for any
25 other first-class car."

26 "It *is* harder, though, and
27 there is a perfectly good reason.
28 They don't use *any* standardized

29 parts — parts that are inter-
30 changeable with other cars of the
31 same size. For heaven's sake,
32 Sally, give up this fool notion of
33 a Vindix, and let me fix you up
34 with a good American car!"

35 "Such as a Kamco Six, I sup-
36 pose? "

37 "That *is* the best automobile
38 made, I'll admit."

39 "You'd *have* to say so, you're
40 vice-president of the company."

41 "I *would* not. It's the truth,
42 and I say it because I'm a rea-
43 sonable man."

44 "Well, I'm a reasonable
45 woman!"

46 "A reasonable—Why, you're
47 not even a woman yet! I'm
48 darned if I think you ever *will*
49 grow up. One thing is certain:
50 you haven't cut your automobile
51 wisdom teeth yet."

52 As may be inferred by any
53 married man, and also by most
54 men who are not married—to
55 say nothing of all the women—
56 the upshot of the discussion was

57 the purchase, on the following
58 day, of the only Vindix at that
59 moment available on the west
60 coast.

61 Carson Kerry had gone too
62 far, anyway. The mere fact
63 that her dead father had recom-
64 mended that she rely on Carson's
65 business judgment did not con-
66 stitute him her "almost guar-
67 dian" in everything else!

68 Sally didn't want him for a
69 husband. She could think of
70 seven hundred and forty-four
71 reasons why, one of them being
72 the best in the world. Love may
73 not always last, but it's wonder-
74 ful as a scaffolding while the
75 building is being put up.

76 Sally broke in her new car her-
77 self. She had often driven her
78 father's Vindix, and the new
79 machine was exactly like it in all
80 essential particulars. The lines
81 of the body were more modern,
82 but from gear shift to gizzard
83 they were mechanical twins.

84 So she spent a lot of time
85 piling up the first thousand miles
86 slowly circling the city boule-
87 vards. Unconsciously—well, al-
88 most unconsciously—she drew a
89 lot of attention from other
90 motorists. Part of it was tribute
91 to the glistening perfection of her
92 perfectly turned out torpedo
93 boat destroyer. No one could
94 see that long, supercilious black
95 snout sneaking up over the crest
96 of a hill, trailing a low-hung,
97 high-sided cockpit, without look-
98 ing a second time.

99 The rest of the admiration she
100 attracted was due to her dress-
101 maker, her hairdresser, her mil-
102 liner, and incidentally to her-
103 self. Sally affected vivid orange
104 shades when she was going for a
105 drive, and they looked per-
106 fectly miserable against the
107 black leather and enamel, as
108 any Princeton man can tell you.

109 She was one of those violently
110 beautiful persons who make men
111 mad enough to want to kill some-
112 body, just for relief.

113 She never flirted. She just
114 looked at people to see if she
115 recognized them, then turned
116 away, leaving them her slaves
117 for life, or, at any rate, for the
118 balance of the day until they
119 could sleep it off.

120 So the young man driving
121 down Cahuenga Pass was not
122 aware that he was especially
123 honored when she gave him a
124 smile with two dimples couchant,
125 and waved a friendly greeting.

126 He was just arriving in Los
127 Angeles from the North and
128 East, and he didn't know yet but
129 that every woman on the south-
130 ern Pacific coast was like that.

131 He drove on; not quite the
132 same man he had been before,
133 but still he drove on. Being
134 human, and masculine, he want-
135 ed to stop. But he didn't. He
136 proceeded thoughtfully on his
137 way.

138 To proceed thoughtfully was
139 one of the things Monte English
140 did most successfully. He could

act, too! But when he did he usually had examined the horizon fore and aft, also to leeward and windward.

Eventually Monte hoped to be Western representative of some flourishing Detroit manufacturer. For the present, he planned to get a job as lowly mechanic in a repair shop until he could accumulate enough entries in a savings bank passbook to warrant him in branching out for himself.

The next time he met Sally, not knowing yet, of course, that her name was Sally, he was towing a broken-down Kamco Six which had turned its right ankle against a too, too solid cement curb.

But she recognized him, even in his overalls; and she smiled again, that same warm, friendly smile as of shipmates who meet in a far country.

This time he guessed why. It was because his own car, which he had leased into bondage along with his mechanical services, was an antique Vindix, a distant cousin of her own resplendent roadster. He had not seen any others since he had been in Los Angeles.

So he waved back and grinned. And Monte had a pretty nice grin himself.

It was strange that he should run across her again the next week. Well, not so very strange at that, if you take into account that he had been a distinct menace to traffic every time he went out, because he was always watching for a long black clipper flying a yellow flag.

She was pulled up on the other side of the street and had raised the hood, just as if she knew what to do with the hub-cap wrench which she held in her hand.

Monte thought that he was justified in helping. Wasn't it all in the line of business? He might get her as a customer for his boss, mightn't he?

"Perhaps I can fix it," he suggested.

She turned around and recognized him even before she looked across the street and identified his car.

"Oh, if you would!" Apparently she never doubted his ability an instant.

He not only would but he could.

"A Vindix is a little complicated for the average American driver, isn't it?" she offered shyly.

"Not really, after you get used to 'em." He gazed admiringly at the sheer beauty of the new car. "Gee, but this outfit is a peach!"

"Would you like to drive it for a mile or so, just to feel it out? No one has driven it except myself, but I know the owner of another Vindix would understand just how to handle it."

She was right. Her car had

225 never been manipulated with
226 such skill. They went twenty
227 miles, not because Monte pre-
228 sumed on her original invitation,
229 but because she insisted that she
230 was learning such a lot just from
231 watching the way he drove.

232 He thanked his lucky stars
233 that this time he had on his
234 street clothes.

235 When they finally pulled up
236 alongside of his own neglected
237 chariot, Sally examined the an-
238 tique with deep interest.

239 "Just where did you get your
240 car?" she demanded.

241 Monte flushed a little. "I got
242 it from a second-hand dealer in
243 New York."

244 "And how did that scratch get
245 on the panel of the front door?"

246 "I haven't had the bus painted
247 since I bought it. I don't know
248 how it got there."

249 "Well, I do! I put it there
250 myself. A suit I wore several
251 years ago had cut-metal buttons
252 on it, and—"

253 "Did you own this car?"

254 "My father did. I thought
255 it looked familiar; and when you
256 said you bought it in New York
257 I wondered if it might be our car.
258 That scratch practically proves
259 it."

260 Monte said something she
261 didn't quite catch. "What did
262 you say?"

263 "Nothing."

264 "Yes, you did."

265 "I said I'd never have it
266 painted again," he admitted.

267 "Don't be ashamed of it. I
268 like to have people like me—
269 even young men."

270 "Even garage mechanics?"

271 "Especially a garage me-
272 chanic! It would be so handy
273 to know just where to apply for
274 aid in case of a breakdown."

275 Of course she was kidding him,
276 but she was so nice about it that
277 he couldn't help smiling back.

278 She took the address and tele-
279 phone number of the garage
280 where he worked. Sally was ab-
281 solutely unscrupulous the way
282 she attached men to her with
283 bonds of service.

284 That evening she and Carson
285 Kerry were going to a party to-
286 gether, and had their usual quar-
287 rel as to which car they should
288 take.

289 "My sedan will be better,"
290 was one of his arguments. "It
291 may be chilly."

292 "If you think you'll be cold,
293 I'll lend you my fur scarf, and
294 we can wrap up your chilblains
295 in the robe."

296 "I'd look fine, wouldn't I,
297 driving a Vindix when every-
298 body knows that I'm the manu-
299 facturer of the best American
300 car made!"

301 "I wasn't expecting *you* to
302 drive," sweetly. "I suppose a
303 Vindix would be difficult for
304 you."

305 "Huh!" scornfully. "I'd like
306 to ride in something that has
307 some slight chance of being re-
308 paired in case of a breakdown."

309 "The Vindix doesn't require
310 repairing—like *some* cars!"

311 Carson ignored her undercuts,
312 and came back with what he evi-
313 dently considered a knockout
314 blow.

315 "You may as well know the
316 truth," he said. "The Vindix
317 Company has gone to the wall!"

318 "The wall?" repeated Sally.

319 "Exactly!" Carson gloated.
320 "It's busted—quit—gone out of
321 business."

322 "Then I'm very glad I bought
323 one while they were still avail-
324 able!"

325 "You won't be so glad you
326 own an orhpan car when you try
327 to get repair parts."

328 "An orphan?"

329 "Yes; that's what they call an
330 automobile of a make that has
331 been discontinued."

332 "I see. Then it's lucky the
333 Vindix is a machine that practi-
334 cally *never* wears out."

335 Carson threw up his hands.
336 "They *all* wear out."

337 "I imagine you base your
338 ideas entirely on what happens
339 to Kamco Sixes. But the Vin-
340 dix—"

341 They finally went to the party
342 in a taxicab.

343 The very next week Sally had
344 reason to recall Carson's out-
345 rageous predictions. A loaded
346 truck swung into her as she was
347 turning a corner. The truck
348 driver had not seen her arm sig-
349 nal. Probably her hand was
350 too small.

351 Anyway, the truck made some-
352 thing resembling a corrugated
353 washboard out of her right front
354 fender; and when she tried to
355 start up again, the front wheel
356 on that side got down on its
357 knees and couldn't get up.

358 The nearest garage man, ar-
359 riving on buzzard wings, shook
360 his head in gloomy prophecy.

361 "The fender can probably be
362 straightened, but that spindle
363 that's broke clean off is going to
364 bother us. Nobody carries it in
365 stock. I might find one at a
366 junk yard, but otherwise it will
367 have to be made from a special
368 pattern mold at the steel mills.
369 That's going to cost money, and
370 may take months."

371 Sally could have cried with
372 vexation. Still, she didn't give
373 up. Instead, she telephoned the
374 garage for Monte English.

375 He was there in ten minutes.
376 In twenty more he had replaced
377 the broken spindle with one from
378 his own car—it fitted perfectly
379 —and had driven her to a near-
380 by fender repair man, who ironed
381 out the wrinkles with a rubber
382 hammer so that you could
283 scarcely notice any damage at
384 all.

385 "But how will you get a new
386 what-do-you-call-it for your own
387 car?"

388 "I'll find one," he promised.
389 "That's the advantage of being
390 in the business."

391 "You'll let me pay for the time
392 that takes, too, won't you?"

65

393 Monte considered. "If it
394 takes long, yes."

395 She made him promise to bring
396 his car around so that she could
397 see it as soon as it was repaired.
398 This inspired Monte to prodi-
399 gies. To find a new spindle
400 proved to be out of the question,
401 but he finally discovered a com-
402 plete front axle assembly that
403 was nearly the same size; and by
404 a little ingenious remodeling he
405 managed to make it fit well
406 enough to do. He kept the dis-
407 carded parts in case of an
408 emergency.

409 When he took his practically
410 paintless ark around to the hotel
411 where Sally was staying, she in-
412 spected it carefully without de-
413 tecting what he had done.

414 "I think that you're wonder-
415 ful," she breathed, in such a tone
416 that he thought he was pretty
417 wonderful himself.

418 "If you have time I wish
419 you'd drive me down to the
420 beach," she suggested, with just
421 the correct shade of wistfulness
422 in her tone. "It's fearfully hot
423 this evening, and I can't go
424 there alone."

425 She could have gone with Car-
426 son Kerry, who was waiting for
427 her in the hotel lobby; but per-
428 haps she never thought of that.
429 Young people are so careless.

430 "You mean in my car?" de-
431 manded Monte incredulously.

432 "Certainly. It's a Vindix,
433 isn't it?"

434 That was the final victory.

435 Monte had been trying to resist
436 her, but what could a man do
437 with a girl like that?

438 "Why, your motor runs better
439 than mine!" Sally marveled
440 when they were on their way.
441 "A trifle smoother, perhaps.
442 These engines improve the longer
443 they run. And this one has had
444 excellent care."

445 Nature had never cooked up
446 an evening such as that one. A
447 full moon, the twinkling neck-
448 lace of Hollywood on the hills to
449 the right, a warm breeze that
450 promised all the impossible
451 things in the world, a girl in a
452 sleeveless orange silk dress that
453 could probably be carried in a
454 vanity case if it were folded up,
455 and a perfume that will doubt-
456 less be illegal when Mr. Volstead
457 gets around to it!

458 "I'm a member of the Santa
459 Monica Beach Club," Sally of-
460 fered, apropos of nothing par-
461 ticular, when they got there;
462 "and it looks like a nice night to
463 take a swim."

464 So they did. Sally, in a bath-
465 ing suit, was a conflict of emo-
466 tions.

467 Nothing happened —nothing,
468 that is, if you discount the one
469 time that Sally was knocked
470 down by a roller and Monte
471 picked her up and held her tight
472 for an instant while she steadied
473 herself. During that second his
474 world reeled.

475 Monte made her come out
476 after that. He said he was

477 afraid it might happen again.
478 He was.

479 On the way home, he talked
480 about machinery, his modest am-
481 bitions, politics and agriculture.
482 Monte's idea was to keep the
483 subject of moonlight, hillsides,
484 springtime, and other things
485 from being mentioned.

486 Carson Kerry had waited only
487 until half past ten for her, so he
488 was not there when they got
489 back. But he was pretty furious
490 the next day, and Sally thought
491 it just as well not to explain
492 that she had not been alone and
493 absolutely unprotected during
494 her evening ramble.

495 There was something else for
496 them to quarrel about, anyway.
497 Sally's aunt was going to be
498 married again, back in St. Louis,
499 and she wanted Sally to be pres-
500 ent. Carson said he was going
501 East himself shortly, and pro-
502 posed that they make the trip
503 in his motor.

504 "My sister will go along as
505 chaperon—unless, of course, we
506 could be married before we left."

507 Sally considered the idea.
508 "I'd like to go; but I'd rather
509 take my own car. You and your
510 sister could ride in your closed
511 elephant and I could drive along
512 a few miles ahead of you—and
513 wait for you wherever we had
514 decided to stop for the night."

515 That phrase "wait for you"
516 made Carson respond to the
517 sting as if there had been dyna-
518 mite under him.

519 "Why, that animated junk
520 pile of yours would never make
521 it. The Vindix was built for
522 European pavements. It takes
523 a he car to travel across the
524 American continent, a car with
525 an engine like—"

526 "I've read your advertising,"
527 Sally interrupted dryly, "but I
528 didn't think you believed it
529 yourself."

530 "I'll prove it to you," Carson
531 offered magnanimously. "If
532 you'll go with me, I'll hire a man
533 to pilot your outfit as long as it
534 will hold together; then we'll use
535 a tow-rope on it the rest of the
536 way. And maybe, after I've
537 shown you that I'm right about
538 *that*, you'll be willing to believe
539 me on one or two other subjects."

540 "Such as?"

541 "Getting married!"

542 If he hadn't mentioned that
543 word "tow-rope" Sally might
544 not have let her indignation get
545 the better of her. As it was, she
546 had to substantiate her faith in
547 the Vindix perambulator. So
548 when they got through a rather
549 violent conversation she had
550 agreed to a proposition which
551 she afterward coldly regretted:
552 namely, to be a party to a double
553 *wedding* if the Vindix did not
554 arrive on its own power in St.
555 Louis in time for her aunt's cere-
556 mony. That was two weeks off.

557 "I'll find a driver for your
558 car," Carson offered.

559 "I'll find my own driver!"
560 Sally retorted, with an asperity

certainly not becoming to an almost engaged girl.

Of course she went to Monte immediately. Quite unexpectedly he refused point-blank.

"I'm just beginning to make good here. I've got to stick until I have enough saved to start in for myself."

"How much do you need?"

"About five thousand dollars."

"I'll give you that much to do as I ask you."

"That would be foolish."

"But five thousand is nothing to me."

"That's what I was afraid of." He said it with bitterness in his heart.

"Please, Monte!" She had called him that when the ocean had slapped her down, there on the beach that night, and it seemed scarcely worth while to correct the slip now. "Please! If you don't, I'll have to marry a man I don't love."

"Nonsense. No girl has to do that."

"Yes, I do. I never go back on my word. Carson knows that."

Monte threw up his job. He knew that he would have to when she first asked him. The money angle he steadfastly refused to discuss. He said he would charge her for his time, but that was all.

Sally reported, upon cross-examination by Carson, that she had hired a driver; but she forbore to tell him the details. Someway, she suspected that he wouldn't like it.

Carson hunted up Monte at his quarters.

"You're the man who is going to drive Miss Sally Sherwood's car to St. Louis, aren't you?"

"Yes."

"Well, I'm Mr. Kerry, of the Kamco Automobile Company. Perhaps you've heard of me."

"I have," Monte admitted.

Carson did not read the storm signals quite right, so he came directly to the point.

"I'll make it worth your while if you don't arrive there until after two weeks from to-day. It's merely a little matter of pride with me. I want to prove that an American car will stand up better under rough conditions than a foreign one. You're an American yourself, so I imagine you're on my side anyway; but I'm sure you will be when I say there will be a five-thousand-dollar check waiting for you at the other end—if you don't get there inside of fifteen days."

Monte wasn't letter-perfect in the language of melodrama, so he did not make any remarks about a poor man's honor. He merely got up and opened the door.

"You won't help?"

"I will not! If you weren't a lot older than I am, I'd save you the trouble of *walking* out!"

That hurt. Carson Kerry did

not like to have anyone notice that he was older than he pretended to be.

"Never mind my age. Let's see you try it!"

Monte did—gently. Carson wasn't hurt a bit—not physically. But the interview did not exactly presage a friendly rivalry between the two men.

It also forced Carson to take other precautions which had not occurred to him before the incident. He took the foreman of his Los Angeles service station into his confidence—at least partially. "I don't want that car to make the trip," he explained. "Whatever happens to it, I don't want to know about; but an ingenious man like yourself ought to be able to dope out something which will eventually cause trouble."

The foreman reflected. "The Vindix is an orphan, ain't it?"

"Yes."

The man smiled. "All right. Leave it to me!"

Monte went home at noon the day before the start, tired out because he had been working all night on Sally's car. Everything had been done that he knew how to do. Mac, the garage mechanic who had helped, agreed to keep an eye on the car so that nothing unforeseen could happen.

Just accidentally, the foreman of the Kamco shop dropped in at the garage that afternoon.

He approached Mac, who was wiping grease off the Vindix.

"Good bus," opined the visiting foreman.

"You said it!"

"Let me hear the motor, will you?"

Mac was proud to show it off, especially to a visiting diplomat, so he stepped on the starter.

The foreman lifted the hood and examined the engine block critically. "They use an old-fashioned carburetor with an open air intake, don't they? But it works like a charm, and that's the answer, I suppose. Shut her off now."

Mac was in the driver's seat to turn off the ignition, so he did not see the visitor drop a handful of pulverized emery into the air intake. The dying motor sucked the sharp deadly particles up into the intake manifold, where they would lie harmless until the engine was started again. Then they would cut and score the cylinders in five minutes so that they would be beyond any repair except a slow reboring job.

"How'd you like to work on the night shift over at our shop, beginning to-night?" the visitor asked.

"I can't come to-night, because—"

"To-night or never. Twenty-five dollars bonus in addition to our regular pay, which is better than any other place in town."

729 "I'll come. Twenty-five bucks
730 is twenty-five bucks."

731 But Mac was conscientious, so
732 he hunted up Monte and roused
733 him from his sleep to explain.
734 Monte could not blame Mac.
735 But when the latter told him
736 that it was the Kamco Company
737 he was going to work for, Monte
738 sat up with an uneasy start.

739 "Did that fellow touch the
740 Vindix while he was in the
741 shop?"

742 "He only lifted the hood to
743 look at the motor. I started it
744 for him."

745 "Started it?"

746 "Wasn't that O. K.?"

747 "Sure! But, Mac, do this for
748 me—don't tell him you've seen
749 me this afternoon."

750 Mac agreed, and went on
751 about his business.

752 Monte tried to assure himself
753 that everything was all right.
754 But he couldn't go to sleep
755 again, so he finally dressed and
756 went over to the garage.

757 Everything seemed to be O. K.
758 —until he started the motor.
759 Then he knew! Before he could
760 shut it off the harm was done,
761 and the engine was ruined be-
762 yond any possible hope of repair
763 in time to start the next morning.

764 Monte's first impulse was to
765 sit down and cry. His next re-
766 action was to call up Sally and
767 apprise her of the disaster. But
768 he stopped himself, with the re-
769 ceiver off the hook. She had
770 implicit confidence in him. To

771 tell her would shatter the slight
772 hold he had on her regard. He
773 mustn't worry her until the last
774 stone had been turned.

775 So he devoted half an hour to
776 intense thought. Then he hired
777 the rest of the crew of the repair
778 shop to work overtime on double
779 pay.

780 By morning the motor from
781 his own Vindix was bolted to the
782 engine bed of the roadster and
783 was running as smoothly as if it
784 had been born there. Monte,
785 tired but happy, thanked his
786 lucky stars that the Vindix
787 Company had not changed the
788 design of that motor for nearly
789 a decade.

790 They started from the hotel
791 about eight o'clock. If Carson
792 Kerry was surprised to see
793 Monte at all, he was doubtless
794 buoyed up by the secret assur-
795 ance of his foreman that the Vin-
796 dix would not make a hundred
797 miles before it would be a hope-
798 less wreck.

799 Sally wanted to ride in her
800 own car for the get-away. But
801 all the available space in the
802 seat of the roadster was taken up
803 by Monte's baggage. There
804 were three grips, and several
805 bulky burlap-wrapped bundles
806 besides. "I should think that a
807 man alone would not require
808 much luggage," Sally observed
809 petulantly.

810 "Perhaps he's carrying his
811 trousseau with him," suggested
812 Carson.

813 "Perhaps I am," Monte con-
814 curred amiably. It was easy to
815 be pleasant, knowing what he
816 knew.

817 The traveling equipment of
818 the Kamco party was carried in
819 long cases fitted onto the run-
820 ning boards on either side, and in
821 a trunk at the rear.

822 "We might transfer some of
823 these things to the other car and
824 make room that way," Sally
825 suggested.

826 But that aroused a storm of
827 protest from both men; quite un-
828 reasonable protest, Sally thought.
829 She was especially provoked with
830 Monte, who had never before
831 opposed her in anything.

832 "All right," she finally con-
833 ceded, in high dudgeon, "drive
834 all by yourself if you want to.
835 I won't bother you again."

836 Carson was tremendously
837 pleased. There is nothing like
838 having a little friction in the
839 ranks of the enemy.

840 So they started out, with Sally
841 in the front seat of the Kamco
842 Sedan and the heavily loaded
843 Vindix trailing behind.

844 That was the relative position
845 of the two cars for the first three
846 days out. It was tacitly under-
847 stood that this was not a race—
848 merely a sort of endurance con-
849 test, with the Vindix on trial.

850 Toward evening of the fourth
851 day, when they were about half
852 way between Flagstaff and Win-
853 slow, on a particularly bad
854 stretch of highway, the Vindix

855 broke a bearing in a front wheel.

856 As soon as she discovered that
857 her car was not following, Sally
858 made Carson turn around and
859 go back. Monte had the wheel
860 off and showed them the broken
861 pieces.

862 "That's too bad," sympa-
863 thized Carson. "The Vindix
864 uses a special light ball bearing,
865 too, doesn't it?"

866 "What can you do?" wailed
867 Sally.

868 "I'll tell you what," declared
869 Carson. "We'll drive on to
870 Winslow and send a man back
871 with a bearing."

872 "Oh, will you?" Sally beamed
873 upon him. "That's nice of you,
874 Carson. You're a good sport."

875 The two men looked at each
876 other. Both of them knew that
877 it would be impossible to find
878 that size bearing in any shop west
879 of Chicago, and maybe not there.

880 The Kamco went on alone,
881 Carson in justifiably good spir-
882 its, Sally slightly subdued, but
883 none the less grateful to Carson
884 for his apparently magnanimous
885 attitude. Perhaps he really was
886 a bigger man than she had given
887 him credit for being.

888 In Winslow, Sally went around
889 with Carson to the various gar-
890 ages in search of the new bearing.
891 As Carson had known before-
892 hand, there was none to be had.

893 "That's the trouble with an
894 orphan," he remarked, with ill-
895 concealed triumph. "You can't
896 buy parts to fit."

897 "But what can we do?"

898 "Why — nothing, I guess. 899 We'll have to go on, if we're to 900 arrive in time for the wed- 901 ding."

902 Sally didn't sleep much that 903 night. She was the victim of a 904 double nightmare: the idea of 905 losing to Carson, and the thought 906 of her driver all alone on that 907 god-forsaken road. She had not 908 forgiven Monte for not letting 909 her ride with him; still, he was a 910 human being, and it was cold 911 and dark out there. Perhaps 912 there were wolves.

913 After breakfast in the morning 914 the Vindix drove up to the hotel 915 entrance! Monte looked slightly 916 tired, and needed a shave, but 917 he did not offer any explanations 918 other than, "I was able to fix 919 it up."

920 That was less mystifying to 921 Sally than it was to Carson, who 922 knew the difficulties. He finally 923 arrived at the conclusion that 924 Monte had managed to make a 925 bearing out of Babbitt metal 926 that would act as a makeshift. 927 Well, if he had, it was bound to 928 burn out again soon, if Monte 929 attempted to follow at the pace 930 Carson was going to set from 931 there on.

932 But Monte tooled along easily 933 in their wake all that day, just 934 out of the dust, apparently un- 935 concerned about the permanency 936 of his repair.

937 There was something wrong 938 with Carson's calculations some- 939 where. That night he thought- 940 fully planted a couple of bottles 941 of his own Scotch, done up in 942 heavy paper, amid the other par- 943 cels in the Vindix. Perhaps 944 Monte would need a little stim- 945 ulant if he had to stay out all 946 night on the road again. He 947 forgot to tell Monte about it, 948 though.

949 He did, however, mention to 950 the sheriff of the next town that 951 he had passed a man in a Vindix 952 roadster who had offered to sell 953 him some liquor.

954 The sheriff was immensely 955 pleased; and when Monte came 956 along a little later, he bought the 957 whisky himself! Good Scotch 958 is hard to get so far from the 959 coast. Monte, shrewdly guess- 960 ing how the liquor came to be 961 there, thought of offering to split 962 the proceeds of the sale with Car- 963 son. But he decided to regard it 964 as a gift without any strings tied 965 to it; so he did not speak of 966 it.

967 His reticence caused a lot of 968 trouble to the Federal agents at 969 Albuquerque, to whom Carson 970 passed the tip. They detained 971 the Vindix for about two hours 972 while they vainly searched it 973 from stem to stern.

974 When Monte picked up the 975 Kamco Six again at Santa Fé, he 976 blandly explained his delay by 977 telling the exact truth about his 978 fruitless arrest. Carson pre- 979 tended to be surprised and indig- 980 nant. As a matter of fact, he

981 really was! He didn't have any
982 more Scotch.

983 In Raton, which is high, they
984 ran into a snowstorm, which
985 changed to sleet and then rain as
986 they descended the eastern slope
987 toward La Junta. There they
988 were warned of dangerous wash-
989 outs ahead, and decided to
990 lay over for weather conditions
991 to improve. That suited Monte
992 all right; but late in the evening
993 he moved his car from the garage
994 where he had originally docked,
995 and put it in an old barn on the
996 outskirts of town.

997 After two days, as the rain did
998 not let up, they decided to go on.
999 Monte bought three sets of
1000 chains and prepared to fly, plow,
1001 or submerge, as emergency in-
1002 dicated.

1003 The roads were all right for a
1004 short stretch in Colorado; then
1005 they changed abruptly to clay
1006 and mud. The speed slowed
1007 down to ten miles an hour or less,
1008 with the Kamco forcing the pace.
1009 The heavy going was hard on
1010 Sally's car; and even with the
1011 best care that Monte could give
1012 it, the Vindix arrived in Kansas
1013 City with rattling gears and a
1014 complaining chassis.

1015 Under ordinary conditions,
1016 Monte would have stayed there
1017 that night to overhaul the car;
1018 but time was getting short.
1019 There was only a day and a half
1020 left to get to St. Louis; and with
1021 the roads the way they were that
1022 would be none too long. Be-

1023 sides, the Kamco was going on
1024 through, and Sally practically
1025 insisted that Monte follow with-
1026 in hailing distance.

1027 It was dark and still raining
1028 when they cleared the outskirts
1029 of Kansas City. The roads, ac-
1030 cording to reports, were moder-
1031 ately good between there and
1032 Jefferson City; and it occurred
1033 to Monte that, if he should go on
1034 ahead, he could perhaps gain a
1035 couple of hours for mechanical
1036 revision somewhere along the
1037 line until the Kamco should
1038 catch up. The Vindix was ca-
1039 pable of greater speed than the
1040 Kamco on any kind of decent
1041 going—a fact that was known
1042 to both drivers.

1043 Therefore, when Monte signi-
1044 fied his intention of passing,
1045 Carson refused to yield the road.
1046 He could do that very effectu-
1047 ally, because they were then on
1048 a dirt and clay pike, crowned
1049 high in the middle. To get very
1050 far down on either side, when it
1051 was wet, would make a car slide
1052 into the ditch—chains or no
1053 chains.

1054 Monte hung on, about ten
1055 yards behind the Kamco, ready
1056 to pass at the first opportunity.
1057 Finally the road widened and
1058 flattened a little. Monte speed-
1059 ed up. So did Carson. They
1060 traveled abreast for a hundred
1061 yards or so, then the road started
1062 to narrow again. Monte was a
1063 few feet ahead and he deter-
1064 mined not to drop behind. Car-

1065 son would not yield, either. The
1066 Vindix skidded a trifle. To cor-
1067 rect it, Monte had to turn toward
1068 the top of the crown. Carson
1069 nearly hit him, but veered off
1070 automatically to the right.

1071 In the slippery and slimy mud,
1072 the wheels of the heavy sedan
1073 did not hold. It began to slide
1074 sideways. Carson speeded up in
1075 the hope of overcoming the skid,
1076 but it was too late. With a sick-
1077 ening slither, the Kamco slipped
1078 into the ditch.

1079 Carson tried to get out under
1080 his own power; but by the time
1081 he had rocked backward and for-
1082 ward a few minutes he realized
1083 that his rear wheels were simply
1084 digging in deeper, and he de-
1085 sisted.

1086 Monte, as soon as he discov-
1087 ered what had happened, backed
1088 up cautiously and got out to
1089 help. For some reason, it did
1090 not occur to him that this gave
1091 him his much needed opportu-
1092 nity to go on ahead for his
1093 mechanical inspection.

1094 "Got that tow-rope you
1095 brought along to use on the
1096 Vindix?" he asked amiably.

1097 The tow-rope turned out to be
1098 a wire cable with a hook at
1099 either end. Monte hitched it on
1100 to the rear of the Vindix and
1101 the front axle of the Kamco.
1102 Then they started both motors
1103 and, on signal from Monte,
1104 dropped into gear simultaneous-
1105 ly. There was a straining pull,
1106 during which the Kamco came

1107 forward about six inches. Then
1108 the cable snapped.

1109 Monte produced a length of
1110 heavy chain from the rear deck
1111 of the roadster, fastened it to
1112 the axle, and they started the
1113 cars once more.

1114 This time the Kamco yielded
1115 to persuasion and was slowly be-
1116 ing drawn from its mud nest,
1117 when suddenly the Vindix ceased
1118 to pull. The motor raced on—
1119 but unavailingly; and the Kamco
1120 wallowed back into the ditch.

1121 Monte thought at first that
1122 one of his chains had broken and
1123 the tires were slipping in the
1124 mud; but a hasty inspection re-
1125 vealed the fact that the wheels
1126 were not turning at all. So he
1127 shut off the motor. He knew
1128 what had happened.

1129 Sally and Carson jumped out
1130 of the Kamco to see what the
1131 trouble was.

1132 "Stripped a differential gear,
1133 didn't you?" asked Carson sym-
1134 pathetically.

1135 Carson could afford to be
1136 sympathetic. The Kamco was
1137 in a ditch, but a team could pull
1138 it out. The Vindix, however,
1139 would never move again without
1140 a new ring and pinion of a size
1141 and ratio not manufactured by
1142 any foundry in the United States.
1143 The two men knew this.

1144 "You can fix it, can't you?"
1145 queried Sally anxiously, but still
1146 with a note of confidence in her
1147 voice.

1148 "He can—just as soon as he

74

can build a factory and install special machinery that has to be imported from France!" Carson assured her. "It ought not to take over six or eight months."

Something in Monte's attitude and expression checked the despair that rose in Sally's bosom. "You don't know Monte as well as I do," she asserted.

It turned out that she was right. Monte knocked boards off a nearby fence and laid them as sort of a platform under the rear axle of the Vindix. With that to work on, he opened the rear axle housing and took out the broken ring gear, the teeth of which had been chewed off nearly flush with the ring.

Carson, watching from the front seat of the enclosed car, failed to suppress a laugh when he saw it.

But the laugh lost its point when Monte unwrapped one of his bulky parcels and produced therefrom a complete differential assembly, which he bolted into place in the roadster housing without any trouble whatever.

The mystery of Monte's baggage was a mystery no longer to Sally. He had brought along with him all the available spare parts he could unfasten from his own car, the elder orphan sister of her Vindix.

When Monte offered to take up the rescue work where he had left off, Sally objected.

"We can't take any chance of breaking the same part again," she pointed out. "Besides, Carson said a while ago that any farmer with a team could pull us out. You go on and send back help from the first farmhouse. We'll be perfectly comfortable in the closed car. It may not be the equal of our Vindix for speed, but at least the upholstery is very deep."

Monte sent back a team from five miles farther on, and then proceeded light-heartedly to Jefferson City. There he washed the Vindix, inspected it carefully, and went to bed with a singing heart.

In the morning, when he called for the roadster at the garage, he found that all of his baggage, save the suit case he had taken to the hotel with him, was gone! He had not noticed when he drove in the night before that it was a Kamco service station.

Sally, at that moment in Carson's car several miles on the way to St. Louis, was eagerly scanning the road ahead for signs of the Vindix. Carson had told her that Monte had left before they did.

So the forenoon passed swiftly and happily and they arrived in mid-afternoon at the home of her aunt in St. Louis.

There, joy was superseded by anxiety. Monte had not checked in, although she was sure she had given him the address. Carson suggested that probably Monte

1233 had gone to a hotel first to clean
1234 up. Sally had her doubts about
1235 that; but, as soon as she could
1236 she went to the telephone to call
1237 up the principal hotels in town.

1238 The house 'phone was out of
1239 order!

1240 Sally was too upset to be
1241 daunted by that, however, so she
1242 slipped out the back way and
1243 went to the nearest drug store to
1244 use a pay station telephone.

1245 There were two booths. One
1246 was occupied; Sally stepped into
1247 the other. Before she could start
1248 calling up the various hotels
1249 which might harbor a missing
1250 Monte, the person in the next
1251 booth began talking. She could
1252 hear perfectly.

1253 "Hello! . . . Kamco Sales and
1254 Service? . . . Give me the general
1255 manager . . . Hello, Jones. This
1256 is Mr. Kerry talking, Carson
1257 Kerry. . . . Never mind the polite
1258 patter, Jones. Here's a rush
1259 order. There's a Vindix road-
1260 ster on the highway somewhere
1261 between here and Jefferson City.
1262 . . . Do you get that? . . . Well,
1263 it's headed this way, and I don't
1264 want it to arrive. Understand?
1265 Send out every car you can get
1266 hold of—trucks, tractors, any-
1267 thing that will move, with in-
1268 structions to block the way.
1269 They can't miss the Vindix.
1270 You know what a funny-shaped
1271 radiator it has. Don't use any
1272 violence, unless absolutely neces-
1273 sary. That's all. Get going."

1274 Sally almost stopped breath-
1275 ing for fear Carson would dis-
1276 cover her; but when he passed
1277 the booth he did not even glance
1278 in that direction.

1279 As soon as he had left the
1280 store, she slipped out and cau-
1281 tiously watched him walk down
1282 the street toward her aunt's
1283 house.

1284 A few blocks away, in the op-
1285 posite direction, was the garage
1286 where Carson had put the
1287 Kamco Sedan. Sally raced over
1288 there. The car was on the wash-
1289 rack, but she ordered it off.

1290 "I've got to use it for perhaps
1291 an hour," she explained.

1292 Between St. Charles and
1293 Wentzville, she found Monte.
1294 The Vindix was in the ditch be-
1295 side the road and Monte was sit-
1296 ting on the running board, his
1297 head in his hands, oblivious to
1298 her approach. The fenders of
1299 the Vindix were bent all out of
1300 shape and the entire front axle
1301 was sagging.

1302 "What's the matter?"

1303 Monte looked up. He was not
1304 even much surprised to see her.

1305 "Axle's broke. A truck hit
1306 me." He made a gesture of ab-
1307 solute despair.

1308 "Can't it be fixed?"

1309 "No chance. Not in time."

1310 "Haven't you got an extra one
1311 with you?"

1312 "I had one; but all my parts
1313 and tools were stolen last night."

1314 "Oh!" The extent of the cal-
1315 amity finally struck Sally with its
1316 full force. "Then we're cooked?"

76

1317 "Yes."

1318 "We could tow it into St. 1319 Louis."

1320 "Your agreement was to get 1321 it there under its own power."

1322 "That's so." She sat down be- 1323 side him. There didn't seem to 1324 be any hope.

1325 "I'm sorry I failed you. No 1326 man ought ever to fail the girl 1327 he—" Monte paused, aghast at 1328 what he had nearly said.

1329 Sally waited for him to go on. 1330 Then she helped him. "Monte, 1331 am I that girl so far as you're 1332 concerned?"

1333 "You know you are. There 1334 isn't any particular point in 1335 denying it now. Yesterday, I 1336 would have had to deny it, be- 1337 cause I'm a poor man and you 1338 are a rich girl. But, since there's 1339 no hope, I'm not ashamed to say 1340 that if I ever marry anyone else 1341 it will be because I've lost my 1342 memory!"

1343 Sally was accustomed to dec- 1344 larations of love, but this one 1345 was unique in her experience. 1346 No one before had ever tried to 1347 phrase devotion and tenderness 1348 with lips that were grimy with 1349 grease, or had expressed un- 1350 speakable desire with eyes ringed 1351 with dried mud.

1352 But she thrilled to it more 1353 than to any speech she had ever 1354 heard. She took his hand—it 1355 was dirty—and held it an instant 1356 between her own two. "If— 1357 oh, I wish—Come on, let's go!"

1358 Monte hesitated. "I guess 1359 I'll stick with the car. Probably 1360 somebody will come along who 1361 will tow it into St. Louis."

1362 "I'll tow it in now with Mr. 1363 Kerry's car."

1364 Monte scowled.

1365 "His tow-rope is broken any- 1366 way; and mine was stolen."

1367 "Perhaps he bought a new 1368 one. Look in the tool box."

1369 Monte did. He lifted the lid 1370 of one of the long running- 1371 board compartments. Then he 1372 stood there, speechless and im- 1373 movable.

1374 "What's the matter?"

1375 "Come here. Look!"

1376 In the box were Monte's bur- 1377 lapped packages!

1378 They worked like mad, Sally 1379 helping with every ounce of 1380 strength she didn't know she 1381 possessed. When the job was 1382 finished her clothes were a 1383 wreck, and she had jammed one 1384 finger so badly that if he hadn't 1385 kissed it she couldn't have stood 1386 the pain.

1387 But in two hours they were 1388 under way again, the most dilap- 1389 idated motorists on the entire 1390 transcontinental highway — and 1391 the happiest. The Kamco Six 1392 they left just where she stood.

1393 "They've got to catch us in 1394 the next thirty minutes," ob- 1395 served Monte. "By that time it 1396 will be dark, and your friend's 1397 piratical agents won't be able to 1398 spot us."

1399 "You don't think they will 1400 try anything more, do you?"

1401 "I not only think it, I'm sure
1402 of it; and here it comes!"

1403 There was a crossroad just
1404 ahead. On each side of it was a
1405 touring car, approaching the in-
1406 tersection. They were idling
1407 along, but as the Vindix ap-
1408 proached at high speed they
1409 suddenly accelerated.

1410 "Hang on!" Monte opened
1411 the throttle wide. "This is the
1412 only way."

1413 The Vindix roadster shot
1414 across between the other two
1415 cars, coming head on. The left-
1416 hand one grazed the rear fender.

1417 There was smashing of glass
1418 as the two vehicles behind them
1419 struck each other.

1420 "I hope they've got a first-aid
1421 kit along," said Monte grimly.

1422 The wedding march was just
1423 beginning when they arrived.

1424 But it stopped. The entrance
1425 of two guests in such a dis-
1426 heveled condition would stop a
1427 wedding ceremony in almost any
1428 stage of its progress.

1429 "You know what Pershing
1430 said at the tomb of Lafayette,"
1431 announced Sally to Carson
1432 Kerry.

1433 "Why, Sally, what has hap-
1434 pened to you?" demanded that
1435 gentleman.

1436 "Me and my little boy friend
1437 here have just brung in the good
1438 ship Vindix. Are we in time for
1439 the wedding? If not, we'll start
1440 one of our own."

1441 "Sally! You wouldn't marry
1442 a mechanic?"

1443 "I wouldn't marry a man who
1444 wasn't one. It's going to *take*
1445 one to keep our car on the road
1446 for the next few years, as spare
1447 parts get scarcer and scarcer."

1448 Carson regarded Monte with
1449 an appraising eye. "I am sure
1450 that Mr. English is not the sort
1451 of man who would propose mar-
1452 riage to a woman of tremendous
1453 wealth, knowing that he is poor
1454 himself."

1455 "You're right, Mr. Kerry,"
1456 declared Monte huskily.

1457 "Of course you're right, Mr.
1458 Kerry," mimicked Sally. "Monte
1459 hasn't, and never would propose
1460 marriage to me; but both of you
1461 have forgotten that this is leap
1462 year. Our two orphan cars are
1463 so thoroughly married already
1464 that it would be hopeless to try
1465 to sort them out; so we've just
1466 got to live together in order to
1467 keep alive the traditions of the
1468 best orphan automobile ever
1469 made. You know just as well as
1470 I do that any man who could
1471 bring an orphan Vindix over the
1472 road from Los Angeles to St.
1473 Louis won't have any trouble
1474 overcoming the minor obstacles
1475 of life—even including the man-
1476 agement of an orphan woman
1477 such as me. Monte, will you let
1478 me be your spare tire forever
1479 and ever, amen?"

1480 An hour later, Monte consent-
1481 ed. By that time, everybody
1482 was arguing on Sally's side, if
1483 only for the sake of peace.

The Analysis

Although this story has no outward resemblance to the story of Ulysses as he makes a series of attempts to reach his wife, Penelope, this story is in direct line of descent from the Odyssey type of story. It is a story which is concerned with setting forth the attempts of a central actor to overcome a number of conditions. Each condition is overcome only to result in the appearance of another condition, which in turn has to be overcome or removed.

This story you will find is modern in that throughout there is the knowledge on the part of the reader that the prize to be won is a girl. This girl is in reality the story's "reason for being." The personality of the girl is made to permeate the story.

The easiest part of a story to write is the Body. This is so because in the Body of a story there are two ways in which interest may be achieved. It may come from the interchanges which lead into the dramatic or narrative turning points of hindrance, or it may come from those turning points of dramatic or narrative hindrance independent of the interchanges. Instead of an interchange the writer may present to the reader a meeting which results in a turning point. The pattern of the story may therefore be either

| Meeting | turning point of hindrance

or | Interchange | turning point of hindrance

In the first case the interest will come almost entirely from the turning point, while in the second place the interest may be extracted from the interchange and the turning point. Keep in mind always when analyzing a story that whenever an actor becomes aware of a condition there is a meeting (a contact), in the sense in which we use the word. Thus on lines 983 to 1008 there is set forth a condition which exists (the bad condition of the roads), and on lines 1009 to 1014 there is set forth the turning point which results from the character's response to that condition or that stimulus. (The car is badly worn.) In this case you have meeting and turning point of hindrance as the pattern.

On lines 790 to 839 there is an interchange between Monte and Sally with Kerry as the observer. This interchange actually closes on line 835, while line 836 to 839 are the crisis of hindrance in the story. These lines form the fifth step of that meeting and project a turning point of hindrance because there is a threat of disaster through the friction existing between Sally and Monte who ought to be partners in the enterprise.

79

The material with which an author is working will almost automatically determine the pattern of his story. The only possible choice which a writer can make for the presentation units of the Body of his story lies between meetings and interchanges. In the Body of the story the interest is in the actor's attempt to overcome conditions or opponents who stand in the way of the successful outcome of his purpose. In general, it may be put down as a rule of craftsmanship that if the hero has to overcome difficulties or conditions the presentation units which the writer employs to show those attempts will be meetings rather than interchanges. When the Body of the story is concerned with the attempts of an actor to overcome an opponent the presentation units will be interchanges between the actor and the opponent.

The experienced writer realizes that although he can depend upon the number of hindrances which he introduces to hold the interest of his reader, he is leaning rather heavily upon plot interest in so doing and is sacrificing presentation interest. Wherever possible then, he will seek to introduce interchanges in order to balance the interest between presentation and plot.

The technical problem confronting him in a story which is made up of an attempt to overcome difficulties is an extremely interesting one from the point of view of expert craftsmanship. Being an experienced writer he realizes, either instinctively or as a technical expert, that any step of a scene may become an interchange. Hence he substitutes the third step of the scene for one of the other steps, thus presenting interchanges which are always more interesting than meetings. Thus for example, on lines 850 to 879 there is presented an interchange which sets forth a condition resulting in a hindrance, which is the fact that a broken bearing is replaceable only in Chicago; and hence the success of the enterprise is threatened. The fifth step of this scene is really set forth in the interchange in Winslow between Sally and Carson. Thus the experienced author is able to present to a reader an interchange which results in a hindrance even though that interchange is really an artificial building up of a fifth step.

It was not so much the interest for writers of the Body of this story which led me to select it, as the interest which its beginning contains for all writers who are sincere students of craftsmanship. The three major divisions of Beginning, Body and Ending are very clearly defined, as well as the sub-division of sequel. The Beginning occupies lines 1 to 673, the Body occupies line 674 to 1421, the Ending occupies line 1422 to 1483 and contains the Conclusive Act on lines 1436 and 1440 together with the Sequel from lines 1441 to 1483.

One of the first questions that is always asked by a person who begins this structural analysis is, "Where does the Beginning end, and the Body commence?" The Beginning contains always the threat of conflict, of difficulties to be overcome, of opponents to be removed or overcome, and of disaster to be averted. Until all this information is placed before the reader, together with the main narrative question which emerges as a result of the actor's response to the main condition, then it is still Beginning. In this story the narrative question emerges on lines 593 to 599, but the Beginning lasts until line 673 because the interchanges between Kerry and Monte on line 606 to 654 and between Kerry and the foreman on line 655 to 673 contain threats of disaster to the enterprise. They are not interchanges which show the attempts of the actor to bring about his purpose although they might conceivably be said to be part of the Body of the story because they involve attempts of forces opposed to the main actor who are attempting to bring about disaster to his enterprise.

It is unimportant however, this making of too rigid classifications; in general it is pretty safe to assume that the Body of the story is made up of the attempts of the actor rather than the attempts of opponents of the chief actor. For this reason I am including these interchanges of which I have spoken in the Beginning of the story, and prefer to regard the Body of the story as being made up of the attempts of the main actor, Monte, to overcome the conditions which confront him from time to time in the progress of the story.

The interesting difference between this story and the two which we have previously examined is that in this story the Beginning occupies 673 lines out of a total of 1483, and that the Body occupies 749 lines and the Ending 62. In this story the Beginning is nearly *one half* of the whole story.

In my work with writers who are interested in analyzing the material of their own and other writer's stories, I have found that at certain stages of their progress they come to a kind of impasse. Settings they can learn to write after very little training. As a matter of fact, in the modern short-story, setting plays a very minor part. Characterization writers learn more slowly than they learn setting; but with the knowledge always before them that characterization can be learned through properly directed observation of the reactions of people to the various stimuli of life. The actual selection of presentation units—which is plotting,—and which is really the most mechanical portion of writing a story, writers seem to find very difficult. It is almost as if they had inhibitions. They learn to plot and present the Body of the story, and to plot and present the Ending of a story, but in a story which has a long Beginning they immediately find difficulty. It is because this story is in that particular category that writers will find it of very much interest.

It will, I hope, prove encouraging to writers to learn that in general the faults that creep into their work are the natural outcome of definite progress which they have made. Unfortunately, in graduating from one set of difficulties, they have reached a point where they find themselves confronted with a new set of difficulties. It is exactly as if a man who, after striving for a long time to jump a three foot hurdle, at last succeeds in doing so easily and consistently, only to discover that he has a harder problem in learning to jump a hurdle five feet high. Instead of being discouraged he should, on the contrary, be very much encouraged by his former success, and because of that success he should be stirred to redoubled efforts.

Those writers who have difficulties with the Beginnings of their stories have made one step forward very definitely. That step is their realization that stories *do* have Beginnings. The hurdle over which they cannot jump is their own failure to realize that there are two distinct types of material which make up Beginnings. In the first type, which I shall call the intrinsically interesting Beginning, or intrinsically interesting narrative problem, that problem is important *in itself*. The explanatory matter is not essential to the reader's understanding of its importance. If you will turn to Case No. 7 in this book you will find reprinted the story *Paradise Island*, by Will Payne. The narrative problem of this story is, "Can Dwyer succeed in killing Langley?" This main narrative problem is an important one, and would be an important one at any time. Whenever a man sets out to kill another man it is important regardless of what led up to it. On the other hand, when a young man sets out to drive a car from Los Angles to St. Louis it is not an important problem. It is important only synthetically, and it falls into the category of the synthetically important Beginning. Its importance is clear to the reader only after he has been presented with a large amount of explanatory matter. It is an artificially contrived narrative problem which shows the main character called upon to accomplish some feat despite the opposition of a force or forces, which is made important because of what depends upon it artificially.

One of the anomalies of the craftsmanship of short-story writing is that the writer who knows quite a good deal about his subject is often likely to be misled by his knowledge of craftsmanship into errors of execution. This is particularly the case with this type of story. The writer knowing either instinctively or from hard-earned experience that the chief interest of the story comes when the opposing forces are caused to clash, tries to reach that point in his story at which this clash occurs at the earliest possible moment, and he does so by compressing the explanatory matter into a summary of the event or fifth step of the presentation unit. *No other method of deadening interest begins to compare in effectiveness with summary.* Yet the writer in his instinctive desire to improve his work was essentially sound when he summarized. In so doing he fell into the pit because his deductions were faulty. Here, if ever, is a case where, if the mountain won't come to Mohammed, Mohammed must go to the mountain. Instead of taking the life out of the Beginning of his story by omitting the interchanges which can always be developed so that they are encounters, in order that the reader may reach the clash in the Body of the story, the writer should *add* life to the Beginning by causing it to contain in its interchanges the same sort of clash that would normally occur in the interchanges in the Body.

The problem of craftsmanship confronting Mr. Adams in presenting this story was that the main narrative question could not be made to emerge for almost the first half of the story. It does not emerge until the end of the interchange between Sally and Monte (lines 563 to 605). The conditions to be presented to the reader are these: Monte English, the hero, a young Easterner, who has just brought a foreign orphan car, a Vindix, across the continent to Los Angeles there meets and falls in love with the heroine, Sally, whose dead father once owned that very car. Sally has just bought a new Vindix against the advice of her "almost guardian," Carson Kerry, agent for the Kamco Six, an American car. It becomes clear that Monte and Sally are in love, Monte resisting because he is too poor to consider marriage to a rich girl. Kerry and Sally quarrel. It develops during the quarrel that Sally's aunt is to be married in St. Louis and wants Sally there. Kerry suggests that Sally marry him and that they go east together. The quarrel culminates in a wager that if the Vindix cannot be piloted from Los Angeles to St. Louis under its own power in time for the wedding of Sally's aunt, Sally will marry Carson Kerry. Although Kerry suggests that he find a mechanic Sally insists upon being allowed to make her own selection: Monte. That is the main condition. Up to this point the story is all Beginning and the main narrative question does not emerge until Sally goes to Monte and asks him to act as her representative in driving the car. For nearly half the story, then, the reader must be held by the writer before he comes to the main narrative question of the story, "Can Monte English succeed in driving an orphan Vindix from Los Angles to St. Louis in two weeks under its own power, thereby winning the girl?"

Although to the inexperienced writer this would be a hurdle very high indeed, to Mr. Adams it presents no difficulties, because he is an experienced writer and knows the most important tenets of the creed of fiction craftsmanship—that interchanges are always the most interesting presentation units, because they can always be developed into complete scenes. His plot sense also tells him that if he uses episodes which are interchanges without clash, they should result in crises in the plot, and that the promise of conflict is an extremely good way to hold the interest of the reader, pending the reader's knowledge of the happenings that will enable him to phrase for himself a main, unifying, central narrative question. This story is in its Beginning a series of interchanges. If the interchanges are in themselves dramatic we can often forego the presence of plot complications, although these can always be additional ornaments to the presentation units.

The first interchange between Kerry and Sally on lines 1 to 75 is a dramatic scene. At its close we learn that Sally does not want this man, Carson Kerry, as a husband. The plot could here have been strengthened had the writer indicated the promise of conflict to the main story by saying that she realized that Carson Kerry was not a man lightly to be dismissed, that he would make trouble for any man with whom she might later fall in love. Then, in the next interchange between Sally and Monte, on lines 76 to 154 this threat of conflict would have carried over and would have strengthened that scene. This second interchange, between Sally and Monte, could have been strengthened in its fifth step had the author pointed out that Sally was in love with this man; but that he had no intention of permitting himself to fall in love with her, or at least to pursue the acquaintance further. Then we would have had two promises of conflict and disaster. However, at the close of the next scene this is made pretty clear on lines 260 to 283, although the importance of it is slightly minimized by the statement that Sally was absolutely unscrupulous. It would have been a little stronger had the emphasis been upon the seriousness with which Sally regarded the meeting. At the close of the next meeting which occupies lines 284 to 342 the reader learns that the Vindix is an orphan car, but does not understand the importance of this in relation to the main problem because he does not yet know what that main problem is. The next meeting is between Sally and the garage man on lines 343 to 374 which results in her sending for Monte. It could have been improved very much had Carson Kerry been there present and insisted or tried to insist upon her sending for somebody else. The two rivals could then have been brought face to face earlier and out of this meeting could have grown an assurance by Monte that if she ever needed him he would be willing to do anything she asked him. This could have occupied the place of the interchange which now occurs on lines 375 to 408. Carson Kerry could, as a result of this, have warned her against seeing more of Monte and that would have added piquancy to the expedition to the beach which now occupies lines 409 to 485. Lines 486 to 562 are the limits of a dramatic scene which occurs between Carson Kerry and Sally. The fifth step of this scene is actually another scene between Monte and the girl. (Lines 563 to 599 with a fifth step of lines 600 to 605.) From then on the reader's interest is clearly held by a knowledge of the main narrative question.

The writer may learn one extremely interesting and basic lesson from reading the Beginning of this story. It is, to present the explanatory matter leading up to the main narrative question in a series of interchanges, making them, wherever possible, dramatic scenes, and pointing out to the reader at the conclusion of each such scene the promise of conflict necessary to avert disaster, to overcome difficulties, or to overcome opponents. 606 to 654 which I have included in the Beginning of the story is a dramatic clash which clearly presents the promise of dangerous opposition. The interchange on lines 674 to 730 presents the promise of disaster. The fifth step of this scene is the interview between Mac and Monte on lines 731 to 751 which makes clear to the reader that Monte is aware of the first condition which he has to overcome. This is the obstacle which stands in the way of his successful performance. Thereafter the Body of the story is made up of a series of such obstacles. These obstacles occur in such a plausible way that the reader is caused to feel that almost any one of them is sufficient to ruin the whole enterprise. He is forever compelled to ask himself, with a sort of breathlessness, "Now what will the main actor do when he encounters *that* condition or obstacle?"

The more numerous the obstacles, and the more difficult these obstacles are, the more sustained is this interest of breathlessness. In selecting and arranging these conditions or obstacles the ingenuity of the writer is taxed. The problem is again one of craftsmanship. Experience comes to the writer's aid. The established writer is identified by his knowledge of one simple basic rule in selecting conditions or obstacles. It is this: "The ideal condition or obstacle to be overcome is the one which presents a state of affairs from which there appears to be no solution but disaster."

In the Body of his story the writer is confronted by a dilemma. It is this: the plot may always be increased in breathlessness by the introduction of apparently insuperable obstacles, but the reader's interest must be also concentrated upon the character of the chief actor. He cannot be a weakling, but must be a person of resource who is able to overcome obstacles. For that reason the chief actor must be confronted with conditions which arises through fate or through the machinations of some opponent. In this particular story this requirement is very admirably met when Monte finds the motor of the Vindix ruined. He substitutes the motor of his own car; but the reader is not allowed long to believe that success will crown his efforts, because in the next interchange between Monte and Sally, the threat of conflict between these two presents a hindrance by threatening the successful outcome of the enterprise. Then later, when all goes well to Flagstaff for four days through the enterprise of Monte, this apparent success is changed to what appears to be failure, by the breaking of the front wheel bearing which it is impossible to replace, according to Kerry. Next, when Monte overtakes the others Kerry is caused to say that the bearing is probably a temporary Babbitt bearing which will not last very long. When later this prediction does not seem to be borne out, there is a hindrance through Kerry's planting liquor in Monte's car and notifying the sheriff. Later, when this is overcome by the sheriff buying the liquor, there is a furtherance, which is not as well chosen as it might be because it is not the action of Monte to overcome the obstacle which was presented by his opponent. Yet it does show his ability to meet almost any condition. Following this there comes the strain upon the Vindix which requires overhauling, when the time limit is rapidly threatening disaster. Then there comes the hindrance which the magnanimity of Monte brings about.

In this case, although the hindrance was caused by the main character, it was not caused by a weakness in his character, but rather by a strength. Also the reader's dislike for Kerry is increased when he gloats over the stripping of the differential gear of the Vindix. Monte's resourcefulness is shown when he fixes the gear with the spare parts of his own old Vindix. This furtherance is instantly removed by the stealing, by Kerry, of the balance of the spare parts, and also by his arranging with his subordinates to smash up the Vindix. Then, instead of Monte getting himself out of the difficulty, an agent of his, Sally, or perhaps we might say an ally, is brought in and she is used to rescue him by bringing along the spare parts in the car owned by Kerry. However, the two cars sent out by Kerry attempt another wreck, and the big moment of the story occurs. Monte averts this disaster by his skillful driving, and avoids collision. At last he arrives in time for the wedding. The main narrative question is answered in the affirmative, "Yes, he can get the Vindix across to St. Louis in two weeks." There are still some loose ends to be taken up, and they involve the winning of the girl; and it is for this reason that the interchanges between Sally and Kerry on lines 1441 to 1479, and between Sally and Monte on lines 1480 to 1483 are introduced.

But interesting as this arrangement is, the most interesting and helpful lesson which the aspiring writer can learn from a study of this story is the one which Mr. Adams has so well mastered. Every condition which the hero is called upon to meet is made to appear to the reader to present an insuperable obstacle. The outcome of the main attempt is always in suspense. For that reason alone, this story will repay a thorough analysis.

ARCHITECTURAL CHART

OF

JAKE BOLTON, 551

BEGINNING	Initial Condition and Main Actor's purpose are set forth.	Jake Bolton and Captain	1– 52
		Captain and Lieutenant	53– 66
		Captain and Lieutenant.	67– 94

BEGINNING — Initial Condition and Main Actor's purpose are set forth.

Jake Bolton and Captain — 1– 52

Captain and Lieutenant — 53– 66

Captain and Lieutenant. — 67– 94

Main Plot Crises apparent. Promises of dramatic Conflict to overcome Difficulties, to overcome opponents, to avert Disaster. Main Narrative Question: "Can Jake Bolton, 551 succeed in making good in the army?"

BODY — Series of attempts of Main Actor to achieve his purpose. Attempts by opponent to prevent that achievement.

Scene. Jake and Subaltern. — 95–126 — Hindrance. Has made enemy who has power to defeat.

Scene (Resumed). Jake and Subaltern. — 127– 223 — Hindrance. Has name and number taken.

Scene. Jake and Colonel. — 224– 235 — Hindrance. Has a bad name.

Interchanges show effect upon actors. — 236– 315 — Hindrance. Name confirmed.

Jake and condition. — 316– 392 — Furtherance. Nickname forgotten.

Jake and Richards and Sergeant. — 393– 417 — Hindrance-Dramatic. Threat of conflict with a dangerous opponent.

Jake and General. — 418– 427 — Furtherance.

Captain and Lieut. (5th step of 418–426.) — 428– 438 — Promise of Disaster. Dramatic Hindrance.

Sikh and Sergeant. Sergeant and Jake. — 439– 482 / 483– 504 — Dramatic Hindrance. Beach unsafe for Jake. Furtherance. Feels safe. Hindrance. Subaltern appears.

Jake and Corporal. — 505– 638 — Hindrance. Name again taken by hostile officer.

Jake and Subaltern. — 639– 751 — Furtherance. But success in encounter is not ultimate success.

Jake, Colonel, and Subaltern. — 752– 868 — Hindrance. Nickname revived.

(5th step. Effect.) — 869– 894 — Furtherance. Does brave deed.

Meeting. Jake and condition. — 895– 981

ENDING — Conclusive Act / Sequel.

Scene. Jake and Staff Officer. — 982–1024 — Main Narrative Question Answered: "No." Character abandons any attempt to make good.

Captain Graham and Lieutenant Townsend. Appended episode gives answer to Main Narrative Question, correcting impression left by 980–1025 — 1025–1053 — Revised answer to Main Narrative Question: "Yes." Jake Bolton has made good.

88

JAKE BOLTON, 551

BY JOHN GALLISHAW

My reasons for reprinting this story are largely personal. Chief among them is my own reaction to statements made by people who have examined analyses which I have made of stories by other authors. These statements were to the effect that the author whose story was analyzed would himself be the last person in the world to be conscious of having striven for definite effect. The only way to prove that such is the case is to select a story which would illustrate the actual building up of a story from a partial plot. I know how this story grew, what was its nucleus, and the various steps in its progress.

I am reprinting *Jake Bolton, 551* not because it is such a good story, but because it lends itself very readily to an illustration of the actual growth of a story from the first conception of the idea until its final appearance in a magazine.

CASE No. 4

JAKE BOLTON, 551

BY JOHN GALLISHAW

1 Captain Graham, the recruit-
2 ing officer, inwardly pleased but
3 outwardly non-committal, sur-
4 veyed appraisingly the wind-
5 tanned, good humored face of
6 the tall recruit, and demanded
7 his name, his occupation, his
8 address, next of kin, and such
9 other particulars as go toward
10 filling out an enlistment-blank.
11 The recruit, it appeared, had no
12 next of kin and no permanent
13 place of abode, and on the
14 official records his name and
15 occupation were set down as
16 Bolton, Jake, trapper and woods-
17 man.
18 The rank and file of the First
19 Colonials, who respect no official
20 record save the pay-roll, paid no
21 attention to this, but hailed him
22 as "Hippo," because of his two
23 hundred and thirty pounds.
24 He took his place easily in
25 the First Colonials. He was a
26 crack shot, since much of his
27 livelihood had depended on his
28 skill with a rifle, and learning
29 to shoot had come to him as
30 unconsciously as learning to
31 walk to ordinary children. All
32 his twenty-five years had been
33 spent in the forest, and all his
34 sustenance had been wrung from
35 it. Hunting had given him the
36 training of a scout, lumbering
37 had developed muscles of steel
38 and a frame of iron, and danger
39 and exposure he took as matters
40 of course. For a soldier no
41 better material could be desired.
42 The doctors found him organ-
43 ically faultless and his eyesight
44 abnormally keen, and passed
45 him as "fit." So Captain
46 Graham, prophesying that in
47 three months he couldn't be told
48 from a regular, detailed him to
49 his own beloved B Company,
50 and noted his name as good
51 material for a non-commissioned
52 officer.
53 "That man," he remarked to
54 Lieutenant Townsend, "is bound
55 to make good."
56 "Making good in the army,"
57 said Lieutenant Townsend, "de-
58 pends entirely on how you get
59 started. It's a case of give a dog
60 a bad name, and you hang him."

"I go by a man's eyes," replied the Captain. "That man has character enough in those straightforward eyes of his to live down any bad name he can ever acquire."

When the preliminary sorting out and posting had been completed, the First Colonials crossed the ocean and went into intensive training under canvas with their fellows at Salisbury Plain. Captain Graham and Lieutenant Townsend again discussed Jake Bolton.

"Bolton worries me a little," said the Lieutenant. "He's pretty independent. He never says 'Sir,' to an officer."

"Who cares," said the Captain easily.

"None of our crowd," admitted the lieutenant. "Our officers are pretty lax on formalities, but I have a hunch that he'll get into trouble with some of those English Officers. You know they can put him on the crime sheet, and he looks like the obstinate kind that won't stir one step to placate them. If those young subalterns once begin asking him his name and number, he's gone."

Lieutenant Townsend's prophecy was soon justified. When Salisbury was knee-deep in liquid mud the trouble began through a particularly youthful-looking subaltern who had imbibed too freely at the officer's mess. He disputed the narrow strip of dry sidewalk with Jake, who was on his way from camp to the town of Salisbury. That was in the first year of the war, when the only requirement for a commission as a second lieutenant in the English army was an uncle. The subaltern, who had the chest of a consumptive, the shoulders of a ginger-ale bottle, the voice of a school-girl, and the manners of a pampered Pekinese, ordered Jake to step off the dry sidewalk that he might pass. The argument was short; a St. Bernard might so have argued with a lap-dog. The big Colonial seized the subaltern by the coat-collar, swung him round behind him, and proceeded.

"They'll soon be wheeling 'em up in baby-carriages to give 'em commissions," was his only comment.

The enraged subaltern followed him closely, demanding at thirty-second intervals, "I say, my man, what is your name and numbah?"

There is one form of torturing prisoners that German ingenuity has so far failed to devise; compared with it, crucifying with bayonets or inoculating with tetanus germs is merciful. It consists in saying to a private soldier, "I say, my man, what is your name and numbah?" Usually in the British army it precedes an inquisition before the commanding officers, resulting in anything from two-days' confinement to camp to fourteen days' field punishment No. 2, which consists of being spread-eagled every day for two hours to the wheel of an artillery-wagon. It is a form of reprisal practised by fledgeling lieutenants on home duty toward men returned from active service, who are guilty of such heinous offences as not saluting or forgetting to button their greatcoats. At Salisbury Plain in 1914 there were many men to whom the question was a veritable sword of Damocles. To this category Jake belonged.

Into the town of Salisbury he strode, apparently unaware of the existence of the subaltern panting behind. More than ever the combination resembled the St. Bernard and the Pekinese. Through the streets of Salisbury Jake proceeded, stopping frequently at places that displayed alluring signs setting forth "Ales, Wines, and Intoxicating Liquors, Licensed to be Drunk on the Premises." Always the officer followed him, and always the yapping cry rang out behind him.

"I say, my man, what is your name and numbah?"

Ever and anon the officer appealed to other Colonials to arrest the man; but they shrugged their shoulders, disclaiming any duty of obedience to an officer not of their own battalion. Some of them told him frankly, "We'll be damned if we'll arrest one of our own men"; but others, more wily, desiring to be beyond reproof, asserted sickness.

Scornfully careless of the riot he created, Jake swung along, pausing only at intervals to refresh himself, and behind the frantic subaltern followed his comrades, taking up the wail: "I say, my man, what is your name and numbah?"

The officer's patience was rewarded when Jake fell asleep on a bench and leaned his bulk against one of the signs, blotting out the part that referred to the liquors. The picture he presented was of a gigantic young man sleeping heavily against a sign which read, "Licensed to be Drunk on the Premises."

An hour later a corporal's guard, sent by the subaltern, found him there, loaded him into a cart, and took him with much indignity to the guard tent on Salisbury Plain, where the subaltern, following persistently, caused the sergeant of the guard to write upon a "crime sheet" the name, "Jake Bolton, 551," and following it the two charges, "drunk" and "insolent to a superior officer."

The next day the colonel of Jake's battalion heard the complaint of the young officer, and although he made clear to the subaltern that he hated any in-

229 terference with his battalion,
230 discipline had to be maintained.
231 He lectured Jake on the neces-
232 sity of respecting the uniform of
233 a superior officer, and sentenced
234 him to four days "C.C." for
235 being drunk.

236 This, translated, means four
237 days confined to camp. To
238 Jake this mattered very little,
239 since all his money was gone and
240 all his headache was not. The
241 four days passed as all days pass,
242 and the headache disappeared
243 the way of all headaches, but the
244 legend of Jake's parade through
245 town endured. Among the First
246 Colonials it is a classic. Some
247 of them have read of "Sherman's
248 March to the Sea," and a few of
249 them of "Paul Revere's Ride,"
250 but in days to come, when
251 Sherman is only a name and
252 Paul Revere is forgotten, the
253 survivors of the First Colonials
254 will tell their children's children
255 of the night that "Name and
256 Number" marched through Sal-
257 isbury, and of his ignoble ride
258 back.

259 Beginning with that night life
260 changed for Jake. By the First
261 Colonials Jake Bolton was there-
262 after no longer hailed as "Hippo"
263 but as "Jake Bolton, 551." He
264 could not live down that nick-
265 name. Thenceforth it was the
266 usual thing to see young
267 Richards, the seventeen-year-
268 old bantam drummer, petted,
269 spoiled, and beloved of everyone,
270 stride behind Jake, piping up at

271 intervals in an absurd falsetto
272 voice, to the huge amusement of
273 onlookers,

274 "I say, my man, what is your
275 name and numbah?"

276 Through ten months of train-
277 ing in the British Isles and in
278 Egypt the legend pursued him,
279 and for officers of battalions
280 other than his own Jake fostered
281 a hatred that was the greater
282 since he found few opportunities
283 to vent it. A less good-natured
284 man might have become soured,
285 but toward his comrades his
286 attitude of easy-going friendship
287 remained always the same. He
288 answered as cheerfully as the
289 others the question, "What is
290 your name and number?" and
291 through the weeks that the First
292 Colonials sweltered in their
293 marquees on the edge of the
294 desert near Cairo the question
295 he had made famous ranked
296 with the one attributed to the
297 Governor of North Carolina.
298 No matter how sultry the day
299 or how thick the flies, there was
300 always a response. Into a
301 marquee where twenty men
302 listlessly smoked cigarettes and
303 swatted flies between whiffs
304 someone would stick his head
305 and inquire in a voice tinged with
306 an exaggerated English drawl,
307 "I say, my man, what is your
308 name and numbah?" No call to
309 arms or official command could
310 ever move them as did that
311 question. The twenty would
312 rise and shout as one man in a

94

313 monotonous sing-song, "Jake
314 Bolton, 551, B Company, First
315 Colonials."
316 At last the First Colonials
317 went to the Dardanelles and no
318 sooner had the battalion landed
319 on the peninsula than Jake ful-
320 filled the promise of his physique
321 and training. He became one of
322 the best soldiers in the battalion.
323 Through the long days, monot-
324 onous and fly-infested, when the
325 well nigh intolerable heat
326 brought complaints and grumb-
327 lings from his companions, he
328 lay on the firing-step of the
329 trench, contentedly puffing at
330 a large pipe. Through ghastly
331 nights when the whine of bullets
332 ticked off the minutes, he
333 crawled through no-man's land,
334 his deer-stalking experience
335 standing him in good stead. On
336 trench raids, in listening posts,
337 lying through mud-soaked hours
338 as silent as a snake and just as
339 dangerous, wriggling through
340 dank, uncut grass of neglected
341 orchards, he was unequalled.
342 At such work he was at home;
343 to him every sound in that
344 ghoulish hunting-ground was
345 pregnant with meaning. The
346 sharp crack of a broken twig
347 that went unnoticed by others
348 he interpreted rightly as the
349 movement of the wily sniper.
350 In accordance with the law of
351 mutation, therefore, he became
352 a sharpshooter, and thenceforth
353 he was free to come and go as he
354 pleased. For the sharpshooter

355 is an arrogant king of the
356 trenches; his attitude toward the
357 ordinary soldier is that of a
358 senior of a small college toward
359 a freshman. He calls no one his
360 superior unless it is another
361 sniper with more kills to his
362 credit. Thenceforth Jake was
363 as nearly happy as mortal can
364 be. Thereafter he was wont,
365 just as dusk made indistinct the
366 landmarks of no-man's land,
367 disguising them with nature's
368 own camouflage, to take his rifle,
369 examine the telescopic sights
370 carefully, clean it painstak-
371 ingly, equip himself with en-
372 ough bully beef and biscuits,
373 and disappear for two or three
374 days. Out there he felt safe from
375 the pursuing question. Swelter-
376 ing heat, sameness of food, lack
377 of sleep, and scarcity of water
378 made no difference to him. He
379 found it all strange, exciting, and
380 stimulating; and while the bulk
381 of the battalion sickened, he
382 waxed strong. In two months the
383 First Colonials had been reduced
384 to one-third of their original
385 strength; the remainder, each
386 doing two men's work, toiled on,
387 too occupied to think of nick-
388 names. Jake's only contact
389 with the others came when he
390 returned for the semi-weekly
391 distribution of rum, or on dig-
392 ging "fatigues."
393 Returning one drizzly night
394 from four hour's digging in a
395 new communication trench, he
396 sought young Richards, who

397 always saved his rum for Jake.
398 The drummer shivered in his
399 blankets, and instead of indulg-
400 ing in his usual bantering, said
401 simply, "I'm sick." Jake felt
402 the throbbing forehead, gave
403 him a drink of his own precious
404 rum, then seizing his own
405 blanket, wrapped the young
406 drummer in it.

407 "I made a mistake," he ex-
408 plained. "It's not your turn.
409 I'll call you when it is."

410 The sergeant to whom he
411 reported for young Richard's
412 "fatigue" regarded him doubt-
413 fully. "There's a staff officer
414 round here, that looks like the
415 baby that did you dirt at Salis-
416 bury. You'd better "sir" him,
417 'cause he's sure out for blood."

418 The first staff officer who
419 came upon Jake working, was
420 the commanding general who
421 was inspecting the lines. He
422 ignored Jake's failure to say
423 "Sir."

424 "If we had a regiment of
425 men like him," he commented,
426 " we'd dig our way to Constan-
427 tinople."

428 Captain Graham, on being
429 told of the happening by Lieu-
430 tenant Townsend, commented:

431 "I guess there's no fear of Bol-
432 ton getting in wrong after that."

433 "Not if we can keep him up
434 here in the front line, away from
435 the English officers," agreed the
436 Lieutenant.

437 But he reckoned without Jake
438 Bolton's liking for rum.

439 Jake's meeting with the
440 general occurred when the First
441 Colonials had been on the Penin-
442 sula only two months, and had
443 advanced only four miles inland.
444 Despite the fact that one
445 hundred and forty miles sepa-
446 rated them from Constantinople,
447 the First Colonials visualized the
448 entire distance traversed by
449 trenches that they had dug. At
450 any rate, the general's statement
451 encouraged Jake and his friends
452 to dig through tangled ravines
453 and hills scarred and torn by
454 shells a winding communication
455 trench, deep and narrow, down
456 the four miles that separated
457 the firing line from the beach,
458 thus forming one of the highways
459 for the supplies of ammunition
460 and food.

461 Through this newly completed
462 trench one moonlight night came
463 a tall Sikh, bearded and digni-
464 fied.

465 "Some nights ago," he said,
466 speaking carefully and slowly to
467 the sergeant, who had been
468 hurriedly summoned by the
469 sentry, "my mule cart was
470 blocked. God was good, and
471 sent to help me some of the men
472 of your regiment. They were in
473 search of mail, which they
474 found not. On the beach
475 which is called Kangaroo Land-
476 ing there are now ten bags of
477 mail for the First Colonials."
478 Having by returning a favor,
479 thus lived up to one of the first
480 principles of the Sikh religion, he

saluted gravely, turned on his heel and disappeared.

"There's a bunch of us fellows that's resting, that'd like nothing better than to go and get that mail," suggested Jake, who had just completed his own and young Richards's stint of digging.

"You've got a funny idea of resting," said the sergeant. "But I guess you know best." He turned to the group sitting on the firing step of the trench.

"I want ten volunteers to get that mail."

Four times that number volunteered, because it meant a trip to the beach, where there was a possibility of meeting artillery men, who usually had plenty of rum. Jake, because of his size, was one of the ten selected.

Marching beside the corporal in charge of the detail, he set off with his usual good nature. During the trip down the sinuous communication trench, save for the occasional sharp crack of an explosive bullet or the whine of one that was spent, there was nothing to indicate that men were fighting. The party emerged upon a broad plateau, flanked by hills, one of which formed an effective barrier to Turkish artillery fire, and served as an excellent location for dugouts. Through slits in the canvas coverings of these, candles guttered in the wind. and their light guided the party past the first-aid dressing station, but did not prevent them from almost blundering into a battery disguised as a clump of bushes, whence some artillery men cursed them. Thence they skirted the Indian transport, warned therefrom by the squealing of mules, shaping their course by the Red Cross that flapped bravely in the fresh breeze above the hospital tent, fronted by a row of silent motor ambulances, finally emerging upon a rocky foreland from which many piers and boats ran out into the angry, wind-swept waters of the Ægean Sea. This was Kangaroo Landing. One side of the beach was piled high with boxes landed recently from the lighters that incessantly plowed a spray-covered course from the piers to the deeper water, where the transports lay beyond the reach of Turkish fire. The other side was given over to a dump in which were piled the kits of the dead, together with those of the wounded, who had been relieved of them before they were taken off to the hospital ship, the red cross of which, oulined in electric light, now shone, steady and unwinking, far out in the bay, now and then obscured by some fantastic, unsubstantial gray shape of a warship flitting to and fro in the moonlight, superintending the landing of reinforcements.

565 A little beyond the heap of 566 piled-up equipments, a lone 567 Australian paced slowly back 568 and forth outside the barbed- 569 wire enclosure that contained 570 the Anzac dead who had been 571 killed in the landing. The 572 lonely sentinel stopped long 573 enough to greet them, indicated 574 the dugout where they might 575 find the ten bags of mail, and 576 resumed his march.

577 Each member of the party 578 selected a bag, hoisted it to 579 his shoulder, and began the 580 return journey. All the lighter 581 bags had been taken by the 582 others, and the heaviest one 583 fell to Jake, who had lingered 584 to chat further with the Aus- 585 tralian. But his bulk and 586 muscle were well equal to the 587 load, and his good nature sur- 588 passed both. Without com- 589 plaint he placed the bag on his 590 shoulder, pushing past the 591 others, and fell in at the head of 592 the line.

593 When the party reached the 594 communication trench the cor- 595 poral took Jake's rifle to lighten 596 his burden, and the cavalcade 597 wound through the trench. Jake 598 hurried as much as the nature 599 of the trench would permit, for 600 he was anxious to witness the 601 opening of the mail bags, and in 602 a short time he and the corporal 603 were a considerable distance in 604 advance of their companions. 605 After fifteen minutes of walking 606 they stopped until their com-

panions overtook them. Jake 607 crouched down in the shadow of 608 the bag and lit his pipe; then, 609 leaning against the bag, puffed 610 contentedly. 611

"I wonder if I get a letter from 612 that girl in Edinburgh," said the 613 corporal, a man of many 614 armours. "By Jingo! I wish 615 I was there now. How'd you 616 like to stroll down Prince's 617 Street tonight, Jake?" 618

"Not me," said Jake, decided- 619 ly. "The peninsula of Gallipoli 620 is good enough for me: good 621 smoking tobacco, lots of fags, 622 nothing to worry you, rum twice 623 a week, and all the bully beef 624 and biscuits you can eat, to say 625 nothing of that damned apricot 626 jam." As he again shouldered 627 the mail sack at the sound of 628 the approaching party he added, 629 "I'm better off at the front than 630 I ever was in training. I have 631 some money storing up in the 632 pay-office in London, and no- 633 body ever says to me out here, 634 " 'I say, my man, what is your 635 name and number?' " He im- 636 itated as best he could the voice 637 of an English officer. 638

They had now reached a point 639 where the parapet was three 640 feet higher than the top of 641 Jake's head. Here the battle 642 had raged fiercely. Wave upon 643 wave of Turks had attacked and 644 attacked again, hurling them- 645 selves upon British bayonets, 646 forming and reforming, rallying 647 with superb intrepidity, in an 648

649 endeavor to drive out of their
650 land the handful of invaders.
651 But dour Scotch and fiery Irish
652 had doggedly met them, and
653 shoulder to shoulder with the
654 lean Australians had succeeded
655 in holding their own and digging
656 themselves in. This trench,
657 hastily dug under fire, the First
658 Colonials had later incorporated
659 in their communication trench
660 to save labor, for here the
661 ground was hard and unyielding,
662 and beset with huge, rocky
663 formations. To avoid these,
664 the trench twisted and curved
665 and turned at sharp angles.

666 Just now, around one of these
667 corners came a young British
668 officer, at the sight of whom
669 Jake heaved a sigh of resigna-
670 tion, as a man might sigh on
671 waking from a pleasant dream.
672 The man who came round the
673 corner of the trench was the
674 subaltern of Salisbury. Jake
675 recognized him immediately.
676 Stick, monocle, faultlessly fitting
677 uniform—there was no mistake.
678 " 'Tis him," said Jake, "just
679 the same as ever, walkin' on
680 eggshells. Sherman was right."

681 The encounter was Salisbury
682 repeated. Jake halted, glaring:
683 the officer halted. If he recog-
684 nized the tanned, determined-
685 looking giant before him, he
686 gave no sign.

687 "I say, my man," he said, with
688 his impersonal, irritating drawl,
689 "put that bag on the parapet
690 and let me pawss."

691 Jake glanced at the parapet,
692 three feet above his head, and
693 then at the officer.

694 "Who are you, anyway," he
695 said, "ordering me about?"

696 "I am your superior officer.
697 Put that bag on the parapet
698 and let me pawss."

699 Jake allowed the bag to slide
700 gently to the bottom of the
701 trench.

702 "Officer or no officer," he
703 said grimly, "you can walk
704 over it."

705 To the credit of the subaltern's
706 intelligence, be it said, he
707 grasped the situation immedi-
708 ately. He walked over the bag.
709 By this time the rest of the party
710 had come up and stood resting,
711 watching the scene with the
712 most intense interest and enjoy-
713 ment.

714 The subaltern, now on the
715 other side of the bag, glaring at
716 them, produced a pencil and a
717 note-book, at the sight of which
718 they sobered. "I say, my man,"
719 he said, indicating Jake with
720 the pencil, "what is your name
721 and numbah?"

722 At this the fatigue party lost
723 its gravity, and led by Jake,
724 yelled in a chorus that reverber-
725 ated down the deep trench,
726 "Jake Bolton, 551, B Company,
727 First Colonials."

728 The officer, frowning, noted the
729 names, first Jake's and then the
730 corporal's and some others' as
731 witnesses, and departed, breath-
732 ing threats of dire punishment.

733 "You'd better knock wood
734 the next time before you begin
735 to boast of how well off you are,
736 Jake," said the corporal.

737 "How did I know I was going
738 to meet him?" demanded Jake.
739 "I hope," he added feelingly, as
740 the corporal readjusted the mail
741 bag for him, "that nothing
742 happens to him—nothing, that
743 is, worse than being cut in two
744 by a shell, or dying of thirst
745 with a bottle of rum three feet
746 away from him." From then
747 until he pulled his blanket about
748 his head for the night, Jake
749 indulged in wild inventions de-
750 signed for the discomfiture of
751 the subaltern.

752 The next morning at nine
753 o'clock the corporal was ordered
754 to report to the colonel as
755 witness and to escort the pris-
756 oner. The prisoner appeared
757 little worried. This was by no
758 means the first time he had been
759 called before the colonel.

760 "The colonel hates that little
761 runt," he said, "hates anybody
762 that butts in on his battalion.
763 Remember the steward of the
764 Oscalona?"

765 This was a reference to a
766 famous occasion when the colonel
767 had refused to interfere in be-
768 half of the steward of a trans-
769 port who had run foul of the
770 wrath of the First Colonials.

771 "The colonel is a good sport,"
772 said Jake as he reached the edge
773 of the dugout that constituted
774 the orderly room in which the
colonel tried all cases of mis- 775
demeanor. Inside, the colonel, 776
the adjutant, and some officers 777
of the headquarters staff, seated 778
at a rough table, were dealing 779
with defaulters. A little to one 780
side stood the subaltern. Jake 781
was ordered to wait while the 782
other cases were dealt with. 783
His offenses were usually original 784
and of special interest. There- 785
fore the colonel, who always 786
looked forward with keen relish 787
to Jake's case, made it a point to 788
finish with other offenders first, 789
in order that he might give Jake 790
full consideration. 791

"Jake Bolton, 551, B Com- 792
pany," called an orderly, and the 793
prisoner and his escort entered. 794
The charge was "Insubordina- 795
tion and insolent behavior to- 796
ward an officer on the night of 797
October third." 798

"Bolton, have you anything 799
to say?" asked the colonel. 800

"Yes, sir, I have this to say. 801
I'll bet five pounds that that 802
little runt there,"—he indicated 803
with a casual nod the subaltern, 804
who glared contemptuously in 805
return—"couldn't lift that bag, 806
let alone put it on the para- 807
pet." 808

The Colonel was proud of his 809
First Colonials, and he had suf- 810
fered much from outside inter- 811
ference. In the regiment it was 812
whispered that on the occasion 813
of the Salisbury complaint he 814
had requested the young officer 815
to keep away from his battalion. 816

817 As Jake had said, he was a good
818 sport.

819 "Have you that much money
820 with you?" he demanded of the
821 astonished Jake.

822 "No, sir," said Jake, "but for
823 the first time since the outbreak
824 of war I have more than that
825 coming to me in London."

826 "Oh, well," said the colonel,
827 with a twinkle, "I'll lend you
828 that much if you wish to make
829 the wager." The Colonel was
830 running true to form.

831 "Mr. Penton," he added, turn-
832 ing to the bewildered subaltern,
833 "should you care to take up
834 Private Bolton on this wager?"

835 "No, Colonel," said Mr.
836 Penton, "I haven't come here
837 to make wagers. I came here to
838 have the man taught a lesson.
839 He was insolent to me. Why,
840 Colonel, he didn't even call me
841 'sir!'"

842 Apparently Mr. Penton was
843 not particularly tactful. Had
844 he been, he might have studied
845 the colonel a little more closely.

846 "Oh," said that officer, very
847 suavely, "that alters the case.
848 You are quite certain of that.
849 You are positive he didn't call
850 you 'sir'? Then I assume you
851 base your charge on that?"

852 "Yes, Colonel," agreed Mr.
853 Penton, brightening, "I base my
854 charge on that."

855 "Well you see, Mr. Penton,"
856 said the Colonel, "I gave my
857 men instructions in daily orders
858 some time in September that

859 they must in no way give any
860 indication to the enemy of the
861 rank of an officer. When the
862 place is alive with snipers and
863 spies, calling you 'sir' comes
864 under that heading. Anyhow,
865 it is hard to expect those
866 Colonials to call you 'sir'; they
867 don't even 'sir' me. Bolton
868 dismiss."

869 Jake's joy at the discomfiture
870 of Mr. Penton was not unmixed.
871 It was tinged with regret, be-
872 cause simultaneously he resumed
873 his old nickname of "Name and
874 Number." The men who had
875 been in the party sent for the
876 mail bags spread the story, and
877 the First Colonials seized upon
878 it, talked of it, enlarged upon it;
879 for every item of gossip is seized
880 upon in the trenches. In many
881 forms the episode was garbled
882 and distorted. It was given out
883 by a corporal with imagination
884 that Jake had died and had
885 refused to enter heaven because
886 St. Peter had demanded his
887 name and number.

888 Although he continued good-
889 natured and added much to the
890 life of the First Colonials, the
891 thought of that persisting
892 question rankled. To escape it,
893 he adopted all kinds of sub-
894 terfuges to avoid his fellows.

895 So things stood when the
896 battalion moved up one
897 night to a particularly dan-
898 gerous section of the firing
899 line.

900 At right angles to the portion

901 of trench which they took over,
902 a narrow sap, or rough ditch, ran
903 out toward the Turkish position,
904 terminating near a ridge that
905 commanded both their own and
906 the Turkish trenches. Which-
907 ever side could gain possession of
908 this ridge could enfilade the en-
909 emies' lines. To hold the sap
910 commanding this ridge was of
911 such vital importance that a
912 bomb-proof over-head covering
913 had been put on it at great cost in
914 human life, and twenty bomb
915 throwers garrisoned it day and
916 night. These twenty men were
917 from a famous Irish regiment,
918 and Jake, who was beloved of
919 the Irish, instead of spending his
920 resting time in his own trench,
921 went out into this sap to ex-
922 change gossip with the Irish,
923 while he evaded the pursuing
924 query of his own regiment, "I
925 say, my man, what is your name
926 and numbah?" In this sap, he
927 felt, he could keep out of trouble.
928 On that day, the Irish, steadily
929 sapping toward the ridge, dis-
930 covered that the Turks had dug
931 to within twenty-five yards of
932 them. One of them, sighting the
933 Turks, seized some bombs and
934 jumped up.
935 "Look at Johnny Tur-rk!
936 Let's bomb him t'hell out of ut."
937 But the Turk would not be
938 bombed out. He stayed where
939 he was despite the deluge of
940 bombs hurled at him. Not only
941 did he refuse to budge, but he
942 sent over some of his own bombs

943 toward the Irish sap. While
944 this exchange of bombing was
945 going on, Jake made his way
946 through all the dirt and dust
947 and smoke to the head of the
948 sap, where only the few yards
949 separated him from the Turks.
950 In one item of armament the
951 British are superior to the Turks;
952 the Turkish bombs explode five
953 seconds after they are thrown;
954 the British take only three
955 seconds. That day in the sap-
956 head the difference of two seconds
957 was of great account. For a
958 short time the British supply of
959 bombs ran out. The man who
960 was frantically trying to pry
961 the cover off a box of them with a
962 bayonet found difficulty in doing
963 it, and suddenly the men in the
964 saphead found themselves with-
965 out bombs.
966 At this unfortunate moment
967 the Turks found the range of
968 the British sap, and one of their
969 bombs landed at Jake's feet.
970 Instead of throwing himself flat
971 on the ground, as most of the
972 others did, or retreating to the
973 part of the sap covered by the
974 bomb-proof roof, he stooped
975 down coolly, picked up the
976 bomb, and threw it back, so
977 that it exploded near the Turks
978 who had sent it. The two extra
979 seconds were just enough to
980 allow him to return it. Then
981 his own supply was resumed.
982 A staff officer, attracted to the
983 sap by the noise of the bombing,
984 stood silent, a little behind him,

102

985 wonder-struck, open-mouthed,
986 gazing at the big Colonial. He
987 took a note-book and pencil from
988 his pocket and approached Jake.
989 "I say, my man," he said,
990 "what is your name and num-
991 ber?"
992 The look on Jake's face was
993 a study. He knew that his
994 proper place was in his own
995 trench and that he had no
996 business in that sap. Also he
997 knew that every time that
998 question had been shot at him
999 before it had meant a reprimand.
1000 For a moment he stood puzzled
1001 and undecided; he felt that some-
1002 how fate was dealing unfairly
1003 with him. The officer repeated
1004 his question, but more loudly
1005 this time, that he might be
1006 heard above the noise of some
1007 twenty of the First Colonials
1008 now crowding into the sap
1009 behind him. They, thinking
1010 that some of their friends were
1011 bantering Jake, shouted the
1012 answer they all knew so well,
1013 "Jake Bolton, 551, B Company,
1014 First Colonials."
1015 "Is that correct?" demanded
1016 the officer of Jake.
1017 The light of insurrection,
1018 which flared for an instant in
1019 Jake's eyes, died out.

1020 "Yes," he answered resign-
1021 edly. Then shrugging his
1022 shoulders, he turned to the man
1023 next to him and said, "What in
1024 hell have I done now?"
1025 In a dugout close to the firing-
1026 line, Captain Graham gazed
1027 through a haze of tobacco smoke
1028 at Lieutenant Townsend.
1029 "Had a visit from a brass hat,
1030 my boy," he said. "Brass hat"
1031 is the irreverent way in which
1032 officers of the line refer to staff
1033 officers.
1034 "Straffing you about the con-
1035 dition of the trenches, I sup-
1036 pose," volunteered the other.
1037 "Wrong. He wanted to make
1038 certain about Sergeant Bolton."
1039 "Who's Sergeant Bolton?"
1040 "He's Jake Bolton, 551, of my
1041 company."
1042 "Oh, you mean my friend
1043 'Name and Number.' I thought
1044 Jake was a private."
1045 "So he was until today, when
1046 he was promoted for bravery in
1047 the face of the enemy. The
1048 brass hat was getting correct
1049 particulars, so that he could
1050 recommend him for a Distin-
1051 guished Conduct Medal. Re-
1052 member now what I said to you
1053 once about that man's eyes?"

THE ANALYSIS

From the point of view of material there are four starting points
for a story: a setting or atmosphere, a character, which is the sum
of the traits of a person, a series of happenings making a partial
plot, or a thematic idea. It is absurd to say that these can long

remain distinct; because all four will merge gradually, each contributing somewhat to the general effect. For example, while in *Jake Bolton, 551* I was interested chiefly in the characteristics of the chief actor, I was also concerned with the thematic idea that any man of character could make good during the war,—this "making good" consisting of being promoted and decorated. (When I talk of a thematic idea I mean what the older story writers mean by the moral of the tale, and what the newer writers mean by the "significance" of a story.) Besides being interested in characteristics and in the theme, I wanted also to render, as much as possible without clogging the story, the atmosphere of the Gallipoli campaign, and of the particular setting against which the action took place. While the action of the story depended primarily upon the responses of the chief actor, the special actions could not have happened so readily elsewhere, although of course they might have taken place on almost any battle front. The initial impulse to write the story came, it must be admitted, from interest in the character of the original of *Jake Bolton, 551*.

What I had to work with as the nucleus of this story was a knowledge of the character of Jake Bolton; and in addition to this I knew of certain actual happenings that focused my attention upon Jake. Those happenings were his meeting with the young subaltern in the trench, and the episode of the bomb which he threw back. Everything else in the story had to be invented or developed.

I have always felt that a writer in presenting a series of happenings to an audience has no right to present an isolated happening, or a series of isolated happenings, from which the audience may be allowed to draw a conclusion, unless that writer feels that this conclusion, so to be drawn, is a sound one. When I talk about the thematic idea behind a story, this is what I have in mind. In the real life version poor Jake was not decorated. Instead, the officer who saw him throw back the bomb, turned upon his heel when Jake Bolton said, "What in hell have I done now?" and walked away in high dudgeon. Later, however, Jake received his reward, although it was not for this special act of bravery.

My materials, then, were the knowledge of Jake's moving characteristics: his obstinacy, his kindliness, and his great willingness to bear burdens. Coupled with this was an understanding of the psychology of the colonial soldier who had enlisted as a private "for the duration of the war." This understanding came from a background of experience in a colonial regiment at Gallipoli, brigaded with British units, in such a manner that although the immediately superior officers were colonials, the higher ranks were held by English officers of the old school. Conditioning my treatment of all this material was an interest in the purely emotional effect of such a terrain as the Gallipoli peninsula, and a desire to reproduce that atmosphere in writing about it.

But in the long run the character of *Jake Bolton, 551*, his unconscious heroism, his simplicity, his kindliness, his unselfishness, and the solid qualities of the man were what interested me. Character, rather than anything else, was the material with which I had to work, and I had before me two complete presentation units in which the character traits in which I was interested were evident.

In considering structure I simply had to take into consideration the fact that character in action as shown by the responses of the actor to the various stimuli which he encounters is what interests the reader; and I had to select and arrange the happenings in such a way that from the presentation units which I used the character I wished to portray might emerge. My problem, then, was largely one of structure.

In building up a story structurally one can obviously take only three points of departure. A writer may have the structural nucleus of a Beginning with no Body and no Ending. He may have the structural nucleus for a Body with no Beginning and no Ending. Or he may have an Ending with no Beginning or Body.

If he has a Beginning it is a narrative problem demanding action of the main character for its solution. It can be phrased as a main or story narrative question. When I come to a discussion of the flashback Beginning I shall go more into detail as to the reasons for its use, but at the present time it is sufficient to say that the main narrative question cannot be presented in the synthetically important story very quickly because it would not of itself hold interest.

If it is an Ending it is a conclusive act which answers a main narrative question. Given a main narrative question or narrative problem a writer can easily find an ending, because to every narrative question raised by a narrative problem, there must be an answer which is either "yes" or "no." Given a decisive or conclusive act his task is not so easy, although it is definite and comparatively simple. He has to find a narrative question to which that Conclusive Act may be the answer.

Thus a writer's task, when he has a Beginning, is a very simple one, because the answer must be either yes or no to the main narrative question. But if he has an Ending only, it may be the answer to any one of a number of different narrative questions.

The material with which I was working could not be classified as either Beginning or Ending. There was no special narrative main situation or problem and there was no special decisive or conclusive act. I had merely two meetings or encounters in each of which my main character ran afoul of the officialdom of the British army as exemplified by officers. I had two cases in which the meetings resulted in the character's being "in wrong." As soon as I came to this definite analysis of my material, the rest of the way was very easy. If a character is "in wrong" he must be "in wrong" in relation to some special attempt to accomplish something. Thereafter there was very little cerebration necessary to invent the thing which was to be accomplished, to which the result of the two encounters or interchanges would be what are technically called hindrances. Obviously, every time he "got in wrong" he must be in a position opposite to that in which he would be "in right." Therefore, a main story situation or main narrative problem instantly phrased itself, "Can Jake Bolton make good in the British army in war time?"

Just as soon as I had phrased this main narrative question, the decisive act was waiting for me. The answer must be either "Yes" or "No." I knew that in this special instance the original of Jake Bolton had not been decorated or promoted; but I felt certain that this was an isolated and special case, that it was not representative; I knew that while it was accurate it was not true to life. So I changed it. This is where my thematic idea conditioned my own response to my material. My theme was that anybody with character could make good in the British army in war time, so this thematic idea gave me not only an Ending but a Sequel or Significance as well. Thus at this point I found myself with a Beginning which was a main narrative purpose, an Ending which was a Conclusive Act, a significant Sequel to that Conclusive Act, and finally, I had my original material of the two interchanges each of which resulted in a hindrance.

I knew enough about the laws of interest to know that story interest, proper, is in the Body of the story,—in the encounters or interchanges which come after the main problem has been presented to the audience together with such explanatory matter as will give the audience a sufficient clue to go on with the story. I then proceeded to write a first rough draft of the material which I had added to the original material, and the special purposes before me as an author conditioned the presentation of that material. I had to present the character of Jake Bolton, and I knew that the most effective way of presenting character is to show how other people react toward the chief actor of the story. For that reason the first 52 lines of the story are concerned with showing Jake Bolton in action, and showing how the Captain and the others react toward him. Lines 53 to 66 I have made an interchange between the captain and the lieutenant because I realized that an interchange is always more interesting than a mere meeting. As a result of this interchange the main narrative question is made apparent to the audience. Further, I knew that a Beginning must contain, besides this main narrative question, the dramatic promise of difficulty, of conflict, and of disaster, all of which are presented in a second mild disagreement between the captain and the lieutenant occupying lines 69 to 94. Knowing that the Beginning of a story must contain the seeds of the conflicts which make up the Body of the story, I planted the threat of a British officer who should encounter Jake Bolton, but I also had to take care of the query of the reader as to why Jake Bolton had not "got in wrong" before he met this officer. That was why I mentioned that his own colonial officers paid no attention to his lack of the usual respectful "sir." Now I was ready to write the Ending of the story, because I knew what the Body was, approximately, and I had already my Beginning completed. So I wrote the interchange now occupying the lines 1025 to 1053 which is an episodic meeting between Captain Graham and Lieutenant Townsend, which contained the revised answer to the main narrative question together with the significance to be drawn from the happenings. This is conveyed by the Captain's remark about Jake's eyes, harking back to his original remark that "any man with character can make good."

Just as I recognized that the seeds of the conflicts which occupy the Body of the story should be planted in the Beginning so I realized that in the Beginning there should be planted the seeds of that significance which should emerge in the Sequel to the act, and for that reason I included in the first meeting between the captain and the lieutenant a discussion as to the main significance of the story, that a man with character could make good in the army. Then, in the closing episode I was able to tie together the Beginning and the Ending by again referring to this character in the man's eyes.

The reason that I made an episodic meeting between the captain and the lieutenant in order to show the effect of the

Decisive Act, which is the throwing of the bomb, is that I wished
to take legitimate advantage of suspense. I might have shown
the officer taking out his note-book and noting the name, immediately informing Jake of his plans for promotion and decoration.
But I preferred to allow the reader to assume that Jake was
again "in wrong," because I felt that a hindrance at the conclusion
of this meeting was better than a Conclusive Act, because the outcome was still in suspense. Further, I was able to utilize the value
of surprise which comes with the swift realization upon the part of
the reader that Jake instead of being "in wrong" has actually made
good in the army through the action of throwing the bomb.

In boiling down the Beginning and the Ending of the story in
the way I did, I naturally reduced the total length of the story so
that the originl meetings which were my structural units were
rather slight to carry the whole interest of the story. So I was
forced to cast about for more meetings which should be encounters
preferably. So I invented a first encounter, the one with the
subaltern at Salisbury, which resulted in Jake's getting a bad name
in the army. I knew instinctively that the first attempt of a
character should result in a hindrance, because if it didn't the
story interest was likely to lag. By having a hindrance at the
conclusion of this first encounter with the subaltern I was enabled to
bring Jake to a point where he had received his bad name, which
came after Jake and the colonel had had an interview regarding the
failure on his part to salute the officer and call him "sir" at Salisbury. This made a hindrance to the main narrative question, and it
brought about the condition which the lieutenant had prophesied
in his meeting with the captain: that Jake would get a bad name.

This condition facing Jake and his reactions to it occupy lines
316 to 392 and resulted in a furtherance, which was that his nickname was forgotten. Realizing, however, that a furtherance was
likely to dull the story I instantly followed this series of reactions of
Jake's with an interchange between him and young Richards which
resulted in a hindrance because of the promise of conflict with a
dangerous opponent which appears when he learns that the officer
is again about.

In the next interchange, which was with the commanding
general, the result is a furtherance, but when in lines 428 to 438,
which make the fifth step of that scene, Captain Graham and Lieutenant Townsend discuss the affair, there is a hindrance because
there is again the promise of disaster.

In the interchange between Jake and the corporal, occupying

lines 607 to 638, there is a furtherance when Jake feels safe, but I caused this to occur because I again wished to do what I did in the latter part of the story,—to surprise the reader by the unexpectedness of the happening, and to get the greatest possible value of what is known as "dramatic irony," which is the ironic feeling that comes to a reader when he realizes that a character has been congratulating himself upon a condition which does not exist at all. Jake is made to feel safe, and instantly he is plunged into a meeting with the subaltern which results in a definite hindrance at the close of the interchange (lines 666 to 751), after his name is again taken by the hostile officer. At the close of the meeting between Jake and the colonel at which the subaltern prefers his charge, on lines 752 to 868, there is a furtherance; but it is instantly followed by a dramatic hindrance, which is apparent when the nick-name is revived. It is this condition which seems to threaten ultimate disaster to Jake, and the chief and most interesting scene in the story is the scene where Jake goes out into the sap and after throwing the bomb, has his interchange with the staff officer. This occupies lines 982 to 1024, and then the main narrative question appears to be answered by the word "No." Very swiftly, however, the reader finds, in lines 1025 to 1053, that the answer to the question is really "Yes" and that Jake Bolton has made good in the army.

It may seem to some people that there is an overload of setting or atmosphere at some places in this story. Probably this is the case; but it was intentional. I had a purpose in so inserting it. I wanted readers to get the feeling of the Gallipoli peninsula, of the drabness, the imminence of death, of the self-sacrifice, of the heroism, and of the hardships dumbly endured. I wanted to show that unforgettable picture, that is to-me-unforgettable picture, of the Sikh who felt that he must repay the kindness done him by the men of Jake's regiment and I wanted to show that lone Australian, pacing slowly up and down in the moonlight, guarding the dead. My judgment was justified, for when the artist was given the story to illustrate, he selected those two pictures.

One other objection may arise in the mind of a craftsman as to my handling of the material of this story. If the story is the story of *Jake Bolton*, *551* and the problem before him is to make good in the army, why is it not made apparent that he is aware of making such an attempt. As a matter of fact my conception of the character of Jake was that he was not aware of any desire to make good. He did his duty as he saw it. He was in no way conscious of being heroic, so in order to keep him true to form,

I had to introduce the two purely lay figures of the captain and the lieutenant. They were the equivalent of the chorus in the Greek drama. They were enabled to say about him certain things which he could not have said about himself, and they were able to phrase the wager—for it was virtually a wager—quickly and incisively. Then, my own experience later in the war, in deciding upon men to be promoted to be non-commissioned officers, led me to insert the comment that a man's progress depended upon his getting a good name, or rather on his not getting a bad name.

There is no setting, not even that of background, for the recruiting office in the first meeting. That is explained by two considerations; first, I wanted to hurry up the Beginning, but chiefly I wanted to keep that setting nebulous, because I did not, at the time I wrote the story, wish to give any inkling as to which particular colonial regiment I was dealing with. As a matter of fact, now that the war is over, I may say that the First Colonials had as originals the members of my own regiment, The Royal Newfoundland Regiment.

This story was written more than ten years ago. Since then I have written many other stories and have collaborated upon still more. What I have learned about craftsmanship would induce me to make one change. It is that I should have made the opponent the same throughout. It would have been a very simple matter to change the staff officer in the final encounter so that he became the subaltern of Salisbury. If I were rewriting the story I think that I should have caused this final encounter to be between Jake and the subaltern, and that he should actually have been "in wrong," but with my thematic idea to guide me I should have caused the general or some person in authority to have overheard and to have reversed the ruling of the subaltern. Naturally I cannot discuss the merits of this story further than to say that it is structurally sound. My reason for reprinting it is not to discuss it in relation to other stories, but to show actually what goes on in the mind of a writer while he is producing a short-story.

BEGINNING

Made up of attempts similar to the attempts usually occurring in the Body of a Story, in order to sustain the reader's attention. The Initial Condition is set forth.

The Main Actor's purpose is apparent.

Section	Lines
Mr. Trimm taking trip. Important and unusual condition.	1– 31
Meeting. Mr. Trimm and condition in Tombs. (5th Step. Effect.)	32– 96 / 97– 121
Meeting. Mr. Trimm responds to condition projected. (Lines 97–121)	121– 136
Interchange. Mr. Trimm and Mr. Walling.	136– 185
Interchange. Mr. Trimm and the Warden.	186– 252
Interchange. Mr. Trimm and Deputy Meyers, resulting in change of attitude by Mr. Trimm; a turning point in his life.	253– 347
Interchange. Mr. Trimm and Meyers. An attempt to hide.	348– 415
Meeting. Mr. Trimm and condition. Attempt to evade notice.	416– 530
Interchange. Mr. Trimm and conductor. Attempt to achieve privacy.	531– 553
(5th step. Effect of interchange 531–553 upon Deputy Meyers.)	554– 556
Interchange. Meyers attempts to put Mr. Trimm at ease.	557– 628
Meeting. Mr. Trimm responds to new condition.	629– 756
Attempt of Mr. Trimm is foiled. New purpose is apparent.	757– 879
Attempt of Mr. Trimm to put new purpose into effect is opposed by impulse, projecting new condition, to which Mr. Trimm, responding, projects main purpose of the story.	880–1141

Main Plot Crises become apparent as the result of the attempts of Mr. Trimm show him to be in an unusual situation, from which he can obtain relief only through overcoming Difficulties, and Dangerous Opposing Forces.
There is no question that Disaster is staring him in the face.

Main Narrative Question: "Can Mr. Trimm escape from handcuffs?"

BODY	*Made up of attempts to reverse the original condition or state of affairs. Various obstacles keep cropping up. The attempt to surmount each of these forms a scene.*	He attempts to pry off handcuffs with contents of pockets. Fails. (5th step. Difficulties increased.)	1142–1309 Hindrance. 1310–1360 Hindrance.
		Boy comes. Meeting. Mr. Trimm runs.	1361–1409 Hindrance.
		He attempts to use harrow tooth as a lever.	1410–1434 Hindrance.
		He attempts to burn cuffs off. Blackens steel and raises blister.	1435–1454 Hindrance.
		He attempts to file off with fence wire. Fails.	1455–1474 Hindrance.
		He attempts to persuade Boy. Boy scared away. (5th step. Effect of interchange upon actors. New plan emerges.)	1475–1525 Hindrance. 1526–1569
		Approaches blacksmith. Finds he is sheriff.	1570–1652 New opponent possible. Dramatic Hindrance.
		Tries to enlist tramp's aid. Tramp refuses.	1653–1992 Hindrance.
		Mr. Trimm kills tramp. Resulting mental haze increases chance of capture.	1993–2045 Dramatic Hindrance.
		Meeting. In search of food, Mr. Trimm encounters dog. Flies.	2046–2073 Hindrance.
		(5th step. Effect of farmer's actions is to cause Mr. Trimm to tighten handcuffs.)	2073–2131 Dramatic Hindrance.
		He attempts to convince Chief of Police of Westfield that he is the banker.	2132–2227
SEQUEL	Conclusive Act.	"Come in and let me get them irons off you."	2228–2231 Main Narrative Question answered "Yes."
	Sequel.	Mr. Trimm, on achieving his objective, no longer considers it important.	2232–2237 Ironic Significance.

113

THE ESCAPE OF MR. TRIMM

BY IRVIN S. COBB

THIS story belongs to the "Odyssey" classification of stories. It is the story of a character who has to overcome a certain number of obstacles in order to be safe. In this story the character, after repeated attempts, abandons his purpose. For that reason alone it is interesting.

Another reason for its inclusion is that it illustrates so definitely the different kinds of conditions which a character may be called upon to remove or overcome. These kinds are two: the passive condition and the active condition.

A third reason for reprinting this story is that it shows that Mr. Cobb, in his first story, recognized those laws of interest which are the determining factors in the success or failure of any story, particularly in the type of story which has a long Beginning. Out of the total of 2237 lines which this story occupies, the Beginning takes up 1141 lines.

CASE No. 5

THE ESCAPE OF MR. TRIMM

BY IRVIN S. COBB

1 Mr. Trimm, recently president
2 of the late Thirteenth National
3 Bank, was taking a trip which
4 was different in a number of
5 ways from any he had ever
6 taken. To begin with, he was
7 used to parlor cars and Pullmans
8 and even luxurious private cars
9 when he went anywhere; where-
10 as now he rode with a most
11 mixed company in a dusty,
12 smelly day coach. In the second
13 place, his traveling companion
14 was not such a one as Mr. Trimm
15 would have chosen had the
16 choice been left to him, being a
17 stupid-looking German-Amer-
18 ican with a drooping, yellow
19 mustache. And in the third
20 place, Mr. Trimm's plump white
21 hands were folded in his lap,
22 held in a close and enforced
23 companionship by a new and
24 shiny pair of Bean's Latest
25 Model Little Giant handcuffs.
26 Mr. Trimm was on his way to
27 the Federal penitentiary to serve
28 twelve years at hard labor for
29 breaking, one way or another,
30 about all the laws that are pre-
31 sumed to govern national banks.

. . . . . .

32 All the time Mr. Trimm was
33 in the Tombs, fighting for a new
34 trial, a certain question had lain
35 in his mind unasked and unan-
36 swered. Through the seven
37 months of his stay in the jail
38 that question had been always at
39 the back part of his head, ticking
40 away there like a little watch
41 that never needed winding. A
42 dozen times a day it would pop
43 into his thoughts and then go
44 away, only to come back again.
45 When Copley was taken to the
46 penitentiary—Copley being the
47 cashier who got off with a lighter
48 sentence because the judge and
49 jury held him to be no more than
50 a blind accomplice in the wreck-
51 ing of the Thirteenth National—
52 Mr. Trimm read closely every
53 line that the papers carried about
54 Copley's departure. But none
55 of them had seen fit to give the
56 young cashier more than a short
57 and colorless paragraph. For

58 Copley was only a small figure
59 in the big intrigue that had
60 startled the country; Copley
61 didn't have the money to hire big
62 lawyers to carry his appeal to the
63 higher courts for him; Copley's
64 wife was keeping boarders; and
65 as for Copley himself, he had
66 been wearing stripes several
67 months now.

68 With Mr. Trimm it had been
69 vastly different. From the very
70 beginning he had held the public
71 eye. His bearing in court when
72 the jury came in with their judg-
73 ment; his cold defiance when the
74 judge, in pronouncing sentence,
75 mercilessly arraigned him and
76 the system of finance for which
77 he stood; the manner of his life
78 in the Tombs; his spectacular
79 fight to beat the verdict, had all
80 been worth columns of news-
81 paper space. If Mr. Trimm had
82 been a popular poisoner, or a so-
83 ciety woman named as co-
84 respondent in a sensational di-
85 vorce suit, the papers could not
86 have been more generous in
87 their space allotments. And Mr.
88 Trimm in his cell had read all of
89 it with smiling contempt, even
90 to the semi-hysterical outpour-
91 ings of the lady special writers
92 who called him The Iron Man of
93 Wall Street and undertook to
94 analyze his emotions — and
95 missed the mark by a thousand
96 miles or two.

97 Things had been smoothed as
98 much as possible for him in the
99 Tombs, for money and the power
100 of it will go far toward ironing
101 out even the corrugated routine
102 of that big jail. He had a large
103 cell to himself in the airiest,
104 brightest corridor. His meals
105 were served by a caterer from
106 outside. Although he ate them
107 without knife or fork, he soon
108 learned that a spoon and the fin-
109 gers can accomplish a good deal
110 when backed by a good appe-
111 tite, and Mr. Trimm's appetite
112 was uniformly good. The war-
113 den and his underlings had been
114 models of official kindliness; the
115 newspapers had sent their bright-
116 est young men to interview him
117 whenever he felt like talking,
118 which wasn't often; and surely
119 his lawyers had done all in his be-
120 half that money—a great deal of
121 money—could do. Perhaps it
122 was because of these things that
123 Mr. Trimm had never been able
124 to bring himself to realize that
125 he was the Hobart W. Trimm
126 who had been sentenced to the
127 Federal prison; it seemed to him,
128 somehow, that he, personally,
129 was merely a spectator standing
130 at one side watching the fight of
131 another man to dodge the peni-
132 tentiary.

133 However, he didn't fail to give
134 the other man the advantage of
135 every chance that money would
136 buy. This sense of aloofness to
137 the whole thing had persisted
138 even when his personal lawyer
139 came to him one night in the
140 early fall and told him that the
141 court of last possible resort had

denied the last possible motion. Mr. Trimm cut the lawyer short with a shake of his head as the other began saying something about the chances of a pardon from the President. Mr. Trimm wasn't in the habit of letting men deceive him with idle words. No President would pardon him, and he knew it.

"Never mind that, Walling," he said steadily, when the lawyer offered to come to see him again before he started for prison the next day. "If you'll see that a drawing-room on the train is reserved for me—for us, I mean—and all that sort of thing, I'll not detain you any further. I have a good many things to do tonight. Good night."

"Such a man, such a man," said Walling to himself as he climbed into his car; "all chilled steel and brains. And they are going to lock that brain up for twelve years. It's a crime," said Walling, and shook his head. Walling always said it was a crime when they sent a client of his to prison. To his credit be it said, though, they sent very few of them there. Walling made as high as eighty thousand a year at criminal law. Some of it was very criminal law indeed. His specialty was picking holes in the statutes faster than the legislature could make them and provide them and putty them up with amendments. This was the first case he had lost in a good long time.

· · · · · ·

When Jerry, the turnkey, came for him in the morning Mr. Trimm had made as careful a toilet as the limited means at his command permitted, and he had eaten a hearty breakfast and was ready to go, all but putting on his hat. Looking the picture of well-groomed, close-buttoned, iron-gray middle age, Mr. Trimm followed the turnkey through the long corridor and down the winding iron stairs to the warden's office. He gave no heed to the curious eyes that followed him through the barred doors of many cells; his feet rang briskly on the flags.

The warden, Hallam, was there in the private office with another man, a tall, raw-boned man with a drooping, straw-colored mustache and the unmistakable look about him of the police officer. Mr. Trimm knew without being told that this was the man who would take him to prison. The stranger was standing at a desk, signing some papers.

"Sit down, please, Mr. Trimm," said the warden with a nervous cordiality. "Be through here in just one minute. This is Deputy Marshal Meyers," he added.

Mr. Trimm started to tell this Mr. Meyers he was glad to meet him, but caught himself and merely nodded. The man stared at him with neither interest nor curiosity in his dull blue eyes. The warden moved over toward the door.

"Mr. Trimm," he said, clearing his throat, "I took the liberty of calling a cab to take you gents up to the Grand Central. It's out front now. But there's a big crowd of reporters and photographers and a lot of other people waiting, and if I was you I'd slip out the back way—one of my men will open the yard gate for you—and jump aboard the subway down at Worth Street. Then you'll miss those fellows."

"Thank you, Warden—very kind of you," said Mr. Trimm in that crisp, businesslike way of his. He had been crisp and businesslike all his life. He heard a door opening softly behind him, and when he turned to look he saw the warden slipping out, furtively, in almost an embarrassed fashion.

"Well," said Meyers, "all ready?"

"Yes," said Mr. Trimm, and he made as if to rise.

"Wait one minute," said Meyers.

He half turned his back on Mr. Trimm and fumbled at the side pocket of his ill-hanging coat. Something inside of Mr. Trimm gave the least little jump, and the question that had ticked away so busily all those months began to buzz, buzz in his ears; but it was only a handkerchief the man was getting out. Doubtless he was going to mop his face.

He didn't mop his face, though. He unrolled the handkerchief slowly, as if it contained something immensely fragile and valuable, and then, thrusting it back in his pocket, he faced Mr. Trimm. He was carrying in his hands a pair of handcuffs that hung open-jawed. The jaws had little notches in them, like teeth that could bite. The question that had ticked in Mr. Trimm's head was answered at last—in the sight of these steel things with their notched jaws.

Mr. Trimm stood up and, with a movement as near to hesitation as he had ever been guilty of in his life, held out his hands, backs upward.

"I guess you're new at this kind of thing," said Meyers, grinning. "This here way—one at a time."

He took hold of Mr. Trimm's right hand, turned it sideways and settled one of the steel cuffs over the top of the wrist, flipping the notched jaw up from beneath and pressing it in so that it locked automatically with a brisk little click. Slipping the locked cuff back and forth on Mr. Trimm's lower arm like a man adjusting a part of machinery, and then bringing the left hand up to meet the right, he treated it the same way. Then he stepped back.

309 Mr. Trimm hadn't meant to
310 protest. The word came un-
311 bidden.

312 "This—this isn't necessary, is
313 it?" he asked in a voice that was
314 husky and didn't seem to belong
315 to him.

316 "Yep," said Meyers, "Stand-
317 in' orders is play no favorites and
318 take no chances. But you won't
319 find them things uncomfortable.
320 Lightest pair there was in the
321 office, and I fixed 'em plenty
322 loose."

323 For half a minute Mr. Trimm
324 stood like a rooster hypnotized
325 by a chalkmark, his arms ex-
326 tended, his eyes set on his bonds.
327 His hands had fallen perhaps
328 four inches apart, and in the
329 space between his wrists a little
330 chain was stretched taut. In the
331 mounting tumult that filled his
332 brain there sprang before Mr.
333 Trimm's consciousness a phrase
334 he had heard or read somewhere,
335 the title of a story or, perhaps it
336 was a headline—The Grips of
337 the Law. The Grips of the Law
338 were upon Mr. Trimm—he felt
339 them now for the first time in
340 these shiny wristlets and this bit
341 of chain that bound his wrists
342 and filled his whole body with a
343 strange, sinking feeling that
344 made him physically sick. A
345 sudden sweat beaded out on Mr.
346 Trimm's face, turning it slick
347 and wet.

348 He had a handkerchief, a fine
349 linen handkerchief with a hem-
350 stitched border and a monogram
351 on it, in the upper breast pocket
352 of his buttoned coat. He tried
353 to reach it. His hands went up,
354 twisting awkwardly like crab
355 claws. The fingers of both
356 plucked out the handkerchief.
357 Holding it so, Mr. Trimm
358 mopped the sweat away. The
359 links of the handcuffs fell in upon
360 one another and lengthened out
361 again at each movement, filling
362 the room with a smart little
363 sound.

364 He got the handkerchief
365 stowed away with the same
366 clumsiness. He raised the man-
367 acled hands to his hat brim, gave
368 it a downward pull that brought
369 it over his face and then, letting
370 his short arms slide down upon
371 his plump stomach, he faced the
372 man who had put the fetters
373 upon him, squaring his shoulders
374 back. But it was hard, some-
375 how, for him to square his shoul-
376 ders—perhaps because of his
377 hands being drawn so closely to-
378 gether. And his eyes would
379 waver and fall upon his wrists.
380 Mr. Trimm had a feeling that
381 the skin must be stretched very
382 tight on his jawbones and his
383 forehead.

384 "Isn't there some way to hide
385 these—these things?"

386 He began by blurting and end-
387 ed by faltering it. His hands
388 shuffled together, one over, then
389 under the other.

390 "Here's a way," said Meyers.
391 "This'll help."

392 He bestirred himself, folding

393 one of the chained hands upon
394 the other, tugging at the white
395 linen cuffs and drawing the coat
396 sleeves of his prisoner down over
397 the bonds as far as the chain
398 would let them come.

399 "There's the notion," he said.
400 "Just do that-a-way and them
401 bracelets won't hardly show a-
402 tall. Ready? Let's be movin',
403 then."

404 But handcuffs were never
405 meant to be hidden. Merely a
406 pair of steel rings clamped to
407 one's wrists and coupled to-
408 gether with a scrap of chain, but
409 they'll twist your arms and ham-
410 per the movements of your body
411 in a way constantly to catch the
412 eye of the passer-by. When a
413 man is coming toward you,
414 you can tell that he is hand-
415 cuffed before you see the cuffs.

416 Mr. Trimm was never able to
417 recall afterward exactly how he
418 got out of the Tombs. He had
419 a confused memory of a gate
420 that was swung open by someone
421 whom Mr. Trimm saw only from
422 the feet to the waist; then he
423 and his companion were out on
424 Lafayette Street speeding south
425 toward the subway entrance at
426 Worth Street, two blocks below,
427 with the marshal's hand cupped
428 under Mr. Trimm's right elbow
429 and Mr. Trimm's plump legs al-
430 most trotting in their haste. For
431 a moment it looked as if the
432 warden's well-meant artifice
433 would serve.

434 But New York reporters are
435 up to the tricks of people who
436 want to evade them. At the
437 sight of them a sentry reporter
438 on the corner shouted a warning
439 which was instantly caught up
440 and passed on by another picket
441 stationed half-way down the
442 block; and around the wall of the
443 Tombs came pelting a flying mob
444 of newspaper photographers and
445 reporters, with a choice rabble
446 behind them. Foot passengers
447 took up the chase, not knowing
448 what it was about, but sensing a
449 free show. Truckmen halted
450 their teams, jumped down from
451 their wagon seats and joined in.
452 A man-chase is one of the pleas-
453 antest outdoor sports that a big
454 city like New York can offer its
455 people.

456 Fairly running now, the man-
457 acled banker and the deputy
458 marshal shot down the winding
459 steps into the subway a good ten
460 yards ahead of the foremost pur-
461 suers. But there was one delay,
462 while Meyers skirmished with his
463 free hand in his trousers pocket
464 for a dime for the tickets, and
465 another before a northbound
466 local rolled into the station.
467 Shouted at, jeered at, shoved
468 this way and that, panting in
469 gulping breaths, for he was stout
470 by nature and staled by lack of
471 exercise, Mr. Trimm with Mey-
472 ers clutching him by the arm,
473 was fairly shot aboard one of the
474 cars, at the apex of a human
475 wedge. The astonished guard

476 sensed the situation as the scroog-
477 ing, shoving, noisy wave rolled
478 across the platform toward the
479 doors which he had opened and,
480 thrusting the officer and his pris-
481 oner into the narrow platform
482 space behind him, he tried to
483 form with his body a barrier
484 against those who came jamming
485 in.

486 It didn't do any good. He
487 was brushed away, protesting
488 and blustering. The excitement
489 spread through the train, and
490 men, and even women, left
491 their seats, overflowing the
492 aisles.

493 There is no crueler thing than
494 a city crowd, all eyes and morbid
495 curiosity. But Mr. Trimm didn't
496 see the staring eyes on that ride
497 to the Grand Central. What he
498 saw was many shifting feet and a
499 hedge of legs shutting him in
500 closely—those and the things on
501 his wrists. What the eyes of the
502 crowd saw was a small, stout
503 man who, for all his bulk, seemed
504 to have dried up inside his
505 clothes so that they bagged on
506 him some places and bulged
507 others, with his head tucked on
508 his chest, his hat over his face
509 and his fingers straining to hold
510 his coat sleeves down over a pair
511 of steel bracelets.

512 Mr. Trimm gave mental
513 thanks to a Deity whose exist-
514 ence he thought he had forgotten
515 when the gate of the train-shed
516 clanged behind him, shutting out
517 the mob that had come with them

518 all the way. Cameras had been
519 shoved in his face like gun muz-
520 zles, reporters had scuttled along-
521 side him, dodging under Meyers'
522 fending arm to shout questions
523 in his ears. He had neither spo-
524 ken nor looked at them. The
525 sweat still ran down his face, so
526 that when finally he raised his
527 head in the comparative quiet of
528 the train-shed his skin was a cu-
529 rious gray under the jail paleness
530 like the color of wet wood ashes.

531 "My lawyer promised to ar-
532 range for a compartment—for
533 some private place on the train,"
534 he said to Meyers. "The con-
535 ductor ought to know."

536 They were the first words he
537 had uttered since he left the
538 Tombs. Meyers spoke to a
539 jaunty Pullman conductor who
540 stood alongside the car where
541 they had halted.

542 "No such reservation," said
543 the conductor, running through
544 his sheaf of slips, with his eyes
545 shifting from Mr. Trimm's face
546 to Mr. Trimm's hands and back
547 again, as though he couldn't de-
548 cide which was the more inter-
549 esting part of him; "must be
550 some mistake. Or else it was for
551 some other train. Too late to
552 change now—we pull out in
553 three minutes."

554 "I reckon we better git on the
555 smoker," said Meyers, "if there's
556 room there."

557 Mr. Trimm was steered back
558 again the length of the train
559 through a double row of pop-

eyed porters and staring trainmen. At the steps where they stopped the instinct to stretch out one hand and swing himself up by the rail operated automatically and his wrists got a nasty twist. Meyers and a brakeman practically lifted him up the steps and Meyers headed him into a car that was hazy with blue tobacco smoke. He was confused in his gait, almost as if his lower limbs had been fettered, too.

The car was full of shirtsleeved men who stood up, craning their necks and stumbling over each other in their desire to see him. These men came out into the aisle, so that Meyers had to shove through them.

"This here'll do as well as any, I guess," said Meyers. He drew Mr. Trimm past him into the seat nearer the window and sat down alongside him on the side next the aisle, settling himself on the stuffy plush seat and breathing deeply, like a man who had got through the hardest part of a not easy job.

"Smoke?" he asked.

Mr. Trimm shook his head without raising it.

"Them cuffs feel plenty easy?" was the deputy's next question. He lifted Mr. Trimm's hands as casually as if they had been his hands and not Mr. Trimm's, and looked at them.

"Seem to be all right," he said as he let them fall back. "Don't pinch none, I reckon?" There was no answer.

The deputy tugged a minute at his mustache, searching his arid mind. An idea came to him. He drew a newspaper from his pocket, opened it out flat and spread it over Mr. Trimm's lap so that it covered the chained wrists. Almost instantly the train was in motion, moving through the yards.

.   .   .   .   .

"Be there in two hours more," volunteered Meyers. It was late afternoon. They were sliding through woodlands with occasional openings which showed meadows melting into wide, flat lands.

"Want a drink?" said the deputy, next. "No? Well, I guess I'll have a drop myself. Travelin' fills a feller's throat full of dust." He got up, lurching to the motion of the flying train, and started forward to the water cooler behind the car door. He had gone perhaps two-thirds of the way when Mr. Trimm felt a queer, grinding sensation beneath his feet; it was exactly as though the train were trying to go forward and back at the same time. Almost slowly, it seemed to him, the forward end of the car slued out of its straight course, at the same time tilting up. There was a grinding, roaring, grating sound, and before Mr. Trimm's eyes Meyers vanished, tumbling forward out of sight as the car floor buckled under his feet. Then, as everything—the train, the earth, the sky—all fused together in a great spatter of white and black, Mr. Trimm was plucked from his seat as though a giant hand had him by the collar and shot forward through the air over the seat-backs, his chained hands aloft, clutching wildly. He rolled out of a ragged opening where the smoker had broken in two, flopped gently on the sloping side of the right-of-way and slid easily to the bottom, where he lay quiet and still on his back in a bed of weeds and wild grass, staring straight up.

How many minutes he lay there Mr. Trimm didn't know. It may have been the shrieks of the victims or the glare from the fire that brought him out of the daze. He wriggled his body to a sitting posture, got on his feet, holding his head between his coupled hands, and gazed full-face into the crowning railroad horror of the year.

There were numbers of the passengers who had escaped serious hurt, but for the most part these persons seemed to have gone daft from terror and shock. Some were running aimlessly up and down and some, a few, were pecking feebly with improvised tools at the wreck, an indescribable jumble of ruin, from which there issued cries of mortal agony, and from which, at a point where two locomotives were lying on their sides, jammed together like fighting bucks that died with locked horns, a tall flame already rippled and spread, sending up a pillar of black smoke that rose straight, poisoning the clear blue of the sky. Nobody paid any attention to Mr. Trimm as he stood swaying upon his feet. There wasn't a scratch on him. His clothes were hardly rumpled, his hat was still on his head. He stood a minute and then, moved by a sudden impulse, he turned round and went running straight away from the railroad at the best speed his pudgy legs could accomplish, with his arms pumping up and down in front of him and his fingers interlaced. It was a grotesque gait, rather like a rabbit hopping on its hindlegs.

Instantly, almost, the friendly woods growing down to the edge of the fill swallowed him up. He dodged and doubled back and forth among the tree trunks, his small, patent-leathered feet skipping nimbly over the irregular turf, until he stopped for lack of wind in his lungs to carry him another rod. When he had got his breath back Mr. Trimm leaned against a tree and bent his head this way and that, listening. No sound came to his ears except the sleepy calls of birds. As well as Mr. Trimm might judge he had come far into the depths of a considerable woodland. Already the shadows under the low limbs were growing thick and confused as the hurried twilight of early September came on.

Mr. Trimm sat down on a natural cushion of thick green moss between two roots of an oak. The place was clean and soft and sweet-scented. For some little time he sat there motionless, in a sort of mental haze. Then his round body slowly slid down flat upon the moss, his head lolled to one side and, the reaction having come, Mr. Trimm's limbs all relaxed and he went to sleep straightway.

After a while, when the woods were black and still, the half-grown moon came up and, sifting through a chink in the canopy of leaves above, shone down full on Mr. Trimm as he lay snoring gently with his mouth open and his hands rising and falling on his breast. The moonlight struck upon the Little Giant handcuffs, making them look like quicksilver.

Toward daylight it turned off sharp and cool. The dogwoods which had been a solid color at nightfall now showed pink in one light and green in another, like changeable silk, as the first level rays of the sun came up over the rim of the earth and made long, golden lanes between the tree trunks. Mr. Trimm opened his eyes slowly, hardly sensing for the first moment or two how he came to be lying under a canopy of leaves, and gaped, seeking to stretch his arms. At that he remembered everything; he hunched his shoulders against the tree roots and wriggled himself up to a sitting position where he stayed for a while, letting his mind run over the sequence of events that had brought him where he was and taking inventory of the situation.

Of escape he had no thought. The hue and cry must be out for him before now; doubtless men were already searching for him. It would be better for him to walk in and surrender than to be taken in the woods like some animal escaped from a traveling menagerie. But the mere thought of enduring again what he had already gone through—the thought of being tagged by crowds and stared at, with his fetters on—filled him with a nausea. Nothing that the Federal penitentiary might hold in store for him could equal the black, blind shamefulness of yesterday; he knew that. The thought of the new ignominy that faced him made Mr. Trimm desperate. He had a desire to burrow into the thicket yonder and hide his face and his chained hands.

But perhaps he could get the handcuffs off and so go to meet his captors in some manner of dignity. Strange that the idea hadn't occurred to him before! It seemed to Mr. Trimm that he

811 desired to get his two hands
812 apart more than he had ever
813 desired anything in his whole
814 life before.

815 The hands had begun natur-
816 ally to adjust themselves to their
817 enforced companionship, and it
818 wasn't such a very hard matter,
819 though it cost him some painful
820 wrenches and much twisting of
821 the fingers, for Mr. Trimm to get
822 his coat unbuttoned and his eye-
823 glasses in their small leather case
824 out of his upper waistcoat pock-
825 et. With the glasses on his nose
826 he subjected his bonds to a crit-
827 ical examination. Each rounded
828 steel band ran unbroken except
829 for the smooth, almost jointless
830 hinge and the small lock which
831 sat perched on the back of the
832 wrist in a little rounded excres-
833 cence like a steel wart. In the
834 flat center of each lock was a
835 small keyhole and alongside of it
836 a notched nub, the nub being
837 sunk in a minute depression. On
838 the inner side, underneath, the
839 cuffs slid into themselves—two
840 notches on each showing where
841 the jaws might be tightened to
842 fit a smaller hand than his—and
843 right over the large blue veins
844 in the middle of the wrists were
845 swivel links, shackle-bolted to
846 the cuffs and connected by a flat,
847 slightly larger middle link, giv-
848 ing the hands a palm-to-palm
849 play of not more than four or
850 five inches. The cuffs did not
851 hurt—even after so many hours
852 there was no actual discomfort

853 from them and the flesh beneath
854 them was hardly reddened.

855 But it didn't take Mr. Trimm
856 long to find out that they were
857 not to be got off. He tugged and
858 pulled, trying with his fingers
859 for a purchase. All he did was to
860 chafe his skin and make his
861 wrists throb with pain. The
862 cuffs would go forward just so
863 far, then the little humps of bone
864 above the hands would catch and
865 hold them.

866 Mr. Trimm was not a man to
867 waste time in the pursuit of the
868 obviously hopeless. Presently he
869 stood up, shook himself and
870 started off at a fair gait through
871 the woods. The sun was up now
872 and the turf was all dappled with
873 lights and shadows, and about
874 him much small, furtive wild life
875 was stirring. He stepped along
876 briskly, a strange figure for that
877 green solitude, with his correct
878 city garb and the glint of the
879 steel at his sleeve ends.

880 Presently he heard the long-
881 drawn, quavering, banshee wail
882 of a locomotive. The sound
883 came from almost behind him,
884 in an opposite direction from
885 where he supposed the track to
886 be. So he turned around and
887 went back the other way. He
888 crossed a half-dried-up runlet
889 and climbed a small hill, neither
890 of which he remembered having
891 met in his flight from the wreck,
892 and in a little while he came out
893 upon the railroad. To the north
894 a little distance the rails bent

895 round a curve. To the south,
896 where the diminishing rails run-
897 ning through the unbroken wood-
898 land met in a long, shiny V, he
899 could see a big smoke smudge
900 against the horizon. This smoke
901 Mr. Trimm knew must come from
902 the wreck—which was still burn-
903 ing, evidently. As nearly as he
904 could judge he had come out of
905 cover at least two miles above it.
906 After a moment's consideration
907 he decided to go south toward the
908 wreck. Soon he could distinguish
909 small dots like ants moving in and
910 out about the black spot, and he
911 knew these dots must be men.

912 A whining, whirring sound
913 came along the rails to him from
914 behind. He faced about just as a
915 handcar shot out around the
916 curve from the north, moving
917 with amazing rapidity under the
918 strokes of four men at the pumps.
919 Other men, laborers, to judge by
920 their blue overalls, were sitting
921 on the edges of the car with their
922 feet dangling. For the second
923 time within twelve hours impulse
924 ruled Mr. Trimm, who wasn't
925 given to impulses normally. He
926 made a jump off the right-of-
927 way, and as the handcar flashed
928 by he watched its flight from the
929 covert of a weed tangle.

930 But even as the handcar was
931 passing him Mr. Trimm regret-
932 ted his hastiness. He must sur-
933 render himself sooner or later;
934 why not to these overalled labor-
935 ers, since it was a thing that had
936 to be done? He slid out of hiding

937 and came trotting back to the
938 tracks. Already the handcar was
939 a hundred yards away, flitting
940 into distance like some big, won-
941 derfully fast bug, the figures of
942 the men at the pumps rising and
943 falling with a walking-beam reg-
944 ularity. As he stood watching
945 them fade away and minded to
946 try hailing them, yet still hesi-
947 tating against his judgment, Mr.
948 Trimm saw something white
949 drop from the hands of one of
950 the blue-clad figures on the hand-
951 car, unfold into a newspaper and
952 come fluttering back along the
953 tracks toward him. Just as he,
954 starting doggedly ahead, met it,
955 the little ground breeze that had
956 carried it along died out and the
957 paper dropped and flattened
958 right in front of him. The front
959 page was uppermost and he knew
960 it must be of that morning's is-
961 sue, for across the column tops
962 ran the flaring headline: "Twen-
963 ty Dead in Frightful Collision."

964 Squatting on the cindered
965 track, Mr. Trimm patted the
966 crumpled sheet flat with his
967 hands. His eyes dropped from
968 the first of the glaring captions
969 to the second, to the next—and
970 then his heart gave a great bound
971 inside of him and, clutching up
972 the newspaper to his breast he
973 bounded off the tracks back into
974 another thicket and huddled
975 there with the paper spread on
976 the earth in front of him, reading
977 by gulps while the chain that
978 linked wrist to wrist tinkled to

the tremors running through him. What he had seen first, in staring black-face type, was his own name leading the list of known dead, and what he saw now, broken up into choppy paragraphs and done in the nervous English of a trained reporter throwing a great news story together to catch an edition, but telling a clear enough story nevertheless, was a narrative in which his name recurred again and again. The body of the United States deputy marshal, Meyers, frightfully crushed, had been taken from the wreckage of the smoker — so the double-leaded story ran — and near to Meyers another body, with features burned beyond recognition, yet still retaining certain distinguishing marks of measurement and contour, had been found and identified as that of Hobart W. Trimm, the convicted banker. The bodies of these two, with eighteen other mangled dead, had been removed to a town called Westfield, from which town of Westfield the account of the disaster had been telegraphed to the New York paper. In another column farther along was more about Banker Trimm; facts about his soiled, selfish, greedy, successful life, his great fortune, his trial, and a statement that, in the absence of any close kin to claim his body, his lawyers had been notified.

Mr. Trimm read the account through to the end, and as he read the sense of dominant, masterful self-control came back to him in waves. He got up, taking the paper with him, and went back into the deeper woods, moving warily and watchfully. As he went his mind, trained to take hold of problems and wring the essence out of them, was busy. Of the charred, grisly thing in the improvised morgue at Westfield, wherever that might be, Mr. Trimm took no heed nor wasted any pity. All his life he had used live men to work his will, with no thought of what might come to them afterward. The living had served him, why not the dead?

He had other things to think of than this dead proxy of his. He was as good as free! There would be no hunt for him now; no alarm out, no posses combing every scrap of cover for a famous criminal turned fugitive. He had only to lie quiet a few days, somewhere, then get in secret touch with Walling. Walling would do anything for money. And he had the money—four millions and more, cannily saved from the crash that had ruined so many others.

He would alter his personal appearance, change his name— he thought of Duvall, which was his mother's name—and with Walling's aid he would get out of the country and into some other country where a man might live like a prince on four millions or the fractional part of it. He thought of South America, of South Africa, of a private yacht swinging through the little frequented islands of the South Seas. All that the law had tried to take from him would be given back. Walling would work out the details of the escape—and make it safe and sure—trust Walling for those things. On one side was the prison, with its promise of twelve grinding years sliced out of the very heart of his life; on the other, freedom, ease, security, even power. Through Mr. Trimm's mind tumbled thoughts of concessions, enterprises, privileges—the back corners of the globe were full of possibilities for the right man. And between this prospect and Mr. Trimm there stood nothing in the way, nothing but——

Mr. Trimm's eyes fell upon his bound hands. Snug-fitting, shiny steel bands irked his wrists. The Grips of the Law were still upon him.

But only in a way of speaking. It was preposterous, unbelievable, altogether out of the question that a man with four millions salted down and stored away, a man who all his life had been used to grappling with the big things and wrestling them down into submission, a man whose luck had come to be a byword—and had not it held good

even in this last emergency?—would be balked by puny scraps of forged steel and a trumpery lock or two. Why, these cuffs were no thicker than the gold bands that Mr. Trimm had seen on the arms of overdressed women at the opera. The chain that joined them was no larger and, probably, no stronger than the chains which Mr. Trimm's chauffeur wrapped around the tires of the touring-car in winter to keep the wheels from skidding on the slush. There would be a way, surely, for Mr. Trimm to free himself from these things. There must be—that was all there was to it.

Mr. Trimm looked himself over. His clothes were not badly rumpled; his patent-leather boots were scarcely scratched. Without the handcuffs he could pass unnoticed anywhere. By night then he must be free of them and on his way to some small inland city, to stay quiet there until the guarded telegram that he would send in cipher had reached Walling. There in the woods by himself Mr. Trimm no longer felt the ignominy of his bonds; he felt only the temporary embarrassment of them and the need of added precaution until he should have mastered them.

He was once more the unemotional man of affairs who had stood Wall Street on its esteemed head and caught the golden streams that trickled from its

1147 pockets. First making sure that
1148 he was in a well-screened covert
1149 of the woods he set about ex-
1150 ploring all his pockets. The coat
1151 pockets were comparatively easy,
1152 now that he had got used to
1153 using two hands where one had
1154 always served, but it cost him a
1155 lot of twisting of his body and
1156 some pain to his mistreated
1157 wrist bones to bring forth the
1158 contents of his trousers pockets.
1159 The chain kinked time and again
1160 as he groped with the undermost
1161 hand for the openings; his dum-
1162 py, pudgy form writhed gro-
1163 tesquely. But finally he finished.
1164 The search produced four cigars
1165 somewhat crumpled and frayed;
1166 some matches in a gun-metal
1167 case, a silver cigar cutter, two
1168 five-dollar bills, a handful of sil-
1169 ver chicken feed, the leather case
1170 of the eyeglasses, a couple of
1171 quill toothpicks, a gold watch
1172 with a dangling fob, a
1173 note-book and some pa-
1174 pers. Mr. Trimm ranged these
1175 things in a neat row upon a log,
1176 like a watchmaker putting out
1177 his kit, and took swift inventory
1178 of them. Some he eliminated
1179 from his design, stowing them
1180 back in the pockets easiest to
1181 reach. He kept for present em-
1182 ployment the match safe, the
1183 cigar cutter and the watch.

1184 This place where he had halted
1185 would suit his present purpose
1186 well, he decided. It was where
1187 an uprooted tree, fallen across an
1188 incurving bank, made a snug

1189 little recess that was closed in on
1190 three sides. Spreading the news-
1191 paper on the turf to save his
1192 knees from soiling, he knelt and
1193 set to his task. For the time he
1194 felt neither hunger nor thirst.
1195 He had found out during his ear-
1197 lier experiments that the nails of
1196 his little fingers, which were
1198 trimmed to a point, could invade
1199 the keyholes in the little steel
1200 warts on the backs of his wrists
1201 and touch the locks. The mech-
1202 anism had even twitched a little
1203 bit under the tickle of the nail
1204 ends. So, having already
1205 smashed the gun-metal match
1206 safe under his heel, Mr. Trimm
1207 selected a slender-pointed bit
1208 from among its fragments and
1209 got to work, the left hand drawn
1210 up under the right, the fingers of
1211 the right busy with the lock of
1212 the left, the chain tightening and
1213 slackening with subdued clink-
1214 ing sounds at each movement.

1215 Mr. Trimm didn't know much
1216 about picking a lock. He had
1217 got his money by a higher form
1218 of burglary that did not require
1219 a knowledge of lock-picking.
1220 Nor as a boy had he been one to
1221 play at mechanics. He had let
1222 other boys make the toy flutter-
1223 mills and the wooden traps and
1224 the like, and then he had traded
1225 for them. He was sorry now that
1226 he hadn't given more heed to the
1227 mechanical side of things when
1228 he was growing up.

1229 He worked with a deliberate
1230 slowness, steadily. Neverthe-

less, it was hot work. The sun rose over the bank and shone on him through the limbs of the uprooted tree. His hat was on the ground alongside of him. The sweat ran down his face, streaking it and wilting his collar flat. The scrap of gun-metal kept slipping out of his wet fingers. Down would go the chained hands to scrabble in the grass for it, and then the picking would go on again. This happened a good many times. Birds, nervous with the spirit that presages the fall migration, flew back and forth along the creek, almost grazing Mr. Trimm sometimes. A rain crow wove a brown thread in the green warp of the bushes above his head. A chattering red squirrel sat up on a tree limb to scold him. At intervals, distantly, came the cough of laboring trains, showing that the track must have been cleared. There were times when Mr. Trimm thought he felt the lock giving. These times he would work harder.

· · · · ·

Late in the afternoon Mr. Trimm lay back against the bank, panting. His face was splotched with red, and the little hollows at the sides of his forehead pulsed rapidly up and down like the bellies of scared tree frogs. The bent outer case of the watch littered a bare patch on the log; its mainspring had gone the way of the fragments of the gun-metal match safe which were lying all about, each a worn-down, twisted wisp of metal. The spring of the eyeglasses had been confiscated long ago and the broken crystals powdered the earth where Mr. Trimm's toes had scraped a smooth patch. The nails of the two little fingers were worn to the quick and splintered down into the raw flesh. There were countless tiny scratches and mars on the locks of the handcuffs, and the steel wristbands were dulled with blood smears and pale-red tarnishes of new rust; but otherwise they were as stanch and strong a pair of Bean's Latest Model Little Giant handcuffs as you'd find in any hardware store anywhere.

The devilish, stupid malignity of the damned things! With an acid oath Mr. Trimm raised his hands and brought them down on the log violently. There was a double click and the bonds tightened painfully, pressing the chafed red skin white. Mr. Trimm snatched up his hands close to his near-sighted eyes and looked. One of the little notches on the under side of each cuff had disappeared. It was as if they were living things that had turned and bitten him for the blow he gave them.

· · · · ·

From the time the sun went down there was a tingle of frost in the air. Mr. Trimm didn't sleep much. Under the squeeze of the tightened fetters his wrists throbbed steadily and racking cramps ran through his arms. His stomach felt as though it were tied into knots. The water that he drank from the branch only made his hunger sickness worse. His undergarments, that had been wet with perspiration, clung to him clammily. His middle-aged, tenderly cared-for body called through every pore for clean linen and soap and water and rest, as his empty insides called for food.

After a while he became so chilled that the demand for warmth conquered his instinct for caution. He felt about him in the darkness gathering scraps of dead wood, and, after breaking several of the matches that had been in the gun-metal match safe, he managed to strike one and with its tiny flame started a fire. He huddled almost over the fire, coughing when the smoke blew into his face and twisting and pulling at his arms in an effort to get relief from the everlasting cramps. It seemed to him that if he could only get an inch or two more of play for his hands he would be ever so much more comfortable. But he couldn't, of course.

He dozed, finally, sitting cross-legged with his head sunk between his hunched shoulders. A pain in a new place woke him. The fire had burned almost through the thin sole of his right shoe, and as he scrambled to his feet and stamped, the clap of the hot leather flat against his blistered foot almost made him cry out.

. . . . .

Soon after sunrise a boy came riding a horse down a faintly traced footpath along the creek, driving a cow with a bell on her neck ahead of him. Mr. Trimm's ears caught the sound of the clanking bell before either the cow or her herder was in sight, and he limped away, running, skulking through the thick cover. A pendent loop of a wild grape-vine, swinging low, caught his hat and flipped it off his head; but Mr. Trimm, imagining pursuit, did not stop to pick it up and went on bareheaded until he had to stop from exhaustion. He saw some dark-red berries on a shrub upon which he had trod, and, stooping, he plucked some of them with his two hands and put three or four in his mouth experimentally. Warned instantly by the harsh, burning taste, he spat the crushed berries out and went on doggedly, following, according to his best judgment, a course parallel to the railroad. It was characteristic of him, a city-raised man, that he took no heed of distances nor of the distinguishing marks of the timber.

Behind a log at the edge of a small clearing in the woods he halted some little time, watching

1396 and listening. The clearing had
1397 grown up in sumacs and weeds
1398 and small saplings and it seemed
1399 deserted; certainly it was still.
1400 Near the center of it rose the sag-
1401 ging roof of what had been a shack
1402 or a shed of some sort. Stooping
1403 cautiously, to keep his bare head
1404 below the tops of the sumacs, Mr.
1405 Trimm made for the ruined
1406 shanty and gained it safely. In the
1407 midst of the rotted, punky logs
1408 that had once formed the walls he
1409 began scraping with his feet.
1410 Presently he uncovered some-
1411 thing. It was a broken-off harrow
1412 tooth, scaled like a long, red fish
1413 with the crusted rust of years.

1414 Mr. Trimm rested the lower
1415 rims of his handcuffs on the edge
1416 of an old, broken watering
1417 trough, worked the pointed end
1418 of the rust-crusted harrow tooth
1419 into the flat middle link of the
1420 chain as far as it would go, and
1421 then with one hand on top of the
1422 other he pressed downward with
1423 all his might. The pain in his
1424 wrists made him stop this at
1425 once. The link had not sprung
1426 or given in the least, but the
1427 twisting pressure had almost
1428 broken his wrist bones. He let
1429 the harrow tooth fall, knowing
1430 that it would never serve as a
1431 lever to free him—which, indeed,
1432 he had known all along—and sat
1433 on the side of the trough, rub-
1434 bing his wrists and thinking.

1435 He had another idea. It came
1436 into his mind as a vague sugges-
1437 tion that fire had certain effects

1438 upon certain metals. He kindled
1439 a fire of bits of the rotted wood,
1440 and when the flames ran together
1441 and rose slender and straight in
1442 a single red thread he thrust the
1443 chain into it, holding his hands
1444 as far apart as possible in the at-
1445 titude of a player about to catch
1446 a bounced ball. But immedi-
1447 ately the pain of that grew un-
1448 endurable too, and he leaped
1449 back, jerking his hands away.
1450 He had succeeded only in black-
1451 ening the steel and putting a big
1452 water blister on one of his wrists
1453 right where the shackle bolt
1454 would press upon it.

1455 Where he huddled down in the
1456 shelter of one of the fallen walls
1457 he noticed, presently, a strand of
1458 rusted fence wire still held to
1459 half-tottering posts by a pair of
1460 blackened staples; it was part of
1461 a pen that had been used once for
1462 chickens or swine. Mr. Trimm
1463 tried the wire with his fingers.
1464 It was firm and springy. Rock-
1465 ing and groaning with the pain
1466 of it, he nevertheless began slid-
1467 ing the chain back and forth
1468 along the strand of wire.

1469 Eventually the wire, weakened
1470 by age, snapped in two. A tiny
1471 shined spot, hardly deep enough
1472 to be called a nick, in its tar-
1473 nished, smudged surface was all
1474 the mark that the chain showed.

1475 Staggering a little and putting
1476 his feet down unsteadily, Mr.
1477 Trimm left the clearing, heading
1478 as well as he could tell eastward,
1479 away from the railroad. After

1480 a mile or two he came to a dusty
1481 wood road winding downhill.

1482 To the north of the clearing
1483 where Mr. Trimm had halted
1484 were a farm and a group of farm
1485 buildings. To the southward
1486 a mile or so was a cluster
1487 of dwellings set in the midst
1488 of more farm lands, with a
1489 shop or two and a small white
1490 church with a green spire in
1491 the center. Along a road that
1492 ran northward from the ham-
1493 let to the solitary farm a
1494 ten-year-old boy came, carry-
1495 ing a covered tin pail. A young
1496 gray squirrel flirted across the
1497 wagon ruts ahead of him and
1498 darted up a chestnut sapling.
1499 The boy put the pail down at the
1500 side of the road and began look-
1501 ing for a stone to throw at the
1502 squirrel.

1503 Mr. Trimm slid out from be-
1504 hind a tree. A hemstitched
1505 handkerchief grimed and
1506 stained, was loosely twisted a-
1507 round his wrists, partly hiding
1508 the handcuffs. He moved along
1509 with a queer, sidling gait, keep-
1510 ing as much of his body as he
1511 could turned from the youngster.
1512 The ears of the little chap caught
1513 the faint scuffle of feet and he
1514 spun around on his bare heel.

1515 "My boy, would you ——"
1516 Mr. Trimm began.

1517 The boy's round eyes widened
1518 at the apparition that was sidling
1519 toward him in so strange a fash-
1520 ion, and then, taking fright, he
1521 dodged past Mr. Trimm and ran

1522 back the way he had come, as
1523 fast as his slim brown legs could
1524 take him. In half a minute he
1525 was out of sight round a bend.

1526 Had the boy looked back he
1527 would have seen a still more curi-
1528 ous spectacle than the one that
1529 had frightened him. He would
1530 have seen a man worth four mil-
1531 lion dollars down on his knees in
1532 the yellow dust, pawing with
1533 chained hands at the tight-fitting
1534 lid of the tin pail, and then, when
1535 he had got the lid off, drinking
1536 the fresh, warm milk which the
1537 pail held with great, choking
1538 gulps, uttering little mewing, an-
1539 imal sounds as he drank, while
1540 the white, creamy milk ran over
1541 his chin and splashed down his
1542 breast in little, spurting streams.

1543 But the boy didn't look back.
1544 He ran all the way home and told
1545 his mother he had seen a wild
1546 man on the road to the village;
1547 and later, when his father came
1548 in from the fields, he was soundly
1549 thrashed for letting the sight of
1550 a tramp make him lose a good
1551 tin bucket and half a gallon of
1552 milk worth nine cents a quart.

·   ·   ·   ·   ·

1553 The rich, fresh milk put life
1554 into Mr. Trimm. He rested the
1555 better for it during the early part
1556 of that night in a haw thicket.
1557 Only the sharp, darting pains in
1558 his wrists kept rousing him to
1559 temporary wakefulness. In one
1560 of those intervals of waking the
1561 plan that had been sketchily
1562 forming in his mind from the

1563 time he had quit the clearing in
1564 the woods took on a definite,
1565 fixed shape. But how was he
1566 with safety to get the sort of aid
1567 he needed, and where?

1568 Canvassing tentative plans in
1569 his head, he dozed off again.

. . . . .

1570 On a smooth patch of turf be-
1571 hind the blacksmith shop three
1572 yokels were languidly pitching
1573 horseshoes—"quaits," they
1574 called them—at a stake driven
1575 in the earth. Just beyond, the
1576 woods shredded out into a long,
1577 yellow and green peninsula which
1578 stretched up almost to the back
1579 door of the smithy, so that late of
1580 afternoons the slanting shadows
1581 of the nearest trees fell on its
1582 roof of warped shingles. At the
1583 extreme end of this point of
1584 woods Mr. Trimm was squatted
1585 behind a big boulder, squinting
1586 warily through a thick-fringed
1587 curtain of ripened goldenrod tops
1588 and sumacs, heavy-headed with
1589 their dark-red tapers. He had
1590 been there more than an hour,
1591 cautiously waiting his chance to
1592 hail the blacksmith, whose figure
1593 he could make out in the smoky
1594 interior of his shop, passing back
1595 and forth in front of a smudgy
1596 forge fire and rattling metal
1597 against metal in intermittent fits
1598 of professional activity.

1599 From where Mr. Trimm
1600 watched to where the horseshoe-
1601 pitching game went on was not
1602 more than sixty feet. He could
1603 hear what the players said and

1604 even see the little puffs of dust
1605 rise when one of them clapped
1606 his hands together after a pitch.

1607 He judged by the signs of
1608 slackening interest that they
1609 would be stopping soon and, he
1610 hoped, going clear away.

1611 But the smith loafed out of
1612 his shop and, after an exchange
1613 of bucolic banter with the three
1614 of them, he took a hand in their
1615 game himself. He wore no coat
1616 or waistcoat and, as he poised a
1617 horseshoe for his first cast at the
1618 stake, Mr. Trimm saw, pinned
1619 flat against the broad strap of his
1620 suspenders, a shiny, silvery-look-
1621 ing disc. Having pitched the shoe,
1622 the smith moved over into the
1623 shade, so that he almost touched
1624 the clump of undergrowth that
1625 half buried Mr. Trimm's pro-
1626 tecting boulder. The near-sight-
1627 ed eyes of the fugitive banker
1628 could make out then what the
1629 flat, silvery disc was, and Mr.
1630 Trimm cowered low in his covert
1631 behind the rock, holding his
1632 hands down between his knees,
1633 fearful that a gleam from his
1634 burnished wristlets might strike
1635 through the screen of weed
1636 growth and catch the inquiring
1637 eye of the smith. So he stayed,
1638 not daring to move, until a din-
1639 ner horn sounded somewhere in
1640 the cluster of cottages beyond,
1641 and the smith, closing the doors
1642 of his shop, went away with the
1643 three yokels.

1644 Then Mr. Trimm, stooping
1645 low, stole back into the deep

woods again. In his extremity he was ready to risk making a bid for the hire of a blacksmith's aid to rid himself of his bonds, but not a blacksmith who wore a deputy sheriff's badge pinned to his suspenders.

.   .   .   .   .

He caught himself scraping his wrists up and down again against the rough, scrofulous trunk of a shellbark hickory. The irritation was comforting to the swollen skin. The cuffs, which kept catching on the bark and snagging small fragments of it loose, seemed to Mr. Trimm to have been a part and parcel of him for a long time—almost as long a time as he could remember. But the hands which they clasped so close seemed like the hands of somebody else. There was a numbness about them that made them feel as though they were a stranger's hands which never had belonged to him. As he looked at them with a sort of vague curiosity they seemed to swell and grow, these two strange hands, while the fetters measured yards across, while the steel bands shrunk to the thinness of piano wire, cutting deeper and deeper into the flesh. Then the hands in turn began to shrink down and the cuffs to grow up into great, thick things as cumbersome as the couplings of a freight car. A voice that Mr. Trimm dimly recognized as his own was saying something about four million dollars over and over again.

Mr. Trimm roused up and shook his head angrily to clear it. He rubbed his eyes free of the clouding delusion. It wouldn't do for him to be getting lightheaded.

.   .   .   .   .

On a flat, shelving bluff, forty feet above a cut through which the railroad ran at a point about five miles north of where the collision had occurred, a tramp was busy, just before sundown, cooking something in an old washboiler that perched precariously on a fire of wood coals. This tramp was tall and spindle-legged, with reddish hair and a pale, beardless, freckled face with no chin to it and not much forehead, so that it ran out to a peak like the profile of some featherless, unpleasant sort of fowl. The skirts of an old, ragged overcoat dangled grotesquely— about his spare shanks.

Desperate as his plight had become, Mr. Trimm had felt the old sick shame at the prospect of exposing himself to this knavish looking vagabond whose help he meant to buy with a bribe. It was the sight of a dainty wisp of smoke from the wood fire curling upward through the cloudy, damp air that had brought him limping cautiously across the right-of-way, to climb the rocky shelf along the cut; but now he hesitated, shielded in the shad-

1728 ows twenty yards away. It was
1729 a whiff of something savory in
1730 the washboiler, borne to him on
1731 the still air and almost making
1732 him cry out with eagerness, that
1733 drew him forth finally. At the
1734 sound of the halting footsteps
1735 the tramp stopped stirring the
1736 mess in the washboiler and
1737 glanced apprehensively. As he
1738 took in the figure of the new-
1739 comer his eyes narrowed and his
1740 pasty, nasty face spread in a
1741 grin of comprehension.

1742 "Well, well, well," he said leer-
1743 ing offensively, "welcome to our
1744 city, little stranger."

1745 Mr. Trimm came nearer, drag-
1746 ging his feet, for they were al-
1747 most out of the wrecks of his
1748 patent-leather shoes. His gaze
1749 shifted from the tramp's face to
1750 the stuff on the fire, his nostrils
1751 wrinkling. Then slowly, "I'm in
1752 trouble," he said, and held out
1753 his hands.

1754 "Wot I'd call a mild way o'
1755 puttin' it," said the tramp coolly.
1756 "That purticular kind o' joolry
1757 ain't gen'lly wore for pleasure."

1758 His eyes took on a nervous
1759 squint and roved past Mr.
1760 Trimm's stooped figure down
1761 the slope of the hillock.

1762 "Say, pal, how fur ahead are
1763 you of yore keeper?" he demand-
1764 ed, his manner changing.

1765 "There is no one after me—
1766 no one that I know of," ex-
1767 plained Mr. Trimm. "I am
1768 quite alone—I am certain of it."

1769 "Sure there ain't nobody look-
1770 in' fur you?" the other persisted
1771 suspiciously.

1772 "I tell you I am all alone,"
1773 protested Mr. Trimm. "I want
1774 your help in getting these—
1775 these things off and sending a
1776 message to a friend. You'll be
1777 well paid, very well paid. I can
1778 pay you more money than you
1779 ever had in your life, probably, for
1780 your help. I can promise——"

1781 He broke off, for the tramp,
1782 as if reassured by his words, had
1783 stooped again to his cooking and
1784 was stirring the bubbling con-
1785 tents of the washboiler with a
1786 peeled stick. The smell of the
1787 stew, rising strongly, filled Mr.
1788 Trimm with such a sharp and an
1789 aching hunger that he could not
1790 speak for a moment. He mas-
1791 tered himself, but the effort left
1792 him shaking and gulping.

1793 "Go on, then, an' tell us some-
1794 thin' about yourself," said the
1795 freckled man. "Wot brings you
1796 roamin' round this here railroad
1797 cut with them bracelets on?"

1798 "I was in the wreck," obeyed
1799 Mr. Trimm. "The man with me
1800 —the officer—was killed. I was-
1801 n't hurt and I got away into
1802 these woods. But they think I'm
1803 dead too—my name was among
1804 the list of dead."

1805 The other's peaky face length-
1806 ened in astonishment.

1807 "Why, say!" he began. "I
1808 read all about that there wreck
1809 —seen the list myself—say, you
1810 can't be Trimm, the New York
1811 banker? Yes, you are! Wot a

1980 elbows an' buckle it around be-
1981 hind at the back; an' I kinder
1982 guess you'll stay right there till
1983 I go down yonder to that town
1984 that I passed comin' up here an'
1985 see wot kind of a bargain I kin
1986 strike up with the marshal.
1987 Come on, now," he threatened
1988 with a show of bluster, reading
1989 the resolution that was mount-
1990 ing in Mr. Trimm's face. "Come
1991 on peaceable, if you don't want
1992 to git hurt."

1993 Of a sudden Mr. Trimm be-
1994 came the primitive man. He
1995 was filled with those elemental
1996 emotions that make a man see in
1997 spatters of crimson. Gathering
1998 strength from passion out of an
1999 exhausted frame, he sprang
2000 forward at the tramp. He
2001 struck at him with his head, his
2002 shoulders, his knees, his man-
2003 acled wrists, all at once. Not
2004 really hurt by the puny assault,
2005 but caught by surprise, the
2006 freckled man staggered back,
2007 clawing at the air, tripped on the
2008 washboiler in the fire, and with
2009 a yell vanished below the smooth
2010 edge of the cut.

2011 Mr. Trimm stole forward and
2012 looked over the bluff. Half-way
2013 down the cliff on an out-cropping
2014 shelf of rock the man lay, face
2015 downward, motionless. He
2016 seemed to have grown smaller
2017 and to have shrunk into his
2018 clothes. One long, thin leg was
2019 bent up under the skirts of the
2020 overcoat in a queer, twisted way,
2021 and the cloth of the trouser leg

2022 looked flattened and empty. As
2023 Mr. Trimm peered down at him
2024 he saw a red stain spreading on
2025 the rock under the still, silent
2026 figure's head.

2027 Mr. Trimm turned to the
2028 washboiler. It lay on its side,
2029 empty, the last of its recent con-
2030 tents sputtering out into the
2031 half-drowned fire. He stared at
2032 this ruin a minute. Then with-
2033 out another look over the cliff
2034 edge he stumbled slowly down
2035 the hill, muttering to himself as
2036 he went. Just as he struck the
2037 level it began to rain, gently at
2038 first, then hard, and despite the
2039 shelter of the full-leaved forest
2040 trees, he was soon wet through
2041 to his skin and dripped water as
2042 he lurched along without sense
2043 of direction and, indeed, without
2044 any active realization of what
2045 he was doing.

· · · · ·

2046 Late that night it was still
2047 raining—a cold, steady, autum-
2048 nal downpour. A huddled figure
2049 slowly climbed upon a low fence
2050 running about the house-yard of
2051 the little farm where the boy
2052 lived who got thrashed for losing
2053 a milkpail. On the wet top rail,
2054 precariously perching, the figure
2055 slipped and sprawled forward in
2056 the miry yard. It got up, pain-
2057 fully swaying on its feet. It was
2058 Mr. Trimm, looking for food.
2059 He moved slowly toward the
2060 house, tottering from weakness
2061 and because of the slick mud
2062 underfoot; peering near-sight-

edly this way and that through the murk; starting at every sound and stopping often to listen.

The outlines of the lean-to kitchen at the back of the house were looming dead ahead of him when from the corner of the cottage sprang a small terrier. It made for Mr. Trimm, barking shrilly. He retreated backward, kicking at the little dog and, to hold his balance, striking out with short, dabby jerks of his fettered hands—they were such motions as the terrier itself might make trying to walk on its hindlegs. Still backing away, expecting every instant to feel the terrier's teeth in his flesh, Mr. Trimm put one foot into a hotbed with a great clatter of the breaking glass. He felt the sharp ends of shattered glass tearing and cutting his shin as he jerked free. Recovering himself, he dealt the terrier a lucky kick under the throat that sent it back, yowling, to where it had come from, and then, as a door jerked open and a half-dressed man jumped out into the darkness, Mr. Trimm half hobbled, half fell out of sight behind the woodpile.

Back and forth along the lower edge of his yard the farmer hunted, with the whimpering, cowed terrier to guide him, poking in dark corners with the muzzle of his shotgun for the unseen intruder whose coming had aroused the household. In a brushpile just over the fence to the east Mr. Trimm lay on his face upon the wet earth, with the rain beating down on him, sobbing with choking gulps that wrenched him cruelly, biting at the bonds on his wrists until the sound of breaking teeth gritted in the air. Finally, in the hopeless, helpless frenzy of his agony he beat his arms up and down until the bracelets struck squarely on a flat stone and the force of the blow sent the cuffs home to the last notch so that they pressed harder and faster than ever upon the tortured wrist bones.

When he had wasted ten or fifteen minutes in a vain search the farmer went shivering back indoors to dry out his wet shirt. But the groveling figure in the brushpile lay for a long time where it was, only stirring a little while the rain dripped steadily down on everything.

· · · · ·

The wreck was on a Tuesday evening. Early on the Saturday morning following, the chief of police, who was likewise the whole of the day police force in the town of Westfield, nine miles from the place where the collision occurred, heard a peculiar, strangely weak knocking at the front door of his cottage, where he also had his office. The door was a Dutch door, sawed through the middle, so that the top half might be opened independently,

2146 leaving the lower panel fast.
2147 He swung this top half back.

2148 A face was framed in the open-
2149 ing—an indescribably dirty, un-
2150 utterably weary face, with mat-
2151 ted white hair and a rime of
2152 whitish beard stubble on the
2153 jaws. It was fallen in and sunk-
2154 en and it drooped on the chest of
2155 its owner. The mouth, swollen
2156 and pulpy, as if from repeated
2157 hard blows, hung agape, and be-
2158 tween the purplish parted lips
2159 showed the stumps of broken
2160 teeth. The eyes blinked weakly
2161 at the chief from under lids as
2162 colorless as the eyelids of a
2163 corpse. The bare white head
2164 was filthy with plastered mud
2165 and twigs, and dripping wet.

2166 "Hello, there!" said the chief,
2167 startled at this apparition.
2168 "What do you want?"

2169 With a movement that told of
2170 straining effort the lolled head
2171 came up off the chest. The thin,
2172 corded neck stiffened back, rising
2173 from a dirty, collarless neckband.
2174 The Adam's apple bulged out
2175 prominently, as big as a pigeon's
2176 egg.

2177 "I have come," said the spec-
2178 ter in a wheezing rasp of a voice
2179 which the chief could hardly
2180 hear, "I have come to surrender
2181 myself. I am Hobart W.
2182 Trimm."

2183 "I guess you got another think
2184 comin'," said the chief, who was
2185 by the way of being a neighbor-
2186 hood wag. "When last seen
2187 Hobart W. Trimm was only

2188 fifty-two years old. Besides
2189 which, he's dead and buried. I
2190 guess maybe you'd better think
2191 ag'in, grandpap, and see if you
2192 ain't Methus'lah or the Wan-
2193 derin' Jew."

2194 "I am Hobart W. Trimm, the
2195 banker," whispered the stranger
2196 with a sort of wan stubbornness.

2197 "Go on and prove it," sug-
2198 gested the chief, more than will-
2199 ing to prolong the enjoyment of
2200 the sensation. It wasn't often
2201 in Westfield that wandering
2202 lunatics came a-calling.

2203 "Got any way to prove it?"
2204 he repeated as the visitor stared
2205 at him.

2206 "Yes," came the creaking,
2207 rusted hinge of a voice, "I have."

2208 Slowly, with struggling at-
2209 tempts, he raised his hands into
2210 the chief's sight. They were
2211 horribly swollen hands, red with
2212 the dried blood where they were
2213 not black with the dried dirt;
2214 the fingers puffed up out of
2215 shape; the nails broken; they
2216 were like the skinned paws of
2217 a bear. And at the wrists, al-
2218 most buried in the bloated folds
2219 of flesh, blackened, rusted, bat-
2220 tered, yet still strong and whole,
2221 was a tightly locked pair of
2222 Bean's Latest Model Little Giant
2223 handcuffs.

2224 "Great God!" cried the chief,
2225 transfixed at the sight. He drew
2226 the bolt and jerked open the
2227 lower half of the door.

2228 "Come in," he said, "and
2229 lemme get them irons off of you

2230 —they must hurt something
2231 terrible."
2232   "They can wait," said Mr.
2233 Trimm very humbly. "I have
2234 worn them a long, long while, I
2235 think—I am used to them.
2236 Wouldn't you please get me
2237 some food first?"

THE ANALYSIS

THE Beginning of this story which contains the main narrative question and the promise of difficulty, opposition and disaster occupy the first 1141 lines. A glance at the chart which precedes this story will show that this Beginning is presented in a series of interchanges almost entirely, but it will disclose an interesting arrangement in that these meetings and interchanges are not, as they are in the other stories preceding this, in chronological order. They are instead, out of chronological order. Had this story been presented chronologically it would have begun on line 32, which opens with Mr. Trimm in the Tombs, and carries through to line 573 where he boards the train. Then lines 1 to 31 would come in, and the story would pick up again at line 574. There are in general two ways in which a Beginning may be presented. It may be presented chronologically or it may be presented in flash back. This is not strictly a flash-back Beginning as I shall point out later in a discussion of a story which is strictly of that type. This is a story in which the Beginning is presented out of chronological order, in that the opening meeting is used to present an important and unusual condition without presenting the narrative problem which emerges as a result of that condition and which unifies the whole story.

What is particularly interesting about this special arrangement is that Mr. Cobb was able to utilize the laws of interest, which are that a meeting is interesting or a condition is interesting in so far as it is important or unusual, and that out of the important or unusual conditions from which he had to choose Mr. Cobb chose unerringly that one which would best hold the interest of the reader. There is another condition which he might have chosen, and that is the condition confronting Mr. Trimm when he realized that the train was being wrecked. But this would not have helped nearly so much as the one Mr. Cobb chose because it was unusual in a way demanding explanation. The one that he did choose, that Mr. Trimm was taking a trip to Sing Sing, was one which might have happened to anybody at any time without very much explanation being necessary to justify it. Besides being important and unusual it was plausible. The other condition would have required a great deal of explanation in order to justify its presentation, and its effect would have been defeated.

Especially illuminating for the student of creative technique is that there are here presented two kinds of conditions. One of these is the one presented in the first 31 lines. This is a *passive* condition and one to which the response must be essentially either passive or in terms of a purpose emerging. It cannot be a response in terms of an interchange, because the passive condition cannot fight. The only possible way in which Mr. Trimm can respond to this stimulus is by reflection. It must be inactive response. It may grow into a purpose, but it cannot grow into an interchange until there is first a purpose apparent. On the other hand, if you will turn to line 1454 in the Body of the story, you will see that at the close of this scene or attempt of Mr. Trimm to burn off his hand-cuffs, a new condition has arisen, and his response to this is in terms of a new purpose projecting an interchange, that is to say, there is an *active* condition to which he is responding, and that active condition actually gives him battle just as if it were an active opponent.

Another thing which makes this Beginning exceedingly worth studying is that throughout the interchanges which make up the Beginning there is a narrative thread running. It is as if a story were being carried along by the main narrative question as to whether or not Mr. Trimm could keep the handcuffs hidden. His attempts unify the interchanges which make up the Beginning although we do not know at that time the main narrative question of the story. From the moment on line 253 when Meyers says, "Well, all ready," until the moment on line 625, when Meyers leaves for the water cooler, the reader is interested in the attempt of Mr. Trimm to keep the handcuffs hidden, and to keep his condition of being handcuffed hidden from the crowd. The technical lesson to be learned from the Beginning of this story is, that if the main narrative question cannot soon be made to emerge, there must be substituted for it some other kind of interest, preferably a narrative interest in some other question than the main narrative question. If there is not narrative interest there must be dramatic interest which comes from conflict and the promise of conflict, or of difficulty, or of disaster, all of which are present in this Beginning.

The Body of this story is again an excellent example of the effectiveness of interchanges which result in hindrances. The

Body of this story occupies lines 1142 to 2227, and is composed of nine attempts or scenes. The central narrative unity given to the story by its main narrative question ties these attempts very tightly together, so that at the close of each one we are aware of definite hindrances, either dramatic or narrative, to the main narrative question. At the close of the sixth scene or attempt, on lines 1570 to 1652 the hindrance is not only narrative but dramatic, because we see in it the threat of a possible opponent in the blacksmith who proves to be the sheriff. Also at the close of the encounter with the tramp, on line 2045, we find that there is again a dramatic hindrance because a new difficulty has arisen which increases that possibility of disaster should Mr. Trimm not escape. He is not only an escaped convict but a murderer as well.

There is a dramatic intensity in this story, which was not apparent in the other stories, and it comes from the importance of the attempts. The main narrative question is both unusual and important because a great deal depends upon it, and we find ourselves, because of the characterization which the author has given to Mr. Trimm in the Beginning of the story, hoping that he will not succeed. As readers, we feel ourselves quite pleased whenever there occurs a hindrance in the main narrative purpose. The Body of this story is therefore both dramatically and narratively interesting. It is both well plotted and well presented.

The Ending occupying lines 2228 to 2237 answers the question very clearly. Mr. Trimm has succeeded in finding someone who will take the handcuffs off him, because the Chief of Police of Westfield is caused to say, "Come in and lemme get them irons off of you." We find in this story the same structural units that we have found in the others, and we find also present the ironic significance in the reversal of the main narrative purpose or situation which occurred in the "Soapy" story, *The Cop and the Anthem*. Mr. Trimm on achieving his object, no longer considers it as important as getting something to eat.

The Beginning of this story will repay analysis because it illustrates so clearly the method by which other interest may be substituted for the main narrative interest which comes from the knowledge on the part of the reader of a main narrative question.

BEGINNING	Initial Condition and Actor's central purpose are both presented through medium of a single dramatic scene.	Scene. Jason Terwilliger and his uncle. Offered $5,000 and his debts paid, Jason agrees to kill Jake Finch, who is represented as a very strong man.	1–178	Main Plot Crises become apparent as scene progresses. Difficulty, Opposition, and Disaster are all implied. Main Narrative Question is "Can Jason succeed in killing Jake Finch?"
BODY	Series of attempts of Main Actor to achieve his purpose, despite difficulties in his way.	Scene. Jason vs. Craving for drink which will defeat his purpose, since success can come only from fitness. Result. Face drawn with suffering.	179–257	Hindrance.
		Scene. Jason and Captain of *Lorelei*. Conquers drink.	258–280	Furtherance.
		(5th step. Effect is to make him feel that he cannot bring himself to point of killing man.)	281–307	Disaster threatens purpose. Dramatic Hindrance
		Interchange. Jason and Frisco Purdy. Jason discovers meaning of Jake Finch. Is offered drink.	308–332	
ENDING	Conclusive Act.	Refuses Drink.	333	Answer to Main Narrative Question is "Yes."

SUNK

BY GEORGE F. WORTS

I HAVE included this story for any number of reasons—all good. It is in every respect a first rate story. After you have read it you will see that my selection of it is justified.

CASE No. 6

SUNK

BY GEORGE F. WORTS

By permission of Mr. Worts and the Editor of Collier's.

Jeffery Terwilliger closed the door of his library and shot the heavy bronze bolt against possible intrusion. He went from window to window, making sure that each shade was drawn to the bottom. He moved over the thick rugs with the ponderous felicity of an aged pelican. When the arrangements of the amber-lighted room were to his liking he walked to the walnut desk, selected a blond cigar from the silver humidor, lighted it, puffed at it with slow deliberation and wheeled upon his nephew Jason, who lay sprawled in a gray plush chair.

The young man returned his hard, disapproving stare with glassy hopefulness. He was unshaven, his lips were dry and cracked, his eyes stained and rimmed with red, his clothing rumpled. His pallor and his shakiness were even more obvious.

"I told you," said his uncle harshly, "never to enter this house again."

The young man nodded sullenly. "I wouldn't be here if it wasn't necessary. I've got to have two thousand dollars."

"Jason, I've given you thousands of dollars, and I'm not going to give you any more. You aren't worth it. I've spent my life making the name Terwilliger stand for industry and decency and you've spent yours making it stand for every kind of dissipation. I won't be blackmailed any longer. When I was your age——"

"You were pearl poaching in the South Seas," his nephew snorted.

"That's a lie! Every dollar I took out of the South Seas was an honest dollar. I worked hard for it. I didn't lean on anyone. At your age I was a man. And you—you've leaned on me ever since you were expelled from college. But you aren't going to lean on me any more."

"You've got to help me," his nephew said desperately. "If I can't get my hands on two

149

61 thousand dollars by to-morrow
62 noon——"

63 "You won't get it from me,"
64 the old man snarled. "God, but
65 you've sunk low. Do you realize
66 you've utterly ruined your life
67 and you're not yet twenty-five?
68 You haven't drawn a sober
69 breath in the past four years."

70 "I'll promise to straighten
71 up."

72 "You've promised that a
73 dozen times. You're lost!"

74 The young man sighed
75 wearily. "Oh, I admit it. I'm
76 sunk."

77 "You've sunk so low that
78 you'd kill me for my money if
79 you thought you wouldn't be
80 caught!"

81 His nephew nodded. "I
82 might."

83 Jeffery Terwilliger stared at
84 him. "I believe it. I believe
85 you've reached the stage where
86 you'd kill for money. Look
87 here! Would you undertake to
88 kill a man for money?"

89 The Terwilliger library be-
90 came terribly still. The old
91 man was standing with his legs
92 apart, his body slightly bent,
93 the cigar half raised to his
94 mouth—a frozen gesture. His
95 nephew was clutching the gray
96 plush arms of the chair.

97 "How much?"

98 "Your debts and—five thou-
99 sand dollars!"

100 "For that price I would kill
101 any man alive."

102 "Understand me. I'm not

joking. I'm offering you a sum 103
of money to kill a man." 104

"I heard you. Who is the 105
man?" 106

Jeffery Terwilliger sank back 107
against the walnut desk and 108
wiped his forehead with a large 109
silk handkerchief. 110

"I didn't think you'd be so 111
willing. I didn't think you'd 112
sunk so low. Or—or are you 113
just drunk?" 114

"I am thinking as clearly as 115
you are. You're always talking 116
about the proud Terwilliger 117
name. Blood is thicker than 118
water! I'll kill your man! Who 119
is he?" 120

His uncle glared. "What 121
difference does it make? As far 122
as you're concerned, he's any 123
man. You will be erasing a— 124
a number. Do you grasp what 125
I mean? You do not know 126
whether he is old, young, tall, 127
short, fat, thin, blond, brunette, 128
white, or black. His name 129
happens to be Jake Finch. He 130
lives on the island of Paulota, 131
which is approximately a five 132
weeks' sail from Papeete. My 133
old schooner, the *Lorelei*, is lying 134
in Papeete harbor. The captain 135
will be ready for you. At Paulota 136
you will look up a trader named 137
Purdy. Purdy will tell you 138
where to find Jake Finch. You 139
can trust Purdy. He knows and 140
he'll help." 141

Jason Terwilliger squinted 142
shrewdly at his uncle. 143

"Let me get this straight. I 144

145 go to Papeete, board your
146 schooner and sail to the island
147 of Paulota. I find there a
148 trader named Purdy."
149 "Frisco Purdy."
150 "All right. I ask Frisco
151 Purdy where to find Jake Finch.
152 Upon finding Jake Finch, I kill
153 him. It sounds easy."
154 "He is a strong man, a
155 powerful man—but not more
156 powerful than you used to be."
157 "But he won't know I'm
158 going to kill him. Perhaps I'd
159 better shoot him in the back."
160 "You can decide the details
161 for yourself. Will you go?"
162 "I will go."
163 "Very well. I'll arrange for
164 your passage. Here is the
165 revolver I want you to use. If
166 you will give me the list, I will
167 pay your debts in the morning."
168 "And the five thousand?"
169 "Will be here when you
170 return."
171 "How'll you know I've done
172 the job?"
173 "It will be written on your
174 face," the old man said. "Re-
175 member: We Terwilligers have
176 always been famous for two
177 traits: keeping our promises
178 intact and our mouths shut."
179 Two days out of San
180 Francisco, Jason aroused him-
181 self from the drunken stupor in
182 which he had lain, fully dressed,
183 since the steamer sailed. It was
184 night. He switched on the state-
185 room light and found, close to his
186 hand on the bunk, the revolver.

187 It was not a slim, gentlemanly
188 revolver; it was blunt and thick,
189 the kind that brutes carry for
190 short-range killing. It was a
191 murderer's revolver.
192 He grasped it by the butt and
193 stood up, with his back against
194 the closed door. At the other
195 end of the stateroom, perhaps
196 ten feet away, was a washstand.
197 There was a water tank above it
198 and a narrow cupboard beneath.
199 With these accessories it was
200 about as high and as wide as a
201 man of average size.
202 Jason lifted the revolver and
203 aimed it at the washstand. The
204 washstand was blurred. His
205 hand was shaking. He could
206 not steady it. If he pulled the
207 trigger, he would probably miss
208 the washstand. In his present con-
209 dition, Jake Finch could kill him
210 before he could kill Jake Finch.
211 He placed the revolver in his
212 suit case, closed the lid and
213 hastened on deck. It was cock-
214 tail hour, and the smokeroom
215 was crowded. Licking his burn-
216 ing lips, Jason elbowed through
217 the crowd toward the bar.
218 But before he reached the
219 bar the image of the revolver
220 shaking in his hand entered his
221 mind. He dared not drink. He
222 must prepare himself for the
223 encounter with Jake Finch!
224 He paced the deck until mid-
225 night, fighting away a thirst
226 that fairly gnawed at his throat.
227 Until morning he tossed, sleep-
228 less, in his bunk. But when the

229 desire for drink became most
230 insistent the shaking revolver
231 and the blurred washstand would
232 come to his mind. Each time
233 this vision brought him up
234 sharply; each time it forced him
235 to realize that his hand must be
236 steady and his brain alert and
237 clear to carry things off with-
238 out consequences fatal to him-
239 self.

240 He endured, in the following
241 week, satanic torments. His
242 throat burned for liquor; his
243 system ached for it; but he
244 determinedly resisted the crav-
245 ing. Meanwhile a murderous
246 hatred of his uncle was growing
247 in him. His uncle was a schem-
248 ing Midas; his uncle had robbed
249 him of the little that had
250 remained of his manhood.

251 When Jason debarked in Pa-
252 peete he had had nothing
253 stronger than coffee to drink
254 since that day when he awoke
255 and found the revolver beside
256 him. And his face was drawn
257 with suffering.

258 He transferred his belongings
259 to the *Lorelei*, and the *Lorelei*
260 went out to sea with the tide
261 that afternoon. Her captain
262 was an old man; incommunica-
263 tive and almost deaf. He told
264 Jason that the schooner was
265 short-handed; that he would
266 welcome Jason's help. And
267 Jason assented with eagerness.
268 He wanted to work, to exhaust
269 himself so that he could sleep
270 again; wanted to strengthen his

271 body for the encounter with Jake
272 Finch.

273 At dinner the captain placed
274 a bottle of whisky on the table;
275 poured himself a drink and
276 raised his eyes to Jason's face.
277 There was a perceptible interval
278 between the unspoken question
279 and Jason's answer.

280 "No," said Jason.

281 The days following were
282 happy for him, but many of the
283 nights were sleepless. The
284 revolver no longer shook when
285 he gripped and aimed it. He
286 practiced on empty bottles
287 tossed overboard, and his
288 marksmanship was good—good
289 enough. He had come to picture
290 Jake Finch as an old man,
291 a hermit; a man whose face
292 haunted him in the darkness
293 of his cabin with an eerie resem-
294 blance to his uncle's, a face whose
295 every line betrayed contempt.

296 As each day drew him nearer
297 to the deed that he had promised
298 to commit, as his health im-
299 proved and his brain cleared,
300 Jason's rebellion grew. He
301 could not have been that
302 creature who had bargained to
303 kill a man.

304 And when Jason went ashore
305 in Paulota he was sick with
306 terror. He could not kill that
307 man. He could not!

308 Three human derelicts on the
309 wharf directed him to Frisco
310 Purdy's zinc-roofed bungalow.
311 And on the veranda he found
312 him—a white-bearded old man

with twinkling young eyes, who blinked at him and nodded incessantly as they talked.

"Jake Finch?" the trader repeated. "There've been dozens of Jake Finches here. Jake Finch is the standing joke of Paulota, and has been for a half century or better. Jake Finch is the name we give to beach combers—the name we give to any man who doesn't amount to a damn. There's three of them down on the dock now— three Jake Finches. Hold on! Where you going?"

"I've got to be getting aboard."

"But you'll stay long enough to have a drink!"

"No; I don't drink."

THE ANALYSIS

The story *Sunk* was first printed in *Collier's* as a "Short-Short-Story." My first interest in it centered in the Ending because it carried over the tradition of the surprise Ending. It was an extremely clever story,—the sort of idea which comes very, very seldom to a writer, and which he seizes upon with joy. But the more I examined this story the more I became impressed with the knowledge of craftsmanship possessed by the writer. Interesting as it is, as a model of compression, it is still more interesting to students of the modern short-story form in showing its author's mastery of the laws of interest. The reader's attention is gained at once. His curiosity and expectancy are aroused. He is anxious to know more about the chief actor, about the problem confronting that actor, the promised encounter, and the actor's solution of the main narrative problem. The structural divisions of Beginning, Body, and Ending are very clearly defined. Lines 1 to 178 make up the Beginning. Lines 179 to 332 constitute the Body. Line 333 forms the Ending. This story is a story of accomplishment. The feat to be accomplished is the killing of Jake Finch by Jason Terwilliger. The main narrative question raised in the Beginning of the story is, "Can Jason Terwilliger succeed in killing Jake Finch?" The answer to the main narrative question, contained in the result of Jason's meeting with Frisco Purdy, is "Yes." The Conclusive Act of the actor by which the reader is made aware of this result is Jason's statement to Frisco Purdy, "No, I don't drink," on line 333.

In the unexpectedness of its dénouement, this story has much of the quality which is so widely associated with the late O. Henry. Just as superficial observers and critics have long been apt to disregard the other artistic qualities of O. Henry in their concentration upon his ability to achieve a surprise Ending, so they will be likely to overlook Mr. Worts's accomplishment in writing the Beginning of *Sunk*.

The Beginning of this story alone would have justified me in reprinting the story. No student of craftsmanship need feel that he is too far advanced to study this Beginning with profit.

The Beginning of every story has one basic purpose. It is to lay before the reader the main narrative problem of the story together with the necessary explanatory matter. A narrative situation, that is, something to be accomplished, is interesting in proportion as it is important or unusual. This narrative situation is both. There is required, however, much more than the mere statement or the mere presentation of the narrative problem, to make up a good Beginning. The explanatory matter required to elucidate that problem must also be laid before the reader. Yet, whether problem or explanatory matter, the material of the Beginning is intended to appeal to the curiosity of the reader and to satisfy that curiosity to the extent of giving him the information which will enable him to follow the story proper without confusion. To give the necessary information, and to render it interestingly and plausibly, is the purpose of every Beginning.

From an examination of the story *The Escape of Mr. Trimm* you learned that as long as the minor narrative interest is sustained it is not essential, although it is desireable, that the main narrative question shall emerge. Therefore, in order to delay the main narrative question, and still to achieve narrative interest, we must introduce a minor narrative question. In this case, the Beginning is presented in a single scene, which has its own minor narrative question, which comes in the first thirty-four lines. It is, "Can Jason Terwilliger succeed in securing $2,000 from his uncle?" This minor narrative question is made to hold the interest until the main crisis is reached on line 119, and in the approximate 400 words contained in those 86 lines from line 34 to 119, Mr. Worts compresses all the information which is needed for his story. In presenting the information leading to the major crisis, Mr. Worts utilizes his knowledge of the laws of interest by presenting the interchange which leads to the crisis as a scene rather than an episode. Thus the reader's interest in the outcome of the clash enables the writer to prolong the dramatic meeting sufficiently to introduce all the explanatory matter for the whole story. The gain from this method is extraordinary. The slow and dull story is ordinarily made so by a surplusage of explanatory matter in the presentation of each minor narrative question. The reader, interested in the outcome of the main narrative question, wants to hurry along. He is prevented from doing so by having to wade through explanatory matter in each scene. Mr. Worts obviates this by presenting all of his explanatory matter in a single scene in the Beginning of the story. When the interchanges or meetings which make up the Body of the story are presented, they are enabled to move right along without any clogging by explanatory matter.

Sunk is a story which will repay analysis by students of the short-story form. The scenic presentation of the Beginning always ensures interest provided always that at the close of each scene there is apparent either a main narrative question or a dramatic crisis consisting of the promise of conflict, or difficulty, or disaster in the meetings or interchanges which are foreshadowed.

Apart from the Beginning there was another reason for including this story. It is in the handling of that portion of the story which is the Body, and which contains the conflict which was foreshadowed in the Beginning, of Jason Terwilliger's attempt to overcome a difficulty which exists, and which must be removed before he can achieve his objective. Lines 179 to 257 contain his first attempt, and it is actually a scene of man against inner man, which is the craving for drink opposed to his desire to fit himself physically for the task he has accepted. It ends in a hindrance, because it shows his face drawn with suffering, which indicates that he is not any nearer to success than he was before. Lines 258 to 280 are an interchange between Jason and the captain of the *Lorelei*, which concludes with a crisis of furtherance on line 280 when he says, "no"—that he will not take a drink. But this is instantly followed by a dramatic hindrance which is the fifth step of that scene, on lines 281 to 307, when he feels that his task is impossible. This is the big moment of the story when disaster threatens the purpose, and it has that essential quality of drama which is the feeling on the part of the reader that whichever action Jason Terwilliger takes he will regret it. It is this dramatic handling of the crisis in the Body of this story which makes the Body worth studying by students of craftsmanship.

The Ending of this story speaks for itself. It has that quality of dramatic suddenness which leaves the reader more or less breathless. It is a complete surprise, and yet upon a thorough examination of all that went before, the reader feels that the author did not in any way cheat him; that personality in Jason Terwilliger which is Jake Finch has been definitely killed by him when, on being asked to take a drink, he says, "No."

This story is an extremely interesting story to be considered in comparison with two others: *Paradise Island* by Will Payne, and *Jetsam* by John Russell. After you have read those I shall discuss each one and point out the resemblances in the material and the differences in the treatment. One lesson which it is the function of this volume to point out is that the same material can be treated by a number of different writers in such a way that we get a number of different stories. But apart from these other stories the story *Sunk* is in itself very much worth your consideration because it illustrates a perfect Beginning from the point of view of craftsmanship.

BEGINNING	Main Actor's central purpose is apparent at once.	Meeting. Dwyer and Ditch.	1– 5	Main Narratve Question emerges. "Can Dwyer kill a man?"
		Meeting. Dwyer and Setting.	6– 111	Main purpose reiterated.
		Interchange. Dwyer and Wife.	112– 171	Main purpose reiterated.
	Initial Condition is then presented by taking the reader back.	Flash-back Scene. Langley and Dwyer. Langley gives Dwyer option of transferring Paradise Island management to a committee or of being exposed. Dwyer and Langley agree to meet that evening, later.	172– 848	The Explanatory Matter is laid before the reader, and he becomes aware of the dramatic plot crises *after* he is aware of the narrative crisis which projects the main Narrative Question of the story.
		(5th Step.) Effect of interchange upon actors is that Dwyer, reflecting, comes to the ditch.	849–1061	
BODY	The only attempt is shown.	Interchange. Dwyer and Langley. Dwyer learns that Langley is protected by information left with his chief. This presents a new condition.	1062–1268	There are no Plot Crises in the Body. At the close of the single interchange comes the Conclusive Act.
ENDING	Conclusive Act, and Sequel	Dwyer abandons his purpose.	1269–1276	The Main Narrative Question is answered "No."

PARADISE ISLAND

Wherever possible I have chosen parallel stories, in order that students of narrative craftsmanship may see that the same essential situation may be developed in different ways by different writers.

Paradise Island contains the same main narrative problem as *Sunk*. They are both stories of a man who sets out to kill another man.

The chief reason, however, for including this story in the volume is that it is a very interesting example of the "flash-back" type of Beginning. A writer's greatest forward step in the mastery of craftsmanship comes when he learns how to write the "Flash-back" type of Beginning.

CASE No. 7

"PARADISE ISLAND"

BY WILL PAYNE

Dwyer halted at the ditch— abruptly, as though an invisible hand had seized his arm. An idea rang in his brain: This would be the place to kill a man. A gully ran through here. But now that Palm Bluff was becoming a city, that would not answer, so they were deepening it and laying a big iron drainage pipe along the bottom, to be covered with earth when the job was finished, leaving the surface of the ground level. At this point the excavation was more than twenty feet deep, sheathed with pine plank to hold the sandy soil. A single plank had been laid across the top bridgewise. An unconnected segment of the new pipe, with a thick iron collar on the end, stuck up through muddy water in the bottom of the cut, and some tools.

Overhead, a seamless loose gray fleece exuded warm mist. One could hardly say it rained; but there was a slow, intermittent drip of water from the leaves. Coming out of doors, one's hands, face and clothing at once grew moist. This plank over the ditch was wet. A man might easily slip on it.

It was the outskirts of town. Only Dwyer's smart new house and three or four humble older ones lay to the north. Beyond them the level ground was still overgrown with tall Southern pine and clumps of palmetto, dissolving into foggy obscurity at no great distance. Only fifty yards to the west the ground broke down into a ragged bluff, its crown thirty feet or so above the sea, which seemed to have stopped and to lie gray, motionless, waiting for something to happen. On that side the picture ended indefinitely in a long, darker smudge formerly called John's Key, but now, thanks to Dwyer, much known as Paradise Island. It was only two-thirds of a mile offshore, but so vague that a stranger might easily have mistaken if for the extended trail

61 of smoke from a Gulf steamer.
62 And this general blur—still
63 and vague, but shut in—seemed
64 to sanction the idea which had
65 exploded in Dwyer's mind; seem-
66 ed to blindfold the world and
67 hold its ears for him. He put
68 up his hand and wiped perspira-
69 tion from his brow. But he
70 shouldn't be stopping here. In
71 fact he had stopped only half
72 a second, hardly missing a step.
73 He set his muddy shoe on the
74 wet plank and passed over, strid-
75 ing toward his new house.
76 The shoe was muddy because
77 the sidewalk had been torn up
78 here for the ditch digging.
79 Otherwise it was a smart article
80 of white canvas and black
81 leather. His fine wool stockings
82 had a pattern worked in the
83 tops. There was an embossed
84 monogram on his silver belt
85 buckle. He wore a silk shirt and
86 belted jacket. Such clothes
87 were becoming to his tall, well-
88 made figure. In profile he
89 would have adorned a coin, in
90 spite of his bald head—for
91 which, indeed, his neatly point-
92 ed, curly golden beard seemed
93 to compensate; but his face was
94 much too narrow, as though it
95 had been squeezed in a press,
96 bringing his eyes close together.
97 On first acquaintance the dis-
98 parity between profile and full
99 face was fairly disconcerting, as
100 though he had two faces, and
101 they were even of different ages.
102 There was a great turmoil

103 within, and a goneness as though
104 a blow in the stomach had taken
105 his wind. Assuredly he had
106 never imagined himself as a
107 murderer. The unspoken word
108 set his heart to quaking furiously
109 now. But he had a baffled feel-
110 ing of the thing's being thrust
111 into his hands—no other way.
112 The new house, of hollow tile
113 and stucco, in Spanish style, had
114 four bedrooms and three baths.
115 The local newspaper, in describ-
116 ing the plans and referring from
117 time to time to the progress of
118 the structure, had dwelt upon
119 the three baths as a crowning
120 distinction. The little blue-tiled
121 sun parlor looked out upon the
122 Gulf and contained a broad
123 lounge with many bright-colored
124 cushions. Mrs. Dwyer, in an
125 embroidered blue silk wrapper,
126 reclined upon it, reading a love
127 story in a magazine. Hearing
128 his step, she hid the box of candy
129 under the cushions. Fat was
130 her arch enemy—a hundred and
131 sixty, she confessed to him; but
132 the bathroom scales said a hun-
133 dred and seventy-four, over
134 which she secretly wept a little
135 in vexation and self-pity. She
136 was a very fair woman, with
137 ash-blond hair and big baby-
138 blue eyes and a beautiful skin.
139 She smiled at her husband as
140 he stepped in, and hid a yawn
141 with a jeweled hand, mention-
142 ing that on such a miserable
143 day it hadn't seemed worth
144 while to dress. He told her

145 that he wouldn't be home for
146 dinner—had to meet some St.
147 Petersburg men; they'd talk
148 over their business while they
149 ate in a private room at the
150 hotel; but he expected to return
151 early.

152 "Oh, by the way, Langley'll
153 be here to see me at half past
154 nine. Said he'd wait if I wasn't
155 home by that time. I expect to
156 be here by then, but it may be a
157 little later. Have him wait. I
158 won't be long."

159 Surely that was a very simple
160 message to leave with one's wife;
161 yet he found himself stammering
162 over it, scant of breath, his heart
163 hammering at his ribs. He
164 looked away lest she see some-
165 thing in his eyes. But she
166 evidently saw nothing, for the
167 next instant her voice came in-
168 dolently to his ears with a laugh:
169 "He's such a funny little
170 mouse of a man! I ought to
171 have a doll for him to play with."

172 No doubt Langley had re-
173 minded other people of a mouse.
174 His hair and tiny, ineffectual
175 mustache were dust-colored. He
176 wore large gold-bowed spec-
177 tacles, and walked with a slight
178 round-shouldered stoop, as
179 though apologizing for his five
180 feet three inches of height. His
181 wrinkled clothes, not exactly
182 shabby, carried out the general
183 effect of insignificance.

184 Trudging down Seaview
185 Avenue at four o'clock of this
186 afternoon, with a big white
187 envelope in the pocket of his
188 flapping coat, thumb and fore-
189 finger absently pecking at the
190 small mustache, he had evidently
191 been lost in thought, and seemed
192 vaguely startled at finding
193 himself in front of an office
194 which, on this overcast day, was
195 flooded with electric light—
196 quite the smartest office in town,
197 with seagreen rugs on the floor,
198 orange-colored wicker chairs and
199 settees and pictures on the walls.
200 The most conspicuous of them,
201 twenty feet long by four high,
202 was brilliantly illuminated from
203 above and showed a long, nar-
204 row, green island in a varnished
205 blue sea. In the foreground
206 stood an immensely long hotel,
207 with towers, minarets and ban-
208 ners, and a huge circular casino
209 built out over the water. A
210 boulevard ran along the beach.
211 Back of it all over the island,
212 roofs, and cornices of villas and
213 cottages peeked out of em-
214 bowering leafage.

215 The legend under the picture
216 said "Paradise Island," and in
217 much more modest letters, "As
218 it will appear when improve-
219 ments are completed." Several
220 people were there, but no one
221 paid any attention to Langley as
222 he ambled through to a smaller
223 room, where a dark, handsome
224 young woman, after stepping
225 back to inquire, said that Mr.
226 Dwyer would see him in a few
227 minutes; then openly mothered
228 him into a wicker chair, where

229 he could wait comfortably. He
230 was flustered and blushing
231 slightly; there had been moments
232 when he had a harrowing pre-
233 vision that this vigorous smiling
234 Miss Hanson was going to take
235 him into her lap and rock him.
236 But although she made him
237 nervous he liked her too.

238 Two men came out from the
239 inner office, talking together as
240 they walked past. A buzzer
241 sounded on Miss Hanson's desk
242 and she turned to Langley with
243 a bright, encouraging nod to
244 signify that he might go in.

245 He drew a quick breath, wet
246 his lips and got up, his heart
247 pounding. Nevertheless, push-
248 ing open the door to the inner
249 room, he could not help giving a
250 woodeny smile, nor the silly
251 gesture of raising thumb and
252 forefinger to peck at his
253 mustache. Athletic Dwyer, in
254 smart golf clothes, stood up
255 genially to shake hands, and
256 hospitably indicated a vacant
257 chair by the desk. Being seated,
258 Langley fumbled in getting the
259 big envelope out of his pocket and
260 swallowed and cleared his throat.

262 "Mr. Dwyer, I've got some
263 newspaper clippings here. They
264 came in this afternoon's mail.
265 I'd like you to glance them
266 over."

267 Looking owlish for all the
268 world, with his round pale eyes
269 staring behind gold-bowed spec-
270 tacles, he pushed the envelope
271 across the desk.

272 Dwyer did not take the en-
273 velope immediately. Instead
274 he looked at his young caller in
275 a sudden arrest and astonish-
276 ment. For there was something
277 in Langley's embarrassed air—
278 well, as though a mouse had
279 abruptly leveled a gun at one's
280 head. Langley's eyes fell before
281 the other man's concentrated,
282 questioning gaze, he moistened
283 his lips and mechanically turned
284 his faded straw hat in his lap.

285 Very soberly, then, Dwyer
286 picked up the envelope, noting
287 at a glance that its upper left-
288 hand corner bore the return
289 card of a Boston newspaper. It
290 bulged with soft contents that
291 seemed to have been hastily
292 stuffed in. When he shook it a
293 dozen newspaper clippings fell
294 out, and a sheet of coarse paper
295 on which was hastily scrawled
296 with lead pencil:

297 *Dr. Jim:* Here's the grave-
298 yard. Be sure to send it back.
299 Don't know what became of D.
300 Will inquire and let you know.
301   Yrs.
302   BEN.

303 Dwyer knew that in news-
304 paper office slang "graveyard"
305 meant the file in which all sorts
306 of contemporaneous biographical
307 material was kept, so that if
308 Peter J. Filkins, of Essex, Massa-
309 chusetts, came into a fortune or
310 broke his neck or got nominated
311 for Congress or otherwise burst
312 into print, a reporter could at

313 once lay hands upon items with
314 which to embellish the story.
315 He merely glanced at the clip-
316 pings, being already quite aware
317 of their purport.

318 From them it appeared that,
319 not long after the war, one
320 Dwyer, doing business under
321 the firm name of E. Pellman
322 Dwyer & Co., had been arrested
323 on a charge of tempting small
324 investors to part with their
325 Liberty Bonds and savings-bank
326 balances in order to participate
327 in vast, mysterious and fab-
328 ulously profitable operations in
329 foreign exchange. But the story,
330 as disclosed by the clippings,
331 ended in mid-air. There was the
332 man's arrest and the charges
333 against him, with names of some
334 of the plucked dupes; then his
335 reply, which consisted of a
336 general denial, and the giving
337 of bail. Small items recorded
338 various postponements of the
339 hearing. But whether or not
340 the man had been brought to
341 trial did not appear.

342 Both Langley and Dwyer
343 knew that at the period covered
344 by these clippings a much more
345 extensive and spectacular swin-
346 dle, conducted by a citizen of
347 foreign birth, was absorbing the
348 attention of the public and of
349 the newspapers, so that this
350 Dwyer case was only a sort of
351 negligible side show. Also, not
352 long afterward, there were excit-
353 ing charges of blackmail and
354 bribery in connection with the

355 administration of justice in
356 Boston. It seemed that in the
357 bigger mess Dwyer had been
358 lost sight of.

359 "I was in Boston at the time—
360 on the *Tribune*," said Langley.
361 "I never saw Dwyer, but we
362 published his picture, I'd fairly
363 forgotten all about it, as you
364 might say. Down here I didn't
365 think anything in particular
366 about your name being Dwyer
367 too—no connection occurred to
368 me. Then the other day"—he
369 hesitated an instant, painfully
370 —"a lady was saying that Mrs.
371 Dwyer spoke of having lived in
372 Boston. Somehow it flashed
373 over me. The same initials,
374 you see, and something about
375 the picture coming back to my
376 mind. Of course you didn't
377 have a beard then, and had a
378 full head of hair. It flashed
379 over me. Well, I was going up
380 to Tampa next day. I sent a
381 wire from there to my friend."
382 He nodded toward the scrawled
383 note. "I asked him to send me
384 what he had, since 1919, on E.
385 Pellman Dwyer. Seems he
386 didn't understand me very well
387 —just sent me on the old stuff
388 in the graveyard. That's how
389 this happened."

390 Haltingly, and in a toneless
391 sort of voice, he made the state-
392 ment; yet with an astonishing
393 air of candor, too, as though, as
394 a matter of course, Mr. Dwyer
395 would understand that he was
396 obliged to find out about his

397 Boston antecedents and come
398 and tell him of the discovery.
399 That candid air really dis-
400 concerted the large man behind
401 the desk.

402 "Why are you showing me
403 these things?" he asked abruptly.

404 Langley elevated his dust-
405 colored eyebrows in faint sur-
406 prise and replied monotonously,
407 "To ask whether you are the
408 same man."

409 Dwyer felt that he ought to be
410 angry, but in a way it was so
411 ridiculous that one couldn't be.

412 "I am not the same man,"
413 he said promptly. "That was
414 my cousin. His first name is
415 Edward."

416 His own first name, as known
417 in Palm Bluff, was Elihu—Elihu
418 P. Dwyer. But it rarely found
419 its way into print. The name
420 that appeared in bold type in all
421 advertisements of Paradise Isl-
422 and was George Ingram & Co.
423 There was a George Ingram,
424 indefinitely understood to be a
425 wealthy, retired capitalist of
426 New York. Twice or thrice he
427 had appeared in Palm Bluff,
428 vanishing again after a week or
429 so. Dwyer was only the "Co.,"
430 and Langley knew that he had
431 privately asked the local news-
432 paper to keep his name out of
433 print, lest Mr. Ingram, who was
434 furnishing most of the capital,
435 should become jealous of a mere
436 lieutenant.

437 With a mild and owlish in-
438 nocence, Langley asked, "Where
439 were you at this time, Mr.
440 Dwyer—at the time this thing
441 happened in Boston?"

442 Dwyer felt something soft and
443 weak but like a leech, not to be
444 shaken off. For the first time
445 he spoke sharply.

446 "See here, Langley, you know
447 what I've done. I've put Palm
448 Bluff on the map. When I came
449 here fifteen months ago this
450 town was dead as a door nail—
451 four thousand inhabitants.
452 That's as far as it had got in
453 thirty years. And that's about
454 as far as it would get in the
455 next thirty." His voice showed
456 anger. "Everybody's running
457 around in circles now barking
458 over the boom in real estate.
459 They know what the boom's
460 done for Miami and Palm Beach
461 and St. Petersburg and other
462 places. A lot of 'em talk as
463 though it just happened in
464 Palm Bluff. But I brought it
465 here! I started it and I've kept
466 it going!"

467 Langley gravely nodded.

468 "I know you did, Mr. Dwyer.
469 I've always said so. Mr.
470 Kendrick says so, too."

471 Dwyer caught at the idea
472 which that name suggested, de-
473 manding, "What does Kendrick
474 know about this?"

475 "He doesn't know anything
476 about it," Langley replied in
477 that monotonous and oddly dis-
478 concerting manner. "He's out
479 of town today. You see, I
480 wasn't expecting an answer from

481 Boston so soon, and I thought
482 when it did come it would tell
483 more about the case—how it
484 ended. So I didn't say any-
485 thing to him—till I knew more,
486 you understand." He gave a
487 little twist to his mustache.
488 "And then, when this came in,
489 I thought I better ask you."
490 Again—obscurely—Dwyer
491 wanted to laugh because it was
492 ridiculous. But he went on with
493 his own statement:
494 "Well, take your newspaper.
495 You know what it was when I
496 came here—ten or twelve pages
497 once a week; not exactly run-
498 ning over with profits. Now
499 you're printing fourteen and six-
500 teen pages twice a week—talking
501 about changing it over to a daily
502 —putting up a new building. I
503 did that, Langley. Same way
504 with other things here. It's
505 the push I gave that started 'em
506 all up."
507 Langley would not have
508 denied it. The newspaper had
509 been launched twenty-five years
510 before, a feeble weekly bantling,
511 mostly patent insides, in a ram-
512 shackle village. The trampish
513 printer who did the launching
514 had a sense of humor, for he
515 called his venture the *Palm Leaf*
516 *Fan.* But he hadn't much else.
517 There had been various changes
518 of ownership. Meanwhile Palm
519 Bluff grew in leisurely fashion
520 —brick pavements, cement side-
521 walks, electric lights, four thou-
522 sand inhabitants. Lewis Kend-

523 rick bought the *Fan.* And
524 progress might have continued
525 in that same leisurely fashion if
526 this mysterious elixir of bloom
527 had not been injected into the
528 veins of the community. Now
529 the most conspicuous feature of
530 each semiweekly edition of the
531 *Fan* was a double-page advertise-
532 ment of Paradise Island, stock
533 in which might be purchased of
534 George Ingram & Co. at only
535 $8.75 a share—if one acted
536 quickly, before the price ad-
537 vanced. Every advertisement
538 reminded the hesitant reader
539 what fortunes had been reaped
540 by sagacious investors in Miami,
541 Palm Beach, St. Petersburg, Los
542 Angeles, New York. Ownership
543 of soil was the road to wealth!
544 George Ingram & Co. advertised
545 Paradise Island not only at home
546 but in other Florida towns
547 where Northern tourists with
548 money to invest congregated,
549 and even in some Northern
550 cities. That, undoubtedly, had
551 touched off the boom at Palm
552 Bluff.
553 "Haven't you an interest in
554 the *Fan?*" Dwyer asked, re-
555 membering something to that
556 effect.
557 "I have three thousand dollars
558 of stock," Langley replied. "I
559 paid fifteen hundred dollars
560 down and Mr. Kendrick gave
561 me two years to pay the balance.
562 He wanted somebody associated
563 with him on the paper and was
564 willing to sell me a small interest

565 that way. I went into journal-
566 ism when I left college, reporting
567 in Bridgeport and Providence;
568 then in Boston. But I always
569 wanted to get an interest in a
570 paper in a smaller place. I
571 had a little trouble with my
572 lungs and came down here, and
573 fell in with Mr. Kendrick."

574 He said it in his toneless, un-
575 emphasized way; and Dwyer
576 felt that he was a sort of slot
577 machine — you dropped in a
578 question, and if he knew the
579 answer it had to come out,
580 mechanically.

581 "Well," the big man observed,
582 "your stock is worth twice what
583 it was when you bought it six
584 months ago. A year from now it
585 will be worth twice as much as it
586 is now." He leveled a forefinger.
587 "And don't forget this, Langley:
588 This is all based on confidence—
589 every bit of it. Now that the
590 boom's here, you've got other
591 fellows advertising real estate.
592 My advertising has brought in
593 more tourists. They're buying
594 more goods and the merchants
595 are advertising more. You may
596 figure that, now the boom is here
597 you can tell me to go to the devil.
598 But you're wrong. It's all based
599 on confidence. Destroy public
600 confidence in me and you blow
601 up the whole thing. People will
602 simply pull out of the game.
603 Everybody in this part of the
604 country knows that I originated
605 the boom here, and have led it.
606 Palm Bluff has got plenty of

607 rival towns. Give 'em a handle
608 against me and they'll set up a
609 howl—make this town a laugh-
610 ingstock. You can't hit me
611 without hitting yourself and all
612 your neighbors."

613 Langley felt that this state-
614 ment was quite true, having a
615 prevision that Kendrick and
616 John Titus, president of the
617 First National Bank, and other
618 solid citizens would be greatly
619 pained at the notion of weaken-
620 ing public confidence in Palm
621 Bluff real estate by exposing
622 Dwyer as a rogue who had
623 swindled small investors out of
624 their Liberty Bonds. That was
625 one reason why he hadn't men-
626 tioned the affair to Kendrick.

627 "Running a newspaper here
628 is a different proposition from
629 running one in a big city,"
630 Dwyer went on. "Newspapers
631 in a big city needn't have any
632 more sense of responsibility than
633 a hyena—and they don't have,"
634 he added bitterly. "They can
635 run around blowing up any-
636 body. That's their occupation.
637 The town's so big, you see.
638 But in a small town like this
639 everything hangs together.
640 You've got to have a sense of
641 responsibility to your neighbors.
642 A newspaper that hurts the
643 town won't be tolerated."

644 Langley nodded gravely.

645 "I understand that, Mr.
646 Dwyer. That's why I came to
647 see you now. Of course, if I
648 was just a big-city reporter I

649 could put this story on the wire
650 and not mind who it hurt."
651 He pecked at his mustache and
652 very soberly made a statement
653 which might have provoked a
654 laugh, coming from such a
655 mouselike person: "All I want
656 to do is to protect the public."
657 Dwyer demanded, "What do
658 you mean by that?"

659 "Well, it's this way," the pro-
660 tector of the public answered
661 judicially: "You've been selling
662 a great deal of stock to the
663 public. The money is supposed
664 to go to build a causeway over
665 to the island, and the hotel, and
666 so forth"—he made a little
667 gesture — "these improvements
668 that you advertise. I believe
669 you've got a good proposition,
670 Mr. Dwyer. You can make a
671 fine winter resort out of Paradise
672 Island. If you do make a fine
673 resort out of it, I don't see any
674 reason why people wouldn't
675 come there—build cottages and
676 estates, and so on, same as at
677 Palm Beach and Miami. If
678 they do, of course, the stock in
679 your company will be valuable."

680 Dwyer listened to this exposi-
681 tion of faith in his enterprise
682 with a certain astonishment.
683 Out on the long, narrow sand
684 bar, overgrown with cabbage
685 palms, palmetto and mesquite,
686 whose name he had changed to
687 Paradise Island, some gangs of
688 colored workmen were clearing
689 up the underbrush and marking
690 streets but it was very, very far

691 from the sophisticated paradise
692 which the big painting in the
693 office represented.

694 "But you can see yourself, Mr.
695 Dwyer," the journalist droned
696 on, "that if you're"—he seemed
697 unable to find the word he
698 wanted and made an awkward
699 little gesture toward the heap
700 of clippings—"if you're the man
701 who did this, you ought to retire
702 in favor of some man the public
703 could have confidence in. There
704 wouldn't need to be any
705 scandal at all—at least not
706 now." His embarrassment in-
707 creased, yet his eyes held soberly
708 to Dwyer's face. "I don't know
709 whether they're looking for you
710 or not; but I don't think I
711 would be required to take Boston
712 into consideration—at present.
713 I think my duty is to the public
714 here—at present. So at present
715 if you would retire here, I would
716 be satisfied."

717 Dwyer stared at him. So
718 that was it! He was simply to
719 eliminate himself—blot himself
720 out of existence with regard to
721 Paradise Island! The astonish-
722 ment arose partly from a feeling
723 of the insignificance of his op-
724 ponent, as though an embar-
725 rassed mouse should sit up on
726 its tail in the path of an elephant
727 and say, with a nervous little
728 gesture, "Now you're to vanish,
729 you know—dissolve into air."

730 "But I'm not the man—not
731 the man at all!" Dwyer pro-
732 tested. "That man was my

733 cousin. I had nothing to do
734 with his affairs; no more"—he
735 made a gesture as though at loss
736 for words—"than the man in
737 the moon!"

738 Langley's monotonous voice
739 came back in propitiation.

740 "In that case, Mr. Dwyer, of
741 course there's nothing more to
742 be said." He brushed his hand
743 over dusty hair. "Where were
744 you in the spring and summer of
745 1919?"

746 And there was the leech again,
747 softly clinging to him, not to be
748 shaken off. Dwyer changed the
749 subject.

750 "When will Kendrick be
751 back?"

752 His mind turned to Kendrick,
753 not as to a straw at which a
754 drowning man clutches, but as to
755 a raft. Because, after all, Ken-
756 drick was a human being—a
757 man who knew his own interests
758 and the interests of his town, and
759 had a proper regard for them.

760 "Kendrick will not consent to
761 a wanton attack on me," he
762 declared firmly.

763 Langley gave another peck at
764 his mustache and squirmed in
765 the chair.

766 "If it came to that," he said,
767 "I'd put the story on the wire
768 anyhow. Other papers would
769 publish it."

770 Fatally true! This mere
771 mouse of a man had the lightning
772 in his hand. In spite of Ken-
773 drick, in spite of everybody, he
774 could launch the thunderbolt

any time he pleased. Other 775
papers would publish it, espe- 776
cially Boston papers, and the 777
reverberations would soon reach 778
Palm Bluff. 779

Langley explained mildly: 780
"You see, Mr. Dwyer, when I 781
left college and went into jour- 782
nalism I had some ideas about 783
it. I've got the same ideas still. 784
In a case of this kind a journalist 785
ought n't to hesitate, no matter 786
what happens to him." He 787
nodded to the clippings. "That 788
man oughtn't to be taking in 789
other people's money this way. 790
In such case a journalist has a 791
duty to the public. He must 792
protect the public that supports 793
him." 794

Half an hour before, Dwyer 795
would have laughed over the 796
speech as a bit of sophomorical 797
egotism, of the kind that might 798
be expected from a reporter who 799
gravely called himself a jour- 800
nalist. Half an hour before, he 801
would have said that the runty 802
young man named Langley who 803
was reporter and associate editor 804
of the *Palm Leaf Fan* had 805
comically round, wide-open, 806
pale-blue eyes that reminded 807
one of an adolescent owl. Just 808
now those same eyes, fixed upon 809
his, looked like a high, thick 810
stone wall. His own eyes fell 811
in a sudden agitation. Blindly, 812
instinctively, he began fighting 813
for time. 814

"See here, Langley, you're all 815
wrong. That's my cousin. We 816

817 must talk this over. It's a long
818 story." He looked quickly at
819 his wrist watch. "I haven't
820 time now. You owe it to me to
821 give me a hearing."

822 "Why, I'll be glad to talk it
823 over with you any time, Mr.
824 Dwyer," Langley assured him;
825 "this evening, if you like."

826 "Why, yes." Dwyer frowned
827 a little, considering. "I've got
828 to meet some men at the hotel
829 for dinner—oughtn't to take
830 very long. Come to my house
831 at half past nine. Will you do
832 that?"

833 "Certainly, very glad to,"
834 Langley replied; and then Dwyer
835 perceived that his opponent, too,
836 was relieved to get away, like a
837 tired boxer at the end of a round.
838 "I'll read these things over,"
839 said Dwyer, with a nod at the
840 clippings on the desk. "It's a
841 long story. . . . If I shouldn't be
842 there at half past nine, wait for
843 me. I won't be long. . . . Of
844 course, you'll say nothing to
845 anybody until you've heard from
846 me."

847 "No," said Langley. "I'll be
848 at your house at half past nine."

849 He slid from the office, hat in
850 hand, and, out on the cement
851 sidewalk of Seaview Avenue,
852 paused to wipe his face with a
853 handkerchief before putting on
854 his faded straw hat, for he was
855 sweating and trembling like a
856 very tired man. He shuffled
857 absently up the avenue, in his
858 slightly stooping posture, and

859 turned off into Hibiscus Street
860 which, naturally, was a dusty,
861 tatter - demalion thoroughfare
862 largely given over to garages.
863 Half a block brought him to a
864 two-story brown frame building
865 with the uncompromising ugli-
866 ness of a big shoe box. The
867 faded sign over the door said,
868 *Palm Leaf Fan. Job Printing.*

869 But this was only the poor
870 cocoon, soon to be abandoned.
871 Over on Orange Street the walls
872 were already going up for a fine
873 new hollow tile and stucco struc-
874 ture, with the best modern im-
875 provements, to which the news-
876 paper would move as soon as
877 it was completed. Langley had
878 spent many a pleasant half hour
879 admiring the architect's sketch
880 and floor plans. He was going
881 to be part owner in it.

882 Of course, like much else in
883 Palm Bluff just now, the new
884 plant, and the daily edition that
885 was to follow within a year, were
886 predicated on the boom. He did
887 not deny Dwyer's claim to being
888 the author of the boom, nor that
889 he was still the pivotal fact in
890 it. He knew how much store
891 Palm Bluff put upon its boom;
892 how much it hoped for from
893 that state of mind which set
894 people to bidding briskly against
895 each other for vacant plots of
896 sand and palmetto which, two
897 years before, nobody would so
898 much as look at. It was a state
899 of mind, and states of mind may
900 change very swiftly. He realized

901 that there were many things to
902 be thought of. His own individ-
903 ual fortune and future were
904 involved in them.

905 Dwyer, meanwhile, was read-
906 ing one of those old newspaper
907 clippings with a fascination that
908 was not without horror. This
909 had always been hanging over
910 his head, but as month after
911 month went by his sense of secur-
912 ity naturally increased. In brief,
913 a friend had assured him that for
914 a certain consideration authority
915 would hold its hand until, in due
916 time, a beneficent statute of
917 limitations barred him from
918 prosecution. But the affair was
919 hazardous. He was like a man
920 lying behind a dike of sand which
921 time might solidify into rock;
922 meanwhile any chance wave
923 would wash it away. After the
924 catastrophe of arrest he might
925 have abandoned all his baggage,
926 plunging into the stream as a
927 stripped and naked man, to
928 emerge at another point, take
929 a new name—and get a job, say,
930 driving a truck or peddling shoe
931 strings. But he couldn't endure
932 abandoning his baggage. He
933 was too soft for that. So he
934 had been obliged to keep the
935 name Dwyer, metamorphosing
936 E. Pellman into Elihu P., just
937 as he abandoned the curly
938 golden wig he formerly wore and
939 grew a beard instead.

940 Staring at the old strip of
941 newspaper, with perspiration on
942 his forehead, he perceived in a
943 luminous instant that he had
944 always been ineffectual, finally.
945 This Boston venture hadn't
946 really succeeded. He was a very
947 presentable man, handsome in
948 profile, he made friends readily,
949 and easily got himself accepted
950 up to a certain point; he had a
951 glib tongue; there was ingenuity
952 in his brain. But somehow, at
953 length, he always stubbed his
954 toe, while men whom he despised
955 as coarse blockheads carried
956 their affairs through.

957 The venture down here had
958 succeeded miraculously. He
959 called himself author of the
960 boom, yet knew well enough
961 that he had appeared just at the
962 psychological moment when cir-
963 cumstances had made every-
964 thing ready for him. In the
965 nature of the case, booms can't
966 be happening always. Probably
967 such another opportunity would
968 never come to him. Certainly
969 it wouldn't if Langley blew up
970 his sand dike now. With that
971 Boston hue and cry at his heels
972 again, and authority, spurred
973 by newspapers, reaching out for
974 him—— He was forty-two
975 and ravenously hungry for
976 long arrears of enjoyments. His
977 advertisements praised Palm
978 Bluff as a new Eden, but he
979 hated the dull hole. What he
980 wanted was to stuff his pockets
981 with money and go where money
982 can be spent to advantage.

983 And there was the instrument
984 of his destruction — Langley;

985 pale-eyed runt of a third-rate
986 newspaper reporter, attached to
987 a country-town semiweekly sheet
988 which docilely printed columns
989 of his puffs of Paradise Island in
990 consideration of a double-page
991 advertisement in each issue for
992 which he paid $112.50. Secretly,
993 or to his wife and a few cronies,
994 he laughed at the journal because
995 it charged so little. Anything
996 that cost only $112.50 must be
997 somewhat contemptible. Yet
998 the *Fan* was dignity itself com-
999 pared with its associate editor.
1000 The most intolerable thing in
1001 the situation was that ruin
1002 should come from such a source.
1003 From the first he had per-
1004 ceived Langley's unmanageable-
1005 ness. A man of sense might
1006 listen to reason and be shown
1007 where his own interests lay, or
1008 even take an outright bribe.
1009 But this was one of your simple-
1010 minded idiots who had got an
1011 idea of duty to the public stuck
1012 crosswise in his feeble nut and
1013 would toddle right along with
1014 it, no matter at what cost to
1015 himself. With intense bitter-
1016 ness, and with a suffocating
1017 surge of rage, Dwyer compre-
1018 hended that immovable and
1019 imbecilic quality in his opponent.
1020 . . . A man you couldn't do
1021 anything with!
1022 He was walking purblindly
1023 homeward, all a-quake inside,
1024 with a seethe of bitter, aimless
1025 anger—Langley! And just when
1026 the prize was fairly at his fingers'

ends! The money was rolling in 1027
now. He had some wild thoughts 1028
of flight; but he had spent a 1029
lot of money so far, taking up 1030
the options on the land, adver- 1031
tising, clearing off the under- 1032
brush. Besides, flight with this 1033
bomb exploding at his heels 1034
would be useless. . . . Trapped! 1035
There had been no plan in his 1036
appointment with Langley. He 1037
had merely fought for time in 1038
which to make a plan. But 1039
how could there be a plan when 1040
you were going to be shot at 1041
daylight anyhow? To be sure, 1042
Langley had offered one—name- 1043
ly, that he eliminate himself, 1044
walk out empty-handed. Dwyer 1045
could have laughed acidly over 1046
that, only the muscles of 1047
laughter seemed paralyzed. . . . 1048
He was quite sure that nobody 1049
here except Langley knew about 1050
this as yet. Nobody would 1051
know, at least, until Kendrick 1052
returned in the morning. As 1053
yet destruction was solely in- 1054
carnated in one ridiculous little 1055
person. Trapped—and only a 1056
gray mouse in gold-bowed spec- 1057
tacles holding the door! Then 1058
he came to the ditch and halted 1059
as though an invisible hand had 1060
seized his arm. 1061
After that it all unfolded in a 1062
fashion as smooth and or- 1063
derly as the operation of a 1064
law of Nature. When Dwyer 1065
returned to his house at a 1066
quarter to ten that evening 1067
Langley was waiting for him— 1068

1069 embarrassed of course, pecking
1070 at his little mustache and mur-
1071 muring as Mrs. Dwyer tried to
1072 entertain him by wholly imagi-
1073 nary references to her social
1074 career in the North. Her sly
1075 smile to her husband confessed
1076 how dull she had found the
1077 young man; and as nearly as she
1078 could remember it, she excused
1079 herself in the way she had once
1080 seen it done on the stage. Of
1081 course she was going to bed.
1082 Unless there was amusement of
1083 some kind, she usually went to
1084 bed at nine. Dwyer had counted
1085 on that.

1086 The host also excused himself
1087 for a moment, then called
1088 Langley into the small and
1089 gaudily colored den back of the
1090 living room, closing the door.
1091 When they were seated—the
1092 guest having awkwardly declined
1093 a cigar—Dwyer spoke with an
1094 air not only candid but cordial.

1095 "I've been thinking it over,
1096 Langley. You were right. But
1097 first I want to tell you about the
1098 Boston business."

1099 At leisure he unfolded a nar-
1100 rative, mostly false, of his en-
1101 tanglement in the foreign-ex-
1102 change speculation; and there
1103 was a secret little delight in his
1104 heart over the coolness and
1005 fluency with which he spoke.
1106 He was in perfect command of
1107 himself as he spun out the yarn
1108 to gain time. It had turned some-
1109 what wetter outside. Through
1110 the open window came a soft,

monotonous drip of the eaves 1111
and a murmurous patter of drops 1112
on the leaves. As dark as a 1113
pocket out there. Hardly one 1114
chance in a million of a soul being 1115
abroad in this edge of the town 1116
on such a night. The three or four 1117
humble houses in the neigh- 1118
borhood would be fast alseep. 1119

Dwyer talked easily, embroid- 1120
ering the tale. And he was now 1121
conscious of an odd, fierce hatred 1122
of the mousy little man opposite, 1123
pecking at his ridiculous mus- 1124
tache, sagely nodding his in- 1125
significant head, looking owlishly 1126
through gold-bowed spectacles; 1127
an object mortally contemptible 1128
in its nature, to be hated and 1129
stepped upon! 1130

Also Dwyer secretly jeered at 1131
the guest for his fatuous sense of 1132
security. There was something 1133
hard and heavy in his coat 1134
pocket. Several times his hand 1135
slipped in to feel of it. He knew 1136
exactly how it was going to be 1137
done. The courteous host would 1138
step outside with his guest, in 1139
the dark. Then three or four 1140
swift, powerful blows with that 1141
thing in his pocket and a body 1142
dumped into the muddy ditch 1143
where the plank was slippery. 1144
And Langley sat there wagging 1145
his head, gaping at him—the 1146
idiot! 1147

"But you were right," the 1148
host continued. "I was the 1149
victim of circumstances, yet it 1150
wouldn't be fair to ask people 1151
to trust me with this money. 1152

I realize it now. I propose an executive committee."

He sketched the scheme: Three local men of the highest reputation would form the committee to take control of the enterprise; every dollar of money received would pass into their hands; they would see that it was all honestly expended in improvements as the advertisements promised; Dwyer would fade out of the scene on some plausible pretext.

Through Langley's general dustiness something like a glow appeared. He nodded his head twice, and there was a perceptible flutter of emotion in his usually monotonous voice.

"I'll be perfectly satisfied with that, Mr. Dwyer—perfectly satisfied," he declared with that unwonted warmth. "There never was what you might call any personal feeling in this. All I wanted was to protect the public. This committee—if it's the right men—will protect the public. That was my object from the start. I'll be perfectly satisfied."

"Well, then, think up a list of names for the committee. I'll think up a list. Come to my office at four o'clock tomorrow. We'll decide on the men. I'll have the other details thought out by that time."

Langley was still perceptibly glowing, with a foolish little smile, as he got up and moved toward the door.

"I'm very glad it's turned out this way," he observed.

The tall powerful man at his heels echoed, "So am I. So am I." But his right hand was in his coat pocket and he was thinking, "Idiot! To suppose I'm going to give up this game for you! Imbecile!"

Langley had the door open. There was a soft drip of water out there, and a vast pitch darkness, cloaking everything. Door knob in hand, the visitor hesitated an instant, with his foolish little smile.

"I didn't intend to speak of my own interests—didn't mean to think about that. But, of course, this means a good deal to me personally." The smile became more awkward. "When I thought it over I had a kind of a hunch you weren't going to give in; maybe would try to bluff me into putting it off. I didn't mean to take any chances, you know—to have anything to hesitate over. So I wrote out my resignation to Mr. Kendrick and an assignment of my stock. I told him if he considered I injured him, or the paper, in what I was doing, he could take it out of what I'd paid him on the stock. I left it on his desk where he'd see it first thing when he gets to town tomorrow."

Dwyer heard himself asking, "Did you tell him why you were resigning?"

Langley gravely nodded.

1237 "I wrote an outline of the case
1238 —enough so he would under-
1239 stand why I was acting—and
1240 inclosed a copy of the dispatch
1241 I meant to send the Boston
1242 *Tribune* after I left you." The
1243 awkward smile reappeared. "In
1244 case, you know that you
1245 wouldn't yield. I didn't mean
1246 to take any chances, you see.
1247 I didn't want anything to hesi-
1248 tate about. I didn't even mean
1249 to put it off till you talked to
1250 Kendrick. It looked clear to
1251 me, so I meant to act. I've got
1252 the original dispatch in my
1253 pocket, ready to send. Of
1254 course, now I can tear up the
1255 resignation and the dispatch.
1256 I'm very glad of that. It means

1257 quite a lot to me personally."
1258 Dwyer, hand still in pocket,
1259 but quite nerveless, looked
1260 blankly down at this comically
1261 mousy person and apprehended
1262 him in a new way; small, homely,
1263 soft, apparently weak, but inde-
1264 structible as truth. That letter
1265 to Kendrick, with copy of the
1266 dispatch, protected him now
1267 like brass armor. . . . Inde-
1268 structible!
1269 "I think the executive com-
1270 mittee will work very well,"
1271 said Dwyer stupidly.
1272 "Yes; I feel sure it will,"
1273 Langley replied in his toneless
1274 manner. "Good night."
1275 The small homely figure shuf-
1276 fled off into the moist dark.

THE ANALYSIS

I mentioned that in *Sunk* the main narrative question was, "Can Jason Terwilliger kill Jake Finch?" In *Paradise Island* the main narrative question is, "Can Dwyer kill Langley?" In each story the same feat of accomplishment is required of the main actor. Since it is clear that every feat is interesting in proportion to its importance, or to its difficulty, or to its threat of disaster, there can be no doubt that the more important or difficult or disastrous a feat is made to appear to the reader the more likely it is to be interesting. The killing of a man is naturally of importance. It will always serve as the main narrative question of a story. A great many stories have been written with this feat as the main narrative problem of the story. Yet these two stories which have this main narrative question, have also something else in common. They neither of them achieve any length in particular from the meetings or interchanges which make up the Body of the story, nor from those which make up the Ending of the story. Obviously then, one of two things must happen. Either the story must be very short or the Beginning must be prolonged. The first is the case with *Sunk*, the second is the case with *Paradise Island*.

With *Sunk* the method of presentation was chronological. After an interchange the main narrative question emerged. This interchange contained the explanatory matter necessary to the reader's understanding of the importance or interest of that main narrative question. In the case of *Paradise Island* the method is reversed. The order instead of being chronological is anti-chronological: it is the flash-back method.

In discussing the *Escape of Mr. Trimm*, we found that Mr. Cobb opened his story at a point which was not in chronological order, but it was not a true flash-back Beginning because the interchange or meeting which was out of chronological order did not present to the reader the main narrative question. In *Paradise Island* the anti-chronological order does present to the reader the main narrative question. It emerges on the fifth line of the story. The first five lines of this story illustrate narrative technique reduced to its elements. Dwyer becomes aware of a stimulus. The stimulus is the ditch. His reaction to that stimulus is to respond in terms of a purpose, that purpose being the main purpose or main narrative problem of the story. Chronologically that story would then be resumed at line 1062 and would carry on to line 1268 which is the Body of the story, so that we would have main narrative question lines 1 to 5, Body interchange lines 1062 to 1268, Conclusive Act and Effect lines 1269 to 1276, but we would have no explanatory matter and we would not know why Dwyer wished to kill Langley. We would have no explanatory matter, and without explanatory matter there is not a complete Beginning.

As it is evident that the quality of the material in both stories is essentially the same, the difference in arrangement must come not from this *quality* but from the *quantity* of the material.

Quantity is the determining factor. In *Sunk* the main problem and its explanatory matter are contained in 178 lines. In *Paradise Island* 1067 lines are needed. Both authors knew and utilized the laws of interest. Both introduced a narrative question within the first 34 lines. In *Paradise Island* the main narrative question comes in the first 5 lines. It is, "Can Dwyer succeed in killing a man?" In *Sunk* a narrative question comes in the first 34 lines. It is, "Can Jason Terwilliger succeed in begging $2,000 from his uncle?" This is a minor narrative question and not a major one for the whole story. It is a minor one for a scene. Now a minor narrative question can be made to hold the interest of the reader for say 500 to 1500 words. In *Sunk*, beginning on line 34, this minor narrative question is used to maintain the interest until the main narrative question is reached on line 119. These 86 lines averaging about 5 words to the line contain about 400 words.

This method could not have been followed in *Paradise Island* because over 1000 lines, or nearly 5000 words are needed to present the explanatory matter which the author wished to place before the reader in order that he might understand the responses of the character when the character became aware of the main purpose actuating him, and was plunged into the meeting growing out of that purpose.

A minor narrative question could not have held a reader's interest long enough to make him read 5000 words without knowing something about a main narrative question. Anything over 1500 words is a heavy strain upon a reader's concentration of interest if a scene is used *merely for information leading to the main narrative problem. After* that main narrative problem has been presented this length restriction does not apply because in addition to the interest which the reader feels from his knowledge of a minor narrative question of a scene, there is present in his consciousness the major narrative question of the story which will hold his interest additionally.

Most stories which are rejected are rejected because the Beginnings are dull, and it is for this reason that the method employed by Mr. Payne in presenting this long Beginning will be so interesting to a student of the short-story form. The problem which faces most story writers is the one which Mr. Payne has here solved through his knowledge of the laws of interest. Structurally, the divisions are very clear. The Beginning occupies lines 1 to 1061; the Body lines 1062 to 1268; and the Ending lines 1269 to 1276. The main narrative question emerges clearly, and the answer is quite definite.

Someone has pointed out that the difference between the untrained recruit and the regular soldier is not in the things that they do but in the precision and unconscious ease with which the regular does them, as opposed to the untrained person. So it is with writers. The writer is really an executive in short-story craftsmanship. A good executive is one who, faced by a problem, makes a decision which is wise and instantaneous. He is able to make this quick and accurate decision because he compares the circumstances of the case confronting him with the circumstances of similar cases, and decides that the general principles involved are the same, therefore the answer must be the same. Even if, at the beginning of his executive experience, not all his decisions are wise, practice will increase the proportion of his successes. So it should be with the writer. If the writer knows that certain treatment of material in previous cases has made a good story every time, he will then be able to employ that treatment whenever the materials are similar. It is essential, however, that a writer shall recognize that the similarity must be a similarity of fundamentals, not a similarity of things which are not fundamental. The aspiring writer, examining *Paradise Island* will not grasp the complete lesson it holds for him in regard to the utilization of the laws of interest until he realizes two things: first, in the typically effective Flash-back Beginning the meetings or interchanges which make up the explanatory matter are made interesting because they are presented after the main narrative question has been made apparent to the reader, and gather a synthetic importance from the reader's knowledge of this main narrative question. Second, that in the effective Flash-back Beginning the main narrative question must be intrinsically important. It will not do to say that the Beginning of any story can be made interesting, provided the main narrative question is projected before the explanatory matter is presented. There would be a technical Flash-back Beginning, but the conclusion drawn would be wrong. The mere showing of something to be accomplished is not in itself enough to form a main narrative question. For example, had Dwyer, as he halted at the ditch, been struck with a determination to ask Langley for the address of a man who manufactered clam chowder, it would involve a main purpose or something to be accomplished. But the reader, asked to read a story in which the whole interest concentrated upon the attempt of a man to discover another man's address, would not read very far. On the other hand, the attempt of one man to eliminate another from the world can be depended upon to hold interest. Therefore, the lesson to be learned particularly from this story is, that when there is a Flash-back Beginning in the true sense the main narrative problem is presented first, and it is followed, out of chronological order by the explanatory matter. But, in order to be effective, this main narrative question must be important, and the secret of importance is that *a thing is interesting in proportion to what depends upon it.*

Another lesson to be learned from this story is, that in the Beginning the meetings or encounters are made interesting in proportion as a writer possesses a knowledge of craftsmanship. Lines 6 to 111 are particularly interesting in this respect. Dwyer becomes aware of a stimulus and reacts toward it; but always in a way that affects the main narrative question. Thus, on line 33, where the writer says, "This plank over the ditch was wet," he follows it by the response of the actor, "a man might easily slip on it" line 34, tying up the reflection of the actor with the main purpose—to kill the man. Again, looking about him at the setting, he sees it as a blurr, and he thinks (see line 62), that this general blurr, still and vague, but shut in, seemed to sanction the idea which had exploded in Dwyer's mind (to kill the man). Again, when the author has presented the appearance of the man Dwyer, he follows it by the contrast between his appearance of competence and the turmoil within as he is affected by his new purpose and then the author follows this by the words on line 109, "but he had a baffled feeling of the things being thrust into his hands, no other way." On line 161, after he has talked to his wife he finds himself stammering, scant of breath, etc., and it is evident that his normal response to every stimulus is conditioned or affected by his purpose in the story.

In that scene between him and Langley which is presented in flash-back there is no lack of clash or of the sense of disaster which overshadows Dwyer during the meeting, and of the further sense of disaster which overshadows Langley because of our knowledge, as readers, that Dwyer has determined to kill him.

Some students of the short-story form do not seem to grasp readily what is meant by a flash-back scene. To simplify this I want them to think that it is the opposite of a *flash-forward scene*, and to illustrate by the case method, I shall ask you to glance at line 1058 of this story and read to line 1068. You will see that it begins, "Then he came to the ditch and halted," and on line 1066 it says, "When Dwyer returned to his house at a quarter to ten that evening."

The time of Dwyer's halting at the ditch was in the late afternoon after he had left Langley. The scene which follows between Dwyer and Langley, beginning on line 1066, occurs at a quarter to ten that evening, and is a flash-*forward* in time. Now if you will turn to line 171 you will see that it is the conclusion of a scene between Dwyer and his wife and that it is followed on line 172 by a description of Langley which goes to line 183. On line 184 there is a flash-*back* in time because it goes from the moment when Langley is speaking to his wife, which is just before dinner, to four o'clock of that same afternoon. This is a flash-*back* scene because it flashes *back* in time. In every other respect the scene is the same as if it had flashed *forward*. Only the introductory sentence tells the difference.

ANALYSIS

The virtue of this flash-back scene is that the author is enabled to introduce a minor narrative question to hold the interest of the reader while he is giving him information which would ordinarily be rendered by the inexpert writer in a summary of what had happened. A scene is always more interesting than a summary, but if the explanatory matter is dependent for its interest upon the main narrative question and this main narrative question must be made to emerge before the explanatory matter can be presented, the tendency of the inexpert writer would be to present the main narrative question and then to *summarize* the explanatory matter. Thus he would defeat his own purpose. He would capture interest, but he would lose it. He would be worse off than if he had summarized and then swung from his summary into a main narrative question.

The flash-back Beginning is therefore a very dangerous method for the inexpert writer. It is dependent for its success entirely upon one factor, and that factor is that the explanatory matter shall be presented in *dramatic scenes*. Otherwise the chief gain is turned into a loss.

This story is chosen because it is an interesting example of the presentation of explanatory matter by the flash-back method. Any writer having difficulty with employing this method will do well to use this story as a model.

Beginning	Initial Condition presented at its high point. The Main Actor's purpose is at once shown. With interest thus aroused, reader has desire to learn what led up to it.	Interchange. Gideon and Doctor.	1– 70 Main condition apparent.
		Gideon resolves to restore money.	Main Narrative Question "Can Gideon succeed in restoring Ten Thousand Dollars to boyhood friend?"
		Character's Flash-back scene. Gideon and Lemuel.	71– 171
		Continuation of Scene with Doctor.	172– 422 Background given to show importance to Gideon.
		Author's Flash-back to earlier in morning. Gideon and wife.	423– 648 Fear of Disaster to project.
		(5th step.) Reflections of Gideon.	649– 732 Opposing Force apparent.
		Interchange. Gideon and Mr. Altyne.	733– 852 Promise of Disaster (841–842)
Body	Single attempt shown is, apparently, a failure.	Scene. Gideon and Lemuel.	853–1235 Hindrance.
		(5th step. Gideon and George.)	1236–1278 Dramatic Hindrance. Disaster close.
		Interchange. Gideon and Mr. Altyne.	1279–1332 Furtherance. Gideon sees method.
Ending	Scene here is almost a Body scene. Conclusive Act, and sequel.	Scene. Gideon and Mrs. Higsbee.	1333–1521
		He made thousands and thousands of dollars.	1505–1521 The Answer to the Main Narrative Question is "Yes."

ONCE AND ALWAYS

BY JOHN P. MARQUAND

THE more stories you analyze the more you will become convinced that the chief value to you, as an author, of a knowledge of craftsmanship is that it will enable you instantly to dispose of structural problems in order that you may be able to devote your interest and enthusiasm to the portrayal of character. When readers speak disparagingly of "ordinary" stories they have in mind the story which is well constructed, but which leaves at the close no sense in the mind of the readers of an actual person having been presented to them by the writer of the story. The narrative problem may hold them, and the arrangement of the crises may sustain their interest, but the interest will be in plot rather than in character. On the other hand, when, as a reader, you feel that a story has distinction, you find almost inevitably, that this feeling of distinction comes because the writer caused the main actor to solve the problem in some unusual way, in a way which marks that character as a distinct personality.

Because *Once and Always* is this type of story, I have chosen it for re-print.

CASE No. 8

ONCE AND ALWAYS

BY JOHN P. MARQUAND

1 Gideon Higsbee's hair was
2 nearly white by now; his sharp
3 face had grown wrinkled; Lemuel
4 Gower had faded long ago from
5 active recollection, like every-
6 thing else in Agamemnon,
7 Maine. And after all, why
8 not. That affair in the Agamem-
9 non House had fallen into the
10 past for thirty years or more
11 before the shade of Lemuel
12 Gower darkened Gideon's con-
13 science in Doctor Follenshope's
14 office just off Fifth Avenue.

15 Through the maze of Mr.
16 Higsbee's thoughts came the
17 voice of Doctor Follenshope,
18 and its tone aroused his in-
18 terest:

19 "And so it wouldn't be fair
20 to either of us if I didn't warn
21 you to expect the worst. With
22 perfect rest we may help matters;
23 but your heart——"

24 A feeling of wonder made
25 Gideon's eyes open slightly, but
26 that was all. He could always
27 control his expression when he
28 chose, and he controlled it then,
29 though something told him that

30 it was no matter—that nothing
31 mattered.

32 "Why not say what you
33 mean?" he suggested. Gideon
34 spoke without a quaver. "You
35 won't startle me, young man.
36 Do you mean I'm going to die?"

37 The doctor nodded, and then
38 looked startled himself, for
39 Gideon Higsbee had begun to
40 whistle softly and to rotate his
41 hand at the wrist. "So that's
42 that," he said at length. "I
43 might have known something
44 would call my bluff."

45 Doctor Follenshope stared.
46 Gideon's face was impassive;
47 his eyes were cool and quiet.

48 "If there's anything on your
49 mind"—it was clear to see that
50 Doctor Follenshope admired
51 him, without knowing why—
52 "any way that I can help——"

53 "Fiddlesticks!" said Gideon
54 Higsbee. "Young man, don't
55 you set me down for a squealer!
56 I've been a gambler all my life,
57 and I guess I can stand it when
58 I'm out on a limb. There's
59 nothing on my mind but what

185

60 was there before. I'm thinking
61 of my wife, that's all—just
62 thinking of my wife."

63 Yet even then, old Gideon did
64 not wholly tell the truth. How
65 could Gideon tell the doctor
66 that his words had awakened
67 the stirrings of conscience which
68 would not be quieted until he
69 had restored ten thousand dol-
70 lars to a boyhood friend.

71 Out of the past Gideon's wife
72 had plucked Lemuel Gower that
73 very morning: Lemuel Gower
74 whom he had almost forgotten.
75 But in Doctor Follenshope's
76 office it all came back to Gideon
77 Higsbee, though not imme-
78 diately, because it had hap-
79 pened so long ago. But after a
80 little concentration he could
81 remember clearly enough the
82 way the three strangers had
83 looked when they descended
84 from the stage in front of the
85 Agamemnon House. Like nearly
86 all the adult male population of
87 Agamemnon, Maine, Gideon had
88 resorted to the lobby of the
89 Agamemnon House late every
90 afternoon, urged by the same
91 habit which brought him to the
92 general store just before going
93 home to supper. Thus he saw
94 the three strangers at close view,
95 and Gideon knew what they
96 were. They were crooks who
97 had probably been touring the
98 county fairs—either gamblers
99 or confidence men. It was
100 written in their predatory
101 glances, and the jewelry they

102 carried was enough to tell any-
103 one with any sense that they
104 used it as a cash reserve. But
105 why should one have expected
106 Lemuel Gower to have any
107 sense? There always had to be
108 someone devoid of it. Lemuel
109 glanced with wonder at their
110 distinguished bearing.

111 "Gid," said Lemuel, in the
112 loud, blank way in which he
113 always spoke, "let's go over
114 and speak to 'em."

115 "No," said Gideon Higsbee.

116 "But, say," said Lemuel plain-
117 tively, "why not, Gid? They're
118 nice pleasant-lookin' fellers,
119 influential bankers, or some-
120 thin', I'll bet. And we're busi-
121 ness men, Gid, ain't we? Come
122 on, Gid, we really otter."

123 Gideon Higsbee smiled. He
124 had no whiskers in those days,
125 and his hair was still light brown.
126 "No, Lemuel," said Gideon, even
127 then with a sigh. "You haven't
128 got a wife—I have."

129 "But, say," said Lemuel, "she
130 wants you to get on, doesn't she?
131 You say you're going to get rich,
132 don't you? Well, say, how're
133 you goin' to do it if you don't
134 grasp opportunity? They're
135 nice fellers, Gid. Mebbe they've
136 come up to see the pulp mill, and
137 if so, it's our business to speak
138 to 'em."

139 Gideon shook his head. The
140 honesty, the Arcadian simplicity
141 of Lemuel Gower might have
142 inspired a pastoral poet, but
143 Gideon was not a poet.

"But why won't you?" inquired Lemuel. "As a rule, Gid, you're the slickest feller. Gid, what are you thinkin' about?"

Gideon was whistling through his teeth and moving his hands in short, sharp circles. "Just thinking of my wife," said Gideon. "That's all — just thinking of my wife."

"Well," said Lemuel, "if you won't speak to 'em, I will."

With his rubber shoes making an honest sound upon the floor, Lemuel Gower walked across the lobby of the Agamemnon House, and Gideon perceived that the three strangers looked up with pleasure. Through the haze of years Gideon recalled that he had watched curiously before he turned away, and he said—he still remembered that he had said it, because even then it seemed to paraphrase nearly all his observations on life—"Once a sucker, always a sucker," said Gideon, and smiled.

Gideon Higsbee's muttonchop whiskers were soft and white as new-flown snow and comforting as a Sunday's benediction. Of old the sirens had their song, but what use had Gideon for alluring music when his whiskers in their carded fleecy innocence were waving on the breeze? Many a strong and case-hardened man had become weak—nay, smilingly lachrymose — at the sight of them, and thus there was no wonder that Doctor Follenshope should also have succumbed. He tilted back his swivel chair. He seemed to find it difficult to discover a beginning in what he had to say.

"I'm afraid it's going to be hard for me to make myself clear," he said.

"Is it, indeed?" said Gideon Higsbee, in a high voice which was somewhat cracked by years. "Well, I guess it won't hurt you to do something hard, young man. You look spry and you're getting paid enough."

"Of course I don't want to alarm you unduly——" began Doctor Follenshope.

"Young man," said Gideon Higsbee, "don't make me laugh. It gives me a crick in the side."

"I'm afraid," said Doctor Follenshope in a slightly altered tone, "it isn't exactly a laughing matter."

Gideon Higsbee raised a wrinkled clawlike hand and snapped his fingers. "Young man," he said, "what I say may be eccentric, but then why shouldn't I be eccentric? What I say may not be gentlemanly, but then am I a gentleman? I make it a rule to laugh when I damn please."

Doctor Follenshope seemed slightly confused and looked at Mr. Higsbee strangely. "Mr. Higsbee," he said, "I make mistakes. We all make mistakes in the medical profession, as no

228 doubt you have made them in
229 yours. People say we have
230 the advantage of being able to
231 bury ours; sometimes it's quite
232 the other way. I just want to
233 say that I might be wrong about
234 you. You may fool us all.
235 Are you listening, sir?"

236 There was a reason for Doctor
237 Follenshope's question. Mr.
238 Higsbee was staring at his hand,
239 which he was rotating briskly
240 at the wrist, and at the same
241 time he was whistling a monoto-
242 nous tune through his teeth.

243 "You don't feel an attack
244 coming on?" asked Doctor
245 Follenshope. "Would you feel
246 better lying down?"

247 Mr. Higsbee still continued
248 to whistle and rotate his hand.

249 "Mr. Higsbee," cried Doctor
250 Follenshope, "this isn't a laugh-
251 ing matter. Do you hear me?"

252 "Yes," said Mr. Higsbee.
253 "I'm not hard of hearing."

254 "But you weren't listening to
255 me—not to a word I was say-
256 ing." Doctor Follenshope's pro-
257 fessional calm was leaving him,
258 and his face was growing pink.

259 "No," said Mr. Higsbee, "I
260 wasn't. I may be eccentric, but
261 then why shouldn't I be eccen-
262 tric? I was thinking. I was
263 snatching the occasion to allow
264 my thoughts to revert toward
265 my wife—toward Mrs. Higsbee.
266 Young man, do you happen to
267 be one of those before whom
268 Hymen has carried the torch?
269 Are you married?"

270 A frown appeared on Doctor
271 Follenshope's placid brow. He
272 glanced hastily toward the
273 door.

274 "Mr. Higsbee," he said, "I
275 must ask you to give me your
276 attention, I'm afraid, whether
277 you wish to or not. Though I
278 happen to be married——"

279 "Then," said Mr. Higsbee,
280 "let me give you a piece of
281 advice. Listen to an old man
282 — I beg of you, listen. Though
283 it may not be applicable in your
284 case, you may pass it on to
285 others. I refer to the principle
286 of the counterirritant, which I
287 believe has been used by your
288 profession from the time of
289 Galen." Mr. Higsbee paused and
290 stroked his whiskers. "Young
291 man, when you find yourself
292 confronted by a serious situation
293 which is harrowing in the ex-
294 treme—think of your wife—
295 always think of your wife."

296 "My wife?" inquired Doctor
297 Follenshope, with a peculiar
298 expression. "I fail to see——"

299 Mr. Higsbee smiled and rub-
300 bed his hands, and, more than
301 smiling, beamed until his
302 shriveled face and glassy eyes
303 were genial as the setting sun.
304 "Ah!" he said. "Then she is not
305 like Mrs. Higsbee—clearly not
306 like Mrs. Higsbee. She does not
307 possess the power of opening
308 you up like an oyster."

309 At this point Doctor Follen-
310 shope betrayed a plodding
311 literal mind. "Like an oyster?"

he inquired, looking at Mr. Higsbee strangely.

"Have you never witnessed," asked Mr. Higsbee, "the struggles of an oyster in the hands of one of those experts who serve you at a counter?"

"No, I haven't," replied Doctor Follenshope, "and what's more——"

"Ah!" said Mr. Higsbee. "Then you should. Let us take one of those known in the trade as a wild Virginia oyster. The man picks him up and grasps his knife. The oyster hastily closes his shell, and with a confidence not wholly based on ignorance—for you could not open him, young man, not without a hammer and a chisel— surrenders himself to his dark and cramped environment. But he is reckoning without a knowledge of his assailant. With an unerring speed, swifter than light, the knife strikes an unguarded crevice. There is a moment's vain resistance, a grating sound, and there you are. The oyster, however wild, lies bare, exposed to the taunts of his victor, ready for the lemon and horse-radish. But you don't follow me?"

"No," said Doctor Follenshope icily, "I certainly don't."

"Young man," said Mr. Higsbee, with a sigh, "I married Mrs. Higsbee at Agamemnon, Maine, thirty years ago. In those days I was wild and free, engaged, in fact, in selling a tonic compounded from roots known only to the Indians at the county fairs. Forced by domesticity from my wild, free ways, I began conducting business in Mrs. Higsbee's home town; in fact, buying into an enterprise. Upon gaining control of it I became aware of a growing though incomprehensible antipathy on the part of the natives, and selling out, I came here; of course, with Mrs. Higsbee. With Mrs. Higsbee still by my side I have struggled from these low beginnings into the possession of some three million dollars. I mention this only incidentally, because I wish to add that in every crisis of my career I have thought of Mrs. Higsbee. It has always made me calm, and why has it made me calm?"

Doctor Follenshope made no answer. He was staring at Gideon Higsbee as though he had never really known him.

"It renders me calm," said Mr. Higsbee gently, "because I feel that nothing is more difficult to cope with than Mrs. Higsbee. For thirty years I have been Mrs. Higsbee's oyster. But I beg your pardon. You said you did not want to alarm me unduly. Don't worry. It's hard to alarm anyone who has been an oyster for thirty years."

For a moment Doctor Follenshope did not speak, but stared at Gideon Higsbee's wrinkled

397 face and snowy whiskers vaguely
398 and uncertainly, at the same
399 time taking off his glasses.
400 Gideon Higsbee leaned back in
401 his chair and crossed his slender
402 hands. Clearly Doctor Follen-
403 shope did not understand him,
404 but then why should he have
405 understood? Others had been
406 puzzled, lots of others, by the
407 fluent ease of Gideon Higsbee's
408 speech, and many had ended by
409 doing things about which they
410 had subsequently wondered.
411 Nevertheless, Mr. Higsbee was
412 surprised at himself. Old as he
413 was and clever as he was, he
414 had very nearly made a con-
415 fession, had very nearly told
416 the truth.

417 And this lack of control filled
418 him with awe, made him feel
419 that his own weakness might
420 step in to defeat him before he
421 could restore that ten thousand
422 to Lemuel Gower.

423 Earlier, that very morning,
424 when he had entered the break-
425 fast room of his brownstone
426 house, his wife's canary had
427 been singing in a most damn-
428 ably carefree way, seemingly
429 out of spite. Mrs. Higsbee,
430 behind a Georgian coffee urn,
431 was opening a pile of letters.
432 Being one of those who never
433 let anything go, Mrs. Higsbee
434 never dropped a correspond-
435 ent, nor allowed herself to be
436 dropped, and the brisk way she
437 wielded her paper knife was
438 enough to prove it. Their son,

439 whom Mrs. Higsbee had insisted
440 on naming Merlin, had pushed
441 his chair back from the table
442 and was reading the paper
443 through a pair of glasses pinched
444 on his nose—a Higsbee nose,
445 slender and beaklike. That Mr.
446 Higsbee could have been a party
447 in producing and rearing a being
448 like Merlin, who, possesed of
449 the sharpest Higsbee attributes,
450 yet was soft and sportive, like a
451 dying species, and who regarded
452 his father with a supercilious
453 scorn, always was puzzling. It
454 was the more puzzling when he
455 looked at Mrs. Higsbee. Her
456 stern, bespectacled visage had
457 preserved its simplicity and
458 forcefulness, despite thick claret-
459 colored carpets and tapestries on
460 the wall. In spite of surround-
461 ings, in spite of time, Matilda
462 Higsbee was as indomitable as
463 when she had first spied him.
464 Gideon had the same feeling of
465 awe and nervousness.

466 "Good morning, my dear," he
467 said.

468 "You're not looking as well
469 even as you did yesterday," said
470 Mrs. Higsbee.

471 Now how was that for a nice
472 way to start the morning?

473 "That's right," said Merlin.
474 'You're not looking well."

475 "My dear boy," said Mr.
476 Higsbee, "how it must hurt you
477 to perceive it!"

478 "Don't talk so loudly," said
479 Mrs. Higsbee. "It makes your
480 face all spotty, Gideon."

481 "That's right, it does," said
482 Merlin.

483 "Merlin," said Mr. Higsbee,
484 "I wonder if you could spare
485 some of your time to pay me a
486 visit downtown. There are so
487 many things I should like to
488 tell you which might not interest
489 your mother."

490 "Tweet! Tweet!" went the
491 canary.

492 "Angel voice," said Mrs. Higs-
493 bee. "Gideon, what do you
494 think I've just heard? I've got
495 the nicest, longest letter from
496 Susie Brickett. It makes me
497 feel as though I was back
498 home to read it, and what do
499 you think?"

500 "Anything you want, my
501 dear," said Gideon. "I've found
502 it best."

503 "It's all about Lemuel
504 Gower."

505 That was like her. It was
506 like the knife finding the chink
507 in the oyster, and things recent
508 or things distant were all the
509 same to her.

510 Out of the past, back from
511 the solitude of Agamemnon,
512 Maine, she had fetched him
513 with swift unerring skill. On
514 purpose or not, it made no
515 difference. There was Lemuel
516 Gower come to disturb his
517 peace.

518 "Gideon," inquired Mrs. Higs-
519 bee, "aren't you feeling well?"

520 "Perfectly, my dear," said
521 Gideon. "Never better."

522 "Lemuel's in financial troubles
523 again. What do you think of
524 that?"

525 Mr. Higsbee drew a deep
526 breath and smiled. "Is that
527 all?" he asked. "Well, I can
528 only say what I've always said,
529 my dear. There's a saying in
530 trade peculiarly applicable to
531 Lemuel Gower, and I ought to
532 know, seeing he was my first
533 associate in business. The
534 phrase is vulgar, but it sums
535 everything up. 'Once a sucker,
536 always a sucker,' that's what I
537 think of Lemuel Gower."

538 There was a slight and rather
539 uncomfortable pause. Mr. Higs-
540 bee became aware that his wife
541 was peering at him around the
542 coffee urn. He drew himself up
543 and stroked his whiskers. After
544 all, was there any wonder that
545 his heart was weak after years
546 of such suspense?

547 "Gideon"—right out of the
548 blue she threw her bolt—"I
549 want to know—you've always
550 edged off it—did you, or did
551 you not, do right by Lemuel?"

552 "Tweet!" went the canary,
553 and Gideon Higsbee jumped at
554 the suddenness of the sound.

555 "My dear," he said, "correct
556 me if I am mistaken, but haven't
557 we discussed this at odd intervals
558 over a period of thirty years!"

559 Unbidden, there came before
560 Gideon's memory, floating cloud-
561 ily, a vision of Lemuel Gower's
562 broad and honest face, his bul-
563 bous nose reddened by the
564 winter's cold and a light of

565 enthusiastic wonder kindling in
566 his credulous gray eyes.

567 "Gideon" — Mrs. Higsbee's
568 voice aroused him from his
569 reverie—"you've always been
570 sharp. How could you get so
571 rich if you weren't? And when
572 Lemuel lost his money first,
573 you started getting rich. Now
574 tell me the truth, did you, or
575 did you not, do right by
576 Lemuel?"

577 Merlin was looking at him;
578 his wife was looking at him.
579 Mr. Higsbee made a distinct
580 effort. "My dear," he said with
581 delicate reproach, "is it possible
582 you still think I conceal any-
583 thing from you? What's the
584 trouble, Merlin?"

585 Merlin had made a gurgling
586 sound behind his newspaper.
587 Mr. Higsbee rose from the table
588 and looked like an old engraving.

589 "I'll not stay and be laughed
590 at in my own house," he con-
591 tinued; "and as for Lemuel
592 Gower, I'd like you both to
593 listen, if you please, once for all.
594 Lemuel and I were associated in
595 business at Agamemnon, Maine,
596 when we were both much
597 younger — the pulp business.
598 I'm specific, because I want you
599 to understand too, Merlin, and
600 afterwards you shall ask my
601 pardon for laughing. At this
602 period Lemuel was approached
603 by three plausible men, who
604 induced him to draw most of his
605 savings in order that they might
606 make a fortune in a stock deal."

607 Mr. Higsbee paused and
608 coughed.

609 "They had, I believe, a private
610 wire from Bangor to New York,
611 and one of them had been a
612 confidential clerk for a famous
613 banker there. This banker, out
614 of the kindness of his heart, had
615 divulged certain pieces of con-
616 fidential information, in which
617 Lemuel was allowed to share.
618 Is it my fault that Lemuel was
619 simple? Answer me, could I
620 help it that Lemuel is a sucker?"

621 Mr. Higsbee tapped his chest
622 gently but firmly, but his
623 whiskers would have been
624 enough. They were as white as
625 the new-flown snow.

626 "And as for me," he continued
627 —he was at his best just then;
628 his self-pity and his enthusiasm
629 clouded his voice—"as for me,
630 what did I do but kindness?
631 When Lemuel was plucked clean,
632 didn't I buy his share of the
633 Agamemnon pulp mill? Was
634 it my fault if I turned around
635 and sold it two months later at a
636 profit? And I'll tell you one
637 thing more——"

638 Mr. Higsbee pointed toward
639 the coffee urn, and something told
640 him he was doing better than he
641 had hoped. Mrs. Higsbee was
642 staring at him, fascinated. Even
643 Merlin's thin mouth had opened.

644 "Yes," said Mr. Higsbee, "one
645 thing more, and take it or leave
646 it, as you please. I hope to die if
647 ever in my life I did a wrong to
648 Lemuel Gower."

817 Gideon as a man might who has
818 speculated largely upon human
819 frailty until he is surprised by
820 nothing. Without unkindness
821 and without vulgarity, Mr.
822 Altyne looked at Gideon with
823 eyes that seemed to pierce the
824 veil of Gideon's whiskers. "With
825 that check you've just been
826 ordering?"
827 "Yes," said Gideon. "Have
828 you anything to say?"
829 "Only," replied Mr. Altyne,
830 "that in my experience I have
831 found that conscience in most
832 men is purely relative, depending
833 upon health. But even if you
834 wanted to sell the whole show
835 out, I'd be right behind you,
836 conscience or no conscience—
837 and I'm not laughing, Gideon."
838 Gideon, himself, was far from
839 laughing; for there had come to
840 him suddenly a thought.
841 "It'd be just like the damn
842 fool not to take the money."
843 And the importance of that
844 act of restitution loomed vast
845 before him, for he knew that
846 only its conclusion would quiet
847 those uneasy stirrings of his
848 conscience that had not let up
849 since the moment when Dr.
850 Follenshope had said. "If
851 there's anything on your
852 mind——"
853 Was there any wonder that
854 the occupants of the ancient
855 barge from the railroad to Aga-
856 memnon stared? It was not a
857 wholly unpleasant experience to
858 Gideon, because they stared not

859 only with vulgar curiosity but
860 with honest admiration. The
861 pale, metropolitan face and
862 watchful eyes of George were
863 eclipsed by Mr. Higsbee's suave
864 and venerable magnificence.
865 The pearl-gray spats upon his
866 patent-leather shoes, his gold-
867 headed cane and smooth silk
868 hat were like a dream come true,
869 like a living, rustic fairy tale of
870 benevolence and wealth. Mr.
871 Higsbee looked upon the oc-
872 cupants of the barge and smiled;
873 he seemed to be bubbling over
874 with an unusual geniality. Mr.
875 Higsbee managed even to smile
876 at the dingy room they showed
877 him at the Agamemnon House,
878 though he shuddered inwardly
879 to think that he had once
880 admired such quarters; and
881 when he and George were on
882 the snow again, plodding up the
883 street, Mr. Higsbee was still
884 cheerful.
885 "George," he said, "I feel
886 better. Oddly enough I already
887 feel better, and I know why it is.
888 It is because I am going to do a
889 kindness here. If you have a
890 chance to do a kindness, do it,
891 George."
892 George shivered slightly. He
893 looked singularly out of place,
894 somewhat like a rare orchid in a
895 cabbage patch. To George it
896 seemed that Mr. Higsbee was
897 becoming very queer, and that
898 the snow-covered houses on the
899 single street, with the turnings
900 and trimmings on their porches,

were overpoweringly grotesque.

"Did you used to live here?" said George, staring unsympathetically about him. "Did you used to live here—honest?"

Mr. Higsbee twirled his cane. "It all depends upon one's standard of ethics, George," he said. "But—yes, I used to live here. Don't scoff at it, George, don't scoff. A town like this is the backbone of our nation, George; and keep your eye on the man you are about to see. He is growing rare, George, very rare."

Gideon remembered the house. It looked like Lemuel Gower. A native frame building out of proportion, with storm windows which glared frankly and openly upon the winter afternoon. Yet Gideon still felt benevolent and joyful, and younger, too, for perfect peace was stealing over him already.

Lemuel Gower looked older, but there he was standing in the musty hall, awkward and angular in his shabby coat, and essentially just the same. There was the same faith, the same childish wonder in his eyes, the same admiring smile upon his rustic lips; and Lemuel was glad to see him—pathetically glad. His corncob pipe fell to the carpet and tears stood in his eyes.

"Is it you, Gideon?" he kept saying. "I want to know, I want to know!" And he ushered them into the sitting room.

Mr. Higsbee seated himself upon a rocking-chair, because it was the only chair that offered even an approximation of comfort, and endeavored to balance his silk hat upon his knee. The feat, however, was somewhat difficult, because the chair kept moving backward, prompting him to kick out his legs and making him aware that his position was not a little awkward. However, even if the chair had gone over backward, and Gideon with it, he would only have had to look at Lemuel to feel completely self-possessed. "And how has the world been using you, Lemuel?" he asked.

It all was just the same. The honest joy of Lemuel made it seem like yesterday since they had last met, and Gideon felt perfectly, patronizingly at ease.

"Gosh, Gid!" said Lemuel Gower. "Gosh! It's good to see you. It's kind of you to come in like this, but I've always told the boys at the store, 'Gid ain't proud,' I've always said. 'If he was to come in now he'd just set on the cracker box like he always did.' How's things going, did you say? Not so good, Gid. But now I've seen you, they're going a whole lot better."

Gideon smiled, not even endeavoring to conceal his smile. The utter guilelessness of Lemuel was so remarkable that he would not have believed it real unless

985 he had remembered. He stole
986 a glance at George, who was
987 sitting in the corner, and was
988 glad to see that George was
989 transfixed and staring.

990 "Oh!" said Gideon. "And
991 what has been the matter,
992 Lemuel?"

993 Lemuel Gower stuffed some
994 tobacco in his pipe and blinked
995 in a puzzled way. "It was
996 speculation, Gid," he said. "It
997 seemed awful good. A letter
998 came to me in the mail from
999 some parties in Chicago. They
1000 had heard of me being a repre-
1001 sentative citizen of the town and
1002 invited me to subscribe to an oil
1003 well that was just due to come
1004 in. I investigated and sub-
1005 scribed, and what do you think?"

1006 Gideon kicked out his feet to
1007 keep his balance and grasped at
1008 his silk hat. "How much did
1009 you put in?"

1010 Lemuel looked innocently sur-
1011 prised. "Why, as much as I
1012 could," he said. "Then I took
1013 a mortgage on the house, and
1014 then—do you know what hap-
1015 pened?"

1016 "Yes," said Gideon. "The
1017 oil well didn't come in."

1018 Lemuel's mouth fell open in
1019 blank amazement. "Gid," he
1020 said, "you do beat me how you
1021 know things. Ain't you the
1022 smartest feller? I always said
1023 you'd have to go to Bangor to
1024 find anyone as slick as you."

1025 Something of Gideon's patron-
1026 izing ease had gone and astonish-
1027 ment took its place. "And now
1028 you're cleaned out?" he asked.
1029 "What are you going to do?"

1030 "Oh," said Lemuel, "I ain't
1031 worryin'. I got my two hands
1032 yet. I guess I'll haul wood for a
1033 spell, and then when I get some
1034 more saved up, maybe another
1035 chance will come. There do
1036 seem to be opportunities up
1037 here if I only took 'em right,
1038 though I never'd be as sharp as
1039 you."

1040 Gideon coughed. The room
1041 seemed close and stifling, and
1042 his head began to ache.
1043 "Lemuel," said Gideon, "do you
1044 remember those three parties
1045 who came here who had a private
1046 wire to New York?"

1047 Lemuel Gower nodded.
1048 "Yes," he said. "That was
1049 another opportunity."

1050 "Another what?" Again
1051 Gideon was obliged to kick out
1052 to keep his balance.

1053 "Another opportunity," said
1054 Lemuel. "It was just my luck,
1055 Gid. The market didn't go
1056 right, and I lost more money."

1057 For the first time in years
1058 Gideon Higsbee's eyes grew wide
1059 with wonder. He had never
1060 asked for Lemuel's opinion on
1061 that old transaction. He had
1062 taken if for granted that Lemuel,
1063 like other disillusioned ones,
1064 would know he had been
1065 cheated.

1066 "Are you joking with me,
1067 Lemuel?" he asked.

1068 Lemuel's blank stare was an

answer in itself. "Why, Gid," he said, "I never joke! Of course I know some conundrums, but I never just plain joke."

Gideon perched himself nearer the edge of his chair. The nap on his silk hat was becoming rumpled. "And you thought those men were honest, those three sharpers who took your money?"

Lemuel raised a protesting hand. He looked surprised and pained. "Now, Gid," he said soothingly, "there's no use in calling 'em hard names. They were mistaken just like me. We all make mistakes."

"Mistaken!" Gideon's voice broke and ended in a squeak. "You crazy idiot! Those three men were crooks—thieves! They stole your money—stole it! Do you hear me?"

It did not seem possible. Not in a farce comedy would it have seemed possible. Lemuel's pipe fell to the floor, but he did not bother to pick it up. He sat transfixed, staring at Gideon Higsbee. "I want to know," said Lemuel. "I want to know. How do you know they were crooks? They were nice, pleasant-spoken fellers."

"How do I know it?" Gideon looked hopelessly about him. After all, how did he know it? "Why, anyone could tell they were crooks! It was the rankest confidence game——"

Words failed Gideon. He paused for breath, and then continued very quietly and very patiently: "Never mind how I know it, Lemuel. Just take my word. I do, and that's what I'm here for now, Lemuel, because I did know. I guess it hadn't occurred to me until the other day, but I guess I cheated you just as much as they did."

"How's that, Gid?" Lemuel Gower placed a bony hand behind his ear. "My hearin' ain't so good as it used to be. You said you did what?"

Gideon paused a moment to collect his thought. It was difficult—more difficult than he had believed. "Lemuel," he said, very carefully, "we were partners in that mill, do you remember? I wanted to get all that mill; I've always wanted to get things. When you told me that you had given those three crooks all your money, I couldn't resist it. I knew the game was fishy and I didn't tell you so. I might have saved your money then."

Gideon Higsbee coughed and felt in his breast pocket. "I'm getting to be an old man, Lemuel, yet I've never done a thing that I've been so much ashamed of as that, and now I want to square the books. You gave those men ten thousand dollars. It was my fault you lost it. Here, Lemuel, take it and shake hands."

At times on a lonely evening Gideon had read of such scenes.

1153 The rich and fortunate man
1154 would smile and at the same
1155 time cough gruffly to hide the
1156 emotions in his voice. His poor
1157 but honest neighbor would be
1158 dumfounded, but would still
1159 give vent to emotions and ex-
1160 pressions of loyalty and grati-
1161 tude. Lemuel Gower, however,
1162 was different from the story
1163 book. He held the check ginger-
1164 ly in his calloused fingers with-
1165 out bothering to look at it; his
1166 other hand was still crooked
1167 behind his ear.

1168 "What's that?" he asked.
1169 "I guess I didn't understand.
1170 I'm rather hard of hearing,
1171 Gideon."

1172 Gideon raised his voice; at
1173 last he was growing irritated.
1174 "I said I was giving you back
1175 the ten thousand dollars you
1176 lost and its interest at 6 per cent
1177 for thirty years. I'm giving it
1178 back because I feel that I wasn't
1179 fair to you. That's what I said."

1180 Still holdng the check in his
1181 calloused thumb and forefinger,
1182 Lemuel Gower extended it to-
1183 ward Gideon. "That's kind of
1184 you, Gid," he said. "What I'd
1185 expect from an old neighbor,
1186 but I couldn't take it, Gid.
1187 Honest, I couldn't."

1188 "Forget about it," said
1189 Gideon heartily. "Put it in
1190 your pocket."

1191 Lemuel Gower looked very
1192 strange. He actually was blush-
1193 ing. He pulled a blue bandanna
1194 handkerchief from his trousers
1195 pocket and mopped his honest
1196 face. "Gid," he said, "it makes
1197 me sort of ashamed of myself to
1198 find you doin' this. I couldn't
1199 take it, Gid, because I was the
1200 one who cheated—honest."

1201 Gideon's silk hat rolled upon
1202 the floor, but Gideon did not
1203 pick it up. Again his voice rose
1204 and creaked and wavered. "You
1205 always were an infernal idiot,"
1206 he said. "You never cheated
1207 anybody—couldn't cheat a fly."
1208 With difficulty Gideon had
1209 pulled himself to his feet, and
1210 Lemuel Gower had also risen.

1211 "But I did cheat you, Gid,"
1212 he said. "It hurts me to say it
1213 in the face of your kindness, but
1214 when I told you about my giving
1215 those three fellers all that money,
1216 it was too late for you to do
1217 anything about it. I meant for
1218 it to be too late, because"—he
1219 stammered and grew redder—
1220 "because I always sort of envied
1221 you, Gideon, you bein' so slick.
1222 I wanted to make some money
1223 without givin' you the chance to
1224 make it too. And mebbe those
1225 men were honest. I like to think
1226 they were. They seemed to me
1227 like nice, civil-spoken fellers."

1228 He seized Gideon's hand and
1229 pressed something into Gideon's
1230 palm. Gideon felt it. It was
1231 the check. "Honest, Gid," said
1232 Lemuel, "take it back, I couldn't
1233 keep it. I'm gettin' to be a old
1234 man, Gid, and my conscience
1235 wouldn't let me."

1236 Out in the snow, in the failing

sun of the afternoon, Gideon Higsbee found it difficult to walk, and leaned heavily on his cane, but even his cane was not enough to steady his tottering footsteps. "George," he said— his voice was hoarse, and both his voice and his hands were trembling—"did you hear what he said? Oh, my stars! Did you hear what he said? He cheated me because he wouldn't say that three confidence men were going to rob him! He wouldn't take a certified check when it was handed to him. Did you ever see anything to beat it, George? Do you wonder that I'm broken up?"

George, himself, looked paler than usual. He stared wide-eyed at the shadows on the snow. "It's contrary to nature," he said. "Here, you better take my arm."

Gideon looked over his shoulder. The gaunt and ugly house of Lemuel Gower was black and stolid against the sun. Gideon raised his cane toward it, and his whiskers bristled.

"But he hasn't beat me yet," said Gideon. "He hasn't beat me yet."

There was something wrong with Gideon when he reached his office the next afternoon. He did not only look tired—he looked more than tired. His whiskers had a bedraggled appearance, which traveling had never given them before.

Yes, there was something wrong with Gideon. Mr. Altyne perceived it at once when he entered Gideon's private room. Gideon had been pacing up and down the carpet, with hands behind his back, but on Mr. Altyne's appearance he stopped and thrust his head slightly forward. "Jim," said Gideon, "he wouldn't take the money."

Mr. Altyne did not look surprised, but then Mr. Altyne never looked surprised. "Well, what of it?" he asked.

Gideon opened his lips and closed them before he finally spoke. "I don't know what of it," said Gideon with a groan. "That's what beats me—I don't know at all. He fooled me, or I feel as if he fooled me. He's so damned honest and damned simple. Can you imagine his not taking the money? I can't sleep for thinking of it. I say, I don't know what he's done, but somehow he's put one over on me."

"It's too bad," said Mr. Altyne, "that you didn't sell him some of that mining stock we got outside."

Gideon did not appear to hear him. "Jim," he said, "I'm not joking. He put something over on me. I tell you he did. I won't feel better until he has that money. Jim, you've got to go up to Agamemnon, Maine."

Mr. Altyne did a very rare thing for him. He smiled and

he no longer had a masklike face.

"Gideon," he began, "you have the most outlandish way of doing a kindness. You hear me? What are you thinking about? What are you doing?"

Gideon was whistling softly and moving his hand in quick, short circles. "Excuse me, Jim," he said. "I was just thinking of my wife—that's all —just thinking of my wife."

It might have been a week later, more or less, that Gideon Higsbee came down to his breakfast room. The canary was singing the same song; Mrs. Higsbee was sitting behind the coffee urn, opening her letters. Merlin had pushed back his chair and was reading the paper.

"Good morning, my dear," said Gideon.

At the sound of his voice Mrs. Higsbee peered at him suspiciously around the coffee urn. "Gideon," she inquired, "have you been up to anything lately?"

"Up to anything!" Gideon Higsbee looked at her and smiled in pained surprise. "Why, what do you mean, my dear?"

"I mean," said Mrs. Higsbee, "that you're looking better this morning, even than you did yesterday, and I've always noticed that you look better when you've been up to something."

"Tweet!" went the canary "Tweet!"

Gideon did a most surprising thing; he rose and tapped Merlin on the shoulder.

"Merlin," he said, "take that bird out of the room. It disturbs me."

"Gideon!" began Mrs. Higsbee.

"Merlin," said Mr. Higsbee, "you heard me speak to you. Take that bird out of the room."

"Why, Gideon!" said Mrs. Higsbee. "I never knew you to behave so! You have been up to something!"

"Simply asserting myself, that's all, my dear," said Mr. Higsbee. "I've really done nothing since you asked me last yesterday morning, except I did sell a block of stock to Doctor Follenshope — mining stock, my dear. He's young; it will do him good to be interested in speculative investments. . . . I'll have my coffee now, please."

There was a moment of silence. Mrs. Higsbee was reading a letter. There were furrows upon her brow. "Gideon," she said at length, "don't make such a noise with your coffee."

"My dear," said Mr. Higsbee over the brim of his cup, "shall I make you a confession which I have delayed for years? I enjoy making a noise over my coffee."

"There," said Mrs. Higsbee, "you have been doing something, Gideon; I know you have, and don't say you haven't."

"Nothing since you asked me

last, my dear," said Mr. Higsbee.

There was another pause, broken again by Mrs. Higsbee, who made a curious sound and moved so suddenly that the coffee urn trembled. "Gideon," she said—"Gideon, what do you think?"

"Only what I should, my dear."

"I just got another letter from Susie Brickett. It's all about Lemuel Gower."

"Oh?" said Mr. Higsbee, and put down his coffee cup and stroked his whiskers. "And what does she say about Lemuel Gower?"

"You needn't take that attitude," said Mrs. Higsbee. "You needn't make fun of Lemuel any more. Lemuel's smart enough. Lemuel's made a lot of money. What do you say to that?"

"Nothing," said Gideon very softly. "Nothing at all, my dear."

"Well," said Mrs. Higsbee triumphantly, "perhaps you will say something when you hear how he made it, after the way you laughed at Lemuel. Three men came all the way up from New York to call on Lemuel because they had heard of him. You know, Lemuel does amount to something in Agamemnon. One of these three men was in one of the big banking houses in New York, in a confidential capacity. . . . What are you laughing at, Gideon? I don't see anything to laugh at."

"There isn't, my dear," said Gideon. "I'm not laughing. I was simply making a noise over my coffee."

"Well," said Mrs. Higsbee, "this man, who was in the big banking house, knew the president very well. The president had given him special information about the stock market, and these three men had a private wire from New York. They asked Lemuel to invest, and Lemuel did. Are you listening, Gideon?"

"Yes, my dear," said Gideon.

"Then why are you whistling and making circles with your hand?"

"I beg your pardon," said Gideon hastily. "I wasn't doing it intentionally."

"Then listen to this," said Mrs. Higsbee. "Lemuel did invest. He had a very hard time; he had to sell his house to find any money; but Lemuel gave them his money right away, because he felt that they were honest; and just as soon as Lemuel gave them the money the stock went up and up. Lemuel made thousands of dollars. I don't know how many thousand. Now what do you say to that?"

Gideon gently stroked his whiskers. He had never looked so youthful, so wholly devoid of guile.

"Do you hear me, Gideon?"

1489 said Mrs. Higsbee. "What do
1490 you think of that? You won't
1491 be able to laugh at Lemuel now."
1492 "My dear," said Mr. Higsbee
1493 —his words had never seemed to
1494 ring more sweetly; his voice had
1495 never been more dulcet—"I can
1496 only think what I thought
1497 before. Once a sucker, my
1498 dear, always a sucker." And
1499 Gideon Higsbee smiled and rub-
1500 bed his hands.

1501 Mrs. Higsbee looked startled
1502 and peered at Gideon around
1503 the coffee urn. "What do you
1504 mean, Gideon?" she demanded.
1505 "Lemuel didn't lose his money.

1506 He made thousands and thou-
1507 sands of dollars."

1508 "What I said, my dear," said
1509 Gideon patiently. "Once a
1510 sucker, always a sucker. But
1511 I've said before, you don't
1512 understand business." Gideon
1513 smiled softly and stared at the
1514 ceiling. "I wonder," he began
1515 —"I wonder——"

1516 "What?" said Mrs. Higsbee.
1517 "Please talk louder, Gideon."

1518 "I wonder," said Gideon, still
1519 staring at the ceiling, "if Lemuel
1520 wouldn't also like to buy some
1521 mining stock."

The Analysis

There are only two ways in which any story may be presented.
In one the order is chronological; in the other the order is flash-
back. The first one shows the situation or main narrative problem
emerging as a result of an interchange or interchanges; and the
explanatory matter necessary to an understanding of that main
narrative problem is presented to the reader before the main
problem itself, or simultaneously.

In the flash-back method the main narrative problem is
presented first, and the explanatory matter comes afterwards.
I am almost prepared to say that the capacity of a writer can be
judged by his ability to use the flash-back method adequately.
In discussing the story *Paradise Island* and the story *The Escape of
Mr. Trimm* I pointed out that there are two kinds of flash-back;
the one which flashes back from the main narrative question to the
explanatory matter, and the one which flashes back from an
important moment which is not the moment when the main narrative question emerges. This second type was the method used
in *The Escape of Mr. Trimm*.

Once and Always is a particularly interesting example of the
use of the flash-back by a competent and experienced writer. The
opening paragraphs from line 1 to line 70 present the chief actor
to the reader at a great moment of his life, the greatest moment,

perhaps, that can occur in the life of anybody, the moment when that person learns that he is in the shadow of death. Just as in *Paradise Island* Langley became important because he was in the shadow of death, so Gideon Higsbee instantly is made important to the reader because he is shown as about to die.

The first four steps of the interchange between Gideon Higsbee and Doctor Follenshope occupy lines 1 to 62. The fifth step, or the reflection of the actor upon what has passed, projects the main narrative purpose of the story, which is Gideon's attempts to restore to Lemuel Gower the $10,000. This step occupies lines 63 to 70. We have here the same type story as in *Paradise Island* in which the main narrative question is presented as an outgrowth of the first presentation unit, which here is an interchange, whereas in *Paradise Island* the main narrative question appears as the outgrowth of a meeting with a stimulus.

The interesting distinction between this story and the story *Paradise Island* is in the arrangement of the flash-back scenes in the remainder of the Beginning, concluding on line 852. Out of a total of 1521 lines for the story, the Beginning, containing the main narrative question and its explanatory matter, occupies 852. The especial difference between this story and *Paradise Island* in its flash-backs is this: in *Paradise Island* when the author flashes back he does it objectively. In this case, the flashing back is done not by the author but by the actor. It is a flash-back in the mind or consciousness of Gideon Higsbee.

This word "objective" would seem to take as its opposite and contrasting meaning the word "subjective." In ordinary criticism those are the two terms which are used. In discussing a poet, for example, we say that he presents his material "objectively" or "subjectively." If the poet describes a brook and makes us aware of that brook without in any way injecting into the description his own personal feeling, allowing the audience to receive whatever sensation it may from the stimuli which he presents, his presentation is "objective." Opposed to this, when he injects his own personality, and makes clear what *he* feels about the brook, then we say that his poetry is subjective.

But in dealing with the craftsmanship of short-story writing this is not an extremely important distinction. The distinction to be made is between the "objective" presentation, when the author presents the material to us, "objectively" in the same way that the "objective" poet does, and the "analytical" presentation by the author, when he indicates what is passing in the mind of an actor. Thus the terms we use in the criticism of short-story craftsmanship are "objective," and opposing the "objective" the "analytical." There are cases, of course, where the short-story writer is "subjective," but what I wish to draw to your attention is the special use of a new term, which is "analytical," as being the opposite of "objective."

Mr. Marquand is especially noteworthy for the ease with which he is able to change from the "objective" to the "analytical," or from the "analytical" to the "objective." On line 63 we learn that Gideon is thinking—that he has something on his mind—and so thinking there flashes into his mind a scene in the Agamemnon House. Beginning on line 172 the author becomes purely "objective" because this is a scene which could have been presented objectively. From lines 658 to 732 the author again becomes "analytical," because this is the fifth step of the interchange and deals with the reflections of the actor, those reflections being analyzed by the author, and rightly so. An example in this story of the flash-back scene which is presented objectively is the scene which begins on line 423 between Mrs. Higsbee and Gideon. It opens with the words, "Earlier that very morning, when he had entered the breakfast room of his brownstone house, etc." The actual interchange of that scene closes on line 648, where he says, "I hope to die if ever in my life I did a wrong to Lemuel Gower." The fifth step of that scene, on lines 649 to 657 projects him forward in time to the close of the scene with Dr. Follenshope, and as a result of that, there come his reflections on lines 658 to 750, as a result of which he presses a button on his desk for the man named George.

What every writer who is interested in analysis will find especially instructive about this story is that all of the Beginning is presented in a series of interchanges, and that those interchanges are almost invariably complete scenes, having purpose and clash to make them both narrative and dramatic, and that their fifth steps swiftly swing the reader either forward or backward into another interchange. Thus, at the close of the first interchange with Dr. Follenshope, Gideon swings the reader back to Agamemnon, Maine, some thirty years before, and out of that there grows the reflection that once a man is a sucker he will always be a sucker. The main character trait of Gideon Higsbee is immediately apparent, because he is shown as summing up the three strangers at once, and realizing that they are confidence men, whereas opposed to him is Lemuel Gower who is impressed tremendously by their distinguished bearing. This capacity of Gideon, which is his distinguishing trait, is the one which is used by the author to solve the narrative problem. It is interesting to see that the next step is a flash forward to the beginning of the interchange with Dr. Follenshope. At the close of this interchange the reader is aware of a dramatic hindrance through the reflection of Gideon that his own weakness may defeat his purpose of restoring the money.

The transition to earlier that morning is a very easy one and swings the reader into the interchange between Mrs. Higsbee and Gideon, when she tries to discover whether or not he has acted justly by Lemuel Gower, and Gideon's reflections upon that defiant, "I hope to die," again plunge the reader swiftly back to the close of the interview with Dr. Follenshope, and through that very swiftly into the interchange with George, and from that into the interchange with Mr. Altyne. At its close this interchange places emphasis upon a dramatic hindrance to the actor's main purpose when the reflections of the actor indicate that there is an opposing force to be reckoned with which may defeat the purpose which has now become paramount in importance. Thus the reader's attention is held by three different kinds of interest,—the main narrative interest of the main problem, with its hindrances at the close of each scene or interchange; the dramatic quality of the interchanges themselves as they disclose character; and the thematic interest of the story which comes from the author's feeling, expressed through the main actor in his story that once a man is a sucker he will always be a sucker, and that a basic trait will determine a character's action at almost any moment in life.

The Body of the story is composed of the interchange between Gideon and Lemuel in which the traits shown earlier in the story are again emphasized so that the reader is absolutely clear as to the kind of people engaged in the controversy. At the close of the interchange he is also aware that there has come the big moment of the story when, through the defeat of his attempt, the main actor is facing a moment of disaster which seems unavoidable and imminent. The quality of urgency is present because the reader knows that at any moment Gideon's heart may fail him completely, and that to achieve his purpose he must consummate this act of restitution in order to die happy.

The craftsmanship of portraying character consists in making clear to the reader the traits of character as shown by the reactions of an actor at any moment in life. The basic trait of Gideon—his ability to judge character,—is shown in his interchange with Mr.

Altyne after he has received his rebuff from Lemuel. He sums up Lemuel's character on line 1301 by saying "He's so damned honest and damned simple," then when Mr. Altyne says, "It's too bad you didn't sell him some of that mining stock we've got outside," Gideon instantly responds in terms of his main trait and there is born in his mind the scheme which is dependent upon his knowledge of Lemuel, who having once been a sucker will always be a sucker, and it is through his basic trait that he is able to bring about the solution to his problem.

Just as in *Jake Bolton, 551*, at the close of the final scene of the Body the main actor appears to have been defeated in his chief purpose, here Gideon appears to have been defeated in his purpose. But there was in *Jake Bolton, 551* an appended episodic meeting or interchange through which the reader learned the actual truth of the matter. Here through the interchange between Gideon and Mrs. Higsbee the reader is made aware of what actually transpired when Gideon sent Mr. Altyne and two other men up to Agamemnon, Maine, to impersonate the three strangers.

Realizing that Lemuel would not accept a straightforward offer because of this queer kink in his mind, and desiring to bring about the end he wished Gideon faked a "sucker scheme" for Lemuel for which Lemuel instantly "fell."

And just as in *Jake Bolton* the two speakers were caused to sum up the philosophy, or theme of the story, that is, what we call its significance, so here on lines 1509 to 1510 the significance is again summed up. It is that, "Once a sucker, always a sucker."

Almost any writer can learn to write the scenes for the Body of his story. The process is simply to get two opposing forces together and to make them clash, making sure that at the end of the clash the fifth step will form a crisis, preferably of hindrance, to the main narrative question. But the difficulty comes when writers try to write the long Beginning. The way out is through the flash-back method, and the flash-back method, as I have said before, consists of presenting the explanatory matter in interesting interchanges. One of the most instructive stories which any writer could read is this story, *Once and Always*. Because it is such a good model, and because it is such an example of character portrayal, I have great pleasure in including it in this volume.

There is a special device of craftsmanship which this story exemplifies, which has not been discussed before in this book. It is the Appended, as opposed to the Contained, Ending. When the Ending is Contained, the reader is shown the Conclusive Act *as it happens.* For example, in *Sunk*, the reader is aware of Jason Terwilliger's refusal to drink. In this story the reader is not aware of Gideon's device to make Lemuel accept the money *until after it has happened*, when he hears of it from Mrs. Higsbee. In the Contained Ending there is no delay between the final attempt of the Body of the Story and the Conclusive Act. In the Appended Ending another meeting intervenes.

ARCHITECTURAL CHART

OF

THE FACE IN THE WINDOW

SEQUEL	(Part 2)	Meeting. Sheriff Crumpett receives letter from Wiley.	1– 85	Effect of Conclusive Act is shown.

| | Interchange. Sheriff and Joseph. | 86– 108 | Significance shown. |

BEGINNING

Initial condition shown.

Interchange. Editor and his staff. (5th step.) Effect upon actors and observers. — 109– 299 / 300– 320 — Dangerous force appears.

Main Actor's purpose is clear.

Interchange. Cora McBride and Duncan McBride. — 312– 514 — Difficulty shown. Desperate straits shown.

Interchange (Mental). Different forces within. — 515– 659 — Promise of Disaster. Main Narrative Question: "Can Cora McBride capture Hap Ruggam?"

BODY

Series of attempts by Main Actor to achieve purpose, with attempts of opponent to prevent achievement.

Attempt to overcome Condition. (A natural obstacle of snow, etc.) — 660– 957 — Narrative Furtherance. Dramatic Hindrance. Tired.

Attempt to overcome Hap Ruggam. — 958–1370 — Furtherance. Gun secured.

Renewed attempt to overcome Hap Ruggam. — 1371–1583 — Cannot kill. Dramatic Hindrance.

Scene. Hap Ruggam attempts to kill Cora. New condition formed. — 1497–1583 — Face appears. Furtherance.

Ruggam reacts to new condition. Collapses. — 1584–1650 — Main Narrative Question Answered: "Yes."

ENDING

Conclusive Act.

Cora captures Ruggam. — 1651–1665 — Apparition explained. Significance shown.

Sequel (Part 1.)

Sheriff's party and Cora McBride. — 1666–1702

THE FACE IN THE WINDOW

BY WILLIAM DUDLEY PELLEY

THE ordinary sequence of the divisions of a short-story is Explanatory Matter and Main Narrative Problem in the Beginning; Interchanges growing out of that problem, making up the Body; the Conclusive Act and its Sequel, making up the Ending. Usually when the "Flash-back" is used, it appears in the Beginning, changing the order of its subdivisions to Main Narrative Problem and Explanatory Matter. In this story the "Flash-back" is used in the Sequel, a sub-division of the Ending.

That, alone, would make *The Face in the Window* an instructive story for analysis; but in addition it contains a development of the different types of struggle that renders it especially illuminating to the student of craftsmanship.

CASE No. 9

THE FACE IN THE WINDOW

BY WILLIAM DUDLEY PELLEY

At nine o'clock this morning Sheriff Crumpett entered our New England town post-office for his mail. From his box he extracted his monthly Grand Army paper and a letter in a long yellow envelope. This envelope bore the return-stamp of a prominent Boston lumber-company. The old man crossed the lobby to the writing-shelf under the Western Union clock, hooked black-rimmed glasses on a big nose and tore a generous inch from the end of the envelope.

The first inclosure which met his eyes was a check. It was heavy and pink and crisp, and was attached to the single sheet of letter-paper with a clip. Impressed into the fabric of the safety-paper were the indelible figures of a protector: *Not over Five Thousand ($5000) Dollars.*

The sheriff read the name of the person to whom it was payable and gulped. His gnarled old hand trembled with excitement as he glanced over the clipped letter and then went through it again.

November 10, 1919.

MY DEAR SHERIFF:

Enclosed please find my personal check for five thousand dollars. It is made out to Mrs. McBride. Never having known the lady personally, and because you have evidently represented her with the authorities, I am sending it to you for proper delivery. I feel, from your enthusiastic account of her recent experience, that it will give you pleasure to present it to her.

Under the circumstances I do not begrudge the money. When first advised of Ruggam's escape, it was hot-headed impulse which prompted me to offer a reward so large. The old clan-blood of the Wileys must have made me murder-mad that Ruggam should regain his freedom permanently after the hellish thing he did to my brother. The newspapers heard of it, and then I could not retract.

213

60 That, however, is a thing of
61 the past. I always did detest a
62 welcher, and if this money is go-
63 ing to a woman to whom it will
64 be manna from heaven—to use
65 your words—I am satisfied.
66 Convey to her my personal con-
67 gratulations, gratitude and best
68 wishes.

69 Cordially yours,
70 C. V. D. WILEY.

71 "Good old Chris!" muttered
72 the sheriff. "He's rich because
73 he's white." He thrust both
74 check and letter back into the
75 long envelope and headed for the
76 office of our local daily paper at
77 a smart pace.

78 The earning of five thousand
79 dollars reward-money by Cora
80 McBride made an epochal news-
81 item, and in that night's paper
82 we headlined it accordingly—
83 not omitting proper mention of
84 the sheriff and giving him appro-
85 priate credit.

86 Having so started the an-
87 nouncement permeating through
88 the community, the old man em-
89 ployed the office phone and
90 called the local livery-stable. He
91 ordered a rig in which he might
92 drive at once to the McBride
93 house in the northern part of
94 town.

95 "But half that money ought
96 to be yourn!" protested the pro-
97 prietor of the stable as the sher-
98 iff helped him "gear up the
99 horse" a few minutes later.

100 "Under the circumstances, Jo-

101 seph, can you see me takin' it?
102 No; it ain't in me to horn in for
103 no rake-off on one o' the Lord's
104 miracles."

105 The old man climbed into the
106 sleigh, took the reins from the
107 liveryman and started the horse
108 from the livery yard.

109 Two weeks ago—on Monday,
110 the twenty-seventh of the past
111 October—the telephone-bell rang
112 sharply in our newspaper-office
113 a few moments before the paper
114 went to press. Now, the tele-
115 phone-bell often rings in our
116 newspaper-office a few moments
117 before going to press. The con-
118 fusion on this particular Monday
119 afternoon, however, resulted
120 from Albany calling on the long-
121 distance. Albany—meaning the
122 nearest office of the international
123 press-association of which our
124 paper is a member—called just
125 so, out of a clear sky, on the day
126 McKinley was assassinated, on
127 the day the *Titania* foundered,
128 and on the day Austria declared
129 war on Serbia.

130 The connection was made, and
131 over the wire came the voice of
132 young Stewart, crisp as lettuce.

133 "Special dispatch . . . Wynd-
134 gate, Vermont, October 27th . . .
135 Ready?"

136 . The editor of our paper an-
137 swered in the affirmative. The
138 rest of us grouped anxiously
139 around his chair. Stewart pro-
140 ceeded:

141 " 'Hapwell Ruggam, serving a
142 life-sentence for the murder of

214

143 Deputy Sheriff Martin Wiley at
144 a Lost Nation kitchen-dance two
145 years ago, killed Jacob Lamb-
146 well, his guard, and escaped from
147 prison at noon to-day.

148 " 'Ruggam had been given
149 some repair work to do near the
150 outer prison-gate. It was opened
151 to admit a tradesman's automo-
152 bile. As Guard Lambwell turned
153 to close the gate, Ruggam felled
154 him with his shovel. He escaped
155 to the adjacent railroad-yards,
156 stole a corduroy coat and pair of
157 blue overalls hanging in a switch-
158 man's shanty and caught the
159 twelve-forty freight up Green
160 River.' "

161 Stewart had paused. The edi-
162 tor scribbled frantically. In a
163 few words aside he explained to
164 us what Stewart was sending.
165 Then he ordered the latter to
166 proceed.

167 " 'Freight Number Eight was
168 stopped by telegraph near Nor-
169 wall. The fugitive, assuming
170 correctly that it was slowing
171 down for search, was seen by a
172 brakeman fleeing across a pas-
173 ture between the tracks and the
174 eastern edge of Haystack Moun-
175 tain. Several posses have al-
176 ready started after him, and
177 sheriffs all through northern
178 New England are being notified.

179 " 'Christopher Wiley, lumber
180 magnate and brother of Rug-
181 gam's former victim, on being
182 told of the escape, has offered
183 a reward of five thousand dollars
184 for Ruggam's capture, dead or

alive. Guard Lambwell was re- 185
moved to a hospital, where he 186
died at one-thirty.' . . . *All* 187
right?" 188

The connection was broken, 189
and the editor removed the head- 190
piece. He began giving orders. 191
We were twenty minutes behind 192
usual time with the papers, but 193
we made all the trains. 194

When the big Duplex was 195
grinding out newsprint with a 196
roar that shook the building, the 197
boys and girls gathered around 198
to discuss the thing which had 199
happened. 200

The Higgins boy, saucer-eyed 201
over the experience of being "on 202
the inside" during the handling 203
of the first sizable news-story 204
since he had become our local 205
reporter, voiced the interroga- 206
tion on the faces of other office 207
newcomers. 208

"Ruggam," the editor ex- 209
plained, "is a poor unfortunate 210
who should have been sent to an 211
asylum instead of the peniten- 212
tiary. He killed Mart Wiley, a 213
deputy sheriff, at a Lost Nation 214
kitchen-dance two years ago." 215

"Where's the Lost Nation?" 216

"It's a term applied to most 217
of the town of Partridgeville in 218
the northern part of the county 219
—an inaccessible district back 220
in the mountains peopled with 221
gone-to-seed stock and half-civ- 222
ilized illiterates who only get into 223
the news when they load up with 224
squirrel whisky and start a pro- 225
gramme of progressive hell. 226

Ruggam was the local blacksmith."

"What's a kitchen-dance?"

"Ordinarily a kitchen-dance is harmless enough. But the Lost Nation folks use it as an excuse for a debauch. They gather in some sizable shack, set the stove out into the yard, soak themselves in aromatic spirits of deviltry and dance from Saturday night until Monday noon——"

"And this Ruggam killed a sheriff at one of them?"

"He got into a brawl with another chap about his wife. Someone passing saw the fight and sent for an officer. Mart Wiley was deputy, afraid of neither man, God nor devil. Martin had grown disgusted over the petty crime at these kitchen-dances and started out to clean up this one right. Hap Ruggam killed him. He must have had help, because he first got Mart tied to a tree in the yard. Most of the crowd was pie-eyed by this time, anyhow, and would fight at the drop of a hat. After tying him securely, Ruggam caught up a billet of wood and—and killed him with that."

"Why didn't they electrocute him?" demanded young Higgins.

"Well, the murder wasn't exactly premeditated. Hap wasn't himself; he was drunk—not even able to run away when Sheriff Crumpett arrived in the neighborhood to take him into custody. Then there was Hap's bringing up. All these made extenuating circumstances."

"There was something about Sheriff Wiley's pompadour," suggested our little lady proof-reader.

"Yes," returned the editor. "Mart had a queer head of hair. It was dark and stiff, and he brushed it straight back in a pompadour. When he was angry or excited, it actually rose on his scalp like wire. Hap's counsel made a great fuss over Mart's pompadour and the part it sort of played in egging Hap on. The sight of it, stiffening and rising the way it did maddened Ruggam so that he beat it down hysterically in retaliation for the many grudges he fancied he owed the officer. No, it was all right to make the sentence life-imprisonment, only it should have been an asylum. Hap's not right. You'd know it without being told. I guess it's his eyes. They aren't mates. They light up weirdly when he's drunk or excited, and if you know what's healthy, you get out of the way."

By eight o'clock that evening most of the valley's deer-hunters, all of the local adventurers who could buy, borrow or beg a rifle, and the usual quota of high-school-sons of thoughtless parents were off on the man-hunt in the eastern mountains.

Among them was Sheriff Crumpett's party. On reaching

310 the timber-line they separated.
311 It was agreed that if any of them
312 found signs of Ruggam, the sig-
313 nal for assistance was five shots
314 in quick succession "and keep
315 shooting at intervals until the
316 rest come up."

317 We newspaper folk awaited
318 the capture with professional in-
319 terest and pardonable excite-
320 ment. . . .

321 In the northern part of our
322 town, a mile out on the Wick-
323 ford road, is the McBride place.
324 It is a small white house with a
325 red barn in the rear and a neat
326 rail fence inclosing the whole.
327 Six years ago Cora McBride was
328 bookkeeper in the local garage.
329 Her maiden name was Allen.
330 The town called her "Tomboy
331 Allen." She was the only daugh-
332 ter of old Zeb Allen, for many
333 years our county game-warden.
334 Cora, as we had always known—
335 and called—her, was a full-
336 blown, red-blooded, athletic girl
337 who often drove cars for her em-
338 ployer in the days when steer-
339 ing-wheels manipulated by wom-
340 en were offered as clinching proof
341 that society was headed for the
342 dogs.

343 Duncan McBride was chief
344 mechanic in the garage repair-
345 shop. He was an affable, sober,
346 steady chap, popularly known as
347 "Dunk the Dauntless" because
348 of an uncanny ability to cope
349 successfully with the ailments of
350 90 per cent. of the internal-com-
351 bustion hay-balers and refrac-

352 tory tin-Lizzies in the county
353 when other mechanics had given
354 them up in disgust.

355 When he married his employ-
356 er's bookkeeper, Cora's folks
357 gave her a wedding that carried
358 old Zeb within half an hour of
359 insolvency and ran to four col-
360 umns in the local daily. Dun-
361 can and the Allen girl motored
362 to Washington in a demonstra-
363 tion-car, and while Dunk was
364 absent the yard of the garage
365 resembled the premises about a
366 junkshop. On their return they
367 bought the Johnson place, and
368 Cora quickly demonstrated
369 the same furious enthusiasm
370 for home-making and moth-
371 erhood that she had for athletics
372 and carburetors.

373 Three years passed, and two
374 small boys crept about the yard
375 behind the white rail fence.
376 Then—when Duncan and his
377 wife were "making a great go of
378 matrimony" in typical Yankee
379 fashion—came the tragedy that
380 took all the vim out of Cora,
381 stole the ruddy glow from her
382 girlish features and made her
383 middle-aged in a twelvemonth.
384 In the infantile-paralysis epi-
385 demic which passed over New
386 England three years ago the
387 McBrides suffered the supreme
388 sorrow—twice. Those small
389 boys died within two weeks of
390 each other.

391 Duncan of course kept on with
392 his work at the garage. He was
393 quieter and steadier than ever.

But when we drove into the place to have a carburetor adjusted or a rattle tightened, we saw only too plainly that on his heart was a wound the scars of which would never heal. As for Cora, she was rarely seen in the village.

Troubles rarely come singly. One afternoon this past August, Duncan completed repairs on Doc Potter's runabout. Cranking the machine to run it from the workshop, the "dog" on the safety-clutch failed to hold. The acceleration of the engine threw the machine into high. Dunk was pinned in front while the roadster leaped ahead and rammed the delivery truck of the Red Front Grocery.

Duncan was taken to our memorial hospital with internal injuries and dislocation of his spine. He remained there many weeks. In fact, he had been home only a couple of days when the evening stage left in the McBride's letter-box the daily paper containing the story of Ruggam's "break" and of the reward offered for his capture.

Cora returned to the kitchen after obtaining the paper and sank wearily into a wooden chair beside the table with the red cloth. Spreading out the paper, she sought the usual mental distraction in the three-and four-line bits which make up our local columns.

As the headlines caught her eye, she picked up the paper and entered the bedroom where Duncan lay. There were telltale traces of tears on his unshaven face, and an ache in his discouraged heart that would not be assuaged; for it was becoming rumoured about the village that Dunk the Dauntless might never operate on the vitals of an ailing tin-Lizzie again.

"Dunnie," cried his wife, "Hap Ruggam's escaped!" Sinking down beside the bedroom lamp she read him the article aloud.

Her husband's name was mentioned therein; for when the sheriff had commandeered an automobile from the local garage to convey him and his posse to Lost Nation and secure Ruggam, Duncan had been called forth to preside at the steering-wheel. He had thus assisted in the capture and later had been a witness at the trial.

The reading ended, the man rolled his head.

"If I wasn't held here, I might go!" he said. "I might try for that five thousand myself!"

Cora was sympathetic enough, of course, but she was fast approaching the stage where she needed sympathy herself.

"We caught him over on the Purcell farm," mused Duncan. "Something ailed Ruggam. He was drunk and couldn't run. But that wasn't all. He had had some kind of crazy-spell during or after the killing and wasn't quite over it. We tied him and lifted him into the auto. His face was a sight. His eyes aren't mates, anyhow, and they were wild and unnatural. He kept shrieking, something about a head of hair—black hair—sticks up like wire. He must have had an awful impression of Mart's face and that hair of his."

"I remember about Aunt Mary Crumpett's telling me of the trouble her husband had with his prisoner in the days before the trial," his wife replied. "He had those crazy-spells often, nights. He kept yelling that he saw Martin Wiley's head with its peculiar hair, and his face peering in at him through the cell window. Sometimes he became so bad that Sheriff Crumpett thought he'd have apoplexy. Finally he had to call Dr. Johnson to attend him."

"Five thousand dollars!" muttered Duncan. "Gawd! I'd hunt the devil *for nothing* if I only had a chance of getting out of this bed."

Cora smoothed her husband's rumpled bed, comforted him and laid her own tired head down beside his hand. When he had dozed off, she arose and left the room.

In the kitchen she resumed her former place beside the table with the cheap red cloth; and there, with her face in her hands, she stared into endless distance.

"Five thousand dollars! Five thousand dollars!" Over and over she whispered the words, with no one to hear.

The green-birch fire snapped merrily in the range. The draft sang in the flue. Outside, a soft, feathery snow was falling, for winter came early in the uplands of Vermont this past year. To Cora McBride, however, the winter meant only hardship. Within another week she must go into town and secure work. Not that she minded the labour nor the trips through the vicious weather! The anguish was leaving Duncan through those monotonous days before he should be up and around. Those dreary winter days! What might they not do to him—alone.

Five thousand dollars! Like many others in the valley that night she pictured with fluttering heart what it would mean to possess such a sum of money; but not once in her pitiful flight of fancy did she disregard the task which must be performed to gain that wealth.

It meant traveling upward in the great snowbound reaches of Vermont mountain-country and tracking down a murderer who had killed a second time to gain his freedom and would stop at nothing again.

And yet—*five thousand dollars!*

How much will a person do, how far will a normal human being travel, to earn five thousand dollars—if the need is sufficiently provocative?

As Cora McBride sat there in the homely little farmhouse kitchen and thought of the debts still existent, contracted to save the already stricken lives of two little lads forgotten now by all but herself and Duncan and God, of the chances of losing their home if Duncan could work no more and pay up the balance of their mortgage, of the days when Duncan must lie in the south bedroom alone and count the figures on the wall paper—as she sat there and contemplated these things, into Cora McBride's heart crept determination.

At first it was only a faint challenge to her courage. As the minutes passed, however, her imagination ran riot, with five thousand dollars to help them in their predicament. The challenge grew. Multitudes of women down all the years had attempted wilder ventures for those who were dear to them. Legion in number had been those who set their hands and hearts to greater tasks, made more improbable sacrifices, taken greater chances. Multitudes of them, too, had won—on little else than the courage of ignorance and the strength of desperation.

She had no fear of the great outdoors, for she had lived close to the mountains from childhood and much of her old physical resiliency and youthful daredeviltry remained. And the need was terrible; no one anywhere in the valley, not even her own people, knew how terrible.

Cora McBride, alone by her table in the kitchen, that night made her decision.

She took the kitchen lamp and went upstairs. Lifting the top of a leather trunk, she found her husband's revolver. With it was a belt and holster, the former filled with cartridges. In the storeroom over the back kitchen she unhooked Duncan's mackinaw and found her own toboggan-cap. From a corner behind some fishing-rods she salvaged a pair of summer-dried snowshoes; they had facilitated many a previous hike in the winter woods with her man of a thousand adventures. She searched until she found the old army-haversack Duncan used as a game-bag. Its shoulder-straps were broken but a length of rope sufficed to bind it about her shoulders, after she had filled it with provisions.

With this equipment she returned below-stairs. She drew on heavy woolen stockings and buckled on arctics. She entered the cold pantry and packed the knapsack with what supplies she could find at the hour. She did not forget a drinking-cup, a hunting-knife or matches. In her blouse she slipped a household flash-lamp.

Dressed finally for the adven-

646 ture, from the kitchen she called
647 softly to her husband. He did
648 not answer. She was over-
649 whelmed by a desire to go into
650 the south bedroom and kiss him,
651 so much might happen before
652 she saw him again. But she re-
653 strained herself. She must not
654 waken him.

655 She blew out the kerosene
656 lamp, gave a last glance about
657 her familiar kitchen and went
658 out through the shed door,
659 closing it softly behind her.

660 It was one of those close, quiet
661 nights when the bark of a distant
662 dog or whinny of a horse sounds
663 very near at hand. The snow
664 was falling feathery.

665 An hour later found her far to
666 the eastward, following an old
667 side road that led up to the Har-
668 rison lumber-job. She had mean-
669 time paid Dave Sheldon, a
670 neighbour's boy, encountered by
671 his gate, to stay with Duncan
672 during her absence which she
673 explained with a white lie. But
674 her conscience did not bother.
675 Her conscience might be called
676 upon to smother much more be-
677 fore the adventure was ended.

678 Off in the depths of the snow-
679 ing night she strode along, a
680 weird figure against the eerie
681 whiteness that illumined the win-
682 ter world. She felt a strange
683 wild thrill in the infinite out-of-
684 doors. The woodsman's blood
685 of her father was having its
686 little hour.

687 And she knew the woods. In-

688 tuitively she felt that if Ruggam
689 was on Haystack Mountain
690 making his way toward Lost
691 Nation, he would strike for the
692 shacks of the Green Mountain
693 Club or the deserted logging-
694 camps along the trail, secreting
695 himself in them during his pauses
696 for rest, for he had no food, and
697 provisions were often left in
698 these structures by hunters and
699 mountain hikers. Her plan was
700 simple. She would investigate
701 each group of buildings. She
702 had the advantage of starting on
703 the northwest side of Haystack.
704 She would be working toward
705 Ruggam, while the rest of the
706 posses were trailing him.

707 Mile after mile she covered.
708 She decided it must be midnight
709 when she reached the ghostly
710 buildings of the Harrison tract,
711 lying white and silent under the
712 thickening snow. It was useless
713 to search these cabins; they were
714 too near civilization. Besides, if
715 Ruggam had left the freight at
716 Norwall on the eastern side of
717 Haystack at noon, he had thirty
718 miles to travel before reaching
719 the territory from which she was
720 starting. So she skirted the
721 abandoned quiet of the clearing,
722 laid the snowshoes properly down
723 before her and bound the thongs
724 securely about her ankles.

725 She had plenty of time to
726 think of Ruggam as she padded
727 along. He had no snowshoes to
728 aid him, unless he had managed
729 to secure a pair by burglary,

which was improbable. So it was not difficult to calculate about where she should begin watching for him. She believed he would keep just off the main trail to avoid detection, yet take its general direction in order to secure shelter and possible food from the mountain buildings. When she reached the country in which she might hope to encounter him, she would zigzag across that main trail in order to pick up his foot-tracks if he had passed her undetected. In that event she would turn and follow. She knew that the snow was falling too heavily to continue in such volume indefinitely; it would stop as suddenly as it had started.

The hours of the night piled up. The silent, muffling snow-fall continued. And Cora Mc-Bride began to sense an alarming weariness. It finally dawned upon her that her old-time vigour was missing. The strength of youth was hers no longer. Two experiences of motherhood and no more exercise than was afforded by the tasks of her household, had softened her muscles. Their limitations were now disclosed.

The realization of those limitations was accompanied by panic. She was still many miles even from Blind Brook Cabin, and her limbs were afire from the unaccustomed effort. This would never do. After pauses for breath that were coming closer and closer together, she set her lips each time grimly. "Tomboy Allen" had not counted on succumbing to physical fatigue before she had climbed as far as Blind Brook. If she were weakening already, what of those many miles on the other side?

Tuesday the twenty-eighth of October passed with no tidings of Ruggam's capture. The Holmes boy was fatally shot by a rattle-headed searcher near Five-Mile Pond, and distraught parents began to take thought of their own lads missing from school. Adam MacQuarry broke his leg near the Hell Hollow schoolhouse and was sent back by friends on a borrowed bob-sled. Several ne'er-do-wells, long on impulse and short on stick-ability, drifted back to more comfortable quarters during the day, contending that if Hap were captured, the officers would claim the reward anyhow—so what was the use bucking the System?

The snowfall stopped in the early morning. Sunrise disclosed the world trimmed from horizon to horizon in fairy fluff. House-holders jocosely shoveled their walks; small children resurrected attic sleds; here and there a farmer appeared on Main Street during the forenoon in a pung-sleigh or cutter with jingling bells. The sun soared higher, and the day grew warmer. Eaves

814 began dripping during the noon
815 hour, to stop when the sun sank
816 about four o'clock behind Ban-
817 croft's hill.

818 After the sunset came a per-
819 fect evening. The starlight was
820 magic. Many people called in
821 at the newspaper-office, after the
822 movies, to learn if the man hunt
823 had brought results.

824 Between ten and eleven
825 o'clock the lights on the valley
826 floor blinked out; the town had
827 gone to bed—that is, the lights
828 blinked out in all homes except-
829 ing those on the eastern out-
830 skirts, where nervous people wor-
831 ried over the possibilities of a
832 hungry, hunted convict burglar-
833 izing their premises, or drawn-
834 faced mothers lived mentally
835 through a score of calamities be-
836 falling red-blooded sons who had
837 now been absent twenty-four
838 hours.

839 Sometime between nine o'clock
840 and midnight—she had no way
841 of telling accurately—Cora Mc-
842 Bride stumbled into the Lyons
843 clearing. No one would have
844 recognized in the staggering, be-
845 draggled apparition that emerged
846 from the silhouette of the timber
847 the figure that had started so
848 confidently from the Harrison
849 tract the previous evening.

850 For over an hour she had hob-
851 bled blindly. It was wholly by
852 accident that she had stumbled
853 into the clearing. And the cap-
854 ture of Ruggam had diminished
855 in importance. Warm food,

856 water that would not tear her
857 raw throat, a place to lie and re-
858 coup her strength after the chill-
859 ing winter night—these were the
860 only things that counted now.
861 Though she knew it not, in her
862 eyes burned the faint light of
863 fever. When a snag caught her
864 snowshoe and tripped her, there
865 was hysteria in her cry of resent-
866 ment.

867 As she moved across from the
868 timber-line her hair was revealed
869 fallen down; she had lost a glove,
870 and one hand and wrist were
871 cruelly red where she had
872 plunged them several times into
873 the snow to save herself from
874 falling upon her face. She made
875 but a few yards before the icy
876 thong of her right snowshoe
877 snapped. She did not bother to
878 repair it. Carrying it beneath
879 her arm, she hobbled brokenly
880 toward the shelter of the
881 buildings.

882 Her failure at the other cabins,
883 the lack, thus far, of all signs of
884 the fugitive, the vastness of the
885 hunting-ground magnified by the
886 loneliness of winter, had con-
887 vinced her finally that her quest
888 was futile. It was all a venture
889 of madness. The idea that a
890 woman, alone and single-handed,
891 with no weapon but a revolver,
892 could track down and subdue a
893 desperate murderer in winter
894 mountains where hardly a wild
895 thing stirred, and make him re-
896 turn with her to the certain pen-
897 alty—this proved how much

mental mischief had again been caused by the lure of money. The glittering seduction of gold had deranged her. She realized it now, her mind normal in an exhausted body. So she gained the walls of the building and stumbled around them, thoughtless of any possible signs of the fugitive.

The stars were out in myriads. The Milky Way was a spectacle to recall vividly the sentiment of the Nineteenth Psalm. The log buildings of the clearing, every tree-trunk and bough in the woods beyond, the distant skyline of stump and hollow, all stood out sharply against the peculiar radiance of the snow. The night was as still as the spaces between the planets.

Like some wild creature of those winter woods the woman clumped and stumbled around the main shack, seeking the door.

Finding it, she stopped, the snowshoe slipped from beneath her arm; one numb hand groped for the log door-casing in support; the other fumbled for the revolver.

Tracks led into that cabin!

A paralysis of fright gripped Cora McBride. Something told her intuitively that she stood face to face at last with what she had traveled all this mountain wilderness to find. Yet with sinking heart it also came to her that if Hap Ruggam had made these tracks and were still within, she must face him in her exhausted condition and at once make that tortuous return trip to civilization. There would be no one to help her.

She realized in that moment that she was facing the primal. And she was not primal. She was a normal woman, weakened to near-prostration by the trek of the past twenty-four hours. Was it not better to turn away while there was time?

She stood debating thus, the eternal silence blanketing forest-world and clearing. But she was allowed to make no decision.

A living body sprang suddenly upon her. Before she could cry out, she was borne down precipitously from behind.

She tried to turn the revolver against the Thing upon her, but the gun was twisted from her raw, red fingers. The snow into which she had been precipitated blinded her. She smeared an arm across her eyes, but before clear sight was regained, talon fingers had ripped her shoulders. She was half lifted, half-dragged through the doorway, and there she was dropped on the plank flooring. Her assailant, turning, made to close and bar the door.

When she could see clearly, she perceived a weak illumination in the cabin. On the rough bench-table, shaded by two slabs of bark, burned the stub of a

982 tallow candle probably left by
983 some hunting-party.

984 The windows were curtained
985 with rotting blankets. Some
986 rough furniture lay about; rusted
987 cooking-utensils littered the ta-
988 bles, and at one end was a sheet-
989 iron stove. The place had been
990 equipped after a fashion by deer-
991 hunters or mountain hikers, who
992 brought additional furnishings to
993 the place each year and left
995 mouldy provisions and uncon-
996 sumed firewood behind.

997 The man succeeded finally in
998 closing the door. He turned
999 upon her.

1000 He was short and stocky. The
1001 stolen corduroy coat covered
1002 blacksmith's muscles now made
1003 doubly powerful by dementia.
1004 His hair was lifeless black and
1005 clipped close, prison-fashion.
1006 His low forehead hung over burn-
1007 ing, mismated eyes. From her
1008 helplessness on the floor Cora
1009 McBride stared up at him.

1010 He came closer.

1011 "Get up!" he ordered. "Take
1012 that chair. And don't start no
1013 rough-house; whether you're a
1014 woman or not, I'll drill you!"

1015 She groped to the indicated
1016 chair and raised herself, the sin-
1017 gle snowshoe still dragging from
1018 one foot. Again the man sur-
1019 veyed her. She saw his eyes and
1020 gave another inarticulate cry.

1021 "Shut your mouth and keep it
1022 shut! You hear me?"

1023 She obeyed.

1024 The greenish light burned
1025 brighter in his mismated eyes,
1026 which gazed intently at the top
1027 of her head as though it held
1028 something unearthly.

1029 "Take off your hat!" was his
1030 next command.

1031 She pulled off the toque. Her
1032 hair fell in a mass on her snow-
1033 blotched shoulders. Her captor
1034 advanced upon her. He reached
1035 out and satisfied himself by
1036 touch that something was not
1037 there which he dreaded. In hyp-
1038 notic fear she suffered that touch.
1039 It reassured him.

1040 "Your hair now," he demand-
1041 ed; "it don't stand up, does it?
1042 No, o' course it don't. You ain't
1043 *him;* you're a woman. But if
1044 your hair comes up, I'll kill you
1045 —understand? If your hair
1046 comes up, *I'll kill you!*"

1047 She understood. She under-
1048 stood only too well. She was not
1049 only housed with a murderer;
1050 she was housed with a maniac.
1051 She sensed, also, why he had
1052 come to this mountain shack so
1053 boldly. In his dementia he knew
1054 no better. And she was alone
1055 with him, unarmed now.

1056 "I'll keep it down," she whis-
1057 pered, watching his face out of
1058 fear-distended eyes.

1059 The wind blew one of the rot-
1060 ten blankets inward. Thereby
1061 she knew that the window-aper-
1062 ture on the south wall contained
1063 no sash. He must have removed
1064 it to provide means of escape in
1065 case he were attacked from the
1066 east door. He must have climbed

225

out that window when she came around the shack; that is how he had felled her from behind.

He stepped backward now until he felt the edge of the bench touch his calves. Then he sank down, one arm stretched along the table's rim, the hand clutching the revolver.

"Who are you?" he demanded.

"I'm Cora McB——" She stopped—she recalled in a flash the part her husband had played in his former capture and trial. "I'm Cora Allen," she corrected. Then she waited, her wits in chaos. She was fighting desperately to bring order out of that chaos.

"What you doin' up here?"

"I started for Millington, over the mountain. I lost my way."

"Why didn't you go by the road?"

"It's further."

"That's a lie! It ain't. And don't lie to me, or I'll kill you!"

"Who are you?" she heard herself asking. "And why are you acting this way with me?"

The man leaned suddenly forward.

"You mean to tell me you don't know?"

"A lumberjack, maybe, who's lost his way like myself?"

His expression changed abruptly.

"What you luggin' this for?" He indicated the revolver.

"For protection."

"From what?"

"Wild things."

"There ain't no wild things in these mountains this time o' year; they're snowed up, and you know it."

"I just felt safer to have it along."

"To protect you from menfolks, maybe?"

"There are no men in these mountains I'm afraid of!" She made the declaration with pathetic bravado.

His eyes narrowed.

"I think I better kill you," he decided. "You've seen me; you'll tell you seen me. Why shouldn't I kill you? You'd only tell."

"Why? What have I done to you?" she managed to stammer. "Why should you object to being seen?"

It was an unfortunate demand. He sprang up with a snarl. Pointing the revolver from his hip, he drew back the hammer.

"Don't!" she shrieked. "Are you crazy? Don't you know how to treat a woman—in distress?"

"Distress, hell! You know who I be. And I don't care whether you're a woman or not, I ain't goin' to be took—you understand."

"Certainly I understand."

She said it in such a way that he eased the hammer back into place and lowered the gun. For the moment again she was safe. In response to her terrible need, some of her latent Yankee cour-

1151 age came now to aid her. "I
1152 don't see what you're making all
1153 this rumpus about" she told him
1154 in as indifferent a voice as she
1155 could command. "I don't see
1156 why you should want to kill a
1157 friend who might help you—if
1158 you're really in need of help."

1159 "I want to get to Partridge-
1160 ville," he muttered after a
1161 moment.

1162 "You're not far from there.
1163 How long have you been on the
1164 road?"

1165 "None of your business."

1166 "Have you had any food?"

1167 "No."

1168 "If you'll put up that gun and
1169 let me get off this snowshoe and
1170 pack, I'll share with you some of
1171 the food I have."

1172 "Never you mind what I do
1173 with this gun. Go ahead and fix
1174 your foot, and let's see what you
1175 got for grub." The man re-
1176 sumed his seat.

1177 She twisted up her tangled
1178 hair, replaced her toque and un-
1179 tied the dangling snowshoe.

1180 Outside a tree cracked in the
1181 frost. He started in hairtrigger
1182 fright. Creeping to the window,
1183 he peeped cautiously between
1184 casing and blanket. Convinced
1185 that it was nothing, he returned
1186 to his seat by the table.

1187 "It's too bad we couldn't have
1188 a fire," suggested the woman
1189 then. "I'd make us something
1190 hot." The stove was there,
1191 rusted but still serviceable; avail-
1192 able wood was scattered around.

1193 But the man shook his bullet
1194 head.

1195 After a trying time unfasten-
1196 ing the frosted knots of the ropes
1197 that had bound the knapsack up-
1198 on her back, she emptied it on
1199 to the table. She kept her eye,
1200 however, on the gun. He had
1201 disposed of it by thrusting it in-
1202 to his belt. Plainly she would
1203 never recover it without a
1204 struggle. And she was in no
1205 condition for physical conflict.

1206 "You're welcome to anything
1207 I have," she told him.

1208 "Little you got to say about
1209 it! If you hadn't given it up
1210 I'd took it away from you. So
1211 what's the difference?"

1212 She shrugged her shoulders.
1213 She started around behind him
1214 but he sprang toward her.

1215 "Don't try no monkey-shines
1216 with me!" he snarled. "You
1217 stay here in front where I can
1218 see you."

1219 She obeyed, watching him
1220 make what poor meal he could
1221 from the contents of her bag.

1222 She tried to reason out what
1223 the dénouement of the situation
1224 was to be. He would not send
1225 her away peacefully, for she
1226 knew she dared not risk the story
1227 she would tell regardless of any
1228 promises of secrecy she might
1229 give him. If he left her bound
1230 in the cabin, she would freeze
1231 before help came—if it ever
1232 arrived.

1233 No, either they were going to
1234 leave the place and journey forth

together—the Lord only knew where or with what outcome—or the life of one of them was to end in this tragic place within the coming few minutes. For she realized she must use that gun with deadly effect if it were to come again into her possession.

The silence was broken only by the noises of his lips as he ate ravenously. Outside, not a thing stirred in that snow-bound world. Not a sound of civilization reached them. They were a man and woman in the primal, in civilization and yet a million miles from it.

"The candle's going out," she announced. "Is there another?"

"There'll be light enough for what I got to do," he growled.

Despite her effort to appear indifferent, her great fear showed plainly in her eyes.

"Are we going to stay here all night?" she asked with a pathetic attempt at lightness.

"That's my business."

"Don't you want me to help you?"

"You've helped me all you can with the gun and food."

"If you're going to Partridge-ville, I'd go along and show you the way."

He leaped up.

"Now I know you been lyin'!" he bellowed. "You said you was headed for Millington. And you ain't at all. You're watch-in' your chance to get the drop on me and have me took—that's what you're doin'!"

"Wait!" she pleaded desperately. "I *was* going to Milling-ton. But I'd turn back and show you the way to Partridge-ville to help you."

"What's it to you?" He had drawn the gun from his belt and now was fingering it nervously.

"You're lost up here in the mountains, aren't you?" she said. "I couldn't let you stay lost if it was possible for me to direct you on your way."

"You said you was lost your-self."

"I was lost—until I stumbled into this clearing. That gave me my location."

"Smart, ain't you? Damn smart, but not too smart for me, you woman!" The flare flamed up again in his crooked eyes. "You know who I be, all right. You know what I'm aimin' to do. And you're stallin' for time till you can put one over. But you can't—see? I'll have this busi-ness done with. I'll end this business!"

She felt herself sinking to her knees. He advanced and gripped her left wrist. The crunch of his iron fingers sent an arrow of pain through her arm. It bore her down.

"For God's sake—*don't!*" she whispered hoarsely, over-whelmed with horror. For the cold sharp nose of the revolver suddenly punched her neck.

1318 "I ain't leavin' no traces be-
1319 hind. Might as well be hung for
1320 a sheep as a lamb. Never mind
1321 if I do——"
1322 "Look!" she cried wildly.
1323 "Look, look, *look!*" And with
1324 her free hand she pointed behind
1325 him.

1326 It was an old trick. There
1327 was nothing behind him. But
1328 in that instant of desperation in-
1329 stinct had guided her.

1330 Involuntarily he turned.

1331 With a scream of pain she
1332 twisted from his grasp and blot-
1333 ted out the candle.

1334 A long, livid pencil of orange
1335 flame spurted from the gunpoint.
1336 She sensed the powder-flare in
1337 her face. He had missed.

1338 She scrambled for shelter be-
1339 neath the table. The cabin was
1340 now in inky blackness. Across
1341 that black four more threads of
1342 scarlet light were laced. The
1343 man stumbled about seeking her,
1344 cursing with blood-curdling blas-
1345 phemy.

1346 Suddenly he tripped and went
1347 sprawling. The gun clattered
1348 from his bruised fingers; it
1349 struck the woman's knee.

1350 Swiftly her hand closed upon
1351 it. The hot barrel burned her
1352 palm.

1353 She was on her feet in an in-
1354 stant. Her left hand fumbled in
1355 her blouse, and she found what
1356 had been there all along—the
1357 flash-lamp.

1358 With her back against the
1359 door, she pulled it forth. With

the gun thrust forward for action 1360
she pressed the button. 1361

"I've got the gun—*get up!*" 1362
she ordered. "Don't come too 1363
near me or I'll shoot. Back up 1364
against that wall." 1365

The bull's-eye of radiance 1366
blinded him. When his eyes 1367
became accustomed to the 1368
light, he saw its reflection on 1369
the barrel of the revolver. He 1370
obeyed. 1371

"Put up your hands. Put 'em 1372
up *high!*" 1373

"Suppose I won't?" 1374

"I'll kill you." 1375

"What'll you gain by that?" 1376

"Five thousand dollars." 1377

"Then you know who I be?" 1378

"Yes." 1379

"And was aimin' to take me 1380
in?" 1381

"Yes." 1382

"How you goin' to do that if 1383
I won't go?" 1384

"You're going to find out." 1385

"You won't get no money 1386
shootin' me." 1387

"Yes, I will—just as much— 1388
dead as alive." 1389

With his hands raised a little 1390
way above the level of his shoul- 1391
ders, he stood rigidly at bay in 1392
the circle of light. 1393

"Well," he croaked at last, 1394
"go ahead and shoot. I ain't 1395
aimin' to be took—not by no 1396
woman. Shoot, damn you, and 1397
have it done with. I'm waitin'!" 1398

"Keep up those hands!" 1399

"I won't!" He lowered them 1400
defiantly. "I w-wanted to m- 1401

1402 make Partridgeville and see the
1403 old lady. She'd 'a' helped me.
1404 But anything's better'n goin'
1405 back to that hell where I been
1406 the last two years. Go on! Why
1407 don't you shoot?"

1408 "You wanted to make Par-
1409 tridgeville and see—*who?*"

1410 "My mother—and my wife."

1411 "Have you got a mother?
1412 Have you got a—wife?"

1413 "Yes, and three kids. Why
1414 don't you shoot?"

1415 It seemed an eon that they
1416 stood so. The McBride woman
1417 was trying to find the nerve to
1418 fire. She could not. In that in-
1419 stant she made a discovery that
1420 many luckless souls make too
1421 late: *to kill a man* is easy to talk
1422 about, easy to write about. But
1423 to stand deliberately face to face
1424 with a fellow-human—alive, pul-
1425 sing, breathing, fearing, hoping,
1426 loving, living,—point a weapon
1427 at him that would take his life,
1428 blot him from the earth, negate
1429 twenty or thirty years of child-
1430 hood, youth, maturity, and make
1431 of him in an instant—nothing!—
1432 that is quite another matter.

1433 He was helpless before her
1434 now. Perhaps the expression on
1435 his face had something to do
1436 with the sudden revulsion that
1437 halted her finger. Facing cer-
1438 tain death, some of the evil in
1439 those crooked eyes seemed to die
1440 out, and the terrible personality
1441 of the man to fade. Regardless
1442 of her danger, regardless of what
1443 he would have done to her if luck

1444 had not turned the tables, Cora
1445 McBride saw before her only
1446 a lone man with all society's
1447 hand against him, realizing he
1448 had played a bad game to the
1449 limit and lost, two big tears
1450 creeping down his unshaved face,
1451 waiting for the end.

1452 "Three children!" she whis-
1453 pered faintly.

1454 "Yes."

1455 "You're going back to see
1456 them?"

1457 "Yes, and my mother. Moth-
1458 er'd help me get to Canada—
1459 somehow."

1460 Cora McBride had forgotten
1461 all about the five thousand dol-
1462 lars. She was stunned by the
1463 announcement that this man had
1464 relatives—a mother, a wife, *three*
1465 babies. The human factor had
1466 not before occurred to her. Mur-
1467 derers! They have no license to
1468 let their eyes well with tears, to
1469 have wives and babies, to possess
1470 mothers who will help them get
1471 to Canada regardless of what
1472 their earthly indiscretions may
1473 have been.

1474 At this revelation the gun-
1475 point wavered. The sight of
1476 those tears on his face sapped
1477 her will-power even as a wound
1478 in her breast might have drained
1479 her life-blood.

1480 Her great moment had been
1481 given her. She was letting it slip
1482 away. She had her reward in
1483 her hand for the mere pulling of
1484 a trigger and no incrimination
1485 for the result. For a bit of

1486 human sentiment she was bung-
1487 ling the situation unpardonably,
1488 fatally.

1489 Why did she not shoot? Be-
1490 cause she was a woman. Be-
1491 cause it is the God-given purpose
1492 of womanhood to give life, not
1493 take it.

1494 The gun sank, sank—down
1495 out of the light, down out of
1496 sight.

1497 And the next instant he was
1498 upon her.

1499 The flash-lamp was knocked
1500 from her hand and blinked out.
1501 It struck the stove and she heard
1502 the tinkle of the broken lens.
1503 The woman's hand caught at the
1504 sacking before the window at her
1505 left shoulder. Gripping it wild-
1506 ly to save herself from that on-
1507 slaught, she tore it away. For
1508 the second time the revolver was
1509 twisted from her raw fingers.

1510 The man reared upward, over
1511 her.

1512 "Where are you?" he roared
1513 again and again. "I'll show
1514 you! Lemme at you!"

1515 Outside the great yellow moon
1516 of early winter, arising late, was
1517 coming up over the silhouetted
1518 line of purple mountains to the
1519 eastward. It illumined the cab-
1520 in with a faint radiance, disclos-
1521 ing the woman crouching be-
1522 neath the table.

1523 The man saw her, pointed his
1524 weapon point-blank at her face
1525 and fired.

1526 To Cora McBride, prostrate
1527 there in her terror, the impact of
the bullet felt like the blow of a 1528
stick upon her cheek-bone rock- 1529
ing her head. Her cheek felt 1530
warmly numb. She pressed a 1531
quick hand involuntarily against 1532
it, and drew it away sticky with 1533
blood. 1534

Click! Click! Click! 1535

Three times the revolver 1536
mechanism was worked to ac- 1537
complish her destruction. But 1538
there was no further report. 1539
The cylinder was empty. 1540
"Oh, God!" the woman 1541
moaned. "I fed you and offered 1542
to help you. I refused to shoot 1543
you because of your mother— 1544
your wife—your babies. And 1545
yet you——" 1546

"Where's your cartridges?" he 1547
cried wildly. "You got more; 1548
gimme that belt!" 1549

She felt his touch upon her. 1550
His crazy fingers tried to un- 1551
button the clasp of the belt and 1552
holster. But he could secure 1553
neither while she fought him. 1554
He pinioned her at length with 1555
his knee. His fingers secured a 1556
fistful of the cylinders from her 1557
girdle, and he opened the cham- 1558
ber of the revolver. 1559

She realized the end was but a 1560
matter of moments. Nothing 1561
but a miracle could save her now. 1562

Convulsively she groped about 1563
for something with which to 1564
strike. Nothing lay within reach 1565
of her bleeding fingers, however, 1566
but a little piece of dried sapling. 1567
She tried to struggle loose, but 1568
the lunatic held her mercilessly. 1569

1570 He continued the mechanical
1571 loading of the revolver.

1572 The semi-darkness of the hut,
1573 the outline of the moon afar
1574 through the uncurtained window
1575 —these swam before her. . . .
1576 Suddenly her eyes riveted on
1577 that curtainless window and she
1578 uttered a terrifying cry.

1579 Ruggam turned.

1580 Outlined in the window aper-
1581 ture against the low-hung moon
1582 *Martin Wiley, the murdered*
1583 *deputy, was staring into the*
1583 *cabin!*

1584 From the fugitive's throat
1585 came a gurgle. Some of the
1586 cartridges he held spilled to the
1587 flooring. Above her his figure
1588 became rigid. There was no
1589 mistaking the identity of the ap-
1590 parition. They saw the man's
1591 hatless head and some of his
1592 neck. They saw his dark pom-
1593 padour and the outline of his
1594 skull. As that horrible silhou-
1595 ette remained there, Wiley's
1596 pompadour lifted slightly as it
1597 had done in life.

1598 The cry in the convict's throat
1599 broke forth into words.

1600 "Mart Wiley!" he cried, "Mart
1601 Wiley! *Mart—Wiley!*"

1602 Clear, sharp, distinct was the
1603 shape of that never-to-be-for-
1604 gotten pompadour against the
1605 disk of the winter moon. His
1606 features could not be discerned,
1607 for the source of light was be-
1608 hind him, but the silhouette was
1609 sufficient. It was Martin Wiley;
1610 he was alive. His head and his

1611 wirelike hair were moving—ris-
1612 ing, falling.

1613 Ruggam, his eyes riveted upon
1614 the phantom, recoiled mechani-
1615 cally to the western wall. He
1616 finished loading the revolver by
1617 the sense of touch. Then:

1618 Spurt after spurt of fire lanced
1619 the darkness, directed at the
1620 Thing in the window. While the
1621 air of the hut reeked with the
1622 acrid smoke, the echo of the
1623 volley sounded through the
1624 silent forest-world miles away.

1625 But the silhouette in the win-
1626 dow remained.

1627 Once or twice it moved slightly
1628 as though in surprise; that was
1629 all. The pompadour rose in
1630 bellicose retaliation—the gesture
1631 that had always ensued when
1632 Wiley was angered or excited.
1633 But to bullets fired from an
1634 earthly gun the silhouette of
1635 the murdered deputy's ghost,
1636 arisen in these winter woods
1637 to prevent another slaughter,
1638 was impervious.

1639 Ruggam saw; he shrieked. He
1640 broke the gun and spilled out the
1641 empty shells. He fumbled in
1642 more cartridges, locked the bar-
1643 rel and fired again and again,
1644 until once more it was empty.

1645 Still the apparition remained.

1646 The man in his dementia
1647 hurled the weapon; it struck the
1648 sash and caromed off, hitting the
1649 stove. Then Hap Ruggam col-
1650 lapsed upon the floor.

1651 The woman sprang up. She
1652 found the rope thongs which had

1653 bound her pack to her shoulders.
1654 With steel-taut nerves, she rolled
1655 the insensible Ruggam over.
1656 She tied his hands; she tied
1657 his ankles. With her last bit of
1658 rope she connected the two bind-
1659 ings tightly behind him so that
1660 if he recovered, he would be at
1661 her mercy. Her task accom-
1662 plished, on her knees beside his
1663 prone figure, she thought to
1664 glance up at the window.
1665 Wiley's ghost had disappeared.
1666 Sheriff Crumpett and his party
1667 broke into the Lyons clearing
1668 within an hour. They had ar-
1669 rived in answer to five successive
1670 shots given a few moments apart,
1671 the signal agreed upon. The
1672 mystery to them, however, was
1673 that those five shots had been
1674 fired by some one not of their
1675 party.
1676 The sheriff and his men found
1677 the McBride woman, her cloth-

1678 ing half torn from her body, her
1679 features powder-marked and
1680 blood-stained; but she was game
1681 to the last, woman-fashion weep-
1682 ing only now that all was over.
1683 They found, too, the man they
1684 had combed the country to find—
1685 struggling fruitlessly in his
1686 bonds, her prisoner.
1687 And they likewise found the
1688 miracle.
1689 On the snow outside under the
1690 window they came upon a black
1691 porcupine about the size of a
1692 man's head which, scenting food
1693 within the cabin, had climbed to
1694 the sill, and after the habit of
1695 these little animals whose num-
1696 ber is legion all over the Green
1697 Mountains, had required fifteen
1698 bullets pumped into its carcass
1699 before it would release its hold.
1700 Even in death its quills were
1701 raised in uncanny duplication
1702 of Mart Wiley's pompadour.

The Analysis

This story contains all told 1702 lines. Of this number 659 lines are presented to the reader before he comes to the attempts or struggles which make up the Body of the Story. Of particular interest to readers is the arrangement of the first 108 lines. The main narrative problem of this story is, "Can Cora McBride capture Hap Ruggam?" The difficulties lying in her way are that she is herself weak and out of condition, and that there is between her and the place where she may hope to find the murderer, a snow covered wilderness. The dangerous opposition is clearly foreshadowed in the fact that Hap Ruggam is a murderer, who having killed twice will not hesitate to kill again, and this in itself constitutes the threat of disaster.

All this would have been made clear to the reader in that portion of the story which begins on line 109 and ends on line 659, but it is obvious that the first 108 lines are a Flash-back from line 1072, and that the happenings shown from lines 1 to 108 took place after the happenings which open on line 109. Yet it clearly is not a typical Flash-back Beginning because it does not open, as such a Beginning should, with the main narrative question, and flash-back to the explanatory matter necessary to a reader's understanding of that main narrative question's importance.

In point of time it comes not only after these, but after the actual Conclusive Act which ends the story by answering the main narrative question. That Act is clear on lines 1651 to 1665 where Cora McBride is shown tying up her victim.

There is only one division of the story which can follow the Conclusive Act; that division is the Sequel. From lines 1666 to 1702 where the sheriff's party find Cora McBride in the cabin, and find also the explanation of the face in the window, the category is Sequel. Lines 1 to 108 are, in point of time, a continuation from line 1702. The flash-back in this case, therefore, consists in splitting up the Sequel, so that a portion of it is presented in the responses of the sheriff to the receipt of the letter from C. V. D. Wylie, in lines 1 to 85, and between the sheriff and Joseph on lines 86 to 108.

The question instantly arising in the mind of a reader is, "What purpose is gained by such a method of flash-back?" The ordinary gain through the typical flash-back method is a gain in interest through presenting the main problem before the explanatory matter. In this case, however, no such gain can occur because the typical method is not used. There is, besides interest, however, another consideration in the presentation of a story. It is the consideration of plausibility. The more extraordinary the conclusion at which a reader arrives, the greater is the author's necessity for preparing his mind for its acceptance. The explanation of the porcupine was a strain upon the credulity of any reader, therefore Mr. Pelley anticipated this lack of credulity by explaining that it was one of the Lord's miracles. And, being wise in the ways of craftsmanship, he caused this explanation to come from the mouth of a character, rather than to make the statement as author. He did what lawyers do in cases where their clients are in danger of being disbelieved. He called in character witnesses. First, he has the letter from the men in which he says he thinks the woman deserves the reward, and has earned it; and then he brings in the testimony of the sheriff, who is a high-minded person, to add further plausibility.

The main condition is set forth on lines 109 to 299 in an interchange between the editor and his assistants. The fifth step is on lines 300 to 320 which shows the effect upon the actors or observers.

Following this comes the interchange between Cora McBride and Duncan. Thus he follows out the regular formula of presenting the condition or state of affairs and following it with the reaction of the main actor toward that condition.

There are, in the final analysis, only three kinds of struggles in which a character may engage. The first is a mental struggle; that is, a struggle between two different traits in the same character, one of which is urging on the purpose and the other of which is opposing that purpose. The second kind of struggle is an attempt to overcome a force of nature. The third kind of attempt is a struggle between man and man. It may be, of course, between man and woman, as it is in this particular story.

All three kinds of obstacles, mental, natural, and human, occur in this story, and lend to the main narrative question its importance and interest. On lines 515 to 659 there occurs a mental interchange, in which the desire of Cora McBride to achieve the capture of Hap Ruggam is opposed by other traits in her character. As a result of this interchange the main narrative purpose is apparent.

The Body of the story is contained in lines 660 to 1650. The attempt to overcome a difficulty which occupies line 660 to 957 is not presented as a struggle between the girl and the elements, but the effect of it was shown quite as effectively by the appearance of the girl after the struggle is over. It is interesting to note that although this attempt is successful insofar as it enables her to reach the spot where the murderer is, the sense of furtherance is almost imperceptible, and is instantly followed by the sense of a dramatic hindrance, when the reader realizes that the girl is exhausted and that tracks lead into the cabin.

In the struggle between Cora McBride and the man, Hap Ruggam, I have made three divisions; one from line 958 to 1370; the second from line 1371 to 1496; the third from 1497 to 1583. I have done this because the first division is an actual complete attempt resulting in a definite crisis of furtherance, on line 1370 when Cora secures the gun. It then ceases to be a scene of physical struggle and it becomes a scene of oral struggle between the man and the woman. From lines 1371 to 1496 this oral struggle continues, and results in a crisis of dramatic hindrance which is very effective because the woman finds that she cannot take away a life. Then line 1497 to 1583 constitute still another scene, because it is the attempt, a quite separate and distinct one, of Hap Ruggam to kill Cora McBride, the result of which is to form a brand new condition or state of affairs on lines 1582 to 1583, when Hap Ruggam has to abandon his attempt because he becomes aware of what appears to him to be the face of Martin Wylie, the murdered deputy, staring into the cabin through the window.

On lines 1584 to 1650 the reader is made aware of the fifth step of that interchange between Ruggam and Cora. It produces a furtherance and changes the condition to one which enables Cora to take advantage of the insensibility of Hap Ruggam to capture him.

The weakness in this story is that the solution is brought about by a coincidence. Strictly speaking, the short-story should show a character in a position where he has to act in order to solve a problem, and the solution should be brought about through some trait in the character, or by some capacity which the character possesses. The grave objection to having a coincidence used for a solution is that it places upon the author the necessity for making this coincidence plausible. Mr. Pelley has used a very clever device in achieving this plausibility, and for that reason I have included the story and have recommended it to those authors who find difficulty with such a problem.

While I am upon this subject of coincidence I might take the opportunity to say that there is a belief on the part of many students of the short-story form that a coincidence should never be used in a short-story. This is not at all the case. You may use coincidence as freely as you like to get your character into trouble, to bring about a main condition, or to create hindrances at the conclusion of the scenes in the Body of your story. The coincidence is not desirable as a solution of the problem, for the reason that most readers who read a story, and who find themselves in a predicament similar to that of the main actor of the story will feel cheated if they find, at the conclusion of the story, that the only way out of such a predicament is by the use of coincidence. That does not open for them a way to solve a similar problem.

But apart from this use of coincidence, the story *The Face in the Window* will be a very interesting model for those authors who wish to develop the promises of conflict which are contained in the Beginning of their story. Particularly so they will find it if they are interested in that particular portion of the story which presents the actor at a point where disaster is imminent, for there is no doubt that it would be very difficult to formulate a condition more dramatically filled with the threat of ultimate disaster than the position in which Cora McBride finds herself, when, at the mercy of this maniac murderer, she is unable to shoot him, because she cannot bring herself to take life.

BEGINNING	Initial condition is set forth.	Meeting. Verena Dayson and Condition.	1– 37	Tragedy implied.
		Flash-back Interchange. City Editor and Mr. Dark. (An author flash-back.)	38– 109	Dramatic Crises of Plot are apparent to reader.
		(5th step of 38–109.) Verena's reaction to condition projected by announcement of Mr. Dark's arrival	110– 400	
	Main Actor's main purpose is presented.	This contains, within it, two flash-backs. (A. Buck and Verena, lines 243–297.) (B. Verena and hypothetical interviewer, lines 298–378.)		Main Narrative Question: "Can Verena recapture her husband?
		Scene. Mr. Dark and Verena Dayson.	401–1119	
BODY	Main Actor engages in series of attempts to achieve purpose.	Scene. Verena and Buck. She attempts to make him jealous. He is unimpressed. Included here (lines 1183–1221) is a flash-back to previous evening. Buck and Mrs. Sennay.	1120–1269	Hindrance.
		(5th step. Effect upon Verena. Goes about her business.)	1270–1400	
		Scene. Verena and Buck. She tries to impress by her new wardrobe. He is indifferent.	1401–1557	Hindrance.
		Scene. Verena and Buck. She tries to impress him by her conversation. He is bored. (5th step. Effect.) Verena and Mr. Dark.	1558–1637 / 1638–1746	Hindrance. Dramatic Hindrance.
BODY	Attempts (Continued)	Interchange. Verena and Mrs. Sennay. Verena and Buck. Verena, noticing that Buck looks liked a roped steer gets idea for solution. New condition projected.	1747–1925	Curiosity aroused.
		Interchange. Verena enlists aid of Mr. Dark.	1926–1961	Curiosity unsatisfied.
		Scene. Final attempt. Verena and Buck.	1962–2200	
ENDING	Conclusive Act. Sequel.	He put out a dazed hand to his wife.	2200–2201	Answer to Narrative Question is "Yes."
		Buck and Verena.	2202–2259	Effect upon actors.

WESTERN STUFF

BY MARY BRECHT PULVER

LEST I seem to be harping too much upon the necessity for writers to possess the ability to employ the "flash-back" method, I shall say that the peculiar variant of this method used by Mary Brecht Pulver is not my only reason for including this story, although I shall discuss this feature of it.

My chief reason for reprinting this story is that it shows the ingenuity of a competent craftsman in dealing with material which at first glance would seem to possess little scope for original adaptation. I refer to the initial Condition or State of Affairs which confronts the main actor in this story—that state of affairs which is commonly called a "situation," but which we refer to throughout this volume as a "condition."

It presents Verena Dayson, the rodeo queen, at the moment when she realizes that her husband has become enamoured of another woman. Because such a condition might be treated as a starting point for a narrative problem of either accomplishment or decision, I am including this story, in which the problem projected is one of accomplishment, in order to use it as a foil against another story, appearing later in this volume, in which the same initial condition is used to project a story in which the main narrative problem is one of decision.

CASE No. 10

WESTERN STUFF

BY MARY BRECHT PULVER

Although it was five minutes to two and the man from the Sunday *Tribune* due on the hour, Verena Dayson, the rodeo queen, still lay face down upon her bed, just as she had flung herself in a straight head-to-toe line, the way a stick is thrown, when she had come into the room ten minutes before, slamming the door so violently the water bottle and glass on the dresser clicked their heels in salute, the pens on the enameled desk leaped in their glass sockets, the wastebasket fell over and the Princesse de Lamballe, in pastel colors on the wall, assumed an angle of forty degrees.

Into her pillow had dived the rodeo queen with the muscular plunge and address of one of the Bar-K boys bull-dogging a Texas yearling. The pillow hadn't a chance. But directly it was thrown and subjected, it ceased to be a steer and became a comforting mother in whose relaxing embrace the queen had now for some time been uttering what she would have described as some wild coyote howls.

"Wrong! Wrong! Wrong!" she lay weeping. "All wrong from A to Zed! What am I going to do now—and how am I going to do it?"

Whatever emotion she expressed would probably not have been lightened had she overheard Mr. Blivens, the city editor, handing out an assignment some twenty minutes earlier.

"I want you," said Mr. Blivens, addressing one of those young minions of his who snapped like rubber bands, in any given direction, "to go down to the McAlpin and interview this rope-and-riding woman, Mrs. Buck Dayson, who's been here all week with the Dayson outfit on their way back to the West from Wembley. They're off the front page now, but what I want is a feature article for the woman's section, from the woman's viewpoint. I understand Buck Dayson and his wife never peel off any inside dope like this

61 —that it's all cooked up, what
62 the public gets. 'Bout as easy
63 to catch 'em off guard as squeez-
64 ing blood from a turnip.

65 "But I've got a line that Mrs.
66 Dayson'll talk. There's some
67 kind of new policy on, I guess.
68 Buck Dayson makes all his own
69 contracts, and has always han-
70 dled publicity; but I hear this
71 Sennay woman who did the pub-
72 licity for the movie actress
73 Blanche Markhouse—that spec-
74 tacular kidnaping of hers—has
75 persuaded him that her services
76 are valuable and is going to work
77 for his show. Any stuff that
78 Violet Sennay might offer is dis-
79 tinctly what we do not want.
80 Slide to it, and catch the lady off
81 first, before Sennay gets in her
82 divine touch. The hour is two.
83 Remember, she's the real rope-
84 and-riding goods, the genuine
85 cowgirl queen born in the saddle
86 —her lifelong game. Never kiss-
87 es a cow under a thousand dol-
88 lars. Still, she must have a
89 human side. Anyhow, go tackle
90 her. She's about as big as a
91 minute, I hear, and is probably
92 a leathery, stringy little piece of
93 dried beef. But you can dress
94 her up. Call the stuff Jelly Bags
95 and Saddle Bags if you like, or
96 a Cowgirl Madonna—there are
97 some kids in the offing. Any-
98 way, slide."

99 "I'll slide," said the minion.
100 His name was Stanley Dark.

101 He was sliding now, coming
102 slowly up in the hydraulic ele-
103 vator to the cream-enamel-and-
104 pink-brocade apartment occu-
105 pied by Mr. and Mrs. Buck
106 Dayson on their short vacation
107 in New York, en route from
108 France and England to the
109 great uncharted spaces.

110 Mr. Dark's announcement of
111 himself by phone had driven
112 Verena from her recumbent po-
113 sition. One glance at her wrist
114 watch, one final yip of misery
115 and she began preparing to re-
116 ceive him. You don't live a life
117 dependent on schedule, on the
118 call boy's summons, without
119 learning to conceal a carking
120 secret sorrow, however terrible.

121 She saw that she would require
122 some camouflage. Her hat,
123 bought earlier in the morning in
124 New York's Rue de la Paix on
125 Fifty-seventh Street, was man-
126 gled; her face a mass of sodden
127 blobs. She straightened her
128 small frankly sun-tanned visage,
129 dusted it with powder, adding a
130 little hasty writing on her lips
131 from a newly procured gold pen-
132 cil—and at once erased this.

133 "What's the use?" she sighed.
134 "It only makes me look like a
135 sugared cruller trimmed with
136 currant jelly. I always feel, any-
137 how, like a fresh-branded steer
138 when I clap the red-hot iron on
139 me."

140 And realizing that she had an
141 extra minute before Mr. Dark
142 would report, she went and stood
143 by the open window and let the
144 May air blow in on her hot cheeks.

145 Below, she could see New
146 York if she craned and bent a
147 little. Above, a narrow panel of
148 pale insipid blue; lower down,
149 vast plunging levels of architec-
150 tural structure, colored with odd
151 geometrical shafts of shifting
152 gray-and-lavender light, with
153 here and there a transverse plane
154 of unobstructed yellow sun; and
155 far, far below, a million teeming
156 pygmy dark forms rushing on
157 remote, ludicrous errands, foam-
158 ing like disturbed ants, from
159 Sixth Avenue and Broadway in-
160 to Thirty-fourth Street. Into
161 her ear poured the voice that is
162 New York—a blend of horns,
163 whistles, sirens, pounding feet,
164 rumbling trucks, street calls,
165 ambulances, fire signals, trolley
166 bells, crashing Elevated, tube
167 and Subway vibration of shaken
168 earth, the architectonic response
169 of vast buildings, keyed to vari-
170 ous chords; a volume of sound
171 in which a feminine crying spell
172 amounted to nothing whatever;
173 a heartless crowd in which one
174 woman's heartache, purposes,
175 acts, dwindled to nil. Yet it was
176 funny, reflected Mrs. Buck Day-
177 son, with a little sniffle, how
178 important they remained—to
179 your own self.

180 Recalled, she tore her eyes
181 away from New York and picked
182 up an oblong black hand bag
183 from her dresser, opened it and
184 drew out a worn and creased
185 paper from one side. It was a
186 draft of a fictitious newspaper
187 interview. Buck had prepared
188 it for her a year ago, in case she
189 should be beset.

190 Buck never allowed her to give
191 out interviews. He attended to
192 this himself, just as he looked
193 after the business end of the
194 whole game so competently—or
195 had before his mind had softened
196 in this strange new way. He had
197 given her this paper right after
198 Wembley—prepared very care-
199 fully, based on his own experi-
200 ences and idea of expediency.
201 Buck was good at this, and thor-
202 ough, as he was in everything.
203 He had worked it out carefully
204 —helped by a man they had met
205 in London and played round
206 with a lot; a Major Niles, with a
207 handsome black mustache—
208 dyed, Buck declared—who had
209 been in oil, he claimed, and cer-
210 tainly a lot of it had stuck to his
211 manner; and who, being a fellow
212 American, given to sprightly red
213 ties and a marvelous vocabulary,
214 had dogged Buck's heels consid-
215 erably—or until he had got fifty
216 dollars off Buck. It was the
217 vocabulary that made Buck
218 patient.

219 Years ago, before they were
220 married, Buck was known as
221 the educated cowboy, and it
222 was a fact that even now he
223 was reading—though slowly
224 —the Five-Foot Shelf.

225 Buck loved big words. He
226 liked to get them off himself,
227 surprising people. It impressed
228 them, combined with his tall dark

229 good looks and careless out-of-
230 doors virility. Take this word
231 "hypothetical" that he had
232 caught off Major Niles last year.
233 Buck had gone crazy over it for
234 a while, and used it everywhere.
235 Verena unfolded the yellow
236 creased paper in her hand.
237 Buck had had it ticked off by
238 a typist at the Savoy.
239 "Hypothetical interview," she
240 read, "between Mrs. Buck Day-
241 son and hypothetical reporter
242 from news daily."
243 "Carry it with you in case the
244 write-up boys catch you when
245 your papa ain't around, honey,"
246 Buck had said; "keep as near as
247 you can to it. It may be a life
248 preserver."
249 What Buck meant exactly
250 was—for she had a good brain
251 and a native shrewdness of her
252 own—that it might preserve
253 what he called the beans of
254 privacy from being spilled. Buck
255 had a fierce love of privacy, a
256 staunch, almost savage desire
257 for the preservation of their
258 family sanctity.
259 "No use letting the public
260 fondle the camp cots and the
261 chuck wagon, honey. We've
262 got a right to an unmolested
263 family life. I'm a family man,
264 and that's the way I want it.
265 It's our work alone—our public
266 stuff they got a right to know
267 about. It's good enough too.
268 Our work stands on its own."
269 It truly did. All through the
270 West, and through those vast

271 reaches where those—to Eastern
272 ears—bewildering terms,
273 "butte," "mesa," "alfalfa,"
274 "arroyos," "canyon," "cactus,"
275 "gulch," and the like, forgather,
276 a region the most conservative
277 Cape Cod citizen will admit
278 holds connoisseurs in these
279 matters, the Daysons, known
280 friendly-wise as Buck and
281 Verena, were famed in rodeos,
282 stampedes, frontier days, as two
283 of the ridingest kids that ever
284 came out of Lochinvar's country.
285 Spectacular of achievement!
286 What need had they of undue
287 intimacy with an inquisitive
288 public? Hence Buck's cautious
289 hypothetical interview.
290 "Remember, honey, the boys
291 mostly begin on the same ques-
292 tion. If you hand it all back pat
293 and copious, fill 'em up pretty
294 good with what I'm told they
295 call a stickful of talk, mebbe
296 they won't have any room left
297 for the other stuff."
298 Verena read:

299 HYPOTHETICAL REPORTER:
300 Mrs. Dayson, what are your
301 impressions of London? Paris?
302 New York?—as the case may be.
303 MRS. DAYSON: My impres-
304 sion of London, Paris, New
305 York—as the case may be—is
306 that it is one of the largest, most
307 remarkable cities I have ever
308 visited. In fact, I think one of
309 the largest, most remarkable
310 cities in the world. We of the
311 West are apt to build a high

312 ideal of the great cities of the
313 world, and my experience has
314 been no different. But I was
315 agreeably surprised in what I
316 have found. Your city im-
317 presses me as attractive, un-
318 usual and filled with interesting
319 sights. It is one of the most
320 interesting places I have ever
321 seen. I am delighted to be in
322 your midst.

323 HYPOTHETICAL REPORTER:
324 Mrs. Dayson, what is your im-
325 pression of our people here in
326 London? Paris? New York?—
327 as the case may be.

328 MRS. DAYSON: It is almost
329 too soon to digest and coördinate
330 my impressions of the many
331 types I have seen here in
332 London, Paris, New York—as
333 the case may be—but I can
334 truly say that I find your street
335 crowds remarkable and very
336 interesting. Your men impress
337 me with their manner, your
338 women have a way that is all
339 their own. I find them all
340 interesting. I am delighted to
341 be in their midst. (*To be added
342 if just leaving country, for Buck
343 had not forgotten the princes who
344 shook his hand at Wembley:*)
345 Individually, I cannot express
346 too highly my pleasure in meet-
347 ing your leading people here. I
348 found their Royal Highnesses,
349 Poincaré, Mayor Hylan—as the
350 case may be—most simple and
351 unaffected in their interest in
352 the work we are doing. I have
353 been received most graciously.

354 I was delighted to be in their
355 midst.

356 HYPOTHETICAL REPORTER:
357 Mrs. Dayson, what are your own
358 impressions of the Far West
359 which you have left behind
359 you?

360 MRS. DAYSON: The Far West
361 is not what it once was. Modern
362 progress, with its hydraulic en-
363 gineering, our wonderful me-
364 chanical improvements, the
365 mighty strides we have made in
366 elimination of time and space,
367 have obliterated those earlier,
368 ruder practices that tradition
369 knows as the Wild West. The
370 amelioration of those primitive
371 conditions which fostered the
372 practices and acts of the pioneer
373 settlers and early cattlemen
374 naturally affected it. Yet that
375 this tradition still exists, if only
376 in a hypothetical state, is at-
377 tested by our own work here in
378 your midst——

379 "The hell!" Verena choked
380 suddenly.

381 The word would have cost her
382 just one dollar's fine off her
383 weekly increment if Buck Day-
384 son had heard it, with his strict
385 ideals of womanly purity of
386 language and ladylike behavior.
387 Only, of course, now Buck was
388 not here to hear it. He
389 usually wasn't—not since his
390 mind had begun to soften.

391 There was a tap on the sitting-
392 room door. Verena tore the
393 hypothetical interview in two.

394 "Buck Dayson," she cried,
395 "I won't pay any attention!
396 You've gone your way—and I'm
397 going mine. I don't know where
398 the trail leads, but I guess it
399 points, first off, to this reporter
400 boy."

401 Even without a hypothetical
402 interview to guide us, most of
403 us would agree with Mrs. Day-
404 son that the West is not what it
405 once was. The coming of barbed
406 wire, irrigation, good roads and
407 automobiles has altered it for-
408 ever. Most of us, of the East,
409 have been out—in the last-
410 named—to have a look at what
411 is left, and we think we know.
412 Where the two-gun he-men of
413 an earlier, hairier era, mixed in
414 over their bald-face whisky,
415 where the pallid glassy-cheeked
416 dealer in faro took his guilty
417 profits in the red-blooded dives
418 of sin in the primitive settle-
419 ments, there stands now rank
420 upon rank of stucco apartment
421 houses like magnificent layer
422 cakes, with at least one five-
423 tube heterodyne and one pair of
424 golf pants per layer.

425 But there still are three strong-
426 holds of the old tradition. Holly-
427 wood—where men still are men
428 —where it's better to smile when
429 you say it, where virility still
430 snatches virtue from the arms
431 of villainy and bad men get their
432 just deserts from diamond-back
433 rattler or a poisoned pool as they
434 make a last crawl on their mis-
435 guided bellies across an equally

436 bad land; dude ranches, where
437 the West is organized as a
438 pattern for Eastern education;
439 and the famous rope-and-riding
440 outfits that follow the line of the
441 big rodeos and stampedes from
442 Calgary to the Mexican border
443 as the season alters, and who
444 conserve the brilliant art of the
445 older days at its best.

446 All this was well known to Mr.
447 Stanley Dark as he rode up
448 pensively on the hydraulic-pres-
449 sure elevator to see Mrs. Dayson,
450 and it bored him a great deal.
451 He had a poor opinion of this
452 Wild West stuff, anyhow. His
453 interests lay much deeper. Al-
454 though he was a hard-working
455 commonplace young reporter
456 outwardly, he led his own
457 magnificent interior life like a
458 great many of us, and with him
459 it was an affair of strong and
460 primal values only. The super-
461 ficial aspects of life did not
462 intrigue him, although he now
463 secured a living by interviews for
464 the Sunday supplement.

465 An aldermanic meeting, the
466 opening of a garbage-disposal
467 plant or the inspecting of a
468 drowned babe in the morgue—
469 he made his bread by this; but
470 what interested him really was,
471 briefly, human passion; primitive
472 feeling as it works itself out in an
473 inexorable track.

474 He had in fact just sent into
475 a competition a little one-act
476 drama of human passions called
477 Lust Below the Willows, and he

478 had it in mind to do shortly a
479 subjective poetic tragedy bearing
480 on the early love-life and frustra-
481 tions of Shakespere's three *Weird*
482 *Sisters*, and the emotional states
483 that had reduced them to the
484 condition in which the Bard
485 was able to use them for his
486 purpose. He was a very wise
487 young man, the son of a minister
488 in a little town called Coshecton,
489 with a widowed mother and two
490 young sisters he adored; but he
491 was very modern, which is why
492 the West bored him. He knew
493 that muscular activity, sunlight
494 and ozone are inimical to the
495 subjective emotional states he
496 so admired.

497 As he tapped on Verena Day-
498 son's door, he took off his hat
499 and sighed, under the pressure
500 of his expectation and boredom.
501 He knew what to expect from
502 Mr. Blivens' little leathery piece
503 of dried beef. She would be all
504 that; and she would wear a badly
505 made divided skirt, vaquero's
506 boots, a white lingerie shirt
507 waist, a green or magenta-
508 colored neckerchief, a bead neck-
509 lace, and perhaps a sugar-loaf
510 hat.

511 But as the door opened, he
512 was startled to see none of this.
513 He was looking at one of the
514 prettiest little girls imaginable;
515 twenty-two or three at most,
516 with a tiny, sturdy, but graceful
517 figure. Above this looked back
518 at him a small, sweet, whole-
519 some sun-cured face whose

520 shapely nose was decorated in
521 a light spatterwork of ingenuous
522 freckles, whose round cheeks
523 were the color of two June wild
524 roses, whose round blue eyes,
525 trimmed with long, dark, curling
526 lashes, frankly moist, were as
527 blue as the Arizona heavens, and
528 the whole framed with a swinging
529 aureole of short, curly, sun-
530 kissed hair whose undulation had
531 no need of the permanent-wave
532 octopus and appeared to have
533 been dipped in liquid gilt. More-
534 over, the ensemble was dressed
535 in strictly Eastern garments,
536 in the most expensive-looking
537 and most horribly arranged
538 combination he had ever seen
539 on a woman. One concedes a
540 certain art, as in an auto-
541 mobile, in assembling the com-
542 ponents of costume.

543 "How do you do?" said Mrs.
544 Buck Dayson. "I guess you
545 must be from the *Tribune*. Mr.
546 Dark? Will you step in and find
547 yourself a chair?"

548 Mr. Dark stepped in with
549 alacrity.

550 "You know," he said, "you
551 are amazingly different from
552 what I expected."

553 "Oh, I'm amazing all right—
554 I can see that myself! Just what
555 were you looking for? May
556 be——"

557 "Well," said Mr. Dark, with
558 a little grin, "I expected to see
559 the Wild West, I guess."

560 "Well, you're seeing the West,
561 all right—and I s'pose you might

562 call it wild." A faint quiver
563 moved Mrs. Dayson's voice.
564 "At least I must be, to see you
565 at all. It has been the policy of
566 my husb—of Buck Dayson—of
567 Mr. Henry B. Dayson—who
568 I am married to, always to take
569 interviews with the reporters
570 and never to let me say any-
571 thing. We decided that before
572 —quite a while ago—when he was
573 around more. But I am going
574 to talk to you now," added Mrs.
575 Dayson firmly, "and you may
576 ask me anything. There are
577 just three things I won't answer:
578 How do I like New York? What
579 do I think of your people here?
580 And what is my impression of
581 the Far West?"
582 That, Mr. Dark explained,
583 was farthest from his intention,
584 and he set forth Mr. Blivens'
585 request for human-interest stuff
586 for women readers as persua-
587 sively as possible.
588 "I was going to call my article
589 A Madonna of the Saddle, but I
590 —I should like to change it to
591 Beauty and Her Beasts. Really I
592 should, Mrs. Dayson." Mr.
593 Dark showed his very good
594 teeth affably. "You see," he
595 swept on, "all that I know of
596 you is the figure which, as you
597 say, your husband has allowed
598 to appear in the public mind.
599 The professional woman rider
600 and rope artist, standing at the
601 top of the profession in skill and
602 salary, with a great tradition of
603 horse-womanship and long train-

604 ing; born, you might say—er—
605 in the saddle, living her life there.
606 Yet there must be—there is the
607 other side of it, the more
608 feminine, the — the usual
609 woman's reactions, the ideals,
610 hopes, tastes of a woman—er—
611 her passions——"

612 In spite of himself, Mr. Dark's
613 pet word escaped and Verena
614 caught at it.

615 "Passions!" she cried. "A
616 woman's passions and tastes and
617 ideals—the usual ones. Yes,
618 Mr. Dark, I've got 'em all, like
619 any other woman." She clenched
620 one hand tightly, with a deep
621 breath, then plunged: "That's
622 why I'm willing to talk now.
623 You want the—the other side
624 of my life and I'm going to
625 give it.

626 "Well, I am a rope artist and
627 Wild West rider, as you say; but
628 I am like other women too.
629 Although I was born in the
630 saddle, you might say, papa put-
631 ting my brother Al and me there
632 when we were only three years
633 old—where I have lived, as they
634 claim, ever since, I also live in a
635 house—when I am there! Buck
636 and I saved every cent we made
637 for five years, to build it, and
638 I'll say it's a good one. It's out
639 at Tulsa, Oklahoma. We had an
640 architect from San Francisco
641 for it. It has four bathrooms.
642 We buy the best of everything
643 too. Blue velvet overstuffed in
644 the parlor—I wish you could see it
645 —where I sit as often as possible

whenever out of the saddle. We have an artesian well and some of the best stock and horses you can find anywheres in the West. No trick stuff, you know. We have a good manager, and Aunt Ida looks after the housekeeping—and our two children. Oh, yes, you may tell that—Buster and Henrietta, three years and eighteen months. Two children —and four bathrooms!" choked Mrs. Dayson bitterly. Her bridges were well ablaze now.

"I know horses and I know riding, but I know other things too. I've got the cutest babies you ever saw, and—and I've played with dolls in my time too. Plenty. When I was growing up I always wanted a house with—with a linen closet and a lot of jam, and little pink aprons to work round in, like anybody. I counted on it and I got it, along with Buck. I mean with my husb—with Henry B. Dayson, who I am married to. We wanted just the same things. We knew that right off when we met at Cheyenne six years ago. We liked each other right off. Buck changed a lot of his dates right away and followed my schedule down the map for three months before we got married. That was the time we rode together early every morning—out over the prairie, while the sun came up, or up into the hills." Here Mrs. Dayson paused abruptly, having apparently a slight constriction of the throat. She swallowed twice and repeated in a rather high, thin, strained tone, "Riding out together in the mornings that way—over the prairie or up in the hills."

Mr. Dark, whose pencil had a minute earlier been fleetly chasing her revelation in his notebook, looked at her, aware of a sudden tension.

It is a fact, as Mr. Dark well knew, or any of us who ply the craft, that words are the poorest possible conveyancers of intent, the weakest imaginable vehicle of emotion or actual psychology —a barrier usually raised between people and a smoke screen rather than a revelation for the soul. That is why Mr. Dark's pencil poised at Mrs. Dayson's commonplace phrase "riding out together in the mornings."

Some very deep emotion seemed to burn in the little rodeo queen. Her blue eyes were dark and soft, and perhaps a little tragic. They shone with the memory of some older loveliness, now denied to her; perhaps the picture of two young figures—a tall, swarthy, supple shape, godlike, superior, bending to a little slim eager companion with a freckled, wild-rose, pink-and-tan face under rough gilt curls. Figures that turned to each other like Clytie to the sun, in an age-old idyl, their horses touching shoulder to shoulder, light feet

730 repudiating the yielding turf,
731 where dew still clung to grass and
732 wild flower in silver meshes;
733 where the air blew sweet with
734 early morning perfume and was
735 filled with whistle and song of
736 lark and quail.

737 Mrs. Dayson resumed after a
738 moment: "It was then that
739 Buck and I planned our lives;
740 to build a house and to do our
741 stuff together; to sell it on itself
742 without any publicity or fussing;
743 Buck to manage our business
744 and fix all contracts. And we
745 have never changed from this
746 until now. Everything," said
747 Mrs. Dayson, "is changed now.
748 Everything we planned as far as
749 up to when we got on the boat
750 at Liverpool is ruined and
751 spoiled. We were on our way
752 out to our house—to Buster and
753 Henrietta. We are not going
754 now. We were on our way to a
755 stampede in the Central West
756 circuit. We are not going now.
757 I may possibly never see the
758 West again. I may never see
759 Buster and Henrietta. I don't
760 know about this. I don't know
761 anything."

762 "Mrs. Dayson—why not?"
763 "Because," said Verena,
764 "Buck, my husb—— Mr. Henry
765 B. Dayson has gone East—or,
766 you might say, loco. Because
767 we are going to stay East, right
768 here in New York for a year at
769 least, and maybe longer, on
770 contract with this new Castle
771 Garden Theater, to perform our

stuff on a platform—on tanbark, 772
mind you—with canvas scenery 773
round us. And that's not all. 774
We have never done such a thing 775
before, but we will begin our 776
contract by a special advertising 777
feature—a kidnaping—of my- 778
self. I'm to go in a taxicab down 779
to Pell Street and be stolen by 780
two Chinamen. Can you beat it? 781
To call public attention to me!" 782

"Mrs. Dayson! How singular! 784
What an idea—for Mr. Day- 785
son!" 786

"Don't lay it to Mr. Dayson. 787
It isn't his." Verena bent closer 788
and two great tears like flat 789
silver disks slipped from beneath 790
her eyelashes. "It belongs to a 791
woman we met on the boat com- 792
ing over; a regular publicity 793
woman, now attached to our out- 794
fit. Her name is Sennay—Violet 795
Sennay—and she always—for 796
everybody begins with a kid- 797
naping, to get attention. But 798
not for herself. I wish to God 799
she would. She—she's cruel, 800
good-looking, b-beautiful, and 801
her clothes——" Mrs. Dayson 802
swallowed hard. "Clothes!" she 803
choked. "What is the matter 804
with me—with mine, I mean, 805
Mr. Dark?" 806

But she didn't wait for an 807
answer. She crumpled own 808
and wept wildly again. 809

"She calls him Buck dea and 810
mong chair, and it's only been 811
three weeks she's known him. 812
Oh, Mr. Dark, what'll do? 813
What'll I do?" 814

815 This, you will admit, is no
816 way to receive the press.
817 Mr. Dark laid down his note-
818 book. His official capacity
819 ceased here. He found himself
820 patting Mrs. Dayson's hand as
821 he would have patted any pretty
822 distressed girl's, as he would
823 have wished his sister's patted.
824 "What you need," said Mr.
825 Dark, "is a friend."

826 The rodeo queen agreed. It
827 was true. She had no friend, no
828 soul in New York to confide in.
829 "It's this repression stuff,"
830 sobbed Verena, "that you're
831 always reading about. You hold
832 in and you hold in till you nearly
833 burst, until a time comes when
834 you cut loose in the wrong place.
835 Think of telling your secrets to a
836 reporter! Oh, I beg of you,
837 don't print this! I should have
838 held my tongue, but I'm so
839 miserable. Forget what I said.
840 I—I shall not say another
841 word!"

842 Whereupon she entered upon
843 a rather lengthy and impassioned
844 monologue provoked by Mr.
845 Dark's kindness and sympathy.

846 Into her monologue she wove
847 many and divers references—
848 Buster and Henrietta, Buck's
849 good looks, his prowess, his
850 previous, loyalty, their happy
851 life, his passion for elegant
852 long words, incidents that had
853 occurred at the Pendleton
854 and Salinas roundups, tricky
855 horses they had ridden, how
856 they bought up all the bad ones

857 so they could really test their
858 stuff; tales of a certain star-faced
859 buckskin used at Wembley, a
860 roan that had tried to kill Buck
861 last year; a white cayuse, a
862 California sorrel. Terms like
863 crow-hopping, fanning, hazing,
864 sunfishing, got all mixed to-
865 gether with the blue velvet
866 overstuffed, some fine French
867 mirrors, Aunt Ida, the artesian
868 well and the bathrooms, with
869 certain concluding mention of
870 clothes and her great handicap
871 here. In feminine fashion, her
872 clothes were the first matter she
873 had thought of.

874 It was, she explained, part of
875 Buck's policy for them both
876 while on tour to wear their show
877 clothes. It was lots of fun, and
878 going around together made it
879 plenty easy. Also, speaking as
880 a cowgirl, she was, if she said so
881 herself, the niftiest dressed rid-
882 ing artist on any circuit. She
883 could afford it, and made a point
884 of it. Still, it got her nothing
885 here in New York. Beside the
886 beauty and sophistication of
887 Mrs. Sennay—who had in addi-
888 tion a line of talk of the kind
889 Buck loved—beside anybody,
890 the way they looked here, she
891 was nothing at all.

892 She related what had hap-
893 pened yesterday afternoon when
894 —alone, as she always was now
895 —she had stepped out to a Sixth
896 Avenue news stand for a paper,
897 wearing a costume that would
898 make any female riding artist

899 ache with envy. A divided skirt
900 and blouse lately cut by an
901 English tailor, over a Laramie
902 pattern, of pale supple pearl
903 doeskin stuff; her very best
904 neckerchief and white sugar-
905 loaf hat, lovely handmade high-
906 heeled teetering Mexican boots
907 of soft pale-gray leather, set
908 with little bronze and turquoise
909 patterns, a rattlesnake belt with
910 a massive hand-tooled silver
911 buckle, pale soft gauntlet gloves.
912 Some little flappers passing
913 made open fun of her. They
914 wore, Verena declared, little
915 short tight shimmies of color-
916 splashed silk and apparently no
917 stockings above high-heeled tot-
918 tering black-satin slippers.
919 There were pieces of fur or
920 colored strips of silk fastened
921 around their necks, and their
922 arms were bare to the shoulders.
923 Colors were mottled on their
924 faces, too, and little gay bowls
925 of cheap felt pulled over their
926 eyes.
927 "I could have laughed," sighed
928 Verena; "honestly, they looked
929 so funny to me, and if they
930 hadn't laughed at me and
931 pointed at me so people stop-
932 ped——"
933 She had defended herself, as
934 she could.
935 "I stopped and said to the
936 worst one right out loud, 'I
937 paid three hundred dollars for
938 my felt hat—how much was
939 yours?'"
940 Not that it made a bit of

941 difference, in the long run.
942 Whether she dressed herself
943 West or East, she was, ap-
944 parently, out of it; out of every-
945 thing that her old life knew.
946 The situation, so banal, so
947 bourgeois and—outside the
948 range of the darker, more exotic
949 forms of emotion—so normal,
950 one might say, almost bored
951 Mr. Dark in its simplicity but
952 for the fact that Mrs. Verena
953 Dayson's pretty blue eyes, moist,
954 appealing, unfortunate, chal-
955 lenged and pleaded with him to
956 consider her case. He patted
957 her hand again.
958 "Well," said Mr. Dark, "it's
959 simply that there's a lot you
960 get out of practice—er—from
961 being in the know. There's a
962 knack about it which—er—I
963 should say you hadn't learned,
964 not that your instinct wasn't
965 sound. I'll tell you what, Mrs.
966 Dayson, there's nothing at all
967 to worry over, really. I know Vi
968 Sennay. Everybody on the
969 newspapers knows Vi. She's a
970 one-story man, though a nifty
971 looker. She hasn't any tricks,
972 no real imagination. Every
973 time she joins up on a case, she
974 pulls a kidnaping, as you've
975 said; after that it's a general
976 diminuendo. Only she's got a
977 lot of appeal, and she's a good
978 dresser and talker. I went to a
979 studio crush she gave once, with
980 a friend. She—she dressed the
981 part. Edgar Saltus stuff—a
982 little. She had her bed on a little

252

platform, with a bearskin thrown over, and three little wooden steps painted orange going up, and one of those wrought-iron torcheres. But you've nothing to worry over, because people all get sick of her. Vi's a home wrecker on Monday, but by Friday she's the landlord collecting three months' back rent, with any fellow."

"Well, but," gulped Verena —"but it's only Tuesday now. I've got to live through the rest of the week. She's got Buck going strong yet. He's going to sign this contract in ten more days; she's got him a practice ground down on a tanbark pen at Mullahey's. She's got Buck caring whether it's black or white ties at dinner. I'm losing my husband, Mr. Dark, and I want to go home—to Buster and Henrietta."

"You'll go," said Mr. Dark confidently, "and I'll tell you why—because I'll help you. We'll put it over together. It amounts to a formula, almost; purely mechanical. You can follow it anywhere you like in the fiction of the day," he explained a little meanly. "You must put on a sketch and meet the lady on her own terms— outdo her, y'understand; put it over—go one better! Roughly speaking, the rescue of a husband divides itself into three parts— raiment, culture, jealousy." Mr. Dark waved his straw hat negligently. "You must outdress Mrs. Vi Sennay, you must outcharm her, you must outflirt her."

"Outdress her! But look at me!"

"I know the very lady to help you—Mrs. Pat Field, a buyer, with Blaine & Holding. She'd be tickled to look you over— put you together. She'd know your type. I'll just make a note to phone and asked her to call today."

"But you said—outcharm her!"

"I mean you must cultivate the sort of stuff Vi talks, her line of vocabulary. I will coach you. I am interested in creative writing and will give you samples to work from."

"But outflirt her? With who? I only know the boys with our outfit. Buck wouldn't get jealous enough to buy a bag of peanuts. And this Mr. Wirtheimer who wants the contract—he's a perfect sixty-six."

"You know me," said Mr. Dark significantly.

"You don't mean—not seriously!"

"Not seriously, of course," Mr. Dark waved his hat again. "But I'm perfectly willing to help you here, to work out this formula, beginning tomorrow. You can't work it alone. I can arrange to give you a good bit of free time in the coming week,

253

as it happens, and—the thing would be rather fun. Another proof of the mechanistic laws governing psychology—the inevitable interweaving of given cause and effect. Your husband, Mrs. Dayson, at present a little fascinated by the novelty Mrs. Sennay offers, thinks of you only in the aspects he's always known. When he sees beside him a comparative stranger, beautifully groomed, cultivated and charming, a little cool and indifferent to him, and especially, admired, courted by another man—well, just wait and watch."

"Yes, but," objected Verena, "what I mean is, Mr. Dark"— and she looked as Penelope might if summoned on Ulysses' peril to pack her suitcase and go and rival Circe—"do you think Buck'll be sure to notice that I'm doing it? Being that he knows me so well, being—I mean that we've been married over five years, and he's got kind of used to me."

Mr. Dark laughed and again referred to watchful waiting. It was, he told her, a practically infallible formula, used a thousand times by creative artists because of its soundness.

"Don't worry; human nature never alters. We'll give it a chance. I'll call you up tomorrow and begin our campaign. In the meantime trust me—with your confidence." As a matter of fact, Verena had forgotten he was a reporter. "I shall arrange a dignified interview for you, coached in language your husband will only be proud and envious of. As a matter of fact, it is because of a certain intellectual sympathy that we shall be drawn together, hereafter, in our little affair. Oh, trust me to manage it, Mrs. Dayson, and don't worry."

She was worried, however, all over, waking early the next morning. Or at least she thought it was morning. That was the awful part of New York. You couldn't tell whether it was night or day, with artificial lights all the time, and the ceaseless outer roar. You couldn't even tell if it was rainy or fair.

What had waked her, thinking it was pouring, was only Buck's nostrils collaborating with the radiator. Buck lay asleep in the companion bed. The dark virile head of the educated cowbcy lay revealed above a cylindric l roll of pink brocade coverlet, a pastel court scene of Louis XIV bove him. An effete setting for Buck of the crow-hopping, sunf hing, squealing broncos.

Lying under her own pink brocade, with her han s, so muscular and capable on the bridle and now impotent in this situation as two wax lilies, tightly clenched in her palm, Verena cried, and swore a little, and reviewed last e ening. Never, never would she forget how Mrs. Sennay looked standing downstairs by the elevator with Mr. Wirtheimer! A picture to linger in anyone's—a man's especially—observing eye.

Buck himself had made unwontedly careful toilet. Ordinarily it was hard to make Buck go even a black tie. Plain business clothes were good enough, he claimed, capped by a tall gray soft hat. But ever since he had known Mrs. Sennay he had been on soup-and-fish after six—things he had bought in Piccadilly, that Wales himself would not have blushed for.

They had planned to go to the Persian Nightingale, on Wirtheimer's suggestion. It was a night club, really, and Verena at first refused on pretense of feeling ill.

But when Buck merely said, "All right, Rena, if your head aches, better stay," she had hastily donned a pink-and-blue-shot taffeta with a lot of lace and a rather bunchy skirt in which she resembled a boudoir lamp, and had tagged along. She had tasted only gall.

Against the foil of Mr. Wirtheimer, the perfect sixty-six, Violet Sennay looked like a Cyprian deity. A tall, supple, voluptuously made woman, with black glossy hair poured tightly on her head, curving in two forward horns upon her fruitlike cheeks. Her dress was perfectly plain—easy, yet also poured, of lustrous black satin, that ended in a little pointed fin. Her perfect arms swung negligently indifferent. On one white wrist was looped a bracelet thread of brilliants; one hand held a long careless sweep of cerise-dyed vulture feathers. Mrs. Sennay's feet and ankles, incased in cobweb black silk hose and pointed black slippers with brilliant-studded heels, invited all eyes to perfection. Her large, rather theatrically shadowed brown eyes, suggested at once mood and mystery. She had floated forward.

"Buck, my dear boy, how you've kept us!" Without a word for Buck's companion lamp shade.

"And yet," reflected Verena, "I'm the one to be kidnaped, taken to Pell Street and rustled by Chinks, stowed away by chuck-wagon boys. How do I know she'll even return the body? No, I won't, I won't, I won't!"

Buck stirred a moment under his cover. " 'S that, Rena?"

A dozen truthful lies fought in Verena for utterance, after the fashion of all women in like plight: "Buck, I'm sick of your carrying on with this woman! Buck, tell me the truth, are you in love with Mrs. Sennay? What's going on here? Buck, are you tired of me? What's in your mind about me? What about our kids, our home?" and the like."

1235 And like other women in like
1236 plight, she feinted and circled
1237 for the answer.

1238 "I d'know," cried Verena with
1239 a gay little laugh. "I just woke
1240 up and got to thinking. I got
1241 to thinking about such a nice
1242 fella I met yest'day. He was
1243 a newspaper reporter, Buck, one
1244 o' these New York boys. I
1245 guess they're all pretty fast too.
1246 Anyway, he wanted to talk to
1247 me for the Sunday paper, and
1248 after a while he asked me out to
1249 lunch today and—I hope you
1250 don't mind—well, I said I
1251 would."

1252 She cocked an eye at the pink
1253 brocade cocoon, to see what
1254 manner of emotional butterfly
1255 it would hatch. Buck only
1256 yawned and burrowed the
1257 deeper.

1258 " 'S right, do," he murmured,
1259 "though I don't know why you
1260 wake me up to talk 'bout it.
1261 You know, wantcha have good
1262 time, Rena, help 'self." And he
1263 was off on his duet with the
1264 radiator. Wouldn't you know?
1265 thought Verena, and yet three
1266 weeks ago—mention of an un-
1267 protected luncheon with a gay
1268 fast New York man and a
1269 reporter!

1270 Nevertheless, she had an al-
1271 most happy morning, shopping
1272 with Mr. Dark's friend, lunching
1273 and preparing a campaign with
1274 Mr. Dark himself.

1275 Two o'clock found her in the
1276 tanbark pen at Mullahey's, with
1277 Dick and Dan bringing out a
1278 cow pony for her. In her rough
1279 riding clothes, working breeches
1280 and shirt, Verena was always
1281 happy. Now she proceeded to
1282 do a few practice turns, just a
1283 little exercise stuff to keep her
1284 in training. Anyone who had
1285 been present would have been
1286 quick to agree that it was a
1287 class of stuff far above the
1288 deserts of the average theater
1289 patron. It was riding for riders
1290 that the rodeo queen proceeded
1291 now to do; an exquisite con-
1292 noisseurship in her art that hung
1293 her name in big electrics of
1294 opinion at Denver, Calgary,
1295 Salinas.

1296 Ordinarily, in any prolonged
1297 stop, Buck and she went through
1298 their training drill together, but
1299 today he was not here. He had
1300 mumbled something about a
1301 conference on the kidnaping with
1302 Wirtheimer and Mrs. Sennay, so
1303 his wife had plenty of room to
1304 kick up dust, ample opportunity
1305 to pull all the tricks she knew.
1306 She went through them all,
1307 evolving every possible trick
1308 from her pony. She raced and
1309 loped and let it buck and crow-
1310 hop. She climbed round and
1311 over it, now in and out of saddle.
1312 She ducked and bent and
1313 doubled. She rode now on its
1314 back, now in one stirrup. She
1315 crawled under its belly as she
1316 raced, dropping from one side,
1317 reaching a hand under for a stir-
1318 rup, coming up on the other,

flying hoofs thrashing, flashing near her head. Round and round she flashed and whirled, courting death carelessly as a part of the day's routine, and when she was tired she uncoiled the rope on her saddle and sent a spinning curvilinear dark serpent into the air.

If Verena Dayson's riding was a legend in the West, her rope work was no less. Buck had taught it all to her. Now, remembering all those long, happy, careful instructions, Verena, as another woman might look over romantic ballroom souvenirs— a wan pressed tuberose, an old glove, a scented note—repeated each supple, graceful, intricate figure in the air, calling up the sweet association of older, more untroubled hours with the big brown-skinned boy she loved. When she had gone through all this—all the parabolas, figure eights, dancing jennys; when she had finished writing hiero- glyphics in the air, she put on that final sketch that set specta- tors roaring, their hats fanning; that had been her particular show stunt at Wembley, that even Buck always watched anx- iously, a little nervously, as performed by her tiny childish figure.

From a chute arranged at one side of the pen Dick and Dan released a steer; a wide-horned, sinister, browned figure that rushed forward, paused, head low, staring, then jerked madly away in a blind race.

Verena halted a moment, then bending low on her pony, her rope swaying out before her in a small perfectly arranged loop, was after it, horse and rider like one creature, centaur fashion; one moment the small loop float- ed in readiness, the dashing steer plunging away; the next, and the lasso curled out in the air, the loop settling over the running creature.

There came a tightening swerve and turn of the pony, and the steer, leaping up, the rope checking it in midrise, was knocked from its feet, fell heavily on its side in as perfect a bust as you could wish. Light as a thistle the rodeo queen lit on the ground in a flying leap, loosen- ing a smaller rope from her belt. With a half dozen motions she had it bound neatly around the steer as a housewife trusses a Sunday fowl for roasting. There were only two women in the country besides herself who could do it.

"Who," inquired Verena, a little breathlessly, as the boys ran up now—"who says I can't rope, throw, tie and deliver— yes, and stamp and take to the parcel post?"

But it was only a rhetorical question, there being no one of any importance to answer it.

It was five o'clock, anyhow, and time for the rodeo queen

257

1403 to begin formally her new pro-
1404 gram. Verena hurried back to
1405 her hotel to dress for dinner.
1406 No walking lamp shade tonight.
1407 She put on with trembling fingers
1408 and a final sense of ecstasy the
1409 lovely things Mr. Dark's kind
1410 friend had helped her choose.
1411 What looked out of the mirror
1412 finally was Titania herself, a
1413 figure of almost unearthly
1414 delicacy, fragility and brillance.
1415 Sparkling silver lace, fine as Jack
1416 Frost spins on the windowpane,
1417 formed the tiny bodice, the
1418 filmy soft-falling long skirt.
1419 From this emerged Verena's
1420 pretty little-girl arms and throat,
1421 covered now with a languorous
1422 siren coat of powder. Her curly
1423 gilt-tipped hair clung decorously
1424 to her shapely head, bound by
1425 a single thread of brilliants. On
1426 one wrist fell a bracelet loop
1427 of brilliants. The other hand
1428 held a great fan of brilliant-
1429 studded silver gauze painted in
1430 faint pink flowers. Little silver
1431 slippers peeped beneath her lace
1432 skirt, the heels set with rhine-
1433 stones. Over a near-by chair
1434 hung a cloak of soft pink velvet,
1435 lined with silver lamé, a great
1436 collar of pink fox. A pink fox!
1437 Verena had whistled aloud when
1438 she saw it. At this moment
1439 Henry B. Dayson entered, and
1440 as Verena looked at him, all her
1441 heart stirred to realize how fit
1442 an accompaniment Buck Day-
1443 son was for any woman at her
1444 very gladdest.

"Buck," screamed her heart 1445
as he spoke to her and turned 1446
away, "notice my dress!" Then 1447
she remembered Mr. Dark's 1448
counsel. 1449

"Oh, Buck," she drawled, "I 1450
was waiting for you, to—to show 1451
you my new costume. Rather a 1452
pretty affair, don't you think? 1453
I think the lines are lovely. It's 1544
after a Boucher print." She 1455
pronounced it Booshay very 1456
carefully. 1457

Buck turned and gave the 1458
dress a careful consideration. 1459

"It's nice," he pronounced; 1460
"It's down-right pretty—if you 1461
like it. You don't sort of look 1462
natural to me. What I mean is, 1463
I like you in your workin' pants 1464
best—or one of your ginghams, 1465
back home, I guess. Some 1466
women take to being hossed up 1467
more than others, I reckon. 1468
But you look good all right, 1469
Verena." 1470

"Well," said Verena airily, 1471
"you ought to know—from your 1472
study of the different kinds of 1473
women. But I can assure you, 1474
Buck, this is a perfect costume. 1475
It's the dern-ee-ay cree, and 1476
that's, after all, what I want in 1477
a New York onsomble. If I'm to 1478
be metropolitan, as you seem to 1479
desire"—Verena curved a pretty 1480
little arm toward the glass—"I 1481
naturally want to do it in the 1482
best possible metropolitan form. 1483
I shouldn't care to have New 1484
Yorkers cherish the hypothesis 1485
that a—that a Western woman 1486

1487 is not adaptable and cannot
1488 conform to sophisticated Eastern
1489 standards. Anyhow, I was
1490 stung enough jack—what
1491 I mean, I think it's very ap-
1492 propriate for a dinner dance or
1493 theater, and if we go to the
1494 Persian Nightingale again to-
1495 night——"
1496 "Look here, Rena"—Buck
1497 stirred uneasily—"would you—
1498 would you mind—the fact is
1499 we didn't get our plans finished
1500 off this afternoon—I mean about
1501 the kidnaping, and Vio—Mrs.
1502 Sennay suggested we conclude
1503 'em at dinner tonight. Wir-
1504 theimer would like it too. He's
1505 got an appointment and has to
1506 leave early, but we three
1507 could finish off. It's a fact it
1508 would be dumb slow for you.
1509 What I mean is"—Buck grew
1510 more uneasy and refused her his
1511 eyes—"what we—I thought was
1512 —being you complained yest'day
1513 of being so tired, I thought you
1514 might like to rest tonight and
1515 have dinner sent up."
1516 "I see," said Verena slowly.
1517 "Well, I admit I've been in a
1518 kind of peaked sickly state
1519 lately, falling off a little, and not
1520 able to lift a feather, as you
1521 might say, and you may be
1522 right. Anyhow, I guess I can try
1523 it—our eating separate tonight
1524 if you want it. Only, I don't
1525 believe I'll be eating alone.
1526 You remember, I spoke this
1527 morning of a charming boy I
1528 met who asked me to lunch.

1529 Well, we've got awfully on rap-
1530 poor together—oh, a lot really.
1531 I mean, he's tremendously inter-
1532 esting as a type, rather stunning
1533 to look at too. But since I'm
1534 to be alone, if you don't
1535 mind——"
1536 She caught up the pink cloak
1537 and crushed the pink fox from
1538 No Man's Land beneath her
1539 pretty bitter little face. Buck
1540 looked at her in honest relief.
1541 "Why, not at all, Rena.
1542 That's the very ticket. Busi-
1543 ness'd be awful dull for you—
1544 you don't wanta know all the
1545 details about this Pell Street
1546 stuff. Go ahead an get this
1547 dude and play with him."
1548 It was not Buck Dayson
1549 speaking—that she knew by the
1550 look of his eyes.
1551 There's a weed that grows
1552 upon the plains, and Western
1553 tradition has it that a horse
1554 grazing thereon goes loco. Buck
1555 Dayson had certainly eaten of
1556 the loco weed. Was there any
1557 cure?
1558 In the next ten days the
1559 rodeo queen followed with the
1560 most careful consistency the
1561 program young Mr. Dark indi-
1562 cated. If there was any subtle
1563 phase of the corrective ritual
1564 young Mr. Dark had proposed
1565 in his friendly interest in young
1566 Mrs. Dayson, as a tonic and
1567 alterative for Mr. Henry B.
1568 Dayson, it has never been re-
1569 corded.
1570 As an artist, a student and

1571 veteran analyst of all subjective
1572 human passions, Mr. Dark, out
1573 of his great fund of experience,
1574 his familiarity with literature
1575 and wide social observation, in
1576 the next few days left no stone
1577 unturned, Verena following
1578 faithfully, in his proposed effort,
1579 mechanistically speaking, to turn
1580 Mr. Dayson, as a matrimonial
1581 delinquent, back to the fold.

1582 With no effect whatever! The
1583 three great levers of human con-
1584 duct which he had indicated here
1585 —beauty, charm and male
1586 jealousy—were pumped on to
1587 the fullest extent, and made as
1588 much impression as a fly alight-
1589 ing on the proverbial wheel.

1590 Some husbands are built like
1591 this. Queen Penelope's startled
1592 cry, summoned to out-rival Circe,
1593 might not have been unfounded.
1594 Mr. Henry B. Dayson was a
1595 husband who knew all about the
1596 girl he had married—a fatal
1597 position, we are often told, yet
1598 unescapable in many instances.

1599 He knew that his Verena was
1600 pretty; he would have knocked
1601 anyone down who claimed other-
1602 wise. Costuming might create
1603 some small advantage, but he
1604 had been well enough suited with
1605 Verena's costumes. Her beauty
1606 was sweet and native, and be-
1607 yond any longer surprising him.
1608 The complete new line of daz-
1609 zling correctly classy raiment
1610 which she proceeded to air
1611 passed completely over him.

1612 Her mind he already knew as
1613 well. They had lived in the
1614 closest intimacy—equally, we
1615 are told, fatal to attraction.
1616 Her boyish candor, her slang,
1617 native spice and pep were as
1618 natural and comfortable to him
1619 as old shoes, as accepted a part
1620 of his life and thinking as his
1621 own mentality.

1622 Verena, in new cultured as-
1623 pects, trained by Mr. Dark to
1624 conversational expressions she
1625 had never used before, to little
1626 touches of sophistication, in-
1627 cluding polysyllables and foreign
1628 expressions, was noticed at first
1629 by her husband in a sort of daze,
1630 then very shortly, figuratively,
1631 slapped and put in place.

1632 "What makes you talk so
1633 dumb, Rena?" he asked one
1634 evening. "You've been goin'
1635 round lately spoutin' like a
1636 gusher. Come to earth, girl, I
1637 don't like it."

1638 As for jealousy, Verena had
1639 long since made the most fatal
1640 error of all. She had revealed
1641 to her husband how much she
1642 loved him. His faith in his
1643 invincibility here would have
1644 required mountains to move—
1645 a great deal larger mountain
1646 than Mr. Stanley Dark. Death
1647 alone, or its threat, could have
1648 aroused him suddenly, as with
1649 many husbands, to a realization
1650 of her special qualities—and the
1651 rodeo queen did not propose to
1652 die to secure her end.

1653 Sitting with young Mr. Dark
1654 disconsolately at dinner one

evening a week later, they reviewed together their lack of progress and Buck's impregnability.

"It must be," said Mr. Dark, running a desperate hand through his dark hair, "that your husband is extra—er—bullheaded, Mrs. Dayson. Er— possibly as a Western man, that type is stronger. Anyhow, no man ought to be so blind as not to perceive—what has been going on here," he added indignantly. It was an outrage, a personal insult actually.

"I don't know. Maybe it's just that Buck ain't ready to see things. Mebbe a man's got to be ready. You forget he's— he's still kind of interested in Mrs. Sennay. He's busy, too, with somebody calling him up all the time arranging things. Anyhow, it ain't working, is it? Suits this Sennay all the better, I guess, what I've been doing; and it'll soon be too late——"

"No," said Mr. Dark. "About that, I've explained—in Vi Sennay's history. The men she plays round with get tired and break off with her."

"But they can't break off with a contract she gets 'em to sign meantime. Day after tomorrow is the time Wirtheimer's set to clinch everything. That's the evening picked I'm to mix in with the Chink boys. Buck told me something else this morning—we're to look for an apartment in Park Avenue. He said I could have Buster and Henrietta all next winter, with a trained nurse. I guess Sennay thinks that would keep me busy. She'll have Buck doin' his rope act in a frock coat with a gardenia soon."

"Well," said Mr. Dark, "something may happen to help us yet. Who knows?"

"At least, I don't," sighed Verena. "What could happen? Our time's up. I s'pose I'll just have to stand round and take my medicine in this like other girls do—let it wear away itself. Only, it's goin' to be a darn hard year. But don't think I'm not grateful. You've been my friend."

"I hope I'll always be your friend," cried Mr. Dark quickly, moved by the pretty distressed little face. "Anything that I can do at all—always! Anything!" he added warmly.

Verena sighed and shook her head. She was due now at what Mrs. Sennay called her studio— her private and anomalous apartment at the top of a house in West Thirteenth Street. Because, at last, they couldn't get along without herself in their plans.

After all, reflected Verena sarcastically, as Mr. Dark put her in a taxi and she rattled away down to Thirteenth Street, whither Buck and Wirtheimer

1739 had preceded her, you can't
1740 pull a kidnaping unless some-
1741 thing is kidnaped; and it might
1742 be, maybe, that—just at the
1743 last moment—the victm might
1744 be allowed a word or two—listen
1745 in—on proceedings. It might
1746 be so! Possibly—perhaps!

1747 Mrs. Sennay lived in a house
1748 with the door painted pea green,
1749 and when you opened it there
1750 were four flights before you
1751 reached her studio. Climb-
1752 ing these four flights slowly
1753 and more and more sarcastic-
1754 ally, Verena felt with every
1755 step an accumulating fund of
1756 rage against Mrs. Sennay—this
1757 blandishing, poised woman who
1758 had come up on the boat, had
1759 flattered and followed Buck,
1760 ignoring her, preëmpting him
1761 for her own, dragging him to a
1762 new life.

1763 It was her first visit to Mrs.
1764 Sennay's studio, and Verena
1765 batted her eyes carefully. It
1766 would probably not be the last.
1767 Mrs. Sennay gave little studio
1768 parties here—and very likely
1769 all next winter! Buck, she
1770 knew, had had a conference here
1771 at least once before—at least
1772 one time that he had mentioned.

1773 A large room with a fanlight,
1774 a baby grand, a piece of armor
1775 and—yes, an alcoved platform,
1776 or dais, with a couch under a
1777 bearskin, three steps painted
1778 yellow and a wrought-iron
1779 torchère. The air was thick
1780 with smoke, for Wirtheimer, a

1781 man named Stendahl, a Miss
1782 Lester, Mrs. Sennay and Henry
1783 B. Dayson were already con-
1784 vened and engaged on tobacco.
1785 But a place was made for her,
1786 and Mrs. Sennay was very
1787 gracious, very sweet.

1788 "Little Rena must hear what
1789 we have decided," she cried at
1790 once. "We've been so full of our
1791 plans and with insuring success,
1792 before our opening here for the
1793 summer, that we haven't been
1794 able to talk competently; but
1795 now we know what to do with
1796 you, *chérie*, you must, you really
1797 must hear."

1798 What little Rena then heard
1799 was really a simple proceeding.
1800 A very kind Eurasian friend had
1801 agreed to turn over to them his
1802 perfectly appointed, really com-
1803 fortable apartment in the
1804 Chinese region for a few hours
1805 for the completion of the plan.
1806 At nine o'clock, in a taxicab, on
1807 the given night Mrs. Dayson and
1808 a friend—no other than Mr.
1809 Stendahl—desirous of a visit to
1810 Chinatown, should have the
1811 conveyance stopped before the
1812 Eurasian's home in order to per-
1813 mit Mr. Stendahl a purchase of
1814 cigarettes. Gone not more than
1815 five minutes, in that brief in-
1816 terval a tragedy should ensue!
1817 Two men would rush from the
1818 Eurasian's home, overpower,
1819 bind the taxi driver and drag
1820 young Mrs. Dayson into the
1821 building.

1822 "To perfect safety, my dear!

1823 The apartment will be entirely
1824 empty except for Lydia Lester
1825 here, who will be there to receive
1826 you. Mr. Wirtheimer's car will
1827 be at the next corner, and at once
1828 you and Lydia, leaving by a side
1829 passage, heavily veiled, will be
1830 placed in it and driven up to
1831 Yonkers, where you will lie
1832 perdu for three days with friends
1833 of mine—perfectly lovely people
1834 named Mitchell. But the police,
1835 notified of course within a few
1836 minutes of this by Mr. Stendahl,
1837 will have their hands full for an
1838 interval—the newspapers furnish
1839 plenty of space—before your
1840 discovery and return on a plau-
1841 sible basis we have worked out."

1842 "How nice!" trembled Verena.

1843 "My dear friends, let us drink
1844 to success!" cried Mrs. Sennay,
1845 whose faultless wrist and arm
1846 looked so well lifted in public
1847 attention.

1848 They drank, because Mrs.
1849 Sennay had supplied not only
1850 tobacco but wherewithal for a
1851 toast, together with dishes of
1852 hors d'œuvres to eat—suitable
1853 to æsthetic studios. Such, for
1854 instance, as sweet ripe olives
1855 filled with garlic and anchovy
1856 paste; dabs of bread spread with
1857 caviar, and the like. We men-
1858 tion these because it is quite
1859 likely that without them the
1860 rodeo queen would never have
1861 had the idea that suddenly came
1862 to her.

1863 She was watching Buck, as
1864 she always did in Mrs. Sennay's

1865 presence, and as Buck put down
1866 his toast—set down his glass,
1867 that is—he reached over and
1868 helped himself to some of Mrs.
1869 Sennay's hors d'œuvres. That
1870 is, in easy plain-man fashion, he
1871 treated it as food. He practic-
1872 ally filled his mouth with the
1873 ripe olives stuffed with garlic and
1874 anchovy. And something very
1875 curious and terrible happened in
1876 his face. To Verena, acquainted
1877 connubially with its least shad-
1878 ing, it took on a blending of
1879 agony, solicitation, surprise,
1880 frustration, utter horror and
1881 panic that made him look
1882 desperately though elusively
1883 familiar.

1884 Buck had large handsome
1885 brown eyes. They rolled up
1886 slightly for a second above the
1887 blank dismay and consternation
1888 in his face. Of what did he re-
1889 mind her? What did Buck look
1890 like? Where had she seen a look
1891 like that before?

1892 She got it in a flash of illumina-
1893 tion. Buck looked like a steer,
1894 jerked to a fall, pinned on the
1895 rope, with herself running up to
1896 tie. She had seen a face—eyes
1897 like that, in their wildness and
1898 anguish, a hundred times before.
1899 Her knowledge shook her be-
1900 cause of an accompanying flash
1901 of inspiration.

1902 "Buck," she asked suddenly,
1903 in a level tone across the smoke,
1904 "do you approve of this? Do
1905 you believe that a couple of art-
1906 ists like us ought to pull a stunt

1907 of this kind—that our work will
1908 go better for it?"
1909 "I do," said Buck, refusing his
1910 eyes again. "I've never held
1911 that policy before, Rena, but I
1912 have changed my views. I am
1913 strongly in favor of a kidnaping
1914 feature. I've told you so before
1915 a dozen times. As an advertis-
1916 ing headliner for Dayson &
1917 Dayson's summer work——"
1918 "Then," said Verena quietly,
1919 "if that's the case, and I'm to
1920 be the goat, mebby Mrs. Sennay
1921 here'll call a cab and let me slip
1922 up to the hotel again. I want
1923 to rest up all I can and get in
1924 good fix, and I'm not needed
1925 here any more."
1926 It was not to rest, however,
1927 that Verena retired. She sum-
1928 moned Mr. Dark. If Mrs.
1929 Dayson, the troubled wife, had
1930 earlier thrown herself upon his
1931 mercy, it was the rodeo queen
1932 who demanded his coöperation
1933 now.
1934 "You said you'd help," she
1935 cried, "always—that's what you
1936 said, and I've got to have help.
1937 It'll take a lot of fixing with
1938 money—the door man, this pro-
1939 prietor and all the damage.
1940 I've got the money, but I want
1941 a man. Besides, I've got to have
1942 some atmosphere. You told me
1943 you acted in a dramatic society.
1944 It's little enough to do. And
1945 last of all, I'm a lady and I'll
1946 want to be chaperoned."
1947 "Chaperoned!" cried young
1948 Mr. Dark dazedly. "I'll help

1949 you—why, yes, I said I would,
1950 but I don't think you need it—a
1951 chaperon—doing cave-woman
1952 stuff."
1953 "Cave-woman stuff!" cried
1954 Verena. "Why, a cave woman
1955 was a gumdrop! She let a man
1956 beat her up and knock her down
1957 all he pleased—just as he
1958 pleased. No, sir, I wouldn't
1959 say cave-woman stuff. Let's
1960 call it all I know—Western
1961 stuff."
1962 If you are a patron of those
1963 forms of light relaxation beloved
1964 of the æsthetic artistic set in
1965 New York, you are already ac-
1966 quainted with the Persian Night-
1967 ingale, that Oriental garden and
1968 rendezvous of delightful dal-
1969 liance with the subtler forms of
1970 evening pleasure, which is set
1971 like a jewel in the smart aloof-
1972 ness of the Sixties and ap-
1973 proached like a guarded citadel
1974 by pass-word and listed member-
1975 ship only. If you are not, it may
1976 be necessary to mention the
1977 famous mural decorations, by the
1978 Arabian Quenjidian, depicting
1979 love scenes—drawn so smartly,
1980 with no perspective—between
1981 a Persian troubadour and a
1982 princess of ancient Ecbatana,
1983 and capped by old legends from
1984 Hafiz; that a great many Ham-
1985 adans, and Ferahans are draped
1986 around appropriately; that there
1987 are bulbuls painted on the china;
1988 that the air is musty, sweet,
1989 heavy with spice, the lights
1990 passionate, a reddish violet in

by a small gray amazon, was clearly realized—a figure bewildered, outraged, yet drawn irresistibly to the door by a small hand that, firm, yet subtly practiced, adjusted the leverage to poundage with just enough skilled compulsion to keep it on its feet.

"Featuring," cried a gay voice at the door, "ladies and gentlemen, Dayson & Dayson; rope-and-riding artists in their big spectacular advertising act — kidnaping in the Western style, or extracting a husband from quarters that do him no good."

Everybody is agreed on this. Only a few near the door heard the passionate exhortation the small gray figure made from her saddle to the roped-and-tied man before her.

"Buck Dayson," she flamed, "you wanted a kidnap—and you got it. I am going home. There's a train at midnight, and our trunks are at the Pennsylvania. Do I go alone? Out to Buster and Henrietta and our house. Out to our two babies— and four bathrooms. Out West, where we rode together in the mornings——"

Language is a poor conveyancer of feeling; but Buck, looking at his little rodeo queen with that memory of cold feet, that now stirring gale of laughter in the Persian room behind— needed none. He was coming

out of it. He put out a dazed hand to his wife.

As I say, there is a conflict of testimony.

Two figures—a cowgirl and a handsome man in evening clothes, it is claimed—got into a waiting car. But the more desperate of the Western desperadoes, it is said, remained standing on the curb. One man claimed overhearing the farewell message:

"—— when we see you next summer, Mr. Dark, out at Tulsa —don't you forget. Never can thank you enough for helping me! It was bang-up help, too, and reg'lar stuff, even if you did put your chaps on hind end to."

With the omniscience of our kind, there is no reason, however, why we should not follow Buck and Verena, two of the ridingest kids the West ever knew, on their flight away from the lures and the voice of New York.

Not that Buck at once forgave Verena. He raged and sulked at the hurt to his dignity as far as Pittsburgh; he gloomed beyond Indianapolis; he was injured and reserved through Illinois; but when they had crossed the Mississippi and the freer airs from stretches of wheat blew on his forehead, he began to relent. He admitted error, he became a little sheepish, he finally laughed, as they neared Kansas.

And Verena, who had hoped

2242 and prayed and battled and lost
2243 —and finally used her last arrow
2244 —like any wife, relaxed with a
2245 fearful joy.
2246 "I guess—I guess," grinned
2247 Buck, "you were right. I don't
2248 wanta see the East again.
2249 Goddy, some of the eats are
2250 awful! I like to try new things.

2251 But Goddy! I guess—I could
2252 say it—you were right, Verena.
2253 I don't know what else I can do."
2254 For answer Verena flung her-
2255 self on him like a Bar-K boy
2256 bulldogging a Texas yearling.
2257 "You could kiss me, I guess,
2258 Buck," sobbed the little rodeo
2259 queen in her relief.

THE ANALYSIS

From a technical point of view this story makes an interesting exhibit. Within the Scene which occupies lines 110 to 400 there are interpolated two Flash-back Scenes. One is a flash-back by the actor. It occupies lines 243 to 297 and is an actual flash-back interchange between Buck and Verena. In this there is nothing of any especial importance to the student, which has not already been discussed; but a rather unusual device is the hypothetical interview which is a somewhat original substitute for a Flash-back Scene. It occupies lines 298 to 378; and the fifth step is also the fifth step of the preceding presentation unit. This fifth step occupies lines 379 to 400.

Another example of a flash-back occurs on lines 1183 to 1221, and is interesting because it is not a flash-back used to give explanatory matter for the Beginning of the story, but is a flash-back which occurs in the Body of the story, where it is used to give information that will make clear to the reader the importance, not of the main situation, but of the scene situation. That scene situation projects Verena's attempt to bring about her main purpose by making her husband jealous through telling him about Mr. Dark.

The writer of this story must have had a great deal of fun in writing it, and every writer must get a great deal of amusement from reading it. The writer takes an old narrative problem, used again and again, and takes the answers which have been used again and again, and pokes fun at them as solutions for such a narrative problem. In the Beginning of the story, which occupies lines 1 to 1119, the condition is made clear to the reader. Verena Dayson, rodeo queen, realizing that her husband is under the spell of a metropolitan publicity woman tells a reporter, who persuades her that to win him back she must outflirt, outdress, and outcharm her rival, Mrs. Sennay. Those three methods of winning back an erring husband have been the solution offered time and again by writers of fiction. The fact that numerous stories have been written and accepted about this central condition is sufficient evidence that plot is not nearly so important in presenting stories as are the scenes which go to make up the story.

But Mrs. Pulver, being a competent and experienced writer, realized that the solution to a narrative problem should be one growing out of the capacity of the main actor that distinguishes her from other actors. The chief capacity possessed by this Verena Dayson, is her ability to ride and rope. So Mrs. Pulver takes each of the tried and true methods and proves that in this special case each one is a failure. In so doing, she is enabled to make each attempt serve as a scene in the Body of the story, and to cause the result of it (its fifth step) to form a hindrance to the main narrative purpose. The first attempt, which is to arouse jealousy is met by indifference on the part of Buck. The next attempt, in which Verena tries to impress him with her specially chosen clothes, finds him also indifferent; and in its fifth step it shows that she seems to have reached the point where disaster is imminent. Then she uses the other method, which is to beat the opponent at her own game, that is to outcharm her. Her newly acquired sophisticated conversation simply arouses the amused tolerance of her husband, who says, "What makes you talk so dumb, Rena?" The fifth step of this interchange is shown in an episode between Verena and Mr. Dark in which, summing up the state of affairs she sees no hope. She then, being in a position where she has virtually abandoned hope, goes to the conference at Mrs. Sennay's and notices that Buck looks like the steer whom she has roped. Then, just as Gideon Higsbee, in *Once and Always*, responded to the stimulus of the suggestion that he should sell some fake mining stock to Lemuel Gower in order to solve his problem, so Verena Dayson responds to the image conveyed by this idea and responds to it in terms of a solution of her problem. And just as Gideon Higsbee enlisted the aid of his friends in his enterprise, so she enlists the aid of Mr. Dark in her enterprise. Nowhere more than in the craftsmanship of short-story writing is it true that "necessity is the mother of invention." When the character has reached the big moment in the story where disaster seems imminent and inescapable the necessity for invention is greatest. All the old methods of escaping from a predicament must be abandoned and a new one, which is inherent in the capacity of the character must be invented either by the character or by the author, which, of course, is the same thing because the author invents the character. For sound craftsmanship this invention must involve a capacity already planted by the author in the early part of the story. This is true in the case of *Western Stuff*. Mrs. Pulver having through the action of her character laughed at all the tried and true methods for solving this old narrative problem, presents a new and entertaining version of a method for winning back an erring husband; and it is essentially one which is based upon the character and capacity of the particular actor in this story, Verena Dayson.

For one other reason this story is also interesting. I spoke before of the difference between objective and analytical writing, and I mentioned that the older formula for criticism was "objective" and "subjective." In this case the treatment is in many cases "subjective" because the personality of the author is apparent. This is true particularly on line 2220, where the author says, "With the omniscience of our kind" thus injecting her own personality into the story.

I have taken pleasure in including this story because it raises and answers many questions which authors will find of interest.

SECTION II

STORIES OF DECISION

WHEN we begin to consider the story of Decision as a distinct classification from the story of Accomplishment we will see the importance of the special nomenclature that we have agreed to use. I have in mind our special use of the word "condition" or "state of affairs" to replace the older and more generally used term "situation." The distinction between the two types of stories lies in the response of the chief actor to the main condition or main state of affairs, and that response projects what we agree to call a "narrative Situation." It is for this reason that I have closed the first section of this book with the story *Western Stuff*, because the condition to which the main actor responds in terms of a narrative problem or narrative situation is the same condition to which the main actor responds in the story *Women are Wiser*, by Frank R. Adams, which opens the second section.

The condition is, in both stories, that the wife realizes that she is in danger of losing her husband. In *Western Stuff* the reaction is instantaneous, and is in terms of purpose. That purpose is to win him back from the other woman. The narrative situation is one of accomplishment. In *Women are Wiser* the narrative problem or narrative situation is one of decision or choice. In *Western Stuff* there is no question in the mind of the main actor as to what course to pursue. In *Women are Wiser* there is a very definite uncertainty as to which course to take, or what decision to make.

People often ask "How may I tell whether a story is a story of accomplishment or a story of decision?" There are several ways in which to tell. Every story has its general large division of Situaation, Explanatory Matter, Struggle, Conclusive Act, and sometimes Sequel to the Conclusive Act. The Sequel is not a distinguishing feature, because it may occur in either story, and it may be the same in either story. But in the Beginning of the story of Accomplishment the main narrative problem is one of accomplishment. In the Beginning of the story of Decision, the main narrative problem is one requiring decision, or might be said to be one of indecision or uncertainty as to what action is to be taken. But confusion may arise in the mind of a reader who finds that in certain stories there is set forth a narrative problem and there is in the mind of the reader an uncertainty, but this uncertainty is followed by certainty, and then a number of struggles arise as a result of the course of conduct decided upon. There is an example of this in the story by William Dudley Pelley, *The Face in the Window*, reprinted in the accomplishment section of this book. In this story the main condition is set forth, and the main actor, Cora McBride, is uncertain as to what course of conduct she will pursue. Had the story ended at the close of line 659, where Cora McBride leaves the house it would be a story of Decision. In the story of Decision no struggles grow out of the Conclusive Act. In the story of Accomplishment it is this Conclusive Act of Decision which projects the struggles of the story. The story of accomplishment only begins when the character decides to do something, in the story of Decision the story then ends (except, of course, for the Sequel). In the Ending of the story of Accomplishment the Conclusive Act is one that tells the reader that the actor has either accomplished his purpose, (that purpose is already known,) or has abandoned that already known purpose. In the Ending of the story of Decision there is a decision arrived at. The character is no longer uncertain, and then the story is over.

In the Body of the story of Decision we find its greatest difference from the story of Accomplishment. The Beginning of either story may have a number of presentation units leading up to the main problem, and each one of these presentation units may, at its crisis, show that there is the promise of conflict, or of a difficulty to be overcome, or of disaster. The difference in the Body of the two types of story is that, in the first, each one of these promises may be developed into a struggle between two people, but in the story of Decision the only possible conflict which can occur is a mental conflict between traits in the same person, one urging him toward one choice, another urging him toward another choice, even though that choice may be inertia. This mental struggle is, of all types of struggle, the least interesting, because it appeals to the intellect and not at all, or to a very slight extent, to the emotions or sensations. Such appeal to the intellect is usually fatal to interest. Theoretically, writers presenting stories of Decision should present a mental struggle leading to that decision. Practically they do not, because the theory defeats their purpose, to write an interesting story, and does not square with the facts.

Many writers who are inexperienced, and who realize instinctively that a story of Decision is almost certain to be an interesting story, are defeated because they try to apply a theory to the presentation of such a story. They clog the interest of the story by presenting as the Body of the story a prolonged mental struggle between different traits in the character of the chief actor. They here are led astray by an instinct which is sound; but are defeated because their knowledge of craftsmanship is insufficient.

The first clarifying step toward mastery of the craftsmanship of the story of Decision, which they would assume to have a Body showing indecision, is a realization that ordinarily the Body Scene is omitted. This is rather a startling discovery to the novices. They do not seem to see the justification for such a method. "If," they say, "the story is concerned with the uncertainty, then that uncertainty ought to be shown in the Body of the story." Here again Necessity is the mother of Invention. There was once a newly enlisted soldier in the colonial army, who did not realize that the rigid discipline of the army made it necessary for him to keep from voicing his opinion of an officer for whose abilities he had very little respect. He voiced his opinions by saying, "That officer is a damned fool." Reprimanded for this, he inquired why he should not say what he believed. "Can't I say he's a fool if I think he's a fool?" he asked. "Not at all," he was told. "You can think what you like so long as you don't say it." "All right," he said, "I think he's a damned fool."

He had devised a way of showing his thoughts. In the story of Decision if you wish to indicate the thoughts of the main actor it is better to *show* those thoughts in a scene in which he expresses them *through his speech*, and that will be an interchange with somebody else. In that way you will avoid the mental scene.

It is, of course, much easier to point out to you through the special cases which make up the remainder of the book just how this is brought about; so I shall abandon a theoretical discussion of it to illustrate by the case method. But before doing so I want to make one or two observations. If the scene in the Body of the story of Decision is eliminated, and if the scenes in the Body of the story of Accomplishment usually occupy a large portion of the space, "Where," you may ask, "is the length so taken away, made up?" It is made up either in the Beginning, or in the Ending, or in the Sequel. But your greatest advance in craftsmanship will come with the realization that in the story of Decision the interest must come chiefly from the *Scenes* of the story rather than from the

Plot. This is particularly true in the story of Decision which is presented chronologically; because when the decision is made the story is over. Therefore the bulk of such a story must be presented in interchanges or scenes which are unsupported in their interest by any knowledge on the part of the reader of the main narrative question, which comes only after there have been presented to him those Scenes which make up the Beginning of the story of Decision. Now let us abandon theory for actual illustration.

ARCHITECTURAL CHART

OF

WOMEN ARE WISER

BEGINNING	Initial condition presented.	Meeting. Faith and condition.	1– 87	Need for Decision apparent.
		Flash-back Interchange. Faith and Roger.	88–136	Difficulties in way of easy decision shown.
	Necessity for Choice is shown.	Scene. Faith and Mr. Brennon.	137–377	Choice No. 1 apparent.
		Scene. Faith and Mrs. Brennon.	378–612	Choice No. 2 apparent. Narrative Question: "What choice will Faith make?"
ENDING	Decisive Act.	Faith telephones Mrs. Brennon.	613–617	Narrative Question Answered. "She refuses to humiliate her husband."
	Sequel.	Interchange. Faith and Roger.	618–679	
		Interchange. Mrs. and Mr. Brennon.	680–733	

CASE No. 11

WOMEN ARE WISER

BY FRANK R. ADAMS

1 The Roger Brennon marriage
2 had stood a five-year breaking
3 strain pretty well. That is, it
4 had not broken.

5 This had taken considerable
6 effort on the part of Faith Bren-
7 non, but presumably all matri-
8 monial pack-loads are carried on
9 the shoulders of women. Men
10 have other things to think about
11 and usually do.

12 That, for instance, was the
13 case of Roger Brennon. He
14 thought about golf, poker, busi-
15 ness, chorus-girls, bootleggers
16 and himself. Naturally he
17 couldn't pay any more attention
18 to the institution of matrimony
19 than an occasional glance in the
20 direction of the engineer to see if
21 she was at her post with one
22 hand on the throttle and the
23 other putting ribbons on her
24 bonny brown hair.

25 Of the things mentioned which
26 occupied Roger's attention the
27 word chorus-girls is generic.
28 It covered a multitude of
29 women with perhaps no real
30 chorus-girl among them. We
31 think of gay ladies as chorus-
32 girls. Heaven knows why. It
33 is a survival, perhaps, of the days
34 when it was considered wicked
35 to be on the stage.

36 There were a couple of reasons
37 why Roger attracted the roving
38 attention of everyone, including
39 women. One of them was that
40 he was an only son and had been
41 accustomed to demand and get
42 a lot of admiration ever since he
43 had worn his first safety-pin.
44 The other reason was that God
45 had made him lovable enough so
46 that you had to care for him in
47 spite of the fact that you knew
48 darn well that he ought to spend
49 all of his leisure moments in the
50 electric chair.

51 It is only in old-fashioned
52 plays and stories that heroes are
53 all virtuous. Recent explora-
54 tions in the labyrinths of the
55 human mind have unearthed the
56 not very astonishing fact that
57 there is about an equal amount
58 of virtue and villainy in every-
59 body. And that everybody pre-
60 fers to wear the mask of virtue

61 until it is torn off. A real crim-
62 inal is an ordinary man whose
63 mask has been destroyed so that
64 he can't fool anyone any more—
65 not even himself.

66 Roger had no illusions about
67 himself. But on the other hand,
68 and Faith knew this, he never
69 asked for mercy. As well as his
70 limitations of character permit-
71 ted, he lived gallantly. Indica-
72 tions were that he would die the
73 same way—and at a compara-
74 tively early age unless someone
75 continued to protect him.

76 Faith had taken over the job
77 from Roger's father five years
78 before.

79 Now it looked as if the elder
80 Brennon was about to reassume
81 some of the responsibility.

82 At any rate Faith had a curt
83 note from him in the mail that
84 morning asking her to call "with
85 reference to the current misbe-
86 havior of your husband and
87 my son."

88 She got the summons shortly
89 after Roger had left for the office.
90 She tried to think back over their
91 breakfast together to see if there
92 had been any symptoms of guilt
93 in Roger's behavior. There
94 seemed to be nothing out of the
95 ordinary. But probably there
96 wouldn't be under any circum-
97 stances. Roger had a duck's-
98 back sort of conscience and an
99 infinite capacity for playing
100 without retrospection whatever
101 game was on at the time.

102 That very morning he had
103 awakened her by acting an elab-
104 orately jumbled fairy-story in
105 which he was the Middle-sized
106 Bear who had found Little Red
107 Riding Breeches sleeping off an
108 enchanted bun in the other half
109 of his twin bed.

110 "What's this?" he had ex-
111 claimed. "As I live, it's the
112 Princess of Peruna under a spell
113 —a rose-colored crêpe de Chine
114 spell. I wonder what will arouse
115 her."

116 Faith had kept her eyes shut
117 and answered faintly, "She is
118 bewitched and can be awakened
119 only by the kiss of the right bozo.
120 Any other who tries will die with
121 a horrible tummy ache."

122 " 'Tis too great a risk," he had
123 decided, after deliberation. "But
124 cold water is a sovereign remedy
125 for witchcraft and methinks I'll
126 drop her in a tub of it."

127 He had picked her up and
128 would have done it, too, if she
129 had not decided then and there
130 to come out of the spell without
131 any further magic rites.

132 Decidedly Roger, as a play-
133 fellow, would be an exceedingly
134 difficult person to be without.
135 Especially after you had once
136 become accustomed to him.

137 He was not much like his
138 father. Faith felt as if she were
139 appearing before the Su-
140 preme Court whenever she en-
141 tered Mr. John Brennon's pres-
142 ence. Mr. Brennon, senior,
143 always reminded Faith of a Pil-
144 grim landing on a Plymouth

145 Rock—and pulverizing it. He
146 was the embodiment of stern and
147 dignified virtue. In the com-
148 munity in which he lived he was
149 the head and personification of
150 militant reform. All of the
151 worthier campaigns for civic de-
152 cency were sponsored and even
153 frequently captained by him.
154 All in all, as Faith had occasion-
155 ally reflected, he was a wonderful
156 influence in the city but un-
157 doubtedly a hard man for his
158 family to live up to. He would
159 pray with you, but even in his
160 prayers there was concealed a
161 punitive lash. The word "com-
162 promise" had never been written
163 into his vocabulary.

164   She called at the house that
165 morning and Roger's mother
166 took her into her husband's
167 private study. Mrs. Brennon
168 used a crutch handily in getting
169 around the house. Out-of-doors
170 she ordinarily was wheeled in a
171 chair.

172   Mr. Brennon had retired from
173 the active presidency of his bank
174 and now conducted most of his
175 business from his home.

176   But he was sitting back of a
177 big desk much as if he were in an
178 office. Bankers and business
179 men in general feel more secure
180 behind an oak or mahogany
181 barricade. Take away all the
182 flat-top desks in the world and
183 the casualties among capitalists
184 would be appalling.

185   To lay down the law, you've
186 got to get behind something.

187 Even ministers, you may remem-
188 ber, are more authoritative in a
189 railed pulpit.

190   John Brennon dominated his
191 study just as he dominated his
192 family and his world. He was
193 the only upright thing in a land-
194 scape that he had personally
195 flailed flat. This was illustrated
196 by the fact that although his
197 wife was in the room she said
198 nothing, but sat, a little twin-
199 kling figure on a straight chair
200 near the wall, much as if she were
201 an office boy awaiting orders.

202   There was a lot of formality
203 about this meeting between
204 Faith and her father-in-law. She
205 felt a little as if the proceedings
206 ought to be opened with prayer.
207 Mr. Brennon was dressed as
208 meticulously as a hanging judge
209 and his pouchy jowls were
210 shaved a faint pink. Under his
211 eyes were undisguisable circles.

212   "Faith," he began, "you have,
213 for five years, been burdened by
214 cares which, before you assumed
215 them, made an old man of me."

216   "If you mean Roger," inter-
217 rupted Faith, "you needn't apol-
218 ogize. He's a very amusing
219 husband."

220   "I rather imagined that mar-
221 riage would sober him down,"
222 Mr. Brennon continued imper-
223 turbably, "but I regret to say
224 that I find it has not. His con-
225 duct with this Winterbottom
226 woman is disgraceful, disgusting
227 and inexcusable."

228   "The Winterbottom woman?"

229 Faith repeated questioningly. "I
230 don't remember—yes, I do, too.
231 Peggy Winterbottom was her
232 name and someone brought her
233 to a country club dance last
234 fall. But we haven't seen her
235 since."

236 "*You* haven't," corrected her
237 father-in-law, "but Roger has."

238 Faith mulled that over in her
239 mind. "Perhaps he has had
240 some business dealings with her.
241 I seem to remember that they
242 said she did something for a
243 living."

244 "Not something — somebody.
245 No. Roger has not been seeing
246 her on any business but her own.
247 Unfortunately she has a hus-
248 band, a traveling salesman, who
249 returned unexpectedly and dis-
250 covered them in—in conference,
251 so to speak."

252 Mr. Brennon paused as if to
253 give her a chance to recover
254 from this shock before feeding
255 her any more indigestible infor-
256 mation.

257 Faith wished that she might
258 be alone for a few moments so
259 that she could be privately
260 hysterical. It was more of a
261 shock to her than she could
262 publicly confess—it probably is
263 to every woman when she first
264 finds that her husband is almost
265 exactly like other men whom she
266 has heard about.

267 But she steadied her voice and
268 assumed a certain composure.
269 "I don't think there is anything
270 I can do about it."

271 "No," Mr. Brennon conceded.
272 "This particular case has been
273 taken care of by me. There is
274 no danger. I have bought off all
275 the parties concerned, even the
276 husband, who seemed to think
277 ten thousand dollars was ample
278 recompense for the loss of a
279 wife.

280 "But your part is the future.
281 You've got to prevent this from
282 happening again. If I did not
283 think that you could do it I
284 never should have mentioned
285 the matter to you at all. You
286 would probably be happier not
287 to know."

288 Faith happened to look up at
289 the elder Mrs. Brennon just at
290 that moment and caught a curi-
291 ous, unfathomable look in her
292 eye, the expression of a woman
293 who has been startled momen-
294 tarily out of a lifetime pose. It
295 interested Faith so much that
296 she almost forgot to pay atten-
297 tion to Mr. Brennon's next
298 words.

299 Mechanically she had said,
300 "How could I do anything that
301 would prevent Roger from doing
302 unwise things?"

303 "Put the fear of God into
304 him," her father-in-law thun-
305 dered. "Make him realize what
306 sort of fool he has been and con-
307 stantly remind him of the wrong
308 he has done to you. It is only
309 because men forget the punish-
310 ment that they transgress."

311 "I'm afraid," Faith began,
312 "that I don't know how to——"

"Fortunately I do," the stern old man interrupted. "And I have all the weapons you need. They cost me enough so that they ought to be put to some good use." He produced a packet of perhaps half a dozen letters held together with a wide rubber band. "These are in the handwriting of your husband and are worth about two thousand dollars apiece."

Faith seemed to have no reaction to express, not even gratitude for the supervision of her affairs under most trying circumstances.

"Are you suggesting that I use them as evidence in a divorce suit?" she finally managed to ask.

"N-n-no," Mr. Brennon replied with final decisiveness, "there will be no divorce scandal in my family. I would never have brought up this subject unless I had thought you were too proud and sensible to consider such a thing. All you have to do is to keep him in order. I suggest that you memorize a few phrases from this mess of expensive rubbish so that you can quote an occasional passage to him whenever you suspect that he has strayed even mentally from the narrow highway of integrity which, heaven knows, I have always tried to train his footsteps to tread."

That was quite rhetorical and Faith had a grotesquely incongruous thought that he had forgotten that there was only one of her and was visualizing an audience.

The interview seemed to be ended.

He gave her the letters and escorted her and his wife to the door. "A delegation from the Women's Civic Improvement Society is waiting to see me. If you want any further advice or instructions in this or any correlative matter, I'll be ready to help you."

As the two women stood in the doorway Mr. Brennon leaned down unexpectedly and kissed his wife with sudden and genuine tenderness.

"I'll be through here in plenty of time for a gallop in the park before luncheon."

Mrs. Brennon led the way from the study, which was on the main floor, toward the stairway. Faith was headed for the door, but the older woman indicated silently that she was to come up.

Imitating her silence but wondering nevertheless, Faith followed her up the staircase. Mrs. Brennon's private sitting-room was so different from the study of the *paterfamilias* that it scarcely seemed possible that they could be under the same roof. There was nothing austere about the wife's apartment, nothing even very modern or in any particular scheme of decoration. The only quality in

397 common that every article in
398 room had was that of comfort
399 and womanly gentleness.

400 The lady of the house disposed
401 of her crutch and seated herself
402 in what was apparently her ac-
403 customed chair. She indicated
404 another near by for Faith. "Did
405 you notice," she queried mus-
406 ingly, "what John said just as
407 we left?"

408 "About a gallop in the park
409 before luncheon?"

410 "Yes. That's his way of tell-
411 ing me that he loves me just as
412 much as he did when I was
413 young and, I'm afraid, lovely in
414 his eyes and when I really could
415 ride a horse instead of a rubber
416 tired perambulator. I just want-
417 ed you to remember what he
418 said because it has quite a lot to
419 do with what I may say to you."

420 "May?" Faith repeated.
421 "Meaning that there is some
422 condition attached?"

423 "Not exactly. But sometimes
424 it is difficult for a wife and the
425 mother of the man she marries
426 to understand each other very
427 perfectly. In the first place, do
428 you feel that you want a divorce
429 from Roger?"

430 "On account of these letters?"

431 "On any account."

432 "I might use them the way
433 Mr. Brennon suggested."

434 "Could you?"

435 "I don't know. Why not?"

436 The older woman, who was
437 also the smaller, spread her
438 hands out in a curious gesture
439 across her skirt. Mothers have
440 done it from time immemorial
441 as an invitation to a child to sit
442 on their laps.

443 Faith had a flash vision of her
444 husband, as a little boy, hugged
445 tight to that forgiving bosom.

446 "You might much better get a
447 divorce," she said gently.
448 "Much better than to hold those
449 letters over Roger's head as a
450 threat."

451 "But I really love him, I
452 think, or anyway I did up to a
453 few minutes ago, and if I give
454 him another trial I might win
455 him back," Faith told her.

456 "Not the way Mr. Brennon
457 suggested. You might keep
458 Roger, but you would lose him.
459 What every woman knows is
460 that her husband is really just a
461 little boy. But what she has to
462 learn is to let him think he is a
463 great big noble man. The min-
464 ute a woman lets a man know
465 she is holding him under her
466 thumb—and he stays there—she
467 hasn't a man at all.

468 "In the hope that you really
469 will understand, I'm going to tell
470 you something that I have never,
471 heretofore, breathed to a soul,
472 especially not to my husband.
473 Will you take my keys"—she
474 extended them—"and unlock the
475 right-hand drawer of my desk?"

476 Faith did as she was told and
477 awaited further instructions.

478 "There are several packages
479 of letters there, most of them
480 tied with bits of old ribbon—

481 those are from my husband both
482 before and after marriage. But
483 there is another with a rubber
484 around it, much like the packet
485 you hold in your hand. That is
486 the one I want. Do you find
487 it?"

488 "Yes." Faith handed it to
489 her.

490 "Mr. Brennon, as you know, is
491 a great influence for good in this
492 city. His example is an inspir-
493 ing one, even to himself.

494 "That last phrase may sound
495 incomprehensible so I will try to
496 explain. Long ago I discovered
497 that he was a human being and
498 not a sort of deputy of God. By
499 that I don't mean that he is a
500 hypocrite. Most of his instincts
501 are right and he really lives up
502 to the standard he sets—most of
503 the time. Any deviations from
504 that standard are more surpris-
505 ing to himself than to anyone
506 else and he has been his own
507 severest judge and jailer.

508 "But there have been many
509 temptations. He is a strong
510 man, a very masculine one, and
511 his self-imposed tasks of civic
512 reform have brought him into
513 contact with women. Some-
514 times some of them confused the
515 cause for which they were work-
516 ing with the man who was at the
517 head of it, and have brought
518 their tribute to the priest instead
519 of laying it on the altar which
520 he serves.

521 "Devotion from a woman is
522 something which a man finds it

523 difficult to trip over without
524 noticing the way she does her
525 hair and takes care of her com-
526 plexion. After a man notices a
527 woman, nature has a high-
528 handed way of ignoring the laws
529 with which men have fenced off
530 the jungle.

531 "The letters in this package
532 are probably quite similar to the
533 ones which you have in yours.
534 The only difference is that these
535 are twenty-five years old. Mr.
536 Brennon has never seen them, at
537 least not since they have been
538 in my possession.

539 "We can take those letters in
540 to him and by merely laying
541 them on his desk we can humili-
542 ate him so that he will crawl to
543 me and to you. What shall we
544 do? We women talk much of
545 emancipation from the control
546 of men. Here are we, two of us,
547 who have the power and the
548 opportunity to wield a lash that
549 will make our husbands forever
550 subject to our slightest wish.

551 "If we use our power we will
552 have no more need ever to ask
553 for anything or to exchange our
554 love for livelihood. All we have
555 to give up is the curious whim-
556 sical devotion which men, as part
557 of their pose, like to bestow on
558 those who they think are stand-
559 ing on the stair just one step
560 lower than themselves.

561 "I have faced the problem
562 alone for a good many years, as
563 you can see, and I have been
564 fearfully weak about making a

285

565 decision. As it is, we are living
566 in a little play with make-up
567 covering our defects even from
568 each other, speaking lines, even,
569 that have been prepared in ad-
570 vance, and with scenery that is
571 beautiful only on the painted
572 side.

573 "What shall I do, what shall
574 we do, you and I—tear off the
575 masks, turn the scenery around
576 to show that it is only canvas
577 and never listen again to lying
578 poetry, or shall we go on with
579 the conscious dream with this
580 little ache in our hearts to tell us
581 that it isn't all quite true? I
582 don't know. What do you say?"

583 Mrs. Brennon had not been at
584 all emotional in stating her case.
585 On the contrary, she had been
586 very matter-of-fact, with her
587 wrinkled old hands lying lightly
588 clasped in her lap.

589 In view of those wrinkled,
590 nearly useless hands Faith's
591 question seemed almost absurd.
592 "You do love him?"

593 "Yes. Quite as much as I love
594 Roger and in much the same
595 way. Women always are older.
596 Nature puts age into our hearts
597 at birth just as she keeps spring
598 always burning in the breasts
599 of men. I don't know why.
600 Marrying a man is much the
601 same as giving birth to him and
602 quite as painful. And they for-
603 get. My dear, that is the worst,
604 they forget. And women must
605 never notice—not if they want
606 them to come back."

607 Faith left the house still carry-
608 ing the package of Roger's let-
609 ters. They were in her hands,
610 unread, when she got home.
611 There, at last, she laid them on
612 her tiny desk.

613 Before dinner she telephoned
614 to her mother-in-law. "I have
615 burned them," she said briefly.
616 "And I'm going to try to be one-
617 half as lovely as you are."

618 Roger was a little late for din-
619 ner. During the interval of
620 waiting Faith had a few bad
621 moments of indecision. Part of
622 it was wondering if perhaps,
623 after all, it might not be better
624 to bind him to her more closely
625 by fear; the other was the pure
626 stage-fright of an actor about to
627 play a part for the first time.

628 Fortunately Roger had some-
629 thing else to occupy his mind so
630 he did not notice her nervous-
631 ness.

632 "Dad has been down to the
633 office all the afternoon," he ex-
634 plained. "He even drove me
635 home. Acted kind of sorry for
636 me and apologetic as if he had
637 been putting a little cyanide in
638 my tonsil alcohol. The last
639 thing he did was to give me a
640 fifty percent increase in pay
641 and drive me around to a flor-
642 ist's and pick out these orchids
643 for you. Something has made
644 him darn sentimental. Got any
645 idea what it is?"

646 Faith shook her head.

647 "And you still love your old
648 man," he questioned, kneeling at

her feet, "even if he has got whiskers?"

"Yes," Faith declared, holding his head tight against her body. In her eyes, which he did not see, was misty light, the light that babes wake up to find in those of the mother who bends over them. "I do, I do," she declared, repeating it as if to reenforce her own faith.

He picked her up bodily—it was convenient to grab her by the knees the way she stood—and swung her over his shoulder.

"All right, then, I'll ride you up-stairs and you can sit on the dresser and catch the bristles as they fall to stuff a sofa-pillow with. I bought a new can-opener today that's just the thing to shave with."

Faith finally began to laugh. Maybe it was the way she had been jounced up and down on his shoulder. Maybe it was sheer relief at realizing that she was going to go on listening to his nonsense until her hands, too, were wrinkled and useless but not very sad. Perhaps——

Half across the city his father came into his wife's room and bent over for a kiss. His eyes were haggard, too, and the circles under them were darker. He clung for a moment to the wrinkled hand that lay in her lap.

"I'm worried, Dear, and afraid," he said. All the high authority, the dominance was gone from his voice. "I'm won-dering if we did the right thing for our boy."

She considered a moment. Then she gently disengaged her fingers from his clasp and touched his head soothingly. "Yes, Dear, I'm quite sure that we have done the right thing for our boy."

Before they went down to dinner he noticed the packet of ancient envelopes fastened with a spiritless rubber band.

"What's this," he asked, with a return to his more familiar, confident mood, "a collection of love letters to the queen by the court jester while the king was in the counting-house?"

"No," she answered. "Perhaps you had better look at them."

He started to remove the elastic. It came apart in his hands and the envelopes fell, disordered, on the table. He picked up one and opened it. He looked at the folded sheets within, then picked up another and another and scanned them rapidly.

"But these are only blank sheets of your new stationery folded up and put in a lot of old envelopes. What on earth did you do that for?"

His wife smiled; finally she laughed as she smoothed her skirt as mothers do.

"That, John dear," she said, "is something I am never going to tell you."

THE ANALYSIS

The production of a story of Decision calls for all the knowledge of craftsmanship which a writer possesses. It calls especially for the ability to write Scenes. It is essentially a problem of enlarging simple outlines into the five to seven thousand word short-story. Writers who have difficulty with the Beginnings of their stories had better stick to some type other than the Decision, that is to an Accomplishment story, because the writing of a decision type story calls for expert knowledge in presenting Beginnings interestingly. You will remember that I mentioned earlier in this book that there were two kinds of curiosity to which the writer might appeal. The one is general curiosity, the other narrative curiosity. Since the use of narrative curiosity is ordinarily denied to the writer who presents the story of Decision chronologically, he must therefore, be able to make the appeal to the other kind of curiosity. In addition to this he must be able to appeal to the dramatic instinct in people which is aroused by the appearance of probable disaster, or conflict.

Mr. Adams's story *Women Are Wiser* falls very readily into its major divisions of Beginning, and Ending. It is one of the Decision type stories which does not bore the reader with a Body scene made up of psychological analysis of the actor's uncertainty. The Beginning occupies lines 1 to 612, the Ending occupies lines 613 to 733, the Decisive Act occupying lines 613 to 617, the Sequel occupying lines 618 to 733. A glance at the chart which precedes the analysis of the story will show that the story is divided into the very same sort of blocks as is the story of accomplishment, these blocks being presentation units. The first block, lines 1 to 87 is concerned with setting forth the condition which confronts the main actor. It contains the probability of disaster, and expecially in that paragraph which tells of the attractions of Roger, and the difficulty of blaming him, it sets before the reader the difficulty lying before Faith in making a choice. It is evident that the choice is not easy because she is very much in love with her husband; at the same time he appears to be a man who ought "to spend all his leisure moments in the electric chair." In the first paragraph of the story the reader's curiosity is aroused. He does not know what the whole thing is about, yet he is not bored, because the introduction is not too long. It sets forth the main condition and it presents the main actor. It shows also the urgency and the immediacy of the need for action. Then there is a flash-back interchange between

Faith and Roger, occupying lines 88 to 136. This is not a typical flash-back Beginning because it does not present the main problem of the story and then flash-back in order to give the information necessary to the reader's understanding of the problem, picking up the chronological order again at the moment when the choice or decision must be made. Instead it goes back and gives a certain amount of information, which is that Faith and Roger are on excellent terms and that he is very necessary to her. This is a flash-back interchange in which the promise of disaster is a turning point at the close of the interchange, but it does not then resume the story at the point where the decision must be made. Before that point is reached, there are two other interchanges. It would have been a typical flash-back had the meetings been arranged in this order: meeting lines 1 to 87, meeting lines 137 to 377, meeting lines 378 to 612, then a flash-back to interchange lines 88 to 136 which would bring the reader back to the main narrative problem. This interchange lines 88 to 136, is now an interchange to avoid the use of summary, a device of craftsmanship of which Mr. Adams is a master.

For the purposes of this book, therefore I shall regard this story as a story of decision presented *chronologically*. At the close of the first meeting which shows that Faith is aware of a certain condition, we do not know that she has to make a choice between courses of conduct. We do not realize that she is uncertain in her mind as to what to do. No uncertainty is shown. When we have read the flash-back interchange we realize the disaster that will occur should she decide to do anything that will smash up the marriage. At the close of the interchange lines 137 to 377, between Faith and Mr. Brennon, we see, however, a very definite choice apparent. The course of conduct is clearly outlined for her by Mr. Brennon. It is that she shall humiliate her husband sufficiently to assure his faithfulness thereafter. At the close of the interchange between Faith and Mrs. Brennon, from 378 to 612, we see that a second choice is possible, and now we are aware that the heroine is torn between two courses of conduct, that she has to make a definite choice.

Because Mr. Adams is a competent and experienced writer he does not bore us with an interchange showing this uncertainty or indecision. Instead he swiftly carries us through to the Decisive Act, which is now lines 613 to 617, when Faith is shown telephoning Mrs. Brennon.

The lesson to be learned from the analysis of this story is that the story of Decision is dependent almost entirely upon the ability of the writer to write interchanges, which are preferably complete scenes. There is a certain amount of leeway available in the opening of a story which may be used by the author and presented in a meeting to indicate to the reader all the information in regard to the character and much of the problem. But this cannot be prolonged. It must be swiftly made a transition to an interchange. It is essential also for a writer who contemplates writing a story of decision to realize that the problem must be one which is of interest to a large number of people. It is essentially a problem of conduct. It must be a clearly defined clash between the affection and a standard of conduct or convention. In this case it is exactly that. Faith is extremely fond of her husband, yet the conventions demand that she shall not permit him to be lax in his duties to her. The decision she makes, and the reason for making that decision are made clear by the author.

This is an extremely interesting example of the Decision story in which the Beginning takes the place of both the Beginning and Body of the ordinary story of accomplishment. Had this been a story of Accomplishment, the first meeting would have set forth the main condition. That meeting and its flash-back would have made up the Beginning, which would be composed of the main problem with explanatory matter necessary to its understanding.

Then the Body of the story would have been made up of the two interchanges between Faith and Mr. Brennon and Faith and Mrs. Brennon. At the conclusion of one there would have been a crisis of hindrance. In this case it is a crisis of choice. At the conclusion of the interchange between Faith and Mrs. Brennan there would have been another crisis of hindrance, at which point disaster would have threatened. In this case there is a crisis of choice, because another choice is apparent; and as in the story of Accomplishment, the close of the Body scenes show a moment when disaster threatens, here again there is such a moment.

The story having no Body achieves its length in the Beginning. It is made up of 733 lines. Of this number the greater proportion, lines 1 to 612, occupy the Beginning. Now I shall ask you to turn to the next story, *Jetsam*, by John Russell.

BEGINNING	Explanatory matter presented to the reader in order that he may understand the line-up of forces which will determine the final choice.	Meeting. Junius Peabody and condition. Finds himself broke at Fufuti.	1– 123	General curiosity aroused. Unusual and striking moment catches reader's attention.
		Flash-back Interchange. Junius and Bendemeer.	123– 139	Hopelessness of condition is shown.
		Interchange. Junius and the Sydney Duck. (His response is to wish to begin again.)	140– 428	Emphasis upon depth of degradation.
		Interchange. Junius and the Sydney Duck Fight over lump Junius has found.	429– 543	New beginning possible. Disaster threatens.
		Interchange with Bendemeer. Is repudiated.	544– 792	Disaster seems sure.
		Interchange. Sydney Duck and Willems, followed by Junius's attack.	793–1037	Now new beginning seems possible.
		Interchange. Junius and Bendemeer. Bendemeer sets forth two definitely exclusive choices.	1038–1256	Narrative Question: "How will Junius choose?"
ENDING	Conclusive Act.	Junius decides upon Nukava.	1257–1263	Answer to Narrative Question is: "He chooses Nukava."
	Sequel.	Meeting. Bendemeer and condition.	1264–1296	Ironic significance clear.

JETSAM

BY JOHN RUSSELL

I HAVE chosen this story because I felt that to leave Mr. Russell out of any collection of stories would be to ignore one of the most competent craftsmen in America today. But I had another reason for including this story—a purely technical interest—which caused me to seize upon the splendid opportunity this story presented of showing how two writers may take the same materials, and using the same Ending, may write different types of stories, and different types of Beginning.

Now turn to the story and I will point out to you just what I have in mind.

CASE No. 12

JETSAM

BY JOHN RUSSELL

It is likely that at some time in his extreme youth Junius Peabody was introduced to those single-minded creatures, the ant and the bee. Doubtless he was instructed in the highly moral lessons they are supposed to illustrate to the inquiring mind of childhood. But it is certain he never profited by the acquaintance—indeed, the contemplation of such tenacious industry must have afflicted his infant consciousness with utter repugnance. By the time he was twenty-seven the only living thing that could be said to have served him as a model was the jellyfish.

Now, the jellyfish pursues a most amiable theory of life, being harmless, humorous, and decorative. It derives much enjoyment from drifting along through the glitter and froth, as chance may direct. It does no work to speak of. It never needs to get anywhere. And it never, never has to go thirsty. But some day it may get itself stranded, and then the poor jellyfish becomes an object quite worthless and fit only to be shoveled out of sight as soon as possible—because it lacks the use of its legs.

Thus it was with Junius Peabody, who awoke one morning of his twenty-eighth year on the roaring coral beach at Fufuti, below Bendemeer's place, to find that all the chances had run out and that the glitter had faded finally from a prospect as drab as the dawn spread over a butternut sea before him. . . .

Mr. Peabody sat up and looked about from under a corrugated brow, and yawned and shivered. His nerves had been reduced to shreds, and even the fiercest heat of tropic suns seemed never to warm him, a symptom familiar enough to brandy drunkards. But he had had such awakenings before, many of them, and the chill that struck through him on this particular morning was worse than any hang-over. It was the soul of Junius Peabody that felt cold and sick, and when he fumbled through his pockets—the subtle relation between the pockets and the soul is a point sadly neglected by our best little psychologists—he uncovered a very definite reason. His last penny was gone.

Under the shock of conviction Mr. Peabody sought to cast up the mental log, in the hope of determining where he was and how he came to be there.

The entries were badly blurred, but he could trace himself down through Port Said, Colombo, Singapore—his recollections here were limited to a woman's face in a balcony and the cloying aroma of anisette. He remembered a stop at Sydney, where he made the remarkable discovery that the Circular Quay was completely circular and could be circumnavigated in a night. After that he had a sketchy impression of the Shanghai race meeting and a mad sort of trip in a private yacht full of Australian sheep-something—kings, perhaps; tremendous fellows, anyway, of amazing capacity. And then Manila, of course, the place where he hired an ocean-going tug to urge a broken date on the coy ingénue of a traveling Spanish opera company. And then Macao, where he found and lost her again, as coy as ever, together with his wallet. And after that the hectic session when

he and a Norwegian schooner captain hit the bank at fan-tan and swore eternal friendship amid the champagne baskets on the schooner's decks under a complicated moon. It was this same captain who had landed him finally—the baskets having been emptied—at the point of a boot on the strand where now he sat. So much was still quite clear and recent, within range of days.

Always through the maze of these memoirs ran one consistent and tragic motive—a dwindling letter of credit, the fag end of his considerable patrimony. It had expired painlessly at last, the night before if he could trust his head, for there had been a noble wake. He recalled the inscrutable face of the tall white man behind the bar who had cashed it for him after a rate of exchange of his own grim devising. And he recalled, too, a waif bit of their conversation as he signed the ultimate coupon.

"You can date it Fufuti," suggested Bendemeer, and spelled the name for him.

"And where—where the devil is Fufuti?" he asked.

"Three thousand miles from the next pub," said Bendemeer, with excessively dry significance.

The phrase came back to him now. . . .

"In that case," decided Junius Peabody, aloud, "—in that case there's no use trying to borrow car-fare, and it's too far to walk. I'm stuck."

Some one sniffed beside him and he turned to stare into a face that might have been a distortion of his own yellow, haggard image.

"Hello," he said—and then, by natural sequence: "Say, you don't happen to have a flask anywhere handy about you— what?"

His neighbour scowled aggrievedly.

"Do I *look* like I 'ad a flask?"

The belligerent whine was enough to renew the identity of the mangy little larrikin whose couch on the sand he had shared. The Sydney Duck, they called him: a descriptive title which served as well as any. Junius did not like him very well, but he had lived in his company nearly a week and he had long forgotten to make effective distinctions. Brandy is a great democrat.

"It's my notion I'm going to have the fantods," explained Junius. "I need a bracer."

"My word, I could do with a nip meself just now," agreed Sydney. " 'In't y' got no more credit with Bendemeer?"

Peabody made an effort.

"Seems to me I was thrown out of Bendemeer's last night. Is that right?"

"You was, and so was me and that big Dutchman, Willems— all thrown out. But it was your fault. You started playin' chuck farthin' among his bottles with a bunch of copper spikes. . . . I never see a man 'old his liquor worse."

"Well, I paid for it, didn't I?" inquired Junius, without heat. "And I believe you had your share. But what I'm getting at is—if he threw me out, the credit must be gone."

This was simple logic and unanswerable. "Maybe y' got something else he'll tyke for th' price," suggested Sydney. "Damn 'im—'e's keen enough to drive a tryde!"

Junius went through the form of searching, but without any great enthusiasm, nor was Sydney himself notably expectant— a fact that might have seemed to argue a rather sinister familiarity with the probable result.

"I did have some cuff links and things," said Peabody vaguely. "I wonder what's become of them."

"I wonder," echoed Sydney. As if some last possible claim upon his regard had been dissipated, he let his lips writhe in mockery. "Ah, and that's a pity too. You got to learn now what it means bein' on the beach and doin' *without* drinks—'cept as you kin cadge them off'n 'alf-caste Chinymen and such. You won't like it, you won't."

"Do you?" asked Junius.

"Me? I'm used to it. But, Lord, look at them 'ands! I'll

229 lay you never did a day's work
230 in your life."

231 "Did you?" inquired Junius
232 Peabody equably.

233 "Garn!" retorted Sydney with
234 a peculiarly unlovely sneer.
235 "W'y, you don't know yet what
236 you've come to, you don't.
237 'Jaimes, fetch me me mornin'
238 drawft!'—that's your style.
239 Only there 'in't no Jaimes no
240 more, and no drawfts to be 'ad.
241 Ho! . . . You're only a beach-
242 comber now, mytey. A lousy
243 beachcomber! And you needn't
244 expect me to do none of your
245 beggin' for you, for I won't—
246 no fear!"

247 Junius observed him with at-
248 tention, with rather more atten-
249 tion than he could remember
250 having bestowed upon any spe-
251 cific object for a long time. He
252 examined the features of the
253 Sydney Duck, the undue prom-
254 inence of nose and upper lip, the
255 singularly sharp ridge of the
256 whole front face—whittled, as it
257 might have been; the thin, pink
258 ears and the jutting teeth that
259 gave him something of the feeble
260 ferocity of a rat. And with new
261 perception he saw Sydney Duck,
262 not only as an unpleasant
263 individual but as a type, the
264 fitting comrade and associate for
265 such as he.

266 "It's a fact," said Junius Pea-
267 body; "I've fallen pretty
268 low. . . ."

269 He looked out again upon that
270 unprofitable dawning. To right

and left stretched the flat, dim 271
monotony of the beach, lined in 272
misty surf and hedged with slim 273
palms like a tufted palisade. 274
From behind drifted the smokes 275
from scores of homely hearths. 276
Down by Tenbow Head the first 277
pearling luggers were putting out 278
under silver clouds of sail. Sea 279
and land stirred once more with 280
the accustomed affairs of busy 281
men, but here between land and 282
sea was the fringe of things, the 283
deserted domain of wreckage and 284
cast-off remnants. Here lay a 285
broken spar half buried in the 286
sand, part of the complex fabric 287
that once enabled some fair ship 288
to skim the waves. And here 289
among the kelp and the bodies of 290
marine animals he saw the loos- 291
ened staves of a barrel limply 292
spread and upthrust like the fin- 293
gers of some dead giant, with an 294
empty bottle near by as if fallen 295
from that slack grip. And here, 296
lastly, he was aware of Junius 297
Peabody, also on the beach, 298
washed up at the far edge of the 299
world like any other useless bit 300
of jetsam: to stay and to rot. 301

"Pretty low," said Junius Pea- 302
body. 303

But Sydney took no offence, 304
and seemed, on the contrary, to 305
extract a certain degree of pleas- 306
ure from the other's recognition 307
of his lot. 308

"Oh, it 'in't so bad," he de- 309
clared, with a quite human im- 310
pulse to reverse the picture. 311
"There's easy pickin' if you 312

know 'ow. Nobody starves 'ere anyw'y, that's one thing. No nigger will let a man starve—a soft lot of flats that w'y, the niggers. Often you fall in with a weddin' or a birthday or some-thin'; they're always 'avin' a feast, and *they* don't care who comes—they 'in't proud. Then you got nobody aharryin' of you up and down and askin' you wot for, that's a comfort—my word! And once in a while there's sure to be a new chum come along with a bit of brass—some flat who's willin' to stand the drinks."

"Like me," suggested Junius.

"Oh, there's plenty like you," nodded the Sydney Duck. "It's the pearlin' brings 'em, though it 'in't so soft as maybe they think, you see. When they're stony they mostly tyke a job till they find a chance to get aw'y again—that's if they're able to do anything at all."

For the first time in his life, probably, Junius Peabody con-sidered his accomplishments with a view to estimating their value in the open market.

"I once won the fancy diving event at Travers Island," he said. "And I used to swim the four-forty in a trifle over six minutes."

"That must 'a' been several seasons back," grinned Syd-ney.

"Not so many," said Junius slowly. "I forgot to add that I was also an excellent judge of French brandy."

He got to his feet and began to divest himself of the spotted remains of an expensive white silk suit.

"What's the gyme now?"

"Morning bath. Have you had yours yet?"

The Sydney Duck laughed, laughter that was strangely un-mirthful and so convulsive that Junius blinked at him, fearing a fit of some kind.

"You're a rare 'un," gasped the Sydney Duck. "I seen a good few, I 'ave, but none as rare as you. Mornin' bawth—and 'ave I 'ad mine yet! . . . On the beach at Fufuti!" He wag-gled his hands.

"Well, if it seems so queer as all that why not blow yourself?" offered Junius with perfect good nature. "You can't tell, you might like it. Come along."

"Garn!" snarled the other.

So Junius turned away and walked down the strand alone. Outward the ground swell broke and came rushing in with long-spaced undulations, and as he stood at the verge, shrinking in his nakedness, the east flamed suddenly through its great red archway and turned all the world to tinted glory. Fair across to him was flung a shining path. It seemed as if he had only to step out along that straight way of escape, and for an instant he had a yearning to try. Never

397 in his life had he followed a single
398 course to a definite end, and
399 what could be better now than
400 to choose one at last, to follow,
401 to go on following—and not to
402 return?

403 He looked down at his body
404 and saw as a revelation the piti-
405 ful wasting of his strength—how
406 scrawny he was of limb, how
407 bloated about the middle, and
408 his skin how soft and leprous
409 white. He made an ugly figure
410 under the clear light of the morn-
411 ing, like the decaying things
412 around him, where the carrion
413 flies were beginning to swarm in
414 the sun. And there came upon
415 him then a sudden physical
416 loathing of himself, a final sense
417 of disaster and defeat.

418 "If I could only begin
419 again—" thought Junius Pea-
420 body, and stopped and laughed
421 aloud at the wish, which is old
422 as folly and futile as sin. But
423 he had no relief from laughter
424 either, for it was the same he had
425 heard from the Sydney Duck, a
426 sort of hiccup. So he stopped
427 that too, and strode forthright
428 into the wash. . . .

429 Something flung against his
430 shin and tripped him. He
431 sprawled awkwardly from a sin-
432 gular impact, soft though quite
433 solid. He could see the object
434 floating on the next wave
435 and was curious enough to catch
436 it up. It was a rough lump of
437 some substance, a dirty grayish-
438 brown in colour, the size of a
boy's football. The touch of it 439
was rather greasy. 440

Junius stayed with the trove 441
in his hands and the tingling of 442
an odd excitement in his mind. 443
His first instinct rejected the 444
evidence. He had a natural sus- 445
picion that events do not hap- 446
pen so. But while he brought to 447
bear such knowledge as he 448
owned, facts read or heard, he 449
found himself still thrilled. 450

There was a sound from the 451
shore and the Sydney Duck hur- 452
ried up behind him to the edge 453
of the water, both hands clawed, 454
his little eyes distended. 455

"You've got it!" He took 456
two steps after a retreating 457
wave, but the next drove him 458
hopping. It was strange to see 459
the fellow drawn by a frantic 460
eagerness and chased again by 461
the merest flicker of foam, lifting 462
his feet as gingerly as a cat. 463

"What have I got?" asked 464
Junius, standing at mid-thigh 465
where the surf creamed in be- 466
tween them. 467

"It's the stuff! Chuck it over 468
—wha-i-i!" Sydney's voice rose 469
to a squeal as a frothing ripple 470
caught his toes. 471

Junius came wading shore- 472
ward, but he did not relinquish 473
the lump when the other felt 474
and paddled it feverishly, bab- 475
bling. 476

"Look at that—look at that! 477
All smooth an' soft—an' kind 478
of slimy, like. Oh, no, we 'in't 479
struck it fair rich this time, 480

481 for nothin'—oh, *now!* . . . My-
482 tey, I tell you—by Gaw', I tell
483 you it's the real stuff!''

484 "But oughtn't there be an
485 odour—a perfume?''

486 "Not yet—not while it's fresh.
487 That comes after. And any'ow,
488 what else could it be—'ey?''

489 Junius shook his head.

490 " 'Ere, I'll show you, you poor
491 flat!'' The larrikin raged about
492 like a man in a strong temper.
493 "Where's a nail? Gimme a nail
494 or a piece of wire—'ell, I'll show
495 you!''

496 He snatched up a strip of
497 planking from the sand and
498 wrenched a rusty spike from it.

499 With swift jerky gestures he
500 gathered a few dry chips and
501 splinters, whipped a match, and
502 set them alight. In this brief
503 blaze he heated the spike and
504 then applied it to the lump. It
505 sank smoothly, leaving a little
506 melted ring around the hole.

507 "Ambergris!'' he yelped.
508 "Worth near two pound an ounce,
509 right 'ere in Fufuti. . . . And
510 the 'arf of it's mine,'' he added,
511 with a startling shift to the most
512 brazen impudence.

513 Junius regarded him, incred-
514 ulous.

515 "What? That's wot! Wasn't
516 I here? 'In't I been pallin' along
517 of you? It's a fair divvy. W'y,
518 damn your soul,'' he screamed
519 in a sudden febrile blast of fury,
520 "you don't think you're goin' to
521 'og my 'arf an' all!''

522 "*Your* half!'' repeated Junius.

523 "Huh—nothing small about you,
524 is there? Why, you weren't any-
525 where near when I found it.
526 Didn't you pass up the swim?''

527 Just here the Sydney Duck
528 made his mistake. Had he pro-
529 ceeded with any finesse, with any
530 understanding of his man, he
531 might have done about as he
532 pleased, and it is likely that
533 little of moment would have
534 transpired on Fufuti beach that
535 morning. But he acted by his
536 lights, which were narrow and
537 direct, and he hit Junius Pea-
538 body suddenly in the smiling
539 face of him and knocked him
540 reeling backward. The next in-
541 stant he was running for the
542 nearest palms with the prize
543 tucked under one arm.

544 Junius sat on the sand and
545 blinked, and at first he felt rather
546 hurt, for he was not used to
547 being treated so, at least not
548 while he was sober. And there-
549 after he grinned, for such was his
550 way of turning aside a casual un-
551 pleasantness, and the thing un-
552 deniably had its humorous
553 aspect. But finally came the
554 throb of a strange new emotion,
555 as if someone had planted a small,
556 hot coal in his breast.

557 It is a fact worthy of note that
558 never before had Junius Peabody
559 known the sting of a living anger.
560 But never before had Junius Pea-
561 body been reduced to a naked
562 Junius Peabody, dot and carry
563 nothing—penniless, desperate,
564 and now cheated of a last

565 hope. That made the dif-
566 ference.

567 "Hey!" he protested. "See
568 here, you know—Dammit!"

569 He struggled up and climbed
570 anyhow into trousers, coat, and
571 shoes, and set off at a shambling
572 trot, with no clear notion of
573 what he meant to do, but keep-
574 ing the larrikin in sight.

575 Sydney dodged in among the
576 trees, found them too scant for
577 cover, paused to fling a yellow
578 snarl over his shoulder, and
579 swung up the shore. He turned,
580 questing here and there, shout-
581 ing as he ran, and presently
582 raised an answering shout from a
583 hollow whence another figure
584 started up to join him, a bearded,
585 heavy-set rogue, whose abnor-
586 mally long arms dangled like an
587 ape's out of his sleeveless shirt.
588 Junius recognized Willems, the
589 third of their party the night
590 before, and he knew where the
591 interest of that sullen big Hol-
592 lander would lie. He had a
593 coalition of thievery against him
594 now. The two beachcombers
595 ran on together, footing briskly
596 past the long boat sheds and the
597 high white veranda of Bende-
598 meer's place. . . .

599 Under this iron thatch stood
600 the man Bendemeer himself, cool
601 and lathy in spotless ducks,
602 planted there, as was his morn-
603 ing custom, to oversee and com-
604 mand all his little capital. And
605 in truth it was a kingdom's
606 capital, the center of a trading

607 monopoly of the old type, and
608 chief seat of as strange and ab-
609 solute a tyrant as the world still
610 offers room for; rich, powerful,
611 independent, fearing nothing be-
612 tween heaven and hell, and at
613 once the best-loved and the best-
614 hated individual in his sphere
615 of influence.

616 Bendemeer, trader, philan-
617 thropist, and purveyor of rotgut,
618 was one of those unclassed
619 growths of the South Seas that
620 almost constitute a new racial
621 type. Nobody could have placed
622 his nationality or his caste or his
623 accent. His name was of a piece
624 with the grim self-sufficiency
625 that gave nothing and asked
626 nothing: an obvious jest, bor-
627 rowed from the Persian song of
628 an Irish poet, but the one touch
629 of fancy about him. Somewhere,
630 somehow, he had taken a cynic
631 twist or a rankling wound that
632 had turned his white man's blood
633 once for all. They tell stories of
634 such cases up and down the is-
635 lands, and mostly the stories
636 are very ugly and discreditable
637 indeed. But not so concerning
638 Bendemeer; against whom was
639 no scandal; only curses and bit-
640 terness. For his peculiarity took
641 the especially irritating form of
642 fair dealings with some thou-
643 sands of brown-skinned natives
644 and no dealings at all with any
645 man of his own color—except
646 to beat him at strict business and
647 then to sell him as much villain-
648 ous liquor as he could at the

649 highest possible price. As he
650 leaned there indolently in his
651 doorway, with arms folded and
652 cheroot between his thin lips, he
653 could measure his own land as
654 far as he could see on either side,
655 a small part of his holdings in
656 plantations and trading stations
657 throughout the archipelago. Off-
658 shore, behind the only good strip
659 of barrier reef and near the only
660 navigable channel on the south
661 coast, lay anchored his *Likely*
662 *Jane*, flagship of a smart little
663 navy. His gang of boys was
664 hustling cargo out of her in surf-
665 boats, and both boys and boats
666 were the handiest and ablest that
667 could be found anywhere for that
668 ticklish work. He had only to
669 turn his head to view the satis-
670 factory bulk of his sheds and
671 dependencies, solid, new-painted.
672 The house at his back was trim,
673 broad, and comfortable, and in
674 the storeroom underneath lay
675 thousands of dollars' worth of
676 assorted trade goods, all of
677 which would eventually become
678 copra and great wealth.

679 This was the man, decidedly
680 in possession of his own legs and
681 able to stand and to navigate on
682 the same, to whom Junius Pea-
683 body appealed in his wretched
684 need. . . .

685 Junius stumbled up to the
686 steps. The burst had marrow-
687 drawn him, his lungs laboured
688 pitifully as if he were breathing
689 cotton wool. It was hot, for the
690 sun had sprung wide like an
691 opened furnace gate, but he had
692 not started a pore.

693 "I've been robbed," he
694 wheezed, and pointed a waver-
695 ing hand. "Those chaps there—
696 robbed——!"

697 Bendemeer glanced aside up
698 the strand after the disappear-
699 ing ruffians and then down at the
700 complainant, but otherwise he
701 did not move, only stayed con-
702 sidering from his lean, leathery
703 mask, with still eyes, outward-
704 looking.

705 "What do you care?" he said
706 idly. "You'll be dead in a month
707 anyhow."

708 Junius gaped toward him diz-
709 zily. The fellow was the local
710 authority, and besides had taken
711 his money. He could not believe
712 that he had heard aright. "But
713 say—they've stolen my prop-
714 erty!"

715 Bendemeer shot a blue ring of
716 smoke into the sunshine. "In
717 that case you've lost it. They're
718 heading for the Rocks, and once
719 they've gone to earth there you
720 never could find them—you'd be
721 torn to pieces if you did."

722 He flicked the ash of his cher-
723 oot in a pause. "I suppose you
724 mean I might help you," he con-
725 tinued. "I might, but I won't.
726 I've seen a good many of your
727 kind before, drift stuff that gets
728 washed up on the beach. You're
729 not worth it. And now, since
730 you have no further business
731 with me, I'd be obliged if you'd
732 kindly get the hell out of my

733 front yard. You're interfering
734 with the view. . . ."

735 Junius Peabody found himself
736 groping away through the sun-
737 light on Fufuti beach once more.
738 A dead calm held the air. Under
739 the steady, low organ note of the
740 reef he could hear only the drag
741 of his own steps, the curious,
742 unforgetable "shr-ring" of boot
743 leather on coral.

744 It was borne upon him then
745 that he had just acquired a lib-
746 eral education, that he had
747 learned more essential facts with-
748 in the last hour than he had ever
749 gained before in his twenty-odd
750 years—a tabloid of life—and too
751 late to be of any use. Such ab-
752 stractions are sometimes valu-
753 able to a man, but they are not
754 the sort that brings a lump in his
755 throat and a winking in his eyes.
756 The thing, the sheerly heartfelt
757 thing that Junius Peabody said
758 to himself, sniffling, was this:
759 "And he didn't—didn't even
760 offer me a drink!"

761 There was nothing to draw
762 him any farther—no help, no
763 promise of success, not even a
764 single witness to shame with a
765 grin or to urge with an expectant
766 stare—nothing outside himself.
767 Fufuti beach lay stark and
768 aching white before him. The
769 two thieves had long since lost
770 themselves among the palms.
771 Down by the water's edge a
772 couple of Bendemeer's boat boys
773 were salvaging odds and ends
774 lost overboard in an upset in

775 yesterday's heavy surf. They
776 did not waste a thought or a look
777 on him. He was many degrees
778 less important than a lot of other
779 rubbish around there. He might
780 just as well, he might much bet-
781 ter, slump down in a sodden
782 heap amid the rest of the jetsam.
783 And yet he did not. . . . And
784 he did go on. For some obscure,
785 irrational human reason, he did
786 go on. Perhaps because of the
787 tiny coal in his breast, blown red
788 by Bendemeer's blasting con-
789 tempt. Perhaps because, after
790 all, no man ever quite achieves
791 a complete resemblance to a
792 jellyfish.

793 On the southern tip of Fufuti
794 stands Tenbow Head, the end of
795 a rough little jut of land known
796 locally as the Rocks. To speak
797 by the book, there is neither rock
798 nor head, but the abyss turned in
799 its sleep once, and shouldered
800 half a mile of Fufuti's shore line
801 to a height of thirty feet—
802 enough for a mountain in this
803 sea of humble atolls. Inciden-
804 tally it smashed the elevated
805 reefs like chalk in a mortar.
806 Tenbow is a wreck of shattered
807 coral terraces clad in the eager
808 growths which profit by its tri-
809 fling rise and which alone do
810 profit. For the rest it remains
811 the island jungle, a section apart
812 and untouched, almost impene-
813 trable.

814 Junius Peabody began his ex-
815 ploration of this cheerful region
816 by falling on his face in a gully

817 and bruising his nose very griev-
818 ously. He found no trail to guide
819 him up the slope. It was pitted
820 like slag, deceitful as old honey-
821 comb. The footing crumbled;
822 tempting beds of moss and fern
823 slipped away at his clutch;
824 twisting lianas caught his ankles
825 and sent him asprawl. The very
826 ground seemed armed against
827 him with a malignant life of its
828 own. He had to creep among
829 jagged teeth that sliced his
830 flimsy garments and his putty-
831 soft flesh. And when a loosened
832 mass slid gently over at a touch
833 and crushed an arm he scarcely
834 wondered whether any personal
835 power had directed. It was all
836 the same.

837 For a long time he lay looking
838 at his pulped fingers and the
839 driven drops of blood from the
840 quick of his nails, sensing the
841 exquisite pain almost as a lux-
842 ury, hugging it to him. But at
843 length he stirred and began to
844 wriggle forward again.

845 "If I'm going to die anyway,"
846 said Junius Peabody, "I'm going
847 to die doing this." Which was
848 an extraordinary remark on all
849 accounts. . . .

850 And so by dint of following
851 something, and still following
852 with unlimited purpose over a
853 limited terrain, he ran it down
854 in the end and came to the
855 hiding place he sought.

856 A rooted instinct of the poten-
857 tially criminal, which prompts
858 them to be ready to flee though

859 no man pursueth, had moved the
860 beachcombers of Fufuti long
861 since to prepare their snug re-
862 treat in the heart of the Rocks.
863 On the inward shore of the
864 promontory they had found a
865 level bit of shelf screened by lush
866 vegetation, with the green-
867 stained cliff for wall and the
868 sapphire waters of the lagoon be-
869 below for forecourt. Hither they
870 repaired in the intervals of lesser
871 lawbreaking and free entertain-
872 ment, always secure of hearth
873 and shelter where the broad pan-
874 danus spreads its shingles. And
875 hither, straight as merry men to
876 their shaw, they had brought the
877 great treasure of the morning.

878 A truly homelike scene was
879 that on which Junius Peabody
880 peered from ambush above. . . .

881 From the convenient branch
882 of a tree the Sydney Duck had
883 suspended by its middle a single
884 stout stick. At one end of the
885 stick he had slung the stolen
886 lump in a fiber net. At the other
887 he had attached a battered tin
888 can of the kind that the benefi-
889 cent enterprise of an American
890 oil company had spread to most
891 of the dark parts of the earth.
892 On this balance of an ancient and
893 primitive design he was engaged
894 in weighing his ill-gotten gains,
895 squatting to the task.

896 "A gallon of water weighs a
897 good eight pound," he declared.
898 "I figger five quarts an' a 'arf.
899 And five is ten and the 'arf is
900 one——"

901 Willems stood beside him in an
902 attitude of stolid skepticism.
903 There was no mistaking the
904 breed of this big derelict. He
905 had managed to assert it on a
906 Pacific isle by fashioning him-
907 self somehow a pipe with a clay
908 bowl and a long stem of the true
909 drooping line. He looked quite
910 domestic and almost paternal as
911 he shuffled his broad feet and
912 towered over the little larrikin.
913 But the fists he carried in the
914 pockets of his dungarees bulged
915 like coconuts, and his hairy arms
916 were looped brown cables. A
917 tough man for an argument was
918 Mynheer Willems.

919 "Yaw," he was saying. "But
920 how you know you got five
921 quarts and a half?"

922 "W'y, any fool could guess
923 near enough!" cried Sydney,
924 with the superfluous violence
925 that was his caste mark. "And
926 you—y' big Dutchman—'in't
927 you swilled enough beer in your
928 time to judge? Besides, the bally
929 can 'olds three gallon—bound to.
930 There's one sure measure. . . .
931 I say we got, anyw'y, eleven
932 pounds of this stuff, and I
933 'appen to know that Bende-
934 meer's fair crazy after it. He'll
935 pay big. We ought to 'ave two
936 thousands dollars Chile to split.
937 . . . Two thousands silver
938 dibs!"

939 It was a cue to friendly feel-
940 ing, that luscious phrase. The
941 two men beamed upon it as
942 Sydney dumped the balance and
943 swung the fiber net. But it was
944 also a cue of another kind, for it
945 brought Junius Peabody on
946 stage. He arrived by the simple
947 process of sliding on a bundle
948 over the brow of the cliff.

949 "That's mine," he announced.

950 The beachcombers stayed
951 stricken, which was pardonable.
952 Surely there never showed a less
953 heroic figure or a stranger de-
954 fiance than that of Mr. Peabody,
955 torn, bedraggled, and besmeared.
956 There was nothing muscular or
957 threatening about him. He took
958 no pose. He offered no weapon.
959 He came on at them limping,
960 with quivering lip and empty
961 hands, even with open hands.
962 And yet the incredible fact re-
963 mained that he did come on at
964 them and continued to come.

965 "It's mine," repeated Junius.
966 "All mine, and I'm going to have
967 it—all!"

968 Amazement held them mo-
969 tionless for as long as it took him
970 to cross the ledge—pleased
971 amazement, as they knew him
972 better. There are few things
973 more congenial to certain gentle-
974 men than a chance to maul an
975 easy victim. And here was the
976 easiest victim that either of these
977 gentlemen had seen in many a
978 day. He was no match for them,
979 could be no possible match.
980 Since he would have it so, they
981 accepted joyously, closed in up-
982 on him from either side and
983 started to drag him down as a
984 preliminary to trampling the

985 lights out of him. . . .
986 But they counted without the
987 absolute simplicity of a man who
988 has found an objective for the
989 first time in his life and has set
990 himself to reach it, regardless.
991 Mr. Peabody did not pause to
992 fight or to wrestle. He let them
993 get a good grip on him and then
994 took the unexpected way by
995 keeping right on—and, pinion-
996 ing their arms, merely walking
997 them over the edge into space.
998 For an instant the three
999 seemed to hang suspended, in-
1000 terlocked amid smashing vines
1001 and taut creepers, and then top-
1002 pled toward the lagoon.
1003 Even before they struck, Syd-
1004 ney's despairing yell rang out.
1005 Their plunge drowned it and
1006 gave way to the cries of startled
1007 sea birds, knifing the air in flung
1008 white crescents and circling
1009 about the troubled spot that
1010 boiled like blue champagne. But
1011 when he came up again the unfort-
1012 unate larrikin loosed shriek after
1013 bubbling shriek and floundered
1014 madly for shore, all else forgotten
1015 in his dominant terror.
1016 Willems was made of sterner
1017 metal. He grappled Peabody as
1018 they rose and sought to use his
1019 long arms, reaching for the
1020 throat. He learned better pres-
1021 ently, however, and he learned
1022 too, how much chance he had
1023 against a man who had once
1024 won a fancy diving title at Trav-
1025 ers Island. Junius took him
1026 down by the feet and held him

1027 down until there was no spring
1028 and no temper left to him, only
1029 a large and limp and very badly
1030 frightened Hollander who want-
1031 ed to get out of the wet. He was
1032 quite willing to paddle after the
1033 Sydney Duck. Meanwhile Jun-
1034 ius gathered up an object in a
1035 fiber net that was floating near
1036 by and swam on to follow his
1037 purpose. . . .
1038 The man Bendemeer was
1039 standing behind his little
1040 zinc bar when a shadow
1041 sifted in through the doorway,
1042 and, looking up, he took a back-
1043 ward step that nearly cost him
1044 his stock of glassware. The man
1045 Bendemeer was not used to step-
1046 ping back from anything, but the
1047 red and dripping ruin that con-
1048 fronted him was beyond usage
1049 of any kind. Junius Peabody
1050 looked as if he had been run
1051 through a mangle. His dress
1052 was fragmentary. Most of the
1053 skin had been flayed from the
1054 more prominent curves of his
1055 anatomy. His left arm hung
1056 useless. He crawled in and
1058 propped himself to keep from
1059 falling, and called for brandy in
1060 a voice scarcely recognizable.
1061 "Peabody—is it?" demanded
1062 Bendemeer, incredulous.
1063 "Will you keep a customer
1064 waiting?" rasped Junius. "You
1065 needn't stare." He laughed
1066 weakly. "You can't order me
1067 off now, Bendemeer. I'm a pay-
1068 ing customer again."
1069 "As how?"

1070 Junius lifted a fist and dropped
1071 the sopping net on the bar.
1072 "Ambergris—eleven pounds of
1073 of it. My property."
1074 Bendemeer inspected the
1075 brownish lump, and as he under-
1076 stood, his thin lips pleated and
1077 his glance quickened. "Oh, ho!"
1078 he said. "Was it *this* they
1079 robbed you of?"
1080 Peabody nodded.
1081 "You got it back from them—
1082 yourself?"
1083 "There's the stuff."
1084 "So I see. But I'm asking—
1085 did you take it away from those
1086 two cutthroats alone, without
1087 any help?"
1088 "I did. And now I've come to
1089 talk business. It's a good prop-
1090 osition, Bendemeer."
1091 The tall, grim white man stud-
1092 ied him with a narrow regard
1093 glinting like a probe and equally
1094 cool, detached, and impersonal.
1095 He had the air of a surgeon who
1096 approaches a clinical experiment.
1097 "I'm inclined to think it may
1098 be," he decided. "Yes—a sport-
1099 ing risk; though I'm certain
1100 enough of the result, Peabody,
1101 mind that. I believe I might
1102 make a bit of a gamble with my-
1103 self, just to see that I'm right.
1104 Come now—what do you want?"
1105 "A thousand silver," said
1106 Junius.
1107 "I haven't so much about me.
1108 Suppose we say a standing credit
1109 for a thousand drinks instead."
1110 Junius stiffened against the
1111 bar.

1112 "It amounts to the same thing,
1113 doesn't it?" continued Bende-
1114 meer: "Why should you trouble
1115 about dollars—mere tokens?
1116 You can't get away from Fufuti.
1117 The *Jane* out there, she's due to
1118 sail this morning on a round of
1119 my plantations. She's the only
1120 ship clearing for a month at
1121 least. . . . By the time you'd
1122 drunk yourself to death I'd sim-
1123 ply have the money back again."
1124 Peabody stared, and a streak
1125 of crimson leaped into his cheek
1126 as if a whiplash had been laid
1127 across it.
1128 "Damn you—!" he cried shak-
1129 ily. "Give me that brandy—
1130 I'll pay for it. Here's the stuff.
1131 It's mine. I went after it and I
1132 got it. I earned it myself, and
1133 fairly!"
1134 "To what end?" Bendemeer
1135 cut in. "So you can pickle your-
1136 self before burial?"
1137 Junius Peabody writhed.
1138 "What's it to you how I spend it
1139 afterward? I'm a free agent. I
1140 can do as I like."
1141 "That," said Bendemeer with
1142 quiet emphasis, "is a lie."
1143 Holding his quivering sub-
1144 ject, impaled on his glance as it
1145 seemed, he reached a black,
1146 square bottle. He shoved a glass
1147 in front of Junius Peabody and
1148 poured a generous measure.
1149 With one hand he kept the glass
1150 covered and with the other
1151 pointed out through the doorway.
1152 "I'll say you lie, and I'll
1153 demonstrate:

1154 "You see my schooner out
1155 there? That's her boat on the
1156 beach. She leaves in half an
1157 hour; her captain's come now for
1158 final orders. She goes first from
1159 here to an island of mine a hun-
1160 dred miles away. I planted it
1161 with coconuts five years ago, and
1162 left a population of maybe a
1163 dozen Kanakas to tend them—
1164 it's going to be worth money
1165 some day. Nukava, they call it,
1166 and it's the edge of the earth, the
1167 farthest corner, and the loneliest
1168 and the driest. There's not a
1169 drop of anything on the place
1170 except water, scant and brackish
1171 at that. But a white man could
1172 live there, if he were fit to live
1173 at all, and wanted to badly
1174 enough.

1175 "Now I'll make you an offer.
1176 I'll buy this lump of stuff from
1177 you, and I'll buy it either of two
1178 ways. A half interest in Nukava
1179 and you go there at once to take
1180 charge as agent. . . . Or else—
1181 here's your brandy and I'll keep
1182 you perpetually drunk as long
1183 as you last."

1184 Junius swayed on his feet.
1185 "Agent?" he stammered. "To
1186 go away——?"

1187 "Now. And once there you
1188 can't escape. You're stuck for
1189 a year on a coral gridiron, Pea-
1190 body, to sit and fry."

1191 "What for? You—! What
1192 for?"

1193 Bendemeer shrugged.

1194 "Because it amuses me. Be-
1195 cause I please. Because—I
know what you'll do. I've been 1196
watching men of your sort all my 1197
life, and I know what they're 1198
worth—drift on the beaches, 1199
scraps, trash, jetsam. Regenera- 1200
tion, eh? Rot and drivel! You 1201
can't save yourself any more 1202
than you could lift yourself by 1203
your own boot straps. It suits 1204
me to prove it to you this way." 1205

He lifted his hand away from 1206
the glass. Peabody's stare 1207
dropped from that cryptic regard 1208
to the waiting brandy before 1209
him, the red liquor, odorous and 1210
maddening. Peabody's lips 1211
moved, and he wet them with 1212
the tip of his tongue and gripped 1213
the bar with straining white 1214
fingers. 1215

"You're wrong," he breathed. 1216
"You lose, Bendemeer. I can 1217
do it—I've just learned I can do 1218
it. And, by God," he added, 1219
prayerfully, "I will." 1220

Bendemeer took up the netted 1221
lump. 1222

"Very well," he said, offhand. 1223
"Just a moment, while I chuck 1224
this stuff in the storeroom." 1225

He turned and tramped out 1226
through the rear without a 1227
glance behind him—and left 1228
Junius Peabody there alone be- 1229
fore the bar. 1230

He was gone perhaps five min- 1231
utes, quite as much as that, an 1232
ample space of time. When he 1233
came back there was no glass in 1234
sight. It had vanished, and the 1235
room reeked with the fumes of a 1236
very flagrant distillation of 1237

1238 French brandy. He looked his
1239 customer up and down and his
1240 lids lowered a trifle.

1241 "Well, how did you like the
1242 flavour?"

1243 The face of Junius Peabody
1244 was like a death's-head, but the
1245 eyes in his sockets blazed with a
1246 light all their own, and, standing
1247 there erect, standing square on
1248 his two legs with his feet braced
1249 apart, he swore—somewhat in-
1250 expertly, it was true, but still
1251 quite heartily; good, crisp pro-
1252 fanity such as one able man may
1253 use with another—until Bende-
1254 meer's puzzled gaze caught the
1255 sparkle of broken glass lying in
1256 a great splash of liquid in a cor-
1257 ner of the floor. "I'm going to
1258 Nukava!" cried Junius Peabody.
1259 "And you see—you see there are
1260 some scraps thrown up on the
1261 beach that are worth something
1262 after all, and be damned to you,
1263 Bendemeer!"

1264 Bendemeer's grip shot out as
1265 if against his volition, and after
1266 an instant's hesitation Peabody
1267 took it. He did not yet know all

1268 the trader had done for him,
1269 perhaps would never know, but
1270 on the inscrutable front of that
1271 remarkable man was a faint
1272 glow curiously unlike a loser's
1273 chagrin.

1274 "So it seems," acknowledged
1275 Bendemeer. "So it seems"—
1276 and smiled a little, rather
1277 oddly. . . .

1278 Bendemeer was still smiling
1279 that way, all by himself, an hour
1280 or so later when he had watched
1281 the *Likely Jane* lay her course
1282 for Nukava with the new agent
1283 on board and had gone down into
1284 his storeroom to put the place
1285 to rights. There was a clutter of
1286 odds and ends of cargo that had
1287 been spilled from an upset surf-
1288 boat the day before. Most of it
1289 had been salvaged by his Kanaka
1290 boys along shore, but a certain
1291 broken tub containing tallow had
1292 lost part of its contents. How-
1293 ever, he was able now to restore
1294 a large lump weighing perhaps
1295 eleven pounds or so, which made
1296 the tally nearly good.

THE ANALYSIS

The Beginning of *Western Stuff* and the Beginning of *Women are Wiser* you will remember had the same initial condition; but one was treated as a story of Accomplishment and the other as a story of Decision. The story *Jetsam* and the story *Sunk* have the same Ending, that is, they have the same Conclusive Act. In each one a man conquers the temptation to take a drink, and in each case the Conclusive Act is a dramatic one. Mr. Worts, however, wrote a Beginning of accomplishment and Mr. Russell wrote a Beginning of decision or choice.

It is almost impossible to write a story of Decision without falling into the necessity for some sort of flashing back. In all cases the competent craftsman will cause this flash-back to be an interchange. If you will look at the chart preceding this story, you will see that of the 1296 lines, making up the total story, 1256 are Beginning. Lines 1257 to 1263 are the Conclusive Act, and lines 1264 to 1296 are the ironic Sequel. This story will repay reading because it is an excellent illustration of the story which opens with setting forth the condition which is unusual and apparently holding the threat of inevitable disaster. Lines 1 to 123 show that Junius Peabody, at 28, finds himself broke at Fufuti. There is a flash-back interchange with Bendemeer and Junius on lines 123 to 139, and immediately following this there is the interchange with the Sydney Duck. As a result of that interchange the response of Junius is to wish for a chance to begin again. On lines 429 to 543 there is an interchange with the Sydney Duck growing out of the finding of the lump which seems to present to Junius the chance to begin again for which he has wished. The fifth step of the interchange with the Sydney Duck is again an interchange with Bendemeer who this time repudiates Junius, who continues on in the hope that he may bring about his wish. Lines 793 to 1037 show an interchange, which is quite exciting, between Junius and the Sydney Duck and Willems as a group. As a result of this interchange Junius recovers the lump. Then the interchange between Junius and Bendemeer on lines 1038 to 1256 results in Bendemeer making clear unmistakably the choice that lies before Junius Peabody of giving up the opportunity to drink or of drinking himself to death. On lines 1154 to 1205 this is made clear. He decides upon reform; and then in the Sequel there is presented, on lines 1257 to 1296, the ironic Significance that after all this the stimulus which caused the initial impulse was only a lump of tallow. Nobody better than Mr. Russell knows the effectiveness of this type of Sequel. As a case in craftsmanship the reader will find this story particularly interesting as a companion story to Mr. Worts' story *Sunk*. He will also find that in its general structure it follows the lines of the story of Decision which Mr. Adams employed in his story *Women are Wiser*, and that in both *Women are Wiser* and in *Jetsam* the Flash-back is not a typical Flash-back in the sense in which we use the word, but it is a Flash-back by the character and not a Flash-back by the author. In this case it is a Flash-back of the character's thoughts presented by the author in an interchange to avoid summary.

These two stories are of the decision type story which show a conflict between the affections on the one hand and a standard of conduct or of conscience on the other. In the case of *Women are Wiser* this is quite clear, in the case of *Jetsam* the decision is really between affection for oneself, or self-indulgence and a desire for a standard of conduct which involves denying this desire. In both cases it is a standard of conduct built up by the world rather than by the individual. It is for this reason that these two stories show a variation from the stories which follow them, in which the decision is between a standard of conduct and an opportunity to profit, a much more common type of story, perhaps because it is a much more easily understood problem than the two preceding, and certainly much more clear-cut from the point of view of treatment. In the story, *Women are Wiser* in particular, there might be some question in the mind of a reader as to whether that course of conduct adopted by the actor was a wise one. In the course of conduct which has been made a possible choice in the stories which are to follow, there is a quite definite standard as to what ought to be done, even though it is not always done by the actor.

OTHER TYPES OF CHOICE ABOUT WHICH STORIES OF DECISION ARE BUILT

The next five stories fall into the type of Decision Story which is concerned with the decision between a standard of conduct and an opportunity to profit. They are a logical outcome of the story of Accomplishment. The story of Accomplishment, in its most usual form, deals with the desire of somebody to accomplish something, to achieve his wish. That is to say it is a story of wish-fulfilment. These stories which I am about to analyze go beyond this, to the moment when there is an opportunity to achieve wish-fulfilment or an opportunity to profit, but which show that the main actor is prevented from seizing this opportunity by some trait of character which has established for him a standard of conduct. A clear-cut example of this is *Gentility*, by Thomas Beer.

BEGINNING

Series of Interchanges giving the background for the reader's understanding of the importance of the choice to be made by Stukely.

Scene. Between all the Kent family and the condition arising from man in attic. Reported chiefly through the responses of Stukely.	1– 578
Interchange. Joe and Rudy Kling.	579– 620
Interchange. Rudy and Kent family.	621– 844
(5th step. Comment of Kents upon Rudy. Interchange Norah and father.)	845– 951
Interchange. Hester and Rev. Gavin Kent.	952–1010
(5th step. Stukely's reflections.)	1011–1088
Interchange. Stukely and Alphenius.	1088–1117
Stukely and Joe.	1118–1148
(5th step. Effect upon Kent family).	1149–1226
Interchange. Stukely and Central Office.	1226–1271
Continued by Norah.	1272–1315
(5th step. Comments of Kent family.)	1316–1443
Interchange. Stukely and Alphenius.	1444–1470
Interchange. Stukely and Rudy Kling.	1471–1629

Stukely's pride in the gentility of the Kent family is established through the series of reflections in which he indulges at the close of the different interchanges.

Choice presented.

Stukely has two choices offered. Narrative Question: "Which choice will he make?"

ENDING

Decisive Act.

Stukely seizes Rudy.	1630–1651

Answer is: "He rejects bribe."

Sequel.

Rudy fights. Mrs. Kent saves situation.	1652–1812

Ironic significance.

GENTILITY

BY THOMAS BEER

I HAVE chosen this story because it indicates so definitely the type of story about which I have just spoken, and because it is so clearly dependent upon the quality of its interchanges for its effectiveness. I am often asked, "Who is the writer that I ought to study," to which I always reply, "There is no one writer that you ought to study. The thing to do is to study all the writers, and from each learn what he does most effectively." There is nobody writing in America today who can present scenes so effectively as Thomas Beer. Those scenes give the illusion of reality perhaps more clearly than do the scenes of any other writer. In general, writers may be divided into two classes: those whose stories are good because of their plot, and those whose stories are good because of their scenes. Mr. Beer is essentially of this second class, his scenes being connected only by a very slight thread of plot. Now read the story.

CASE No. 13

GENTILITY

BY THOMAS BEER

Stukely merely yawned at his mother's first scream. A mosquito resumed its threatening song somewhere in the darkness not far from his wet face and he waved an arm slowly, until Mrs. Kent screamed again with an abandoned violence that might mean something positive, for she usually woke herself. He swung a leg from bed as feet bumped the floor of his sister's bedroom and Joe Fancher said, "Uh-huh, woman, I heard it." On the third wail Stukely jumped for his bath robe and the baby raised a distinguished yell of anger at the hall's eastern end. Light shone under the door while Stukely pulled his hot body into thin silk and wound the robe's cord around his waist. Another week of this indecent heat and he would be down to a hundred and sixty pounds or less. Silk stuck to his chest as he blundered to the doorway and entered brightness, jarring Norah, in some drapery of green stuff that sparkled dramatically.

"Do look where you're going, Stuke!"

"How did I know you'd be right outside my door, idiot?" he snorted, and shoved past her slimness toward his mother's room.

"My dear Grace," said the Rev. Gavin Kent in a composed but annoyed cadence of his barytone, "you very seldom scream as loudly as that, even over a rat in the cellar. There must have been something!"

Mrs. Kent apologized in rapid little gasps, inside the dark bedroom.

She said, "No, no, Gavin! I thought I heard something, but it wasn't anything. I was just dreaming, of course. I'm so sorry! I'm so sorry, Joe! Do turn the light out and go back to bed, dear. I'm ever so sorry!"

"Goodness gracious mamma," Joe Fancher yawned, filling the hall with the folds and loops of a whole sheet, "I wasn't sleepin' any. Yeh, this Norah was doin' all the sleep in our room. I was

317

61 kinda recumbent on the couch,
62 wonderin' if it's any hotter'n this
63 down in Gawgia. Stuke, your
64 mamma says she meant nothin'
65 whatsoever by yellin'. You can
66 go back to bed if it's any good to
67 you, son."

68 Doctor Kent observed from
69 the unseen bedroom, "It's fright-
70 ful for June. . . . Is that the
71 new bath robe Norah's been
72 making for you, Joe?"

73 "No, rev'rend. This is just a
74 sheet, sir. Winter'll come an'
75 I'll be twenty-five or so when
76 your no-account daughter has
77 that bath robe finished on me.
78 Yeh, the kid'll be talkin' an'
79 reachin' for a cigarette when it's
80 all done. . . . Want some ice
81 water, mamma?"

82 "Oh, no thank—I really would
83 like some, Joe," said Mrs. Kent
84 pathetically and suddenly, "if
85 it's not too much——"

86 "Not any, ma'am," the long
87 man drawled, and wandered
88 majestically in his sheet down
89 the green stairs, fading into the
90 blackness of the living room be-
91 low as a rooster gave an inspired
92 cry on the next farm and the
93 rooster Androcles answered from
94 Doctor Kent's henhouse.

95 "Daybreak," said the old man
96 with a sigh, "and it's the longest
97 day in the year. Grace, you'd
98 best go down to Southampton,
99 My dear, if this heat keeps up."

100 Norah Fancher grinned at her
101 brother in the hallway, lighted
102 by three little bulbs, and leaned
103 on the wall in a fluctuation of
104 the green robe strewn with spots
105 of silver embroidery. Their
106 mother heroically remarked that
107 she wouldn't think of going to
108 Uncle George's house at South-
109 ampton. The tomatoes would
110 be ripe soon and Joe and Stukely
111 would need help, and the new
112 nursemaid wasn't broken to the
113 eccentricities of Joseph Fancher,
114 Jr.; and if she went to South-
115 ampton the Rev. Gavin Kent
116 must come with her. If the high
117 farm was impossible for her, it
118 was just as hot for him; and any-
119 how, this was Sunday and it
120 might be better to wait until
121 Monday to travel. She said all
122 this with diminishing vigor and
123 concluded, "I do hope it will be
124 cool at Southampton when we
125 get there."

126 Then she went to sleep with a
127 short moaning noise and at once
128 began her delicate repressed
129 snore, a gently modulated, sooth-
130 ing little noise that always made
131 Stukely proud of her; she was a
132 lady even when asleep. He
133 gathered his blue silk robe be-
134 tween his knees and sat down on
135 the planks of the ancient floor to
136 wait for Joe Fancher and the
137 iced water, wondering whether a
138 snore could be controlled by sur-
139 gery or mental suggestion, and
140 whether roosters were glad to
141 wake with the first threat of
142 dawn or if it was something of a
143 burden on their sense of duty.
144 And did the roosters yell down

318

ninety miles to New York progressively or were there roosterless intervals where some cock woke in silence and started the traveling noise on his own account? Then he looked at a drop of sweat that trickled on his right thumb's brown curve from the soaked blue sleeve. The drop fell on the planks beside his foot and was immediately covered by a slipper of worn gray leather. The boy put back his black head and stared up at Doctor Kent, a tremendous figure in white pajamas, which his gaunt body left unrumpled, immaculately neat.

"Stuke?"

"Don't step on me, dad," Stukely whispered.

"My dear boy," said the retired rector of St. Philip's Church, "I had no intention of doing so. I can't find my glasses, and I'm so blind without them—— What I was going to say—Is that you, Norah? Don't be alarmed, my dear girl!—was that I'm afraid there's somebody in the spare bedroom." He paused and finished with civility, "I can hear him, you know, through the wall where the old door's papered over."

Norah Fancher clasped her hands on her green breast and said delightedly, "Father, you're really wonderful! I think if the house caught fire you'd apologize for waking us. Stuke, go see what it is. If it's a burglar tell him he ought to wait for cool nights."

"Quit bein' frolicsome," Stukely grunted, getting up from the floor with its illusion of coolness. Norah had painted it a somber gray and imitated the broken squares of a paved walk on its length. His father caught his arm and the boy said, "Oh, come off it, daddy! How can anybody get in there with the door locked? It's the new rat; the one Joe saw in the cellar yesterday—I mean day before yesterday. I don't see how you have the gu-courage to wear pajamas on a night like this."

"It's his conventionality," Norah sighed.

"My dear boy," said the old man, nervously holding his son's right biceps, "wait until Joe comes up with——"

"I can face this rat all by myself, sir," Stukely assured him, and strolled twelve steps down the gray floor to the painted door of the spare bedroom. He yawned and turned the key under the glass knob which looked so pleasantly like ice against the green wood, and was even a little cool in his palm when he shut his hand on it. But the door did not stir. Directly a rasping fall of sand slid down his back and he said loudly, "Oh, yeh—other way," in what sounded the falsest voice of known time. The door had been unlocked and he had locked it. Now he must

229 unlock it and carelessly go into
230 the black room full of masked
231 men, armed unpleasantly. His
232 blue bath robe seemed perilously
233 thin. And why had Joe gone
234 downstairs just when a former
235 sergeant of marines was demand-
236 ed by this situation. After three
237 years of friendship Joe might
238 have stuck to him in an emer-
239 gency instead of sneaking down-
240 stairs after iced water. The key
241 turned. The door swung briskly
242 inward and Stukely set a hand
243 on the wall's dry paper, hunting
244 for the button of the lights.
245 Two bulbs flared through the
246 yellow silk of a tall lamp beside
247 the bed, and the room was empty
248 from the vermilion floor to the
249 wooden ceiling on which Norah
250 Fancher's hand had drawn a
251 number of fat golden fishes.
252 Smells of hot cloth and lavender
253 welled from the bed and from a
254 shallow cupboard set in the deep
255 wall between two windows.
256 "G-golly," said Stukely, "but
257 the place smells to heaven!
258 Nothin' here, daddy." He spoke
259 in the tone of comfortable benev-
260 olence, while five drops of sweat
261 went wandering the middle of
262 his chest and relief swelled his
263 lungs. "If any rat wants to stay
264 in here, he's trying to lose
265 weight. I'll open the windows.
266 It might start a draft through."
267 The vermilion floor seemed
268 sticky underfoot. Stukely wres-
269 tled with the weight of fine
270 chintz curtains in each window

271 and undid the locks. Outside a
272 sedate grayness glowed behind
273 the heavy timbers of the water
274 tower beside an oak whose foli-
275 age rustled vaguely in the pas-
276 sage of an exhausted wind. The
277 river below the orchard made a
278 little sound as though the water
279 tired of pebbles and flat rocks.
280 Earth yawned, he thought, at
281 the promise of another weary
282 day, more heat, more breathless
283 air. He stretched over the sill of
284 the second window and reached
285 an idle hand to the iron spikes
286 which made a ladder up one cor-
287 ner of the water tower's skeleton.
288 His fingers could not quite touch
289 the iron, and the boy drew him-
290 self back across the ledge of win-
291 dow sill without interest in the
292 failure.
293 "You know the tower's too
294 close to these windows," he said
295 listlessly; "if anybody did want
296 to get in, dad, this would be the
297 way."
298 "I suppose so," said Doctor
299 Kent, blinking up at the gilded
300 fishes; "and I suppose this room's
301 hotter because the ceiling's noth-
302 ing but the floor of the attic.
303 Yes, a house built in 1803 offers
304 inducements to rats. But what
305 a fine piece of building it is,
306 Stuke! I have to praise my own
307 investment, you know. We've
308 been here three years, and liter-
309 ally nothing in the way of re-
310 pairs. . . . Is that you, Joe?
311 I decided that I heard a burglar
312 in here. It was just a rat, but he

313 conveyed an impression of weigh-
314 ing hundreds of pounds. I think
315 he must be a very big rat, really
316 to make such a noise."
317 "Some rats," Joe assured him
318 in the sleepiest drawl, "are tal-
319 ented 'bout noises. Oncet in
320 that war they had in France I an'
321 forty to a hundred other guys
322 were kep' awake all night in a
323 very damn uncomfortable trench
324 by just one rat. He was tryin'
325 to saw off an old post outa sight
326 in the dark with his teef."
327 "Teeth, lamb," said Norah;
328 "don't be so Southern just be-
329 cause it's——"
330 Joe rounded his turquoise eyes
331 in his brown face and gave the
332 beautiful woman a long, offended
333 glare. He trailed his sheet over
334 the vermilion floor and said as
335 he walked, "Girl, grandmamma
336 raised me to be polite to women,
337 but you've no call to be rude at
338 me. For one cent, Mex'can, I'd
339 tear your hair offa your dumb
340 head. I married you for pity,
341 anyhow. . . . Here's a lotta
342 flood, rev'rend. . . . Ace, give
343 your poppa a drink."
344 Stukely took a glass from the
345 tray and got it firmly in his
346 father's grasp. The Rev. Gavin
347 Kent was helpless without spec-
348 tacles that marred his fine long
349 face by daylight. He bent his
350 curly head to drink iced water
351 and a tiny feather floated down
352 to rest on his white curls.
353 "Regards from the angels,"
354 Joe drawled, hitching up the

355 green trousers of limp silk that
356 covered his long legs. He drew
357 a fold of the sheet higher up his
358 white chest, hiding the crooked
359 purple scar that roamed his ribs,
360 and blinked up toward the ceil-
361 ing. Then he yawned and
362 rubbed tanned fists in his eyes.
363 "Yuh! Gimme credit, poppa.
364 I behaved all decorous, like the
365 father of a fam'ly oughta. Many
366 an egg would have loped out in
367 the corridor bare-nekkid on a yell
368 like that, but I fetched this sheet
369 wiv me."
370 "It's extremely becoming,"
371 Norah said, with her wild black
372 hair close to Joe's shoulder;
373 "you look like Demosthenes or
374 one of those classic people mak-
375 ing an oration about something,
376 except that your nose isn't as
377 Greek as theirs."
378 "My nose," Joe asserted, wrin-
379 kling it, "is better'n most noses,
380 female! Many dames have told
381 me it's an int'resting kinda nose.
382 As for a sheet as clothes, no.
383 The Greeks didn't have many
384 fires to run to or they'd ha' never
385 wore anything so sorta clingy.
386 Go back to bed. You've been
387 makin' noises like a sawmill in
388 trouble all night. Your mamma
389 snores like a lady, but you're no
390 gentleman when you're asleep.
391 G'on back to bed. I'm gonna sit
392 in the creek until it's time to
393 milk. . . . Rev'rend, it's my
394 sad dooty to say that old Her-
395 mione's days as an asset on this
396 farm are over. She's a good,

397 kind, well-meanin' cow, but too
398 sorta ven'rable. I expect she's
399 twenty or so. Bought her with
400 the place, didn't you, sir?"
401 "Hermione," said Doctor
402 Kent, "is that obstreperous
403 black cow that used to give
404 Stuke so much trouble when he
405 was learning to milk. Yes, I
406 bought her from Mr. Kling with
407 the farm. Well, we've had her
408 three years. I don't know, Joe,
409 what one does with a venerable
410 cow. As a useless relic, I have
411 a sentiment for Hermione, of
412 course, a natural fellow feeling—
413 tempered, perhaps, with our hu-
414 man superiority. At least I
415 can't be eaten or sold to the tan-
416 nery at Poughkeepsie, if there is
417 one there. Can we pension
418 Hermione?"
419 "Good gracious, rev'rend," Joe
420 murmured, kicking the sheet
421 around his feet, "it's no question
422 of slayin' this dame. No, she's
423 a very orn'mental cow. All your
424 fool friends from New York al-
425 ways admire her a lot. She
426 reminds me of grandmamma
427 comin' outa church whenever
428 daddy had wrung tears from his
429 sinners down in Gawgia or out
430 in Eutropius. Yeh, Hermione
431 an' grandmamma are similar.
432 Very dignified an' kinda
433 haughty. All I meant was that
434 we gotta getta new cow, sir.
435 'At means you don't have
436 mamma write any checks for
437 homes to shelter blind Episcopal
438 choir boys this monf. Hear me,

rev'rend? This place has got to 439
pay in more cash if you're gonna 440
have mamma write any moh 441
three-hundred-dollar checks for 442
blind choir boys, sir. We're a 443
dairy an' veg'table farm, poppa, 444
an' not a distillery." 445
The Rev. Gavin Kent shuffled 446
his slippers on the vermilion 447
paint and said, humbly, "Yes, 448
Joe, I—er—am afraid that was 449
rather reckless of me. You and 450
Stukely make the farm pay so 451
nicely that——" 452
"Good gracious, poppa," Joe 453
crooned, "you can't help bein' a 454
gentleman. Babe, take that 455
feather offa your poppa's ear. 456
Makes him look friv'lous. No, 457
rev'rend, you give away nuffin' 458
moh until middle of July. After 459
mamma's dividends come in, you 460
can have a spree an' send checks 461
to char'ties. Right now we have 462
to get us a new cow. I knew a 463
cow in France named"—a cloud 464
of feathers drifted prettily past 465
Doctor Kent's white curls and 466
the melodious flow of Joe's voice 467
slowed for a second. His eyes 468
changed suddenly to emeralds un- 469
der the bleached arcs of his eye- 470
brows, and he stared upward, go- 471
ing on—"Peritonitis. She——" 472
"It doesn't sound a very 473
French name, Joe," the old gen- 474
tleman objected. "Peritonitis?" 475
"Near as I can come to it, 476
poppa. My b'talion kinda 477
adopted her. She was all sad by 478
the roadside, with an elderly 479
dame along who sold her for a 480

481 hatful of francs. We were new
482 to Frawg money then an' the old
483 dame looked so sorta des'late
484 that it touched us a lot. Cal-
485 c'latin' afterward, we made out
486 that Perry cost us about three
487 thousand dollars American mon-
488 ey. I chipped in a pretty grand-
489 lookin' sorta purple bill that
490 looked fine in Porky Olsen's hel-
491 met. Yeh, I was seventeen in
492 those days, an' extravagant.
493 Only 'at old French dame was
494 downright immoral, 'cause this
495 cow had given down her last shot
496 of milk when Robert E. Lee and
497 the late Ulysses Grant were ar-
498 guin' around Richmond. Other-
499 wise she was an awful nice cow
500 an' useda lick my face real
501 friendly. It was the French lady
502 whose conduct was vulgar."

503 Stukely heard all this easy
504 chatter while cold sand seemed
505 to slide down his broad shoulders
506 under the moist silk of his bath
507 robe. He looked up at the open
508 square trap in the ornamented
509 ceiling. It shouldn't be open,
510 and feathers would not float
511 down from the ancient pillows
512 stored in the low attic unless
513 something had disturbed them.
514 A feather roved and made a
515 white point on the crust of Joe's
516 cropped pale hair. . . . Yes,
517 this burglar had heard the
518 shrieks and had jumped into hid-
519 ing through the ceiling. He
520 might be squatting above them,
521 scowling down, with a revolver
522 rested comfortably on his knee.

"The morality of the French 523
lady's dealings with the marine 524
corps," said the Rev. Gavin 525
Kent in his best manner, "is 526
open to question. Perhaps you 527
should say her *mores* are——" 528
"Her—huh, sir?" 529
"*Mores*," the old gentleman 530
intoned. "The word implies the 531
social customs of a race, such as 532
chewing gum, eating mission- 533
aries, attending or not attending 534
religious services, polygamy, 536
polyandry, human sacrifice and 537
cheating innocent strangers in 538
bargains. Probably she thought 539
herself justified by local custom 540
in taking anything she could get. 541
Morality is the individual's sense 542
of honorable conduct; the *mores* 543
are merely habits." 544

Joe balanced from white foot 545
to foot, watching the trap above 546
Doctor Kent's white head, and 547
evenly crooned, "Poppa, my 548
daddy's very eloquent when he 549
gets goin', but I gotta say you 550
have him plastered flat wiv a 551
ton of bricks on his belly when 552
it comes to sudden information. 553
. . . Yeh, it horrified the 554
Frawgs to see us chewin' gum, 555
but they d'vour snails in jelly. 556
Out in Eutropius, when I was 557
young—Norah, honey, run along 558
back to bed, dear." 559
"I shall do nothing of the 560
kind," said Norah, brushing her 561
hair's black masses back from 562
her face with its enormous eyes. 563
"D-daddy, you'd better go to 564
bed, though. You'll be too tired 565

for church in the morning. W-won't he, Stuke? Please go to——"

Her voice became the thinnest whisper as fresh feathers floated in a whirling shower.

"Oh!" said the old man after a hot second. He sat upright on the mattress and blinked at Joe's restless movement three yards from him. "I see! What's happened, Stukely? No, I shan't go to bed, Norah! Stuke?"

Joe Fancher dropped the sheet and hitched his green trousers higher up his flat waist.

He said lightly, "Poppa there's a guy up in the attic, sir. Babe, take your daddy out in the passage an' gimme my gun from my room. You up there," he drawled, his voice rising to a falsetto rasp, "I was five years in the m'rines an' I gotta mean disposition an' a medal for revolver shootin'. I'm a preacher's kid an' when I get nasty, oh, you ain't any idea, son, how nasty I get! Yeh, come down an' be fast or——"

"I'll come down," a man said weakly; "but don't rough me up, pal. I ain't doin' any harm." He coughed close to the trap and went on drearily, "If the old gentleman'll get out from underneath, why——"

Stukely drew his father from the mattress and Joe dropped his hands on the painted green of the bed's foot, grinning upward, with his small ears wriggling on the round of his head. All the muscles of his white chest bobbed in a single motion as a black suitcase tumbled from the ceiling. Then he watched black shoes and radiant socks descend. A little person dropped through the square trap and knelt on the bed, plucking feathers from his blue coat. Norah produced a long giggle that lifted into a squawk before she pressed her hands on her mouth.

"Why," said Doctor Kent, straining his dull eyes, "it's a mere child!"

"Yeh, poppa," Joe mused, "the mountain snorted an' a mouse come out. . . . Stranger, tell us your *mores* after scarin' nine pounds offa me like that. I'd get me a hairbrush an' wallop you for two cents, fella!"

The small person said in a terrible whimper.

"You leave me be! This is my folks' house, and I s'pose they've rented it to you guys or sumpin. Only I wasn't doin' nothin'. Only you scared me, yellin'. My name's Rudy Kling, an' this is my room. . . . Where's mamma?"

Stukely became extremely shy and embarrassed. Joe towered six feet at the bottom of the bedstead. The Rev. Gavin Kent was quite as long and his son had only an eighth of an inch to gain. They must seem terrific to this minute creature crouched on the mattress. Norah suppressed another giggle.

"Oh," said the Rev. Gavin Kent, "are you a member of Mr. Otto Kling's family who formerly lived here?"

The little thing gave out a horrid sound and asked, "They ain't all dead, mister? Aw no!" with his soiled hands flattened on the mattress.

"No, no," the old man said hastily; "no! In fact, Mrs. Puddy had a postal from your mother only the other day. Mrs. Puddy, you know, across the road. No, they're all very well. But I don't understand——"

Joe Fancher put a brown thumb on the little man's shoulder and affably commanded, "Tell your yarn, Aloysius, an' don't improve it any moh'n you can help. You're kin to this Mr. Kling that Rev'rend Kent bought him this farm offa? Go on, fella an' be plain wiv me. I'm a hard hound 'at bites babies."

"I'm Rudy Kling. I ain't been home in five years since pop kicked me out last time. I—I came home," the soiled person babbled, moving back from Joe's finger; "this used to be my room. Th-the front door was open. I just walked in an' came on up. I was huntin' for the gas when the lady screamed. I see you guys have put in electric light. And then I heard you all talkin' and knew sumpin was wrong.

When you've been in jail twice you ain't so anxious to be in again and"—he gulped—"I jumped up through the trap. . . . Wher've my folks gone to?"

"California," Doctor Kent said, slowly blinking. "We've been here three years and three months. How old are you?"

"Twenty-four, sir," the little man said, and was silent on the mattress, with his nose twitching and his fingers working gently. A rosy color had come back into his round face; he was suddenly a rather pretty fellow, Stukely saw. His thick hair was black and waved around his forehead in a becoming untidiness that made him childish. But he had been twice in jail and his romantic socks announced in determined red and green stripes that he was hopelessly vulgar. The socks were inexcusable and inexpensive.

"You've not been home in five years?"

"No, sir," said Rudy Kling in the same dreary voice; "I came home five years back. Only I got in a muss over a poker party an' pop kicked me out. Oh, I ain't sayin' he was hard on me! Naw! I ain't any good. The Puddys or anybody will tell you that. My brothers got all the good there was in the fam'ly. I'm a kind of a left-over. I'm the youngest."

"Ran off pretty young, fella?"

733 Joe asked, gathering up his sheet.
734 "Yeh, I was fourteen. And
735 then my wife used to beat me up
736 pretty bad," the young man said
737 dolorously, rubbing his pert nose
738 with a green silk handkerchief,
739 "so pop let me come home.
740 Only I got in this fight over a
741 poker game an' knocked Ralph
742 McCarthy's eye out with a chair.
743 I expect you'd know him if
744 you've been here three years.
745 His folks have a farm over
746 by——"
747 Joe said soothingly, "Yeh,
748 fella. His glass eye's a pretty
749 fair match for his real one.
750 You're real frank."
751 Rudy Kling looked up at the
752 tall man with a sort of scorn and
753 wailed, "It wouldn't be any good
754 lyin' to you guys. You're all
755 gentlemen. I can string it out
756 pretty fair with tough eggs, but
757 it's no good lyin' to classy peo-
758 ple." He looked briefly at
759 Norah's green gauzes and said,
760 "I'm sorry I made you yell,
761 lady."
762 "Oh, that was my mother,"
763 Norah brightly mentioned. She
764 considered the trivial person fav-
765 orably and inquired, "So you've
766 been in jail a good deal?"
767 "Twice," Mr. Kling answered
768 sulkily; "but not lately. I had
769 a good job at a track. I'm a
770 pretty fair jockey, only I ain't
771 enough nerve for big races."
772 Stukely shivered. Dawn rose
773 in color behind the water tower's
774 plain gauntness and new light

775 mingled with the glow of lamps
776 in this stifling room. He had a
777 sleepy feeling of something quite
778 unreal under the gilded fishes of
779 the blue ceiling. This shameless
780 person was Joe's age—four years
781 older than himself; but his trivial
782 body had been in jail and beaten
783 by some awful wife and jounced
784 on race horses. And he had no
785 nerve and said so! He was en-
786 tirely strange. Of course any-
787 body got scared now and then.
788 But you didn't sit and say so to
789 people in night clothes or sheets.
790 "Any chance I could get a
791 drink of water, pal?" Mr. Kling
792 asked Joe Fancher. "Them
793 feathers in the attic nearly——"
794 "Take him downstairs, Joe,"
795 said Doctor Kent, in the oddest
796 tone, "and give him some water.
797 . . . What time are the Puddys
798 likely to get up?"
799 "Any minute, poppa. Puddy
800 thinks unfriendly of the sun if
801 it's later'n three o'clock in sum-
802 mertime."
803 "Then," said the old gentle-
804 man, "Puddy will be able to
805 identify Mr. Kling. If Mr.
806 Puddy identifies you," he said
807 directly to the intruder, "we
808 have no reason to detain you,
809 sir. Good morning."
810 Mr. Kling picked up his little
811 suitcase. It could hold nothing
812 much, and Stukely wondered
813 whether it had been chosen to
814 match its owner's lack of bulk.
815 Rudy slipped from the mattress
816 and gave Norah a look of sharp

817 interest, as he asked, "I don't
818 suppose you know where my
819 folks moved to in California?"
820 "It happens that I do. Your
821 father is so kind as to send me
822 Christmas cards each year. They
823 live at Los Altos. It's below
824 San Francisco somewhere. Los
825 Altos—can you remember?"
826 "Yeh," said Mr. Kling; "I
827 was through there oncet with a
828 circus. . . . Honest, mister, the
829 front door was open."
830 "I fear that it was," Doctor
831 Kent nodded. "I'm afraid that
832 I left it open. Good morning.
833 . . . Joe, please take Mr. Kling
834 over to see if Mr. Puddy is able
835 to identify him."
836 "Puddy can identify me all
837 right. Always hated the sight
838 of me," the trivial person sighed.
839 Norah swished her green skirt
840 and gave the intruder a nod of
841 farewell as he followed Joe's
842 sheet through the doorway.
843 He ducked his head and van-
844 ished.
845 With a tremendous sigh the
846 Reverend Gavin Kent sat down
847 on the mattress and said softly,
848 "Ugh! I hope, really, that he
849 wasn't as offensive as his voice,
850 Norah."
851 "Dad, he was perfectly charm-
852 ing! He had purple socks with
853 jade embroideries on them, and
854 he looked exactly like a doll
855 baby. His hair's the same as
856 Stukely's, only he oils it, and his
857 eyelashes are an inch long. I
858 don't think he's more than five

feet high. He'd break if Stuke 859
or Joe slapped him." 860
"Oh, no, he wouldn't, Norah," 861
Stukely protested sleepily; "he's 862
hard as wire. One of those 863
rather pretty kids, daddy. Weak 864
face." 865
"I adore you, lamb," said 866
Norah, "when you get frightfully 867
mature! You're twenty and he's 868
twenty-four. Pretty kid!" 869
The Reverend Gavin Kent 870
fumbled his old silver case from 871
the pocket of his white jacket 872
and tapped a cigarette on its 873
shimmer. He musically re- 874
marked, "My dear daughter, 875
Stuke is unusually mature for 876
twenty. Joe thinks so, and Joe 877
is the least immature boy of 878
twenty-four now alive in the 879
United States. It interests me 880
to hear that our visitor is mus- 881
cular. He sounded so feeble. I 882
expect he was acting a little." 883
"Of course he was, daddy," 884
Norah agreed; "he laid it on 885
thick. So should I in his shoes! 886
If I were only an inch high and 887
saw two big brutes like Joe and 888
Stuke standing over me—and 889
Joe looks simply terrific when 890
his eyes get green—I'd simply 891
have groveled on the floor and 892
kicked my heels. He's a coward 893
anyhow. And he—— Oh, pre- 894
cious angel bunny!" 895
"I beg your pardon, daugh- 896
ter?" 897
"She's talkin' to Junior, dad," 898
Stukely explained; "he's just 899
rolled in, sir." 900

Joseph Fancher, Jr., rolled on the door sill and waved a determined fist at his relatives, saying ferociously, "Yattakow!" A muddled white garment incased his fat legs. He was otherwise bare and visibly cross, after a crawl down the corridor from his low crib beside the eastern windows and his nurse's door. He said "Yattakow!" again, and inflated himself for a howl of rage, shutting his black eyes.

"Yes, darling," Norah gurgled; "Uncle Stuke'll give you a glass of water. Thank heaven there is some! Hurry, Stuke! Yes, lamb! There," she said, settling the dark infant on her green lap, "drink that and tell us what you think. There was a nice burglar here and your fond grandpapa let him go because our manners are perfect in the Kent family. He just told us a lot of awful lies and Papa Joe has taken him outdoors so that his hair oil won't smell any more. . . . Yes, spill it on mother, darlin' ducky."

"So you think he was lying, daughter?"

"Certain of it, daddy. . . . Oh, Hester," she said to an apparition in a blue gown outside the door, "baby got out of his crib. Just put him back and go on giving him this water. He doesn't want it, of course, but it soothes his egoism. Here, angel, nursie wants you."

The nursemaid picked up her charge with indeterminate, pretty noises of reproach and said "Yes'm. Some noise woke me up. . . . Did he bump himself gettin' out of bed? My!" while Junior clung to his glass of water and chirped triumphantly when he contrived to kick Norah in the face.

"Ah, Hester," said the Reverend Gavin Kent, "you were acquainted with the Klings of course. Yes? Was there a Rudy Kling in the family?"

"Rudy? I should certainly say there was," the girl said, bundling Junior in her arms; "my, yes! Yesterday when I was down home to see mamma's sore foot we were talkin' about him. 'Cause the doctor stuck some co-cocaine into her toe when he lanced it—yes."

"He's a pretty little thing with big black eyes, Hester?"

The nursemaid giggled, "Yes'm. He looked awful sissy, but all the big fellas were scared of him 'cause he fought so hard. Yes'm. He was just a dreadful boy. . . . No, baby. . . . The other Kling boys were nice fellas, but Rudy was a tough. He—— Now, Junior, be good!"

Junior plunged his whole arm into the glass, found that it wouldn't come out with his fist doubled and raised a horrid lamentation in which traces of the word "Mamma!" mingled with mere breath. Mrs. Kent appeared as a wraith in lavender,

985 and the howling baby retired
986 with all his social apparatus
987 down the hallway.

988 "The day," said the Reverend
989 Gavin Kent, "has begun, Stuke.
990 And what the thoughts of Mr.
991 Kling were while he listened to
992 our conversation from the attic
993 we shall probably never know.
994 Probably we're nothing but an
995 episode in his career. Is it ego-
996 tism to wonder whether he relied
997 on our gentility in surrendering?
998 His story was silly. Few people
999 would have gone through the
1000 form of believing it. I think it
1001 was Ludovic Halévy who re-
1002 marked that well-bred people
1003 are utterly helpless in their deal-
1004 ings with rogues. . . . Meantime,
1005 my dear boy, you might run
1006 down and look at the silver for
1007 safety's sake."

1008 "Yes, sir," his son said,
1009 through a yawn; "time to milk
1010 anyhow."

1011 He crossed the hallway
1012 drenched in fresh heat and echo-
1013 ing with notes of admiration
1014 from Junior's nursery. The
1015 black-haired baby was being
1016 adored for his latest cleverness.
1017 Historically, Stukely thought,
1018 several million babies had stuck
1019 their doubled fists in glasses of
1020 water and hadn't been able to
1021 pull them out again. A stream
1022 of babies passed in his misty
1023 speculation, each with a doubled
1024 fist in a glass. He pulled off his
1025 soaked bath robe and stood with
1026 a lazy wind playing on his

1027 brown body through slats of his
1028 closed shutters. In Babylon, in
1029 otiose Corinth, in Roman villas
1030 beside white Naples, in the grim
1031 Middle Ages and throughout the
1032 rational eighteenth century, ba-
1033 bies had gone on sticking their
1034 fists in glasses, and innumerable
1035 women had adored them for do-
1036 ing what seemed, on any calm
1037 consideration, one of the most
1038 obvious things you could do.

1039 He hauled limp cotton trou-
1040 sers up his legs and hunted out a
1041 shirt of no intrinsic value from
1042 his closet. . . . Perhaps people
1043 were often admired for doing
1044 rather obvious things. It was
1045 really nothing extraordinary that
1046 Joe and he managed fifty acres
1047 of farm and made the land pay.
1048 Lots of people had done that be-
1049 fore. His mother's unexampled
1050 talent for screaming at sudden
1051 noises was really rarer than the
1052 common sense needed to manage
1053 cows, eggs, tomatoes and apple
1054 trees. It might have to be class-
1055 ified as an entirely useless accom-
1056 plishment. The boy laced on
1057 his canvas shoes in a drowsy
1058 speculation. What accomplish-
1059 ments were always useful? He
1060 had taken three prizes at school
1061 in French composition, and now
1062 he sprayed apple trees content-
1063 edly. Numbers of thoughts
1064 flowed together without relation
1065 in his mind as he descended the
1066 green stairs into the living room,
1067 lined with books. Nobody had
1068 touched the silver ranged in the

old sideboard of the dining room. He yawned ten times, picked a pipe from the table below Bishop Stukely's portrait beside the open front door and idled into the pillared porch. The dewy roofs of Gossetville twinkled down the shallow valley's hot reaches, and the red hair of young Alphenius Puddy, the hired boy, twinkled near at hand. Alphenius diligently left his father's farm when the multitude of Puddys rose in summer, but he usually craftily waited for Joe or Stukely to appear before he began to milk the twelve cows. However, Norah liked the boy's hair and he sometimes worked. This morning he had an appearance of prim virtue, sitting on the low step of the porch, and he said with discretion, "I'll help you carry him in, Stuke. Only he's certainly awful drunk."

"Who's drunk, Alphenius?"

"Well," said Alphenius in soprano, defensively, "he's lyin' down in the yard with nothin' on him but some p'jama pants, an' his head in a bucket. I says 'Are you drunk, Joe?' only he just kicked at me an' kind of cussed."

"But where's Rudy Kling, Alphenius?"

Alphenius remarked in a surprised barytone, "How d'I know, Stuke? Somebody saw him in Coney Island last summer. Maybe he's in jail."

"Then Joe didn't bring him over to your father's?"

"Naw," said Alphenius, with indignation; "pop'd kick him off the place if anybody fetched him in. He was sellin' that cocaine stuff to the kids in——"

His stomach became an icy balloon in Stukely's middle. He went loping down the flagged walk to the white fence of the barnyard and vaulted its solid height. Immediately Joe said hollowly, "Gettahell 'way from me, y'——" And the voice trailed into wasted vowels. He lay stretched on ruts of the yard with his naked shoulders twitching, and his head was hidden in a tin pail.

"Joe," said Stukely dizzily, "wh-what on earth are you—— Joe!" The body heaved in its vivid trousers.

Joe said, "'At you, babe? Find me my gun, boy. Gonna——" A lovely line of scarlet picked its way down his brown neck and seemed to hesitate among the dimpling muscles of his shoulders. Stukely dropped back his head and howled three times so that his throat burned. Joe said "Gracious! Quit 'at yawp, ace!" and then said nothing more for a whirling time. The clocks of Gossetville struck four.

At ten it occurred to Stukely that he would die if he didn't get to sleep. Farmers flooded up and down the pillared porch, ducking their heads when lightning showered violet flares through the rain that fell with a vexatious steadiness. The bloodhound from Poughkeepsie sat in dignity on the hearth of the living room under Bishop Stukely's portrait and moved its ears whenever rolls of thunder banged in the valley.

Norah observed the beast with sympathy and told it, "Poor dear! Did the nasty rain wash all the scent away? Stuke, maybe it's thirsty."

"The hell I care," said Stukely, lighting a cigarette.

"My dear boy," his father intoned, "as this is primarily— and secondarily—all my fault, don't be so miserable. . . . Grace, darling, please don't scream so loudly!"

"Gavin," said Mrs. Kent, "I simply abominate lightning! And Joe's door is shut. Stuke, is he really fond of chicken broth? You're so much more observant than the rest of us. I must ask the doctor about soup when he comes back this evening."

"Mother," Norah assured her, "his digestion is not affected at all. He's had three cups of coffee and four pieces of toast. Being hit on the head with a horseshoe doesn't affect the stomach. I think Rudy was too frightfully clever to jam a pail over his head afterward. But I don't understand what he wanted with that sheet. It's not a good one. Joe uses it on his cot on hot nights. . . . Precious angel bunny," she told the baby, "go bite the niceums bloodhound. Rudy improves the more you hear of him. He sells cocaine to kids in schools. He knocks people's eyes out and if Joe wasn't indestructible, of course he'd have fractured his skull."

Mrs. Kent screamed with restraint, picking up Junior from beside the bloodhound's tail, and gaspingly said, "No, baby! I must say that I think you were all a little idiotic last night. You find a terrible creature in the house and——"

"My dear Grace," said the Reverend Gavin Kent, dusting ash from his black coat, "I was the idiot. The children looked to me for an attitude. I chose to turn this person loose. If I had known that he sold cocaine to people, of course—— There's the telephone."

Several neighbors leaked in through the open door and gazed at Stukely picking up the telephone. A brisk person remarked that he was the central office in New York City, and then demanded Mr. J. Fanchetti.

"If you mean Joseph Fancher," Stukely growled, "he was knocked on the head with a horseshoe this morning and he's ill in bed."

"Yeh," said the telephone, "him. We got a call from your

1237 chief of police up there about
1238 this thing. This man Klung
1239 he speaks of——"
1240 "Kling," said Stukely, in bit-
1241 terness.
1242 "Yeh, this man Klieg is de-
1243 scribed as very small, kind of,
1244 with dark hair an' eyes. Kind
1245 of a round face. Age about
1246 twenty-three or four."
1247 Stukely yawned, "That's cor-
1248 rect. Yes?"
1249 "Well," the telephone said,
1250 "he's wanted for assault. It's in
1251 yest'day's papers. This lady he
1252 'saulted is able to describe him
1253 this mornin'. She's come to.
1254 He married her under the name
1255 of Thomas Edwards in Boston
1256 last week. Only she says he's
1257 got R. J. K. tattooed on his right
1258 arm. He'll have two em'rald
1259 rings set in platinum, and——"
1260 "Set in what?"
1261 "Platinum," the telephone re-
1262 peated with an air of authority;
1263 "one gold lip stick with a rooby
1264 in the bottom of it. One dia-
1265 mond lavaleer——"
1266 "A what?"
1267 The telephone groaned; then
1268 asked: "Is there a lady there?"
1269 "Norah," Stukely urged,
1270 "come and listen to this—this
1271 stuff."
1272 Norah assumed the telephone
1273 and told it briskly, "Tell me all
1274 about it. Poor Stuke's so sleepy
1275 he can't stand up straight. . . .
1276 This is Mrs. Fancher. . . . No,
1277 not Franceshi. . . . Yes, with
1278 a horseshoe. . . . Kling, not

1279 Klieg. . . . How characteristic
1280 of him! . . . Oh, no, we only met
1281 him last night. . . . He was hid-
1282 ing in the attic. Attic, the
1283 top of a house, you know. . . .
1284 Garret is the same thing. Yes,
1285 you're quite right. . . . Married
1286 her? Was she old and rather
1287 idiotic? . . . I thought so. . . . .
1288 Set in platinum? . . . Stuke,
1289 give me a pencil. . . . Diamond
1290 lavallière. . . . Real pearls or syn-
1291 thetic? . . . Yes, she'd naturally
1292 say they were real. . . . Yes,
1293 he's very well known around
1294 here. He sold cocaine. . . . Oh,
1295 five years ago! . . . No, his fam-
1296 ily moved to California. We're
1297 living in their house. We found
1298 him hiding in the attic at three
1299 this morning. . . . That's what
1300 the neighbors tell us. They
1301 found that he'd been selling co-
1302 caine to children in the schools
1303 here. His father ordered him
1304 out. . . . Oh, yes, the police tele-
1305 phoned everywhere. We have a
1306 bloodhound from Poughkeepsie,
1307 only it doesn't work. The rain,
1308 you know." She beamed over a
1309 shoulder at the bloodhound.
1310 "Yes, I can. He was wearing a
1311 dark blue suit, purple socks and
1312 a green tie. . . . Yes, green. . . .
1313 And is his wife going to recover?
1314 That's nice. . . . Yes. . . . Thanks,
1315 awf'ly. . . . Good-by."
1316 "What's all that?" Joe
1317 drawled from the green stair-
1318 case. He scowled as Mrs. Kent
1319 screamed, and said, "Mamma,
1320 don't! My head's like a tea-

kettle awready. Yeh, babe gets his talent for yellin' offa you. I'm all melancholy and you leave me 'lone. What's that on the telephone, girl?" He sat down on the stairs abruptly and touched the cap of white bandage that hid his fair eyebrows with tremulous fingers. "Is Rudy gummed up down in New York?"

Norah fluttered her fresh gown up the green treads, saying gayly, "Yes, lamb. He married some imbecile hag in Boston and then robbed her and beat her a good deal on Friday. So the poor dear was trying to hide. . . . Come back to bed, you unutterable idiot!"

"Yeh, some dizzy dame marries this fella an' he bungs her frame. He's a nice man. Where's all our p'licemen we had here?"

"They're out looking for Rudy, Joe," said Stukely, yawned twice and finished: "In cars an' things. . . . Go back to bed, for heaven's sake!"

"Won't either!" Joe growled, getting his head on Norah's shoulder. He closed his eyes and drawled, "This fella sold dope, somebody was sayin'. . . . Aw right. And he was up in the attic makin' noises like a rat. I bet he's got him some dope hid out in the attic right now. Babe, you shinny up in the attic and look for dope. It'll do you good, bud. I'm so mis'rable I

want everybody to be unhappy too. Rev'rend, next time you wanta be all kinda magnanimious and let Rudy outa this house, you're gonna be surprised how nasty I'll act. I'll be mean and ungentlemanly."

"My dear boy," said the clergyman, "you won't—wouldn't be half as mean as I should."

"G'on, fella," Joe snorted; "it ain't in you! You ain't had any experience. Girl, unless you quit usin' sandalwood on your hair, I'll quit you cold an' marry a fat blonde. Babe, go look for dope in the attic. Nice an' hot up there an' you'll like it. Honey, get me back in bed. I'm a rooined woman."

Stukely trotted up the stairs, dragging Alphenius Puddy with him. Joe's weight seemed terrific as the long man sagged back on Stukely's shoulder and stumbled into the bland splendors of Norah's gilded Spanish bed. He recited absently:

"There, little pimple, don't y'cry!
Gonna be a sore boil by and by."

Norah urged, "Don't be so coarse, darling. You've no idea what words you used when the doctor was stitching your poor head."

"Yes, I have, female! I s'lected them careful 'cause poppa was in the room. Stuke knows I can do lots better'n that. . . . Alphenius, you worfless an'mal, go and help Stuke

1404 hunt dope in the attic. If you
1405 work hard, boy, an' keep at it
1406 steady, you'll be as bad as this
1407 Rudy when you're his age, even
1408 if your folks are Baptists."

1409 "Yes-sir," said Alphenius, in-
1410 vestigating Norah's dressing ta-
1411 ble. "What's cocaine look like?"

1412 "Toof powder," Joe moaned;
1413 "Toothbrush Fallon in my com-
1414 p'ny kep' his in a toof—tooth—
1415 teef-powder box, over in that
1416 war they had in France. He
1417 was extremely good for nothin'
1418 an' died grand, all full of cocaine,
1419 shootin' at trees. He was a
1420 tough kid outa Kentucky. They
1421 got a mon'ment to him in his
1422 home town where he was run
1423 out by the sheriff back in 1912.
1424 It's kinda sarcastic. The cap-
1425 tain was just gonna put him in
1426 arrest when the Dutch started
1427 firin'. She's an ill wind 'at
1428 don't blow somebody's dirty
1429 laundry down the creek. . . .
1430 Babe, go look in the attic. If
1431 Rudy Kling wasn't just hidin'
1432 out here, he came for somethin'.
1433 In his class of s'ciety dope's as
1434 good as cash. Me, walkin'
1435 ahead of this pinyap like I was
1436 ten years of age an' not too
1437 bright at that! I could expire
1438 of shame if my dome wasn't
1439 fallin' in on me. I told you
1440 those green p'jamas were bad
1441 luck, girl! Only you'll dec'rate
1442 or die. Get outa here, ace, an'
1443 snoop for snow in the attic."

1444 Stukely went dutifully into
1445 the spare bedroom, blinking at a

1446 final flare of lightning through
1447 the wet windows. His dazed
1448 legs mounted the bed and he
1449 raised his dirty hands to the
1450 trapdoor. Then he stopped to
1451 scratch an ear and wonder
1452 whether cocaine was a durable
1453 drug. He had never seen any.
1454 Would it degenerate, stored in
1455 an attic for five years?

1456 "I wonder if cocaine keeps?"
1457 "I dunno," said Alphenius,
1458 industriously gathering a feather
1459 from the vermilion floor. "Will
1460 I go ask Doctor Kent, Stuke?"

1461 "You might just as well, Al-
1462 phenius. Your assistance is
1463 mostly spiritual anyhow," Stuke-
1464 ly yawned; "you're an awf'ly
1465 good witness for a dollar a day."

1466 "I know I am," the hired boy
1467 assured him; "Joe says I encour-
1468 age him a lot clippin' trees. I'll
1469 go ask your father about the
1470 cocaine."

1471 He politely closed the door.
1472 Stukely pondered the value of
1473 sarcasm as applied to the adol-
1474 escent mind and then paused to
1475 yawn some more. He would
1476 gratify Joe by a cursory look
1477 around the attic and then he
1478 would sleep. He would sleep im-
1479 mensely, probably for the rest
1480 of the day. If Alphenius came
1481 to tell him that the cows needed
1482 milking or that chickens had
1483 died of lightning, why, Alphenius
1484 might be slapped on a prominent
1485 ear. He lifted his arms to the
1486 sides of the trapdoor and mutely
1487 stared into the white face with

1488 its black eyelashes fluttering.
1489 Rudy Kling looked down at him
1490 silently and licked his lips twice.
1491 A wave of thunder passed above
1492 the house and one feather from
1493 the stored pillows came flutter-
1494 ing out of the black attic past
1495 the tiny man's head.
1496 "Oh, I see," said Stukely;
1497 "yeh—yes! You banged Joe an'
1498 then you ran around behind the
1499 house an' climbed up the tank
1500 onto the roof. Yes, nobody
1501 ever thought of that, of course!"
1502 "Aw, keep your shirt on,
1503 kiddy! Let's talk business, pal,"
1504 Mr. Kling murmured; "don't
1505 get excited, either. . . . Who's
1506 downstairs?"
1507 "About half the men in the
1508 county," Stukely whispered.
1509 "All right. Now," the pretty
1510 man said rapidly, "when it gets
1511 dark get a car—you got one,
1512 ain't you?—get a car up the
1513 north fence by the bunch of pop-
1514 lars. I'll be on the roof. Toot
1515 the horn oncet. I'll get down
1516 an' you drive me inta C'necticut.
1517 Two hundred to you when we
1518 get there, pal, and I'll tell you
1519 where's there's easy a couple of
1520 hundred dollars of snow in the
1521 house here. Be a gentleman
1522 and——"
1523 "Are you crazy?" the boy
1524 asked after a gulp.
1525 The white face stooped down
1526 a little farther. Mr. Kling said
1527 in his whining whisper, "No,
1528 I've been in an' out of this house
1529 five times since you guys have

1530 been livin' here! You never lock
1531 up right. I could have swiped
1532 your silver an' your sister's kid
1533 any time without wakin' up a
1534 soul. I had near a hundred
1535 ounces of coke hid here when my
1536 old man kicked me out. I still
1537 got nine or ten. You can sell it
1538 to a feller over in Brooklyn.
1539 Sands Street. I forget the num-
1540 ber. Now have the car up the
1541 north fence, pal, about eight
1542 o'clock."
1543 "What did you want with
1544 Joe's sheet?" Stukely inquired.
1545 "To lie on, pal! Gee," said
1546 Mr. Kling morosely, "you guys
1547 don't ever clean this garret! I'm
1548 all over feathers! And the trap
1549 in the roof leaks too! If you was
1550 real farmers, you'd look after
1551 things better. . . . Now, kiddy,
1552 don't get excited and tell anybody
1553 I'm up here, 'cause it'll be hell
1554 in the papers if I'm caught
1555 in this dump, see?"
1556 He licked his lips again.
1557 Stukely yawned. He was not
1558 asleep. This was real and inter-
1559 esting, but he drowsed with his
1560 hard fingers on the edges of the
1561 trap and wearily wondered what
1562 the tiny rogue meant.
1563 "You're a lot of swells out of
1564 New York, pal."
1565 "I don't know," said Stukely;
1566 "Uncle George is awf'ly rich—
1567 mother's brother. Father had
1568 Saint Philip's Church until he
1569 retired, and, of course, we know
1570 a lot of smart people. But——"
1571 "Stuff a gun with it," Mr.

1572 Kling commanded; "you're
1573 swells. Your sister's named
1574 Norah and she's married to that
1575 yella-headed devil that talks like
1576 a nigger. Get me in front of a
1577 judge an' I'm an old friend of the
1578 lady. Picked her up at a dance
1579 parlor in the city years back. I
1580 phoned the lady I'm in trouble.
1581 She leaves the door open for me,
1582 see? . . . See? . . . See?"

1583 Stukely said, "Yes, I see.
1584 That's awf'ly interesting."

1585 "All right. And I'm good-
1586 lookin'. Tell me nobody'd be-
1587 lieve it and I'll tell you they
1588 will, pal! It'll be all over the
1589 papers. . . . What d'you say?
1590 It's a gentleman's offer. Two
1591 hundred——well, I'll make it
1592 two hundred and fifty to run me
1593 into C'necticut. And I'll tell
1594 you where the dust is. All you
1595 need is a chisel and ——"

1596 "And suppose you just bang
1597 me on the head when we're up
1598 the road a couple of miles an'
1599 then drive into Canada, h'm?"
1600 Stukely asked.

1601 "Aw, pal, I ain't even got a
1602 gun with me!"

1603 "Careless of you. . . . Excuse
1604 me," Stukely said after a yawn,
1605 "but why should I trust you?
1606 They want you in New York
1607 for——"

1608 "What the hell d'you think
1609 I'm doing here? Playin' pin-
1610 ochle? I ran for this place.
1611 You got me. What's the good
1612 in turnin' me over, pal? You
1613 won't make a cent, see? This
1614 way you'll be in three or four
1615 hundred at the very least," Mr.
1616 Kling insisted, "and——"

1617 "And if I go down and tell
1618 them you're here," Stukely
1619 broke in, "you'll be cad enough
1620 to lie about my sister?"

1621 "Pal," said Mr. Kling, brush-
1622 ing a feather from his ear, "don't
1623 talk any of that morality on me!
1624 I'm a cad and all that hooey.
1625 All right; only I'm not goin' to
1626 jail another stretch. You guys
1627 are gentlemen. If you want your
1628 sister in the papers for bein' in
1629 love with a——"

1630 Stukely slapped him over the
1631 mouth and got his hands in the
1632 man's drooping coat miraculous-
1633 ly at the same time. The light
1634 body came down from the ceiling
1635 on him in a remarkable limp-
1636 ness, then changed to a tangle of
1637 fighting muscles as the bedstead
1638 cracked and collapsed. A suffo-
1639 cating shower of dust and feath-
1640 ers followed Rudy Kling's tum-
1641 ble and his infantile suitcase
1642 smacked on Stukely's head, then
1643 rattled on the red floor, spilling
1644 two fat pears and a pair of horn-
1645 rimmed spectacles as the fall
1646 jarred it open. Stukely saw this
1647 revelation over the man's shoul-
1648 der. He seemed to be waltzing
1649 with Mr. Kling on the gray mat-
1650 tress, over bedposts and incon-
1651 venient pillows.

1652 Alphenius Puddy opened the
1653 door and stood civilly gaping
1654 with a slab of chocolate cake in
1655 his hand.

1656 "Call yourself a gentleman!"
1657 "Oh, don't be so damn silly!"
1658 said Stukely. "Alphenius, go
1659 and call——"
1660 Alphenius turned into the
1661 hallway and said timidly, "Oh,
1662 Mis' Fancher! Oh, Jo-oe! Hey,
1663 Stuke's fightin' a fella up here!"
1664 Mr. Kling stumbled, or Stuke-
1665 ly stumbled. There was an in-
1666 determinate clatter and a whirl-
1667 ing movement that left Stukely
1668 sprawling on the tiny man in a
1669 corner by the windows. He was
1670 embarrassed by Mr. Kling's size.
1671 Eventually it seemed best to sit
1672 on him, although a constant
1673 writhing made the matter un-
1674 comfortable, and it was supreme-
1675 ly irritating that a number of
1676 men who came in sat on their
1677 heels and watched Stukely sit
1678 on the noisy body. Alphenius
1679 Puddy got up on the dresser of
1680 blue enamel and ate some cake.
1681 His large father said, "Well,
1682 we got him," in an utterly fatu-
1683 ous tone of complacency, as
1684 though he had attended to all
1685 this.
1686 "Well, do something about it,
1687 please!"
1688 A hairy long youth from the
1689 orchard second on the left up on
1690 the north road practically sug-
1691 gested, "Otto, you take his legs.
1692 Sam, you catch his arm. Keep
1693 away, Doctor Kent! Hey, Rudy,
1694 quit, will ye? Be a gentleman!
1695 Hold his head on the floor,
1696 Stuke! Aw, Rudy, behave!"
1697 Stukely tried to drag his hand

1698 from the teeth set in its side and
1699 woke fully in the pain. The tiny
1700 man was biting his hand, biting
1701 it violently too!
1702 The boy said, "Stop that!
1703 Stop it or I'll hurt you! Say,
1704 stop it!" while he wondered
1705 whether he should hammer the
1706 mad black eyes with his free fist.
1707 No, he was too big. Wouldn't be
1708 fair. Ouch! He said "Oh, stop
1709 it!" and then something bright
1710 descended with a thump on the
1711 flushed face inclosing his hand.
1712 The teeth parted. Stukely got
1713 up in a cloud of blue shirts and
1714 stared incredulously at his moth-
1715 er holding a silver-backed hair-
1716 brush in both hands.
1717 "Good heavens, Grace!" said
1718 the Reverend Gavin Kent, lifting
1719 his yellow spectacles.
1720 "Gavin," Mrs. Kent panted,
1721 "I do not care! Will some of you
1722 please take this person out of our
1723 house? H-he has absolutely no
1724 manners!"
1725 "Grace," the old gentleman in-
1726 toned, "the poor creature is
1727 crazy with fear. Get up, young
1728 man. Nobody will hurt you."
1729 Alphenius Puddy, on the
1730 dresser, said to someone in the
1731 hallway, "Mrs. Kent, she soaked
1732 him on the nose. He was bitin'
1733 Stuke."
1734 "If he doesn't behave him-
1735 self," Mrs. Kent cried, gripping
1736 her weapon, "I shall certainly
1737 hit him again!" She screamed
1738 a little and added, "And I hope
1739 that his nose is broken! Norah,

337

1740 you must see after this that your
1741 father does not leave the front
1742 door open again. It's entirely
1743 your fault, Gavin! I'm sorry to
1744 seem disagreeable, but you must
1745 be careful about locking up. You
1746 see what happens!" She lifted
1747 her lavender apron with its
1748 futile pockets and jammed its
1749 hem into her mouth, repressing
1750 a shriek, then took it out and
1751 said, "I shall be hysterical unless
1752 someone takes this man away."
1753 Rudy Kling rose from the
1754 vermilion floor with a hand on
1755 his nose and gazed at Mrs. Kent
1756 in silence.
1757 After a moment he gabbled,
1758 "Yeh! It's that lady—it's your
1759 daughter left the door open for
1760 me. I and——"
1761 "How can you have the im-
1762 pudence to say that? Gavin,
1763 he's trying to make a scandal!
1764 It's like that horrible man who
1765 was caught at the Milliman's
1766 house in Lenox and said that
1767 their governess had let him in.
1768 How dare you?" said Mrs. Kent,
1769 tightening her slim fingers on the
1770 hairbrush. "If you say that
1771 again I shall hit you! Norah,
1772 please be serious!"
1773 "Mother," Norah gurgled
1774 through her fingers, "I—I can't
1775 be! . . . Please, take him away.
1776 . . . I—he—it——"

1777 Stukely sat down on the
1778 wrecked bed in a murmur of
1779 voices and studied a crescent of
1780 blue marks on his hand. He had
1781 a sense of something incredibly
1782 wonderful, a performance in a
1783 dream. Yes, he had seen his
1784 mother, the daughter of a bishop,
1785 hit a man in purple socks on the
1786 nose with a hairbrush. The
1787 room cleared on some order from
1788 Joe Fancher in the hallway.
1789 Everything was gone, and in the
1790 vacancy Joe drawled feebly,
1791 "Mamma, I've never said any-
1792 thing of you but that you're a
1793 gentleman. Yeh, and it takes a
1794 lady to be that. No common
1795 sorta female can! It's more'n
1796 most men can manage, at that!"
1797 "Good heavens," said Mrs.
1798 Kent, "this terrible creature was
1799 simply gnawing Stuke! And the
1800 poor boy wouldn't hit him be-
1801 cause he was so little, or one of
1802 those idiotic reasons that men
1803 have for things, and somebody
1804 had to do something, and if
1805 you dare to tell me, Gavin, that
1806 it wasn't ladylike, I shall
1807 scream!"
1808 "My dear," the Reverend
1809 Gavin Kent said violently, "I
1810 never admired you so much in
1811 all my life!"
1812 Mrs. Kent screamed.

THE ANALYSIS

Gentility has a total length of 1812 lines. Of these 1629 are
occupied by the Beginning, only 23 by the Decisive Act, and 161

by the Sequel. The Ending, you will remember, includes both the Decisive Act and the Sequel. The story of Decision resembles the story of Accomplishment in this respect.

A glance at the chart will show that this story is presented entirely in interchanges with the single exception of lines 1011 to 1088 which show the reflections of Stukely upon the interchanges that have just passed. Attention is instantly concentrated upon the central character, Stukely, and it then shows how he reacts to the Scene which is contributed to by the whole Kent family, from lines 1 to 578. Lines 579 to 620, which are an interchange between Joe Fancher and the burglar, Rudy Kling, follow immediately after Stukely has become aware that there is a burglar in the attic. This interchange between Joe and the burglar occupies lines 579 to 620. Lines 621 to 844 are again an interchange between Rudy and the Kent family. The fifth step of the lines 845 to 951, is the comment of the Kents upon Rudy's statement, and includes the interchange between Nora and the Reverend Gavin Kent. Following this is the interchange between Hester and the Reverend Gavin as a result of which Stukely's reflections are presented. All these interchanges are made to contain the probability of conflict or clash, and to show the dangerousness inherent in the apparently innocuous burglar. The interchanges between Stukely and Alphenius, lines 1088 to 1117, between Stukely and Joe Fancher, lines 1118 to 1148, are also intended to make this same feeling of danger and disaster apparent. The fifth step is the effect upon the Kent family in lines 1149 to 1226. The interchange between Stukely and the central office, the interchange between Nora and the central office, again lead to the comments of the Kent family on lines 1316 to 1443. Then the interchange between Stukely and Alphemius presents to Stukely a moment of danger into which he enters bravely. After this the interchange on lines 1471 to 1629, between Stukely and Rudy Kling, set forth very definitely the main narrative problem of the story which shows that Stukely has to choose between accepting a bribe in order to keep his sister from scandal, or to preserve the gentility of the Kent family, which is the same thing, and the other course of turning Rudy over to the police. Accepting a bribe would preserve the gentility which he appears to value so highly, and turning Rudy over to the police will involve conflict with a man who has shown that he is a dangerous opponent.

The Decisive Act is contained in lines 1630 to 1651. The Sequel is contained in lines 1652 to 1812, which show that Mrs. Kent whom he considered the acme of gentility, is the one person who, in this rough and tumble scrap, does exactly the right thing, a thing which he would have hesitated to do and which he would not in the slightest degree have connected with his mother.

I have reprinted this story because it is such a clear example of the story of Decision told chronologically without any attempt whatsoever at flash-back, dependent entirely for its interest upon the interchanges. The main narrative problem is not apparent until lines 1471 to 1629. All the material preceding that has to stand upon its own feet, and a reader of this story will do well to realize that there is no hope for a person trying to write a story of Decision until he is able to write interchanges which are in themselves interesting. As in the previous stories the narrative question is one of choice. The narrative question can always be phrased, in the Decision story, "What course will the main character adopt confronted by various choices, or by two choices at least?"

It is obvious that the Beginning, therefore, must be concerned with making clear to the reader these choices that lie before the main actor. Because this story does this so well I am sure that it will repay analysis by writers interested in writing the story of Decision.

BEGINNING	Main condition is shown as placing Main Actor in a dilemma.	Gretchen Innes and Burke. Flash-back. Interchange Maurice Greer and police. 284–521 (5th step 522–584) Gretchen tells of being with Greer at time of murder.	Reader learns of the difficulty, struggle, and probable Disaster which any choice is likely to cause.
		1– 907	

BODY	Mental struggle.	Fifth step of preceding interchange shows mental struggle between two desires in Gretchen. 908– 980	Choices each have something to commend them.

ENDING	Decisive Act.	Interchange. Gretchen and District Attorney. Choice made. 981–1048	Answer to Narrative Question is: "She will make public avowal."
	Sequel.	Interchange. Barney and others. 1049–1148	
		Interchange. Barney and Burke Innes. 1149–1167	
		Interchange. Gretchen and Abbie. 1168–1237	
		Interchange. Gretchen and Burke. 1238–1344	
		5th step. Comment of Observers. 1345–1366	
		Interchange. Gretchen and Burke. 1367–1442 Significance.	

THE HAUNTED LADY

BY ADELA ROGERS ST. JOHN

IN compiling this volume I have tried, wherever possible, to include companion stories; because such stories are extremely illuminating.

Sunk and *Paradise Island* are companion stories in that the main narrative purpose of each is the same.

Sunk and *Jetsam* are companion stories in that their Conclusive Acts are the same.

The most interesting parallelism in the volume, however, is that between *The Haunted Lady* by Adela Rogers St. John, and *The Trouble with Men* by Lucian Carey.

That parallelism, alone, would have been sufficient justification to include in this volume *The Haunted Lady;* but I have another reason for including it, which is that it is an excellent example of a story of Decision which achieves its length not so much from the Beginning as from the Ending; and particularly from that portion of its Ending which in our nomenclature we refer to as the Sequel—that portion which follows the Decisive or Conclusive Act.

CASE No. 14

THE HAUNTED LADY

BY ADELA ROGERS ST. JOHN

The man looked up, startled by the muffled crash of glass shattering upon the exquisite blendings of a Bokhara prayer-rug. It was a very small crash, yet it echoed in the warm intimacy of that charming, book-lined room. It spoke so inevitably of some shameful, violent, secret thing—some unheard-of, shameful thing that had no right to be there.

The man's eyes—fine, clear, gray eyes that were just a little stern—rested upon his wife for a moment, and then went back to the pages of his book. He simply could not sit and stare at her, because she had obviously forgotten him and it couldn't be fair to violate her privacy like that.

But, though he was no longer looking at her as she sat there, taut as a wire that has been stretched and stretched little by little to the breaking-point, he could still see her. His eyes could not strike through the memory of her face to the printed words that he tried to find—her face that was so small and sweet and secret. And he could still see that gallant struggle of hers to keep her firm tight mouth from twitching, and the way her bright color lost ground and wavered to a moon pallor along her high cheek-bones.

The glass had fallen from her hand upon the Bokhara rug—a rug they had once chosen together in their happy rambles about the world. And it was plain that it had fallen because the hand trembled so it could no longer hold it.

She was not reading. Lately, she had ceased to read on these evenings when they stayed home together. Instead, she sat quite still in a big velvet chair that was her favorite, her dark blue eyes fixed half angrily upon some phantom in the fire. When his eyes glimpsed her in the brief space of turning a page, it seemed to him that her jaw, always too sharp and powerful

61 for beauty, was etched raw
62 against the darkness. For when
63 her own reading-lamp was off,
64 her corner of the room lay in
65 shadow.

66 And yet, she used always to
67 read. In those days, if she put
68 down her book, it was to caress
69 and maul the great Dane, who
70 always lay as close to her small
71 feet as he could get, in the hope
72 that she would remember his
73 existence and vouchsafe him a
74 word or two. Or to come and
75 sit upon the arm of Burke's
76 leather chair and indulge in one
77 of her whirlwinds of talk—
78 colorful, pungent, witty talk,
79 full of a bright malice and a gay
80 sophistication. But usually he
81 had to take her book away from
82 her, when the fire had quite
83 died down and he himself was
84 the victim of one prodigious
85 yawn after another.

86 But now—these silences in the
87 dusk of the lampless corner.
88 This broken glass.

89 And on the nights when they
90 did not stay at home together—
91 Gretchen, who had always been
92 so aloof, so easily bored, so
93 impersonal; Gretchen, who had
94 disdained so much and so many;
95 Gretchen, of whom lesser people
96 were wont to say: "Per-
97 sonally, I do think that young
98 Mrs. Burke Innes is an awful
99 snob. She does think herself
100 grand, doesn't she?"
101 But young Mrs. Burke Innes
102 didn't think herself grand, nor

was she a snob, though she had 103
some slight justification for being 104
socially a little exclusive; after 105
all, she had been Gretchen Hunt- 106
Douglass, and Burke Innes's 107
money, which allowed him to 108
spend his life in the pursuit of 109
sport upon the tennis-court and 110
the polo field, was at least three 111
generations old. It was only 112
that Gretchen looked upon the 113
multitude with a clear, cool 114
gaze and too often found them 115
wanting in everything worth 116
while. A self-sufficient woman, 117
Gretchen Innes. 118

But now—this sparkling, in- 119
cessant talk, almost gushing, 120
with people she had been wont to 121
forget existed. Almost as though 122
she were bidding for favor, for 123
popularity. This surrender of 124
her cool, aloof disdain. This 125
broken glass. 126

But he went on reading or try- 127
ing to read, pretending to read. 128
It was part of his code—and men 129
who had met him in the heat and 130
danger of a polo game or in the 131
strain and high tension of a 132
championship tennis match de- 133
clared that Burke Innes was the 134
finest sportsman in America—it 135
was part of his code that a man 136
must never interfere with an- 137
other man's game. Even more 138
particularly a woman's, and 139
that woman his wife, whom he 140
loved. 141
Suddenly she said: "Burke!" 142
The great Dane got up, rigid, 143
his eyes fastened upon her. But 144

145 she put him down with a firm
146 little hand on his swelling
146 neck.

147 The man laid down his book
148 with a smile. He was almost
149 good-looking when he smiled.
150 The sweetness of it softened the
151 stern lines of his tanned, lean,
152 sharp face. The gray eyes lifted
153 under the line of black brows
154 that met above his nose and
155 that, without a smile, made him
156 look a little fierce.

157 "Yes, my darling?" he said.
158 "I can't stand it any longer,"
159 said Gretchen, and she pushed
160 back the lion-cub mop of hair
161 from her forehead.

162 At the tone of her voice, the
163 man opposite, who loved her
164 better than all the world, felt
165 his heart turn over within him.
166 For as a rule Gretchen had the
167 most charming of voices, low
168 and crisp, with a thousand
169 dainty lights and shades.

170 He had first fallen in love
171 with her voice, that day almost
172 ten years ago when she had come
173 out on the tennis-courts just as
174 he had finished a hard set. He
175 had heard her voice before he
176 saw her, and it had struck deep
177 into his heart, telling him that
178 the woman with such a voice
179 might possess all those things he
180 had been seeking in a woman.
181 Now, tonight, her voice was raw
182 and panic-stricken and it broke
183 because the breath back of it
184 failed. But that was not what
185 made Burke's heart quail and

almost stop beating. It was the 186
shame and guilt with which the 187
voice was laden. 188

He didn't say anything. He 189
could not look at her. To see 190
Gretchen's eyes—those dark 191
blue eyes that were so full of 192
pride, so secret of inner thoughts. 193
To see shame upon that brave, 194
imperious mouth. 195

"I can't stand another night 196
of it," she said swiftly, as though 197
she wanted to be rid of them, 198
those shameful words. "I can't. 199
I shall go mad. I sit here—I sit 200
here—night after night, thinking 201
about it, strangling with it. I 202
go to bed and lie there, suffocat- 203
ing, haunted with it. I am 204
haunted. I tell you, I shall go 205
mad." 206

Burke Innes got up and stood 207
half turned from her. There 208
was something inflexible about 209
him—something inflexible be- 210
sides his lean, hard strength. A 211
man of honor, a man of principle, 212
a sportsman playing life's game 213
according to a rigid code. In no 214
way did he betray his thoughts, 215
his feelings. 216

The voice went on passion- 217
ately. "I should have told you 218
then. But I couldn't. I thought 219
it would kill me to tell you. I 220
think I was living in a mist. 221
And, Burke, though I know you 222
love me and I love you, I do not 223
always know what you will 224
think. Besides, I didn't want 225
the decision to rest upon your 226
shoulders. I couldn't—couldn't 227

bear to hurt you. I thought you need never know."

Burke Innes made a swift gesture of appeal. His iron control wavered just that much. The menace of this unknown shame and guilt that weighted his wife's voice, the menace which he now realized had been hovering above him for weeks, months, had approached near and become a monstrous night-mare. If she would only give a name to this horror. But he would not ask her. It was fair that she should be allowed to tell him whatever she had to tell in her own way.

"Do you know where Maurice Greer was between twelve and four the night his wife was murdered? Do you know? Do you want to know?"

He turned then and looked full at her. Amazement had sent him white beneath the heavy tan. Amazement. Nothing more yet. Just sheer, incredulous amazement.

Gretchen Innes had risen and stood facing him. Her face was working, but her voice sounded angry.

"He was here—with me."

The great Dane growled, deep in his throat, whimpered, began to whine dismally. Gretchen touched him with the toe of her silver slipper and he was quiet.

The man and woman stood looking at each other. Maurice Greer. For an instant the man flashed before Burke Innes. That smooth, fair Greek head, with a touch of the faun about it, and the dark, smiling eyes, the wistful mouth. And the face of the wife who had been murder-ed, with its unwholesome ugly beauty, its heavy eyelids, its half open, painted lips.

In the still room, the man whose wife had said to him: "He was here—with me," tried slowly, painfully, to understand just what those words meant.

At four o'clock on a certain night in June now almost a year ago, Maurice Greer had tele-phoned to the police station. They had gone to the Greer bungalow in Montecito which the police knew well because, in spite of the tangled grounds that surrounded it, neighbors had sometimes phoned to protest against the hilarity and jazz which disturbed their slumbers.

It was a glorified bungalow, set well back from the highway rambling about among the live oaks and the yuccas and the stiff little palms, and on the long, uncovered veranda they found Maurice Greer, walking up and down, up and down.

Even as the car swung into the drive, they saw him make a swift turn and walk back, and turn again swiftly and walk, as though something drove him close.

He was hatless, and his blond hair was as smoothly groomed as though he were just starting for some exclusive little dinner party. His dinner clothes were immaculate and worn as only Maurice Greer could wear them. He was smoking a cigaret, with all the ease and nonchalance for which he was famous.

But for all that, he looked, in the half light from the porch lamps, haggard and desperate.

Inside, they found Veronica Greer.

"I—haven't touched anything," said Maurice Greer, in a desperate, nonchalant voice.

They had seen her often enough——handsome, black-haired Veronica Greer. Some of them had even known her before she was Veronica Greer, when she was little Veronica Talamantes, last of a distinguished old Spanish family, beautiful with that ripe, luscious beauty of the Spanish-Californian, noted already in her teens for her escapades and indiscretions. Already a little cold-shouldered, there where her fathers had once ruled as kings over hundreds of thousands of acres.

But on that June night she lay quite still, her black hair, that was her greatest beauty and that she still wore long flung about her like some lace mantilla such as her grandmothers might have worn.

She had been shot through the heart and probably had never known that her swift, passionate, reckless young life was ending.

There was a gun—a gun that Maurice Greer explained he always kept in the house. The bungalow was distant from its nearest neighbors. He was away a great deal in the evening. His wife was nervous.

Followed, inexorably, those awful days after the tragedy, which for sheer horror and ugliness and humiliation always so far surpass the tragedy itself.

The coroner had fixed the hour of Mrs. Greer's death as sometime between two and three in the morning. The servants, whose quarters were some distance from the house, had heard voices sometime after midnight. They did not know exactly what time. Hilarious voices. Then angry voices. They didn't recognize the voices. They didn't pay any attention, because there were often voices in the bungalow. Also they had heard vaguely a sound which might have been a shot, but which they took for an automobile exhaust on the highway. Mrs. Greer had had a guest for dinner, but he had left duly by the front door and his hat and coat had been presented to him by the Japanese houseman. The guest was fortunately able to account for his movements from that time on. The servants knew nothing of any-

396 one who had come after his
397 departure.

398 Mr. Greer had not been at
399 home for dinner. They did not
400 know what time he had returned.
401 He was driving his own car.

402 Maurice Greer said that he
403 had telephoned the moment he
404 came home, and the telephone
405 at the police station had rung at
406 exactly ten minutes after four.
407 He had left the Samarkand,
408 where he had been playing
409 bridge with some Easterners
410 who lived there, at a little after
411 eleven. He had disappeared,
412 swiftly, in the big black car.
413 At four o'clock he had tele-
414 phoned the police station.

415 Five hours.

416 The thing had torn Santa
417 Barbara wide open.

418 No one believed—at least no
419 one who knew them—that
420 Maurice Greer had shot Ve-
421 ronica. If he had been going
422 to shoot her, he would have
423 done it years before. There had
424 been cause enough.

425 In fact why Maurice Greer,
426 who might have married almost
427 anyone, had ever married Veron-
428 ica Talamantes, no one in Santa
429 Barbara had ever quite under-
430 stood. It was even rumored
431 that he might have married the
432 famous heiress, Janet Grant.
433 Janet herself knew that no-
434 thing but the fact that he had
435 never asked her had kept him
436 from it. He was that kind of a
437 man—a throw-back to all that

438 was romantic, all that was
439 poetical, able somehow to melt
440 the hearts of women with that
441 tender, wistful, unscrupulous
442 smile of his.

443 And with all that, he had
444 suddenly married Veronica Tala-
445 mantes, whom lesser men had
446 never taken the trouble to
447 marry.

448 The truth was that he had
449 loved her. And he had married
450 her, as she knew, because being
451 what he was himself, Maurice
452 Greer could not find it in some
453 secret, chivalrous corner of his
454 heart to judge or condemn any
455 woman. One night Veronica
456 Talamantes had spoken broken-
457 ly, bitterly, of the odds that life
458 had stacked against her. And
459 that strange chivalry in Mau-
460 rice that made him every wo-
461 man's champion, except against
462 himself, sent him to his knees be-
463 fore this girl whom all the world
464 condemned, this bedraggled, bit-
465 ter damsel in distress.

466 But it was not long before
467 he knew himself tricked and
468 cheated.

469 There were people in Santa
470 Barbara who said that Veronica
471 could not help herself, that her
472 heritage of bad blood was too
473 much for her. And they, of
474 course, were not surprised when
475 they heard how she had been
476 found that June dawn, in the
477 cluttered, perfumed room.

478 But that Maurice, after six
479 years of playing the game as

Veronica played it, after six years of taking his fun where he found it while she did the same, should suddenly have shot his tawdry, unfaithful, unloved wife —that was too silly. Everyone said so. Everyone except the police.

They merely said, very politely: "Of course, Mr. Greer there won't be any trouble about your telling us exactly where you were between eleven and four that night."

Maurice Greer laughed. "Our old friend the alibi, eh?" he said, his eyebrows making a very sophisticated but rather pathetic question mark in his forehead.

"If you don't mind," said the district attorney—it had been taken over by the district attorney by that time— "I should like to know especially about the hours between two and four. It was after two that Mrs. Greer was shot."

"An alibi," said Maurice Greer, musingly. "I should have thought of that. I dare say there are a number of people who would have lied for me. Good society melodrama, this. I understand society melodrama's very popular in the movies just now." He lighted a cigaret and made the other man a little bow. He was always a bit of an actor. "I'm sorry, my dear sir; I have no alibi."

And that was that.

"Of course," said Mrs. William Wosley Grant when she heard of it: "it's all perfectly ridiculous. I've read of such things, but I certainly never thought one would happen to us. He was with some woman. Anyone can see that. Evidently with some woman he had no business to be with. Maurice always found that kind the most interesting. But it's silly of him not to tell now. As if a woman who would receive Maurice Greer, with his reputation, between two and four in the morning, deserved any protection. At least I hope she'll have the decency to own up."

But she did not own up.

Of course at first there seemed no real necessity. Maurice Greer wouldn't be convicted. Everyone was sure of that. Possibly that was why he was convicted.

Maurice Greer was convicted and sentenced to spend the rest of his life behind the walls of San Quentin, instead of in the pursuits of pleasure which had hitherto occupied him. Even then, the woman did not own up.

"The thing I hate most," said Mrs. Grant vindictively on the afternoon when she had allowed her well-known weakness for Maurice to influence her to the extent of permitting Janet to go and say good-by to him, "is thinking that Veronica may

563 know of all this and be laughing
564 at us. The little beast."

565 Janet Grant, heiress to all the
566 Grant millions and the social
567 prestige that went with them,
568 only continued to look out the
569 window, her homely, freckled
570 little face pinched. At last she
571 said: "I wonder who the woman
572 is."

573 The world—the whole news-
574 paper-reading world—also
575 wondered. For seven days.
576 Then it forgot.

577 Only Janet Grant wondered
578 about the women who wait at
579 prison gates. Would a man be
580 glad to see even the wrong
581 woman then, if she had proved
582 herself? Janet did not forget.
583 And one other woman could
584 not.

585 And so Burke and Gretchen
586 Innes stood face to face in the
587 warm intimacy of their firelit
588 library—Burke and Gretchen
589 Innes, whom everyone knew to
590 be the happiest of married
591 couples: Burke, with his rigid,
592 old-fashioned code of honor and
593 conduct, his standard of clean
594 sportsmanship; and Gretchen his
595 wife, whose name was like a star
596 among the Japanese lanterns of
597 the women of her set.

598 Between them lay those five
599 words, "He was here—with me."

600 So, having remembered all
601 those things which it was neces-
602 sary for him to remember, Burke
603 Innes thrust his hands deep into
604 the pockets of his gray house-

605 coat and said very quietly to his
606 wife: "Then he was here when
607 his wife was shot. Where"—he
608 was fighting hard to keep his
609 voice level and steady, that it
610 might remind him that he was a
611 gentleman and not a savage—
612 "where was I?"

613 "Don't you remember? You'd
614 gone to Los Angeles to play in
615 the tournament for the state
616 championship."

617 "Oh, yes. And while I was
618 away—Maurice Greer came
619 here——"

620 Gretchen set her jaw, look-
621 ing at him angrily, miserably.
622 Words were so hard for
623 Gretchen. She hated words.
624 They were so inadequate. Why,
625 they had been married for years
626 before she ever found the aban-
627 don to say to Burke the million
628 love thoughts—wild, gorgeous
629 love thoughts—that all the time
630 had seethed in her heart and
631 head for him.

632 And besides, it had been their
633 way, a secretly mutual, secretly
634 understood way, to avoid talk
635 of serious things. Now she must
636 attempt to throw a bridge of
637 words across the hell that
638 yawned between them, and she
639 felt it to be a flimsy, treacherous
640 thing that would cast her head-
641 long into the depths.

642 Finally she said, "Burke, per-
643 haps I could make you under-
644 stand——" Her voice died, of
645 hopelessness and agony and
646 shame.

647 Those dark brows of Burke
648 Innes's drew down heavily
649 over his eyes. "I didn't know
650 you and Maurice Greer were
651 friends."

652 "We weren't. Of course we
653 weren't. How silly——"

654 "Then——"

655 He waited for her. Gave her
656 every chance. Would not con-
657 demn her unheard. Would not
658 hurry her. But something of
659 what that waiting cost him
660 wrote itself in the sharp lines
661 that carved themselves from
662 his nostrils to his lips.

663 Gretchen flung across the
664 room because she could not
665 stand there before him, even
666 though his eyes were upon the
667 Bokhara rug at his feet.

668 How like Gretchen to pretend,
669 now, to be angry. She had
670 pretended, so, to be angry when
671 the birth pangs tore her, and
672 angrier still when death hovered
673 so very close above her small,
674 disordered head. It was self-
675 defense, that anger of
676 Gretchen's.

677 He wondered, in deepest
678 misery, what had betrayed them
679 into this horrible place.

680 Maurice Greer—of all men.
681 The sort of man they called a
682 sheik. All Burke's young, clean
683 manhood revolted from the
684 thing. Why, he was probably
685 soft all over from lack of exer-
686 cise. It would be easy to take
687 him in one hand and break him
688 in two.

689 He dragged his mind back
690 from that flaming desire. For
691 Maurice Greer was in prison.
692 He had gone to prison because
693 some woman did not speak when
694 he might not.

695 "I can never make you under-
696 stand," said Gretchen's voice,
697 harshly despairing. She sat on
698 the arm of the chair, one silver
699 toe moving back and forth across
700 the body of the great Dane.
701 "I'm such a fool at talking. And
702 nobody can explain the unex-
703 plainable. But I'll try. For
704 God's sake, listen—listen.

705 "They plead temporary in-
706 sanity as a defense for murder,
707 don't they? Well, there are
708 other things that ought to have
709 temporary insanity as a de-
710 fense, too. They ought, they
711 ought.

712 "Years ago, before I knew you,
713 Maurice and I were—oh, no-
714 thing. Only, one night at a
715 dance he kissed me. That's
716 all. And I liked it and so did
717 he. He was the only man before
718 you that ever made me *feel*—
719 I think, Burke, he was the only
720 man who ever kissed me. I
721 wasn't a girl who let men kiss
722 me——"

723 The little appeal choked her,
724 but she stiffened herself again.

725 "Well, when Maurice kissed
726 me it thrilled me so that I was
727 afraid—because it was new, and
728 I did not like him. I did not.
729 I went home and lay awake all
730 night, remembering it and not

353

liking him. But whenever I saw him, my breath always stopped and I felt that dizzy little thrill, and I knew he could move me, terribly. I think he must have known it, too.

"But then—you came. And you were my love and my man, and I had been created for you and I had been waiting for you always, and you loved me, and my real life began then.

"But when you have kissed a man like that, it's an unfinished thing. It's like a snake lying in a shell waiting to hatch. You forget it, but it lies there. When we met there was always just a little something between us—a little secret understanding. I know it now.

"And on that night I had been sitting for hours under the pomegranate trees. You know, Burke, how heavenly it can be down there? I could see the moon on the water, a silver mantle of romance. And the garden was so sweet.

"The rest—is harder to tell, Burke. Harder. But I had been reading some silly poetry, and some sillier sophisticated stories. And there came to me a foolish, foolish thought such as women have sometimes. I wondered if I had missed part of the glory of life and love because I hadn't had—many loves. I wondered if I had been listening all the time to one melody, when there were many melodies if only a woman cared to open her ears to them. I felt—this was my greatest sin, darling—I felt as if our love were dull and domestic and drab because it was safe and sane and righteous. And it seemed to me that all the romance in the world was dead and I would never know it again. And that made my heart ache with the queerest, saddest ache I had ever known. It was all because of that silly poem I had been reading about a woman of—many loves.

"I don't think I had been dozing—just dreaming. Anyway, when I saw it all again, the world didn't seem real at all. It was a world crying for romance—crying.

"He saw me sitting there and he stopped his car by the wall below the pomegranate trees. He jumped the wall and came in. I remember he didn't wear any hat and his hair was smooth and glistening in the moonlight. He looked so young and handsome and fair—not as though he could possibly be evil. He kissed my hand, there in the garden."

Again Burke had to listen to the death of that hot, breaking, shameful voice.

"Cheap. Cheap and common and shameful it was. But, Burke, I forgot I was a married woman. I even forgot you. I even forgot"—but that name she could not name in this one story—"I just remembered that old, unfinished kiss and I was a silly girl again.

"I cannot explain to you about Maurice. No woman could explain Maurice to a man. Only there is something that stirs your pulses, and swamps you in a fire of tenderness. And——"

The poor, worn voice whispered now, the shameful secret of it all.

"And, Burke, maybe women have a beast within, just as men have. Only he is more tightly chained and there is less chance for him to break forth and wreak havoc—havoc. But because women do not know he is there, when he does clamor, they have less defense, because they do not know.

"When he kissed me again——

"I must have been mad. I tell you I must have been mad. Don't you see? I am not cheap. I am not common. I am not untrustworthy. My whole life says I am not. Am I then to be judged by one moment of madness?

"And then I hated him. I hated him. I hate him now. I could kill him. When a man has been drunk and finds some low woman beside him, doesn't he hate her and hate himself, and want to kill her and himself?

"Because that is the way I felt about Maurice, when he left me.

"I had my name to think of, my son, you—and I hated him. I hope he rots in a prison cell. But I wish he would not haunt me so—in prison. In prison. I thought at least you would never have to know. But he has made me tell you—by haunting me."

The broken glass cried out beneath her restless feet.

"Then you and he didn't agree about this—silence?" said Burke.

His voice was cold. His face was severe enough now, his lean, dark face that could be so forbidding in spite of its youth.

And she saw accusation in his eyes.

Gretchen went scarlet, painfully, horribly. Shame was upon her, enveloping her. Shame was in the aching breath he saw her draw, in the hands that twisted and untwisted.

"I never saw him again," she cried at him. "I hope I will never see him again. I can see in your face that you—can't forgive me, but I tell you——"
She stopped.

Quietly he said: "I'll have to think this thing out, Gretchen. I want you to think it out. We must see what we can do about it. I must go away, until we can think this thing out."

She started toward him. The pain in his dark face. The suffering in his gray eyes. And she could not comfort him.

900 The door closed behind him,
901 not loudly, but with a horrible
902 finality.

903 Gretchen staggered.

904 "He's—gone" she said to the
905 great Dane, who rose and came
906 close to her, pressing himself
907 against her knees to console her.
908 Above the wind that shook
909 the tree tops she heard the car
910 purr away—away.

911 But all the time, strangely,
912 the mist seemed to be clearing
913 from her brain. Well, this was
914 the end—the end of everything.
915 She had told him. That was
916 necessary. And now he had
917 gone away, and there had been
918 accusation in his eyes.

919 But she was no longer
920 haunted. Not as she had been.
921 Only for the first time, now,
922 she began to think of Maurice
923 Greer without that murderous
924 film of scarlet hatred.

925 He had not told. He had
926 taken a life sentence in prison
927 rather than tell. It must be
928 terrible to be shut up in prison,
929 to face the long years of life
930 from behind those steel bars.

931 And she had shut him there.
932 The old arguments filed past
933 her. But she knew them now
934 for what they had always been
935 —part of her hatred, part of her
936 revenge.

937 "Oh God, what a rotter I've
938 been!" she cried to the silent
939 night.

940 Then a new fear walked in, to
941 keep her ghastly company.

942 If she told now! Perhaps,
943 after a while, Burke might for-
944 give her. Perhaps time might
945 soften that judgment that had
946 looked out of his eyes. He had
947 loved her greatly. Perhaps some
948 day he might forgive her, as
949 other men had forgiven their
950 wives, and they might wipe
951 out the past and be happy as
952 they had been.

953 But if she cried her shame to
954 the world, she made that impos-
955 sible. If she dragged that proud
956 name of his into the gutter, if
957 she took upon herself this
958 scandal that had rocked the
959 whole nation, she would shut
960 herself from him forever.

961 He could never forgive the
962 woman whom the world would
963 know as Maurice Greer's alibi.

964 And still that inner conviction
965 grew and grew.

966 She shuddered away from the
967 coldnesses, the insults, most of
968 all from the fellowship, the
969 equality of cheap women whom
970 she had loathed and who would
971 welcome her now as one of
972 themselves, whether she would
973 or no.

974 But none of these things
975 mattered, now that the mist
976 was gone. Clear-cut as a gallows
977 against the sun, the things that
978 she must do stood forth. Only
979 when it was done could her soul
980 know peace with itself.

981 The district attorney of Santa
982 Barbara County was a little
983 surprised the next morning when

356

a slightly flustered stenographer came in to tell him that Mrs. Burke Innes wanted to see him at once. He told the stenographer to show her in and was almost instantly aware of a lady standing in the doorway.

A very arrogant, imperial lady, in a short white skirt with an indefinable distinction about it, and a woolly orange sweater, buttoned up high about her throat, and an impudent orange hat, pulled far down over her right eye.

But for all her perfection of grooming, all her smart arrogance, the district attorney somehow got the impression that this lady had not slept, had certainly not closed those dark blue, angry eyes all night long. And he felt that the scarlet bow of her mouth had been painted on over gray lips.

"I want to tell you something," she said in a cold, crisp voice.

Now the district attorney had heard many astounding confessions in that unpretentious office. As a rule, he spurred men and women on to those confessions. That was his business.

But looking at this haughty orange and white lady, with the impudent orange hat pulled down over her right eye, he felt a desire, an imperative desire, to keep her from speaking. He did not want to hear what she had to say. He had never felt like that before.

"Maurice Greer," said the lady—and now the scarlet bow of her lips was plainly painted like a scarlet letter upon her white face—"Maurice Greer was with me on the night his wife was murdered. He was with me from midnight until four o'clock. He was with me between two and three, when she was killed. He did not kill her. Will you be kind enough to make out the necessary papers or—or whatever is correct legally, and I will do whatever it is essential for me to do."

She looked, this orange and white lady, with that impudent orange hat pulled so rakishly over her right eye, like a woman who knows that she has just signed her own death warrant.

The group of men lounging in the club dressing-rooms turned at the sound of the shrill whistle and the horrified "My God!" that followed it. There were five or six men in the dressing-rooms. It was noon of the day of the finals in the men's singles.

Big Jim Turner was there, looking at the comic section of the morning paper and giving forth riotous guffaws like a fourteen-year-old schoolboy. With him were the Renny brothers, slim and a little shy, their mild blue eyes and straw hair indicating nothing of their demon swiftness and accuracy upon the tennis-courts; and wizened, dried-up little Phil Dellivan, beginning to go bald, but still a wizard in the art of the unexpected.

With Burke Innes, they were the ranking tennis stars of the State—a state, moreover, that had produced some tennis champions.

Burke Innes had been there himself only a moment before, long and lean and dark and dangerous—the personification of the best in American athletes. He always looked younger, too, in his tennis clothes, and almost handsome, because of his fine shoulders and slender waist.

The large fat man who had whistled came forward. In his hands he held a futuristic afternoon extra, bright pink paper from which black and green headlines screamed.

"I say," he gasped, "this is terrible!"

The youngest Renny brother was looking over his shoulder and his face had gone pale. Even Jim Turner, upon whom things dawned slowly off the tennis-court, had finally been jarred into nervousness.

"What is it?" he said.

"Burke Innes's wife," said Barney. "I wouldn't have believed it. This is terrible!"

"You said that once already," said Little Phil. "Is she dead?"

"No. Worse. Much worse."

He read it, wheezing with excitement between paragraphs. There was a little comprehending, shamefaced pause when he finished.

"Where's Burke?" said Little Phil.

"He was here just a minute ago," said Jim Turner. "I guess we better put off the matches."

"He had a paper," said the older Renny brother. "I saw him take it from the boy. I didn't know——"

"It wouldn't be fair for him to play today," said Jim Turner slowly. "Especially the finals. Gosh, it must have taken a lot of nerve for a woman to do that. To walk right up and tell on herself."

"What else could she do, for God's sake?" said Little Phil. "Let a guy spend the rest of his life in jail for something he didn't do?"

"I wonder what we'd better do about the matches," said Barney, perspiring freely; "this is terrible. The biggest crowd we've ever had, too. Mrs. Grant's here already—giving a luncheon. And I tell you, this will be just like throwing a bombshell. The Burke Inneses of all people. She was always so strict, too. Now Maurice will be out, and I wonder if he'll marry Janet Grant. I suppose everybody'll make a hero out of him."

At exactly that moment Burke Innes strolled in. He had the

afternoon paper in his hand. His face was set like a mask, but his eyes were alight, unreadable but brilliant.

"Great crowd we've got, Barney," he said in his level, steady voice; and then to Jim Turner, "And I'm going to beat you this afternoon if it takes a leg." And he smiled.

"Then," said Barney, wiping his forehead, "we aren't going to call the matches off?"

Burke Innes looked at him coldly.

"Why," he asked, "should you call the matches off?"

Gretchen Innes folded a black and gold kimono and laid it carefully in the shining black leather suitcase. Then she folded one of the chiffon nightgowns that Abbie had laid out so carefully on the bed. She was just smoothing it absently when Abbie came in.

As she came in, Abbie said, "That was Mr. Innes on the phone, Miss Gretchen."

Gretchen's hand turned to stone.

"Yes?" she said, and she felt that the beating of her heart must shake her voice.

"He said it wasn't necessary for him to speak to you," said Abbie in a matter-of-fact way. "He just wants you to come right on over to the Country Club as soon as you can. He said to be sure to come, because he's playing Jim Turner in the finals this afternoon and he wants you there."

"Is that all he said?"

Abbie laid a little pile of silk and lace on the floor. "You need some more of those brassieres, Miss Gretchen," she said, "but I guess these'll do till you get home. Oh, he said tell you be sure to come. Not to let anything interfere." Then, as her mistress did not stir, "Here's your hat," said Abbie. "You haven't got time to change. Anyway, that looks all right for a tennis match."

Mrs. Burke Innes pulled the orange sport hat far down over her right eye and tucked the unruly lion-cub mop under it, so that only the edges of it showed.

"My gloves, Abbie," said Mrs. Burke Innes, and her voice had the desperate determination of a woman who has pulled herself up to it by her boot straps— "my gloves."

She drew them on, angrily controlling the hands that would have trembled.

"My bag," said Mrs. Burke Innes, and Abbie thought she had never seen anything so defiant and yet so frightened as the way Mrs. Innes swung the bizarre trifle over her wrist.

"Will you be in for dinner, Miss Gretchen?" asked Abbie.

"I don't know, Abbie," said Mrs. Burke Innes. "Oh—I don't know."

But to herself she was saying,

over and over, "Has he seen the papers? Oh God, has he seen the papers?"

The Country Club stands were packed so that not an inch of boards showed between the smart sport skirts and the smarter white flannels and tweed golf trousers. Everybody who was anybody, whether they knew anything about tennis or not, had come to the tournament.

As Barney had predicted the afternoon paper had exploded in Santa Barbara and Montecito like a bombshell. Every now and then between games, that rushing, sibilant roar, like the hissing of many serpents, swept the fashionable throng.

That Burke Innes should play had seemed the crowning surprise of the day that had witnessed the biggest shock they had ever known.

"That's Burke Innes's idea of good sportsmanship," said Mrs. Grant with a sniff. "I might have known that. I hope he realizes that Maurice Greer was something of a sport himself."

But when, just in the pause between sets—Jim Turner had won the first set and Burke Innes by magnificent service and sheer, blinding speed had captured the second one—when a lady came across the strip of lawn from the clubhouse and entered her box alone, the whole stands were literally flabbergasted, literally struck dumb for the space of an entire minute.

They watched her in bewildered silence, this arrogant orange and white lady, who flung her white coat so nonchalantly over a chair and settled herself so unconcernedly in another. Her sharp little chin was held very high, and she did not seem to see the hundreds of faces that stared at her— stared and stared.

They could not see, of course, how her heart-beats were actually shaking her whole body, or how each breath cost her such a struggle that she believed she could never, never take another.

They could only watch her haughtiness and her indifference, and then the silence broke in a gasp, and the gasp was followed by that hissing, rushing sound as of many waters.

Gretchen did not see them. She knew they were there, like horrible creatures in a nightmare. But she was really conscious of only one thing—the lean, dark, hard figure on the tennis-courts in the sun.

Had he seen the paper?

"Well," said Mrs. Grant, rubbing her nose in a way that was characteristic but hardly aristocratic, "I didn't think she'd dare."

"Why not?" said Janet Grant bitterly. "I'd be glad to be able to do what she's done."

The match ended.

1319 And then Burke Innes did one
1320 of those things that a Burke
1321 Innes never does. One of those
1322 theatrical, dashing things that
1323 might have been done—oh, by
1324 a Maurice Greer, for instance.
1325 But, being Burke Innes, he did
1326 it well, so boldly and impres-
1327 sively that everyone in the grand
1328 stands held their breath.

1329 For he came off the court
1330 where he had played so bril-
1331 liantly, and went straight to his
1332 wife and bowed gallantly above
1333 her little white and orange glove.
1334 Being the victor, it had almost
1335 the air of a knight coming to
1336 receive the reward of conquest.

1337 And he said, loud enough so
1338 that many people about could
1339 hear and thus repeat later: "If
1340 I won, my dear, it's only because
1341 I wanted to pay tribute to the
1342 standard of gameness and good
1343 sportsmanship that you have set
1344 me today?"

1345 "Ah," said Mrs. Grant, when
1346 some excited bystander had car-
1347 ried the speech to her box, where
1348 she still lingered, "that is very
1349 clever. He is trying to becloud
1350 the issue. He means to stand
1351 by her and make us like it.
1352 That's all very fine, but I shan't
1353 do it. I think Maurice is quite
1354 the most heroic of them all, and
1355 I shan't do it."

1356 "Well," said her daughter,
1357 with the first defiance of twenty-
1358 five years, "I shall."

1359 And so it happened that Janet
1360 Grant slipped her arm through

1361 Gretchen's, and they walked,
1362 laughing and talking very
1363 brightly indeed, the length of
1364 that inquisitorial grand stand,
1365 with Burke Innes strolling beside
1366 them.

1367 In the car Gretchen said
1368 explosively, "You did that so
1369 wonderfully, Burke! But—what
1370 about just you and me?"

1371 Her husband smiled at her.
1372 "You're funny, Gretchen," he
1373 said.

1374 "Maybe," said Gretchen, "but
1375 —does that mean, Burke, that
1376 you've forgiven me?"

1377 "It looks rather like it, doesn't
1378 it?" said Burke Innes, very busy
1379 piloting the big roadster out of
1380 the grounds through the crowds
1381 of expensive automobiles.

1382 "Then you've—seen the
1383 papers?"

1384 "Of course."

1385 "And you forgive me in spite
1386 of my telling the district
1387 attorney——"

1388 "In spite of your telling the
1389 district attorney!" said Burke
1390 Innes, turning utterly astonished
1391 gray eyes upon her. "Good
1392 God, Gretchen, did you think I
1393 could ever have forgiven you if
1394 you hadn't done that?"

1395 "You mean—you wouldn't
1396 have forgiven me if I hadn't
1397 proved Maurice's alibi?" she
1398 gasped at him.

1399 "There was never anything
1400 else to forgive," said Burke
1401 Innes. "I can't talk a lot of
1402 rot, you know. But no man is

1403 capable of judging the tempta-
1404 tions and defeats and victories
1405 of a woman's soul, Gretchen.
1406 And—women are so much better
1407 than we are. I wasn't so dumb
1408 I didn't understand your tempo-
1409 rary insanity defense, Gretchen.
1410 Every man could understand
1411 that if he didn't hang on to his
1412 man-pride too tight. I felt sorry.
1413 But—men and women aren't
1414 different, they're just human
1415 beings. I tried to do as I know
1416 you would have done if I'd—
1417 made that mistake. I shall
1418 always be sorry, but I knew
1419 every word you said was true,
1420 and that you had loved me—
1421 and only me—always.
1422 "But of course I could never

1423 have forgiven you for that—
1424 missing alibi. That was why I
1425 left last night. Because of
1426 course that was just a matter of
1427 clean sportsmanship."
1428 "Burke," said Gretchen and
1429 he knew that she was weeping
1430 at last, "I do think you're a
1431 funny man."
1432 The car swung around the
1433 curve and into a shadow cast by
1434 the low-hanging oak trees. The
1435 man leaned down and crushed
1436 her very close to him, so that her
1437 small, weeping face was hidden
1438 on his shoulder.
1439 "And I do think," he said,
1440 "that you're a very game wo-
1441 man, Gretchen, and the best
1442 sport I know."

THE ANALYSIS

The Haunted Lady occupies altogether 1442 lines. Of these lines 1 to 907 are the Beginning of the story. Lines 908 to 980 show a mental struggle which is the Body of the story. This mental struggle is in the mind of the character between two possible choices set forth in the Beginning. One choice is to refrain from telling the District Attorney in the hope that she may profit by retaining the love of her husband, who will forgive her after a while. The other is that she must adhere to a standard of conduct by telling the District Attorney and, as she thinks, thus sacrifice the possibility of her husband's forgiveness.

The Ending, containing the interchange which shows the Conclusive Act, together with the other interchanges which show the Sequel, occupies lines 981 to 1442. Lines 981 to 1048 contain the Conclusive or Decisive Act which shows the decision that she has arrived at—to tell the District Attorney.

Particularly interesting to the student of craftsmanship is the fact that the Ending occupies 462 lines of which 394 are Sequel; the Beginning occupies 907 lines, and the Body occupies 73 lines only. This is an interesting example showing that in the story of Decision the length can never come from the Body. It must come from either the Beginning or the Ending.

It is extremely interesting to notice that this story in its Beginning contains, on lines 284 to 521, a Flash-back interchange between Maurice Greer and the police, which is interpolated within the interchange between Gretchen Innes and Burke Innes, occupying lines 1 to 907. The fifth step of this Flash-back interchange is on lines 522 to 584, after which the interchange between Gretchen and Burke Innes is again taken up. In fact, it is almost impossible to write a story of Decision in which the Beginning occupies any length, without resorting to the flash-back method in some way. This is not a Flash-back in the typical sense because it does not come after the main problem has been made apparent to the audience. It is a Flash-back to avoid summary.

The interchange on lines 908 to 980 is a mental one between the two traits in the same character. This is a rather unusual thing to be included in the story of Decision. Ordinarily this is omitted.

The interchange between Gretchen and the District Attorney on lines 981 to 1048 is the interchange used by the author to show that the actor has come to a decision and has acted upon it. As in the other stories of Decision quite outstanding is the evidence that such a story depends entirely upon the capacity of the writer to present interchanges and to make people who are taking part in those interchanges seem like actual human beings. The story of Decision depends for its success upon characterization; and characterization is merely the portrayal of definite traits of character in action as the actors respond to various stimuli. Particularly interesting are the first 22 lines of the story because they show just how a competent author is enabled by a knowledge of craftsmanship to set at once before the reader a character trait. She causes Burke Innes to respond to the stimulus, which is the crash of the glass, by looking up, but she causes him to withdraw his eyes because his basic character trait is that he is sportsmanlike, and it would not be fair to violate the privacy of his wife. This character trait, planted at the Beginning of the story, gives an authenticity to the significance of the story which is presented in the Sequel.

In discussing the composition of the Concord Hymn, President Emeritus Charles W. Eliot of Harvard spoke of the action therein described and its "infinite reverberations." In this story the Decisive or Conclusive Act, by which the main actor answers the main narrative question of the story has "infinite reverberations," and the story is not finished until these "infinite reverberations" have been made clear to the reader. There are more people involved than the main actor; and furthermore, no story is really ended until all the questions, either of narrative or other curiosity, raised in the Beginning or Body of the story have been answered. In this way the story varies from the scenes within the story. In the Scene ordinarily only one conflict is foreshadowed, and only one problem is presented to the reader. Only one possibility of disaster is apparent, only one minor narrative question is raised. At the end of that scene this minor narrative question is answered. In the main story, however, many questions are raised in the reader's mind. They may be answered one by one through the scenes in the Body of the story. That is the ordinary way. In this case, however, they must be answered in the Ending of the story, because the Body of the story does not present such an opportunity to the writer. There is virtually no Body to this story.

The question that arises at once in the mind of the aspiring author at this point is, "How can I keep such meetings or interchanges interesting enough to hold the reader when I am denied the use of suspense which usually comes with clash with an opposing force, which makes up the Body of the story of Accomplishment?"

The author of *The Haunted Lady* answers this query of the aspiring author by showing that while suspense *ordinarily* comes from clash, it is fundamentally concerned with the outcome of a meeting between two hostile forces, or forces regarded as hostile. The uncertainty as to this outcome keeps up the interest of the reader. This interest will be intensified in proportion as this hostility has been emphasized or this threat of disaster made apparent; but it will always be as it affects the main actor in the story.

Taking each group of forces in this story you will see that such hostility has been foreshadowed by the author in the consciousness of the main actor. The effect upon the main actor is the chief interest of the reader. This is kept in suspense. While the effect upon Burke Innes is that he goes on playing the game as always, Gretchen Innes does not know whether or not he has heard the news of the confession. Upon this depends the outcome of the story from the point of view of Gretchen. On lines 861 to 963 the author makes clear to the reader that Gretchen believes that Burke "could never forgive the woman whom the world would know as Maurice Greer's alibi." On lines 522 to 538 the hostility of Mrs. William Woolsey Grant is evident when she says, "As if a woman who would receive Maurice Greer, with his reputation, between two and four in the morning deserves any protection." Thus there is added the promise of disaster to disaster already foreshadowed.

The episode with the maid is merely stage business, purely preparatory for the interchange with the group representing the "whole world," who would thereafter know Gretchen as "Maurice Greer's alibi." But throughout all these interchanges the uncertainty as to the outcome as it affects the main character's happiness is still in doubt. It is not until the final interchange between Gretchen and Burke Innes that the reader is made aware beyond question, as Gretchen is made aware also beyond question, that to a person of Burke Innes's standards of sportsmanship the very action by which Gretchen thinks she has ruined her whole life and her whole future happiness is in reality an action which guarantees that future happiness.

This story is an extremely valuable one for the person who is interested in writing stories of "character," who wants to show the reactions of actors under the stress of great emotional crises. It is unnecessary, of course, to reiterate that a story of decision must deal with a great emotional crisis in the life of an actor. This story illustrates that the Ending may be prolonged provided that there is suspense in the interchanges, or growing out of questions raised in the story; but this suspense must be a legitimate suspense and must have a definite bearing upon the main narrative problem of the story. For such readers this story will have an additional interest, however, because it is a companion story to the one which I am about to present to you, *The Trouble with Men*, by Lucian Carey.

		Condition stated by author, projecting interchange.	1–128
		Interchange. Philip Maple and Gertrude Woolcott.	129–288
BEGINNING	Initial condition presented, together with the responses of Main Actor, which show that she realizes that condition forces her to make choice.	(5th step. Effect upon actors.)	289–306
		Interchange. Gertrude and Frieda. Possible choice.	307–464
		Interchange. Archie and Gertrude. Frieda observes.	465–515
		(5th step.)	516–541
		Interchange. Gertrude and John Powell.	542–656
		Interchange. Gertrude and Archie.	657–721
		Effect upon actors.	722–765
		Interchange. Gertrude and Frieda. (Begun by phone, and continued in house.)	766–948
ENDING	Conclusive Act.	Gertrude proceeds to admit guilt.	949–952
	Sequel.	Archie and Gertrude. He has overheard.	953–981

Unusual and interesting series of happenings project the necessity for a decision, which once made only proves to be the inception of a new and greater dilemma.

(Choice presented.) — 766–948 Choice presented.

Choice made. Answer to Narrative Question is "She will admit guilt even though innocent, to preserve love."

Ironically, sacrifice is unnecessary.

THE TROUBLE WITH MEN

BY LUCIAN CAREY

I SHOULD not wish any reader of this volume to get the impression that the only reason for studying this story is that it is a companion story to *The Haunted Lady*.

The problem of craftsmanship confronting Mr. Carey was a very difficult one indeed. In order to reach his initial condition or basic problem of Decision he had to present to his readers all the series of events which were contained in the story by Mrs. St. John.

That he was able to do so without loss of interest is a high tribute to his craftsmanship. The story presents material for study which will be amply repaid.

CASE No. 15

THE TROUBLE WITH MEN

BY LUCIAN CARY

The Woolcotts lived in East Harwich, which is one of those Long Island places favored of actors, bankers, scenario writers and people who go in for tournament golf.

You couldn't call East Harwich a Bohemian community because Bohemians are people who live in attics and drink red ink in basements, whereas actors, bankers, scenario writers and people who go in for tournament golf live in country houses and drink a combination of grain alcohol, water and creosote labeled Scotch. You couldn't call it suburban because a suburb is a place from which all the able-bodied men depart on the 8:10 train, and almost nobody commuted from East Harwich. You couldn't call it a fashionable summer colony because people would think you didn't know about Southampton. East Harwich is just Long Island-after-the-War. Which means that it is the home of melodrama.

Archie Woolcott was one of those chaps who used to be described as a he-man, meaning a big, honest, sentimental fellow who is scared to death of women and has the same romantic notions about life at thirty-five that he had at fifteen. He had no doubts about what is right and what is wrong, or what is probable and what is improbable. If he had been born in the time of Richard the Lion-hearted, he would have spent his life happily mounted on a draft horse and wearing a couple of hundred pounds of steel plate and chain mail. He was built to handle a mace, or the favorite medieval form of meat cleaver called a gisarme. As it was, Archie Woolcott went in for the only bone-breaking sport there is left. He rode to hounds and averaged a collar bone a season.

Gertrude Woolcott was the kind of clever woman who has sense enough to marry a man like that. She loved his size and strength. He wore so well that

61 air of masterful protectiveness
62 that means so much to a woman
63 so long as she runs the whole
64 show. She loved his boyish
65 helplessness. When some other
66 woman teased him into kissing
67 her he always imagined he was
68 in a serious predicament and
69 hurried home to tell Gertrude
70 all about it and beg her to
71 extricate him. But above all
72 she loved his being so completely
73 in love with her. He had had
74 in the beginning a childlike
75 trust in her, and this trust had
76 grown with the years. It was
77 deeply gratifying to be so
78 needed.

79 For the rest, she had her
80 children, her garden and her
81 abiding interest in other people's
82 troubles.

83 This summer the troubles had
84 been those of the Maples. Philip
85 Maple was an actor who always
86 played the lover in polite com-
87 edies. He was handsome, agree-
88 able, and he had a voice with
89 a throb in it. When he made
90 his entrance the round of ap-
91 plause was followed by a sound
92 like that of a summer breeze
93 blowing through a poplar tree.
94 It was the sound of the people
95 in the audience whispering to
96 their neighbors that Philip
97 Maple made love as effectively
98 off the stage as he did on it and
99 naming the lady for whom he
100 was then exercising his gift.
101 The mere list of conquests which
102 were attributed to him by his

103 audiences would have required
104 a newspaper page to print. Only
105 his most intimate friends knew
106 the disillusioning truth, which
107 was that there had never been
108 other than one woman in his
109 life and that woman his wife.

110 Jane Maple had been born to
111 the theatre; for several seasons
112 she had ruled there as the first
113 of comediennes. But she had
114 lost her place. She was a dipso-
115 maniac who had ruined a first
116 night once too often. And she
117 refused to do anything about it.
118 She would not take a cure; she
119 would not consult a psycho-
120 analyst; she would not brook
121 interference with her desire for
122 oblivion. Gertrude Woolcott
123 had reluctantly decided that
124 there was nothing to do about
125 Jane. She would inevitably
126 drink herself to death. The only
127 question was whether Philip
128 would survive the process.

129 Gertrude had been enjoying
130 the luxury of a silent house of a
131 night in late August. Archie
132 had been spending the week in
133 Virginia searching for a hunter
134 up to his weight. He had wired
135 that he was coming home the
136 next day. The children and the
137 servants were asleep. Gertrude
138 was deep in a new and engrossing
139 novel when the telephone beside
140 her bed buzzed. She reached for
141 the receiver without taking her
142 eyes from the page.

143 "I'm sorry if I've waked you
144 up," Philip Maple said, "but

145 I want awfully to see you."
146 Gertrude glanced at the little
147 clock on her table. It was a
148 minute before midnight.

149 "Where are you?" she asked.
150 "I'm at home—I could drive
151 over in fifteen minutes."

152 "Very well," Gertrude agreed.
153 "I'll meet you in the garden."

154 She allowed herself ten
155 minutes to finish the chapter
156 in her novel; dressed in five
157 minutes, and slipped out of a
158 French window into the garden
159 a moment before the lights of
160 Philip Maple's car swung into
161 the drive.

162 He got wearily out of the car.
163 Gertrude knew at once that
164 something quite devastating had
165 happened. They walked side
166 by side to the summerhouse at
167 the back of the garden. Philip
168 lit a cigarette. Gertrude re-
169 flected that it was a night for
170 something to happen—a hot
171 August night with no stars
172 visible, and the moon riding
173 high and pale in a misty halo,
174 and in the distance flashes of
175 heat lightning against the clouds.

176 "You know I've been in
177 Washington all week trying out
178 the new play," he said. "I got
179 home half an hour ago. The
180 house was in the most terrible
181 mess. I should guess that six
182 or seven people have been hold-
183 ing a drinking bout for days.
184 Empty whisky bottles on the
185 drawing-room mantel. Dirty
186 glasses beside every chair in the

187 library. The butler's pantry
188 full of dirty dishes. One room
189 after another turned upside
190 down. Every door, every
191 drawer open. Every rug and
192 coverlet and table top burned
193 where a cigarette stub had
194 dropped. I don't know whether
195 the servants left or if she fired
196 them."

197 Philip paused, his head in his
198 hands. "You see," he con-
199 tinued, "I haven't told you the
200 worst. I couldn't bear to. She's
201 been running around with the
202 lowest crew she could find on
203 Broadway—race-track touts and
204 bootleggers and dope fiends.
205 She's been trying morphine.
206 I've been afraid she'd be ar-
207 rested any night in—in some
208 raid."

209 Gertrude put her hand on his
210 bowed head. She wanted to
211 comfort him. And yet she felt
212 that he must at last face the
213 fact that his wife was a hopeless
214 dipsomaniac who ought to be
215 shut up in a sanitarium.

216 Philip threw up his head, and
217 in the pale light of a far-off
218 flicker of lightning Gertrude saw
219 that the tears were running down
220 his cheeks and his mouth was dis-
221 torted with pain.

222 "Why," he cried, "why does
223 she want to humiliate me so?"

224 "She doesn't want to humil-
225 iate you, Philip. She can't help
226 herself."

227 "Why can't she help herself?
228 What does it mean when a wo-

man as fine as Jane, a woman with nice instincts and delicate sensibilities, a trained artist, falls so low?"

Gertrude stroked his sleek head. She had no answer except the answer that Jane had gone insane.

"Why," Philip went on, "two years ago she was playing in 'Captain Brassbound's Conversion'—playing the part that Shaw wrote for Ellen Terry. And how she did play it! There isn't an actress living who could play the lady as she could. She just was that sort—a lovely creature, with grace and wit and manner. And now——"

"I know," Gertrude said. "I remember." What Philip said of her was true. The change in Jane was incredible.

"She's ruined herself," he cried bitterly, "and I don't care. I don't care what she does or what she is. Let her go to the devil. I don't care."

"But you do care, Philip," Gertrude said gently.

"I hate her," he said through shut teeth. "Oh, God, how I hate her!"

"You hate her because you still love her," pronounced Gertrude emphatically.

"What else can I do?"

"You can think of her and treat her as a person who is desperately ill—mentally ill. You can face the truth, and when you do face it you will no longer feel humiliated, and you will no longer hate, but you will quite simply and courageously do the thing that you have to do."

They talked about that endlessly. Gertrude went over and over the same ground with him, trying to make him see that he could no longer salve his pride by concealing the facts about Jane. She had to lead him back again and again to the idea of permitting Jane's condition to become public. It was four o'clock in the morning when he looked at his watch and apologized for keeping her so late.

Gertrude felt that she had won her case—that if Jane Maple had come home Philip would lock her in her room and look at once for a lawyer and a physician and begin the process of having her committed to a sanitarium. Meanwhile she was tired. Back in her own room she picked up her novel. But she could not read. She remembered that she had the next day a luncheon engagement in town with Frieda Remington. Frieda was her best friend. And Archie would be coming in on his way home from Virginia. Gertrude fell asleep. . . .

Gertrude entered the lobby of the St. Francis promptly at one o'clock, but for once Frieda's bright head was there before her.

"My dear," Frieda cried, and her face took on the deepest

313 concern, "you haven't heard."

314 "I haven't heard anything
315 awful," Gertrude said.

316 Frieda put her hand on Ger-
317 trude's arm as if to steady her
318 against a shock. Gertrude saw
319 that Frieda had a hastily folded
320 newspaper in the other hand.

321 "Jane Maple is dead."

322 "Wha-a-at!" Gertrude cried.

323 "Come," Frieda said, "let's
324 get a table in a corner where we
325 can talk."

326 "Suicide?" Gertrude asked.

327 "Apparently not," Frieda said.

328 "Come—let's get a table."

329 "Let me see that paper."

330 "Wait till we've found a
331 corner," Frieda insisted.

332 "Let me see that paper!"

333 Frieda reluctantly unfolded
334 the newspaper. It was an early
335 edition of one of the more lurid
336 afternoon papers. Clear across
337 the top in big black letters ran
338 the headline:

339 *Jane Maple Shot. Husband*
340 *Held!*

341 Gertrude skipped to the first
342 paragraph of the story as they
343 walked into the café of the St.
344 Francis.

345 Philip Maple had telephoned
346 the police of the East Harwich
347 station at half past four in the
348 morning to notify them that he
349 had found his wife with a bullet
350 through her heart. The police
351 surgeon declared that Jane
352 Maple had been dead for from
353 three to four hours when he

354 examined her body at five o'clock
355 in the morning. Philip Maple
356 said that he had been out of
357 town; had returned shortly be-
358 fore midnight to find the house
359 empty; had gone out again.
360 When he got back after four
361 o'clock in the morning he had
362 found his wife dead. But when
363 he was asked to tell where he had
364 been between midnight and four
365 o'clock he refused. The police
366 had promptly arrested him.

367 Gertrude looked at Frieda.

368 "You don't think he shot Jane?"

370 "I can't believe it," Frieda
371 said, and hesitated. "But," she
372 concluded, "why won't he tell
373 where he was?"

374 "Because he's a man and
375 therefore a fool," Gertrude said
376 sharply.

377 "You think he was with some
378 other woman?"

379 Gertrude felt suddenly calm.
380 Philip's refusal to tell where he
381 was had made everything as
382 difficult as possible. His impulse
383 had been to shield her from
384 scandal. He had made it certain
385 that when the truth came out
386 some people would think she had
387 been having a love affair with
388 him. But she was innocent. If
389 she told the truth quite boldly
390 and simply, no one who mattered
391 would doubt her.

392 "I know he was with another
393 woman, Frieda," she said. "He
394 was with me."

395 Frieda's eyes got big and
396 round.

397 "Heavens!" she said.

398 "He called me up about mid-
399 night and asked if he could come
400 over. I met him in the garden.
401 He was terribly upset because
402 Jane had been having a wild
403 booze party while he was in
404 Washington. I was trying to
405 make him see that he'd have to
406 get Jane committed to a sani-
407 tarium."

408 Frieda's eyes narrowed
409 thoughtfully.

410 "You know, Gertrude, I can't
411 help thinking that if you told
412 the whole story people would
413 believe you."

414 "I think they would," Ger-
415 trude said. "And what if they
416 did think I was guilty? As long
417 as Archie knew it was all right,
418 and the people I care about, I
419 could stand anything the news-
420 papers said."

421 Frieda impulsively reached
422 across the table and took Ger-
423 trude's hand in hers.

424 "Of course," she said, "no-
425 body who knows you would
426 doubt you. And"—she laughed
427 —"nobody who knows Philip
428 Maple doubts that he was com-
429 pletely wrapped up in his wife.
430 I don't suppose he ever talked
431 to another woman about any-
432 thing else."

433 Gertrude smiled back at
434 Frieda. It was a relief to put
435 the tragedy of the Maples out of
436 her mind for a moment and smile
437 at Philip Maple's reputation.

438 "No," she said, "I don't sup-
439 pose he ever did talk about any-
440 thing else. His only interest in
441 other women was in being patted
442 on the head a little while he
443 talked himself out about Jane.
444 Isn't it absurd that people
445 always pick out that sort of man
446 to make into a Don Juan?"

447 "It's partly because he's an
448 actor and plays the lover so
449 gracefully in the theatre," Frieda
450 said.

451 "I know. And men more
452 than women make that mistake
453 about him. Most men feel so
454 awkward about making love
455 that they take it for granted a
456 man who can do it gracefully
457 would make love to every wo-
458 man he saw. I shouldn't be
459 surprised if Archie thinks Philip
460 couldn't be trusted along
461 with——"

462 Frieda stopped Gertrude with
463 a gesture.

464 "Here comes Archie now."

465 Gertrude turned and saw her
466 tall, broad-shouldered, bronzed
467 husband threading his way be-
468 tween tables toward them. He
469 had a newspaper in his hand,
470 and he looked grim.

471 "Have you heard?" he asked
472 as he reached the table. "I
473 must say Maple is more of a man
474 than I ever thought he was.
475 He's a gentleman."

476 "What do you mean, Archie?"
477 Frieda asked.

478 Archie sat down and looked
479 pityingly at Frieda. "I mean
480 that he's in an awfully tight

374

place, and if he's willing to
stand the gaff rather than tell
on the lady I respect him—
which is more than I ever expected to do."

Gertrude and Frieda ex-
changed a significant glance.

"You take it for granted he
was with a lady?" Frieda asked.

"I take it for granted he was
with a lady," Archie said, with
irony.

"He might have been with a
lady quite innocently," Gertrude
said.

"From midnight until four in
the morning?" Archie asked.
"Not Philip Maple."

Again Gertrude and Frieda ex-
changed a glance.

"Of course," Archie went on,
"it is sort of up to the lady to
come forward." He interrupted
himself to order lunch for the
three of them. "Not," he continued when the waiter had
gone, "that I can blame her for
hesitating to ruin her reputation."

"I don't think her reputation
would necessarily be ruined,"
Gertrude said.

"Neither do I," Frieda added.

"A lot you women know about
life," said Archie.

For the first time in the ten
years of their marriage Gertrude
doubted her ability to manage
Archie. She felt herself up
against a conviction in him so
naïve, so spontaneously arrived
at, so unthinking that she could

not imagine herself arguing
against it successfully. And
when Frieda spoke again she
knew that the same thought
had been running in Frieda's
mind.

"It's possible," Frieda said,
"that Philip won't need the alibi.
After all, it will be possible to
show that he was fond of his wife,
and there is no evidence against
him."

When, late that afternoon,
Gertrude got a chance to talk to
Frieda she was forced to agree
that the only wise thing to do
was to wait. The legal process
would take weeks, perhaps
months. A good lawyer might
put off the trial until spring.

It was a sunny afternoon in
April when Gertrude Woolcott
went down to Broad Street to
see the great John Powell.

Gertrude looked at the man
who had devoted his life to
defending men accused of
murder. He had a magnificent
head, with large features, thick
white hair and the voice of a
man who has talked much in
public. He smiled and when he
smiled Gertrude trusted him.

"I've come to tell you that I
am the woman Philip Maple was
with the night his wife was
shot."

He gave her a slow, appraising
glance in which there was not the
slightest surprise.

"I suppose you knew," she
said.

565 "No," he said. "Philip has
566 never told me."

567 "I wish he had told in the first
568 place," Gertrude said. "It
569 would have made everything so
570 much easier."

571 "You mean you are willing to
572 testify in court?"

573 "Yes," said Gertrude, "I am."

574 "Have you thought what it
575 will mean to your reputation?"

576 "I am quite innocent," Ger-
577 trude said.

578 "Being thought innocent isn't
579 the same thing," John Powell
580 said. "The prosecuting attorney
581 is trying to make capital out of
582 this case, as prosecuting at-
583 torneys usually do. He will see
584 that your testimony has ruined
585 his case and he will turn on you
586 and do everything he can to
587 make you appear in a bad light.

588 Gertrude threw up her head.

589 "I'm willing to stand it—if
590 it's necessary," she said.

591 John Powell leaned back in
592 his chair and put the tips of his
593 fingers together and frowned
594 thoughtfully with half-shut eyes.

595 "It isn't—*necessary*," he said
596 suddenly.

597 "You mean he will be acquit-
598 ted, any way?"

599 "I think so. And if he should
600 be convicted I could get an
601 appeal on the strength of new
602 evidence and win the appeal."

603 "But suppose you do get him
604 off—what will people think?"

605 "People will think what they
606 always think when a man is tried

607 for murder—they will think a
608 clever lawyer got him off."

609 "Then I want to testify,"
610 Gertrude said.

611 "What sort of man is your
612 husband?" John Powell asked.

613 "He's a big, athletic man who
614 rides to hounds and trusts me
615 completely."

616 "Does he know?"

617 "Not yet."

618 "Will he still trust you when
619 you have testified in court?"

620 "I—I think so," Gertrude
621 said.

622 John Powell gave her a shrewd
623 look.

624 "It's important to you that he
625 should continue to trust you," he
626 said.

627 "Yes," Gertrude admitted
628 with a little involuntary catch
629 in her voice.

630 "I see it is," John Powell said.

631 "I love him," Gertrude said,
632 and tears came to her eyes in
633 spite of herself. "And—and—
634 he loves me."

635 "Is he a man of the world?"

636 "Not a bit," Gertrude said
637 and smiled. "He's a romantic
638 boy—a boy who has never
639 grown up—a he-man."

640 John Powell shook his head
641 slowly.

642 "I'm sorry," he said. "I'm
643 afraid he will doubt you. And
644 I feel it's only fair to warn you
645 of what you are getting in for.
646 Because, of course, I am going
647 to accept your offer. In the
648 interest of my client I've got to."

649 "Very well," Gertrude said,
650 and her voice trembled.

651 "I shall call you as a witness
652 to-morrow morning."

653 "To-morrow morning," echoed
654 Gertrude, and her heart sank.

655 John Powell nodded, and Ger-
656 trude went home to tell Archie.

657 There happened to be no
658 guests at dinner. But Gertrude
659 put off telling him. There hap-
660 pened to be no one in that even-
661 ing. But still Gertrude put off
662 telling him. They sat in the
663 library. She read a novel.
664 Archie was studying the pedi-
665 grees of several hunters. Every
666 five minutes she looked up at
667 him over her book and opened
668 her mouth to speak. And each
669 time her heart failed her.

670 At midnight she went and sat
671 on the arm of his chair and
672 stroked his hair.

673 "Archie," she said, "I've been
674 trying to tell you something for
675 months."

676 Archie leaned back and took
677 her free hand in his.

678 "What, old thing?" he asked.

679 "That I was the woman Philip
680 Maple was with the night Jane
681 was shot."

682 His face hardly changed its
683 expression, but she felt the
684 muscles in the hand that held
685 hers contract, felt his whole
686 body stiffen.

687 "He came to talk to me about
688 Jane and what he should do. It
689 was the most innocent thing in
690 the world. I was advising him,

691 trying to make him see that he
692 would have to put Jane in a
693 sanitarium. He was so upset.
694 We talked from midnight till
695 four in the morning."

696 Archie rose and paced up and
697 down the room, avoiding her
698 eyes.

699 "You will have to testify in
700 court," he said.

701 "I've already told John Powell
702 that I would testify. I saw him
703 this afternoon. I am going on
704 the stand to-morrow."

705 Archie walked back and forth.
706 Jane watched him breathlessly.
707 He paused. He came over to
708 her. He held out his hand. She
709 took his hand in hers. He wrung
710 her hand as if she were a man.

711 "I—I always knew you were
712 a gentleman, Gertrude," he said
713 huskily.

714 Gertrude burst into tears. He
715 didn't believe she was innocent.
716 He would never believe. He
717 would never say so, but he would
718 never believe. His trust in her
719 was gone. He could only praise
720 her for the masculine virtue of
721 taking the consequences.

722 The moments on the witness
723 stand did not prove as withering
724 as John Powell had predicted.
725 The district attorney did not
726 turn on her and try to make it
727 appear that she was a guilty
728 woman. Her testimony so thor-
729 oughly smashed his case that his
730 shoulders drooped in defeat. He
731 dismissed her after a superficial
732 cross-examination.

377

733 Gertrude drove home from the
734 court-room with Archie.

735 "I must say," he said, "I was
736 proud of you."

737 He did not smile. He did not
738 smile in the week that followed.
739 He made an attempt to treat
740 her as he always had and
741 succeeded in being courteous.
742 Gertrude could not name a single
743 difference in his manner or his
744 attitude. But the old, simple,
745 loving harmony was broken.

746 Gertrude could only weep.
747 She who had been so wise about
748 other people's troubles had no
749 answer to her own. There
750 seemed no way to penetrate
751 Archie's reserve. Frieda prom-
752 ised to talk to Archie if she got
753 half a chance. But Gertrude
754 could not imagine Archie's dis-
755 cussing the subject of their
756 relations with a third person.
757 His code forbade it. His idea
758 of what a gentleman should be
759 required him never to mention
760 his strong or intimate emotions.
761 Now, when he needed most to
762 talk, he withdrew even from
763 Gertrude. She came on him in
764 odd corners of the house sitting
765 staring into space.

766 Gertrude stood it for ten days.
767 And then one night Archie did
768 not come home. She lay in bed
769 beside her telephone listening.
770 He had never in ten years stayed
771 away without telling her in
772 advance where he was going.
773 The children and the servants
774 were long since asleep. The
775 house was very still, so still that
776 Gertrude felt she could hear a
777 mouse run across the floor if
778 there had been any mice. Twice
779 she got up and walked all
780 through the house to see if
781 Archie could have got back
782 without her hearing him.

783 She was trembling with
784 anxiety, with fear of she knew
785 not what, when she heard a car
786 drive in. She turned off the
787 light beside her bed and went to
788 the window and looked out. It
789 was Archie. Gertrude slipped
790 back into bed and waited. She
791 heard him come in; after ten
792 minutes he came upstairs; he was
793 moving about in his own room,
794 the room next hers. When the
795 sounds ceased and she guessed
796 that he had gone to bed Gertrude
797 turned on the lamp to look at
798 the little clock on her table. It
799 was four o'clock in the morn-
799 ing.

800 Where had he been? Gertrude
801 could not guess. She was still
802 making wild surmises when she
803 went to sleep.

804 Gertrude was awakened at
805 ten the next morning by the
806 buzzer of the telephone. It was
807 Frieda.

808 "Oh," Gertrude cried, "I must
809 see you."

810 "I'm coming right over,"
811 Frieda said, and something in
812 her voice heartened Gertrude.
813 It was a hint of laughter.

814 "What's happened, Frieda?"
815 she asked.

816 "I'll tell you when I see you,"
817 Frieda promised.

818 "Tell me now," Gertrude beg-
819 ged.

820 Frieda's answer was to hang
821 up the receiver.

822 Gertrude lay in bed listening
823 for Frieda's car, listening for any
824 sound that would indicate Archie
825 was awake in the next room,
826 listening for anything that would
827 break the tension of anxiety.

828 Frieda came running up the
829 stairs and burst into Gertrude's
830 room.

831 "Oh, my dear," she cried, "do
832 you know where your husband
833 was last night?"

834 "No," Gertrude said. "I only
835 know he didn't come in till four
836 o'clock this morning."

837 Frieda burst into laughter.

838 "Sh-h-h!" said Gertrude,
839 "you'll wake him up."

840 "He was with me, my dear.
841 And he talked! Oh, how he
842 talked."

843 "What did he say?" Gertrude
844 cried. "Tell me what he said."

845 Frieda's answer was to laugh.
846 Gertrude could have slapped her.

847 "I don't see what's funny,"
848 she said testily.

849 "I'm sorry, Gertrude. But it
850 it is funny. And it makes every-
851 thing simple. I know what you
852 must do, now. You see, he can
853 forgive you for having an affair
854 with Philip Maple. There's no
855 convincing him you didn't. But
856 he can somehow accept it. The
857 thing he can't forgive you for is

lying to him about it. He wants 858
to forgive you, but he can't." 859

"Do you suppose he still loves 860
me?" Gertrude asked. 861

"Of course he does, you little 862
idiot. He's crazy about you— 863
as he always was and always 864
will be. I told him he was a fool. 865
I told him I knew you were in- 866
nocent. And all he would say 867
was, 'It doesn't stand to rea- 868
son.'" 869

Gertrude burst into tears; 870
Gertrude wept until Frieda be- 871
came impatient and shook her. 872

"Come out of it, Gertrude," 873
she said sharply. "Come out of 874
it and use your head." 875

"I have used my head," 876
Gertrude cried. "I've thought 877
and thought and thought. And 878
there just isn't anything to do 879
with a fixed idea like that. He 880
just can't believe that a man 881
and a woman could be together 882
alone from midnight till four 883
o'clock in the morning in- 884
nocently." 885

"Oh, I don't know," Frieda 886
said. "I twitted him about it 887
last night. He talked to me 888
until a quarter to four." 889

Gertrude shook her head. 890

"I know," she said. "But 891
having the experience himself 892
won't convince him. He thinks 893
Philip Maple is different. He 894
thinks Philip Maple is simply 895
irresistible to women." 896

"Then let him think it," 897
Frieda said. 898

"What?" Gertrude gasped. 899

"What on earth do you mean?"

"I mean take him at his word. He says the thing he can't forgive you is telling him you are innocent. Tell him you are guilty."

"Tell him I'm guilty!" Gertrude cried.

"Why not? He believes it, anyhow. Let him feel that you trust him enough to confess to him."

Gertrude tried to consider the idea seriously.

"Don't you see, Gertrude? It's one of the oldest situations in the world. I have read a dozen stories about it. The woman is always guilty. The chivalrous man practically admits her guilt by refusing to tell her name. He would rather be hanged for murder than give her away. And then when she is given away everybody is sure she is guilty. It's the tradition. It's the thing men believe—about other men. You can't fight it. Well, my answer is, don't fight it. Let them keep their romantic notions. Let them go on believing that a woman can't be with a man at an unconventional hour unless there's a guilty passion in it."

Gertrude thought, and the more she thought the more inclined she was to accept Frieda's view of it. The only difficulty was she couldn't quite imagine bringing herself to the point of going through with it.

"It's what you'd tell me if I were in your predicament, Gertrude."

"I know it is," Gertrude said suddenly.

"Go and tell him—go and tell him quickly."

"I will," Gertrude said. "I will tell him now."

She rose and washed her face and powdered her nose.

She was interrupted in this last process by a knock on her door. It was Archie.

"Come in," she said.

Archie stood in the doorway.

"I—I——" he began.

"Have you been listening?" Gertrude cried.

Archie swallowed twice. In his code it was the last crime to listen in on a private conversation.

"I have," he said. "And I——"

With a little rush, Gertrude was in his arms. He took her in his arms gladly.

"Oh, Archie," she cried, "I was going to tell you I was guilty."

"I know," he said gently. He kissed her. "I was a fool."

Tears rolled down Archie's cheeks for the first time since he was a little boy. Gertrude sobbed in his arms. But she sobbed happily. She had got the old, harmonious, loving relationship back.

The Analysis

Of the total number of lines in this story(981), lines 1 to 948 comprise the Beginning, lines 949 to 952 comprise the Decisive Act, and with the Sequel, lines 953 to 981, make up the Ending.   There is no Body scene in this story.   In comparison with the story by Mrs. St. John this story will show that whereas her story ended with the confession to the district attorney, this story does not begin until after that confession has been made and the effect of that confession upon the actor is shown.   What Mr. Carey set out to prove was that this problem as presented by Mrs. St. John was presented from a man's angle,—a purely abstract standard of conduct— whereas in this story the story is presented from a woman's angle, specific and personal considerations triumphing over abstract, which is rather a curious anomaly, considering that the man's angle story was written by a woman and the woman's angle story was written by a man.

Lines 1 to 128 set forth a condition which is stated by the author in a way to project the interchange which comes between Philip Maple and Gertrude Woolcott.   This, it seems to me, might have been presented as an interchange between Gertrude Woolcott and either her husband or Frieda, purely on the ground that an interchange is usually more interesting than a statement.   In this case, the author is enabled, because he is a competent writer, to keep the statement from dullness, but an author using statement rather than interchange always runs the risk of dullness.

Once, however, this initial condition is stated, the story is, as every story of decision must be, a series of interchanges, first between Philip Maple and Gertrude on lines 129 to 288 then with Gertrude and Frieda, then with Archie, Gertrude, and Frieda as an observer, then with Gertrude and John Powell.   Following this is the one between Gertrude and Archie; and this, with its effect upon the actor shown in lines 722 to 765, would be the corresponding structural units in this story that occur in Mrs. St. John's story from lines 981 to 1442.   But Mr. Carey, taking this as his point of departure, in the interchange between Gertrude and Frieda, caused Frieda to set forth to Gertrude the choice which is now presented to her by this unexpected condition.   Lines 949 to 952 show the conclusive Act, while lines 953 to 981 show the Sequel, which fortunately makes everything come out right for everybody.

There is always a challenge to the inventiveness of a writer when somebody says, didactically, that such and such things cannot happen. I think it was Frank Norris who said that there were only three cities in the world in which romance was possible, and scoffed at the idea of romance being the theme for a story written about Nashville, Tennessee. To this O. Henry took exception, and wrote a story about Nashville. Writers are always saying that this situation has been worked out, that nothing more can be extracted from it. Then along comes Mary Brecht Pulver and takes the oldest situation in fiction, which is of the woman trying to regain the erring husband, and upsets the apple-cart by showing that something else can be got out of this apparently worked-out vein. Then, following her, comes Mr. Carey, and, taking another old situation, of the woman who has to choose between telling or not, works out of it an entirely new solution in the light of modern psychology.

It is interesting to see that these two writers consciously recognized that they were working over old situations and put in the mouths of their characters this statement in self-defense. On lines 1011 to 1015, Mrs. Pulver causes Mr. Dark to say that, "It amounts to a formula, almost purely mechanical. You can follow it anywhere you like in the fiction of the day." On lines 915 to 917 Mr. Carey causes Frieda to say to Gertrude, "Don't you see, Gertrude, it's one of the oldest situations in the world? I have read a dozen stories about it."

Because it is in this way a companion story to Mrs. Pulver's in showing that there is no condition or situation which a competent craftsman cannot work out to some new solution, this story will be most interesting to that group of writers who feel discouraged when they are told that there is nothing new to write about. Here is evidence that it doesn't matter a bit whether or not there is anything new, a writer with originality can always give a new twist to something which has always been regarded as old, and apparently abandoned as worthless.

SHADOWED

BEGINNING	In a series of interchanges, all the factors of the problem are presented. Necessity and urgency are indicated.	Interchange. Stroude and Mountaineer.	1– 181	Possible choice shown.
		(5th step. Stroude reflects upon what has passed.)	181– 285	Wavers toward return.
		Meeting. Stroude considers wife's ambitions.	285– 354	Wavers toward remaining.
		Interchange. Stroude and wife.	355– 755	Two possible choices clear.
		Interchange. Stroude with Laflin and Wilk.	756– 973	Opportunity to profit. Agrees to remain.
		Interchange. Stroude and wife, over Laflin's remark, leading to reading of letter, which introduces a new stimulus. Sacredness of promise recalled.	973–1097	Standard of conduct. New forces enter.
BODY	Struggle.	Interchange. Mental struggle. Standard of conduct versus opportunity to profit.	1098–1183	
ENDING	Conclusive Act.	Interchange with wife. Says he will go.	1184–1218	Answer to Narrative Question is: "He will keep his promise."
	Sequel.	Interchange. Boyce and Stroude.	1219–1258	Significance shown.

SHADOWED

BY MARY SYNON

I AM including *Shadowed* because it is a type of Decision story, presented chronologically, which comes nearer to having a Body equivalent to the Body of the Accomplishment story than any other type. Where the story of Accomplishment has furtherances and hindrances at the conclusion of the interchanges, in the Body, this story has a Beginning which is architecturally the same as the Body of the story of Decision. The difference is that at the close of the interchanges the fifth step shows a wavering between choices upon the part of the main actor. Crises of character decision take the place of narrative crises of furtherance and hindrance.

The character, at the close of each scene, appears to be about to come to a certain decision, and is plunged into a meeting with another person before that decision can be crystallized into action. At the close of this new interchange he appears to be about to come to another decision.

Thus, at the close of the different meetings the advantages or disadvantages of each choice is made apparent; and eventually there is a Conclusive Act.

The illuminating discovery which a writer will make from a study of this story in that *mental wavering should never be shown through dull analysis of thoughts.*

CASE No. 16

SHADOWED

BY MARY SYNON

All the way down from the Capitol, Stroude knew that he was being followed. From the moment he had come out of the Senate office-building upon the plaza, fragrant with forsythia in the March moonlight, he had been conscious of the man who trailed his sauntering footsteps. He had led him down a winding way past the Marshall statue and into the deserted wideness of Pennsylvania Avenue. He had thought to lose him when he stepped into the lobby of a big hotel, pausing for a word there with men he knew, men who made their greetings casual or portentous, according to their knowledge of the turning of the inner wheels of Washington; but he found the other man some twenty paces behind him as he crossed Lafayette Square, and his amused acceptance of the situation curdled to annoyance at the possibility of having to deal with an irresponsible crank determined on an interview.

The day had been more than ordinarily difficult, one of the hardest Stroude had known since the turmoiled times of war. He had suffered under the sense of impending crisis, knowing that his future hung on to-morrow's balance; and his temper, always drawn like a taut bow, had been ready to snap a hundred times through the afternoon's battle in the Senate chamber. Now, in the doorway of his house, that limestone palace of Georgian severity which loomed in stately classicism among the older residences of the neighbourhood, he poised the arrow of his wrath as he turned to confront the man behind him. "What do you want?" he snapped at him.

The man came nearer. By the dim light of the hall lantern Stroude saw his shambling listlessness, and his hand went to his pocket with a thought of relief that the other sought only alms. The man, seeing the gesture, put up his hand arrestingly. "Remember me?" he inquired, almost too nonchalantly. His

61 voice, for all its soft slurring of
62 the consonants, was threaded
63 with a fibre of steel which edged
64 the menace of his quiet poise.
65 "Why not?" Stroude asked
66 sharply, his shoulders lifting as
67 if for defense.
68 "Then I reckon you're none
69 too glad to see me?"
70 "You haven't come here to ask
71 me that. You might as well tell
72 me first as last what you want
73 from me."
74 "Nothing you'll call the sheriff
75 about," the man told him. He
76 faced the Senator squarely, re-
77 vealing even in the half-darkness
78 a certain racial resemblance to
79 him which made them equals on
80 the instant. For all Stroude's
81 grooming and the stranger's
82 shabbiness, they were strangely
83 akin in their antagonism, bound
84 not by family ties but by
85 broader, more basic associations.
86 Each of them, tall, thin, lithe,
87 gazed on the other with un-
88 flinching blue eyes. Each of
89 them kept watch with wildcat
90 tenacity. From each of them
91 emanated the recklessness of
92 personal courage that takes no
93 count of law beyond its own
94 code. In their sudden springing
95 to guard, the predominant char-
96 acteristics of the two men, the
97 Senator and the shambling
98 shadower, flared up stronger than
99 their setting, and although the
100 lights of the White House gleamed
101 golden across the Square, they
102 were mountaineers facing each

103 other in the hate of vendetta. The
104 years and the place fell away from
105 Stroude, leaving him stripped to
106 the bone of his clan's creed.
107 "We've settled our own affairs
108 before," Stroude said. "We can
109 do it now."
110 As if the words gave him
111 advantage, the other man seized
112 them swiftly. "Let's do it,
113 then," he replied. "I've come
114 here to get you to do something
115 you won't want to do. Will
116 you fight me for it?"
117 "Not till I know the stake."
118 "Didn't you get her letter?"
119 "Whose?"
120 "There's only one woman I'd
121 be coming to you about, I
122 reckon."
123 "I've never heard from her
124 since the day she went back to
125 you. That was twenty-six years
126 ago last May."
127 "The fourteenth."
128 "Why should she have written
129 me now?"
130 "She's dying." The man's
131 voice sounded in a softer timbre.
132 "A month ago the doctor from
133 the moonlight school told her
134 that she had only a little while to
135 live. She's been pining ever
136 since, not about dying, for she's
137 as brave as any man, but for
138 something I couldn't guess until
139 she told me. She wants to see
140 *you.* She wrote you a letter,
141 but she was afraid you might
142 not get it, and so she sent me.
143 'Tell him,' she said, 'that I
144 won't rest easy in my grave over

there on the side of Big Stony, if he don't come to me before I die. He told me once,' she said, 'that he'd come when I'd call. I'm calling now.' That's her message." His tone lifted from its softer depth. "Are you coming to her?"

"I can't."

"Why not?"

"I've a thousand duties. I've— It's ridiculous."

"Then you're not coming?"

"How can I, Martin? I'm not my own man. I'm here for my State, for my country. I have work to do. I can't let any personal obligation interfere with it. Besides——"

"It couldn't hurt your wife, not even if she knew it. And Dell's dying."

"I'm sorry, Martin. I am, honestly. Will you tell Dell that I——"

"I'll tell her nothing but that you wouldn't come. Nothing else matters. And I think you owe her that, at least."

"But——"

The other man turned away, crossed the street and walked back across the Square. Stroude could see him swinging on between the bushes, and the remembrance of another trail which Boyce Martin would climb rushed over him. More plainly than the crocus-bordered path to the White House shone the moonlit path up to the cabin on Pisgah where Dell Martin had been used to wait for his own coming, the cabin where she waited for death. The memory of that way, twisting among laurel and rhododendrons, stabbed him more sharply than had Boyce Martin's words; but with the old habit of setting aside disturbing thoughts, he tried to thrust the memory from his brain as he unlocked the door of his house.

A servant, coming forward at the sound of his key in the lock, gave him a message with a careful precision which bespoke respect for the executive management that directed his tasks. "Mrs. Stroude wishes you to be told, sir, that she is at the theatre, and will see you when she comes in. And she made an appointment, sir, for Senator Manning and two other gentlemen to see you to-night on their way from the Pan-American dinner. She said it was very important."

He thanked the man, and went upstairs to the library, switching on light after light to dispel its shrouding gloom. He tried to read, but the pages of the periodicals he took up ran into dullness. He chewed his cigar savagely, finding it flavourless. He strove to concentrate on his impending interview with Manning and his companions, realizing its portent, but he could not focus his attitude. Impatiently he thrust away the work which always waited his attention on his homecoming—findings of committees, digests of newspaper editorials, confidential reports on public interest in various measures, letters from men who had constituted themselves his captains. He frowned at the framed photograph of his wife, the only decoration she had placed upon his table; and he grimaced at the portrait of himself which Rhoda had set above the immaculate mantel. He was weary with work, he told himself, crossing the room and flinging wide open the windows which looked down on the Square.

The thrill of the night wind, prematurely warm as it crossed the Potomac, and burdened with elusive odours of a southern March, caught him unawares. For a moment he stood drinking deeply of the immortal beauty of the recurrent springtime. Memories he had thought long dead and buried went over him. Pictures more vivid than those on the walls framed themselves in the darkened greenery of the little park: a girl in a faded gingham dress waving him welcome on a hill road, a girl with eyes brighter than mountain stars telling him her love, flinging away all thought or care of herself, giving him everything and glorying in the gift, even to the last sacrifice of her departure from him. Not as she was now, Boyce Martin's wife dying in that far-away little community of his native hills, but as she had been when she had defied their little world to come to him, Stroude saw her. In the thought of what she had been to him, he flung out his arms. "After all these years," he muttered, "after all these years!" And as if drawn by a power stronger than his will, he crossed to the table, and picking up the telephone, called the information desk of the Union Station. "What time does the Mountain Mail on the C. & O. go out now?" he asked. "One o'clock? One-fifteen." He hung up the receiver, and saw again the photograph of his wife.

He studied it with suddenly arrested attention. What would she think of his desire to leave Washington at a time when, according to her fundamental ideas, his presence was imperative for the fulfilment of his ambition? Or was it her ambition? He gazed at the pictured countenance, seeing the determination of the uplifted chin, meeting the challenge in the steady eyes. Rhoda was certainly her father's daughter. Old Peter Armond's indomitable will and shrewdly calculating brain lived on in her. For the fourteen—or was it fifteen?— years of their marriage she had managed Stroude's career as cleverly as ever her father had directed one of his lieutenants, and he had acknowledged his debt to her with a certain attitude of amusement. Now,

313 facing the last triumphal stage
314 of its development, he felt an
315 angry distaste of Rhoda's
316 maneuvering. It might bring
317 him, he conceded, to the goal,
318 but he wished he might have
319 traveled a simpler path.

320 He had been an obscure
321 Congressman of fiery political
322 rectitude when he had met
323 Rhoda Armond. She, and her
324 group, and the circumstances
325 the Armond connection had con-
326 jured for him, had made him
327 into a statesman. Or was it
328 only that they had made it
329 possible for him to plant his
330 own standards on the heights?
331 At any rate, he owed her some-
332 thing, he thought. She was his
333 wife, even though her attitude
334 toward him was that of a director
335 of destinies. She had given him,
336 after all, what he had desired
337 from her. She had made the
338 upward road smooth, and she
339 had dowered him with loyal faith
340 in his ability. It wasn't fair to
341 compare her attitude toward him
342 with Dell's. He had never given
343 to Rhoda what he had given
344 Dell. Poor little Dell! But
345 what good could he do her now
346 by going to her? Twenty-five
347 years would have changed her
348 as they had changed him. They
349 had had their day, and the sun
350 of it had set long since. "I
351 won't go; I can't," he said, and
352 turned back to the work on his
353 desk, not looking up until his
354 wife entered the room.

355 She came, a tall, consciously
356 beautiful woman, bringing with
357 her an aroma of power as subtle
358 and as pervasive as the perfume
359 of her toilet. She gave to
360 Stroude the greeting of a per-
361 functory kiss on his brow, and
362 stood off for his admiration. It
363 was, however, not the product
364 of her personality as much as
365 her satisfaction in the work
366 which struck him as he watched
367 her. Rhoda's thought of herself
368 as well as of him, was that of a
369 sculptor of his masterpieces.
370 Stroude accepted it with the
371 affectionate tolerance of a long
372 marital relationship, feeling
373 somehow sorrier for Rhoda than
374 she would ever feel for herself,
375 since she would never know
376 what she had missed from life.
377 "I was playing your game to-
378 night," she told him.
379 "Isn't it yours too?" he
380 smiled.
381 "In a way, yes," she acknow-
382 ledged, "but this involved real
383 sacrifice, and I want reward. I
384 went to the theatre with the
385 Covingers."
386 "Was the play deadly?"
387 "No, but the Covingers are."
388 "He isn't a bad sort, and——"
389 "Oh, I know that he'll have
390 the delegation from his State,
391 and that it's one of the big
392 States; but oh, my dear, have
393 you ever had to listen to his
393 wife?"
394 "She isn't so terrible, Rhoda."
395 "Oh, of course, if you will look

396 at people as characters rather
397 than as social factors, you won't
398 see the awfulness of the Mrs.
399 Covingers of Washington. But
400 really——"

401 "Did Manning hint at why he
402 had to see me to-night?"

403 "At nothing but the import-
404 ance of seeing you. He is bring-
405 ing, he said, Mr. Laflin and
406 Senator Wilk."

407 "He probably said Senator
408 Wilk and Mr. Laflin, but you
409 know the field well enough to
410 put them in the order of their
411 importance. Laflin's the new
412 factor, a shrewd wolf raised in a
413 wild forest."

414 "Does it mean"—she leaned
415 forward, tapping the table with
416 her fan in eagerness—"that they
417 are going to ask you to take the
418 nomination?"

419 "They haven't the entire giv-
420 ing of it, my dear."

421 "Don't be silly, Burton. You
422 know that they are the architects
423 of presidential nominations."

424 "But even architects——"

425 "Oh, Burt, don't quibble.
426 You know that you're the logical
427 man for the place. You're
428 squarely based in party
429 politics——"

430 "Safe, and steady." His tone
431 was whimsical.

432 "But picturesque enough to
433 be a good campaigner."

434 "Barefoot boy from the
435 mountains. Good American
436 stock with fine traditions. Reads
437 rhetorically, doesn't it?"

438 "And a border State gives
439 you strategic advantage."

440 "Someone has coached you
441 well."

442 "I was coached before I ever
443 knew you, Burt dear. My father
444 taught us politics as religiously
445 as my mother taught us sewing.
446 It wasn't as practical, perhaps,
447 as yours, but——"

448 "There haven't been many
449 men more practical in their
450 politics than Peter Armond,"
451 Stroude said dryly.

452 "Even if he did grow
453 wealthy," his daughter defended,
454 "you know how high he kept his
455 standards."

456 "I can guess," Stroude said,
457 but his tone gave her no handle
458 to catch for controversy, and she
459 swung into off-side statement.
460 "Mrs. Covinger let slip some-
461 thing that may be vital to us,"
462 she told him.

463 "If it's vital, she let it slip
464 with due deliberation," he de-
465 clared. "Don't under-estimate
466 her brains, Rhoda, even if she
467 wasn't raised by the Armond
468 code. What did she say?"

469 "I don't believe I'll tell you."

470 "Yes, you will."

471 "We do run in double harness,
472 don't we? Well, she said that
473 Covinger wasn't going back to
474 New York until to-morrow
475 night, as there was a tremend-
476 ously important conference at
477 noon to-morrow. Seven men
478 will be there, and they will
479 decide the fate of the nation.

480 That's exactly what she said.
481 She's bombastic, you know."

482 "Seven? Then they're letting
483 Covinger in?"

484 "You knew about it?"

485 "Not that it would be to-
486 morrow."

487 "Is that why Senator Manning
488 is coming to-night?"

489 "Probably."

490 "Then that means—" Her
491 voice broke in excitement.

492 "That our fate hangs in the
493 balance."

494 "Does it?"

495 "It looks like it." He smiled
496 at her through the smoke of his
497 cigar. Her eyes shone with
498 myriad points of light. "Not
499 planning what you'll wear at
500 the inauguration, are you?" he
501 teased her.

502 "No," she said, "but wonder-
503 ing what you'll say. It's wonder-
504 ful, isn't it?"

505 "Don't count your chickens
506 yet, Rhoda," he warned her.
507 "We, both of us, know the
508 thousand slips between the cup
509 of consideration and the lip of
510 nomination. We've gone through
511 it all for other offices."

512 "But we've won every time,"
513 she said solemnly. "You've
514 never been beaten, Burt. Don't
515 you see what an advantage that
516 is, now? You've been going up
517 and up, and up."

518 "The Senate's a rather high
519 plateau, at that."

520 "But not the high mountain.
521 Oh, Burt, think of it! It seems
522 almost unbelievable, and yet
523 I've always known you were
524 destined for it. I knew you'd
525 be great. Why, even in those
526 first days here, you promised it.
527 You knew it, too. You had
528 the look of a man who was
529 dedicated to something beyond
530 the immediate, the look of one
531 who is going to travel far and
532 high. I believe that was one of
533 the reasons why I loved you.
534 And you—" She leaned over the
535 table, and spread out the brilliant
536 feathers of her fan, gazing at their
537 splendour and not at her husband
538 as she went on: "Did you love
539 me when you married me?"

540 "Why else do men marry wo-
541 men?" he countered, letting the
542 smoke veil his eyes.

543 "To put other women out of
544 their lives, sometimes," she said.

545 "Well?" He drew hard on
546 the cigar.

547 "I never knew until to-day
548 who she was," she said. "I
549 opened a letter by mistake.
550 You may see from the envelope
551 how easy it was for me to think
552 it was addressed to me when I
553 found it in my mail. It was
554 directed merely to Washington,
555 and the post office sent it to the
556 house here."

557 "I quite understand," he said,
558 and held out his hand for Dell
559 Martin's letter.

560 His wife drew it from the gay
561 bag she had borne, and gave it
562 to him. For a moment he looked
563 at the pitiful missive, contrast-

393

564 ing it with the appointments of
565 the table before him. "She's
566 dying," Rhoda said, "and she
567 asks you to go to her."

568 "Yes," he said, "I know it."

569 "But——"

570 "How did I know? Her
571 husband followed me down from
572 the Hill to-night. He demanded
573 that I return with him."

574 "Then she married, after——"

575 "She was married," he said,
576 "when I met her."

577 "Oh!" She snapped shut the
578 great fan, twisting its tortoise-
579 shell handle between her lithe
580 fingers. "When was that?"

581 "Before I knew you." He
582 sank down into his chair, staring
583 forward as if he were a judge
584 considering a decision. "I was
585 twenty-two years old, teaching
586 school in the mountains, and
587 studying law with old Judge
588 McLaurin, when I met Dell
589 Martin. She had been married
590 to Boyce against her will, as
591 plenty of the girls in the hills are
592 married. She was lonely, and
593 wretched, and lovelier than a
594 wild rose. I was young, and
595 reckless. I fell in love with her,
596 and I made her love me. Boyce
597 found it out. He drew me into
598 a fight, and I won it. He shot
599 me then. Dell came to nurse me,
600 and I wouldn't let her go. Boyce
601 wouldn't get a divorce, and she
602 couldn't, but she stayed with
603 me. We had two years of utter
604 happiness. I'd have gone
605 through hell to win them."

606 A stick of the tortoise-shell
607 handle of the fan broke in
608 Rhoda's hands. "But you left
609 her?"

610 "No," he said. "She left me.
611 She saw before I did that it
612 couldn't go on. She saw in me
613 the ambition that I thought I
614 had buried in my love for her.
615 She knew that if I stayed with
616 her, I'd never be anything but a
617 miserable shyster, living from
618 hand to mouth, despising myself
619 and all I did, coming perhaps
620 in time to hate her because she
621 had been the cause of my degra-
622 dation. She went to Judge
623 McLaurin, and asked him to tell
624 her the truth. He told her, old
625 Covenanter that he was. Then
626 she went up the mountain to
627 Boyce, and asked him if he wanted
628 her to come back to him. She
629 knew that it was the only action
630 I'd consider final. He told her to
631 come. She told me that she was
632 leaving me. I pleaded with her
633 all that night, but she went with
634 the dawn. I couldn't hold her.
635 I went up Pisgah with her till
636 we came to the trail to Boyce's
637 cabin. We could see the wood-
638 smoke curling up above the
639 masses of shining green leaves
640 and pink clusters of the laurel.
641 'You're going away from me,'
642 she said, 'far away, and you'll
643 climb a higher mountain than
644 Pisgah.' I begged her to come
645 with me, but she shook her head.
646 'I'm giving you up for your sake,'
647 she told me. 'But you need me,'

I pleaded. 'Not now,' she said. 'But some day I shall, and then I'll call you. And no matter where you are, you'll come, won't you, Burt?' I promised her that I would. The last I saw of her was as she climbed the trail to Boyce's cabin. From that day to this,"—he touched the crumpled little white letter, —"she has sent me no word."

"It's strange, isn't it," Rhoda said, her voice not quite steady, "that a woman may live with a man through long years, and never really know him at all?"

"Should I have told you?"

"I don't know," she said. "I suppose I'd have married you, even if you had. It's not deception, perhaps, when you've never seen her nor written to her since you married me; and yet— Are you going to her, Burt?"

"To-morrow's the conference. I must be there if I am to be the man chosen."

"Do you want to go?"

"I wonder," he mused, "if you'll understand me when I tell you that, other things being equal, I should go to-night. It's with no sense of failing you, and with no idea of helping her, but I promised her—that I'd come if she called."

"Even if there weren't the conference," Rhoda said, "you're a marked man now. You couldn't go back to a little village in the mountains without it being

known, and the reason for it blazoned. It wouldn't do, would it?" She could not quite succeed in making her tone judical. Her own eagerness palpitated back of the assumed impartiality. "You've wanted the presidency too long to throw away the chance of it."

"I've never wanted it," he said.

"You don't mean," she demanded, her vexation rising into view, "that I've urged you to seek something you haven't desired?"

"It's more complex than that," he shrugged. "I suppose it's simply that I married the Armond hope as well as you. Old Peter set a standard for your family which has kept you all up on your toes. If the dead see, he must chuckle sometimes over its way of working."

"Why?" she flared, letting her annoyance catch at a point of difference less vital than the main issue. "He gave his whole service to his country. He was one of the really great men of his generation, wasn't he? You've never known my father as I knew him. You've always let yourself be influenced by the demagogic attacks on him. You've thought that because he made a great fortune he couldn't be an idealist. Haven't you seen that, if he had been a materialist, he wouldn't have trained his family as he did?

395

732 Why, it's been his torch that
733 I've tried to keep alight, and if I
734 have done anything for you,
735 Burton, it has been by that
736 torch's flame."

737 "You've done a very great
738 deal, Rhoda," he said. "I'm
739 not questioning the number or
740 the brightness of the candles
741 you've burned in my game.
742 I'm only questioning the value
743 of the game itself. Power's like
744 money. If you give up all else
745 to possess it, then it possesses
746 you."

747 "But——"

748 "I know. I should have
749 chosen long ago. I'm not turn-
750 ing back now. I owe you that,
751 I think. If I'm anything at all
752 beyond a struggling lawyer in a
753 little city—" He broke off
754 suddenly as the young servant
755 came to the library curtains.

756 "Senator Manning and two
757 other gentlemen," he announced.

758 They came almost on his
759 heels, three men with the aspect
760 of dignitaries: Manning tall,
761 thin, almost cadaverous, with
762 the eye and the hand of a
763 Richelieu; Wilk heavy, ponder-
764 ous, inscrutable as a great
765 Buddha; Laflin, a blend of
766 college professor and Wall Street
767 lawyer, hiding a predatory keen-
768 ness behind horn-rimmed spec-
769 tacles. Characteristically,
770 Stroude felt, they fell into place,
771 Wilk into the nearest easy-chair,
772 Manning into an Italian seat
773 which put him in the centre of a

774 softly lighted stage, and Laflin
775 back in the shadows. After a
776 moment of casual conversation
777 Rhoda rose to leave them.
778 Stroude halted her. "I have
779 an idea," he said, "that these
780 gentlemen have come to me on
781 an errand which concerns you as
782 well as myself.—Do you mind if
783 she stays?"

784 "Not at all," said Manning
785 suavely. Laflin nodded, and
786 old man Wilk grunted assent.
787 Rhoda went over beyond Laflin
788 as far outside the group as she
789 could, and just out of her
790 husband's line of vision; but he
791 turned his chair a little, that he
792 might encompass her in his sight
793 as Manning began to speak.

794 "It makes it a little easier for
795 us," he said, "that you have
796 guessed something of our mis-
797 sion."

798 "I couldn't help knowing,"
799 Stroude swung back, "when
800 every other man in the Senate
801 has known it for days."

802 "Not definitely," boomed
803 Wilk. "There's always talk, of
804 course, and often more smoke
805 than fire."

806 "Sometimes it's only a screen
807 for the protection of a real issue,"
808 Manning went on, "but in this
809 case the fire is burning. You
810 know, I am sure, that the con-
811 ference to determine the best
812 candidate for the next term of
813 the presidency is to be held here
814 in Washington to-morrow."

815 "At noon," smiled Stroude.

816 "Your information," Manning
817 said, "is speedy as well as
818 accurate. The time was not
819 determined until seven o'clock
820 this evening. Seven men know
821 it."

822 "And their wives," cut in
823 Laflin, peering at Rhoda.

824 "We have canvassed the field
825 thoroughly before coming to
826 you," Manning continued with
827 his air of authoritative spokes-
828 manship. "We have eliminated,
829 for one reason or another, all
830 the men who have been under
831 consideration. Bannister is too
832 old. Maxwell is too radical.
833 Vandringham is too theatrical.
834 Stearns is too variable. Dur-
835 ham is too light. Landreau
836 lacks the necessary tradition.
837 Penn comes from the wrong loca-
838 tion. Jarvis jumped the party.
839 The process brings us to you."

841 "How about Corliss?"

842 "I don't mind telling you,"
843 Manning said, "that Carmichael
844 is fighting desperately for Cor-
845 liss, and that, without Covinger's
846 help, he *might* be able to swing
847 the conference. Mr. Laflin,
848 Senator Wilk and I have never
849 swerved from our determination
850 to have you. Carmichael has
851 Bennett and Franklin with him.
852 Covinger is the determining
853 vote. You have him."

854 "Are you sure?"

855 "Certain. He's attending on
856 Parker's proxy. We won that
857 point this afternoon. He's
858 solidly with you."

859 "Even against Corliss? Cor-
860 liss is from his State."

861 "Even against him."

862 "Why?"

863 "Well, it seems that Corliss
864 has an old scandal against him
865 which frightens Covinger. He's
866 afraid that it might make an
867 election issue. By the way—
868 You're not interested in these
869 affairs, Mrs. Stroude?"

870 "Very vitally," she said, "and
871 there's nothing you need fear
872 to discuss before me."

873 Manning cleared his throat,
874 and old man Wilk stirred un-
875 easily in his chair. Laflin's
876 mobile mouth twisted.

877 "Go on," said Stroude.
878 "What's the charge?"

879 "Carmichael says," Manning
880 stated, "that there's an old story
881 back in your own State, Stroude,
882 that might explode. We've all
883 known you a good many years,
884 all of us but Laflin, and we've
885 never heard a whisper of it. I
886 have told him that I do not
887 believe it. So has Senator Wilk."

888 "What's the story?" Stroude's
889 fingers, lighting a match, did not
890 tremble.

891 "Well, if you insist——"

892 "I do."

893 "Carmichael says that you
894 stole another man's wife."

895 "There was no theft about it.
896 She came with me. Later she
897 went back to her husband. I
898 left the place, started to practise
899 law, and married. My wife
900 never heard the story until to-

night." He looked down at Dell Martin's letter, not yet read by him, topping the documents on the table in front of him. "It's an old story," he said, "and one not likely to explode unless——"

"Unless what?" Laflin demanded from the gloom.

"Unless I choose to revive it by an overt act," Stroude retorted. "It all happened more than twenty-five years ago in a tiny community in the mountains. I know the people there. They're my kind, my stock. They won't talk to strangers coming in. There's only one way the newspapers could get the story. I'd have to lead them to it."

"That's true," old man Wilk grunted. "I know the mountains."

"Then it's settled," Manning said with evident relief. "I fancy a story as old as that, cut off altogether by the time between, could not be a very appalling Banquo's ghost." He arose a little wearily. "You'll be at the conference to-morrow?" He named the time and place. "It's necessary that you should be. Without you, Covinger may switch. You may have to combat Carmichael directly. You'll be ready?"

"If I'm—if it's necessary," Stroude said.

The other two men stood up, Wilk unwieldily, Laflin with quick ease, smiling at Stroude as he held out his hand. "This was a real star-chamber session," he said, "according to the best rules of old Peter Armond. Wouldn't the old pirate have loved to sit in a ten-minute game of four men who decided the next President?"

"What do you mean?" Rhoda's voice rang out in challenge, and Manning and Wilk rushed to speech to head off Laflin, but he went on in almost boyish unconcern: "Old Peter trained me, you know, and I've always had a soft spot for him in my heart, although I've known what a wolf in sheep's clothing he was. We have to hand it to him, though, that with all his grafting and his materialism, he was a great party builder. He was the first of the Warwicks in American national life. We're just rattling around in his shoes, but we'll do our best to put you over."

He moved off, almost pushed by Manning's eagerness to depart, but his voice seemed to linger in the room after the three of them had gone. Stroude sat toying with a paper-knife. Rhoda, deep in the shadows, did not stir. A clock in the hall boomed twelve. Stroude, sighing, put his hand over Dell Martin's letter. Then Rhoda spoke. "Is Mr. Laflin telling the truth about my father," she asked Stroude, "or what he thinks is the truth?"

"The truth."

"That he wasn't an idealist—a patriot?"

"Well, if he was——"

"I understand. And you've known it always?"

"Since before I knew you."

"Then do you mean"—she came back to the chair beside the table—"that through all these years my standards have meant nothing to you? That you have known them to be false?"

"They aren't false," he said. "The standards are true enough."

"But the man who gave them to me wasn't?"

"Well, he didn't live up to the code."

"Your own code?"

"I've tried to hold to it."

"The one Judge McLaurin taught you?"

"The very one. The one Judge Foxwell taught *him*. *He* got it, I believe, from John Marshall. Don't think about it, Rhoda. Those old boys lived in different days. Sometimes I think that I'm an anachronism." He sought to smile at her, but the smile faded before her intensity. "Don't let a chance word of Laflin's bother you," he counseled. "He didn't know you, of course, as your father's daughter, or he'd have cut out his tongue before saying what he did."

"It doesn't matter who said it," she declared. "It's not that alone that hurts; it's the knowledge that I've meant so little to you that cuts deep—now. I used to think, Burt, even when I knew that you didn't love me, that I was giving you something fine and splendid. I let myself believe that the Armond tradition was the beacon which was lighting your way. I thought that if I couldn't give you anything else, I was at least giving you that torch. And now, I find out that the light I was holding for you was only marsh fire. You've never needed me!" Her voice rose to accusation.

"Oh, yes," he countered, but he could not put verity into his tone.

"No," she said. "You don't owe me anything for the playing of the game. I've loved that for itself."

"But you thought you were giving me the other——"

"And I wasn't. It's really a joke, isn't it? A buccaneer teaching his family the Golden Rule, and the family passing it on!"

"It isn't a joke, Rhoda. I've always taken it in the measure of your intention."

"And been sorry for me?"

"Yes."

"I've never sought pity."

"None of us do."

"It's funny, isn't it," she mused, "that one woman who loved you set you free, so that another woman whom you didn't love might take away that freedom?"

"I've had as much freedom as most men," he said, but his eyes went back to the crumpled missive. Rhoda's glance, following his, saw its significance. "Read it," she challenged him. He hesitated an instant, as if doubting his desire to read it before her watchfulness, then drew the letter from its envelope.

Pale tracing on common paper met his gaze. *"Burt,"* he read, *"you're a great man now, and maybe you've forgotten me. I've never forgotten you. Every morning and every night I've prayed for you. Boyce has been good to me, better than I deserved; but oh, Burt, all that my life has been since I left you is just a hope that eternity will bring us together again. I used to believe it would, but I'm getting afraid, now that it's coming near. Won't you come to me for just one hour before I go? You told me once that hell wouldn't keep you if I——"*

Before the pathos of the call something in Stroude's soul trembled. He didn't love Dell now, he told himself as he came to the end of the page. He hadn't loved her in twenty years. There was no thrill of remembered passion rising from the white page to stir his heart, but there was something deeper, more poignant than romance in the plea which this woman in the mountains had sent him across time and distance. Through those long years she had never wavered in her belief in him and in the promise he had made to her. Out of the depths of his spirit he had told her that he would come to her if she should ever need him. It was a promise given not only to the woman who had heard and heeded it, but to the God of his faith and his fathers. If he failed to keep it, no matter what the cost, he would be violating more than an old love. He would be tearing down his own code. Through whatever glory might come to him he would know himself as a man who failed in the one virtue on which he had always prided himself, the keeping of his word. It was an oath he had taken to Dell Martin, just as he would take an oath to uphold the Constitution of the United States if—if he climbed the mountain of Rhoda's vision!

Realization of the immediacy of his problem came to him with the sight of his wife's fan, broken, lying beyond the letter in his hand. He looked up to find Rhoda's eyes studying him. But he must not fail her, he told himself, snatching at the straw of conventionality in the current of emotion. The very fact that he had not given her love put him under obligation to her. Because of her, because of the expectations she had harboured for him, because of the time and thought and labour she had spent for the advancement she had thought he sought, because of her very disillusionment now, he could not fail her. He must go to the conference, even if it meant the breaking of a vow he had made before the altar of his one great love. It was part of the price, he reasoned, that all men pay for power; but he felt that something within him was dying as he turned the page of Dell Martin's letter.

"—*if I called for you*," he picked up the thread. "*That was why I didn't call when I needed you before, when our boy was born. I couldn't let you know about him. You'd never have let me go if you'd known. But it doesn't matter now, does it? And oh, Burt, I need you so! If you'll only hold my hand again, I won't fear the crossing. And perhaps when you come to die, you'll find the going easier if you have the memory of this hour you'll give me. Won't you come?*" It was signed waveringly, "*Dell.*"

He folded it back into the envelope, and put it in his pocket. "You aren't going?" Rhoda asked him, her voice strangely strained.

"Yes," he said, "I'm going."

"But to-morrow——"

"It's the long years afterward I'm thinking of," he told her.

"And the nomination——"

"Sometimes the things we put out of our lives," he said, "are the only things we really keep."

"That's ridiculous," she said. "I can't understand you at all to-night, Burton. Why should a man give up the highest honour a nation can give him——"

"There are other kinds of honour, Rhoda."

"To go to a woman he hasn't seen for twenty-five years?"

"She is the—" he began, then halted quickly in the fear of the hurt his word might give her.

"I understand," she said.

She picked up her broken fan, and moved toward the door, but before she reached it, turned back. Her face was stonily calm. "Shall I telephone Senator Manning in the morning that you will not be there?" she asked him.

"If you will," he said.

As his car bore him past the shadowy white pile on the other side of the Square, Stroude sighed. A man does not live with a dream—even the dream of another—through season after season without catching some gleam of its radiance; but in Boyce Martin's straight look as he met him at the train gate, Stroude began to drink of his justification.

"You Stroudes always kept your word," the other man said.

"We aim to," said Stroude, unconsciously slipping back into the vernacular of his youth. "It was her letter," he explained. "I

1237 never knew about the boy."
1238 "I know," said Martin. "I
1239 —I've loved him as if he'd been
1240 the child I've never had. That's
1241 why I came for you." He held
1242 out his hand, and Stroude
1243 grasped it. "You're one of us,
1244 after all."
1245 As the train slid past the
1246 Potomac and threaded the low
1247 pines of the Virginia river-lands,

1248 Stroude pondered the moun-
1249 taineer's tribute. In the light of
1250 it he saw the path to Dell
1251 Martin's cabin leading higher
1452 than the way across the Square.
1253 For the first time in many years
1254 he felt the surge of freedom ris-
1255 ing in his soul. A thousand
1256 shackles fell away as the last
1257 lights of Washington slid down
1258 on the horizon.

THE ANALYSIS

A glance at the chart will show you that this story contains 1258 lines. Of these the Beginning is made up of 1097 lines, the Body 86 lines, the Ending 75 lines, 35 for the Decisive Act and 40 for the Sequel.

The first interchange is between Stroude and the mountaineer and occupies lines 1 to 181. At the close of this interchange a possible choice is shown, and Stroude appears about to make a decision; but as he reflects, which is the fifth step occupying lines 181 to 285, he wavers toward the return. Then there is the consideration of a condition, which is shown as a meeting, when Stroude becomes aware of the stimulus, which is to consider a state of affairs involving his wife. Then he wavers toward remaining in Washington. Following this is an interchange between Stroude and his wife, and at the close of it, after lines 355 to 755, two possible choices are clear. The interchange between Stroude and Laflin and Wilk, occupying lines 756 to 973, shows at its close an agreement to remain. The decision is practically consummated, but, after the interchange between Stroude and his wife brought about by Laflin's remark which leads to the reading of the letter in which he recalls the sacredness of his promise, there comes, in lines 1098 to 1183, a mental struggle between his standard of conduct as opposed to his opportunity for wish fulfilment or profit, which makes up the Body of the story.

At the conclusion of the struggle he says, on line 1189, "Yes, I am going." That is the Decisive Act, and in the Sequel there is an interchange between the Senator and Boyce Martin in which Martin voices the reason that caused Stroude to make this decision. It is that, "You Stroudes always kept your word," (line 1231).

This story would have been improved had this trait been indicated in the interchange between Stroude and the mountaineer early in the story.

This story is particularly interesting because it is told in straight chronological form. There is no flash-back whatsoever; but the analytical reader will observe that it is made up of an extremely important situation, that it is a clear-cut case of an opportunity to profit as opposed to a standard of conduct, and that the interchanges are prolonged and dramatic because they are important. One other special reason for its inclusion is that it shows a variation from the other stories of this type in that the decision is made after the actor has become aware of a stimulus of which he was not aware at the opening of the story. At the opening of the story he knew that the woman had sent for him, but it was not until on lines 1168 to 1183, when he read the letter, that he became aware that the woman was depending upon him to keep his sacred promise. Then that trait in his character which made that standard of conduct more important to him than his opportunity to profit came to the front and defeated the other trait.

	Interchange. Claypool and waiter.	1– 38
	(5th step. Claypool's reflections. Interchange with waiter.)	39– 95
Main Actor is shown in characteristic responses. Condition which calls upon him to decide is presented.	Interchange. Krohn and Claypool. Krohn offers opportunity to profit.	96–493
	Martin Claypool accepts.	484–487
	Interchange. Claypool and Krohn, regarding tailor.	494–574
	Meeting. Claypool sees and buys loud goods.	575–637
	Interchange. Claypool and tailor.	638–907
	(5th step. Reflections. Claypool aware of photograph.)	908–963
Upon reflecting Claypool reverses decision. Decisive Acts.	Interchange. Telephones Tailor.	963–972
	Interchange. Telephones Krohn.	973–988

BEGINNING

Main Narrative Question: "What choice will he make?"

Choice apparently made. Loophole left by writer.

Decision made.

SHODDY

BY RICHARD CONNELL

THE story *Shoddy* is an especially interesting variant of the type story illustrated by *Shadowed*. It is the story of a man who has apparently made up his mind and has come to a definite decision, but who becomes aware of a new stimulus as a result of which he reverses his original decision.

It is extremely interesting in the way in which it carries along two separate stories, linking them cleverly together. One is the story of Martin Claypool and the poor tailor; the other is the story of Martin Claypool and Mr. Krohn.

CASE No. 17

SHODDY

BY RICHARD CONNELL

Martin Claypool went directly from his suite on the world's largest—and most costly—liner to the suite engaged for him in London's largest—and most costly—hotel. He always took a suite wherever he went.

He sent for a waiter, and with a gold-mounted pencil ticked off the dishes for his dinner on the right-hand, or price, side of the menu: Beluga caviar, fillet of sole Marguery, a squab Lucullus, asparagus, an alligator-pear salad, a bit of old Stilton, hothouse grapes. He said to the waiter, "And a bottle of your best wine."

"Yes, sir. What sort, sir?"

"The best," said Martin Claypool.

"Does the gentleman prefer a sauterne? Or perhaps a claret?"

"Bring me the best you have."

The old waiter regarded Martin Claypool appraisingly. "A half bottle of Château Yquem '06," he murmured reverently, "and a half bottle of Romanée '11?"

"Yes, yes," said Martin Claypool impatiently. "That's it."

"And a liqueur, sir?"

"Yes, yes."

"What sort, sir?"

"Let me see now——"

"We have some prime '76 brandy, sir."

"That will do."

When the waiter had bowed himself away Martin Claypool stretched the long legs which supported his powerful frame, and paced his suite. He took from a thin platinum case a very long and strong cigar, lighted it. It had no band on it, because he had had it made specially for him.

In front of the long glass in one of his bedrooms he paused to survey himself. He patted the spot where vest and trousers met, reflectively. Not so bad for a fellow past forty. The golf had helped. If he could keep the circumference of his waist two inches smaller than his chest he'd be doing better than most men of his years and habits, he mused. He rubbed his head.

407

61 Hair going fast, despite the
62 violet-ray treatments of that
63 high-priced specialist. Still, he
64 had a good fresh color. Plenty
65 of vigorous years ahead of him—
66 years of progress and success.

67 He adjusted the black pearl
68 pin in his necktie—a rather florid
69 necktie. He was reminded of
70 something. He took off his suit
71 —it was gray, pronouncedly
72 striped with white—and changed
73 to his dinner clothes. The shirt
74 he put on had been made to order
75 for him in St. Louis. It was
76 heavily pleated. He had had
77 two dozen made, at thirty-six
78 dollars each.

79 His dressing finished, he was
80 poking the ends of his black tie
81 under the wings of his collar
82 when his dinner arrived. He
83 gazed approvingly at his image
84 in the mirror. Before he sat
85 down to dinner he telephoned to
86 Mr. Krohn. Yes, Mr. Krohn
87 could come to his suite at nine.
88 Good! Good-by.

89 "Telephone service here is al-
90 most as bad as in St. Louis," he
91 remarked to the waiter.

92 "Yes, sir. Sorry, sir," said
93 the waiter, who up to that
94 moment had always thought of
95 St. Louis as a man.

96 Krohn was prompt. Pre-
97 cisely at nine he came in, bowed
98 to Martin Claypool, held out a
99 long-fingered hand. Krohn was
100 a lean, sallow man, meticulously
101 dressed, and of no particular age
102 or nationality.

103 "Delighted to see you, Mr.
104 Claypool," he said.
105 "Pleased to meet you, Mr.
106 Krohn. Sit down and have a
107 cigar."
108 "Thanks."
109 "How about a little drink?"
110 Krohn shook his head. "I
111 leave spirits to the Americans.
112 They suit their temperament,"
113 he said. "Glass of port after
114 dinner is my limit. But please
115 don't let me deter you."
116 Martin Claypool mixed him-
117 self a highball. Then he turned
118 to Krohn.
119 "Now then," he said, "let's
120 talk turkey."
121 "I beg your pardon?"
122 "That means, in American,
123 let's get down to business,"
124 laughed Martin Claypool.
125 Krohn inclined his dark head.
126 "By all means," he said. "There
127 is really no great hurry though.
128 You see, Mr. Claypool, I've just
129 come from China, where time is
130 nothing."
131 "And I," said Martin Clay-
132 pool, "have just come from
133 America, where time is money—
134 and money is everything."
135 "But now that you are here,
136 you plan to look round a while,
137 I hope. It's your first visit to
138 England, isn't it?"
139 "Yes."
140 "You'll be taking a bit of vaca-
141 tion then, I expect; see London
142 —Paris." Mr. Krohn pro-
143 nounced "Paris" with a sug-
144 gestion of a leer.

145 "No," said Martin Claypool
146 "You deserve a rest, Mr. Clay-
147 pool. I've heard how tremen-
148 dously you work."

149 "That's no lie," said Martin
150 Claypool. "I've always worked
151 hard all my life. I wouldn't be
152 on top today if I hadn't. But I
153 don't intend to slacken my pace
154 now, Mr. Krohn. No, sir! I'll
155 save my sightseeing till I'm
156 sixty-five or so and am thinking
157 of retiring. My present trip is
158 strictly business. I'm booked to
159 sail for home a week from
160 tomorrow."

161 "You Americans are wonder-
162 ful," remarked Mr. Krohn. "It's
163 a pleasure to do business with
164 you. You see straight and you
165 go directly to the point."

166 "Have to," said Martin Clay-
167 pool, drinking his highball.
168 "Competition. It's devil take
169 the hindmost where I come
170 from, Mr. Krohn. We don't
171 bunk ourselves about what we
172 are in business for. I don't,
173 anyhow. I admit I'm not in
174 business for my health. I'm in
175 the game to make money. The
176 more money I make, the better
177 I like it."

178 "That's common sense," said
179 Mr. Krohn.

180 "Common-sense College is
181 where I got my schooling," said
182 Martin Claypool, pouring him-
183 self another drink. "It's a tough
184 school. I wasn't born with any
185 silver spoon in my mouth, Mr.
186 Krohn. Nothing was ever hand-
187 ed to me on a platter. I had
188 to grab it. Yes, sir!" He raised
189 his glass, smiled expansively.

190 "I was born a poor boy," he
191 said. "I'm not ashamed of it.
192 I didn't stay poor. My dad was
193 a puddler in a steel mill. I went
194 to work in the mill myself when
195 I was a kid. See this chest and
196 these shoulders? Well, I didn't
197 get them from lying round a
198 country club and eating cream
199 puffs. I earned them, like every-
200 thing else I have. I've had no
201 bed of roses, I'll tell you. I've
202 known what it is to be hungry.
203 Yes, and I've seen the day when
204 I had but one shirt to my back
205 and not a dime in my pockets.
206 I know what poverty means."

207 "Really?"

208 "Yes, sir. I guess that's why I
209 know the value of money. Don't
210 let anybody kid you, Mr. Krohn.
211 Money is the only thing that
212 counts. People don't ask you
213 where or how you got it. All
214 that interests them is that you
215 have it. The more you have, the
216 better they like you. Why, do
217 you know that there are plenty
218 of families in St. Louis today who
219 wouldn't have let me in their
220 back doors when I was a lad
221 juggling steel rails for a living,
222 who today invite me in their
223 front doors and are damn glad
224 to see me too?"

225 "Indeed?"

226 "Yes, there's a lot of differ-
227 ence between Martin Claypool,
228 puddler, and Mr. Claypool, head

of Martin Claypool, Inc., Locomotive Builders. Yet I'm the same man. The answer is—I've done something. I've built a big corporation out of nothing. I've developed and perfected the best engine in the world. I'm mighty proud of that."

"You have every right to be, Mr. Claypool."

"I wanted money—and I got it," finished Martin Claypool. "And I'm going to get more too." Mr. Krohn's thin lips formed a knowing smile. "I shouldn't wonder," he said. He studied Martin Claypool, whose great torso was sprawled in an easy-chair. "Mr. Claypool," he said, "shall we—what is it now?—talk turkey?"

"Shoot!" said Martin Claypool.

"The Kiang-su-Kiang-si Railroad Syndicate has left everything in my hands," said Mr. Krohn.

"Good!"

"The money to buy rolling stock for the new road has been provided."

"Good!"

Mr. Krohn inserted a long cigarette in a still longer holder, lighted it and said, "The question which I now must decide is: Where shall I buy the locomotives?"

"That's easy," said Martin Claypool. "The Claypool locomotive is the best in the world."

Mr. Krohn nodded. "I think," he said, "that you'll find few who will dispute that. Even our Chinese directors know its reputation and are in favor of buying Claypools. It's the best, beyond doubt. That's just the trouble."

"What do you mean?"

Mr. Krohn smiled blandly. "It's too good," he said.

"You want the best, don't you?" demanded Martin Claypool. "Any fly-by-night outfit can sell you a bunch of junk that won't last five years."

"True," said Mr. Krohn. "But, Mr. Claypool, isn't there a difference in your mind between 'too good' and 'good enough'?"

Martin Claypool regarded Mr. Krohn with his shrewd blue eyes. "You've got some sort of proposition," he said. "What is it?"

Mr. Krohn smiled admiringly. "It would have taken weeks of negotiation, hinting, circumlocution, to get this far in an interview with a Chinese," he said.

"Well, I'm no Chinaman," remarked Mr. Claypool. "Put it in plain words."

Mr. Krohn hitched his chair nearer Martin Claypool. "What I mean is this," he said in a confidential tone: "If you supply standard Claypool locomotives, made according to the rigid specifications you sent us, at the price we can pay, you can't make much profit on the transaction."

313 "Don't expect to," said Mr.
314 Claypool promptly. "I'll tell
315 you just how it is, Mr. Krohn.
316 Business is slack in my works
317 now. I want to keep them run-
318 ning full time. That's why I
319 sent a bid to you. I want to get
320 into the Far East market. I
321 want the people out there to
322 learn by experience how good
323 the Claypool locomotive is.
324 There'll be more railroads built
325 in China—a lot more. I'm out
326 to win that business, even if at
327 first I only break even."

328 "But," said Mr. Krohn,
329 "you'd like to make money—a
330 lot of money—out of this pres-
331 ent deal—now wouldn't you?"

332 "Does a cat like cream?"

333 "There's cream in this, Mr.
334 Claypool."

335 "Show me!"

336 "Your bid was four million
337 dollars, wasn't it?"

338 "Yes."

339 "Suppose you could deliver
340 those engines to us at a cost to
341 you of, say, three million?"

342 "No chance," said Martin
343 Claypool. "I can't cut the price
344 of labor and material."

345 "No," said Mr. Krohn, closely
346 watching his face, "but you can
347 change the kind of labor and the
348 kind of material." Martin Clay-
349 pool frowned. "Of course," said
350 Mr. Krohn hurriedly, "I don't
351 wish to suggest——"

352 "I get you," said Martin
353 Claypool. "You mean I could
354 cheapen the quality of the Clay-

355 pool locomotive. That's it,
356 isn't it?"

357 "Well, since you believe in
358 plain speaking—yes." Martin
359 Claypool's frown deepened. "You
360 see," said Mr. Krohn, "I've a
361 plan by which you could make
362 around a million dollars."

363 Martin Claypool ceased to
364 frown. "Let's hear it," he said.

365 "Remember," said Mr. Krohn,
366 "we are dealing with a lot of
367 rich Chinese who know nothing
368 about the practical side of rail-
369 roading. They accept me as an
370 expert. Now listen. If I say the
371 engines you ship me are O. K.,
372 well, they are O. K. and no ques-
373 tions asked."

374 Martin Claypool gestured with
375 his cigar that he got that much
376 and wanted to hear more.

377 "My technical staff is under
378 my thumb," went on Mr. Krohn.
379 "No trouble there. They didn't
380 go to China because they love
381 the country or the work. They
382 went there for the same reason
383 I would or you would—to make
384 money. The Chinese officials
385 won't interfere. There's a pleas-
386 ant custom in China called the
387 squeeze, and the highest man-
388 darins are not above taking a
389 squeeze when they can. They
390 expect us to do the same. It's
391 business ethics out there. When
392 in Rome, you know—eh, Mr.
393 Claypool?"

394 "About that million," said
395 Martin Claypool.

396 "That's up to you," said Mr.

411

397 Krohn. "You make the loco-
398 motives—make them as cheaply
399 as you can—make them so they
400 look right and will run a while.
401 You'll get the contract on the
402 specifications you have sub-
403 mitted. Well, somehow, the set
404 of specifications in my office will
405 get mysteriously lost. The Chi-
406 nese will never know the differ-
407 ence. If the engines don't stand
408 up well, we'll blame it on the
409 climate and on the fact that the
410 native engineers don't know how
411 to treat them. We'll give them
412 the merry devil for abusing the
413 Claypools. Sound scheme,
414 what?"

415 Martin Claypool chewed his
416 cigar. A hard smile came to his
417 face. "A million, eh?" he said.
418 "That's worth thinking about.
419 You and I have something in
420 common, Mr. Krohn. We both
421 play the game for all we can get
422 out of it."

423 "Quite so."

424 "I'm thinking about your
425 proposition. I'm looking at it
426 from a practical point of view.
427 I'm not one of these moon-struck
428 idealists. I'm out for the dough,
429 first, last and all the time; and
430 what's more, I'm honest enough
431 to admit it. These big million-
432 aires can yap about service, but
433 you'll notice they didn't start to
434 yap till they'd served themselves
435 pretty well first. I know these
436 philanthropists. You have to be
437 a hard-headed trader first, and
438 get yours. You can't give away

439 what you haven't got. That's
440 sense, isn't it?"

441 "Right!"

442 "As you point out," went on
443 Martin Claypool, "the Chinese
444 market is different. They half-
445 way expect to be stung. Now
446 the only reason I make the Clay-
447 pool locomotive so well is because
448 I have to if I want to get busi-
449 ness in America. If I can do
450 business in China with an in-
451 ferior article, and clean up—
452 well, why not?"

453 "An eminently sensible point
454 of view," agreed Mr. Krohn
455 warmly.

456 "Now," asked Martin Clay-
457 pool abruptly, "where do you
458 come in?"

459 Mr. Krohn waved his long
460 cigarette delicately. "Thirty per
461 cent of your saving would sat-
462 isfy me," he said.

463 Mr. Claypool's teeth tightened
464 on his cigar. "Twenty per cent
465 seems right to me," he stated.

466 "I run risks," said Mr. Krohn,
467 the temperature of his voice fall-
468 ing many degrees.

469 "So do I."

470 "There are many people I will
471 have to—satisfy," said Mr.
472 Krohn, more coldly.

473 "Twenty per cent," repeated
474 Martin Claypool.

475 "Twenty-five," said Mr.
476 Krohn, his voice touching zero.
477 "Other firms would give more."

478 "Well, then," said Martin
479 Claypool, "call it twenty-five.
480 That means about three-quarters

481 of a million to me. Not so bad."

482 Mr. Krohn thawed. "Not at
483 all bad," he said.

484 "We won't sign anything
485 now," said Martin Claypool.
486 "I'll have to do some figuring
487 and cabling."

488 "I'll be at your service when-
489 ever you are ready," said Mr.
490 Krohn. "The formal contract is
491 waiting for your signature." He
492 bowed low and started for the
493 door.

494 "Mr. Krohn?"

495 "Yes, Mr. Claypool."

496 Martin Claypool's manner
497 held a hint of embarrassment in
498 it. "I'd like to ask you a per-
499 sonal question," he said.

500 "Certainly."

501 "I've been noticing the fit of
502 that coat of yours," said Martin
503 Claypool. "Now I thought I'd
504 stock up on clothes while I'm in
505 London. Could I ask who your
506 tailor is?"

507 "Well"—Mr. Krohn hesitated
508 —"that's a rather delicate ques-
509 tion to ask a Londoner. We
510 guard the secret of our tailor's
511 name as zealously as you, in the
512 States, might the name of a boot-
513 legger who had genuine Scotch.
514 But since it's you, Mr. Claypool,
515 I'll let you in on my secret; and
516 mind you, it's a secret worth
517 knowing."

518 "Thanks."

519 "I get my clothes from an
520 artist," said Mr. Krohn, smooth-
521 ing a flawless coat. "He's a
522 queer old bird with a tiny shop

523 in Albemarle Street. Been a
524 tailor fifty years, and his father
525 and grandfather were tailors be-
526 fore him. He does all the cut-
527 ting and fitting himself; and
528 what beautiful work! He could
529 have built up a huge business,
530 but he keeps to a small clientele
531 so, as he says, he can give every
532 garment his personal attention.
533 Old guild spirit, I suppose you'd
534 call it. His prices——"

535 "They don't matter if he's
536 good," put in Martin Claypool.

537 "He's the best I know about,"
538 said Mr. Krohn. "And, inciden-
539 tally, his prices are not high. He
540 has excellent materials, or you
541 can take your own cloth to him
542 to make up. Now I don't ordi-
543 narily send people to him, but I
544 happen to know that he needs
545 work badly now. He's getting
546 old, you see, and can't produce
547 very fast. He'll be glad to get
548 your order."

549 "I expect to give him a big
550 one," said Martin Claypool—"a
551 complete outfit."

552 "I'll give you a letter of intro-
553 duction to him," said Mr. Krohn.

554 "Lord save us, do I have to
555 have a letter of introduction to
556 a tailor?"

557 "You do to this one," said Mr.
558 Krohn, sitting down at a desk
559 and picking up a pen.

560 "Back home they hound you
561 for business," observed Mr.
562 Claypool.

563 "This old fellow will be a
564 new experience for you then,"

565 said Mr. Krohn, writing. "You
566 can safely leave everything to
567 him. His taste is excellent.
568 Here you are."

569 "Thank you," said Martin
570 Claypool. "J. Tavistock,——
571 Albemarle Street. I'll drop in
572 and see this paragon tomorrow."

573 "You won't regret it," said
574 Mr. Krohn. "Good night."

575 London was having one of its
576 fair days when Mr. Claypool
577 woke next morning. After a
578 regal breakfast of bloaters and
579 other cheering things, he wrote
580 some business letters and then
581 sauntered out. He strolled down
582 the Strand, gazing idly into shop
583 windows.

584 "Bum lot of stuff," he decided.
585 "Not up to Fifth Avenue."

586 He had passed St. Paul's,
587 bound east, when he stopped
588 sharply in front of a shop win-
589 dow—rather, he was stopped.
590 It was a large shop, with a garish
591 new sign which announced that
592 it supplied you with cloth Direct
593 From the Mill at Prices that
594 Will Astound You!

595 Martin Claypool's eyes had
596 been arrested by a piece of tweed
597 on display in the window. Its
598 pattern was the sort calculated
599 to start a runaway, or stop one.
600 The prevailing tone was saffron
601 —a gaudy, bellicose saffron. It
602 had been surveyed and marked
603 off into square lots by lines of a
604 rich, poisonous green. It was as
605 rough and shaggy as the coat of
606 a collie; and, indeed, at a quick

607 glance, it looked somewhat like a
608 collie that had fallen into a kettle
609 of alphabet soup. Small vermi-
610 celli-like excrescences of divers
611 bilious hues leaped out from it to
612 smite and burn the eyes of pas-
613 sers-by. At a distance anyone
614 daring enough to wear a suit of
615 it must inevitably look like a
616 hairy man suffering from acute
617 jaundice complicated by some
618 strange and violent form of
619 measles.

620 It somehow fascinated Martin
621 Claypool. "It certainly would
622 make the boys at the country
623 club sit up and take notice," he
624 said. "A bit loud, maybe; but
625 a man in my position can get
626 away with anything."

627 He went into the shop. The
628 price of the fearsome stuff was,
629 indeed, astoundingly low. Mar-
630 tin Claypool bought enough for
631 a suit. The clerks followed him
632 with their eyes as he went down
633 the Strand with his purchase
634 under his arm, as if they expected
635 to see him arrested for carrying
636 incendiary material in the public
637 streets.

638 He found Albemarle Street
639 after questioning six bobbies.
640 Before his number he stopped
641 uncertainly. It was a plain, neat
642 brick house of two stories, with
643 a small bare shop window. On
644 the door he located a tiny name
645 plate, a venerable brass sign
646 worn by years of polishing, and
647 there in old-fashioned script was
648 the name, J. Tavistock.

⁶⁴⁹ Mr. Claypool knocked and ⁶⁵⁰ waited. Presently a small faded ⁶⁵¹ man with white hair came to the ⁶⁵² door. He did not look at Mar- ⁶⁵³ tin Claypool's face. He looked ⁶⁵⁴ at the lapels of his coat. They ⁶⁵⁵ seemed to sadden him.

⁶⁵⁶ "I've a letter to Mr. Tavis- ⁶⁵⁷ tock," Martin Claypool an- ⁶⁵⁸ nounced.

⁶⁵⁹ "Yes, sir. I'll take it. Step ⁶⁶⁰ in, please." His voice was small ⁶⁶¹ and faded too.

⁶⁶² He conducted Martin Clay- ⁶⁶³ pool into a dim parlorlike room, ⁶⁶⁴ furnished with two chairs and a ⁶⁶⁵ desk. It was all very solemn, ⁶⁶⁶ Mr. Claypool thought.

⁶⁶⁷ "Now, sir?" said the small ⁶⁶⁸ faded man.

⁶⁶⁹ "Are you Tavistock?"

⁶⁷⁰ "Yes, sir." He read the letter. ⁶⁷¹ It brightened him. He bowed ⁶⁷² to Martin Claypool. "Now, ⁶⁷³ sir?" he said again.

⁶⁷⁴ Martin Claypool was enter- ⁶⁷⁵ tained. He was accustomed to a ⁶⁷⁶ more aggressive type of sales- ⁶⁷⁷ manship. "The general idea," ⁶⁷⁸ he said, "as you may gather ⁶⁷⁹ from the letter, is that I came ⁶⁸⁰ here to have you make me some ⁶⁸¹ clothes."

⁶⁸² "Very good, sir."

⁶⁸³ "I'll want a lot of them," said ⁶⁸⁴ Martin Claypool. "First, some ⁶⁸⁵ business suits—a dozen, any- ⁶⁸⁶ way. Then three or four evening ⁶⁸⁷ suits. Then golf clothes, sport ⁶⁸⁸ clothes, riding habits—you know ⁶⁸⁹ —a complete gentleman's out- ⁶⁹⁰ fit."

⁶⁹¹ "I'll do my best for you, sir," ⁶⁹² said the tailor. "Will you step ⁶⁹³ this way, please?"

⁶⁹⁴ He conducted Martin Clay- ⁶⁹⁵ pool to a back room, larger than ⁶⁹⁶ the front one and a bit brighter. ⁶⁹⁷ It was furnished with a long mir- ⁶⁹⁸ ror; that was all. The tailor ⁶⁹⁹ stood for some minutes, his ⁷⁰⁰ white head cocked on one side, ⁷⁰¹ studying Martin Claypool's im- ⁷⁰² pressive proportions with a pen- ⁷⁰³ sive pale-blue eye. Then from ⁷⁰⁴ drawers he took little books of ⁷⁰⁵ cloth.

⁷⁰⁶ "For lounge suits for you, sir, ⁷⁰⁷ I'd advise this and this and ⁷⁰⁸ this," he said, indicating sam- ⁷⁰⁹ ples. "Now this blue would be ⁷¹⁰ good, and I rather fancy this ⁷¹¹ brown herringbone and this gray ⁷¹² flannel for your type."

⁷¹³ "A bit quiet, aren't they?" ⁷¹⁴ remarked Martin Claypool.

⁷¹⁵ "They are on the quiet side, ⁷¹⁶ sir," said Tavistock. "But a ⁷¹⁷ big man like you, sir, should ⁷¹⁸ favor the conservative patterns. ⁷¹⁹ Now here's a splendid suiting— ⁷²⁰ this nut brown—to go with your ⁷²¹ complexion."

⁷²² "You're the doctor," laughed ⁷²³ Martin Claypool. "Guess I'd ⁷²⁴ better leave it to you, eh?"

⁷²⁵ Tavistock nodded. "Yes, sir." ⁷²⁶ He did a lot of minute measur- ⁷²⁷ ing. "I'll start to work at once, ⁷²⁸ sir," he promised. "I'm not ⁷²⁹ very—well, rushed at the mo- ⁷³⁰ ment, you see."

⁷³¹ "Now about the prices," ⁷³² began Mr. Claypool.

733 "I send out my bills once a
734 year," said Tavistock. "The
735 garments will be sent to you
736 directly they are finished."

737 "Good!" said Martin Clay-
738 pool. He was starting to leave.
739 "Is this your package, sir?"

740 "Well, I almost did forget
741 that. You'll make me up a sport
742 suit from some material I
743 bought?"

744 "If you wish, sir." Martin
745 Claypool unwrapped his new-
746 bought tweed. As it emerged
747 from the paper like some great,
748 hirsute, leprous caterpillar, Mr.
749 Tavistock audibly gasped. "Is
750 this the material, sir?" he asked.
751 His voice shook a trifle.

752 "That's it," said Martin Clay-
753 pool.

754 The tailor backed away from
755 it. He retreated to a corner and
756 looked on the defensive, as if he
757 expected the tweed to spring at
758 him and do him bodily harm.
759 "I—I really think, sir, if you
760 don't mind my saying so, that
761 you wouldn't like this," he
762 faltered.

763 "But I do like it," said Martin
764 Claypool.

765 "I mean, it wouldn't make up
766 very well."

767 "It might be a bit noticeable,"
768 granted Martin Claypool.

769 "Noticeable, sir? Of, yes—
770 yes, indeed. It would positively
771 call attention to you, sir. I
772 really wouldn't like to see you
773 in it."

774 "Well," laughed Martin Clay-
775 pool, "I'm the one who will have
776 to wear it. You need never see
777 me in it. I won't wear it outside
778 the state of Missouri."

779 "I'm sure, sir," said Tavistock
780 gravely, "it would be a serious
781 mistake to wear it anywhere."

782 "I'll take the blame for the
783 error then," said Martin Clay-
784 pool. "Let's see now; I'll want
785 a belted coat and patch pock-
786 ets——"

787 He saw the slight form of the
788 old tailor stiffen. "I'm very
789 sorry, sir," Tavistock said, "but
790 I could not make it for you."

791 "Why not?"

792 The old tailor approached the
793 goods, stretched out a wary and
794 reluctant finger and touched the
795 tweed.

796 "You see, sir," he explained,
797 "it isn't only the pattern that
798 makes it unsuitable; it's the
799 quality of the goods. Why, sir,
800 it's—shoddy!"

801 He said the last word as if it
802 were something almost too
803 terrible to mention.

804 "Oh, it didn't cost much and
805 I don't expect it to last for-
806 ever, you know," said Martin
807 Claypool, feeling somehow net-
808 tled. "Besides, I won't hold
809 you responsible for its wear;
810 only for its cut."

811 Tavistock shook his head.
812 "I'm sorry, sir," he said
813 firmly, "but I just couldn't
814 put my shears into a piece
815 of goods like that. And I
816 certainly could not put my

817 name on a suit made from it."
818 Martin Claypool had attained
819 his position in life by generally
820 getting his own way. He grew
821 more impatient.

822 "Look here," he said, "do
823 you want my order, or don't
824 you?"

825 "Of course I do, sir. To be
826 frank with you, sir, I need the
827 work badly. Times are hard in
828 England now, you know. My
829 business has fallen away to al-
830 most nothing. Now couldn't I
831 show you some real homespuns
832 or tweeds with a good bit of life
833 in them for that sport suit?"

834 Martin Claypool compressed
835 his lips. His jaws set stubborn-
836 ly. His associates knew this was
837 a sign to stop arguing.

838 "No," he said. "I want a
839 suit made of that material."

840 Tavistock sighed and shook
841 his head. "I'm very sorry, sir,"
842 he said. "You'll find tailors in
843 London who will make it up for
844 you. I can't."

845 "Can't, eh?" Martin Claypool
846 snapped. "What do you mean
847 —you can't?"

848 "Mr. Claypool," said Tavis-
849 tock in his faded voice, "I've
850 been a tailor all my life. I
851 haven't grown rich, but I've
852 been proud of my work always.
853 I inherited a tradition from my
854 father, who had it from his. In
855 a hundred years the name Tavis-
856 tock has never been put on a
857 suit of poor fit or poor material.
858 I hope it never will be."

859 "Oh, never mind putting your
860 label in this suit if that's what
861 is worrying you," said Martin
862 Claypool, half amused, half
863 angry. He always tried to win
864 a contest of wills.

865 "That isn't the point, sir,"
866 said the tailor. "You see, sir, if
867 I may say so, I look upon my
868 work as—well, as a sort of art.
869 You wouldn't ask a painter to do
870 a cheap and nasty picture, would
871 you, sir?"

872 "He'd do it if he needed the
873 money," said Martin Claypool.
874 "That's the thing that counts in
875 this world—the old brass. I
876 know the world. I've found
877 that out."

878 "If you'll pardon my saying
879 so, sir," said the old tailor, "I'm
880 a great deal older than you; and
881 I have a notion which may be
882 old-fashioned, but which I have
883 found to be true, and that is that
884 a good name is better than great
885 riches. Good day, sir."

886 The little tailor bowed stiffly.
887 Martin Claypool felt an unrea-
888 soning surge of rage. He
889 surged angrily toward the door.
890 The tailor's voice stopped him:
891 "One minute please, sir."

892 Martin Claypool stopped,
893 turned. "Changed your mind,
894 eh?" he grunted.

895 "No, sir. I merely wanted to
896 ask you to take this away." The
897 tailor pointed at the scrofulous
898 tweed. "I really shouldn't want
899 to have it about my shop, sir."

900 Martin Claypool gathered up

the cloth and stalked out. He was not a man of even temper. He was mad now, mad all through; and yet he was critical enough of his own emotions to realize that his anger was out of all proportion to its cause.

"There are thousands of tailors in London," he growled, as he strode toward his hotel. "I don't need to bother with that old fool. Why should I let him upset me? He's nothing but a stick-in-the-mud, a failure. Him and his art! Cutting out pants an art? Bunk!"

Once in his suite, he flung the tweed on a chair, where it clung like a flat serpent.

"Why should that old fossil of a vest cutter get my goat so?" Martin Claypool demanded of himself. "Better get to work and forget him."

From an elaborate pigskin portfolio he took papers, blue prints, photographs and studied them. "Let's see now——" He wrote down figures. "Suppose now, I substituted. . . . Let's see now—six times nine is fifty-four—— Big saving there. Not so good, of course. Apt to break any time. Good enough for a lot of Chinks though."

He picked up a photograph from the pile in front of him. It was a picture of the newest Claypool locomotive. He ran his eyes over its powerful lines. His eyes stopped at the name plate, set in the side. He could read it, clearly:

CLAYPOOL. Built and Guaranteed by Martin Claypool, Inc.

He got up and walked across the floor and poured himself a glass of water. The piece of tweed tripped him and he kicked it aside. Then he stooped, picked it up, ran his fingers over its surface, held it to the light. He dropped into a chair, still holding the cloth in his hand, and sat there, staring at it. He was thinking now of the first locomotive he had built and of how he felt when he saw it steam past him, and read the name—his name—engraved on the plate in its giant side. He must have sat there, staring, motionless, for an hour. He sprang up suddenly, reached for the telephone.

"Hello, Tavistock! This is Mr. Claypool. . . . Yes, that's right, Claypool. Go ahead with that order of mine. Forget about that sport suit. I've been examining the tweed and I find it isn't up to standard. . . . You're welcome. Good-by."

He called up another number: "Mr. Krohn? This is Martin Claypool. Listen, that deal we discussed last night is off. . . . Yes, all off. I'll take your contract, but I'll fill it with A-1 locomotives, real Claypools, or nothing. . . . Yes, I'll pass up that money. All right, Krohn,

982 you can give the order to a
983 Swede, or a Czech or the devil
984 if you want to. But get this,
985 Krohn—if you ever buy a Clay-
986 pool locomotive you are going to
987 get the real thing. No shoddy.
988 No, sir!"

The Analysis

A glance at the chart will show that his story contains 988 lines. There is in this story no Body scene, because there is no clash of traits shown within the character. The Beginning occupies lines 1 to 963 and the Ending occupies lines 963 to 972 and 973 to 988. The Ending is particularly interesting because it shows *two* Decisive Acts; one in regard to the problem set before Martin Claypool by the tailor, the other the problem set before Martin Claypool by Krohn.

In the Beginning the bulk of the presentation units are interchanges. Lines 1 to 38 is an interchange between Martin Claypool and the waiter, lines 39 to 95 are the fifth step of that interchange and show Claypool's reflections. This is the one weak spot in the Beginning of the story. Here the basic trait which determines the main outcome ought to have been planted and it ought to consist of a pride in the name of Claypool. It could have been brought about by some such device as having him known to the waiter or having him sign his name and having the waiter look awed or extremely respectful because of what is conveyed to him by the name Martin Claypool on the check. Then, this pride in name being emphasized, we would have been prepared later for the Decisive Act of the story.

The interchange between Krohn and Claypool is quite definitely one intended to set forth the possibility of profit for Martin Claypool. The interesting thing about it as a variant from the other stories we have discussed is that Martin Claypool definitely comes to a decision then and there. The fifth step of that scene is the interchange between the two in regard to the name of the tailor, and here again the effect upon Martin Claypool of the mention of his own name could have been emphasized a little more strongly than it is, his pride in his name being an extremely important factor in his character to account for the solution of the story. The interchange which follows, between Claypool and the clerks, in which Claypool buys the loud goods is one in which he is made to be rather proud of his own ability, as Martin Claypool, to carry off any situation, and in this respect it is good, as it prepares the way for the final decisive act. In the interchange between Claypool and the tailor, the fifth step brings about his reflections which come nearer to being a Body scene than anything else, and they project his awareness of the stimulus, which is the photograph of the Claypool locomotive with the name-plate, which brings to his mind, as a perfectly new stimulus, the thought that he is proud of that name.

Then there follow swiftly the two conclusive Acts; one the calling of the tailor on the telephone, the other the calling on the telephone of Krohn.

This story is the last of the series of this type story of Decision. It is illuminating because it shows that it is of the second type of characterization story. In the first type the story interprets character, and it shows that that character is, throughout, the same. In this case, the story shows a development of character. In the first case the characteristics of the actor remain unchanged. The story deals with the manipulation of events by the character, through the exercise of a trait already in his character. In the second case, there is an actual growth of characteristics. Certain traits, not hitherto a part of the actor's character, emerge and determine the outcome. We may see, therefore, already four distinct types of story. One, the Accomplishment story, which requires only that the happenings shall be interesting and highly exciting, but not greatly significant.

Two, the second type Accomplishment story, in which the moment in life shall be both interesting and exciting, but shall in addition, have a certain significance of characterization. This is the type of the Mary Brecht Pulver and of the John Marquand stories, in which the outcome is brought about through the accomplishment of an actor who evidences in that accomplishment a certain definite and individual trait of character, or a capacity not inherent in anybody who might be confronted with that problem.

The third type is the Decision story in which the great moment of the story is one in which there is a conflict of emotions, and the basic character trait emerges.

Then there comes this fourth type, which Mr. Connell has presented, in which the character becomes aware of a new stimulus, and there is presented to the readers an evidence of certain traits in his character not hitherto known to the reader, and it is through the exercise of those new characteristics that he solves the problem of conduct facing him. We often hear statements to the effect that the American short-story is not as important or poignant as the Continental short-story. The chief evidence upon which such critics base their comparison is that the American short-story so often has a happy ending and the Continental short-story so frequently has an unhappy ending. The critics say that the American short-story goes deep into the life. They make the distinction between "realism" and "romance" which in a final analysis is no distinction at all. As a matter of fact the Continental short-stories do not go very deep, for the simple reason that they take a single great moment and show how a character reacted at that moment. When they so render the responses of a character they say that their rendering is true to life. They fail to realize that readers cannot actually know the character of any person from a single reaction at a single great moment. Writers and critics tell you that a certain reaction of a character at a single great moment is true to life because "it actually happened." In adducing such evidence they fall into the error of confusing accuracy with truth to life. Accuracy is simply the exact rendering of a fact. Truth goes beyond accuracy and presents as sincerely as possible the relationship of one fact to all other facts within the limitations laid down by the artistic purpose of the teller of the story.

The isolated fact that a certain character, at a great moment of his or her life, found his purpose achieved, or on the other hand found his purpose frustrated, may be accurate; but it is not essentially true to life. Therefore, to say that accomplishment, which is a happy ending, and frustration, which is an unhappy ending, are opposed as representing truth and untruth is not at all a fair conclusion. One single instance of either accomplishment or frustration is not a real test of character. To show the conduct of a person at a given moment is not so important as to show the characteristic of the person that dictated his conduct. Conduct is merely a surface indication of character, and like all surface indications, is likely to be misleading.

The critics who make this distinction between American and Continental stories have failed to realize that usually American stories which they say do not go deep, are stories which deal with accomplishment, whereas the stories which really go beyond accomplishment or "wish fulfilment" into the depths of character, are stories which deal with a real test of character when a choice has to be made between an opportunity to profit and a standard of conduct. The important short-story in America is that which is important anywhere. It is the short-story which deals not with Accomplishment as material, but with Decision. As the most important moment in a short-story is one of decision, so it is in any form of fiction, whether that be play or novel or short-story or moving picture. The moment when a character has to choose is what is known in the movies as the "big moment" of the story. The decision is between a possibility of achievement and has opposed to it frustration; but the frustration is brought about through a generous act of abnegation on the part of the character, and not through the stepping in of fate as in the Continental short-story. Therein lies the essential difference between the American and the Continental attitude toward life. There may be in this country frustration; but it is frustration which is brought about by a character's actions or by some basic trait under his control. The characters are not regarded as supine puppets moved about by fate. There is, however, in our newer knowledge of psychology, a justification for feeling that a character can act only in a certain way, and that at great moments only basic traits determine conduct. It is for that reason that I am including in this volume the next two stories, as companion stories, *The Roads We Take*, by O. Henry, and *The Mummy*, by John Galsworthy.

ARCHITECTURAL CHART

OF

THE ROADS WE TAKE

BEGINNING	{ Main Actor's necessity for choice is presented.	Series of Incidents, setting forth condition.	1–110	Readers' interest captured by unusualness of happenings.
		Interchange. Effect upon Bob Tidball and Shark Dodson.	111–252	Choices apparent.
ENDING	{ Decisive Act.	Shark Dodson shoots Bob Tidball.	253–265	Choice made. Answer to Narrative Question is clear.
	Sequel.	Dodson rides away on Bolivar.	266–270	Cupidity triumphs.
BEGINNING	{ Necessity for choice presented.	Interchange. Dodson and Peabody, showing choices apparent.	271–318	Choice is required.
ENDING	{ Decisive Act.	Shark Dodson insists upon settlement.	319–328	Answer is clear. Cupidity triumphs

THE ROADS WE TAKE

BY O. HENRY

THERE is great scope for conjecture in wondering how successful O. Henry might have been in this modern age with our newer knowledge of the pyschological laws of character superimposed upon his capacity for observation and his talent in presentation.

O. Henry was especially interested in a philosophy of character which John Galsworthy has since summed up very succinctly by saying that "Behind conduct lies the main trend of character." By this he meant that the basic trait of a person's character determines that person's responses to the great moments of life.

Very early in his career O. Henry wrote a story called *Roads of Destiny*, in which he showed that when a boy came to three forks in a road the outcome was the same. Showing his progress along each successive road, O. Henry caused him in all three cases to be shot by a bullet from the same pistol. This story was a groping toward this theory of predetermination, with the exception that, here, Fate determined the outcome.

In the stories which I am including under what I call the "basic trait" category, *The Roads We Take* and *The Mummy*, it is not an outside Fate, but a basic trait of character in the main actor which determines the outcome. As an example of this type of story, *The Roads We Take* will be very informative, especially in comparison with *The Mummy*.

CASE No. 18

THE ROADS WE TAKE

BY O. HENRY

1 Twenty miles west of Tucson
2 the "Sunset Express" stopped at
3 a tank to take on water. Be-
4 sides the aqueous addition the
5 engine of that famous flyer
6 acquired some other things that
7 were not good for it.

8 While the fireman was lower-
9 ing the feeding hose, Bob Tid-
10 ball, "Shark" Dodson, and a
11 quarter-bred Creek Indian called
12 John Big Dog climbed on the
13 engine and showed the engineer
14 three round orifices in pieces of
15 ordnance that they carried.
16 These orifices so impressed the
17 engineer with their possibilities
18 that he raised both hands in a
19 gesture such as accompanies the
20 ejaculation "Do tell!"

21 At the crisp command of
22 Shark Dodson, who was leader
23 of the attacking force, the
24 engineer descended to the
25 ground and uncoupled the engine
26 and tender. Then John Big
27 Dog, perched upon the coal,
28 sportively held two guns upon
29 the engine driver and the fire-
30 man, and suggested that they
31 run the engine fifty yards
32 away and there await further
32 orders.

33 Shark Dodson and Bob Tid-
34 ball, scorning to put such low-
35 grade ore as the passengers
36 through the mill, struck out
37 for the rich pocket of the express
38 car. They found the messenger
39 serene in the belief that the
40 "Sunset Express" was taking on
41 nothing more stimulating and
42 dangerous than aqua pura.
43 While Bob was knocking this
44 idea out of his head with the
45 butt-end of his six-shooter Shark
46 Dodson was already dosing the
47 express-car with dynamite.

48 The safe exploded to the tune
49 of $30,000, all gold and currency.
50 The passengers thrust their heads
51 casually out of the windows to
52 look for the thundercloud. The
53 conductor jerked at the bell
54 rope, which sagged down loose
55 and unresisting, at his tug.
56 Shark Dodson and Bob Tidball,
57 with their booty in a stout
58 canvas bag, tumbled out of the
59 express car and ran awkwardly

427

60 in their high-heeled boots to
61 the engine.

62 The engineer, sullenly angry
63 but wise, ran the engine, accord-
64 ing to orders, rapidly away from
65 the inert train. But before this
66 was accomplished the express
67 messenger, recovered from Bob
68 Tidball's persuader to neutrality,
69 jumped out of his car with a
70 Winchester rifle and took a
71 trick in the game. Mr. John
72 Big Dog, sitting on the coal
73 tender, unwittingly made a
74 wrong lead by giving an imita-
75 tion of a target, and the mes-
76 senger trumped him. With a
77 ball exactly between his shoulder
78 blades the Creek chevalier of
79 industry rolled off to the ground,
80 thus increasing the share of his
81 comrades in the loot by one-
82 sixth each.

83 Two miles from the tank
84 the engineer was ordered to
85 stop.

86 The robbers waved a defiant
87 adieu and plunged down the
88 steep slope into the thick woods
89 that lines the track. Five
90 minutes of crashing through a
91 thicket of chaparral brought
92 them to open woods, where the
93 three horses were tied to low-
94 hanging branches. One was
95 waiting for John Big Dog, who
96 would never ride by night or
97 day again. This animal the
98 robbers divested of saddle and
99 bridle and set free. They
100 mounted the other two with the
101 bag across one pommel and

102 rode fast and with discretion
103 through the forest and up a
104 primeval, lonely gorge. Here
105 the animal that bore Bob Tidball
106 slipped on a mossy boulder and
107 broke a foreleg. They shot him
108 through the head at once and
109 sat down to hold a council of
110 flight.

111 Made secure for the present
112 by the tortuous trail they had
113 traveled, the question of time
114 was no longer so big. Many
115 miles and hours lay between
116 them and the spryest posse that
117 could follow. Shark Dodson's
118 horse, with trailing rope and
119 dropped bridle, panted and
120 cropped thankfully of the grass
121 along the stream in the gorge.
122 Bob Tidball opened the sack,
123 and drew out double handfuls
124 of the neat packages of currency
125 and the one sack of gold and
126 chuckled with the glee of a child.

127 "Say, you old double-decked
128 pirate," he called joyfully to
129 Dodson, "you said we could do
130 it—you got a head for financing
131 that knocks the horns off of any-
132 thing in Arizona."

133 "What are we going to do
134 about a hoss for you, Bob?
135 We ain't got long to wait here.
136 They'll be on our trail before
137 daylight in the mornin'."

138 "Oh, I guess that cayuse of
139 yourn'll carry double for a
140 while," answered the sanguine
141 Bob. "We'll annex the first
142 animal we come across. By
143 jingoes, we made a haul, didn't

we? Accordin' to the marks on this money there's $30,000—$15,000 apiece!"

"It's short of what I expected, said Shark Dodson, kicking softly at the packages with the toe of his boot. And then he looked pensively at the wet sides of his tired horse.

"Old Bolivar's mighty nigh played out," he said slowly. "I wish that sorrel of yours hadn't got hurt.

"So do I," said Bob, heartily, "but it can't be helped. Bolivar's got plenty of bottom—he'll get us both far enough to get fresh mounts. Dang it, Shark, I can't help thinkin' how funny it is that an Easterner like you can come out here and give us Western fellows cards and spades in the desperado business. What part of the East was you from anyway?"

"New York State," said Shark Dodson, sitting down on a boulder and chewing a twig. "I was born on a farm in Ulster County. I ran away from home when I was seventeen. It was an accident my comin' West. I was walkin' along the road with my clothes in a bundle, makin' for New York City. I had an idea of goin' there and makin' lots of money. I always felt like I could do it. I came to a place one even' where the road forked and I didn't know which fork to take. I studied about it for half an hour and then I took the left-hand. That night I run into the camp of a Wild West show that was travelin' among the little towns, and I went West with it. I've often wondered if I wouldn't have turned out different if I'd took the other road."

"Oh, I reckon you'd have ended up about the same," said Bob Tidball, cheerfully philosophical. "It ain't the roads we take; it's what's inside of us that makes us turn out the way we do."

Shark Dodson got up and leaned against a tree.

"I'd a good deal rather that sorrel of yourn hadn't hurt himself, Bob," he said again, almost pathetically.

"Same here," agreed Bob; "he sure was a first-rate kind of a crowbait. But Bolivar, he'll pull us through all right. Reckon we'd better be movin' on, hadn't we, Shark? I'll bag the boodle ag'in and we'll hit the trail for higher timber."

Bob Tidball replaced the spoil in the bag and tied the mouth of it tightly with a cord. When he looked up the most prominent object that he saw was the muzzle of Shark Dodson's .45 held upon him without a waver.

"Stop your funnin'," said Bob, with a grin. "We got to be hittin' the breeze."

"Set still," said Shark. "You ain't goin' to hit no breeze, Bob.

227 I hate to tell you, but there
228 ain't any chance for but one of
229 us. Bolivar, he's plenty tired,
230 and he can't carry double."

231 "We been pards, me and you,
232 Shark Dodson, for three years,"
233 Bob said quietly, "We've risked
234 our lives together time and
235 again. I've always give you a
236 square deal, and I thought you
237 was a man. I've heard some
238 queer stories about you shootin'
239 one or two men in a peculiar
240 way, but I never believed 'em.
241 Now if you're havin' a little
242 fun with me, Shark, put your
243 gun up, and we'll get on Bolivar
244 and vamoose. If you mean to
245 shoot—shoot, you black-hearted
246 son of a tarantula!"

247 Shark Dodson's face bore a
248 deeply sorrowful look.

249 "You don't know how bad I
250 feel," he sighed, "about that
251 sorrel of yourn breakin' his leg,
252 Bob."

253 The expression on Dodson's
254 face changed in an instant to
255 one of cold ferocity mingled with
256 inexorable cupidity. The soul
257 of the man showed itself for a
258 moment like an evil face in the
259 window of a reputable house.

260 Truly Bob Tidball was never
261 to "hit the breeze" again. The
262 deadly .45 of the false friend
263 cracked and filled the gorge with
264 a roar that the walls hurled back
265 with indignant echoes.

266 And Bolivar, unconscious ac-
267 complice, swiftly bore away the
268 last of the holders-up of the

"Sunset Express," not put to the 269
stress of carrying "double." 270

But as Shark Dodson galloped 271
away the woods seemed to fade 272
from his view; the revolver in 273
his right hand turned to the 274
curved arm of a mahogany 275
chair; his saddle was strangely 276
upholstered, and he opened his 277
eyes and saw his feet, not in 278
stirrups, but resting quietly on 279
the edge of a quartered-oak desk. 280

I am telling you that Dodson, 281
of the firm of Dodson & Decker, 282
Wall Street brokers, opened his 283
eyes. Peabody, the confidential 284
clerk, was standing by his chair, 285
hesitating to speak. There was 286
a confused hum of wheels below, 287
and the sedative buzz of an 288
electric fan. 289

"Ahem! Peabody," said Dod- 290
son, blinking. "I must have 291
fallen asleep. I had a most 292
remarkable dream. What is it, 293
Peabody?" 294

"Mr. Williams, sir, of Tracy & 295
Williams, is outside. He has 296
come to settle his deal in X. Y. Z. 297
The market caught him short, 298
sir, if you remember." 299

"Yes, I remember. What is 300
X. Y. Z. quoted at to-day, 301
Peabody?" 302

"One eighty-five sir." 303

"Then that's his price." 304

"Excuse me," said Peabody, 305
rather nervously, "for speaking 306
of it, but I've been talking to 307
Williams. He's an old friend of 308
yours, Mr. Dodson, and you 309
practically have a corner in X. 310

311 Y. Z. I thought you might—
312 that is, I thought you might
313 not remember that he sold you
314 the stock at 98. If he settles at
315 the market price it will take
316 every cent he has in the world
317 and his home too to deliver the
318 shares."
319 The expression on Dodson's
320 face changed in an instant to
321 one of cold ferocity mingled
322 with inexorable cupidity. The
323 soul of the man showed itself
324 like an evil face in the window
325 of a reputable house.
326 "He will settle at one eighty-
327 five," said Dodson. "Bolivar
328 cannot carry double."

The Analysis

One of the characteristics of the story of Decision is that it almost always forces the writer to open with a series of incidents presenting the main condition confronting the actor. The chart of this story will show that it is made up of practically parallel stories; one the story of Shark, Dodson and Bob Tidball, the other the story of Dodson and Peabody. The complete story occupies 328 lines, of which the first 111 lines are occupied with setting forth the incidents which portray the main condition. Then the fifth step of this awareness of the actor is an interchange between Tidball and Shark Dodson at the close of which the two choices are apparent; one, of abandoning his partner, the other, of assisting him. The Ending occupies lines 253 to 270 and shows a Decisive Act, lines 253 to 265, in which he shoots his partner, and the Sequel (266–270) which is that he rides away on Bolivar. And here we have cupidity as the character trait which is triumphant.

Now, we notice when we come to the parallel story that there are no series of incidents setting forth the conditions, but that they are set forth in an interchange. This is because they have already been set forth in the opening part of the story. This interchange is between Dodson and Peabody, and it shows the choices which he may make. Again the Decisive Act follows swiftly, and shows that he insists upon settlement, and that cupidity is again triumphant. This is what I should call a transitional story in the development of the character or choice story which is based upon the assumption that "behind conduct lies the main trend of character." It is a companion story to the one which follows:—*The Mummy*, by John Galsworthy.

431

THE MUMMY

	Main Problem Presented.	Meeting. Eugene Daunt at 66 finds himself facing death.	Main Narrative Question is: "What course will he take?" 1– 50
		(Flash-back Beginning shows previous choices in similar circumstances—a development of the type of parallel character decisions, of which *The Roads We Take* is an example.)	
BEGINNING	A series of parallel meetings or interchanges at the close of which the Main Actor is faced by a problem of conduct similar to the Main Problem of conduct confronting him.	Interchange. Eugene and Mollie. At 28 he finds that he must make effort or marry Mollie.	His effort takes form of going on yachting 51–232 cruise. (a game)
		Interchange. Eugene and Mollie. At 38 he finds that he must make effort or elope with Mollie.	His effort takes form of going to Boer War. (a long day's 233–391 hunting)
		Meeting. Eugene, at 49 becomes aware of curtailed income.	His effort consists of playing billiards sys-392–417 tematically. (a game)
		Interchange. Eugene, at 54, and recruiting officers.	Effort takes form of stalking innocuous 418–484 persons.
		Meeting. Eugene, at 57, and condition of poverty.	Effort takes form of 485–519 making bets.
		Interchange with Mollie. He must make effort or accept her proposal.	Turns again to play-520–590 ing billiards.
		Meeting. Eugene and condition of shakiness.	Turns to raising 591–705 dogs.
		(End of flash-back.)	
ENDING	Conclusive Act.	Eugene, at 66, is finally down and out Throwing contest.	Answer to Narrative Question: He meets great crises as he has hitherto met minor crises. He avoids effort by 706–836 turning to some form of sport.

THE MUMMY

BY JOHN GALSWORTHY

THIS story is included because it shows the "basic trait" type of story at its highest point of development. The quality of the "basic trait" type of story that distinguishes it from other types is that it is a series of parallel scenes tied together by character traits. At the end of each scene there is a struggle of character traits; and always the same type trait is triumphant. It is what the older school of teachers used to call the "dominant trait."

The immediately distinguishing feature of this story as opposed to the O. Henry story is that this story is a real "flash-back" decision story. It opens with the moment when the character has to act. There is no evasion or delay possible. This urgency is an essential quality of interest in the good story of Decision.

The obvious disadvantage of opening at such a moment of urgency is that in the ordinary story of Decision the Conclusive Act comes immediately after the moment when the character becomes aware of the urgency. Such a story would be extremely short. The only way in which length can be added to such a story is to make a "flash-back" between the moment of urgency and the moment of Decision.

Because this story shows the method of presenting such a "flash-back," I am extremely anxious that every reader shall examine it with the greatest care.

433

CASE No. 19

THE MUMMY

BY JOHN GALSWORTHY

In the end shelter of that Devon watering-place Eugene Daunt had been sitting for two days and nights. At sixty-three, and with his lack of adipose, any but the southwest wind in late October must have "sewn him up" long before. He sat, huddled in his worn blue overcoat with belt tight-drawn, peaked golfing cap over his eyes, and his skinny brown hands deep-thrust into his pockets, dozing or staring before him.

This end shelter was out of range of lamplight, and few passed it even in the daytime. For these reasons he had chosen it. He had ceased to wonder how much longer he could "stick it." His nodding thoughts were free from the tortures of effort. The cards were hopelessly against him, and he just wanted to be let alone. Nothing so definite as suicide was in his drowsing mind. Suicide meant effort, and he had always avoided effort, except in the playing of games. He played this last game—conserving the ebbing vitality of his body, ribby as a greyhound's. Neither was he bitter, sitting there. Natural that the "Johnnies" of whom he had borrowed scantily these last five years should be "fed up." He would have been "fed up" himself. Natural that his old landlady should have come to him crying—"poor old soul"; a wonder she hadn't, long ago! He had shifted two watering-places down to the coast, to sit it out where he was not known. On his lean brown face lurked a sort of grin. He looked a little like a Red Indian; had there ever been one who needed their stoicism more — or needed it less?

Only child of an Indian civilian, Eugene Daunt had been born in India, and taken home at the age of five. While at a private school he lost both parents, killed in an accident, and fell under the protection of his father's sister, an unmarried lady who lived at Baymouth, and

435

60 doted on him. He remained at
61 this private school till he was
62 fourteen. He was given to dys-
63 pepsia, and apt at games, good-
64 looking, assured, stoical; he won
65 races, made scores, had indiges-
66 tion whenever there was an
67 examination. It was thought
68 that he would go into the army
69 or the diplomatic service. On
70 leaving school, however, he was
71 such a comfort to his aunt, and
72 it was so difficult to find a tutor
73 who did not give him instant
74 dyspepsia, that he was found
75 suddenly too old to go in for
76 either. His aunt rejoiced; she
77 would have missed him too
78 much, and he was now perma-
79 nently free for the sports, handi-
80 caps, drives, and matches of the
81 neighborhood, whence he could
82 bring home those cups, cigarette
83 cases, and other rewards of
84 which she was so proud. She
85 had a verandaed house called
86 Eglamont, in a pleasant garden.
87 Eugene had his own rooms and
88 key, his spirits and tobacco, his
89 fox terrier and spaniel, a day's
90 hunting when he wished; he shot
91 well, and was welcome with his
92 gun, to the landed neighbors; or
93 on the local yachts where he
94 looked to the life in a yachting
95 cap. He had no patrimony, but
96 his aunt had enough for two. A
97 singularly placid woman she
98 concerned herself entirely with
99 seeing that time made no changes
100 in the life of him on whom she
101 doted. No girls, however much

102 he impressed them, lean in his
103 very good clothes, detached him
104 from her roof. It was less dan-
105 gerous to prefer, platonically at
106 least, the society of barmaids and
107 married women. So the years
108 passed by him, embalmed in her
109 affection, in sport, and cigar-
110 ettes; till at the age of twenty-
111 eight, he fell in love with the
112 wife of a naval commander with
113 whom he yachted and played
114 billiards. She was a gray-eyed
115 young woman, with great good
116 humor, and an admirable figure.
117 They had leased a house within
118 a stone's throw of "Eglamont"
119 before the naval commander re-
120 tired to the China station for
121 two years. Not, indeed, till
122 after his departure was Eugene
123 aware of his feelings. Loyal to
124 one with whom he had played
125 games, he took himself in hand
126 at once, and would sit gloomily
127 pulling his fox terrier's ears and
128 smoking cigarette after cigarette,
129 sooner than go and see her. In
130 1890 the phrase "playing the
131 game" had not as yet come in,
132 and he was confined to fortifica-
133 tion by the term "not sporting."
134 The young woman, however,
135 whose name was Mollie, had
136 Venetian red hair; and he was
137 startled one morning by her ap-
138 pearance with a letter in her
139 hand. She had come to read
140 him a message from her husband.
141 After that it seemed natural that
142 she should often come. The
143 effort of saying: "Look here, you

144 know, you mustn't; I'm gone on
145 you," exhausted his defenses;
146 nor was it easy to remember a
147 man who, after all, was too old
148 for her, and would not be back
149 for two years. They remained,
150 however, on platonic terms, part-
151 ly because of their loyalty to the
152 absent commander, and partly
153 because he was not accustomed
154 to any form of energy outside
155 sport. So he would sit in his
156 long chair, a cigarette between
157 the yellow-stained fingers of one
158 hand, and his fox terrier's ear
159 between his yellow-stained fin-
160 gers of the other hand, staring
161 at her and casting out between
162 his filed-looking teeth, his short
163 laughs and answers to her rally-
164 ing talk. So it might have gone
165 on for the two years, if her hair,
166 one evening, had not been too
167 much for Plato.
168 Eugene woke up next morning
169 genuinely shocked—he had not
170 been "sporting." And yet, it
171 was impossible to resist her. For
172 a fortnight the affair proceeded,
173 till one morning she arrived with
174 a telegram in her hand, and on
175 her face an expression remorse-
176 ful, elated, tearful, glad. The
177 commander had died on a boat
178 expedition up a Chinese river.
179 The news was three weeks old.
180 "Gene," she said, "isn't it
181 awful, and isn't it—isn't it won-
182 derful, in a way! After all, we—
183 we haven't committed—and we
184 can—we can be—" She
185 stopped; his face was copper-

colored. He stammered out: 186
"Poor Bink! Poor old chap!" 187
She went away dreadfully up- 188
set. Next day he had violent 189
dyspepsia. 190
During the following weeks of 191
seclusion under his aunt's care, 192
he had time to see the matter in 193
all its bearings; it had become 194
evident to him that he was on 195
the edge of being married. It 196
would need inertia almost 197
amounting to effort to avoid that 198
fate. Had he enough? Think- 199
ing of her hair, he felt a sinking 200
in that part of him nourished 201
just then solely on Benger's 202
food. In the third week it came 203
to him by inspiration that he 204
knew a "Johnny" about to start 205
on a six weeks' yachting cruise. 206
That evening, eluding his aunt, 207
he made his way to the "Lion's 208
Tail" and over a game of bil- 209
liards proposed to the "Johnny" 210
and was accepted. That night 211
he was free from pain for the first 212
time. 213
Leaning over the side in the 214
sun, on his friend's yacht, a week 215
later, he felt a kind of regretful 216
deliverance. He wrote from 217
Fowey:— 218

"Dear Mollie, 219
"I have been very seedy, but 220
am feeling as right as rain again. 221
This is a nice little hooker. We 222
shall be hanging about in her 223
most of the summer. The 224
weather is jolly, at present. I 225
hope you are fit. It was a 226

227 shock to me to hear about poor
228 old Bink. Poor old chap! What
229 awful luck!

230   "With the best,
231   "Yours ever,
232   "Gene."

233   He did not return to Bay-
234 mouth till October. He hardly
235 knew whether to be glad or sorry
236 that she had left. A letter in-
237 formed him that she could not
238 live on her "moldy pension" and
239 had started a milliner's shop.
240 He admired her pluck, her ener-
241 gy. She sent her love and hoped
242 that his "poor tummy" was
243 stronger. She mentioned thea-
244 tres—she was evidently having
245 quite a good time. Just one
246 sentence began: "Gene, don't
247 you ever——" It had been
248 crossed through. He felt that
249 she had "sand."
250   He settled down to the
251 sports of the season; and time
252 passed like a game that is
253 played.
254   He was thirty-eight, a little
255 more dried, with a gray hair or
256 two, when she came down to
257 Baymouth again with her second
258 husband, an old sportsman of
259 fifty with any amount of brass,
260 and a dicky chest. He was no
261 end glad to see her, looking "so
262 jolly fit" with her hair as red as
263 ever. "The old sportsman"
264 played quite a good game of
265 bridge—just then coming in.
266 They resumed their relations
267 quietly under his nose. She had

268 never stopped loving him all this
269 time, she said. He was touched
270 and flattered, and would sit in
271 his long chair with a cigarette
272 between the yellow-stained fin-
273 gers of one hand, and the ear of
274 his spaniel between the yellow-
275 stained fingers of the other hand,
276 staring up at her, and emitting
277 his rather high cackles, while she
278 laughed lovingly at his taci-
279 turnity.
280   The Boer War began—he had
281 thought "those Johnnies" could-
282 n't ride or shoot "for nuts"; he
283 became surprised. It got on his
284 mind a good deal. In December
285 he noticed a great change in
286 Mollie; she grew excitable. And
287 then one day, clinging to him,
288 she said it couldn't go on, they
289 would have to "kick over"; she
290 couldn't bear that old man any
291 more. Gene must take her away
292 —he must! Divorce and all, it
293 wouldn't take a year until they
294 could be married. Extremely
295 copper-colored, he smoothed her.
296 "Easy on!" he muttered.
297 "You're off color, old girl.
298 What's the matter with the old
299 sportsman? He seems a harm-
300 less sort of old Johnny."
301   She flung off his hand. Oh!
302 yes; what did he know—what
303 did he care? He had no blood in
304 him! She was altogether unjust.
305 He told her not to be a little
306 juggins. She clung to him—she
307 called him a "mummy." He
308 said: "If you don't shut up,
309 I'll spank you!" She raved at

310 him. Couldn't he see—couldn't
311 he feel—she was only thirty-
312 three—to be taken away from
313 Gene—to be tied to that old
314 man—with his—and his—and
315 his——!

316 He smoothed her again; told
317 her to go "steady over the
318 stones!" They were very well
319 off as they were.

320 "Yes," she said suddenly,
321 "but he suspects."

322 "Oh!" he said, and sat down
323 in his long chair. He had seen,
324 suddenly, an effort before him.
325 He had a pain in his diaphragm.
326 He lighted a cigarette. His
327 teeth at that moment looked
328 very filed.

329 The effort before him took
330 shape in the watches of the
331 second night. Enlist! After all,
332 what would it be? Only, as it
333 were, a long day's hunting, the
334 exertion of it nothing compared
335 with that of running away with
336 Mollie to an ultimate marriage.
337 He had four days' severe dys-
338 pepsia—then took an early train
339 to Exeter, and joined the Im-
340 perial Yeomanry. They wanted
341 fellows of his stamp who could
342 ride and shoot. His aunt was
343 horrified; it seemed to her the
344 end of the world. He rallied
345 her. It would be a "picnic."
346 She admired his patriotism.
347 They wanted him at once, he
348 said. He left without having
349 again seen his young and ardent
350 woman. He wrote to her from
351 Plymouth, on his way out:—

352 "Dear Mollie,

353 "I was awfully sorry not to
354 see you to say good-by. The
355 Johnnies in my troop ride pretty
356 well, but they can't shoot for
357 nuts. We're all as keen as mus-
358 tard to give these Boer jokers a
359 knock. I hope you'll have a
360 good winter, and get some hunt-
361 ing. I shall think of you riding
362 the chestnut. Well—so-long,
363 Mollie.

364 "Yours with the best,
365 "Gene."

366 He rather enjoyed the cam-
367 paign, and developed a talent
368 for stalking. He had drilled
369 three of those "jokers" when he
370 himself received a bullet through
371 the calf. While in hospital he
372 developed enteric, and when
373 convalescent was discharged and
374 invalided home. Leaner and
375 browner than ever, he lay in a
376 long chair with a cigarette in his
377 yellow fingers, staring at some
378 conversationalist of the female
379 sex with his steel-colored eyes,
380 and occasionally emitting a little
381 high laugh. He felt "full of
382 steam," and enjoyed the voyage
383 "like smoke."

384 "Well, Aunt Susan," he said
385 on reaching Baymouth. His
386 aunt shed tears of rapture. He
387 renewed his life as if it had never
388 been broken. The young woman
389 and her husband were no longer
390 there. And ten more years
391 passed like a game that is played.

392 He was forty-nine when his

393 Aunt Susan died. It upset him; 394 she was a "good old soul." 395 "That old josser," her lawyer, 396 worried him awfully about busi- 397 ness. She seemed to have been 398 living on her capital. All he 399 would have would be the pro- 400 ceeds of the house. It was sold 401 under his feet. He and his fox 402 terrier were compelled to move 403 out. They moved to lodgings 404 close to the "Lion's Tail." He 405 experienced almost at once the 406 lack of Aunt Susan; he had to 407 think of money. It was "an 408 awful bore." His billiards and 409 bridge became systematic. He 410 could no longer afford to hunt 411 unless a friend mounted him. 412 Still, he got along—there were 413 few evenings when he did not 414 make his five to ten shillings 415 over the green baize—large and 416 small. And five years passed 417 as a game that is played.

418 He was fifty-four when the 419 Great War broke out. It roused 420 him as nothing had ever roused 421 him yet. Those German "jos- 422 sers" wanted a good hiding. 423 Sitting in his long chair with a 424 cigarette between the yellow fin- 425 gers of one hand and his cocker 426 spaniel's ear between the yellow 427 fingers of the other, he nerved 428 himself for an effort. Two or 429 three months passed in the pro- 430 cess, then he journeyed up to 431 London, and presented himself 432 at the headquarters of an Offi- 433 cers' Training Corps. He asked 434 for a commission on the strength

of his service in the Boer War. 435 They were sorry—they wanted 436 men of his stamp, but he was 437 too old for a commission. He 438 persisted that he could ride and 439 shoot. They looked at him, and 440 somebody remarked: "Yes, but 441 can you think?" 442

He went very copper-colored, 443 looked at them deeply, and left 444 the room. If those "poopsticks" 445 thought they were going to win 446 the war by thinking—! He 447 traveled back to Baymouth, and 448 enrolled himself as special con- 449 stable. It was his duty to 450 guard a culvert. He did it sit- 451 ting on a shooting-stick, with a 452 cigarette between the yellow fin- 453 gers of one hand, and the yellow 454 fingers of the other hand playing 455 with the ears of his cocker 456 spaniel. 457

Think! He had plenty of 458 time to think, out there week in, 459 week out, in various weather. 460 He would listen to the dripping 461 stillness, or the soughing of the 462 wind in the neighboring spinney, 463 and wish that one of those "Hun 464 Johnnybirds" would appear and 465 give him sport. Now and again 466 he stalked some innocuous per- 467 son who came near his culvert; 468 but there was never anything 469 "really doing." In sheer bore- 470 dom he took to thinking about 471 how to improve his income. 472 What little he had could easily be 473 doubled, he was sure, by any 474 "juggins who knew the ropes." 475 He set himself to know them, by 476

477 reading newspapers. And three
478 years passed as a game that is
479 played. During those years he
480 doubled his income—on paper—
481 but owing to circumstances that
482 no juggins could have foreseen,
483 he was receiving less of it than
484 before he began to increase it.
485 He was literally compelled to
486 seek for a paid job. They gave
487 him something in connection
488 with a hospital. In 1919 the
489 hospital was closed; the war
490 being over, there was nothing
491 for anybody to do, and his in-
492 come was now just half the
493 insufficient amount it had been
494 before he increased it. In fact,
495 it was about a pound a week;
496 and prices double what they had
497 been. He shot his dog Quiz—
498 —"poor old chap;" sold his gun,
499 and changed to a back bedroom
500 in a by-street, where he could
501 sit in what sun there was, and
502 settle down to live on "fags" and
503 billiards. "Bet you a lunch"
504 was his formula, varied by "Bet
505 you fifty cigarettes"—he seldom
506 lost. His clothes were still those
507 he had worn in the days of
508 Aunt Susan, pressed under his
509 heavy leather trunk, and only
510 put on when he went out to the
511 "Lion's Tail" at noon. The
512 mornings he spent in an old blue
513 dressing-gown, smoking cigar-
514 ette after cigarette, and conning
515 some derelict paper picked up
516 in the bar. He never pitied him-
517 self, but he would now and again
518 go copper-colored, thinking of

519 his income and the newspapers.
520 On the parade, in the spring
521 of 1921, a lady sat down beside
522 him. He recognized her at once
523 —his old flame Mollie, and
524 "pretty long in the tooth," too!
525 He made no sign of recognition—
526 he hadn't forgotten her calling
527 him a "mummy" last time he
528 had seen her, and that his clothes
529 were not what they had been.
530 But suddenly she turned and
531 said: "Why, it's Gene! So
532 you're still here!" It seemed to
533 him odd. Where else should he
534 be? And how was he? She her-
535 self hadn't been at Baymouth
536 since. She was a widow again.
537 "Oh, and aren't we old! Why
538 you're quite white, Gene; and so
539 should I be, if I didn't——"
540 He grinned. Old Mollie had
541 always been a "sport."
542 "And to think you nearly
543 knocked me out twice, Gene!"
544 She looked him over slowly:
545 "Poor old Gene, you look rather
546 'on your uppers'!"
547 He became copper-colored,
548 showed his filed teeth, and said:
549 "What damned cheek! You
550 always were a cheeky kid!"
551 Something came into her eyes
552 —a sort of light.
553 "You must come and dine
554 with me, Gene. I'm at the
555 Courtfield."
556 He answered stiffly: "Thanks."
557 He still had an old dress suit,
558 and one white shirt with cuffs
559 intact. In the next few days he
560 used it several times. She could

441

561 never elicit from him where he
562 lived. He just grinned, or
563 emitted his high laugh. He
564 began to perceive that she had
565 "tumbled to" his one dress shirt,
566 and pitied him. He did not like
567 it. One evening after dinner,
568 while he was sitting in a long
569 chair with a cigarette in the
570 yellow fingers of one hand and
571 the other hand dangling to the
572 floor, she proposed to him. He
573 grinned and called her "a little
574 juggins." Next day he was
575 down with a severe attack of
576 dyspepsia. There was some-
577 thing disgusting to him in her
578 wanting at her age to marry
579 him out of pity. If she thought
580 he was "such a tail-down
581 Johnny," she was jolly well mis-
582 taken. For a fortnight he stayed
583 in his room, reading old *Pink
584 'Uns*, and living on Benger's and
585 cigarettes. Only when he had
586 none left did he emerge. To
587 his relief, she was gone. He had
588 seldom played billiards better
589 than in the week that followed.
590 Then a real disaster befell him.
591 His hands suddenly began to
592 shake—he couldn't play "for
593 nuts." It meant that he must
594 live on a pound a week. He
595 began to sit stiller than ever,
596 thinking of what he could do.
597 "Bear-leading some young cub"
598 —something in a riding school;
599 he even thought of wheeling a
600 bath chair, of billiard-marking,
601 of clerking to a bookmaker. But
602 all such occupations would neces-

603 sitate his leaving Baymouth; he
604 was too well known. The exer-
605 tion of such uprooting was be-
606 yond him. Besides, he had no
607 interest anywhere else, and for
608 such careers interest was neces-
609 sary. In a sort of coma, time
610 went by. Five shillings bor-
611 rowed here and there, "tick"
612 with his old landlady—"poor old
613 soul;" the sale of little odd bits of
614 salvage from Aunt Susan's days,
615 eked out his existence for the
616 next six months. And then he
617 plunged. A "josser" of his ac-
618 quaintance who bred dogs was
619 going out of business. Selling
620 out his one remaining stock of
621 value, he bought it. With the
622 paid help of a "joker" out of a
623 job, he put up extra kennels. It
624 was the most definite work he
625 had ever done. In memory of
626 his shot spaniel, Quiz—"poor old
627 chap!"—he bred cockers. For
628 over a year nearly everything
629 went well—he spent most of his
630 capital, and had three large lit-
631 ters of pedigree pups. He passed
632 hours among the "little beg-
633 gars," a cigarette between his
634 lips, his yellow fingers crump-
635 ling their ears or feeling their
636 points, while their little avid
637 tongues licked all of him within
638 reach. They were a great pleas-
639 ure to him, not the less so for
640 their promise of ten pounds
641 apiece, and twenty pounds if
642 over distemper. He debated
643 whether to have them inoculated
644 and sell them with a guarantee.

Nature took the matter out of his hands before he had made the effort of decision. The violent distemper of that season came down like a wolf on his pups; all but two died. "The poor little black beggars!" For the first time since he went to school he almost shed tears. He had sat up with them night after night, had buried them one after the other. It was "rotten luck." When the holocaust was over he was compelled to sell the kennel, lock, stock, and barrel, to pay the bills he had run up. He had fifty pounds left. The efforts of that past year and its final disaster had produced in him a perfect fatalism. For fourteen months he lived on the fifty pounds, his watch, his family seal, the remains of his wardrobe. He never mentioned his condition, and would sit whole afternoons on the high seat in the billiard room of the "Lion's Tail," watching the game being played, and thinking: "They can't play for nuts." What people thought of him sitting there, lean and white-haired, with his drawn copper-colored face and thirsting eyes, with his grin, and his well-cut clothes shiny from age, he neither knew nor cared. He had to sit somewhere. And here he got cigarettes, and once in a way a drink was offered him. His friends he had exhausted; he had borrowed from them and was never able to repay; his acquaintances began to shun him for fear that he would borrow. He was "down and out."

One morning his landlady, "poor old soul," came to him crying. She owed money. He couldn't—she supposed—pay her just a little? He called her an "old juggins," and told her to buck up. That afternoon he put his toothbrush, shaving brush and razor in the pocket of his old blue overcoat, sold his old bowler and his spare shirt for seven-and-six, bought two hundred fags and a ticket down the coast. The "poor old soul" would be able to let his room, at least.

In the shelter, huddled into the corner out of the increasing wind, he passed his shaking hand over the bone and skin of his face, then diving it into his pocket, brought out a paper packet. Still ten cigarettes, but he felt too sick and empty to smoke them. If the sun would come out, he would get into it and have a sleep. He was "fed up." Some "jokers" in his place would make for a workhouse, or take a brick and heave it through a window, get "quodded" and fed. Not much! Easier, more dignified, to sit on, here. If only the sun would come out and warm him! These "dam-cold" nights his heart was giving him "beans." He thought with a grin of his Aunt Susan—the "old girl" would have a fit if she could

729 see him; so would "old Mollie,"
730 or his landlady, "poor old soul!"
731 He shivered, so that his teeth
732 rattled. People would notice
733 him. He would get under the lee
734 side of a fishing boat till it was
735 dark. He stood up with diffi-
736 culty, and began to move slowly
737 toward the beach. With hands
738 deep thrust into his pockets, he
739 tried to look like any other
740 "Johnny" crossing that little
741 space. He sat down exhausted
742 between two boats. An "old
743 josser" was looking down at him
744 from the parade; he took up a
745 pebble, and with a shaking hand
746 threw it at a log of driftwood
747 ten yards or so away. Nobody
748 would notice a chap throwing
749 pebbles. He threw them at
750 long intervals. His hand shook
751 so that he could not aim—could
752 not hit "the darned thing." It
753 angered him. Who would bet
754 him he didn't hit it five times
755 out of fifty? He groped slowly
756 for the pebbles, amassed a little
757 heap, and counted fifty. Yes,
758 he would hit "the darned thing"
759 five times in fifty. He began.
760 He missed his first sixteen shots,
761 then hit the log twice running,
762 and, taking out a cigarette, he
763 rested. He smoked slowly—he
764 was two pebbles up. The sun
765 had come out, and shone full
766 on him over the edge of the old
767 boat. He turned his face to it;
768 then taking up a pebble, began
769 again. His hand shook worse
770 than ever; he missed eleven

771 times, then "got it plumb cen-
772 ter." Three hits in thirty shots
773 —just up to his points. Again
774 he took a cigarette and rested.
775 Two hits to make in twenty
776 shots—odd if he couldn't win
777 that bet! Time was when he
778 would have hit that "joker"
779 every time. His cigarette went
780 out. He leaned against the boat,
781 and closed his eyes. Cold sweat
782 oozed from him; things sank
783 around him. He rested, half-
784 conscious; came to again, and
785 saw the log with the sun on it.
786 He groped up a pebble, and
787 feebly flung it. A hit—by
788 George! The devil would be in
789 it now if he couldn't make the
790 other in nineteen shots. On his
791 face, bony and copper-colored in
792 the sinking sunlight, a grin was
793 fixed. He flung and flung. Miss
794 after miss after miss—thirteen
795 running! "Curse! Couldn't
796 throw for nuts! Get the damned
797 thing or bust!" Miss after miss
798 after miss. Three more pebbles!
799 He paused.

800 The setting sun still shone;
801 a sea-gull with brightened wings
802 was passing within gunshot. As
803 a boy he remembered he had
804 shot a sea-gull—before he had
805 learned to be a sportsman.
806 Three more shots. He was
807 tempted to get up and lob them.
808 But could he get up? Besides,
809 he must "play the game" with
810 the darned old log! He had once
811 claimed a ball "out" at tennis,
812 when he knew that it was in.

813 It was the sort of thing one
814 didn't like remembering. He
815 raised his arm. Look at it
816 shaking—how could a Johnny
817 throw with an arm like that?
818 The pebble flew wide. Two
819 more! He remembered a "beak"
820 at his private school who used
821 to bowl round-arm. Nobody
822 had bowled round-arm for forty
823 years and more. Give it a
824 chance! He swung his trem-
825 bling arm three times in prac-
826 tice, then took up the last pebble
827 but one. Now for it! His
828 whole body swung with his arm.
829 Whump! A faint exultant
830 whoop came from his lips. A
831 stab went through his breast-
832 bones—it "hurt like steam!" He
833 fell back, collapsed under the
834 tarry boat, still as a mummy.
835 . . . And so next day they
836 found him.

The Analysis

Had this story been told chronologically, it would merely have
been a narration of happenings in the life of a character; and
instead of being a short-story it would have been a narrative of
character. So arranged, it would have opened on line 51, and
going through to line 705, it would have picked up the story at line 1
and then gone on to line 50, resuming again at line 706 and through
to the last line 836.

On the page following the reprint of the story there is the usual
chart of the story showing the arrangement of the Flash-back
Beginning. The following chart will show how the Flash-back was
accomplished.

Chronological	Flash-back
Lines 51–705. Events from boyhood to 66.	Lines 1–50 form main situation.
Eugene Daunt at 66 is finally down and out. Lines 1–50.	Lines 51–705. Events from boyhood to 66.
He turns to throwing contest; meets great crisis. Lines 706–836.	Lines 706–836 form Ending.

The flash-back in this type story is accomplished by writing the
final scene, and then splitting it in two, putting one half of it at the
opening of the story to make the main narrative situation, and
putting the other half of it at the end to make the Conclusive Act.

445

Thus, the answer to the first scene's question is also the answer to the main narrative question of the story. The Flash-back Beginning then occupies the intervening space, and this Flash-back Beginning is entirely a series of interchanges at the conclusion of which a basic trait emerges; and just as in the O. Henry story cupidity emerged as a basic trait, here turning from effort to the playing of a game emerges as the basic trait of Eugene Daunt. The story opens at a moment when there seems to be no possibility of evading the issue by turning to the playing of a game. Then, in the flash-back showing him at the age of twenty-eight, he meets the condition there confronting him by going on a yachting cruise which is the equivalent of playing a game. At the next crisis he goes to the Boer War, which to him is "a long day's hunting." Next, at the age of forty-nine, he turns to the playing of billiards. At the age of fifty-four he, when he is rebuffed, turns to stalking innocuous persons at the culvert. At the age of fifty-seven he meets the condition by making bets. In 1921 he again turns to billiards, and when his hands become shaky he turns to raising dogs; and finally he meets the basic condition by a throwing contest, and thus as always he meets the issue by evading it and turning to the playing of a game instead of making an effort.

Before closing our consideration of the special type of Decision or Choice story of which *The Mummy* is such an excellent example, let us examine Mr. Galsworthy's structural handling of the scenes within the portion of the story which is the Flash-back for Explanatory Matter of the Beginning. We will find that the first four steps of the different scenes almost always occur. There are exceptions, of course. Sometimes two steps are closely merged; sometimes the order varies; occasionally one is omitted; the proportion of space taken up will vary. But these exceptions are undoubtedly the result of the author's definite choice. The purpose of these different Cases in Craftsmanship is to point out to aspiring authors the use which established craftsmen have made of their knowledge of such simple steps. If, thereafter, the aspiring author chooses to ignore them, he will do so consciously, rather than through ignorance.

It is from a close study of the use which Mr. Galsworthy makes of the fifth steps in each of his presentation units that those interested in craftsmanship will gain most. This fifth step is employed always to show the effect of the happenings making up the presentation unit upon the chief actor. It has other functions, of course; but this is the one which is our special concern just now. *The*

Mummy is a story of character, as opposed to a story of action. The purpose is to show the character of the chief actor rather than to hold interest by exciting clashes in the interchanges. In the story of action the fifth step would be employed to show that the actor's chief purpose in the story had been strengthened or weakened by the happenings making up the presentation unit immediately preceding it. In the story of action, or as it is sometimes called the story of "incident," the interchange is all-important. In the story of "character" the interchange is important only as it leads into a condition where the basic trait of the chief actor clashes with some other trait, and emerges triumphant. It is not necessary to show the clash of traits in this fifth step; it is only necessary that the basic trait shall emerge.

You will see the difference between the scenes in the two types of story—the Accomplishment story, and the Decision story,—if you will turn to the scene in *Once and Always*, by John P. Marquand, where Gideon Higsbee attempts to persuade Lemuel Gower to accept his check. That scene takes 309 lines to present its four steps. (Lines 927 to 1235.)

Now if you will turn again to *The Mummy* to the scene where Eugene Daunt, at fifty-four, applies for a commission on the strength of his service in the Boer War, you will see that the four steps occupy only 28 lines. (Lines 418 to 445.) The important unit is not the first four steps, as in *Once and Always*, but the fifth step, which shows that Eugene Daunt has turned to the nearest approximation of sport which he can devise, the stalking of innocuous persons near the culvert he is guarding.

This fifth step occurs in all the types of stories. In the story of Accomplishment it dwells especially upon crises of Hindrance or Furtherance, and by so doing knits together the presentation units into a plot.

In the story of Decision or Choice it dwells especially upon the choices to be made by the actor, and here again, gives to the story its unity as a whole.

In that special type of Decision Story which is occupied with a series of decisions involving the Basic Trait of an actor it ties together the presentation units.

My reason for dwelling at such length upon this fifth step at the close of scenes, is that it must be kept clearly in mind for a comprehension of the two stories which are to conclude this collection of Cases in Craftsmanship.

These two stories are interesting variants of the story of Decision.

ARCHITECTURAL CHART

OF

RICH MAN—POOR MAN

BEGINNING	Main condition set forth.	Scene. Jay and Marianne. Jay, a wealthy man, learns that his wife, Marianne, has been having an affair with another man. He upbraids her, saying it was all brought about by her love for perfume and gold color.	1–186	Scene. Jake and Mary Smith. Jake, a common laborer, learns that his wife has been having an affair with another man. He upbraids her, saying it was all brought about by her love for perfume and the color, yellow.	1–399
ENDING	Conclusive Act.	He leaves her, declaring:— "Had I been a poor man, a common laborer, this could never have happened to us."	187–195	He turns his wife out, declaring:— "This wouldn't 'a happened, if I'd only been a rich guy."	399–405

(These parallel stories are linked together by the ironic significance of the similarity of their happenings, and the conclusions drawn by the two men from those happenings.)

RICH MAN—POOR MAN

BY MELANIE KOLL

I HAVE chosen this story, together with its companion story, *Claire and the Dangerous Man*, because it presents an interesting variant of the Decision Story. In all the other Decision stories which I have included in this volume, the Decision has been that of a single person. The presentation units in the O. Henry story, *The Roads We Take*, and in the Galsworthy story, *The Mummy*, were tied together and unified by the same trait in the main actor. They consisted of parallel scenes given a central unity by a basic trait. This story is especially interesting because it presents parallel scenes, each of which shows an actor responding to a condition by making a choice. In this case, however, there are two people who make choices. For each there is a single great moment; but the same condition confronts each one, and the parallelism extends to a similarity in the decision made. Besides this there is an additional parallelism, in that the ironic significance of their similarity is that each actor draws from the happenings an exactly opposite significance. Whereas the two stories which we have just examined were composed of parallel scenes tied together by basic character traits, here we find that the pattern is parallel scenes tied together by ironic significance.

CASE No. 20

RICH MAN—POOR MAN

BY MELANIE KOLL

In the long oval mirror of her dressing-table Marianne watched the ivory-paneled door quietly open and give place to the tall, slender man now framed in the doorway. He came into the room, the black and white of his sharply etched dinner clothes the solitary contrasting note in the dainty feminine boudoir of ivory and gold.

"I knocked twice. Perhaps you didn't hear?"

Marianne breathed more easily. His voice was cool and crisp as always. Perhaps, then, he hadn't learned. . . . That cat of a Doris—the little beast, to phone her, Marianne, under the guise of friendship, to warn her that Jay had learned of that wild, mad—

"I should like ten minutes of your time."

Her eyelids narrowed—*that* voice didn't sound quite so casual. But she twisted up the corners of her mouth in a smile. She must be charming, lovely—

"Of course, dear." Did she fancy it, or had he winced, ever so slightly, at that last word. "I've plenty of time. Really, so much time to kill, always, that it's getting to be harder and harder to find ways to do it." She laughed ruefully. "I play such rotten bridge—have such beastly luck. Only, one must do as the others do, or just simply cease to be. You know what I mean." A silence followed; then she rattled on: "I'm dining at the Delavans' tonight, but I've plenty of time. Quite all ready for dinner, except my gown." She indicated a wickedly shimmering thing, lying there like a great golden serpent. "Isn't that a dream? Such a perfectly exquisite duck of a dream! It's just come. Madame Louise says it's quite the smartest gold-lace dinner-gown she's ever created." Playing for time, praying for time, she ran on, her mind darting now this way, now that, striving to recall each tiny telltale bit. "I'll ring for Celeste and tell

451

her not to come back for ten minutes—"

"I've already told her."

"So good of you." Her voice drawling, lazy, indolent, her eyes sharp, keen, alert. "Eleanor's just gone. We had such a nice hour over the teacups. Eleanor's just returned from China, and she brought me some of the most perfectly marvelous tea. I do adore good tea—with plenty of rum drops in it. Since she left, I've been idling away a half-hour trying out some new perfumes. A Frenchwoman's come out with an article in one of the magazines, about matching up one's perfumes to one's moods." She half smiled, as if at some mysterious, tantalizing recollection, as she turned to the row of gold-topped crystal bottles, fingering them lovingly. "You know how I adore perfumes, don't you? I'm horribly extravagant—"

"I didn't come here to talk perfumes."

She turned quickly, a tall, lovely figure, in her golden draperies. "Of course not. Why, you don't even like them, do you?" Stupid of her to have forgotten that. She bit her lip, vexedly. It was Alfred who liked them—not Jay. "But you've not even admired my gown. Gold lace doesn't come under the ban of your disapproval also, does it?"

That maddening, provoking little pout of hers—funny how it used to make his pulses beat faster, faster. Now it left him quite cold. "I wonder why you love gold color so?" he asked curiously. "This room, all gold and ivory, that gown there, your negligée—" He pointed to the exquisite clinging thing she wore so gracefully. "Is it because gold color is so like—gold—and gold means wealth, power, luxury?"

"Why, Jay!" Her tone was sweet, pained, surprised. "What a horrid thing to say—even if you don't really mean it!"

He nodded impatiently. Heavens, couldn't she understand that he was scarcely in the mood to say anything he didn't mean—tonight. "I stopped at the club on my way home this evening."

"Yes?" Hard to keep her voice quite steady now.

"I went there, to meet a man on business. While I was there, I heard—"

"A lot of gossip, didn't you? You men scorn women for gossiping, but when it comes to scandalmongers, give me a crowd of women any time, in preference to you club men."

"Drop it. This is between you and me, Marianne. No use generalizing, discussing male *versus* female. This is just—us. You see, I—I learned of the whole rotten mess there. No use arguing, Marianne. I don't

144 wish to hear any more of the
145 details. I—"

146 "But, Jay, you don't under-
147 stand—"

148 "A trifle too well, I'm afraid!"
149 —wearily.

150 "You were away—so much—"
151 Why, her voice was pleading
152 now. How—how—queer! "And
153 while I was away, slaving to
154 give you—things—jewels, furs,
155 cars, the place in the country,
156 *perfumes*, all this—you—you
157 were lonely."

158 "Oh, I was, I was."

159 "Till you met Alfred—and
160 then— Yet you wouldn't have
161 a child—why, you shrank from
162 the very thought of bearing one.
163 If you hadn't, then you'd have
164 had no empty idle hours to fling
165 away to—Alfred. No,"—as she
166 started to speak,—"let me fin-
167 ish. You wanted luxury, and I
168 gave it to you—on a great golden
169 platter. You never wanted me
170 for myself, just for what I could
171 give you."

172 "You said you loved me,
172 Jay."

173 That tricky little lilt in her
174 voice that had always played
175 the devil with him, made him
176 weaken, heretofore! But the
177 time for that was over—well
178 over. "We'll not discuss that
179 now, if you please."

180 "But why—"

181 "Get the divorce on any
182 grounds you please. I'm leaving
183 here—going to live at the club.
184 Simpson will pack my things."

"Jay, Jay, you're going with- 185
out a regret, aren't you?" 186

He turned and gave her a long 187
look. "My dear Marianne," he 188
said, more gently than he had 189
yet spoken, "I am leaving, with 190
one *big* regret—that I happen 191
to be a wealthy man. Had I 192
been a poor one,—a common 193
laborer,—this could never have 194
happened to us." 195

"Whew!" said Mary Smith, to 196
her neighbor Mrs. O'Keefe. 197
"Them onions is something 198
fierce on the eyes, ain't it the 199
truth?" 200

Mrs. O'Keefe, watching Mary 201
slice endless onions into the fry- 202
ing-pan, nodded majestically. 203
"They sure air that," she agreed. 204
"Say, Mary, if I was you, darlin', 205
I wouldn't run around so much 206
with that no-account Al—" 207

"Now, Mrs. O'Keefe, I can 208
look out fer myself, I can. I—" 209
She stopped abruptly, as a 210
man slouched into the room. 211
Tall he was, and thin—his face 212
red with the perspiration beading 213
it, his shock of black hair awry. 214

"Evenin', Mrs. O'Keefe." He 216
nodded to her indifferently. 217
Then, curtly: "Say, I wanta 218
talk to Mary alone." 219

"Sure, I was joost goin', any- 220
how. I only joost dropped in to 221
have a dish o' tea." 222

"Then come some other day 223
an' have it, Mrs. O'Keefe." 224

"We've ahlready had it, bless 225
you—and foine tea it was, too— 226

227 some noo Chiny tea they give
228 away now, wid ivery dollar's
229 worth of groceries at McNulty's
230 store. Well, Mary darlin', I'll
231 be on me way. Me own stew's
232 on the stove, and I'd best be
233 lookin' after it, or 'tis burned
234 'twill be, and himself swearin'
235 mad, to be eatin' it burned,
236 more's the pity."

237 As the door creakingly closed
238 after her, Mary turned to her
239 husband, a little frown of dis-
240 approval wrinkling her white
241 forehead. "Jake, ain'tcha got no
242 manners at all, that you'd ask
243 Mrs. O'Keefe to be leavin' like
244 that," she reproached him, face,
245 neck, arms, glistening with beads
246 of moisture as she stood over
247 the blazing stove.

248 "See here, Mary, I ain't come
249 home today to be perlite nor to
250 talk to Mrs. O'Keefe. I come
251 home to—"

252 "Well, whatever it is, make
253 yerself comf'table while ye're
254 doin' it. Set, why don'tcha?"
255 She ran past him on her way to
256 the door, out of the kitchen into
257 the bedroom and back again,
258 while he filled a thick glass with
259 water from the faucet, gulped it
260 down and wiped his mouth with
261 the back of his hand. When
262 Mary returned, he was still
263 standing there, a puzzled, un-
264 certain look on his none too
265 clean countenance.

266 "Why don'tcha set, Jake?"

267 He made a wry face—sniffed
268 the air. Then he brought a

clenched hand down heavily on 269
the table beside him. "Thet 270
damn' smell again!" 271

"I know. It's them onions." 272
She nodded sympathetically. 273
"Somethin' fierce, ain't it?" 274

" 'Tain't them onions, an' well 275
you know it. It's thet damn' 276
perfumery you been wastin' 277
money on again." 278

"Now, Jake!" The pout in 279
her voice, like that in a little 280
child's. 281

"You know how I hate that 282
stuff." 283

"But, Jake, I only put it on, 284
to take off that there onion smell. 285
Sure I like perfume—I'm crazy 286
about it, but I wouldn't use it, 287
when you don't like it, except 288
only fer them onions. Honest, 289
Jake." 290

"Honest, nothin'," he snarled. 291
"You're a fine one to use thet 292
word '*honest*', ain't you, now? 293
You, thet ain't got a honest bone 294
in yer whole lyin' body." 295

She stiffened at that, and a 296
look of fear crept into her gray 297
eyes. But she spoke coolly 298
enough. "Say, look out! Who 299
you think ye're talkin' to, any- 300
ways, Jake? I ain't standin' fer 301
no—" 302

"Ye're standin' fer whatever 303
I want you should stand fer, see? 304
'Cause I got the goods on you— 305
get thet? I dropped in at Mike 306
Casey's fer a drink, comin' home 307
—an' I heard—" 308

"What do I care what you 309
heard? Talk about women's 310

311 gossipin'. Men is twicet as bad.
312 What do I care fer any rotten
313 gossip they told you?''
314 "You'll care all right, before
315 I'm through. You—you—"
316 The muscles of his face worked
317 strangely.
318 "What's eatin' you, Jake?
319 Spit it out, fer heaven's sake."
320 "Ye're yella, you are. Sure
321 you are. Thet's why you was
322 always wantin' yella walls in
323 here, wearin' yella dresses—even
324 got a yella apern on now!"
325 He glared furiously at the inno-
326 cent yellow gingham. "You
327 betcher sweet life, yella's yer
328 color all right, all right."
329 Her chin went up defiantly.
330 "Sure, I like yellow, sure I do.
331 I love it. For why? 'Cause it's
332 all happy—like the sunshine—it
333 ain't a mean, cold color—it's
334 happy—happy—like I wanta be.
335 I always feel good when I'm
336 wearin' yellow—it's a happy
337 color."
338 "Yeh? Well, you ain't gonna
339 feel so happy, when I get through
340 with what I'm tellin' you," he
341 sneered. "I just heard all about
342 you an' Al—"
343 "What you hear?" She nobly
344 feigned a nonchalance she was
345 far from feeling.
346 "Heard o' yer carryin's-on, I
347 did. Heard o' yer goin' round
348 with thet dancin' skunk, while
349 I been slavin' like a dog to give
350 you all the stuff you keep hol-
351 lerin' fer—like thet damn' per-
352 fume!" he growled.

353 "Jake, I get so lonely here."
354 She strove to keep the sobs out
355 of her shaking voice. "When
356 I'm through with my work—an'
357 there ain't so much work, even,
358 to fill up my time, what with
359 only two of us to do fer—"
360 "Well, why's it only two?
361 You never wanted a kid." His
362 tone was surly.
363 She flared up then. "Don't
364 you dare shoot lies like that at
365 me, Jake. You know it's a lie!
366 I'm crazy to have kids, lots of
367 'em, only I ain't ganna have 'em
368 till I can bring 'em up decent an'
369 proper, an' you ain't never made
370 enough money fer that. When
371 you do, why—"
372 He threw back his head and
373 gave an ugly laugh. "When I
374 do, hey? Well, get this—an' get
375 it right: When I do, you ain't
376 gonna have no share in my pile,
377 see? You ain't gonna have no
378 kids o' mine to spend it on, see?
379 For why? 'Cause I'm quittin' you
380 flat—now—right here. Maybe
381 I ain't got such a swell name,
382 like yer friend Al Carter.
383 I got a plain name, Smith, Jake
384 Smith; but anyhow, it's always
385 been a clean name, an' no fe-
386 male's gonna dirty it up, see?
387 No one's gonna have the right
388 to throw mud on it, neither, get
389 me? I said I was quittin' you,
390 didn't I? Well by God, I ain't!
391 After them pretty little stories
392 I heard about you an' him,
393 you're the one what's gettin' out
394 o' here—not me! You kin go to

455

395 yer mother's, any place—an' I'll
396 send yer clothes after you.
397 Only"—his face worked convul-
398 sively as he spat the words at
399 her: "Only—get the hell out o'
400 here—an' hurry!" He stood
401 there, tense, taut, as the door
402 slammed shut, upon Mary's exit.
403 "This wouldn't 'a' happened,
404 if I'd only been a rich guy," he
405 muttered bitterly.

The Analysis

A reading of this story will show very quickly that here there is a story dependent not upon its reality but upon its cleverness for the thrill of pleasure which the reader receives from it. It is a refinement of craftsmanship. It is a story which calls forth the same sort of applause that is called forth by the expert magician or juggler in the vaudeville show. Professional golfers who make pitch shots of thirty or forty yards and always land the ball in a bucket cause us the same glow of respectful admiration—and envy. The formula is simple. A condition confronts an actor, requiring decision. He makes a decision. Parallel with this is another actor confronted by a similar, almost identical condition. The "kick" comes from the ironic resemblance of the two decisions.

I remember once hearing about a very distinguished old English General who had a great reputation as a bon vivant. He professed to be able to identify any drink by taste. He made a large wager that in the course of an hour his hosts could not bring him any beverage which he could not identify blindfolded. He was blindfolded, and one after another he identified Burgundy, Moselle, Champagne, Rye Whiskey, Scotch Whiskey, Ale, Stout, Beer and many others. At last his hosts brought him water. He sipped doubtfully; again more doubtfully. Then he put down the glass, saying, "Gentlemen, I have lost my wager. I cannot identify this beverage; but I venture to say, whatever it is, it will never be popular."

I feel much the same way about this type of story. I can identify it; but I venture to say that it will never be popular. Its interest is in its unusualness. It is rather too rich fare for general and continued consumption in large quantities. But as an excursion from the tried and trodden paths of the stories of Decision involving a single person it is an interesting and instructive variant.

BEGINNING

Skeletonized interchanges. Bahmer and Ruth set forth the condition. 1-134

George Bahmer is confronted with a condition calling upon him to make a decision. **BEGINNING**

(5th step. Interchange. Ruth and Claire. Ruth aware of a new sort of life.) 135-272

Reader becomes aware of the factors involved in the choice to be made.

Bahmer and Ruth. Interchange. 273-313

Interchange. Claire and Bahmer. (Gibson present.) 374-543

Interchange. Bahmer and Claire. He attempts to establish friendly footing. 544-609 Rebuffed.

Interchange. Another try. 610-831 Rebuffed.

Interchange. Bahmer and Claire. Re Bright Treasure. 832-904 Claire less cautious.

Claire is confronted with a condition calling upon her to make a decision. **BEGINNING**

Meeting. Bahmer responds to new atmosphere as did Ruth Wilson. 905-974 Claire off guard.

Interchange. Bahmer and Claire. After party. 975-1084 Forgiven after rebuff.

Interchange. Bahmer and Claire. He declares love. 1085-1874 Need for choice is apparent.

Claire makes reservations. 1875-1932 She cuts off affair. Conclusive Act.

Effect upon Actors. "George Bahmer had been merely a minor incident in a busy life." (Line 1988-1990.) Sequel. 1933-1990

ENDING

Bahmer delivers final dismissal. 314-317 Narrative Question Answered: "He will cut off affair." Decisive Act.

Effect of interchanges upon actors. "Ruth had been only an incident." 318-373 Sequel.

371-373 Significance.

ENDING

458

CLAIRE AND THE DANGEROUS MAN

BY FANNIE KILBOURNE

BECAUSE it is such an interesting example of the type of Parallel Decision Story; and because its author's consummate craftsmanship gives it the breath of life and reality I am including *Claire and the Dangerous Man*. Unlike the story *Rich Man—Poor Man*, it does not depend for its success exclusively upon the ironic significance of the fifth step of the parallel decisions. This ironic significance, tying together the Decisive Acts of Claire and of George Bahmer, is additional value given by the author. The difference between the two stories is that in one there were parallel *scenes*, while in the other there are parallel *stories*.

CASE No. 21

CLAIRE AND THE DANGEROUS MAN

BY FANNIE KILBOURNE

Sooner or later Claire was sure to meet George Bahmer. Every young New York business woman meets some George Bahmer —the out-of-town man who comes to New York once or twice or half a dozen times a year on business; who buys tickets for the musical shows at speculator prices; who goes to the revues and the night clubs, usually with some girl only a little older than his daughter, whom he tells, of course, that his wife doesn't understand him.

Claire knew all about George Bahmer before she met him. Or, if not all, enough, at least, so that she might have been on her guard. She knew, of course, that he came from Chicago, that he was traveling representative —and a very successful one— for the huge tannery that supplied most of the leather for Gibson shoes, that he and D. E. Gibson worked together, hand in glove, to their mutual profit and satisfaction. As the still fairly new advertising manager for Gibson shoes, Claire knew this. As a young woman, she knew also that George Bahmer was, so far as young women were concerned, a dangerous man.

And it was to the obviously nice girls that Bahmer was the most truly dangerous. This, despite the fact that he knew a nice girl when he saw one, and behaved toward her accordingly. The others, of course—the soft-cheeked, pearled and furred little ladies who bought their forty-five-dollar slippers at Gibson's— concealed the nerve and guileful acumen of a slick confidence man behind a perfumed smoke screen of wide eyes and sweet, cooing voices. A prosperous Chicago man was an opportunity, never a menace, to these luxurious Persian kittens.

But of what George Bahmer could do to a nice girl, and how, all unintentionally, he could do it, Claire had already learned. Little Ruth Wilson, for instance, one of the youngest of the

Gibson stenographers, a downy chick just hatched out of business college, as truly naïve as a three-year-old, clapping chubby hands at the pretty lights. She wore gun-metal chiffon stockings and powdered heavily over the honest pink of her cheeks and reddened her lips and stiffened her eye-lashes with mascaro in an earnest effort to look sophisticated. An effort as hopeless as it was whole-hearted. Not a chance in the world of its fooling an old stager like George Bahmer. He enjoyed her for the very freshness that she tried so hard to hide. Two-thirds of the fun of taking her to dinner at the Ritz had been watching her try to make him think she'd been there before.

D. E. Gibson, who was as conventional as a small-city banker, would have given the child a fatherly warning if he had known that she was going out with George Bahmer; might, if she had failed to heed it, even have fired her eventually. So she had a wonderful young time, feeling secretive and surreptitious and wicked. And all the time she was really as safe as she could have been with an amused and indulgent grandfather.

For the five days Bahmer was in town Ruth lived the social life she had read about in her highly colored magazines and always dreamed of knowing.

She learned the thrill of being led to a restaurant table by an obsequious head waiter, of taking a taxi for a short three blocks. She saw Bahmer carelessly pay more for two theater tickets than she would have dared spend for a winter coat; caught a furtive, awed glimpse of his check at the Palms afterward—supper for two, and half a dozen dances that cost a month's rent on the four-room flat she and her mother lived in, up in One Hundred and Twenty-third Street.

Bahmer had had fun, too, in giving her things; lavish, highly proper gifts—candy in a mahogany box with dull metal fasteners; such sweets as she had never tasted, little candied violets, chocolates that seemed to be wrapped in flexible iridescent glass and were so rich that even her unspoiled young sweet tooth had been satisfied with one or two; perfume, priced by the drop and sold by the ounce, and an atomizer, delicately lovely enough to stand alone in a jeweler's window.

Ecstatic over it all, the youngster had had to tell somebody and had, oddly, chosen Claire. Or perhaps there had been nothing odd about this. She would have been afraid to tell any of her fellow stenographers in the office, who would, she felt sure, have been jealous and might have been, accordingly, indiscreet in sharing her confidences till they might eventually have come to Gibson's ears. But there was a warm friendliness in Claire's smile and a steadiness in her eyes, a combination both inviting and reassuring. One knew that she would listen and not tell.

"He says he likes to give me things," the child confided, "because I don't hint for them. Why, he says you'd be surprised at the way most girls do. 'Platinum diggers,' he calls them." She giggled breathless appreciation. "He says gold diggers are all out of date. Girls don't use anything as cheap as gold any more, except maybe to fill a back tooth." She giggled excitedly again. "But he doesn't mind, because he knows how to deal with them. He just lets them hint and hint, and pretends he doesn't know what they're getting at. Then, just before he's ready to go home, when they've about given up hope, he gets them something grand that they've never even mentioned. He says it's lots of fun to do it that way."

"It must be," Claire agreed dryly.

"And he's been so sweet to me. You just wouldn't believe it! Even mother thinks he's grand now, though at first she didn't like the idea of my going out with him, him being married and all."

"'And all,' meaning how many children?"

"Two. Both boys. One is twelve and the other is at Andover. That's a school."

Claire nodded. She could see exactly how piquant such freshness must be to a jaded palate. Bahmer had respected the youth and innocence, too; had gone back to Chicago without any more than a little hand holding, perhaps; or, at the very most, a good-by kiss in the downstairs hallway of her flat building; going back in the comfortable consciousness of having behaved both handsomely and decently.

And yet, in those five days he had ruined little Ruth Wilson as devastatingly as any movie villain could have done. For in that brief time he had made her own life almost unendurable to her.

It would have required something of character which little Ruth did not have, to go back contentedly from casually summoned taxis to the twice-a-day jam in the Subway, from lobster *à la Newburg* sizzling over a chafing-dish flame, and avocados in subtly blended dressing to watery tomato soup and a minced-ham sandwich on a stool at a soda-fountain lunch. The two-dollar-a-week raise which had seemed so well worth working and hoping for had become a niggling insult, the merest waiter's tip. Saturday-evening jaunts with the young man she had been thinking of marrying, an eighty-five-cent table-d'hote in some crowded Italian restaurant, and balcony seats in one of the big movie theaters—once a glorious weekly climax whose prospect had cast an anticipatory glow over even Thursday and Friday, was now something merely to be openly ashamed of.

And as for the young man himself whom she had been thinking of marrying—a mechanic who actually proposed setting up housekeeping on a weekly wage that wouldn't have paid for the embroidered shawl Bahmer had bought her as the merest souvenir; an uncouth barbarian who thought tea in the afternoon or a decent manicure was sissy; whose manners, after Bahmer's suave ease, seemed those of a frolicsome baboon! Oh, unquestionably, little Ruth's own life had been ruined for her.

Claire watched her during the three months that intervened before Bahmer's next visit, convincing herself that she was in love with him. Claire's hints, even her frank counsel, fell on deafened ears. Little Ruth would have none of it. By the time Bahmer was due again she had completely convinced herself that she was the victim of a grand passion. As the day of his arrival approached she became fairly ecstatic with anticipation.

And when Bahmer actually did arrive he didn't see Ruth at all—didn't really see her, that is. A friendly nod as he passed her typewriting desk in the big outer office on his way into Gibson's sanctum, and that was all. There had been a mistake in a shipment of pastel kids, and Bahmer, the busiest and most absorbed of business men, had no time for pretty girls. By his next trip he would have forgotten Ruth altogether.

Claire happened, by the merest chance, to see a bit of the end of the incident. She had worked late in her own office and had slipped out through the deserted salesroom. It was sleeting, and she paused in the entryway just outside the door, to find a nickel for the Subway, to put up her umbrella. And as she stood there in the early winter darkness she recognized two other figures, also pausing in the shelter under the shop's ornate entrance. The girl was Ruth, the man was obviously Bahmer.

"If I've done anything to make you angry," Ruth was saying in a tight, strained little voice, "won't you tell me?"

Hastily Claire fitted her key into the lock, slipped back into the empty dark salesroom. She had no desire to play eavesdropper, but she was not quick enough to miss Bahmer's answer,

313 half amazed, half irritated:
314 "But I've told you, over and
315 over, I'm not angry at you;
316 I've never even thought of such
317 a thing."
318 Had he been honest enough
319 to go on and assure her that he
320 had never even thought of her
321 at all? Claire wondered. She
322 found herself speculating sym-
323 pathetically on the probable
324 remainder of this little scene.
325 Would Bahmer be wise enough
326 to realize that what little Ruth
327 was in love with was not himself
328 but the glimpse of a different sort
329 of life he had shown her? Would
330 he be kind enough to be sorry
331 for the havoc he had wrought?
332 Had he liked her well enough
333 to feel guilty now, for a fleeting
334 moment or so, because though
335 he was so rich in all the things
336 she wanted, he could really do
337 little to change things for her?
338 Even if he were both wise and
339 kind, even though he sincerely
340 liked the child, Claire couldn't
341 see just what he could do to
342 help matters now. He might, of
343 course, call Ruth's attention to
344 certain precious things she had
345 —her youth, for instance. But
346 that sort of reasoning seldom
347 helps much. Probably it was
348 just as well for him to step
349 right out of the picture, de-
350 finitely and abruptly, leaving
351 little Ruth to start at once,
352 picking up the pieces, making
353 such adjustment as she could to
354 whatever she could make out of

355 her own life. He would have to
356 do that sooner or later, anyway,
357 and there never was much point
358 in trying to taper off the inevit-
359 able.
360 Well, kind and wise or not,
361 that was about what he would
362 probably do. And he would
363 probably forget pretty much
364 about the whole incident, long
365 before Ruth would. Not that he
366 would necessarily mean to; but
367 he was a man of many and
368 varied interests. Granted all the
369 sympathy that could possibly be
370 expected, one incontrovertible
371 fact would remain. The fact
372 that Ruth had been only a minor
373 incident in a busy life.
374 As to Bahmer's previous New
375 York visits, Claire had had
376 neither leisure nor interest for
377 speculation. He had been com-
378 ing on some three or four times a
379 year for the past fifteen years.
380 Undoubtedly there had been
381 plenty of Ruths as well as plenty
382 of others. Except for feeling
383 awfully sorry for the Ruth she
384 knew, Claire would never have
385 given a moment's thought to
386 George Bahmer one way or an-
387 other. As it was, however, she
388 knew well enough, when he asked
389 her to go to the theater with him,
390 that even at his best and most
391 chivalrous he was a dangerous
392 man.
393 A considerable spice of mis-
394 chief was mingled with Claire's
395 acceptance of the invitation—
396 because D. E. Gibson was

465

present when it was tendered. The invitation had been, in fact, tendered to D. E. first. But D. E. was feeling the first premonitory twitches of neuritis and was pretty sure that by theater time he would have to be tucked up with an electric pad under his shoulder.

Bahmer had looked from D. E. to the slim, trim young advertising manager who had been called in to explain the exact kind of white ooze leather the new French designer had in mind. There was nothing the matter with the young French designer's mind or what he might have in it, but when he tried to put this into English he needed help. The Frenchman had gone back to his studio in the rear of the office floor; Claire had been just leaving D. E.'s office. Bahmer looked at Claire and spoke to Gibson.

"I don't suppose you've enough pull with Miss Deming." he suggested, "to dare urge her to go with me in your place? I'm afraid to ask her myself."

Claire smiled—she had a very naïve, very white-toothed smile. And it was, right now, a very genuinely amused smile.

The sight of the conflicting emotions which suddenly came to battle all over Gibson's face was downright funny. It was a conflict with which Claire had already become familiar, but which never ceased to amuse her —the battle of the old-fashioned gentleman and the new-fashioned business man.

Gibson was approaching sixty, and for forty of his sixty years he had been a shoe man. Starting out as a salesman for prison-made footwear in the days when men still wore boots and all ladies wore black kid, winding up as owner of one of the smartest shoe shops on Fifth Avenue—a thoroughly successful business man—he had kept his business senses alert and his business mind flexible. No Canute, he, to stand on the shore of fashion and command the waves to fall back—not D. E. of Gibson shoes. He was canny enough to build him a good seaworthy craft and sail to success with the wind and the tide.

As a gentleman, though, he had done his best to play Joshua and make the sun stand still. In regard to women, for instance, he had made his opinions at about the time he had stopped making boots, and he had never allowed himself to see any reason for changing one of them. Such inconsistencies as being a successful business man had forced upon him had never made a dent on the firmness of his beliefs. He had been forced to hire young women stenographers, but he had not allowed this to interfere with his conviction that woman's place is in the home.

A young and even attractive woman advertising manager had,

of course, been engaged by the business man who couldn't quite blink at ability when he saw it. But it caused the old-fashioned gentleman to do considerable blinking. It was difficult, for one thing, to pay her practically the same salary he would have had to pay a young man, and yet to remain convinced that the sun was standing still.

He was blinking hard right now, which was what was amusing Claire. As a gallant and fatherly employer of a young girl, he knew that it was his duty to protect her from just such men as George Bahmer. But as owner of D. E. Gibson shoes, if George Bahmer wanted to take the advertising manager to the theater, D. E. wanted her to go. Every now and then, of a May or November, even a very successful shoe retailer is likely to need a little temporary financial backing. This, Bahmer had always been able to persuade the tannery to advance. The tannery had lost nothing by it, of course. With the shoes which Gibson bought with this advance went the requirement that they should be made of leather from the tannery. It was a mutually profitable arrangement, but one which would have been quite as profitable to the tannery if made with any competing retailer. George Bahmer was Gibson's friendly and important intermediary. Oh, just as a matter of prudence, Gibson earnestly hoped Claire would accept Bahmer's invitation. And as he looked at her, so fresh and girlish in her new tan spring suit, his conflict was writ large on his face.

Bahmer spoke to Claire direct, "Won't you take pity on a solitary out-of-towner?" he asked. "Going to the theater alone is such a dreary business."

There was a really charming humility in his voice. Dangerous men, of course, usually do have charming manners. That is what makes them so dangerous. Claire glanced at D. E.

"Thank you," she said. "I'd be very glad to."

Bahmer chose the Frivolities, of course. Claire had been sure he would. Just as she had felt sure that, during the first intermission, he would attempt to establish a more personal, more provocative relationship between them. His manner coming up in the taxi had been perfectly that of pleasant, impersonal business friendliness. But Claire, being a woman, knew that she was much more attractive after she had taken off her coat. Her black dinner dress was simple and three years old, but it had come from an excellent shop originally and it made her neck and bare arms startlingly white, just as her flame-colored scarf accentuated the blackness of her hair. Besides, she knew Bahmer in advance, or thought she did.

True to her prophecy, the curtain had scarcely descended for the first time when Bahmer turned to her in the soft rustling stir that always comes with the lights.

"You know," he said, "the moment you came into D. E.'s office this morning I knew that you were a person I'd simply got to know."

"Is that so?" said Claire. There was not the slightest hint of rebuff in her pleasant voice. It was courteous, even friendly. But it would have been impossible to convey more perfectly in three short words a complete and utter indifference as to what Bahmer thought about her, one way or the other.

Bahmer waited. The opening of a game of this sort is as full of conventional signals as a bridge play. His remark had been like leading the nine of spades, indicating his strongest suit and expecting the lead returned.

When Claire did not return it, "You struck me as being entirely different from any woman I had ever seen."

Going on like a good sportsman, to establish his suit despite his partner's obtuse play. But she went right on being obtuse. After a bit Bahmer began to suspect that she was playing by different signals. Not till very nearly the end of the show did it dawn upon him that Claire was simply not playing the game at all.

During the Roaring Forties number—one of those gaudy affairs with a lot of radium paint and flashing lights, New York's sky line in the background and some hundred chorus girls in the fore, tiny electric stars twinkling in and out in their slipper heels —Bahmer stole several side glances at the girl in the seat beside him. He was no fool and, though Claire's eyes were always fixed on the stage, he began to suspect that her thoughts were not. There was something too dutiful about the fixedness of her gaze. Bahmer was suddenly sure that her interest was a thousand miles away.

"Don't you care for this sort of show?" he asked.

"Yes, indeed," Claire answered. "I think they're great fun once in a while. This is a very ingenious number, isn't it?"

"It strikes me that way," said Bahmer; "but you're bored to death with it. What's the trouble?" And then suspiciously: "You haven't seen the show before, have you? I thought it was a safe bet; that's why I didn't ask you first. It's only been running three nights."

"I know," said Claire. "I meant to play the appreciative guest better. I'm so sorry you found me out."

⁶⁴⁹ "You have seen it before,
⁶⁵⁰ then?"

⁶⁵¹ "Why, you see," Claire ex-
⁶⁵² plained, "we shoe the Frivolities
⁶⁵³ and I've been to such a lot of
⁶⁵⁴ rehearsals, especially this parti-
⁶⁵⁵ cular number. Our designer had
⁶⁵⁶ considerable trouble about the
⁶⁵⁷ lights in the slipper heels." She
⁶⁵⁸ laughed. "You know," she said,
⁶⁵⁹ "even as clever a number as this
⁶⁶⁰ looks better to you the first six
⁶⁶¹ or eight times you see it."

⁶⁶² Bahmer laughed too. "What
⁶⁶³ a rotten shame—to take a bus
⁶⁶⁴ driver out on his day off and give
⁶⁶⁵ him a nice long bus ride! I'll feel
⁶⁶⁶ rotten about this to my dying
⁶⁶⁷ day unless you let me square it
⁶⁶⁸ with you."

⁶⁶⁹ It came perversely to the tip
⁶⁷⁰ of Claire's tongue to assure
⁶⁷¹ Bahmer that he needn't square
⁶⁷² it with her, that she had only
⁶⁷³ gone with him in the first place
⁶⁷⁴ as a matter of business policy,
⁶⁷⁵ that she hadn't expected to
⁶⁷⁶ enjoy the evening especially
⁶⁷⁷ herself. But of course she didn't
⁶⁷⁸ say it. She couldn't so outrage
⁶⁷⁹ ordinary human friendliness,
⁶⁸⁰ even with a dangerous man.

⁶⁸¹ "I haven't minded really,"
⁶⁸² she assured him. "Part of the
⁶⁸³ show is colorful enough to bear
⁶⁸⁴ any amount of repeating."

⁶⁸⁵ "No." Bahmer insisted, "I
⁶⁸⁶ want to take you to something
⁶⁸⁷ you'll enjoy, not just something
⁶⁸⁸ that you won't mind. Won't
⁶⁸⁹ you let me take you to some
⁶⁹⁰ show that you really want to

⁶⁹¹ see, some other night while I'm
⁶⁹² here?" And as she hesitated,
⁶⁹³ "Please do," he urged. "If
⁶⁹⁴ you've got a free evening, please
⁶⁹⁵ do. Something that you'd plan
⁶⁹⁶ to go to sometime anyway."
⁶⁹⁷ And as she still didn't answer,
⁶⁹⁸ "Surely there are some other
⁶⁹⁹ shows that you want to see,
⁷⁰⁰ aren't there?"

⁷⁰¹ "Oh, yes, of course there are,"
⁷⁰² Claire admitted. "But any one
⁷⁰³ of them might bore you to
⁷⁰⁴ tears."

⁷⁰⁵ Bahmer did not make the
⁷⁰⁶ obvious gallant retort that no
⁷⁰⁷ evening spent with her could
⁷⁰⁸ possibly be a bore. He had had
⁷⁰⁹ too many such remarks fall dead
⁷¹⁰ that evening. Instead:

⁷¹¹ "An evening alone in New
⁷¹² York is worth two cents on the
⁷¹³ dollar," he said. "I'd rather
⁷¹⁴ take a chance on being bored."
⁷¹⁵ And again, insistently, "What
⁷¹⁶ do you want to go to the most?"

⁷¹⁷ "Well," Claire admitted, "I've
⁷¹⁸ been planning all winter to see
⁷¹⁹ Bright Treasure."

⁷²⁰ "Which night?" Bahmer
⁷²¹ asked crisply. "I'll be here till
⁷²² Saturday."

⁷²³ He expected Claire, of course,
⁷²⁴ to have great difficulty in finding
⁷²⁵ a free evening among her many
⁷²⁶ engagements. Girls always did
⁷²⁷ it that way, though he was
⁷²⁸ cynical enough to have observed
⁷²⁹ that they seldom missed finding
⁷³⁰ one eventually.

⁷³¹ "I'm free any evening till
⁷³² Saturday," Claire answered.

733 "Suppose we make it for which-
734 ever night you can get the best
735 seats."

736 And then, where he was quite
737 unprepared for coquetry, it
738 seemed to Bahmer, at least,
739 that he found it.

740 After the Frivolities, "Can't
741 we go somewhere and have a
742 bite to eat," he asked, "and a
743 dance or two? You dance,
744 don't you?"

745 "Yes," said Claire, "but I'm
746 afraid not tonight, thank you.
747 You see, I'm working awfully
748 hard on my job and I'm worse
749 than useless the next day if I
750 stay up to all hours."

751 Obviously coquetry, that,
752 Bahmer felt sure. He knew
753 women, and women didn't pass
754 up invitations to night clubs
755 except in ways calculated to call
756 forth more invitations.

757 As he was leaving Claire out-
758 side her apartment on West
759 Eighth Street she said, "You
760 won't need to go to an agency for
761 the Bright Treasure tickets, un-
762 less it's more convenient. I'm
763 sure you can get seats at the box
764 office. It isn't one of the big
765 hits."

766 Bahmer looked at her quiz-
767 zically. "You're a funny girl,"
768 he observed. "I thought girls
769 always wanted to see the big
770 hits."

771 Claire smiled. "Girls usually
772 choose the shows that they think
773 will please the men who are
774 going to buy the tickets," she

775 told him. "You brought this on
776 yourself, you know."

777 Bahmer watched her as she
778 fitted her latchkey into the
779 apartment-house door. No
780 swanky, hall-boyed, all-night-
781 service apartment house, hers.
782 He had expected her to hand
783 him the key, let him unlock the
784 door for her, the usual helplessly
785 feminine gesture of appeal.

786 "You don't like me very well,
787 do you?" he guessed shrewdly.

788 Claire met his eyes with a
789 distinctly uncoquettish direct-
790 ness. "Yes, I do," she said
791 frankly, "though I didn't expect
792 to. I think you'd be a very
793 nice person, if you'd let yourself
794 be."

795 Bahmer was no more surprised
796 at this answer than Claire her-
797 self. For it was absolutely true.
798 Spoken straight out from some
799 instinctive reaction. Despite all
800 her warnings, all her foreknow-
801 ledge of Bahmer, for the moment
802 she completely forgot about be-
803 ing on her guard against him.
804 Though he looked exactly as she
805 had known he would look. And
806 behaved exactly as she had
807 known he would behave. Good-
808 looking without being particu-
809 larly handsome, well-tailored
810 and well-groomed. Pleasant-
811 mannered, genial, generous, but
812 well protected with a firm glaze
813 of cynical, worldly-wise suspi-
814 cion.

815 Queer that Claire should feel
816 so suddenly sure about that

cynical glaze; so sure that it had nothing more to do with the real man underneath it than a brittle, hard coating of ice has to do with the current below. Something of this reluctant liking must, even before she recognized it herself, have crept into her manner despite her prudent intent. If she had succeeded in being quite as impersonal, as almost rudely reserved as she had planned to be, Bahmer could not possibly have been so determined to see more of her.

Bright Treasure was a charming play, witty and gay and about real people. Bahmer had lost no time; had bought tickets for the very next evening. Between acts, tonight, he did not attempt to flirt with Claire. And because he did not, Claire found herself impelled, more and more, to be herself with him—gracious, companionable, friendly.

"I knew a man once exactly like that father," Bahmer observed after the first curtain. "I used to wonder how he could expect his sons to amount to anything when he never gave them a chance to make so much as a mistake on their own."

"How did the sons turn out?" Claire asked.

"I don't know," Bahmer said, "I lost touch with them years ago, but I can guess. And I can guess just about what's going to happen to those two lads." He nodded toward the stage.

So he guessed, and Claire guessed. And they quarreled, about their respective guesses, keenly and good-humoredly. And then, through the following acts, watched the dramatist shrewdly and deftly outguess them both.

They stopped at a little Sixth Avenue rotisserie on the way home and had ginger ale and toasted cheese sandwiches.

"You know," Bahmer admitted, across the table, "I'd never have thought I'd like that play, if it had been described to me, but it was really very interesting. Let's go to another."

"I think I've already seen most of the plays that I know are especially good," said Claire, and obligingly mentioned the two or three she had enjoyed the most.

Bahmer was not interested in these, however. "I want something you'll go to with me," he said frankly. "You said you were free till Saturday. Isn't there something else that we can do together?"

Claire hesitated. Why not? She could not ask a more thoroughly delightful companion than Bahmer had been tonight.

"Come on, please do," he urged. There was something boyish, appealing, in his eagerness. It was as though he had suddenly realized that he could not buy her companionship with expensive gifts or costly enter-

902 tainment and, for some reason
903 or other, wanted it on her own
904 terms.

905 "Please," he begged, "can't
906 you think of something?"

907 "Well, they're having a block
908 party somewhere down on the
909 East Side tomorrow night," she
910 said. "A friend of mine who's
911 been doing some settlement work
912 with the children is going to
913 have a bunch of them sing
914 Neapolitan folk songs. She says,
915 though it hasn't been announced
916 that that new young Neapolitan
917 tenor at the Metropolitan is
918 going to sing. A lot of his
919 relatives live there. I thought
920 it would be great fun to go
921 down and look on. At worst,
922 it's sure to be different and
923 colorful."

924 "Great," said Bahmer. "Can't
925 we have dinner somewhere
926 first?"

927 Claire smiled. "Would you
928 like to try my pet cafeteria?"
929 she asked. "You have to
930 juggle a tray, but the food
931 is wonderful and there are
932 sure to be some nice people
933 there."

934 Oddly out of place Bahmer
935 seemed at the Round Table next
936 evening. No ready check boy
937 took his hundred-and-seventy-
938 five-dollar coat. There was no
939 obsequious head waiter to guide
940 him to the choicest table. He
941 hung his coat on a peg between
942 a sweater and a rubber raincoat,
943 obediently found a tray and a

944 knife, fork and spoon wrapped
945 in a paper napkin, and lined up
946 behind Claire at the steaming
947 counter.

948 The half dozen young people
949 already seated around a table, to
950 whom she casually introduced
951 Bahmer, accepted him quite as
952 casually. Two young men across
953 from each other continued a
954 good-humored argument about
955 the recent Pulitzer Prize award;
956 a cordial, yellow-curled girl next
957 to Bahmer directed him to the
958 ice-water cooler, showed him
959 where the empty glasses were
960 kept.

961 Little Ruth Wilson, vainly
962 trying to convince Bahmer that
963 she was used to dining at the
964 Ritz, had made no more gallant
965 effort than Bahmer himself made
966 tonight to fit in well at this
967 cafeteria dinner table. He felt
968 oddly flattered when he essayed
969 a joking comment and every-
970 body laughed. Still more flat-
971 tered when a young cover artist
972 specifically included him in an
973 invitation to dinner in her studio
974 the next evening.

975 "You'd better get something
976 to eat first," Claire cautioned
977 him privately, later in the even-
978 ing, as the two of them wedged
979 their way into a crowded trolley
980 to escape from the colorful,
981 foreign-babbling, lantern-strung
982 block party on the lower East
983 Side.

984 It had been a hilarious even-
985 ing, all colored lights and con-

fetti, laughter, singing. Claire and Bahmer had given themselves over to the fiesta atmosphere like two children at a circus, joining in on the familiar choruses, drinking pop through straws stuck in the bottles, buying chestnuts out of the braziers, clinging together, arm in arm, against the jolly pressure of the jostling crowd.

"Polly means well," Claire continued her warning for the next evening, "but she's as likely as not to forget to order the meat."

Polly proved the next night to have remembered the meat, but her whole dinner had obviously been hastily assembled from the nearest delicatessen, and there wasn't enough dessert to go around. Nobody minded though. A gay young hodgepodge of an evening—dancing, laughing, wise-cracking. A smooth-faced youngster who was doing a magician act in a near-by vaudeville dropping in after his number to show them a new trick he was working on; a young professor from the big downtown university haranguing about the mysticism of the East Indian fakir; a little dancer from the Frivolities, arriving late, to dance and sing in a high, sweet, haunting voice that filled the bare studio like perfume. All fairly poor still, but all young and eager and ready for fun.

At the door of Claire's apartment house that evening Bahmer paused.

"Tomorrow's my last evening here," he said. "Won't you have a farewell dinner with me?"

"Mr. Gibson was back in the office today," said Claire. "His neuritis proved to be a much shorter affair than usual."

"That's good," said Bahmer. "Well, how about tomorrow evening?"

"What I was trying to suggest delicately," said Claire, "was that by tomorrow evening Mr. Gibson will be both able and eager to do the honors for the firm."

For several moments Bahmer did not answer. Then: "I see," he said stiffly. "Dining with me is the same thing as working overtime."

"Oh, I didn't mean that at all!"

Claire forgot all about Bahmer's being a dangerous man, in the quick remorseful response to the unmistakable hurt under the stiffness of his voice.

"Why, I'd love to have dinner with you if you want me to."

"Is there anywhere you'd especially like to have it?"

There had been something so unmistakably genuine in that hurt, it struck at the very root of Claire's natural kindliness. She quite forgot to be cautious and on her guard, in her eagerness to make amends.

"Wouldn't you like to come

here for dinner?" she asked. "I've a little kitchen in my new apartment; we could get dinner ourselves." It was her friendliest gesture. To its possible indiscretion Claire was temporarily blind.

"I'd like it better than anything in the world," the man answered. "If you'll let me be the commissary."

Claire nodded assent.

"I can get down here by 5:30," she said. "We'll do the marketing then."

At 5:30 Bahmer was waiting for her on her doorstep. "Let's have a steak," he proposed. "And I'll cook it. Lord, I haven't cooked a steak in twenty years!"

Claire cocked a dubious eye. "Smothered in onions?" she asked hopefully.

Bahmer looked at her in admiring unbelief. "Did I hear you right?" he asked incredulously. "Is there a woman in the world who would actually suggest onions?"

"I love 'em. Let's be natural and vulgar."

"Come on!"

They shopped in the great market that occupies a full block. Bahmer personally chose the steak, watched it cut off, directing its exact thickness.

"Green peas?" At the vegetable stand they bought, too, a head of lettuce as firm as a young cabbage; tomatoes, Claire pinching them with critical, housewifely fingers. They went to three different stands before they found a box of strawberries, fresh and large and red enough to suit.

"We don't want any cake with them, do we?"

"We do not," Bahmer agreed gratefully. "How about some crackers and cheese to top off with, with the coffee?"

So they stopped at a delicatessen. Here, after buying the cheese—an expensive pineapple affair—Bahmer ran quite wild. Ripe olives, wild-grape jelly, sweet butter, imported *antipasto*, spiced currants. All the expensive delicacies, and such quantities of each! He brushed aside Claire's protests as so many mosquitoes.

"You're buying a dinner, you know, not stocking a hotel."

"We want enough. Besides, you can eat up whatever's left, some other day."

She stopped him at last and, both loaded with knobby packages, they made their way back to the apartment.

It is difficult to retain any vestiges of formality between two people getting dinner together in an apartment-house kitchen. As Claire and Bahmer shelled peas and scraped potatoes and peeled tomatoes and opened up a jiggly little card table in front of the living-room fireplace, Claire forgot more and more completely to keep up any protective screen of formality. Forgot, more and more, that she was dining alone with a dangerous man.

As he tinkered with the gas broiler which exploded mildly each time instead of lighting, Claire found herself looking curiously at Bahmer, her rubber apron tied around his neck, his whole attention centered on twisting and turning the metal tube which regulated the mixture of air and gas. There was nothing about this man to suggest the George Bahmer she had heard about, the George Bahmer she had, in fact, found at first. Surely this was no cynical man about town, wise in the ways of business men and platinum diggers, complacently ignorant of everything else in life. No self-protective materialist, content to find new ways to eat, drink and be merry and forget that tomorrow we may die.

This man getting dinner in her little kitchen seemed oddly younger, oddly hungry for the very interests the other Bahmer would have passed by, unseeing or contemptuous. A very simple person, this Bahmer seemed, with all the doors of his mind standing wide open, hospitable to any vagrant wind of thought.

The steak broiled to a turn, they lighted the fire against the chill spring evening and sat down at the jiggly legged card table.

"I'm going to get a good solid table as soon as I can afford the kind I want," Claire observed. "I seldom get a meal here, except breakfast, but it's fun to, once in a while, and with this table it's like eating at sea in a hard wind."

Bahmer glanced about her living room's partial bareness— low, deep-seated wicker chairs, obviously comfortable but obviously cheap, and only two of them; the floor bare, except for one small domestic rug in front of the fireplace; a single, parchment-shaded light with an added wire length so that it could be moved about to serve wherever needed most. No room, of course, where a well-broiled steak is being served in front of an open fire is likely to seem lacking in genial hominess, but there was no blinking the fact that this room, on close inspection, was cheaply and scantily furnished.

"I used to think it would be more fun to get furniture a piece at a time," Bahmer observed. "Everything you get means something then."

Claire nodded. "I'd have to do it that way anyway. I couldn't wait any longer to have a home, but I can't put much money into it right now."

"You get a good salary at Gibson's, don't you?"

Odd, Claire realized, that such a question, coming from a Bahmer, could be asked with a frank

1239 friendliness that robbed it of
1240 any hint of impertinence.

1241 "Very good," she answered
1242 quite as frankly. "But I haven't
1243 had it so awfully long and I'm
1244 not at all sure of Mr. Gibson.
1245 He's dubious about women in
1246 responsible positions, and I'm
1247 not sure whether he'll be willing
1248 to make my job anything I'll want
1249 to stay in indefinitely. I want to
1250 have enough available money so
1251 that I'll be free to do whatever
1252 seems best when the time
1152 comes."

1253 Bahmer nodded. "That's the
1254 way to do it, all right," he said,
1255 "If you can stand out against
1256 the temptations on all sides."

1257 Claire laughed. "I spend my
1258 days breaking down other
1259 people's sales resistance and the
1260 rest of the time bolstering up
1261 my own. I like almost every-
1262 thing that money will buy, but
1263 I'm not going to have my life
1264 decided for me by the things I've
1265 bought."

1266 "There are mighty few people
1267 who have the sense to figure that
1268 out," he said, "until after they've
1269 bought them and it's too late."

1270 It was half-past eight before
1271 they finished off with crackers
1272 and cheese.

1273 "I made my dinner take as
1274 long as I could," Bahmer con-
1275 fessed, "because I wanted it to
1276 be too late to ask you if you
1277 wanted to go anywhere after-
1278 ward. I'd so much rather stay
1279 right here."

1280 "So would I," said Claire
1281 contentedly. " 'Be it ever so
1282 humble——' "

1283 "What about the dishes?"
1284 Bahmer asked.

1285 For a moment Claire stared
1286 at him as he had at her when she
1287 had suggested onions—amazed,
1288 incredulous.

1289 "Now," she said, "I know
1290 you're nice! But we don't need
1291 to bother about them, thank
1292 heaven! I've a maid who comes
1293 in Saturday mornings to clean
1294 up, and she'll do them."

1295 So they carried them out to
1296 the little kitchen, then drew the
1297 lone two comfortable chairs be-
1298 fore the fire.

1299 "Smoke?" Claire asked.
1300 "There are plenty of cigarettes
1301 over there in the box."

1302 Replete with the good dinner,
1303 almost drowsy in the warmth of
1304 the fire, they sat for some little
1305 time in an incongruous sort of
1306 companionability, Bahmer puf-
1307 fing away at a cigarette, Claire
1308 leaning forward now and then
1309 to poke the logs. In this odd
1310 sense of comradeship she forgot
1311 entirely the Bahmer Gibson
1312 knew, the Bahmer of little Ruth
1313 and the platinum diggers. Ac-
1314 cepting in his place the other
1315 Bahmer who, her common sense
1316 told her, must surely be just an
1317 illusion. But such a likable il-
1318 lusion—young, even a bit in-
1319 experienced, eager, adventurous,
1320 open-minded, frankly hungry for
1321 life. An illusion who seemed,

oddly, so much more real than the reality; with whom she could be friends unreservedly, could be herself.

It was to this friendly illusion of a man that she turned, her eyes suddenly ashine with interest when he chanced to speak of London.

"You've been to London several times!" she exclaimed. "I wonder if you've ever been to my London." She sighed. "I don't suppose you have though. I've asked so many people, and nobody ever has."

"What is your London?" Bahmer asked curiously.

"Oh, I don't suppose it really exists at all," Claire confessed. "That's why nobody's ever been there. It's just a jumble of things I've read and things I've imagined and funny ideas I got when I was a little girl. You know the kind of things."

Queer that she should feel so sure he would know. But he seemed to. He nodded. "Dick Whittington, thrice Lord Mayor of London," he suggested.

"And Vauxhall where Dobbin went with the Sedleys and Becky Sharp!"

"And Fleet Street and the Cheshire Cheese."

"And London Bridge and Kensington Gardens and Piccadilly Circus—of course they won't look the way I think they will, but——"

" 'Oranges and lemons, say the bells of Saint Clement's,' " Bahmer quoted.

" 'I'm sure I don't know, says the big bell of Bow,' " Claire finished.

They laughed, a half-amused, half-embarrassed laugh, then went on shamelessly, building up this fairy city, the London of history and phantasy, the London priceless and precious, that is owned inalienably by those who have never been to London.

"The Tower," said Bahmer— "that was the place I used to dream most about going."

"Didn't you believe you'd see the two little princes somewhere on the stone stairs in their velvet suits?"

"And Sir Walter Raleigh and Lady Jane Grey." A little pause.

"And didn't you see any of them," Claire asked half fearfully, "when you really did go to the Tower?"

"I've never been to the Tower," said Bahmer.

For a moment Claire was silent with sheer incredulity. "And you've been to London several times?"

"I had planned to go, of course, the first time," said Bahmer, "but, you see, I was there on my honeymoon and my— Mrs. Bahmer had been there two or three times before. She knew a good many people who lived in London, and it mortified her to death the provincial things I wanted to do."

477

Bahmer laughed a little wryly. "I was a provincial who had never been anywhere before," he said, "so, of course, I didn't want anyone to think I was. I used to think I'd slip off alone and go to the Tower, at least, by myself. But I never got a chance. We were entertained a lot, and then I had some business to see to and—well, I just never seemed to find a good chance. You see, all Mrs. Bahmer's friends were fashionable people, or trying to be fashionable, and they set great store on knowing the right people and going to the right places. I didn't know anybody at all, and all the places I wanted to go to were the wrong ones." Claire nodded understandingly. "I thought then that I'd go over to England sometime by myself and be a provincial and do all the wrong things and have a glorious time. But——"

He did not finish the sentence. After a minute or two Claire asked curiously, "Why didn't you?"

"Well, my next time was fifteen years later. And fifteen years is a long time. I'd forgotten all about the little princes and Sir Walter Raleigh. I'd forgotten that I had ever wanted to see the Tower of London."

Claire turned a little in her chair, looked at the man beside her as he sat staring into the fire. And suddenly her riddle was solved. The riddle of this other Bahmer, eager, friendly, open-minded, hungry for life. This illusion who had helped cook dinner in her little kitchen and seemed so oddly real. Why, of course he was real! More real than the cynical man about town whose place he had, for this one evening, taken. It was he who was sitting here right now, an ardent and romantic boy in a middle aged man's expensive clothes, wearing a worldly-wise, sophisticated face like a mask, staring into the fire through disillusioned eyes that meant no more than cloudy window glass—the man that Bahmer might have been.

No wonder he seemed young and inexperienced. He had never grown up. He had just been left behind. Somewhere, along the streets of London, a quarter of a century ago, Bahmer had walked off and left him; walked off and briskly on his way to become the ultra-successful salesman, the man who would learn to deal with men and handle women, the man who would forget that you can't buy friendship with a loan or love from a platinum digger.

"I suppose," said Claire, "that you were awfully in love with your wife."

There surely must have been some potent force to make him leave that charming boy behind. "She was very pretty," said

478

Bahmer, "and I was attracted to her." He paused. "She'd had a lot more advantages than I had, and that flattered me," he added honestly. "Then I had two or three rivals, and you know how competition stimulates trade. But I see now that that's quite different from being in love."

"It may be that the only way you can keep your dream of any place is by never going there. You've still got your Tower with Sir Walter Raleigh and the little princes. Maybe you'd have lost that if you'd ever seen the real one."

Claire went flying back to London on the quick wings of apprehension; in sudden realization that this quiet, firelighted apartment was no place for her and the Bahmer of today—the sporty Chicago man who tells you that his wife doesn't understand him. It had been a mistake, mentioning his wife at all. This couldn't be helped now, of course. Claire could only do her best by a hasty flight back to London and the other Bahmer, with whom she felt so unguardedly at ease.

"I came across a poem once," she went on hurriedly, "that I feel sure was written by somebody who had never been there either. There were two lines, I remember, that went something like: 'London, London, they counted me a fool—I could draw your sky

line plain before I went to school.'"

Across the hearth Claire felt Bahmer's eyes on her, and she rose hastily, crossed the room, chattering determinedly.

"I think I cut it out of the magazine and saved it," she rattled on. "One verse goes something like this:

" 'As I went up to London,' I
   heard a stranger say,
  As though it were a casual thing
   for casual lips to say.
'As I went up to London'—I'll
  wager many a crown
He never took the road that I
  shall take to London Town.'"

She came back into the firelight with a large manila envelope, shook its clippings into her lap—bits of magazine verse from here and there, saved over a dozen years or so. She did not find the poem she was seeking among them, and as she bent her smooth dark head over the others it was with a mere pretense of attention. She was becoming with every moment more conscious of Bahmer's interest. She kept her eyes lowered over her lapful of clippings, avoided meeting the steady intensity of his gaze. But she could not avoid feeling it sweep over her, warm, vibrating, as real as the glow of the fire. She knew that in another moment he was going to rise and come across the little distance

1573 between his chair and hers.
1574 She picked up one of the bits of
1575 verse at random, passed it across
1576 to him.

1577 "Here's a good one," and as
1578 he took it tentatively: "Read
1579 it aloud, won't you?"

1580 Obediently Bahmer settled
1581 back and adjusted his glasses.
1582 Fortunately Claire's chance
1583 choice had fallen on a ballad—
1584 a long one. So she had a bit of
1585 respite as Bahmer dutifully read
1586 the lengthy rollicking account
1587 of Forty Singing Seamen in
1588 an Old Black Barque. Before
1589 he reached the "Could the grog
1590 we dreamed we swallowed make
1591 us dream of all that followed?"
1592 Claire was ready with another
1593 clipping.

1594 "Here's a spooky thing; read
1595 this!" And when he reached its
1596 concluding "I cheer a dead
1597 man's sweetheart—never ask me
1598 whose," she was ready with
1599 another. But despite the sing-
1600 ing beauty of this last choice,
1601 she could feel her reader growing
1602 restive.

1603 "My soul," she thought, in
1604 whimsical panic, "this is like
1605 that old story of grandpa's,
1606 about the time the wolves chased
1607 his cutter and he kept throwing
1608 out things to them—the lap
1609 robe, his coat, his overshoes, his
1610 shoes. I can't keep throwing out
1611 poems all night! Besides grand-
1612 pa said that after a while the
1613 wolves began to get on to him
1614 and by the time he got down to

1615 gloves they wouldn't even stop
1616 to fight over them."

1617 It had been a mistake, she
1618 realized now, these few evenings
1619 she had spent with Bahmer.
1620 Possibly she should never have
1621 accepted even that first semi-
1622 business invitation; probably she
1623 should have declined his second
1624 suggestion with a chill unfriend-
1625 liness that would have been un-
1626 mistakable, whatever bearing it
1627 had on her position as advertis-
1628 ing manager for D. E. Gibson
1629 shoes. But if these were mere
1630 possibilities and probabilities, it
1631 was a flat certainty that she
1632 should never have invited him
1633 here tonight. The informal
1634 comradeliness of the little
1635 kitchen, the unconventional
1636 friendliness of dinner on the
1637 jiggly card table and now the
1638 warm intimacy of a shared
1639 hearth fire.

1640 Someway, though, she could-
1641 n't take the situation quite
1642 seriously. Even her sense of
1643 humor continued to function
1644 quite unawed. As Bahmer ap-
1645 proached the end of the verse
1646 she pawed about for another
1647 to succeed it, and inside was
1648 laughing at herself for doing
1649 it.

1650 "I'm like the heroine in the
1651 old-fashioned novels who used
1652 to try to hold off the villain by
1653 plying him with wine. Didn't
1654 she just pretend to drink hers
1655 and keep coaxing him on till
1656 suddenly he went off into a safe

drunken sleep?" Claire bent lower over her lapful of clippings to hide her little one-sided secret smile. "I used to doubt that story, even on wine. And fancy trying it with poetry!"

Claire could smile her little one-sided smile, could make fun of herself, because she simply couldn't make herself think of Bahmer as a villain. Not even when suddenly he stopped reading, rose, scattering the clippings recklessly over the floor, crossed the bit of firelight to her chair.

"I can't go on," he said. "I'm mad about you."

So it had come. For a moment Claire considered a brisk "Nonsense, you're not really at all, you know. It's just the combination of a porterhouse steak and an open fire."

But she thought better of this before she said it. Giving a man a chance to argue about a thing of this sort is poor policy. He only convinces himself further by his own eloquence. So instead:

"I'm awfully sorry," she said simply.

He stood close beside her chair, but did not venture to touch so much as the sleeve of her trim, tan office dress.

"I didn't believe there was a girl like you in the world. I used to think there might be, years ago, when I was just a boy. Beautiful and clever and brave and good—the kind of girl who would want the same kind of life I would; that I could go anywhere with. But I decided, years ago, that it was just a dream, that women didn't come that way."

"I used to think——" Of course it was the Bahmer who used to be, who was talking now! That was why his voice was so youthfully eager, so young in its intensity. Why, too, he stood so still beside Claire, so stiff in a boyish respect. It was a very young man talking, younger even than Claire herself, the young man he had walked off and left behind somewhere in London.

"Why, we could do anything in the world together," he went on eagerly. "There's a lot in life besides just making money and spending it. As you say, you don't have to let life be decided by the things you've bought. What do you get out of a great lot of things, anyway! Here I belong to three different golf clubs, and what does it get me? I can't shoot a decent game over any one of them. Don't even know that I want to. I notice that the men I know, who can go around in ninety, have to put up five dollars a hole to keep them interested." Claire stirred uneasily in her low chair. "What is there in having a decent house and servants to run it, when it's nothing but a place that you're

481

1741 glad to travel to stay away
1742 from; and dinner parties that
1743 the only men you'd really like
1744 to eat dinner with aren't invited
1745 to because they don't fit with
1746 the crowd?"

1747 "It's your own crowd that
1748 they don't fit with, isn't it?"
1749 Claire asked mildly.

1750 "My own crowd!" Very
1751 young, too, was the outraged
1752 intolerance of his voice. "My
1753 own crowd! A bunch of men
1754 who all happen to live in the
1755 same suburb, in about the same-
1756 priced houses, who've all found
1757 some way of making fifteen
1758 thousand a year or over. And
1759 a bunch of women who've
1760 all been about the same kind
1761 of pickers when it came to
1762 husbands—financially, that is.
1763 That's exactly all my crowd has
1764 in common. Why, we have to
1765 have two or three stiff cocktails
1766 before we can stand each other
1767 through an evening!"

1768 Claire said nothing; there was
1769 really nothing she could say.

1770 "Traveling!" Bahmer went
1771 on with mounting bitterness.
1772 "Everybody thinks I travel a
1773 good deal. Oh, I'm abroad two
1774 or three times a year, I grant
1775 you. Paris, Cannes, Deauville
1776 —it's very broadening. I come
1777 back knowing all about whether
1778 to make up Dresden calf or
1779 Sudan lizard." He stopped
1780 short. "I've had more of what
1781 I used to think traveling would
1782 be, sitting right here in this chair

1783 tonight and talking to you about
1784 London."

1785 It was the defrauded cry of
1786 the immaterialist who has spent
1787 most of his life in the wrong
1788 camp.

1789 Claire stared into the fire un-
1790 happily. No one-sided smile
1791 tipped her lips now. The sense
1792 of humor which would have kept
1793 right on functioning through
1794 passionate love-making had flown
1795 away. Vanished, too, was the
1796 poise and common sense which
1797 could have dealt so completely
1798 with a dangerous man; could
1799 have been so safely cynical about
1800 the middle-aged philanderer who
1801 tells young women that his wife
1802 doesn't understand him. For
1803 Claire was an immaterialist, too,
1804 and she recognized plain truth
1805 when she heard it.

1806 She was suddenly afraid as
1807 she sat staring into the blaze—
1808 afraid, not of Bahmer but of
1809 herself; of the sense of aching
1810 pity that swept over her; of the
1811 wild, irrational impulse to let
1812 him take her in his arms, to
1813 comfort him, to try to make
1814 up to him for all that life had
1815 done him out of.

1816 It was a foolish, reckless
1817 impulse, she knew; it could lead
1818 to nothing but eventual sorrow
1819 for them both. But she knew,
1820 too, without having to think it
1821 out, that she was rich in all that
1822 Bahmer wanted out of life—
1823 youth, simplicity, adventure,
1824 companionship, the power to

1825 love. She felt a poignant guilt,
1826 to sit at so rich a banquet and
1827 turn a hungry man away.
1828 She could feel prudence, com-
1829 mon sense, all the little wisdom
1830 she had, slipping away as Bah-
1831 mer stood there beside her, not
1832 touching so much as the hem
1833 of her dress. Her knuckles
1834 whitened as she held fast to the
1835 arms of her cheap low wicker
1836 chair, trying to hold herself
1837 back, as from a perilous preci-
1838 pice, and knew that she was
1839 being swept closer to it every
1840 moment.
1841 "I love you so!" Bahmer was
1842 saying tensely. "I never
1843 dreamed that being in love
1844 could be like this. I just can't
1845 go back tomorrow, go on with-
1846 out you, knowing that there is a
1847 woman like you in the world. I
1848 didn't mind before, when I
1849 didn't know there could be any-
1850 thing else—oh, I can't go on
1851 without you now! I love you so!"
1853 Claire's hands loosed their
1854 hold on the chair arms; that
1855 terrific, tender sense of pity was
1856 too much. Wisdom could not
1857 stand against it. She lifted her
1858 eyes to the man beside her.
1859 Suddenly the telephone
1860 shrilled, loud, insistent, at the
1861 other end of the room. For
1862 a moment their eyes clung.
1863 The telephone rang again,
1864 raucous, peremptory. Claire
1865 waited defiantly for a moment
1866 —a moment of insurrection—
1867 then habit triumphed.

1868 "Just a moment, I'd better
1869 answer it." She rose, crossed
1870 the room.
1871 "Yes," her voice shook a little,
1872 "yes, this is Miss Deming. . . .
1873 Good evening, Mr. Gibson." A
1874 considerable pause.
1875 "Why, yes, I think it probably
1876 would be best for me to," Claire's
1877 voice steadying. "I'll wire the
1878 Boston papers. If the cuts are
1879 all made I'm sure we could."
1880 Another pause, a bit of com-
1881 monplace arranging. "Tomor-
1882 row morning? Yes, of course I
1883 can." A brief silence. Then:
1884 "I think there's a Boston sleeper
1885 around twelve or one tonight
1886 though. It would be better if I
1887 could get that. I will, if I can.
1888 . . . All right. I'll wire you
1889 back sometime tomorrow."
1890 Claire came back into the
1891 firelighted circle. She had been
1892 away but a brief three minutes,
1893 but she looked at Bahmer as
1894 though half surprised to find
1895 him there. Her voice was
1896 steady, her eyes cool and di-
1896 rect.
1897 "I'm awfully sorry, but I've
1898 got to dash. The Boston branch
1899 store has got into a mess of some
1900 kind. Gibson wants me there
1901 in the morning. Would you
1902 mind telephoning the station for
1903 me and see if I can get a reserva-
1904 tion while I throw some things
1905 into my bag?"
1906 There was a long pause. Then:
1907 "I——" Bahmer began.
1908 But Claire was already in the

1909 next room. In the opening and
1910 shutting of bureau drawers she
1911 did not hear his tentative be-
1912 ginning.

1913 "You know I suspect that
1914 Boston manager of having some-
1915 thing up his sleeve," she ob-
1916 served chattily. "Because he
1917 strikes me as being too smart a
1918 man to be so incompetent. He's
1919 always doing the most stupid
1920 things, and yet he's certainly not
1921 a stupid man. It's queer."

1922 "I——" Bahmer began again.

1923 "Mr. Gibson's giving him
1924 every chance in the world to
1925 make something good out of
1926 the branch, and yet he——"

1927 "I——" Bahmer began once
1928 more.

1929 "If you can't reserve a berth
1930 on that sleeper, will you find
1931 out what time the first train
1932 leaves in the morning?"

1933 Bahmer's lips parted, but this
1934 time no sound came forth. He
1935 stood staring blankly at Claire's
1936 door, as though incredulously
1937 facing the fact that he was
1938 speaking into a dead instru-
1939 ment, that his connection had
1940 been cut off. For several mo-
1941 ments he stood perfectly still,
1942 looking at the blankness of the
1943 door. From its other side came
1944 the sounds of brisk, competent
1945 packing. Claire herself had
1946 fallen silent now, but a silence
1947 that was as far from invitational
1948 as her casual words had been—
1949 the absorbed silence of a business

1950 woman, preoccupied with the
1951 business on hand.

1952 After a few moments Bahmer
1953 crossed to the telephone, called
1954 the railway station. And after
1955 all, it was probably as wise and
1956 kind a way as could have been
1957 contrived for closing up the
1958 incident. Clare might, of course,
1959 have tried to soften the blow a
1960 little; might have pointed out to
1961 Bahmer that what he was in love
1962 with was really not herself at all,
1963 only the glimpse of another sort
1964 of life that she had shown him;
1965 might have called his attention
1966 to certain precious things he had
1967 —his boys, for instance.

1968 But that sort of reasoning
1969 seldom helps much at the time.
1970 Sooner or later he would have to
1971 start picking up the pieces, mak-
1972 ing such adjustments as he could
1973 to his own life. And there is
1974 never much point in trying to
1975 taper off the inevitable.

1976 And, wise and kind or not,
1977 what Claire did was exactly
1978 what she would inevitably do.
1979 And she would probably pretty
1980 much forget the incident long
1981 before Bahmer would. Not that
1982 she would mean to, but she was
1983 a young woman of many and
1984 varied interests. Granted all
1985 the sympathy that could possibly
1986 be expected, one incontrovertible
1987 fact would remain.

1988 The fact that George Bahmer
1989 had been merely a minor incident
1990 in a busy life.

THE ANALYSIS

In the chart of *Claire and the Dangerous Man* I have placed the two distinct stories side by side to show their parallelism. There is first the story of Bahmer and the little girl Ruth Wilson. Side by side with it is the story of Claire and Bahmer, Claire occupying the same relation to Bahmer that Bahmer did to Ruth.

It is interesting to notice that the same technical treatment occurs in this story that occurred in *The Roads We Take*, by O. Henry. He presented the two stories of Shark Dodson. In the first story there was set forth a series of incidents before arriving at an interchange. The information therein contained sufficed for the second story, so that in presenting the second one the author was able instantly to present an interchange. This is true of this story. In the story of Bahmer and Ruth Wilson the information is presented in a series of skeletonized interchanges (Lines 1 to 134). The fifth step (Lines 135 to 273) are presented in an interchange between Ruth and Claire. The reader realizes that Ruth is aware of a new sort of life infinitely more desirable than her present one. This projects the interchange between Ruth and Bahmer (Lines 273 to 317). Had the author not intended to introduce the story of Claire and Bahmer she could have omitted the interchange between Ruth and Claire, and gone directly to the interchange between Ruth and Bahmer which makes it clear to Bahmer that he must take decisive action. This action he takes. The significance of this action, that Ruth had been only a minor incident in a busy life, is adroitly planted to form the ironic parallel with the other story, which follows it in structure as it does in significance.

The story of Claire and Bahmer is composed almost entirely of interchanges, as a glance at the chart will indicate. And here an interesting fact is disclosed. The author combines the technique of both the accomplishment and the decision type stories. For she keeps before the audience always the fact that Claire is setting out to play with fire, which has always before this burned other girls who played with it. The narrative question "Can she succeed?" informs all the interchanges. Although she is successful, the threat of disaster ultimately is always before the reader, to form a Dramatic Hindrance at the fifth step of each interchange. There is present, too, the Big Moment when this threatened disaster is imminent and apparently inescapable. I rather think that the author thought of this as a story of accomplishment—I deduce this from the title—and that the parallel story of Bahmer and Ruth

Wilson was merely added to give a fillip to the story of Claire. But such conjecture is idle. The lesson to be drawn from this story as from the other stories in the book is that there are only two possible Main Narrative Questions. One is "Can A Succeed?" If this is kept always before the reader, the story is one of Accomplishment. The other is "What will A do at this crisis of his life?" If this is what interests the reader, the story is one of Decision or Choice.

But whether the main Narrative Question is one of Accomplishment or one of Decision, one inescapable and inexorable conclusion is apparent. The capacity of a writer is the measure of his or her ability to write scenes. If an author can write good dramatic scenes, plotting will be an easy matter. It consists of juggling the scenes about until the most interesting and effective order of their presentation is apparent. Above all a writer, to be successful, must realize that whether the story is a Decision Story or an Accomplishment Story, there are only two ways to tell the Modern Short Story: Chronologically, or in a Flash-back.